WORLD PHILOLOGY

WORLD PHILOLOGY

Edited by

Sheldon Pollock, Benjamin A. Elman,
and Ku-ming Kevin Chang

Harvard University Press
Cambridge, Massachusetts
London, England
2015

Printed in the United States of America

First Printing

Library of Congress Cataloging-in-Publication Data
World philology / Edited by Sheldon Pollock, Benjamin A. Elman, and Ku-ming Kevin Chang.
pages cm
Includes bibliographical references and index.
ISBN 978-0-674-05286-4 (hardcover : alk. paper)
1. Philology—History. I. Pollock, Sheldon I., editor of compilation.
II. Elman, Benjamin A., 1946–, editor of compilation.
III. Chang, Ku-ming Kevin, 1968–, editor of compilation.
P61.W67 2014
400—dc23 2014009973

Contents

Foreword vii
Fan-Sen Wang

Acknowledgments xi

Introduction 1
Sheldon Pollock

1. From Book to Edition: Philology in Ancient Greece 25
Franco Montanari

2. The Bride of Mercury: Confessions of a 'Pataphilologist 45
James E. G. Zetzel

3. Striving for Meaning: A Short History of Rabbinic Omnisignificance 63
Yaakov Elman

4. Early Arabic Philologists: Poetry's Friends or Foes? 92
Beatrice Gruendler

5. What Was Philology in Sanskrit? 114
Sheldon Pollock

6. Reconciling the Classics: Two Case Studies in Song-Yuan Exegetical Approaches 137
Michael Lackner

7. Humanist Philologies: Texts, Antiquities, and Their Scholarly Transformations in the Early Modern West 154
Anthony Grafton

8. Mughal Philology and Rūmī's *Mathnavī* 178
Muzaffar Alam

9. The Rise of "Deep Reading" in Early Modern Ottoman Scholarly Culture 201
Khaled El-Rouayheb

10. Early Modern or Late Imperial? The Crisis of Classical Philology in Eighteenth-Century China 225
Benjamin A. Elman

11. The Politics of Philology in Japan: Ancient Texts, Language, and Japanese Identity 245
Susan L. Burns

12. "Enthusiasm Dwells Only in Specialization": Classical Philology and Disciplinarity in Nineteenth-Century Germany 264
Constanze Güthenke

13. The Intelligence of Philological Practice: On the Interpretation of Rilke's Sonnet "O komm und geh" 285
Christoph König

14. Philology or Linguistics? Transcontinental Responses 311
Ku-ming Kevin Chang

Notes 333
Bibliography 385
List of Contributors 437
Index 439

Foreword

FAN-SEN WANG

There seems to be no better place than the Academia Sinica in Taiwan to host a conference on the global history of philology and support the publication of a book on world philology. Its Institute of History and Philology, where I work, is one of the very few institutions in the world that unites history and philology in its mission. Moreover, the institute was founded with an intentionally internationalist character, being the first to apply Western philology and historical methods to Chinese material and then to contribute to global scholarship with its findings. Its vision and orientation aim at a comparative history of important philological traditions around the world.

The institute's remarkable sense of scholarly internationalism was attested already by its founding director, Ssu-nien Fu (1896–1950). He proclaimed that his institute would work on "materials not bound by countries," and would draw its methods "from unlimited regions, in order to . . . take part in the scholarly successes that have so far been accomplished in other countries." The head of the historical section of the institute, Yinke Chen, had trained in history and philology at Harvard and Berlin. He applied his knowledge of Sanskrit, Tibetan, and Mongolian, among other languages, to decipher Chinese historical texts that were rendered problematic by medieval transliterations of the names of foreign persons and places. Later devoted to Tang history, Chen articulated a view of the multiple ethnicities, languages, and religions of the medieval states and dynasties that made up China. His command of a great variety of historical languages, all acquired abroad, and his sensitivity to the multiethnic nature of Chinese history implicitly embodied the common sense of German classical philology, or *Altertumswissenschaft,* and medieval European history.

The enthusiasm for Western philology among the founders of the institute was part of an international phenomenon that took place when non-Western civilizations were confronted with Western modernity in the nineteenth and twentieth centuries. Edward Said made famous the importance of philology in the formation of Ernest Renan's Orientalism and its impact on the colonial world. But countries that were never under the direct rule of Western powers, such as Japan, also welcomed the methods of Western philology. As Susan L. Burns and Ku-ming Kevin Chang point out in this volume, the first Japanese students to study philology in Europe, and indeed the first two Japanese holders of the chair in philology at the University of Tokyo, Kazutoshi Ueda (1867–1937) and Yaichi Haga (1867–1926), took on the tasks of constructing the national language and literature of Japan, and of surveying local languages and compiling dictionaries, with the philological methods they had learned abroad. Japan's national language movement soon inspired Chinese intellectuals to create a unified Chinese language, especially after the foundation of the Chinese Republic in 1912. If this interest in the construction of a modern national language arrived in China secondhandedly through Japan, Fu and Chen at the institute were eager to apply their firsthand knowledge of European philology to the renewal of Chinese learning. The effort to study local languages and to compile dictionaries was also reproduced by Ueda's student Naoyoshi Ogawa (1869–1947) in Taiwan, then a Japanese colony but the Academia Sinica's new home after 1949. These cases in Japan, in China, and at Fu and Chen's institute all testify to the formidable impact of philology on non-Western scholarship.

Philology, traditional and new, could also, contrarily, serve as a bulwark of traditionalism and nationalism. Japanese nativists supported their cultural essentialism with traditional philology in the eighteenth and nineteenth centuries, and, even more strikingly, the Western-trained Haga argued that modern Japanese literature could be established without relying on imitation of the West. Though internationally minded, Fu and Chen were also motivated by a strong nationalism that resulted from the humiliation of their country by Western powers and Japan, though they differed from conservative intellectuals who resorted to the ideology of national essence *(guocui).* Even today there are philologists in different societies who assert the superiority of their own language and its traditional scholarship.

Both modern and traditional philology, like other disciplines, run the risk of becoming "sterile, ineffectual, and hopelessly irrelevant to life," the kind of scholarship Said criticized in one of his last essays ("The Return to Philology"). From the 1880s on there had been criticism in Germany, the center of European philological scholarship, of the kind of philological work that (according to Fritz Ringer) was characterized by "technical practice" and "endless facts" without "theories" and "ideas." Similar problems can be found in philological work in Taiwan based on the conviction that good philology and history must reject interpretation in order to be scientific and objective, which was further based on the assumption that historical "facts," when adequately arranged, speak the truth by themselves. This assumption was advanced most strongly by, ironically, none other than Fu. His followers continued Fu's scientistic or "positivist" credo, to the extent that they lost sight of the theoretical depth and cultural wealth of the European philology that he advocated. Fu himself never believed that language or literature could exist in linguistic isolation or in a theoretical vacuum; he also offered many theoretical interpretations, even speculations, about the material he worked on. Attention to facts alone cannot suffice, and indeed, it can impoverish humanist research.

For non-Western countries, is modern philology worth celebrating? Wouldn't accepting philology amount to succumbing to Orientalism? Not necessarily. The best antidote to the perils of traditionalism, sterile philology, or even Orientalism seems to be what this book embodies: that is, philology's commitment to historical reflexivity, nonprovinciality, and methodological and conceptual pluralism. They are also the qualities that Sheldon Pollock argues the new philology of the twenty-first century needs. Indeed, even the author of *Orientalism* suggests that there are ways to overcome the limitations of Orientalism, nationalism, traditionalism, and the fixation on words and facts. In Said's terms, a philology-based humanism supports the search for knowledge, justice, and even liberation.

The publication of this book is especially welcome at a time when the Academia Sinica and philology as a discipline are working to give this science a new life. The Academia Sinica has become a very different institution since its relocation to Taiwan in 1949, thanks to political and intellectual developments after World War II. The institution is more diverse, incorporating many more disciplines in the social and natural sciences. It is also more international in terms of the training and the academic activities of its faculty. The society that supports it has gained a new political and cultural identity, in part by securing something the generation of the institute's founders, Fu and Chen, longed for: democracy. Meanwhile, as Pollock shows in the introduction, philology as a scientific discipline has lost its glory in the Western countries where it originated, and the prestige of traditional philology has dwindled in East Asia. The question of the future of philology confronts my institution as seriously as it does practitioners in other parts of the world. Cheng-sheng Tu, accomplished historian and once successor to Fu's position as the director of the institute, has recently called for a search for a new paradigm to replace the old tradition that is now lost. I am pleased that my institution can join the contributors to this book in promoting the study of philology's history as a way of exploring its future. By supporting this book's publication, the Academia Sinica hopes to help infuse new life into philological studies in the new century.

Acknowledgments

A number of the essays in this volume were first presented at the conference "The Global History of Philology," which was organized by the Institute of History and Philology at the Academia Sinica, Taipei, Taiwan, on October 28–29, 2008. The contributors wish to express their gratitude to the host institute, and especially Dr. Fan-Sen Wang, its director then, for its hospitality on that occasion, and to the Chiang Ching-kuo Foundation for its funding for the conference. Several essays in this book were also presented on November 4–5, 2010, at the international conference "Asia in the Early Modern World: Intellectual History in India, China, Japan, Korea, Islam, and Europe," sponsored by the National Institute for Advanced Humanistic Studies at Fudan University, Shanghai. Thanks are also due to Professor Zhaoguang Ge, Director of the Institute.

This book has received generous financial support from Taiwan's Academia Sinica, for which the contributors are deeply grateful. Benjamin A. Elman and Sheldon Pollock received supplemental support from the Andrew W. Mellon Foundation. The editors also wish to thank Sharmila Sen, of Harvard University Press, for her advice and support throughout the publication process; Heather Hughes, also of Harvard University Press, for her diligent oversight; and Leslie Kriesel for her superb editing.

Introduction

SHELDON POLLOCK

THIS COLLECTION of new essays by practicing philologists interested in intellectual history and intellectual historians interested in the practice of philology is the first book to examine the discipline across the vast space and time it has actually occupied. There are undoubtedly difficulties in translating the term "philology" into the idioms of Eurasia's various learned traditions, and these are compounded by the complexities of its conceptual history in the West itself. Yet the problem of how to make sense of texts—the lowest common denominator of philological practice—has been at the heart of those traditions for centuries. Indeed, in a real sense it constitutes the origins of those traditions.

It is the temporal depth and geographical breadth of this problem, with the emergent parallels and differences across cultures—made manifest here by juxtaposition rather than by systematic comparison, which would be premature—that the contributors to this book are concerned in the first instance to delineate. At the same time, a number of us have become increasingly intrigued by the hypothesis that an early modern transformation in philology may be detectable across much of the world; the essays on Song and Qing China, Japan, India, and the Ottoman Empire complement the essay on Renaissance Europe in this regard. This may have begun, according to our still provisional hypothesis, as early as the first quarter of the second millennium; it is in full view almost everywhere by the seventeenth century, when scholars like Benedict de Spinoza in Europe, Melpputtūr Nārāyaṇa Bhaṭṭatīri in India, and Yan Ruoju in China sought actively to transform philological thinking.[1] What additionally concerns us is how to understand the relationship between this early modern philology and its modern academic descendant; how the latter came to be what it now is; how philology has related to adjacent disciplines (or subdisciplines) such as poetics, hermeneutics, and historiography; how all these relations may have changed over time.

In addition to sketching the broader history of philology in various world regions and in particular its development over a long early modern era, whether synthetically or on the basis of a case study of a representative person, text, or problem, this book seeks better answers to, or at least better formulations of, a range of other questions. How coherent in fact is philology as a conceptual category across time and space, or is it impossible to unify without introducing serious distortion in any given tradition? How do we assess philology's relation to other forms of thought, such as scientific or legal thought, and explain the changes in its intellectual status? And—what is perhaps most important, if most elusive—how far may a reconstruction of philological practices in the past relate to a reconstruction of philological practices in the future?

1

The past thirty years have witnessed perhaps the most remarkable attempt in the two centuries since Wilhelm von Humboldt founded the first modern university (in Berlin, 1809–1810) to rethink the order of academic disciplines, which had in fact been largely instituted in Humboldt's day.[2] The self-flagellation of anthropology; the newly announced "death" of comparative literature; the critique of "autistic" economics; the institutional implosion that led to the wholesale disbanding of departments of linguistics; the frontal assault on some of the ruling ideas (or what were taken to be the ruling ideas) of Oriental studies; the insurgency of the so-called perestroika movement in political science; the boundless proliferation of the "studies" phenomenon, from American to women's, with everything in between (cultural, development, ethnic, film, gender . . . strategic and terrorism studies): all these debates and more, including now the digitization of everything, have left our inheritance of the nineteenth-century university in a shambles.

For no discipline, however, has the reversal of fortune been more dramatic and total than for philology, though its fall from grace has extended over a far longer period than that just described. Philology was the queen of the sciences in the nineteenth-century European university, bestriding that world like a colossus in its conceptual and institutional power. It set the standard of what scientific knowledge should be and influenced a range of other disciplines, from anthropology to zoology.[3] Indeed, the philological seminar of late eighteenth-century Germany offered the model for Humboldt's university as a whole.[4] Philology's fall to its current position at the bottom of what might be called the Great Chain of Academic Being has been variously charted, but it can be linked in part to a fissiparous tendency characteristic not only of the growth of knowledge but also of institutional ambition and academic rent-seeking. This occurred over the course of the first half of the twentieth century, when philology's subdisciplinary children, including national literary histories, literary criticism (and later, "theory"), comparative literature, and (kin of more proximate origin) linguistics, believed themselves sufficiently mature to rebel and leave home. What resulted was not just institutional but intellectual fragmentation, which often took (or was thought to take) the form on the one hand of theory without practice—literary studies—and on the other of practice without theory—philology. A second factor in philology's collapse is tied to the first: weakened by subdivision, both philology and its components, instead of hanging together, have now all been hanged alone after the contemporary attack, unprecedented for its depth and extent, on the humanities as representing little more than a market inefficiency in the newly corporatized Western university. Philology does not produce patents, say the administrators; indeed, say the students, what is the point of learning to read well when all you need to know is how to count?[5]

This is not an entirely new story, of course, and not entirely a story of external forces. Humanists in general and philologists in particular have been perceiving, or maybe imagining, a crisis ever since there were humanists and philologists. Think of the "proficient philologist" Ismael Boulliau's pointed declaration in 1657: "The age of criticism and philology has passed and one of philosophy and mathematics has taken its place"; or Robert Burton's broader jeremiad of 1621:

> Our ordinary students . . . apply themselves in all haste to those three commodious [i.e., profitable] professions of law, physic, and divinity, sharing themselves between them, rejecting these arts in the meantime, history, philosophy, philology, or lightly passing them over, as pleasant toys fitting only table-talk, and to furnish them with discourse.[6]

Then too, philologists themselves are partly to blame for their current abasement. If their professional title is now a term of abuse, "what you call the dull boys and girls of the profession,"[7] it is because philologists, worn down by a century of disdain, have in fact become dull. By narrowing their sights to the smallest of questions, the only ones left them thanks to institutional fragmentation, they have nearly turned the discipline's vaunted "rigor" into rigor mortis. But although what we are now observing may have aspects rather of repetition than revolution and may result in part from self-inflicted wounds, recent developments are as worrisome as they are historically unprecedented.

Most alarming is the fact that knowledge of historical languages is being lost globally in a way strikingly similar to the global loss of biological diversity. In India, for example, which as recently as the midnight of freedom from colonial rule in 1947 could boast of world-class academic achievement in dozens of classical literary languages, from Assamese to Kannada and Persian to Telugu, it is today next to impossible to identify scholars who have deep competence in any.[8] The same is increasingly true even in Europe, the first world region to institutionalize the discipline. In 1969, the Romance philologist Erich Auerbach, widely viewed as the consummate practitioner of the discipline in the post–World War II era, warned of the imminent disappearance of philology, describing its loss as "an impoverishment for which there can be no possible compensation."[9] And the situation today bears out his warning, with academic posts in philology—classical, East Asian, Romance, Semitic, South Asian—disappearing in every country in the European Union with every passing year. A small but exemplary case is Syriac—the language that bridged the Greek and Arabic worlds—which is no longer taught anywhere on the continent.

This volume, while unique in other respects, is not the only attempt to provide a perspective on these developments. A small but significant collection of books, journals, and articles has slowly built up over the past few decades that at once intimates this growing mood of insecurity and seeks to offer reassurance through conceptual (if not historical, let alone transregional) rethinking. In 1990—to take the last quarter century or so as our frame of reference—a cross-section of prominent European literary historians, premodern and modern, was assembled to ask what precisely was to be understood by the term "philology," and the very tentativeness of their answers ("impressionistic and ill-informed explanations," said one observer, a caution "how *not* to think about these issues") demonstrates how little serious attention, of a theoretical, self-reflective sort, scholars had been paying up to that point.[10] Indeed, it had been rare, almost undignified, for philologists to pause and reflect, at least in writing, on what philology actually was, how it came to be whatever that was, whether it should continue to be what it was. Even the great Auerbach never did.

In the same year as the question "what is philology?" was finally raised, European medievalists published an important, if more modest and practical, collection proclaiming a "new philology," which has had continuing reverberations in the renewed appreciation of premodern manuscript culture for modern philological practice.[11] But there were grander visions too. In each of the last three decades impassioned calls for a "Return to Philology" have been sounded in essays of that name, though "philology" has been understood so discrepantly—as tropology in the one case, text editing in the second, interpretation in the third—as to entirely belie the uniformity of their purpose.[12] Edited collections with European focus began to appear regularly, including—whether as a sign of the advancement of analysis or its paralysis it is difficult to decide—a recent one on "metaphilology." There have been books that offer new sectional overviews, from a five-volume work of critical studies on the history of classical philology to a series of biographies of Romance philologists ("Auerbach studies" constituting a veritable subfield of its own), as well as appreciations of philology as a whole and in its intersections with other forms of literary theory.[13] Leading journals have dedicated special issues to exploring the discipline, or rather, attempting to discipline a very disparate set of textual practices.[14] The Centre de recherche philologique (also known as L'École de Lille), founded in the 1960s by the Hellenist Jean Bollack, sought to give institutional shape to the particular theory of philology embodied in Bollack's scholarly oeuvre: the tradition of reception was to be actively reconstructed as the framework of reengaged close reading, where "closeness" refers to continuous reflection on the process of understanding while reading. This theory forms the background for Christoph König's chapter in this book and is splendidly realized in his explication of a Rilke poem.[15]

More recently, reflections on such reflections have begun to appear. An edited volume, *Was ist eine philologische Frage?* (What is a philological question?), seeks to shed light on this recent "fascination" with philology by distinguishing three different tendencies.[16] One masks an antitheoretical *ressentiment* among some now reengaging with philology, who show a kind of Schadenfreude over the fall of Big Theory in the course of the last decade and seek a return to that past "rigor" whose very historicity and theoretical grounding remain theoretically and historically opaque to them. A second offers a minimalist understanding of philology as the craft of collecting, editing, and commenting on texts, especially via the use of new technology. A third tendency is maximalist, and aims to rethink the very nature of the discipline, transhistorically and transculturally—the category to which the present collection aspires to be assigned. No explanation is given in the volume, however, for why this last trend has arisen now, since it is not the result of a new theoretical vacuum or of some recent technological innovation. But it cannot be unconnected with the threats to philology noted above, the imperilment of the very capacity to read the languages of the texts philology seeks to understand, and the institutional endangerment—and broader societal disregard and disdain—that constitutes the source of that threat.[17]

2

The fate of philology in the modern Western academy—the quite different stories in India, the Arab world, and China will be touched on in turn—is closely linked with its own sense of its nature and purpose, its disciplinary self-understanding. A close correlation can be observed: the more ambitious philology's intellectual aspirations have been, the more prominent has been its institutional presence—and the reverse. One can chart the history of this correlation, and philology's concomitant rise and fall, from the time it was first understood as a distinct academic discipline.

Philology's emergence as an independent form of knowledge is usually marked by the moment Friedrich August Wolf, future editor and critic of Homer and member of Humboldt's new institution in Berlin, declared on enrolling in the University of Göttingen in 1777 that he was a "philologist" *(studiosus philologiae),* thereby becoming the first official student of the subject in Europe. Things are of course more complicated than this legend suggests, given that a philological seminar had been founded in Germany as early as 1737, and Wolf's teacher himself, the remarkable classicist Christian Gottlob Heyne, was already busy at Göttingen transforming the "classical philology" *(Altphilologie)* of recitation, reconstruction, and disputation into a genuinely historicist and hermeneutical discipline.[18] And this is to say nothing of the philological work of Enlightenment thinkers such as Spinoza, or the Italian humanists before them, let alone the scholars of Alexandria in the third century B.C.E., such as Eratosthenes, who described himself as a *philologos,* uniting and transcending the skills of the *grammatikoi* and the Stoic *kritikoi.* Obviously, the development of the discipline in modern Europe has a conceptual history much longer than its institutional one.

Wolf's importance for disciplinary history lies in his quest to secure the autonomy of philology by separating it from theology. It was no longer to be a mere propaedeutic, but an independent form of knowledge—whereby Wolf confirmed the great emancipatory power of philology, as a critique of authority and a rejection of all metaphysical grounding.[19] Two decades later the Romantic philosopher (and budding Sanskritist) Friedrich Schlegel sketched out, though never published, a remarkable "philosophy of philology" (1797), in which the discipline encompassed far more than Wolf's new triad of grammar, text criticism, and historical analysis. For Schlegel, philology comprises nothing less than "all erudition in language"; it has "an extraordinary and almost immeasurable" extent (indeed, an *ungeheuer,* "monstrous," extent) demanding conceptual limitation.[20] In this Schlegel may have been anticipated by Giambattista Vico, who a half century earlier had claimed (in *New Science,* 1725) that philology comprised not just the "awareness of peoples' languages and deeds" but "the science of everything that depends on human volition: for example, all histories of the languages, customs and deeds of various peoples in both war and peace." But Schlegel's definition aimed to make an epistemological point rather than simply to offer an alternative organization of knowledge.[21] "The philologist ought to philosophize as a philologist," he proclaimed, and the conclusion he drew as a philological philosopher was profound: philology and interpretation as such are identical; interpretation actually precedes and informs all other aspects of philology, including grammar and criticism.[22] The pithiest encapsulation of this grand vision of philology, as not any of its subfields but a kind of total knowledge of human thought as expressed in language, we owe to August Boeckh, student of Wolf and author of the much-quoted but now little read *Encyclopedia and Methodology of All the Philological Sciences* (1877, but containing material from possibly as early as 1809). Philology for Boeckh is "knowing what has been known," or "(re-)cognizing [what the human mind has produced—that is] what has already been cognized."[23] Disciplinary self-understanding of this magnitude, found in Wolf, Schlegel, Boeckh, and others (most prominently Wilhelm Dilthey)—a topic examined here in Constanze Güthenke's chapter—undoubtedly correlated with philology's ability to achieve the kind of academic dominance mentioned earlier.

In the later decades of the nineteenth century scholars began to descend from these lofty heights toward a more modest, and reasonable, middle ground. For Nietzsche, the most visionary and critical philologist of his age, philology was the practice of "slow reading": "the leisurely art of the goldsmith applied to language," and thus "the highest attraction and incitement in an age of 'work,'" where getting things done at once is all that matters: "Philology itself, perhaps, will not 'get things done' so hurriedly: it teaches how to read well." What precisely "reading well" meant was a question that preoccupied Nietzsche throughout his life. He came to see it, as Schlegel did, as a style of hermeneutics above all, but one more critically and reflexively conceived than Schlegel's. As he described it in one of his last published works, philology is *ephexis,* constraint (or restraint), in interpretation, the means by which we learn to guard ourselves both from falsification and from the impulse to abandon caution, patience, and subtlety in the effort to understand. And this pertains not just to reading the Greek or Latin classics, but "whether one be dealing with books, with newspaper reports, with the most fateful events or with weather statistics, not to mention the 'salvation of the soul.'"[24] Peter Szondi, perhaps the last great self-professed theorist in this tradition of hermeneutical philology (he died in 1971), restricted its scope yet further, to the form of knowledge specific to literary texts.[25]

The abandonment of this strong middle ground in a march to the bottom began already in the early twentieth century, signaled most prominently by the long entry on "philology" in the eleventh edition of the *Encyclopedia Britannica* written by the American Sanskritist and protolinguist W. D. Whitney. Notwithstanding his almost Vico-like definition of the discipline as "that branch of knowledge which deals with human speech, and with all that speech discloses as to the nature and history of man," Whitney concerned himself in his exposition (and throughout his life) exclusively with "the instrumentality of [thought's] expression," that is, language, while entirely ignoring "the thought expressed," that is, literature and other forms of textuality.[26] And in this he was fully representative of historic developments under way.

Now that it was split down the middle in the manner scholars like Whitney demanded—however impoverished (if even possible) may be the study of literature without language and the reverse—the grand nineteenth-century mansion of philology was soon to see one of its "two principal divisions" expropriated by the new science of linguistics.[27] The other was quickly carved up and seized, all the most desirable rooms, by those new subdisciplines: national literary histories, comparative literature, and more recently literary theory. What was left was turned into a tenement and rented out to a congeries of regional or national philology departments (East Asian, Middle Eastern, Romance, Slavic, South Asian, and of course English and classics), with worse quarters given to those thought to be lower on the cultural-evolutionary scale. It is hardly surprising, in consequence of all this fragmentation—to say nothing of the stains philology incurred from its contributions, however forcible and *unphilological* they may have been, to nineteenth- and twentieth-century nationalism and racialism[28]—that philology should have been so thoroughly denigrated and brought to its present nadir. To the degree it even remains alive today in the eyes of outsiders—a "protohumanistic empirical science . . . that no longer exists as such," according to one observer, no doubt speaking for many—philology leads a pale, ghostly existence. All it has left are the fragments others have left behind: text criticism, bibliography, historical grammar, corpus linguistics. As a disciplinary category it is used in common parlance to refer almost exclusively to the study of the Greek and Latin classics—though even Classics itself has finally repudiated the association.[29]

The claims of philology outside of the West have largely followed the history just recounted, especially wherever colonialism worked to predetermine that history by importing and enforcing Western presuppositions. In South Asia, the study of historical languages underwent thorough, if uneven, Europeanization. This started in the latter half of the nineteenth century, with British (as well as German) scholars staffing the colleges and universities founded in midcentury, and inculcating British (and German) philological notions, but of an ever-limited sort. Before long Indians, almost all of them students of Sanskrit, were being trained in England (and Germany; rarely in France and the United States) in the text criticism of Karl Lachmann (and never that of Joseph Bédier). This they often applied, with considerable acuity, to Indian works, though not always in a way sensitive to the lives of Indic texts, which, given the persistence of orality, vast circulation of manuscripts, and unbroken vitality of tradition, often show dramatic differences from those of Greek and Latin.[30] They also wrote new forms of literary criticism, profoundly shaped by Romantic standards, and new literary histories, profoundly shaped by European national narratives. This whole style of philological scholarship, of both the more capacious and the narrower sort, had little continuity with precolonial practices, which were largely ignored anyhow except for the printing of premodern commentaries.

That such Europeanization was uneven can be observed in vernacular language scholarship. In their text criticism scholars often continued older practices of selecting the best manuscript and noting occasional variants, with very little explicit theorization. Exemplary is the career of the Tamil scholar U. V. Swaminatha Iyer (Caminataiyar, 1855–1942). Without exposure to Western philological methods when he made his spectacular discovery of the corpus of ancient Tamil literature, he edited according to principles largely derived from tradition (inventing others as he proceeded), while being stimulated, though in a way less easy to trace, by the "science of nationality" model of contemporary European philology.[31] One is reminded of the procedures of the Italian humanists, who (as Anthony Grafton remarks in his essay here) "did not devise their practices *de novo,* as a whole, but worked them out on the fly," while deriving "substantial elements of their methodology from the ancient texts they read and taught." In Tamil, however, as in all other vernacular philologies of South Asia, the general tendencies noted earlier have ultimately prevailed. With the loss of its social and institutional context, engagement with historical languages has faded to the vanishing point or, where still in existence, has ceded almost entirely to a descriptive linguistic model,[32] or been reduced to ethnochauvinism and nationalism.

Trends somewhat dissimilar to those in South Asia are visible in the twentieth-century Islamic world, where the liveliness of philological reflection is to some extent to be explained by the dominance of religious textuality (especially hadith) in everyday life. A large number of philology manuals were produced in Egypt, for example, sparked by lectures of the German scholar Gotthelf Bergstraesser in 1931–1932; these compare Western and traditional methods, favoring sometimes the putative scientificity of the former, sometimes the cultural normativity of the latter. Thus, in some cases older practices were continued; in others, Europeanized styles of philology came to dominate. Mehdi Mohaghegh in Iran and the Ottoman (later Syrian-Egyptian) scholar Muhammad Zahid al-Kawthari produced superb editions by continuing some of the practices outlined in works like al-Dīn al-Ghazzī's sixteenth-century treatise on the "proper manner of perusing books" (described in Khaled El-Rouayheb's chapter), typically choosing one manuscript as the basic text and supplementing it as needed with others. Juxtaposed to these were scholars such as Ihsan ʿAbbas (Lebanon), Saʾid Nafisi (Iran), and Ahmed Atesh (Turkey), who for the most part were trained by French or German scholars. Even more significant than questions of the presence (or absence) of the past in modern philology is the scope of that philology: the excitement in the first half of the twentieth century at rediscovering the literary and historical works that had fallen out of the late-medieval syllabus has given way in the present to stark traditionalization and sectarianization, with Shiites publishing only Shiite works, Saudis Salafi works, and so on.[33]

An exception to this general tendency is found in East Asia, unsurprisingly to the degree we attribute causal force to colonialism in the transformation of preexisting philological tradition. In China (despite Marxism and Maoism) and Taiwan (though colonized by Japan), modern scholarship has shown considerable continuity with the doctrine of evidential studies in the Qing, which was developed to gainsay the hermeneutics promoted in the Song (discussed in the essays of Benjamin A. Elman and Michael Lackner, respectively), whereby scholars avoid theoretical speculation and continue to accept traditional authority. At the same time, intellectual historians have been expanding the domain of what counts as philological inquiry by assessing Chinese exegesis as hermeneutics, emphasizing the role of commentaries, or reconnecting earlier philology to its social and political contexts.[34]

Japan presents a rather similar picture of continuity (as Susan Burns shows in her chapter). When first encountering European philology, early twentieth-century Japanese scholars counterposed to its new theories and methods those appropriated from their own past, especially the so-called nativist philology (*kokugaku,* literally, "our country's learning") of the eighteenth-century scholar Motoori Norinaga, who argued that the earliest literature had to be read, both grammatically and conceptually, as pure expressions of the Japanese world, entirely devoid of Chinese influence. (There are substantial ironies in this doctrine, given that Japanese nativists were getting their philological ideals from the Japanese Confucians, who were accessing the philological works of Qing China.) In Japan, Taiwan, and now the People's Republic of China, philological studies continue to command remarkable prestige and academic preferment in traditional scholarship. The post-Maoist appeal to the Qing philologists' slogan "To search truth from facts" now graces the title of the lead Communist Party journal, once called "Red Flag." At all events, it is clear that the history of Westernization in philology, in both its intellectual substance and its institutional fate, was uneven across the non-West, and contingent to a large extent on the force of colonialism and other paths of modernization.

3

The current threat to the institutional survival of philology in most places and its vastly diminished disciplinary self-understanding; the need to understand the history of these factors in the modern world and their variability across regions; and, last, the urgency to frame some kind of response, are among the factors that have inspired this book project. But we have also been driven by a far more basic, even innocent question: What has philology been over time and space, in the rest of the world no less than in Europe, and before the modern era just surveyed? Given the densely tangled history sketched above of the notion of "philology" in the West, compounded by the built-in problems of translation in the widest, most conceptually challenging sense of that term, globalizing the intellectual history of philology and the history of its practices is no simple matter.

One of the purposes of this book is precisely to explore the diversity and complexity of philological phenomena across time and space. The editors began their inquiry expecting neither that global intellectual history would turn out to be completely homogeneous nor that it would inherently resist all synthesis. We started instead from the assumption that our presentation of philology must comprise as wide as possible a sample of the reading practices discernible in history, and that these practices, to the degree they exhibit family resemblances, should be grouped into the same category; that "philology," accordingly, might constitute a single coherent object of analysis. But we were prepared to abandon hopes for such coherence and pluralize our object—and, as a concession, to entitle the book "World Philologies"—if it were to disintegrate under historical scrutiny.

From surveying the various definitions of philology in the West over the past two centuries, we have gained a sense of the shifting shape of the discipline, and some remarkable parallels with that history from elsewhere in the world are offered in this book. One apparently intractable problem, however, is that, whereas every textual tradition has developed practices no one would hesitate to include in the category "philology" however variously we define it, a comparable covering term is not always available in traditions outside the Greek and Roman. Some do come close: *ṣināʿat al-adab,* "the art of literary culture," in early Abbasid lands; *kaozheng,* or "evidential scholarship," in late imperial China; and *kokugaku,* "national studies," in early modern Japan combine many of those concerns into a single category that also includes a second-order reflection on how philology is to be done. But if elsewhere we have difficulty locating this sort of integral conceptual object, we nonetheless always find parts of what we can readily understand as, precisely, parts of philology: concern with problems of grammar and usage, with the history of manuscript (or printed) sources and their discrepant readings, and with problems of interpretation.

In the Hellenistic tradition, the concepts of edition *(ekdosis)* and of variant (*graphe;* the now-common Latin term *varia lectio* dates only to the Renaissance) were explicitly enunciated (as Franco Montanari shows in his chapter) and formed the core of what, in various times and places in Europe, would come to be called *philologia.* The term is famously foregrounded in Martianus Capella's fable of the marriage of Mercury and Philologia (recounted here by James Zetzel), but already we face complications, for Martianus Capella's philology, whose handmaids were the seven liberal arts (grammar, dialectic, and the rest), was not that of the Hellenists, who were restricted to the purely text-critical side of the discipline. If such nominalization is elusive in other traditions outside those already noted, the kinds of practices themselves that both Greek and Latin philology comprised are richly attested. Consider Persian or Sanskrit learning in the seventeenth century. It was precisely for the purpose of *ekdosis* though an analysis of *variae lectiones* that ʿAbd al-Laṭīf of Gujarat collected manuscripts of Rūmī's *Mathnavī* (discussed by Muzaffar Alam in his chapter) or, a few decades later and a few thousand miles eastward, Nīlakaṇṭha Caturdhara gathered manuscripts for his edition of the *Mahābhārata,* India's great epic (described by Sheldon Pollock in his chapter). If no term for "philology" is specifically employed, this is certainly what ʿAbd al-Laṭīf would have understood by the cluster of notions he names *muqābala* (comparison, collation), *taṣḥīḥ* (correction), and *tanqīḥ* (purging, inquiry), and Nīlakaṇṭha by the process he describes as "gathering many manuscripts from different regions" and "critically establishing the best readings." That neither of these scholars had a word, let alone a theory, for the philological enterprise as a whole—and that neither tells us any more about their methods than the Latin commentators described by Zetzel—may be surprising, but it is considerably less significant for intellectual history than the fact of their enterprise itself.

We have seen how the scope of philology expanded in Europe in the late eighteenth century, moving beyond *Altphilologie* to become, for Schlegel, the very science of criticism itself, of understanding the world mediated by language. The struggle over the scope of philology, between what at one extreme is essentially the historical study of individual vocables and at the other "all erudition in language," would take on specific contours in nineteenth-century Germany with the controversy between *Wortphilologie,* or the philology of words (promoted by the classicist Gottfried Hermann), and *Sachphilologie,* or the philology of things (promoted by the classicist August Boeckh).[35] But we can observe something like this tension in many other times and places, despite the fact that different terms of debate (and sometimes no explicit terms at all) were used. A case in point is offered by the early Arabic intellectual tradition (examined by Beatrice Gruendler in her chapter), where the battle lines were clearly drawn between grammar and literary criticism. The former was represented by the scholars of the Qurʾān (and of the pre-Islamic poetry they collected in order to illuminate its sometimes obscure language—an early and quite astonishing instance of linguistic ethnography) and hence of the high Arabic language *(ʿarabiyya)*. The latter was embodied in the patrons, readers as well as poets, of the "new poetry" of the early Abbasid period. But it is also entirely plausible to reframe this struggle as a contest over the scope of philology, how to evaluate and hierarchize the modalities of textual understanding—and of course, how to evaluate and hierarchize those whose job it is to produce such understanding. Especially striking is how these antithetical views were finally "aufgehoben" and synthesized in a new, more capacious discipline that actually integrated linguistic and literary knowledge: the "art of philology" *(ṣināʿat al-adab)* or "the literary arts" *(al-ʿulūm al-adabiyya),* the latter of which even included creative writing. Here we are directed toward an even richer conception of the discipline that includes what might be called the study of "authorial philology."

With that phrase we point to the integration of philological knowledge or principles into the very production of a text—how, in other words, the presuppositions employed by scholars for editing and interpreting texts come to be used by authors for creating them. The Hebrew tradition provides a striking example of this that speaks at the same time to the more general nature of its philological project. Early Hebrew intellectual history shows remarkably little concern with questions of the grammar of the Bible or even its textual transmission, whether written or oral. Scholars were focused exclusively on the problem of interpretation, above all the resolution of inconsistencies and contradictions in a text that was viewed as perfect and "omnisignificant" (as Yaakov Elman characterizes it here), and that, equally important, was held to be a source of knowledge of law. Understanding the Bible was a matter of understanding what it asks the reader *to do* and not just *to know.* (Here Hebrew exegesis bears a striking resemblance to other hermeneutical philologies, especially Roman law and what in India is known as Mīmāṃsā, the discipline of interpreting the sentences of the Vedas that eventually became the exegetical science of Indian jurisprudence.) This sort of early Hebrew philology became "authorial" when its assumptions informed the very composition of texts like the book of Chronicles, which is constructed precisely in a way that aims to reconcile the contradictions and explain the inconsistencies that mark sections of the Pentateuch.

In East Asia, by contrast, the primary impetus for and focus of the philology of ancient texts were presented by the peculiar puzzles thrown up by

Chinese and Japanese script, especially in the early modern period when these puzzles were intensified by historical caesuras and the new historicism, so to call it, that they provoked. Scholars in the late Ming (1368–1644) and early Qing (1644–1911) concluded (as detailed by Benjamin A. Elman here) that they had lost the empire to barbarians (the Manchus) because they failed to read the classics properly. In order to solve old problems of unintelligibility they set about devising new philological principles (the groundwork for this cleansing philology was, however, laid in the Song-Yuan era, 1000–1350, which Michael Lackner discusses in his chapter). In the early Tokugawa period Japanese scholars, following interactions with Confucian China and Korea via books and manuscripts, took up Japan's earliest texts with the aim of reconciling them with the metaphysics of Song thinkers—and eventually, of establishing their cultural autonomy. But they too were confronted with a veritable "linguistic labyrinth" (as Burns calls it), and to negotiate it philology proved crucial.

In many ways the Sanskrit tradition of India presents counterpoints to all these tendencies. No term was ever coined that comprised all the disparate textual practices so highly developed in that culture, including grammar, phonetics, prosody, lexicography, poetics and tropology, and hermeneutics (as well as the text criticism already illustrated by Nīlakaṇṭha's editorial work). No irreconcilable conceptions or principles ever divided grammarians and literary critics; all textual specialists were schooled in all the philological arts. Texts (at least culturally important texts) were recopied over the generations in ever-modernizing scripts, or passed down orally, so that no gulf between writing and reading ever developed. Texts that could not be recopied, or were thought unworthy of recopying, or were not transmitted orally did become illegible. Inscriptions in the Brahmi script, for example, including the Asokan edicts of the third century B.C.E. that mark the start of Indian literacy, remained illegible to Indians for a millennium (until the British civil servant James Prinsep deciphered them in 1836). But no one seems to have been much concerned with this loss, not even the Buddhists, who had appropriated Asoka in their legends. Other ancient languages that had no cultural or religious base gradually became more or less illegible too, such as Prakrit outside of the Jain community (for which Prakrit, in one of its registers at least, was the medium of scripture).

Thus, absence of nomenclature is neither as surprising nor as consequential for a global history of philology as it may appear at first glance. Sometimes, as it seems necessary to argue in the case of the Sanskrit tradition—where the arts of language played the foundational role in intellectual life that mathematics played in Greece—philology may have so permeated the thought world that it did not need to be, or perhaps could not be, identified through a separate conceptual category. Sometimes, moreover, the creation of a technical term or second-order discourse would appear to be a function of specific social conditions of possibility. Consider in this regard the theorization of, and indeed the very term, "translation." Despite the fact that in India, to stay with that case, there is evidence of frequent and varied translation into and out of Sanskrit and other languages, we find no reflection on the practice in any South Asian intellectual tradition before colonialism (even in the Indo-Persian world, despite the massive translation project undertaken by the early Mughal court), not even the terms by which to describe it. In Europe, by contrast, translation did become an object of analysis in its own right, but only in the Renaissance and only owing to the pressure of new institutional forces. It was restrictions imposed by the Church on producing new versions of the Bible, Latin or vernacular, that prompted Erasmus in the early sixteenth century to explain not just his purpose in retranslating the New Testament but his methods and very concept of translation (he wanted, inter alia, to make the text *latinius,* "more Latin," than the Vulgate).

Analogously, people might simply engage in an array of philological practices until for one or another institutional or political reason they are forced to explicitly conceptualize as a totality what they are doing. This occurred in the German university world, where Wolf, as earlier noted, was led to invent the discipline of "philology" in 1777 because he needed to declare an academic major; or, more grandly, in China in the mid-seventeenth century, when Ming intellectuals, confronted with the fall of the empire, developed "evidentiary scholarship" to ensure proper reading of the classics lest the texts ever fail them again. But philology pre-exists such conceptualization, since—at least the evidence of this book suggests this conclusion—wherever there are texts there is philology in some sense, both readerly and authorial. Had we more time and space we could have shown the evidence of such preconceptualized, or underconceptualized, philology in everything from Babylonian and Assyrian text commentaries at the beginning of the first millennium B.C.E. to the hip-hop corpus analyses of today.

4

This volume begins with the Hellenistic age since, obvious historical and cultural differences between ancient philology and the modern conception notwithstanding, the foundations of philology in the West, at least as a scientific discipline of text criticism, were laid during that period, from the third to the first century B.C.E. As Franco Montanari argues, it was first the practices of book production, especially correction of manuscripts, that eventually transformed into the practices of philology: the corrector of a copy of Homer became, in time, the corrector, or editor, of Homer. How exactly the Alexandrian critics went about their business, whether by comparison of sources or pure conjecture, is a question that has divided Hellenists for generations.

Essential for intellectual history, however, is the invention of the two key concepts mentioned earlier: *ekdosis* and *varia lectio.* The idea of *ekdosis* was fundamentally defining the correct text of a work as such, overcoming and correcting the differences found to exist between the copies in circulation. The basis for this approach was to compare different exemplars of a given text and to choose the reading held to be the correct one. This was indeed put into practice, albeit within the limits imaginable for a process that was still in its infancy. But it would be a mistake to view the whole issue as a matter of quantity, either of the copies subjected to comparison or of the readings examined comparatively, or of the quality of the results obtained. What is essential to recognize is the historical importance of the underlying principle: the realization that a text needed to be cleansed of the defects inflicted on it by the very manuscript tradition through which it had been preserved, and that in order to achieve this it was necessary to assemble suitable tools and techniques (which gradually became consolidated and enriched over time). This intellectual innovation laid the basis for text philology as it has developed in the West over the following two millennia.

The evidence for how Romans thought about understanding texts falls into two broad classes: remarks found in ancient commentaries and the like, and the actual manuscripts. These two sets of evidence hardly ever overlap; only rarely can we perceive any influence of discussions of textual problems on the transmitted texts. In his chapter James Zetzel concentrates on the evidence found in the commentaries on and *paradosis* of the two most widely read and discussed school authors, Virgil and Cicero. He asks, first, how ancient scholars went about assessing the correctness of the manuscripts in which they read literary texts, and, second, what they actually did to such texts. (Did they alter texts in accordance with their critical beliefs, for example?) While grammarians took a very radical and interventionist stance in their theory, they were extraordinarily conservative in their actions. If we contrast ancient philological techniques with those of Christian philology in the fourth and fifth centuries, we can see the relationship between the worth ascribed to texts and the willingness of scholars to alter them: the more important "truth" was, the less cautious scholars were in correcting it.

In the Hebrew tradition, which Yaakov Elman analyzes here, the dominant form of philology, the chief concern of rabbinic scholarship, was interpretation, not grammar or transmission. While the earliest rabbinic work, formally speaking, is the Mishnah (early third century C.E.), it and other works of the third through fifth centuries contain teachings that date to the second century B.C.E., as has been confirmed by anti-Pharisaic polemics recorded in the Dead Sea Scrolls and the book of Jubilees; thus the most continuous Jewish philological tradition for which we have records is the rabbinic one. However, its roots can be found in the Bible itself, with later books commenting on earlier ones—the "authorial philology," as described above, of the sort found in Chronicles.

By the second century C.E., two trends in biblical philology had emerged: a striving to make every jot and tittle of the biblical text meaningful ("omnisignificance"), which often involved ignoring what was called "the plain meaning" of the text, and the striving to understand the biblical or even rabbinic texts in a somewhat more restrained way, which animates the Aramaic translations of the Bible. Another constraint surfaces in rabbinic interpretation of legal texts: the need to make them conform with current circumstances, practices, conceptions, or values. Generally speaking, plain-sense interpretation remained the province of those charged with the determination of legal and ritual requirements, that is, the writers of *responsa* and codes. In regard to biblical interpretation and exposition, however, homiletic approaches of various sorts remained the preferred methods.

In the Arabic tradition, which would come to exercise such profound influence on both Hebrew and Persian scholarship, philology in the sense of the linguistic sciences (*naḥw,* "grammar," and *lugha,* "lexicography") constituted the first scientific approach to Arabic poetry, which it used as data in the project of codifying the high Arabic language *(ʿarabiyya)* during the early Abbasid dynasty (late eighth and ninth centuries C.E.). This earned Arabic philologists status in both scholarship and society. But during the same period, as Beatrice Gruendler shows, poetry itself evolved aesthetically, revisiting old models in unconventional ways and adopting a rhetorical style and daring imagery. As a result, philologists no longer accepted it as sufficiently pure for their purposes; they did not understand its intricacies, and they voiced (at times disingenuous) criticism of contemporary poets. The "new style" *(badīʿ)* found instead admirers among the elite (scribes, courtiers, and the aristocracy), where the first poetics of this style arose, before poetics emancipated itself as an independent discipline. But the tension between the old philology and poetics was only temporary. By the twelfth century, poetics and the composition of poetry were integrated into what came to be defined as the "philological arts" *(al-ʿulūm al-adabiyya),* though a century later poetics would again be incorporated, within the branch of rhetoric *(balāgha),* into a standard theory of language.

We enter a rather unfamiliar world when we consider Song-Yuan China and the two different philological techniques it evinces. One, typified in Zhang Zai (1020–1078), is a hermeneutic approach to the Chinese classics; the other is found in diagrammatic interpretations of canonical writings. According to Michael Lackner, whereas the former was characterized by rewriting the classics through the innovative form of a mosaic, the latter invented visual tools to elucidate the syntactic and semantic structure of crucial passages and texts.

Philology in traditional India found its most sophisticated theoretical expression in two independent disciplines, grammar and hermeneutics, both fully matured by the end of the first millennium B.C.E. Indian philological practice, however, is manifest most distinctively in commentarial writing. Sheldon Pollock charts the historical contours of commentary on literary and scriptural texts, a remarkably late invention, relatively speaking, of the early second millennium, and an obscure one in terms of its historical conditions of possibility. Sanskrit commentary embodies every dimension of philology discussed so far, though never is any such discipline named, let alone constituted as a distinctive form of knowledge. What exactly it meant to edit and to read a text in premodern India are interesting questions for intellectual history; but do the answers have any bearing on the development of a truly critical renewal of the discipline? The consequences of the philology of India in the past for Indian philology in the future is a subject we are only beginning to explore.

Between 1400 and 1650 the multiple textual traditions of Western Europe underwent radical changes. The rise of secular schools and libraries and the introduction of printing transformed the conditions of textual study. The Reformation and Counter-Reformation revolutionized biblical studies. Texts and traditions about which Western scholars had known relatively little, and that indirectly—Greek and Jewish ones in particular, but Islamic and others as well—became directly accessible. Anthony Grafton recounts this history, describing the principal tools that scholars developed as they tried to understand, master, and explicate these textual traditions. In particular—in an early instance of the importance of the history of philology for the practice of philology—he differentiates between the tools that scholars derived from the textual traditions themselves and the new ones that they devised as they confronted a transformed world of canons and texts.

Few episodes in world philology provide a more exact parallel to the model of classical textual criticism and exegesis than what we find among some scholars of Persian literature in Mughal India, specifically the seventeenth and eighteenth centuries, a period of extraordinary yet previously unstudied innovation. These practices, which, as noted earlier, included the editing *(taṣḥīḥ)* of literary texts and the composition of commentaries *(tahshiya wa tashrih),* are examined by Muzaffar Alam with special reference to a remarkable edition of the *Mathnavī* of Jalāl al-Dīn Rūmī (d. 1273) prepared in the mid-seventeenth century by ʿAbd-al-Latif ʿAbbasi of Gujarat. We possess not only the scholar's edition but also an autobiographical account of his tireless travels through the Islamic world in search of manuscripts of the text. This is a world of philology with deep linkages among family, learning, literature, and Mughal service, which parallels very closely the situation elsewhere in the period, especially in imperial China.

Philology in the largest sense, as we saw, is about the practices of reading as such. And in Ottoman scholarly culture of the early modern period these practices were subject for the first time to careful analysis, as can be observed in a manual examined by Khaled El-Rouayheb on "the proprieties of studying" written by an Ottoman polymath of the seventeenth century. El-Rouayheb situates this manual synchronically as well as diachronically by relating it both to seventeenth-century Ottoman scholastic culture and to what Franz Rosenthal in a classic work called "the technique and approach of Muslim scholarship" in earlier centuries.

The historical and philological consequences of evidential research studies *(kaozheng xue)* in late imperial China (1600–1800), which Benjamin A. Elman explores, contributed to the emergence, in the decades of the late Qing and early republic (1890–1930), of a virulent form of cultural iconoclasm and revolution that saw its roots, hence its legitimacy, in earlier studies. But such perspectives misrepresent the actual motives that Qing scholars clearly laid out in their own writings. In the end, the scholarly intentions and cultural consequences of evidential research are analytically distinct. As literati scholars, they remained committed to classical ideals. Representing the last great native movement in Confucian letters, they sought to restore the classical visions of state and society. The early modern consequences of their cutting-edge philology, however, yielded to a corrosive modern decanonization and delegitimation that went beyond the intellectual limits they had imposed on their own writings.

The intellectual movement in eighteenth-century Japan known as *kokugaku* took up the philological examination of the earliest texts written in Japan, most significantly the mytho-history known as the *Kojiki* and the poetic anthology the *Man'yōshū.* Both works date from the early eighth century, before the emergence of *kana,* or the Japanese syllabaries, and thus are written entirely in Chinese characters, using styles of inscription that were later abandoned. As Susan Burns explains, the *kokugaku* scholars (or "nativists," as they have come to be named) argued that correct reading of the early texts was the key to understanding what they conceived of as an original Japan that had existed before the influence of Chinese culture in the form of language, texts, ideas, and institutions. The nativist movement of the eighteenth century is explained by focusing on the work of the scholar Motoori Norinaga. In his groundbreaking study of the *Kojiki,* Motoori argued that the ancient text was fully readable as Japanese, and that it recorded intact ancient transmissions from the age of the deities and thus revealed Japan's original culture. Although Motoori's work was challenged by later nativist thinkers, in the modern period scholars of the new discipline of national literature made him a model for students of "classical studies" and "textual studies." Only in the postwar era have the ideological underpinnings of Motoori's work come under scrutiny.

As noted earlier, in nineteenth-century Germany, philology, especially classical philology, achieved unprecedented institutional dominance. To a degree this success can be attributed to the quality of philological scholarship itself, of course, but, as Constanze Güthenke shows, equally if not more important were the major programmatic works—those of Friedrich Schlegel, Friedrich Schleiermacher, and Wilhelm Dilthey, in particular—that argued for philology as the foundation of the science of interpretation. The models of disciplinarity and the institutional practices championed by German classical philology were eventually exported across disciplines and national cultural systems. But so were the contradictions, or at least tensions, inherent in these models, between, for example, empirical depth and conceptual breadth, the particular and the universal, and scientificity and creativity. The problems and possibilities of philology in the age of Romanticism thus remain, in many ways, the problems and possibilities of philology as such.

That philology can be a source of some of the most creative thinking about literary interpretation is demonstrated in Christoph König's chapter, in which he examines what a theory of philological practice might look like today, with an analysis of a sonnet by the modern German poet Rainer Maria Rilke. The philological practice of attributing meaning to literary texts should be examined historically, he argues, in viewing conflicts of interpretations within the discipline's European tradition of scholarship, and systematically, within a hermeneutic tradition. The main question he raises is how to reinterpret the term "philology" if the aim is to master the métier and to "understand" the individual text at the same time.

The book concludes with Ku-ming Kevin Chang's study of the different trajectories of philological developments in Germany and Anglo-French countries. Linguistics, or *linguistique,* as the science of living languages was an Anglo-French reaction to the dominance of German philology, which excelled in the study of written languages. He investigates the context in which these two intellectual forces were introduced simultaneously to the most successful institution of Chinese history and languages in the first half of the twentieth century, the Institute of History and Philology at Academia Sinica, by scholars who had solid training in both Western and Chinese scholarship.

On the evidence offered by the essays in this book, then, its title seems entirely justified: terminological dilemmas notwithstanding, we can legitimately speak of philology in the singular as a unitary global field of knowledge. If we were to redefine philology in a way that most closely corresponds to that historical phenomenology and captures its true capaciousness, we would think of it most simply as the discipline of making sense of texts, whatever sense we may wish to attribute to "sense," and however much the corpus of "texts" to be included in this discipline may change over time. Philology is neither the theory of language (that is now the domain of linguistics) nor the theory of truth (that is philosophy), but the theory of textuality as well as the history of textualized meaning. If philosophy is thought critically reflecting on itself, then philology may be seen as the critical self-reflection on language.[36] Under this description, and with the materials offered in this book, we recognize that philology has been at once as historically deep as any other form of systematic knowledge and as global as language itself. Both in theory and in practice across time and space, accordingly, it would seem to merit the same centrality among the disciplines as philosophy or mathematics.

If this is not the place philology occupies in today's university, the university of tomorrow may look different. The decades-long critique of disciplines may finally be gaining traction, to the degree that recent attempts at reconstruction, reform, or renewal of the university made all over the world—most prominently in China, India, and the European Union, but also in the United States—while often prompted by market imperatives, actually aim to produce a new, truly global institution. What are the minimal requirements that successful applicants for admission to the twenty-first-century temple of disciplinarity will have to meet in order to qualify as core knowledge forms? One is historical self-awareness. Twenty-first-century disciplines cannot remain arrogantly indifferent, as the teleological social sciences often appear to be, to their own historicity, constructedness, and changeability—this is an epistemic necessity, not a moral one—and accordingly, the humbling force of genealogy must be part and parcel of every disciplinary practice. Another is nonprovinciality. Disciplines can no longer be merely local forms of knowledge that pass as universal under the mask of science; instead, they must emerge from a new global, and by preference globally comparative, episteme and seek global, and by preference globally comparative, knowledge. A third requirement is methodological and conceptual pluralism. Understanding by what means and according to what criteria scholars in past eras have grounded their truth claims must be part of our own understanding of what truth is, and a key dimension of what we might call our epistemic politics.

No aspirant for inclusion in the twenty-first-century disciplinary order could satisfy these historical, global, and methodological-conceptual requirements better than a renewed philology. Philology, as these essays demonstrate, is constitutively concerned with the history of its own practices; transregional in its existence, and, in its modern Western avatar, comparative in its objects of study, perhaps the first systematically comparative discipline;[37] and based squarely on the confrontation with multiple forms of understanding. If, like mathematics, philology is a method, it is also, like mathematics, a discipline, aiming—or having the as yet untapped potential to aim—toward "analytic perspectives that disaggregate complex phenomena into potential general variables, relationships, and causal mechanisms," and able to grow in intellectual, hence institutional, strength the greater the historical scope of operation it is encouraged to embrace.[38]

One of the more disabling constraints on the creation of a new philological disciplinary formation is that, while philology may historically have been as global as language itself, that very fact, far from stimulating the research and writing it would seem to merit, has gone largely unregistered. For most parts of the world almost nothing substantial has been produced that would enable students to develop a global appreciation of this history, to know how philology has made our world, not just in Europe but everywhere. Once we begin to appreciate its vast historical life—and this book could easily have had a companion volume of studies of philology in Mesopotamia (where it may in fact have begun),[39] Egypt, Africa, medieval Latin Europe, vernacular India, Korea, Southeast Asia—we will see that philology has been everywhere that texts have been, indeed, in a way we have yet to fully grasp, everywhere that language has been. It is the project of charting the life of this sort of philology in all its various manifestations that this book aims to initiate.

From Book to Edition

Philology in Ancient Greece

FRANCO MONTANARI

The Birth of Philology in the Hellenistic Age

THE SCIENTIFIC discipline that for many centuries has been known by the name of "philology" is believed to have first arisen in Greece during the Hellenistic age, that is to say, over the period from the third to the first century B.C.E. This view recurs with some regularity in studies and overviews of the history of philology, and can be said in general to represent an established and accepted fact.[1] When, however, we seek to define its exact meaning and limits, above all in relation to philology (not only classical) in the modern age, a number of problems arise and nonnegligible divergences come to light.

From a historical perspective, we may speak, in this regard, of the Alexandrian scholars and the Alexandrian period (early Hellenistic age) as the essential and decisive stage, which began under the reigns of Ptolemy I Soter (305–283 B.C.E.) and Ptolemy II Philadelphus (285–246 B.C.E.) and extended up to the second century B.C.E., centering on Alexandria with its institutions (chiefly the Library and the Museum) and its remarkable cultural ferment. The major personalities were Zenodotus of Ephesus (c. 325–260), Eratosthenes of Cyrene (c. 280–195), Aristophanes of Byzantium (c. 260–185), Aristarchus of Samothrace (c. 215–144), and the great scholar-poets Callimachus (c. 310–240) and Apollonius Rhodius (c. 300–220). The second century B.C.E. also saw the rise of the kingdom and city of Pergamum, which became a flourishing cultural center and rivaled Alexandria, also excelling in the field of philology and text interpretation: the figure of one of the greatest Pergamene representatives, Crates of Mallos,[2] is usually mentioned for his controversies with Aristarchus, the "supreme authority as critic and interpreter" of the Alexandrian school.[3]

A second stage can be identified for the period extending from the generation of the first pupils of Aristarchus up to the work of the scholars of the Augustan age, such as Didymus, Aristonicus, and Theon—in other words, up to the end of the Hellenistic age. The attention of grammarians focused, first and foremost, on poets, obviously awarding priority to Homer, but also directed toward the works of lyric and scenic poets; prose writers also were objects of study, above all historians and orators (from a papyrus of the third century C.E. we have a fragment of Aristarchus's commentary on Herodotus);[4] finally, interest also began to center on "contemporaries" in a broad sense, that is, the major poets of the Hellenistic age. To assess the weight and importance of this cultural phenomenon it should be borne in mind that, by the age of Augustus, scholarship covered an extremely wide range of literary genres and took into consideration a vast chronological time span (from Homer to the Hellenistic age). For the purposes of this essay, I will focus on the Alexandrian period up to the second century B.C.E., a period we regard as the decisive phase that led to essential innovations.

On the cultural and intellectual plane, we can endeavor to bring the problem into sharper focus (setting aside numerous other aspects) by inquiring into the type of activity the Alexandrian *grammatikoi* (the ancient term for "scholars") effectively undertook, what purposes they had in mind and what they aimed to accomplish by examining the texts of their cultural heritage, and what genuine change and intellectual progress effectively ensued from their ideas and activities. I believe that the question hinges fundamentally on the form and content of what was defined as the *ekdosis,* "edition," of a text carried out by an ancient scholar.

What the Alexandrian philologists' production of the *ekdosis* of a literary work really meant and truly involved is a problem that raises at least two main points, closely linked and mutually illuminating. That is to say, it is crucial to determine (1) how the *ekdosis* was performed, what material form it took, and how it was concretely built up—in other words, what a grammarian actually did when he set to work on producing an *ekdosis,*[5] and (2) what was the real nature of the readings attributed by the erudite tradition to Alexandrian grammarians: conjectures *ope ingenii* and based only on subjective criteria, or variants deriving from collation of copies and thus the result of a selection, or a mixture of both proceedings? Indeed, this is the most crucial and central node of the work of the Alexandrian scholars. We will see that it is vital to be aware that we face a problem of principles and method, not of quantity of the data or quality of the results.

The ancients had a very clear idea of the concept of "textual reading," and their technical terminology in this field made reference to the basic ideas of "reading" and "writing." In Greek, the most widespread term in the erudite material known to us (scholia and grammatical works) is *graphe* (what is written) and the related verb *graphein* (to write), but the ancients also made use of *anagnosis* (what is read, a reading) and the associated verb *anagignoskein* (to read). In Latin one also finds *scriptura,* based on *scribere* (to write), but the most frequent term is certainly *lectio,* with the verb *legere* (to read). The concept of "variant," expressed by *varietas* or more commonly by *varia lectio,* appears only later, in the Latin of humanism, and it has become established in modern philological terminology, where the term generally used is *varia lectio/variae lectiones.*[6]

Ekdosis: Correcting a Copy, Editing a Text

The Hellenistic age has rightly been seen as a civilization based on books, a society in which the spread of written copies of poetic-literary works gradually increased and became customary. Possession of books and personal reading took on a much greater role than in the past, even though the use of written books had already begun to be significant in the preceding two centuries. As stated by Rudolf Pfeiffer: "it is obvious that we have reached the age that we called—hesitatingly—a 'bookish' one; the book is one of the characteristic signs of the new, the Hellenistic, world. The whole literary past, the heritage of centuries, was in danger of slipping away in spite of the learned labors of Aristotle's pupils; the imaginative enthusiasm of the generation living towards the end of the fourth and the beginning of the third century did everything to keep it alive. The first task was to collect and to store the literary treasures in order to save them for ever."[7] The idea that scholars should be concerned with preserving the magnificent culture and education *(paideia)* of previous centuries was certainly not restricted to the material aspect of book production and the collection of exemplars. The decisive cultural impetus came from Aristotelian and Peripatetic circles:[8] intellectuals and men of culture realized that preserving the cultural heritage of a priceless and incomparable past could not be achieved without an understanding of its true worth and a proper interpretation of its content, and this called for the creation of appropriate and effective tools. In a logical order, which was also a chronological development, the first problem concerned the actual text of the great writers of the past, and the place of honor could not fail to be assigned to Homer, who had constituted the basis of the Greek *paideia* since the very beginning.

In the period from Zenodotus to Aristarchus and his direct pupils (i.e., roughly in the third and second centuries B.C.E.), the Alexandrian *ekdosis* confirmed its place within ancient culture as a typical product of Hellenistic philology along with the continuous commentary *(hypomnema),* the monograph *(syngramma),* the collection of words peculiar in form or significance or rare and obsolete (*lexeis* or *glossai*), and other exegetical-erudite products. Zenodotus was chosen by King Ptolemy as the first head of the Library of Alexandria. In the source from which this piece of information is derived, he is defined as the first *diorthotes* of Homer.[9] The term *diorthotes* is highly significant and is confirmed in another source, which states that during the reign of Ptolemy II Philadelphus (285–246 B.C.E.) two philologist-poets, Alexander Aetolus and Lycophron, "dealt with" plays (the former with tragedy, the latter with comedy),[10] while Zenodotus "dealt with" Homer and the other poets.

I have deliberately paraphrased the Greek verb with a neutral and imprecise phrase, "dealt with," although in actual fact it is a precise and specific Greek term, that is, *diorthoo,* namely "straightening up, revising," more precisely "correcting": it is the verb from which is derived the designation *diorthotes,* used to characterize Zenodotus, literally "corrector." The term that indicated the operation of correcting a text was, naturally, *diorthosis* (correction, emendation), which is used here in connection with both Zenodotus and Aristarchus. As Pfeiffer pointed out in this regard: "it is not improbable that Zenodotus, examining manuscripts in the library, selected *one* text of Homer, which seemed to him to be superior to any other one, as his main guide; its deficiencies he may have corrected from better readings in other manuscripts as well as by his own conjectures. *Diorthosis* can be the term for either kind of correction. It is hard to imagine any other way."[11]

Klaus Nickau, who has produced fundamental studies on Zenodotus,[12] is in agreement with the vision put forward by Pfeiffer on an important point, which in my view is to be made the basis of subsequent lines of reasoning: Zenodotus selected a copy he considered to be suitable and worked on it in various ways. Helmut van Thiel likewise believes the Alexandrian *ekdosis* consisted of the copy chosen by the grammarian from among those available, provided with a series of annotations.[13] Martin West suggests that the particular eccentricity of Zenodotus's text could not have been due merely to his judgment and opinions, but must in part have reflected an eccentricity of the tradition he followed: he may have worked on a rhapsodic exemplar produced in an Ionian context (perhaps brought with him to Alexandria from Ephesus, his native city), which thus reflected a line of tradition idiosyncratic and different from that which subsequently became widely accepted and was predominantly of Attic origin.[14] Of course, this is no more than a mere hypothesis, which, however, is based on the same vision with regard to the manner of working of the first *diorthotes* of Homer: choosing a copy and performing a *diorthosis,* that is, carrying out corrections, emendations on the copy in question, in order to produce his own *ekdosis.*

By pondering on these themes over the years, I have come to the conclusion that the problem of the characteristics of the Alexandrian *ekdosis* can be profitably addressed by starting from its material form as a book, on the basis of the following presupposition: in order to understand the nature of what we call a grammarian's *ekdosis* of a text and what it contained, it is crucial to examine the way it was materially constructed. I have therefore tried to emphasize the importance of the relationship between the bookshop artifact on the one hand and the text as an object of philological editing, with its various paratextual elements such as annotations and critical signs (see below) on the other.[15] We must take into account and award suitable prominence to what we know regarding the creation of new copies of texts, in the scriptoria by professional scribes or privately by individuals, along with insights that can be gleaned from surviving examples. To look at the problem in this perspective, the papyri are an essential source of information that cannot be disregarded; we will thus start from the papyri to search for data helpful to illuminate these issues.

It is an accepted and well-documented fact that, in book production, new copies of literary works were normally reread and corrected through additional further comparison with the antigraph, at times even on the basis of a collation with other exemplars. Numerous types of evidence for this can be adduced on the basis of papyrus fragments of literary texts, and papyrologists are fully aware of the phenomena of corrections introduced in order to improve an exemplar in the framework of book production. Naturally we are particularly interested in the most ancient evidence, although we are hampered by the fact that the papyri datable to the period between the last decades of the fourth and the first half of the third century B.C.E. (the era of Zenodotus) are very limited in number.

Notwithstanding, some small corrections of material errors can already be observed in the two most ancient surviving literary papyri, the *Persians* of Timotheus (*PBerol.* inv. 9875) and the renowned *Derveni Papyrus,*[16] dated to the last decades of the fourth century B.C.E. (recall the dates of Zenodotus: c. 325–260). Such examples suggest that the corrections were not the result of a systematic revision but were made by the scribe, perhaps *in scribendo.* Though not a highly striking phenomenon, these occasional corrections of small errors certainly represent the most ancient and visible evidence of a concern for a correct text, or better, of the intention to correct a text in which an error could be perceived.[17] A few decades later we already find some considerably richer and more significant evidence.

One noteworthy witness is the Homeric roll *P.Ilias 12,* of which substantial parts are preserved, pertaining to books 21, 22, and 23 of the *Iliad,* dated between 280 and 240 B.C.E., thus still in the Zenodotean era or shortly thereafter, and in any case decidedly pre-Aristarchean.[18] Apart from the fact—not particularly strange, given its chronological position—of having numerous plus-verses,[19] this exemplar of the *Iliad* shows a particularly abundant quantity of corrections performed on the base text (in agreement or at variance with the so-called *vulgata,* that is, the Homeric text that prevailed in the transmission) and of marginal signs (which are numerous, if one takes into account that the left-hand margin of the columns is often lost, and that the signs are considerably problematic). This is a witness that should certainly be the object of an in-depth reexamination from all points of view, including from the perspective of paleography, above all to determine the time gap between the base text and the subsequent interventions.

Of a slightly more recent date, but equally significant, is *P.Odyssey 31,* dated to between 250 and 200 B.C.E., which contains parts of books 9 and 10 of the *Odyssey.*[20] There are plus-verses and marginal signs, most of which are probably of a stichometric character, but the most important fact is that the roll underwent a twofold process of collation and correction: the first scribe would seem to have had two exemplars available, and he often corrected his text on the basis of another manuscript, after which a second hand inserted readings that are in agreement with the *vulgata.*

This is of great importance for the question we are examining here: we have two Homeric exemplars from the mid-third century B.C.E., therefore definitely and decidedly pre-Aristarchean, which in addition to various kinds of—often somewhat problematic—critical signs and the expected plus-verses, also show clear evidence of collation with other copies and a conspicuous number of interventions performed on the base text at various times and in different ways.[21] Michael Haslam has pointed out that of the over forty known Homeric manuscripts datable up to the middle of the second century B.C.E., in which the readings of the *vulgata* coexist with "eccentric" readings, quite a few certainly show traces of having been collated with another exemplar and consequently present interventions consisting of corrections and annotations of variants: "the Homer of readers in the 3rd and early 2nd century . . . was appreciably more flaccid than the Homer of subsequent readers." This was the situation that Zenodotus and his earliest successors found themselves facing.[22]

Another significant piece of evidence from the third century B.C.E. is the Milan papyrus with epigrams by Posidippus, which is rightly held to be of major importance in view of the quantity of corrections and annotations the text presents. The majority of the corrections were made by the same scribe, clearly *in scribendo* (in general amounting to one and never more than three letters, and all aimed at correcting minor slips in the drafting stage), but subsequently two other hands intervened with further emendations. The third person to make changes to the text in column 11 recorded a variant on the reading of line 30, noting it in the upper margin.[23]

The papyrus fragments of the following centuries, and in particular of the three centuries of our era (with regard to which the papyrus findings are most abundant) provide rich and valuable documentation of exemplars with interventions of deletion, addition, and correction of all types. Elsewhere I have examined and described various examples;[24] here I will mention only one case, which I consider to be particularly significant: *POxy.* 2404 + *PLaur.* inv. III/278, a fragment of a papyrus roll (late second–early third century C.E.) containing a part of paragraphs 51–53 (*POxy.* 2404) and of paragraphs 162–163 (*PLaur.* III/278) of Aeschines's oration *Against Ctesiphon.* It seems quite evident that this copy has been collated with a second exemplar and has been the object of detailed and systematic correction, seeking to identify the textual structure by distinguishing *cola* and periods and to correct copying errors for the benefit of the reader, and to emend the text in places judged unsatisfactory by means of various methods of deletion and by writing the alternative readings above or beside the wrong interpretations.[25]

I wish to emphasize at this stage why I have drawn attention to these manuscripts and their characteristics, with a choice of significant examples, to which others could easily be added.[26] The point is not that they may be considered exemplars of a grammarian's *ekdosis:* there is absolutely no evidence for such a suggestion. Rather, in my view they are of value because they highlight the importance of the techniques adopted in the workshop for book production and the effect such craftsmanship had on the development of a philological practice that sought to ameliorate and emend texts regarded as unsatisfactory due to the (real or supposed) errors they contained. The papyri provide ample evidence of the different methods used to "improve" an exemplar of a book, in other words to correct the (new) copy of a text. It was considered appropriate to add, remove, or modify letters or words that had been omitted or written erroneously, or cancel what was regarded as erroneous and replace it with what was judged to be correct by writing the correction above the line, in the margins, and in the intercolumnia. At times specific markings were used to indicate the position referred to; often the correction was introduced in replacement of the previous words once these had been materially eliminated; sometimes the correct letters or words were simply written between the lines or in the interlinear space above the form judged to be incorrect, as a way of indicating, as it were, a self-evident deletion without the need for other material indications. On occasion, a horizontal or oblique line could be drawn through the letters or words to be deleted, or these letters or words could be marked by dots or lines above or below or enclosed within round brackets or even erased with a sponge.[27] Thus there was a veritable toolkit for *diorthosis*. Often the interventions were carried out by the *diorthotes* (corrector) of the scriptorium (the book production atelier), whose task was to reread and correct the text, also by comparing the copy with the model, in other words, through a practice of collation. Turner and Parsons write:

> One of the questions the palaeographer should ask about any literary manuscript is whether it has been adequately compared against its antigraph (the exemplar from which it was copied), a task which, in a publishing house, was the duty of the *diorthotes* (corrector), or whether it has been collated with a second exemplar (a procedure often carried out by private individuals to secure a reliable text). . . . But several of our surviving papyrus manuscripts, and especially those which are beautifully written, contain such serious unnoted errors that it is clear their "proof-reading" was of a summary, superficial kind, if done at all. . . . Those ancients themselves who set store by having a dependable copy (persons like Strabo and Galen) were aware of this weakness and adopted a routine to counter it: they themselves (or their secretaries) checked the copy to be used against another exemplar. If, therefore, the text had been checked against its first exemplar, and was later collated with a second, it may well bear the marks of this double checking.[28]

Best practice in book production consisted in a comparison between copies and corrections of mistakes, carried out by a professional or occasional corrector, who had adequate resources for deleting, adding, replacing, and marking various aspects and features of the text in order to improve it and increase its reliability. Even a private copy could be subjected to the same kind of treatment, with the use of the same tools and procedures, for personal reasons springing from cultural or research interests. Analogies with what we understand by "philological practice" are evident and need to be stressed: the methods and techniques adopted in the craft of book production honed the skills that were applied and developed by grammarians. A procedure that probably did not appear particularly strange or extravagant among those who used books every day developed into an extraordinarily innovative principle: the *diorthosis* of the corrector of the publishing house became the *diorthosis* of the philologist, *diorthotes* not of an individual copy of Homer but *diorthotes* of Homer. Effectively, concerns and emendations of specifically commercial book production took on a critical and philological-grammatical nature.[29]

The corrector of a publishing house aimed to produce an exemplar that would represent the best possible workmanship, a good copy suitable for sale on the book market or to a client, perhaps destinated to be the personal copy of a scholar or an educated man, who did his own corrections and annotations (we will note the case of Galen). In contrast, the grammarian's underlying objective in correcting the text of his personal copy was more ambitious, because he sought to find the true and proper form of the work he was dealing with. He worked on a copy with the aim and intention of achieving, as it were, the model exemplar, which would display what in his view was the genuine form of the literary work in question. This conception led to the possibility of indicating doubts or a textual aporia, a perspective that certainly did not belong to the mental system and operational horizon of the craftsmen of the scriptorium.

Thus in Zenodotus, drastic and univocal deletion (a typical action of the craftsman in book production, meaning "don't write these words in the new copy") for the first time was accompanied by the sign of philological uncertainty, namely the *obelos,* a simple horizontal stroke on the left of the line. This "critical sign" *(semeion)* marked a decisive intellectual change: attention began to focus on the work in its own right rather than merely on perfecting an individual copy. It is vital not to underestimate or downplay the invention of this critical sign, which had a momentous impact because it could also be applied systematically to poems of great length and cultural importance such as the *Iliad* and the *Odyssey.* By means of his simple *semeion,* the *obelos,* Zenodotus was able to indicate his suspicion that a given line might not be a genuine line of Homer, but that he was not sufficiently sure to be able to proceed with clear-cut and definitive deletion of the element in question. Later, the discipline gradually progressed and further developed the system of *semeia* and the markings of exegetic reflection and erudite comment. By the time of Aristarchus the system of *semeia* had become complex and refined, but it had all begun with Zenodotus's small *obelos* and its radically new meaning for a reader of his texts.[30]

I believe that the philological work of the Alexandrian grammarians, starting from the first generation, represented something new in cultural history and marked significant intellectual progress. The reality and significance of this "revolution" become more evident and tangible if we grasp a fundamental chain of circumstances: the aspects and procedures of book production had molded a material and, in a sense, "craft-oriented" base of tools and working procedures that were adopted and utilized by grammarians for different purposes and in a different perspective. Thus the tools and methods of book production became the tools and methods of scholarship by virtue of an innovative and decisive intellectual change, which signaled a transition from the aims of pure craftsmanship, namely correcting an individual copy in the scriptorium so as to create a good product, to an intellectual aim of a philological nature, namely producing the exemplar that would contain what was held to be the correct text of the work. Thus, no longer would the copy be *an* exemplar of the work: rather, it would be *the* text of the work in itself, and this implied a sharp difference between "correcting a (single) copy" and "editing a text itself."[31]

Let us recapitulate. Zenodotus worked on an exemplar of Homer that was available to him and that he deliberately chose for the specific purpose of producing his *ekdosis.* However, he had more than a few reservations about it, concerning both the *numerus versuum* and a certain quantity of readings. He had doubts about the authenticity of some lines, and adopted a sign indicating his suggestion that they should be expunged, the *obelos,* which he marked beside the lines; the technical term for this operation was *athetein,* the operation was the *athetesis.* But he also believed that some lines should be deleted from the text as definitely spurious and to be completely rejected. Such lines would have been present in his base text, and he must have used one of the graphic methods mentioned above for lines that were clearly and definitely intended to be deleted and omitted from the text (with or without verbal annotations accompanying the deletion sign[32]). Zenodotus's *ekdosis* was a corrected copy, and for this reason the operation has been called *diorthosis,* correction, and he has been called *diorthotes,* corrector, of Homer.

It is not unlikely that the paratextual apparatus on the working copy may have given rise to problems of comprehension and readability, especially with the accumulation of interventions over time, and in places where the multiple interventions on the text became interlaced with one another. The copy bearing the work of *diorthosis* resulted materially in the philologist's own *ekdosis,* and we can conceive of this as a product of years of study that led over time to a series of interventions on the same exemplar. Together with critical *semeia,* explanatory annotations must have been present in the working copy starting from Zenodotus onward, and probably continued to be used by grammarians in their editorial and exegetic work. I therefore feel it is far more plausible to assume that the *ekdosis* became available for consultation by scholars, poets, and intellectuals as soon as the grammarian himself, or someone working on his behalf, had had a copy made that followed the indications in the base text on which *diorthosis* had been performed. An exemplar would thus be created that was a correct and "fair copy" of the work,[33] but still bore the name of the grammarian who was the author of the copied *diorthosis,* with the marginal annotations that would still be necessary once the text had been properly prepared. In short, first there was a working copy belonging to the *diorthotes,* with all his interventions and annotations, after which it was possible to proceed to reproducing it as a "fair copy" of his *ekdosis.* Thus it was a stepwise production, which we should obviously imagine to have been done not only for Zenodotus but also for his successors. This would also explain the conservation and transmission of the interventions and textual choices made by the grammarians.[34]

Zenodotus's choice of the base text of Homer seemed highly debatable and was open to criticism, which is why Aristophanes of Byzantium and Aristarchus chose exemplars with noticeably different characteristics.[35] Consequently, a line of tradition predominantly of Attic origin gradually spread, partly by virtue of the base text of working copies used by grammarians who were active at a later period than Zenodotus. That base text of post Zenodotean grammarians proved decisive above all as regards the *numerus versuum,* whereas the readings suggested by individual grammarians generally did not become standard in the *vulgata.* The plus-verses present in the Zenodotean text were not his own interpolations but were typical of exemplars current in his day:[36] they disappeared because the work of Aristarchus led to general recognition of a text that had a very similar number of lines to our *vulgata.*

It is significant that, after Zenodotus, grammarians like Aristophanes did not go so far as to carry out the drastic act of line deletion: in other words, that Aristophanes stopped performing material deletions on his own copy with the graphic techniques mentioned above. The *obelos* became the prime tool for expressing a cautious doubt concerning parts of the text of the working copy: *ou graphein* (do not write, eliminate from the text) disappeared, leaving only *athetein* (suggestion that the line may be spurious and then should be expunged).[37] Aristarchus followed the same procedure. This explains why many of the lines Zenodotus had decided to eliminate from the Homeric text—but that were present in the copies chosen by later grammarians—were preserved in the *numerus versuum* that became the generally accepted tradition after the Aristarchean age and thus remained in our *vulgata*.[38] The abandonment of the drastic practice of material deletion highlights the increasing sense of caution that had developed, and accounts for the fact that many of the lines "deleted" by Zenodotus were in effect no longer deleted[39] and thus were not obliterated from the tradition.

The work of Aristarchus marked the period in which Alexandrian philological production included the drafting of extensive commentaries *(hypomnemata).* The great continuous commentary, which followed the text step by step, greatly facilitated and enriched the communication and preservation of the arguments and motivations put forward by the grammarians, so the material that has come down to us from this tradition is much more substantial. Yet the *ekdosis* as an annotated working copy by no means went out of use, as clearly testified by the information on the Aristarchean edition(s).[40] However, the *hypomnema* on arguments pertaining to text criticism and exegesis constituted an important resource. In practice, the need to write on the copy chosen as the base text was no longer so strongly felt, especially as regards philological-exegetic arguments. Previously, before the rise of separate commentaries, there had been a greater need to write on the working exemplar, but with Aristarchus the particularly elaborate system of critical signs placed next to the lines[41] as well as the variants and the readings to be adopted must have been present in the margins and interlinear spaces, while the philological-exegetic treatment was mostly developed in the commentary. Marginal annotations continued to be utilized whenever they were felt to be of practical use, for example, for short notes and textual proposals.

Variants and Conjectures

An interesting testimony concerning these problems can be found in the recently discovered *De indolentia* by Galen, an author of major importance in the history of ancient philology, not only on account of his activity and thought but also by virtue of the information Galen's text provides. It has begun to be studied and appreciated from this point of view, but certainly much fruitful investigation remains to be done.[42] The new text is preserved in a manuscript that, overall, has many incorrect forms and results in considerable uncertainty of interpretation, also affecting the points of interest here, but it is worth commenting on the material and singling out several pieces of information.[43]

In the work in question Galen relates that in the 192 fire of Rome he lost, among other things, all the books he possessed; he talks extensively about his activity as a scholar and about his books. Those lost included texts "corrected in my own hand" (par. 6); there were also rare books that were not available elsewhere, and books that, while not rare, constituted unrepeatable exemplars due to the particularly accurate and carefully written text, such as the Plato by Panaetius and two Homers by Aristarchus, and others of this kind (par. 13). There follows a rather tortuous passage, which may contain a reference to copies with marginal annotations and bearing the name of the person who had (originally) made the marginal jottings.[44] A little further on, Galen relates that he also lost books he himself had worked on, in which he had corrected various errors in order to compose an *ekdosis* of his own. The task he had set himself, he says, involved careful attention to textual readings, to ensure that nothing was added or left out and that all the appropriate signs were present to distinguish the structural parts of the text,[45] as well as the punctuation—the latter being so important, especially in obscure works, that it could even substitute for the exegete himself (par. 14).

It has been rightly emphasized that here a new aspect of the personality of Galen emerges: already known as an exegete and commentator, he can now also be seen as a text editor (not only of medical works but also of the works of numerous philosophers). Thus he was the author of editions *(ekdoseis)* designed for his own personal use: in preparing them, he worked on the text in order to identify lacunae and interpolations and to highlight the structural framework of the work with appropriate diacritical signs, as well as to indicate the punctuation as an important aid to text comprehension.[46]

Elsewhere Galen cites a number of *ekdoseis,* including that of Hippocrates by Bacchius (a partial contemporary of Zenodotus), dating from the third century B.C.E., and by Dioscorides and by Artemidorus (from the age of Hadrian, one generation earlier than Galen). Especially for the *ekdosis* by Dioscorides, Galen offers important insight into its material form: it presented diacritic signs and punctuation, the *obelos* was used to indicate doubtful authenticity, and variants were marked in the blank spaces (lower and upper margins and the intercolumnia).[47]

The information Galen provides on the *ekdoseis* of medical texts that he himself had performed or that had been carried out by his predecessors is in agreement with the arguments put forward so far. The philologist selected a copy on which to work and thus produced his own edition by correcting it; he then personalized this copy, on which all his markings were visible, by writing his own name on it, after which the copy was allowed to circulate for essentially private use, or for school and teaching purposes (like the Homer of Zenodotus or of Aristarchus). On request or for various reasons, the copy itself could then be copied, that is, reproduced as complete exemplars of the work, corrected and presented as "fair copies." This could be done either by the editor himself or by someone entrusted with the task. In paragraph 14 Galen mentions precisely the case of books transcribed as fair copies after undergoing correction (*diorthosis;* see above).[48]

Our reconstruction of the manner of carrying out the Alexandrian *ekdosis,* based on observation of well-documented and purely material and technical facts, helps to clarify, on a more solid basis than usual, the problem of the real nature of the readings attributed by the erudite tradition to the Alexandrian grammarians. Were they conjectures *ope ingenii* based solely on subjective criteria, or deliberate choices among variants attested by documentary sources and deriving from the collation of copies, or a combination of both? Was there a practice of comparing a variety of exemplars of the Homeric text to identify the differences and thereby offer an opportunity for choice? This is a problem of fundamental importance—indeed, it is one of the most disputed issues in the history of ancient philology, not only for the history of the Homeric text in antiquity—inasmuch as these questions are crucial in evaluating the work of the Alexandrian philologists and their role in intellectual and cultural history.

Let us now take another look at the passage from Pfeiffer cited at the beginning: "it is not improbable that Zenodotus . . . selected *one* text of Homer . . . its deficiencies he may have corrected from better readings in other manuscripts as well as by his own conjectures. *Diorthosis* can be the term for either kind of correction. It is hard to imagine any other way."[49] Considering the terminology used, it is in fact almost impossible to imagine any other way, which means that the Alexandrian philologists' production of an *ekdosis* must have involved both conjectural emendations and choice among variants detected through the collation of copies: "Zenodotus' text is shown to be based on documentary evidence," says Pfeiffer.[50]

The two aspects, namely conjecture and comparative assessment of copies, have received differing emphasis, with some scholars suggesting that the idea and practice of comparing different copies and choosing among variants generated by collated texts was alien to the Alexandrian critical-philological mindset, at least until Aristarchus, perhaps until Didymus. They maintain that the Alexandrians conjectured exclusively (or at least mostly) with the aim of changing, without too many scruples, a text judged to be unacceptable on the basis of a series of subjective criteria, such as supposed inconsistency, inappropriateness, moral principles, material repetitions, preference for textual concision, standardization, and uniformity. I would argue that it is not appropriate either to assert that *all* the readings espoused by the Alexandrian grammarians were merely arbitrary conjectures or, alternatively, to claim that they were *all* readings derived from collated exemplars. One may far more reasonably think of a mixture of conjectures and critical assessment of variants, complete with the work of interpretation this implied. Naturally, given the evidence available to us today, it will be very difficult to distinguish case by case whether a reading represented a personal and subjective conjecture or rested on a documentary source, unless we resort to hypotheses and deductions that may not always be reliable and show a high degree of arbitrariness. But this is our own problem in interpreting individual cases and readings—it is not a problem regarding the modus operandi and the method of the Alexandrian philologists. The two levels must not be superimposed, and the fact that we have a serious lack of definitive criteria to distinguish coherently between what springs from a conjecture and what represents a variant by no means implies that one of the two categories is misleading and should be excluded.

The idea that the Alexandrian philologists offered only arbitrary conjectures ("Konjekturalkritik") and did not carry out any collation of copies (no documentary basis) has had a number of supporters.[51] This tendency leads *recta via* to a (quite unfair) underestimation of the importance and the value of the work performed by the Alexandrians. Arguments against it have been adduced by various scholars.[52]

On the question of the "Konjekturalkritik" often and abundantly attributed to the Alexandrians, it can easily be observed that this is a theory based on the false presupposition that we have general criteria for distinguishing between conjectures and genuine variants, when we are faced with the overall set of readings contained in the erudite sources. But in actual fact no such criteria exist (except in a distinctly rationalistic and perhaps somewhat naïve illusion). Furthermore, in the sources there is no explicit testimony referring to conjectural interventions, and it is impossible to demonstrate that a given reading is the fruit of a conjecture by the philologist to whom the textual choice is attributed (see above). On the contrary, there is actually a considerable amount of plausible evidence of the Alexandrian philologists' knowledge of variants deriving from a comparison among copies.[53]

In addition to the arguments already illustrated above, based on the papyri and on the general practice of book production, Antonios Rengakos rightly invokes the testimony offered by the poets of early Hellenism, that is, of the Zenodotean age, who reveal knowledge of different preexisting Homeric readings: "do Hellenistic poets offer cases which prove beyond doubt that they made use of different Homeric manuscripts? In other words, do their works display *Bindefehler* which point to the older Homeric tradition? The answer is clearly 'yes.'"[54] Indeed, we may confidently maintain that some of the Homeric variants testified in the lines of the philologist-poets of the Zenodotean age derived from the consultation of manuscripts and collation of copies.

To this should be added cases in which it can be demonstrated, by finding veritable conjunctive errors, that the variants chosen by the Alexandrians already existed in a more ancient Homeric tradition.[55] Indeed, Pfeiffer himself explicitly supported this argument, reaching the following conclusion: "these three examples from the fifth to the third centuries, in which Zenodotus' text is shown to be based on documentary evidence, show how unjustly he was charged by ancient critics, and by those modern scholars who followed them, with making arbitrary changes for wrong internal reasons."[56]

Besides this indirect evidence, direct evidence can be found, and I believe that it is decisive. Explicit testimony is supplied by the scholia, where one finds several undeniable references to the fact that Aristarchus consulted a number of different *ekdoseis* and found them to contain divergent readings: in other words, he certainly availed himself of the direct tradition of the copies he had at hand. The most evident and irrefutable case is that of sch. *Il.* 9.222 *b,* where Didymus reports that Aristarchus accepted a reading *(graphe)* because he found that it appeared in this form in many *ekdoseis.* Equally significant is sch. *Il.* 6.4 *b,* where Didymus states that Aristarchus at first accepted a certain reading, but later changed his mind because he had found another reading that he deemed to be preferable.[57]

This is a clear testimony that, when engaging in text criticism, the Alexandrians—starting with Zenodotus, the most refined method being reached with Aristarchus—based themselves not only on text-internal conjectural proposals but also on external and diplomatic resources, consisting in choice among variants they found or noticed in a nonunivocal tradition composed of the copies they had available and were thus able to consult. It would seem, therefore, that the burden of proof is on whoever seeks to strip the Alexandrian grammarians of any knowledge of variants deriving from collation of copies, attributing to them only arbitrary conjectures, rather than the opposite: the fact is that we have, at the very least, convergent evidence in favor of knowledge of variants—and I would go so far as to say that we have real proof.[58]

Martin West warns against a travesty of the situation: "The misapprehension, which goes back at least to the time of Wolf, is that Zenodotus, Aristophanes and Aristarchus were all editors in the modern sense, who wanted to establish a good text of Homer and who approached the task as a modern editor does, by collecting manuscripts and comparing their readings."[59] But what is likely to have been the aim in carrying out emendations (even only arbitrary conjectures!) on the Homeric text? Are we thus to believe that Zenodotus had a conscious premeditated idea of "modeling" Homer according to his own taste, that is: "I'm going to set about reworking Homer and I'm going to make it the way I think it ought to be"? This paradoxical possibility is by no means easy to accept, but actually this is the only alternative to the view that "he wanted to establish a good text," which is the natural goal of anyone who starts working on a text, whatever the value of the result.

The fact that Zenodotus used the *obelos* in the margins to signal the critic's suspicion that certain verses were un-Homeric[60] obviously means that Zenodotus felt he had to tackle the problem of how to discriminate the authentic from the spurious. "The critic's suspicion that certain verses were un-Homeric" suffices, for once a critical approach toward the way the text presents itself has been acquired, the problem at hand resides in the opposition between authentic/correct versus spurious/damaged and in seeking to identify the proper text. By addressing the issue of the authentic text and how to devise the critical-methodological tools to obtain it, Zenodotus achieved a major breakthrough: it was a crucial intellectual step, identified above as residing in the difference between "correcting a single copy" and "editing a text."

I fear that misunderstandings arise from the fact that there is no clear definition of the guidelines for our judgment on the work of the Alexandrian philologists. By adopting our own point of view concerning the "competence" on which they based their opinions and arguments, so as to ascertain whether and when they were right or wrong in comparison with the "truth" according to scientific philology, we risk producing unfounded and pointless judgments. Naturally, evaluation of the quality of their choices is the proper perspective for the interpreter and editor of Homer as a modern philologist. In contrast, maintaining conscious awareness of historical distance and taking care not to overlay our criteria on their behavior is the proper perspective for the historian of philology as a cultural and intellectual phenomenon and for the reading of Homer in ancient civilization.

Perhaps it is hard to admit that Zenodotus's aim (however incoherent and unsophisticated) was precisely "to establish a good text of Homer," inasmuch as the testimony that has come down to us indicates that his text was far from good, from our point of view—in fact it was dreadful, and incoherent seen through the filter of the requirements and knowledge of modern scientific philology. And even as regards the successors of Zenodotus, including the great Aristarchus, we can hardly claim always to agree with their text choices. The viewpoint from which a Homeric scholar approaches his task is the need to decide whether the text Zenodotus, Aristophanes, or Aristarchus judged to be the best is indeed the one to print in a present-day critical edition,[61] and whether their interpretations should be espoused as valid in a scientific commentary. A historian of ancient philology, by contrast, starts out by seeking to understand their methods, arguments, principles, and knowledge—in a word, their historical and intellectual position.

The tendency to scoff at the opinions of the Alexandrian philologists in terms of modern Homeric studies should by no means translate into discrediting their historical significance, which needs to be correctly positioned and contextualized. It is a mistake to blur the distinction between the two planes.[62] It is impossible to escape the fact that by inventing the *obelos* and setting himself the task of emending and restoring the text he had at hand, Zenodotus had lit upon an idea that, however embryonic and crude it may appear, would undergo further development among his successors, eventually becoming the germ of the discipline we call classical philology. But even if one were to suppose that he acted purely on the basis of conjectures, could it be denied that conjecture is one of the emblematic and representative tools of philology aimed at restoring the correct text?

A further comment by West is surprising: "Consider what we know of Aristarchus' methods, for which we have plenty of material in the scholia. Of course he had the text of his teacher Aristophanes before him. He also *kept an eye on* that of Zenodotus,[63] and took up critical positions against it. But the arguments he used were always based on the internal evidence of contextual coherence or general Homeric usage. Not once does he appeal to the authority of manuscripts."[64] Be that as it may, the picture implies he made a certain *small* comparison among copies, but that he took great care to avoid consulting any other exemplar than his own, together with that of Zenodotus and that of Aristophanes, although these alone already presented him with various divergences: a paradoxical Aristarchus who, despite his concern for the Homeric text, made every effort *not* to look at other copies he may have come across, *not* to note the points where they departed from his own copy, and *not* to ask himself any questions about those differences.[65] It seems to me far more likely that he noticed the differences, in both the number of lines and individual readings, and decided to write them down and express his opinions.[66]

However, a subtle ambiguity needs to be eliminated: when speaking of "other" or "various" copies of Homer that were actually available and utilizable, one should not be misled into thinking that hundreds of exemplars were concretely at hand and ready for consultation, thereby transforming the idea of a comparison into an exaggerated undertaking that becomes totally implausible. Obviously, it would be a pure anachronism to assume that the Alexandrian philologists had conceived the idea of a *collatio codicum* of the entire known manuscript tradition, after a *recensio* in the style of the so-called Lachmann method: but who would dare advance such a ludicrously naive proposal? In actual fact the problem should be considered in a rather different fashion, embracing a perspective that is perfectly reliable in historical terms. More specifically: can one begin to speak of comparison among copies only when a certain number (how many?) is reached, or was it sufficient to compare a few, to detect variants when the textual tradition was not univocal, and then address the problem of which text was correct and which ones were wrong?[67]

Overall, we must recognize that we owe to the Alexandrian grammarians an idea of text philology aiming to establish a good text, to restore the correct text, freeing it from errors and damages. From the age of Zenodotus onward, progress was gradually made in refining the method, which achieved its highest accomplishment with Aristarchus. The grammarians realized that a text had its own history of transmission, during the course of which it deteriorated in various ways; it could be restored to its correct form either via conjecture or by choosing the correct reading from among those offered by a nonunivocal tradition.[68] The recognition of transmission-induced damage that had affected the authentic text, along with steps and procedures to restore it, is proof of how the mutual dependency of textual criticism and textual interpretation became established and operational.[69]

Conclusions

This essay started by stating that we would concentrate on the elements we regard as essential for an appropriate vision of intellectual and cultural history, namely the birth of an idea, an approach to literary texts and their interpretation, an initial seed, which came to represent the dawn of that discipline we now call (classical) philology.

To bring to a conclusion the various points outlined in the preceding pages, it is worth noting once more that we are dealing with a problem of principles and methods, not of the quantity of the data (number of collated copies or of variants discussed) or of the quality of the results (right or wrong from our point of view). We are not concerned with establishing the minimum number of copies to be subjected to comparison or of variants to be considered before one can even begin to speak of philology, nor with determining how many "correct" readings or "good" interpretations are needed before it makes sense to speak of philology.

Rather, in a historical perspective, all that was needed for there to be a decisive step forward in intellectual achievement was the very fact of understanding and addressing the problem, even if only partly, erratically, and incoherently: a literary text had a multifaceted history of transmission, during which it could become distorted at various points; the correct text (i.e., what is authentic versus what is spurious and what was the original wording) could then be restored by conjecture or by choosing the best reading among those offered by a divergent tradition.[70]

The idea of the recognition of damage and of finding a way to repair it reveals that the organic unity between interpretation and textual criticism had become established. Although much progress still remained to be made, and Wolfian scientific philology, the modern critical edition, and the scientific commentary were still in the distant future, our viewpoint—far from being an anachronism—is the historical evaluation that a nodal step had been taken in the period from Zenodotus to Aristarchus.

The Bride of Mercury

Confessions of a 'Pataphilologist

JAMES E. G. ZETZEL

Preview

THE ANTAGONISM produced by similarity is often sharper than that produced by difference, and close relatives can be more hostile to one another than complete strangers:

We do everything alike, we look alike, we dress alike,
We walk alike, we talk alike and what is more
We hate each other very much.

Roman philology (like other varieties) appears in two forms that, like the siblings in Howard Dietz's song, are simultaneously very much alike and completely antithetical, and while those forms are themselves variable, the antithesis is pretty constant.

A Tale of Two Sisters

According to Martianus Capella in the fifth century C.E., the god Mercury decided to marry a mortal woman (who was made immortal for the marriage) named Philology. In her train, as servants, followed the Seven Liberal Arts (grammar, dialectic, and the rest), each of whom offers a seemingly endless potted discourse on herself in books 3–9. The tale lingered on as an influential allegory and encyclopedia for centuries. But innocent Martianus seems to have got it just a little wrong: Philology was not one woman, but twins. Throughout the tradition of Roman philology—and not just Roman philology—Philology is always twins. Their interests may change (sometimes texts, sometimes grammar, sometimes commentary; sometimes new books, sometimes old ones), but philology always comes in pairs, one good and one evil. But like all twins in fairy tales, they are always indistinguishable—at least until it's too late. What is more, each of them always denies the existence of the other. They claim to be one and the same person and to have unique access to the right way to deal with words and texts. In fact, they always have different goals and address different audiences. One often calls herself Lady Literature: she manages a salon (to give it a polite description) for people of high culture and intellectual aspirations—that's the one Martianus thought Mercury was marrying. The other is often Mistress Grammar the dominatrix, whipping her devotees into submission. One twin is Philology; the other is named (with apologies to Alfred Jarry) 'Pataphilology. But which is which? Although their tastes and proclivities are often very different, it's not easy at any given moment to identify them or to be sure which to believe. Mercury may know; but Mercury isn't talking.[1]

What Is Philology?

"I have no idea where to go for Latin books—the ones that are copied for sale are *so* full of mistakes." So Cicero to his brother, writing in November of 54 B.C.E.[2] Varro, Cicero's slightly older contemporary, described the duties *(officia)* of grammar as consisting of four parts: reading *(lectio),* explanation *(enarratio),* correction *(emendatio),* and (last but not least) evaluation *(iudicium). Emendatio* is further defined as "the correction of errors in writing or language."[3] The grammar of Varro's definition is that not of a scholar, but of a schoolteacher; the process is the daily grind of the schoolroom. Students and teacher first read aloud the text being studied; we then explain what is going on (plot summary); then we all get out our styluses and correct the text we have written on our tablets; and finally (raise your hand, please, and wait until I call on you) we offer some assessment of the merits of the text. And after that, we move on to the next reading or even the next class, taught by Ms. Rhetoric (another lady of multiple identities) in 3B.

In an age of manuscripts, the task of the grammarian—very few people claimed the title "philologist" before the eighteenth century[4]—is a very basic one: to get the words of the text right, or at least intelligible, in the interests of teaching correct language. It is an axiom of textual criticism that no two manuscripts are ever identical: if it were possible, or even remotely likely, that someone could copy a text without making a single error, we philologists would be distinctly underemployed. But although the task of Philology as Mistress Grammar—simply to proofread and correct handwritten books—is a lowly one, the correction of texts, even at an elementary level, presupposes some sense of the "correctness" of language. We emend even typographical errors on the basis of sense, of syntax, of fact—and while the process is often mechanical or automatic, the serious proofreader may find herself suddenly in the midst of a linguistic morass and require not just a fine sense of what "grammatical" language (in this case, Latin) is, but also a sense of the history of the language and its levels of style and diction: Mistress Grammar morphs into Lady Literature, Philology into 'Pataphilology—or vice versa—at a moment's notice. For us, at least, to "correct" a copy of Plautus requires a different knowledge of Latinity from that required to correct a copy of the *City of God.* And once that question is raised, Philology heads for the empyrean: what are the principles that govern syntax and style? What are the canons by which we can judge the correctness of texts? Does language (or, heaven forbid, does Philology herself) have principles and binding rules?

The goal of this essay is to explore some of the problems of Roman philologists in evaluating the language and correctness of Latin texts. My argument is that in Rome, Philology is always at odds with herself. I begin from the question of origins: Roman philology has two, one native and one imported, and they entail very different approaches and lead to very different results. When Philology deals with Latin literary texts, she goes all Greek and applies methods that are, in context, often very inappropriate. When she deals with Roman legal and religious texts, she puts on her toga and becomes very straitlaced. Beyond that, successive sections will explore different aspects of the doubleness of Philology, moving gradually from the particularities of Roman intellectual history to Roman concerns that are also relevant to the study of language and texts in general. Philology, in Rome as elsewhere, is sometimes torn between explaining texts and improving them *(enarratio, emendatio);* she is sometimes stretched between normative and descriptive grammar, between providing instruction to shaky little Latinists and exploring the rich varieties of inherited syntax and declensions, between teaching and scholarship.

At the end of the paper, I will return to the end of the Roman tradition, which is also, as I will show shortly, its starting point: the problem of distinguishing between the criticism of law and the criticism of literature—although this time, so-called sacred texts, the good(?) book. I am not, I should stress, claiming that the two shapes that Philology takes at any given moment can be connected to form consistent or coherent biographies: what we see as "grammar" at one moment may look suspiciously like "literary criticism" at another. But that, of course, is my point. These twins are always hard to tell apart. But before becoming didactic, I will begin with a couple of funny stories.

Two Jokes

1. A Priest, a Rabbi, and a Minister . . .

A philosopher, a philologist, and a grammarian were all puzzling over the same text, Cicero's (largely lost) dialogue *De re publica.* The philosopher was amazed at the speech against justice. The grammarian was interested in Cicero's use of forms and words that had since become obsolete. And the philologist in this case was struck to find that one Roman king had no known father and another no mother, and that the office subsequently called "dictator" was among the *antiqui* called "magister populi." He also observed that Romulus died during a solar eclipse and that the right of appeal to the people existed even under the rule of the kings.

This story is told by Seneca, in *Epistles* 108.30–32. His point, as one might expect, is that philosophy is the only thing that matters, not the interpretation of texts, and he uses the age-old form of a joke to make his ethical case. But if one is trying to disentangle the history of philology in Rome, the story yields something very different. How can you tell the difference between a grammarian and a philologist? The answer (seriously, folks) seems to be that, for Seneca at least, the grammarian is interested purely in the history of the language, while the philologist is interested in the words as indices to genuine historical knowledge: language as revelatory of the history of Rome, not of the history of Latin. That is not how a modern classicist would describe philology; nor, indeed, did all Romans necessarily agree with Seneca's distinction.[5] But although Seneca is telling a joke, he is not joking: philology is fairly useless for the conduct of a moral life, but it teaches us to understand how texts convey information about the so-called real world. Grammar is purely about language; philosophy is purely about conduct. Philology just might be the missing link between the two.

2. The Absentminded Professor and the Banana Peel

In 168 B.C.E., the Attalid kingdom of Pergamum sent as an ambassador to Rome one Crates of Mallos, a renowned Stoic scholar of both philosophy and language.[6] When in Rome, the philosopher caught his foot in a drain, slipped, fell, and broke his leg; while recuperating, he passed the time giving lectures on philology. As a result, eager Roman disciples began to apply some of his methods to their own literature, collecting, editing, and reciting the poetry of earlier generations.

Suetonius tells this story as prelude to his collection of biographies of famous Roman grammarians; it is meant to explain the origin of grammar in Rome.[7] What exactly Crates *did* to texts is unclear in Suetonius's account—but then, the methods of Alexandrian as well as Pergamene criticism are still much disputed. Suetonius wants to minimize the importance of Crates; his own not unreasonable choice for the first *real* grammarian in Rome is the Roman knight L. Aelius Stilo from Lanuvium (an influential intellectual in the late second and early first centuries B.C.E.), who brought increased social prestige to what had been mere semi-Greek schoolmastering. Suetonius's discomfort with the story of Crates in fact makes it all the more important—even though he wanted to minimize it, and even though it did not fit the narrative he wanted to construct, Suetonius could not omit it.[8]

Two Origins

Most modern critics are skeptical about the real importance of Crates down the drain, for several reasons.[9] In the first place, Suetonius's examples of Crates's influence in Rome are both vague and diffuse: they amount to no more than a set of attempts (over more than half a century) to tidy up some of the major literary works of the archaic period. Second, and perhaps more important, is that this vagueness about both the date and the nature of the work done by Crates's followers points to the true origin of the story's importance: the eagerness both of Romans and of modern scholars to find a significant individual, and particularly a significant Greek, behind any Roman intellectual activity.

The third and best reason, however, not to think of the Pergamene Crates as the onlie begetter of Roman philology (or grammar) is very simple: he wasn't. The editing and explanation of early Roman texts began a generation before Crates ever set foot in Rome; the true first work of Roman philology is one of the first great works of Roman legal scholarship, the *Tripertita* of Sextus Aelius Paetus Catus, consul in 198 B.C.E. His work included both a text and an explanation of the Twelve Tables of the Law (the third part concerned more recent forms of legal action), arguably the first attempt in Rome at an edition of any text and, to judge from later traditions of legal commentary, pretty evidently a work of what we would call philology as much as of legal reasoning—to the extent that it is ever possible to distinguish between the two in Rome.[10]

At this point, a caveat: the evidence about the actual content of Sex. Aelius's work is approximately as nonexistent as the evidence about Crates's effect on budding Roman literary scholars. But although we have precious little of Sex. Aelius, we have a great many fragments of the Twelve Tables, the majority of which probably derive from his exegesis, at one or more removes, and it is striking that while many of them are embedded in discussions about disputed *meanings* (either of laws or of words), there is not a single discussion about a disputed *text.* Indeed, in certain cases—very clearly in the fragments dealing with financial penalties—it is perfectly clear that later scholars quote as genuine words of the fifth-century B.C.E. law code words that could not possibly have stood there, and which they knew could not have been written in the fifth century—even setting aside the obvious fact that later commentators and jurists rarely preserve archaic spelling.[11] If Sex. Aelius or anybody else actually constructed a text of the Twelve Tables and paid attention to the variants or changes that we know existed, they do not acknowledge the possibility of textual variance. Even if a text of the laws was constructed, and even if it contained emendations or changes, textual deviations were unspoken and unspeakable.

Lawyers, to be sure, tend to be conservative. But there is a reason for that, particularly in the Roman tradition. Statute law was not common in Rome; the fundamental law of delict, the Lex Aquilia, was (and is) obscure in meaning and abrupt in language.[12] And yet it remained the basis for a huge amount of active litigation for centuries. The text was not modified; the meaning was.[13] It is no accident that the most productive form of juristic writing was in fact the commentary, leading up to Ulpian's vast commentary on the Edict, a great deal of which was excerpted in Justinian's *Digest.*[14] Sex. Aelius provided a text of the Twelve Tables—the founding document of Roman law—that, in all likelihood, made no attempt to change or improve the wording as he found it, and that even a century after his time, bright young students were expected to memorize.

But the tradition of legal philology embodies a form of conservatism that is strangely familiar in its weirdness: to judge from some of the later exegesis of these laws, even if the text was in fact modernized, that strenuously denied. The law is unchanged and perfect, and even if it, we claim that we have not. The text is not constructed philologically, it is accepted with all its flaws. The bulk of Sex. Aelius's work was in the commentary, employing two fairly evident and long-enduring techniques. One was to explain the meaning of a text already 250 years old in his day: glossing obsolete words, paraphrasing archaic language. The other, quite clearly, was the application of legal fiction to the text: to interpret the ancient law in such a way as to make it useful in his own time. Legal revisionism hides itself under the guise of the fiction of textual perfection: we claim to revere the letter of the law, but we adjust its meaning—and deny that we are adjusting the text as well. The common law tradition largely does this by judicial decisions; the Roman tradition did so by commentary.[15]

We know both more and less about the work of the other Philology, work done by Romans under the influence of Crates of Mallos.[16] The three examples Suetonius gives are not uniform: Lampadio divided Naevius's *Bellum Punicum* into seven books; Vargunteius gave readings of Ennius's *Annals;* and Laelius Archelaus and Vettius Philocomus both read and explained (orally) the *Satires* of Lucilius. Suetonius offers these instances as early clues to the new direction in the study of grammar and language in Rome, but they are not particularly helpful. Cleaning up, publicizing, and commenting on texts are indeed philological activities of a sort—they are rudimentary forms of textual editing and textual commentary. But nothing is said about what, from a modern classicist's point of view, is the central activity of philology: the theory and practice of textual criticism, the scholarly purification and enhancement of corrupt texts.

Is there a difference between the activities of Sex. Aelius and those of the followers of Crates? As suggested earlier, Suetonius's story fits into a well-established, if fictional pattern of Roman cultural history as written in the late republic and early empire: benighted and ignorant Romans paid no attention to cultural activities or their cultural inheritance (crude though it might be) until the Light from Greece shone upon them. The earliest Roman poet (Livius Andronicus) was a Greek captive from Tarentum; philology comes with Crates; philosophy with Carneades and the Philosophers' Embassy in 155 B.C.E. The activities of the now philologically enlightened Romans duly reflect Greek practices—the copying and preservation of old texts; their restoration and organization; commentary and linguistic exegesis. All these are at home not just in Crates's Pergamum, but above all in Ptolemaic Alexandria.

So far, so good; but what on earth Philology was supposed to do in Rome with her shiny new scholarly toolkit is hard to imagine. In the third and second centuries B.C.E., the great scholars of the Alexandrian Museum—Zenodotus, Callimachus, Aristophanes of Byzantium, Aristarchus—had a clear and present purpose: they gathered (sometimes using fairly unscrupulous methods) the literary remains of archaic and classical Greece.[17] They clarified and defined the text of Homer—and it is perfectly clear from the papyri that texts before Aristarchus were very different from the later vulgate. They collected and organized the texts of Greek lyric poetry. They put together texts as complete as possible of the three great tragedians and of Aristophanes. They dealt with texts that were often rare and often in dialects very unfamiliar in Alexandria in the third century B.C.E. And, together with the work of compilation and editing, they wrote monographs and commentaries on the language and literature of the poets they studied. Whatever their methodological principles—and that is still a matter of dispute—they did a pretty good job on necessary and difficult work, and the texts of Greek literature that we possess are very largely dependent on the work of Alexandrian (and occasionally Pergamene) critics.

But the techniques of Greek philology that Crates presumably began to expound while recovering from his encounter with the drain were not obviously applicable to Roman literature. It may have been a service parallel to that rendered by the Alexandrians for Homer when Lampadio divided Naevius's *Bellum Punicum* into seven books, but if he did anything to improve the words of the text itself, we do not know it. Ennius had died only a year before Crates came to Rome, and the *Annals* was one of his last works; there is no reason to believe that the text was particularly in need of rescuing. Lucilius, the third author mentioned by Suetonius here, did not stop writing or die until near the end of the second century. With the possible exception of Naevius's poem, the texts referred to in connection with the influence of Crates will not have profited from this kind of tweaking.

Philology is never irrelevant to the reading and transmission of texts, but the kind of philology required to read or edit *recent* literature—which was, for several centuries, the case at Rome—is substantially different from the kind required to read *ancient* literature. Explanation of dialect or obsolete words; textual problems derived from repeated transcriptions (not to mention oral transmission); the unfamiliarity of ideas or social context—none of these presents much of a problem if you are editing a book written ten years ago in your own language.[18] The Alexandrians had an enormous task in clarifying the text of Homer or Hesiod; Roman scholars did indeed have to work to create a text of Plautus, and perhaps of other early drama, but by and large the issues facing the Alexandrians or Crates were not the same as the issues facing someone like Aelius Stilo at the end of the second century B.C.E. or Varro in the first century B.C.E. or Asconius and Cornutus in the first century C.E. Difficult literature always needs explanation, but the kind of explanation is not always the same.

Setting aside for the moment the problem of Plautus—where some genuine evidence exists—one can view the contrast between Greek and Roman philology either (as above) as a difference in chronological distance between critic and text (and hence in the quality of the text itself) or, perhaps equally productively, as a difference in the kind of texts being encountered. And that returns us to legal philology. The earliest Greek texts to be shaped by philological criticism were poems, not documents, but that is precisely what the earliest Roman philologists encountered. Aelius Stilo, unlike Sex. Aelius the lawyer, did apparently work on Plautus, but his primary interest was in religious and legal texts: most of the surviving fragments are glossographic, and most of the words they concern come from laws or hymns.[19] Indeed, the texts that most interested philologists and lawyers alike in the Roman republic were ceremonial or legal. And while it is a drastic thing to emend the sacred text of Homer, it is surely more so to try to correct the text of a statute or a prayer—it is not, after all, a matter of literary aesthetics or authenticity, but of crime and sacrilege. One can comment on a hymn or a law; one can suggest meanings for it; but one cannot alter—or at least cannot admit to altering—one jot or one tittle of the law, at least until all be fulfilled. In Rome, in other words, Philology cut her teeth on texts that by definition cannot be changed, while Greek philology was designed for changing them. The remnants of ancient work on the text of Plautus are the exception that proves the rule.[20] We know (and in parts can infer) from an invaluable chapter of the *Attic Nights* of Aulus Gellius (3.3) that the surviving text of Plautus—the twenty-one plays once contained in the Ambrosian palimpsest and the twenty preserved in the Palatine manuscripts—are based on the selection of plays made by Varro in the middle of the first century B.C.E. We also know that Varro selected those twenty-one plays because they were the only ones that all earlier critics of whom he knew thought were genuine of the 130 plays at one point in circulation under the name (or one of the names) of Plautus.

The establishment of a canon of authentic works is a good Alexandrian task, and it is obvious—as it is obvious in the case of Shakespeare—that many plays were attached to the name of the greatest comic poet of Rome even though his role in writing them may have been marginal or nonexistent. But what of the methods for determining authenticity? Varro's canon is the most conservative possible, based on unanimous consent. What method the earlier critics used we cannot tell, and we know that Varro himself was pretty certain, on the basis of his sense of style, that at least one play that he *excluded* from his canon, the *Boeotia,* was genuine. And what, if anything, did these critics do to the text? We cannot tell. All extant manuscripts contain doublets, pairs of alternative versions of the same passage that could not both be original; the Ambrosian has fewer of these than the Palatine. But every sign points to the conclusion that the text, insofar as it was consciously edited, was put together by accretion rather than selection, by collection rather than by critical judgment; and what critical judgment there was, and remains visible in the Ambrosian palimpsest, was exercised by readers in later antiquity.[21] Critics of literature, as far as we can see, tidied texts and transmitted them. They glossed them and interpreted them. They judged their authenticity. But they did not edit them.

Two Philologies

Literature and law require two different ways of reading; constructing a text and composing a commentary ideally imply two different ways of writing. Editing a text—certainly editing a text using modern, Lachmannite methods—entails not merely clarifying but improving inherited materials.[22] Textual criticism is inherently interventionist and tends to be normative, even though the norm itself may vary: every editor judges the inherited text by external criteria, whether they be the rules of grammar and rhetoric, historical accuracy, or aesthetic beliefs. Much modern textual criticism invokes standards of truth, sense, and (occasionally) decency to claim objectivity for what is, and must be, a deeply subjective process: the text given by no modern edition matches exactly any of the evidence on which that text is constructed. Even the most mechanical recension is not mechanical: we make a priori judgments—necessary and often reasonable—about which variants are significant and which are not and whether shared errors are the product of similar conditions or common descent. But the goal is clear: textual philology aims at reconstructing what the author must have written rather than enshrining or embalming the errors transmitted by what the editor deems to be (and often were) ignorant or inattentive copyists.

Commentary, on the other hand, aims to clarify, not to improve.[23] The commentator builds a hedge around the text: in late medieval manuscripts and early modern books, the text is quite literally surrounded and protected—or imprisoned—by the commentary. Like the lawyer, the commentator interprets; she does not alter or improve. She explains errors, perhaps offers suggestions about what the text should have been, but she makes a strong divide between what is and what might be; and that is precisely the divide that textual philology aims to erase. In terms of modern practice, of course, this distinction is overstated. Commentaries are attached to texts, and the exegesis explains editorial choices—textual philology is still at work. But while modern commentators incorporate the interventionism of editors, in Rome, it would appear, the reverse was true: editors seem to keep their improvements in the margins just as much as exegetes do.[24]

The reconstruction of the methods of Roman philology is neither simple nor uncontroversial, because the evidence is scarce and not always to the point.[25] Very few ancient manuscripts survive that display either commentary or textual activity. We have a slightly greater number of medieval manuscripts that record (in what are called "subscriptions") their descent from copies that were corrected or "edited" in antiquity, of which the most famous is the set of notes found in many manuscripts of the first ten books of Livy's *History*.[26] We have hundreds of surviving comments on particular textual variants or problems preserved in ancient antiquarian writings (notably the *Attic Nights* of Aulus Gellius) and in the ancient commentaries on major authors, above all the shorter ("Vulgate") and longer ("Servius Auctus") form of the fifth-century C.E. commentary of Servius on Virgil. But rarely do the commentators refer to manuscripts; we are almost never certain whether a reading is conjectural or a choice among transmitted readings; we are not allowed to see any system in the way a scribe or editor or owner is using multiple manuscripts to construct a text.[27] When, in the earliest of the subscriptions, the second-century archaist Statilius Maximus says in his manuscript of Cicero's second speech *On the Agrarian Law* "I corrected the text against (the manuscripts of) Tiro and Domitius and Laecanianus and three other old copies," we do not know if he simply noted interesting readings that he happened upon, or was systematic in collation, or (as is often the case in modern editions too) was just copying someone else's notes.[28]

The one clear example of a corrector at work, a man possibly named Caecilius adding variants to his manuscript of Fronto's correspondence in the sixth century C.E., marks some readings as coming from another manuscript *(in alio);* he makes corrections (crossing out or erasing); he adds alternatives (readings not clearly preferred to what is in the text). What he does not do is identify which manuscript he used on any given occasion.[29]

He does not regularly distinguish between variants and conjectures, nor does he distinguish between what he thinks of as corrections and what he thinks of as alternatives. In other words, we have very little idea what he thought he was doing, other than adding material of interest to himself. Some of it is readings, some comments, some summaries. That is not surprising: the margins of our own books are similarly lacking in philological rigor when we write notes to ourselves. We know what we meant, or at least we hope so. Other readers, in the same position that we are when we look at an ancient manuscript, are rather more at a loss.

While ancient and modern readers might be in the same position, the more serious questions concern the scribes and correctors and critics who studied ancient texts: did they know, in modern terms, just what they were doing, any more than a reader would? Are the categories of judgment remotely comparable to those that evolved, in fact, in the late eighteenth and early nineteenth centuries?[30] By most accounts, the most philological of the ancient Roman grammarians was Marcus Valerius Probus, working at the end of the first century C.E.[31] According to Suetonius, he was interested only in the correction/improvement of texts, and in no other part of grammar. According to the obscure and corrupt fragment *De Notis* preserved in an eighth-century manuscript from Monte Cassino, he used critical signs in the margins of texts.[32]

Here at last, we may hope, is some kind of "scientific" criticism. Alas, hope is illusory and truth is elusive. Most of the so-called critical signs are not textual but exegetical. And the readings attributed to Probus look very much as if they are emendations inspired by external criteria, or at the very best, readings he admired because they conformed to his own aesthetic tastes. Famously, on *Aeneid* 1.21–22, he put a critical sign in the margin and commented: "it makes just as much sense if you omit these two lines."[33] At *Aeneid* 12.605, he argued in favor of reading *floros* rather than *flauos* as the adjective describing Lavinia's hair not because of better manuscript attestation—we have no evidence at all as to whether *floros* was in any manuscript (and it still isn't)—but because it is the more archaizing reading.[34] Which is the better text is still arguable, but the grounds of decision are striking: Probus believed that it was appropriate for Virgil to appear more archaic than most of our manuscripts (or his too, in all probability) make him seem.

Probus is the best attested of the early critics, but he is not the only one. Other first- or second-century readers (Augustus's librarian Hyginus; the Stoic critic Cornutus; various readers cited in the *Attic Nights* of Aulus Gellius) brought to the text their own critical understanding of what it should be, and they often make that understanding quite explicit: to make Virgil seem more Homeric; to make Virgil or Cicero more archaic; to justify their own taste for precious and peculiar lections. Modern critics bring similar a priori assumptions to the editing of texts—that is, after all, what a critic does—but modern critical rhetoric is in fact more disingenuous than ancient: we loftily claim to be restoring a "true" or "faithful" text, while they, at least some of the time, reveal their principles and assumptions. Those principles are not always, or even often, better than ours, and unlike modern editors, the ancient critics were rarely hampered by any serious interest in the evidence of manuscripts. But that they do offer a consistent and coherent philological rhetoric is clear, and in some respects it is no better or worse than others.

What is striking within this tradition is not that scholars have their own particular axes to grind or that they conceal those axes in a cloak of objectivity, but that the scholarly tradition is, so far as we can tell, almost entirely independent of the transmission of the text. Commentators know about the readings approved by Probus, but no manuscript regularly preserves his ideas. Correctors of manuscripts sometimes claim to have corrected their copy using a particular earlier copy or with the aid of a particular teacher, but there is no evidence either that the signed copies of Virgil or Cicero circulating in the second century were genuine, or that they contained anything other than the same-old transmitted text—corrected against its exemplar, as was standard practice in antiquity and the Middle Ages, but not against anything else. Some Roman texts obviously were edited, in some respect, but very rarely is there any indication that scholars had a hand in establishing the wording.[35] And who knows? Maybe we're lucky that Philology (or was that 'Pataphilology?) kept her hands off the scribes, or vice versa.

Philology and Grammar

Philology, by her very name, seems to stake a claim to objectivity and truth; Grammar is not so sure of herself. There are, in antiquity as at present, two audiences for grammatical writing: schools and scholars. Most of us, then as now, teach adolescents. We teach the rudiments of language, "proper" speech and punctuation, how to read, and how to write. In our spare time, however, we indulge in the higher flights of philological fancy. We can, now as then, speculate on the multiple meanings of a given text or on the choice among multiple readings. We can dispute dis(re)putable etymologies. We can track down rare and valuable manuscripts and collate them (or at least dig a few recherché readings out of them). We can, like the weird grammarians described by the grammarian Virgilius Maro in the seventh century, spend days debating the vocative of *ego*. And the best part of it is, none of it matters to anyone except the three or four other people interested in the vocative of *ego*.[36] And that was even more true then than now. Lady Literature disdains her other self, Mistress Grammar, and the recondite researches of philology did not, for the most part, find their way into school commentaries, much less into school texts. They did not affect the way most people read, or learned to read. They were the idle pastime of the idle rich.[37]

But that, of course, is only one point of view—very much the point of view of Mistress Grammar. But suppose we were to ask both Philology and 'Pataphilology about their own goals and methods. The results could be tabulated something like this:

	Philology	'Pataphilology
Methods	Scientific	Scientific
Aims	Truth	Truth
Audience	Those who can appreciate me	Those who can appreciate me
Interest	To honor the real text, stupid	To honor the real text, stupid

In other words, if one were using some kind of Turing test to determine the "real" Miss Philology, it would fail. Both of them think they are doing the Right Thing. Both of them think that what they do is the Real Philology. But if we set aside the problem of identifying "real" philology, then there are real differences apparent between the philologists upstairs and the grammarians downstairs, and that was no less true in Rome than it is now. Here is a different table of differences:

	Philologists	Grammarians
Audience	Amateurs	Teenagers
Approach	Descriptive	Normative
Linguistic orientation	Anomalist	Analogist
Goal	Antiquarianism	Job placement

One pole of this antithesis, the grammarian, is better known than the other, if only because that is what the ancient people who did things to words and texts called themselves. Many of their works survive, many to be found nowadays in the seven volumes of Keil's *Grammatici Latini*. The grammarian is a functionary, a drudge (perhaps not harmless) hired (by the government or by parents) to train the young for Success. The goal is to make them proficient in the language, to use whatever means necessary to make them able to write eloquently and above all grammatically, in such a way as to be accepted in the higher reaches of society and government. Hence, the function of grammar in the classroom is *normative:* speak like this, not like dat. Learn the difference between -*b*- and -*v*- (*habeo* is not the same as *aveo,* stupid). When Virgil does it, it's a figure of speech; when you do, it's a mistake. We find this, over and over, in the grammatical observations in the commentary of Servius (the vulgate Servius) on Virgil.[38] The constant need to shape correct language in his little charges, moreover, makes the true classroom teacher an *analogist:* he pushes hard for the regularity of language, as irregularities lead to awkward faux pas in speech.

The classic school grammar—a standard text for more than a thousand years—is the grammar of Donatus, the *Ars Maior* (a relatively full exposition of the basics [letters, words, syllables], parts of speech, and virtues and vices of language) and the *Ars Minor* (a catechism concerning just the parts of speech). Its purpose is not to explore the varieties of Latinity or the variations of morphology, but to make sure that the students come out of Latin 101 with an adequate knowledge of basic grammar.[39] Compare that to a more philological text, the selections from the third-century scholar Julius Romanus preserved by the grammarian Charisius: an alphabetical list of adverbs, drawn from such obscure sources as Sisenna's *Milesian Tales* and the early comic poets. A work like that—or the vast dictionary of Festus, or parts of the third-century Bobbio scholia on Cicero's speeches—is aimed not at pimply youths but at would-be members of the upper classes who want to learn to write or talk (terrifying thought) like Apuleius and Fronto. Philology is what grammarians can't afford to spend class time on: it's not on standardized tests and, then as now, how your school does on the College Boards may affect your funding or the number of applications you receive. Teach to the test.

Normative grammar aims to instruct on the correct way to write Latin. Not *a* correct way: *the* correct way. No matter that Latin changed drastically over the centuries from Plautus to Juvenal, the repertory from which about 99 percent of grammarians' quotations are drawn. Every teacher has the obligation, the need—if he wants to keep his job or get promoted—to demonstrate his authority on the basis of authoritative texts. He controls good Latin, and good Latin controls social advancement.[40] So too, grammar is almost by necessity analogist: those paradigms have to be clear and comprehensible. Let's not look at the various perfect stems of *mordeo,* "to bite," as

Gellius does (6.9.1–4). Pick a form, any form, and make sure it looks like the correct forms of other second-conjugation verbs. Let's not consider the alternative paradigms *iter, iteris,* and *itiner, itineris,* as Romanus does (Charisius 134.12K). Pick one story and stick to it, even if it makes no sense at all. As the teaching of Latin extended to the northern savages who had no acquaintance with the tongue, grammar had of necessity to become ever more analogist, ever more normative, ever more disciplinarian.[41] Smack.

If one considers some of the great sources for the Higher Philology in Rome, it becomes immediately apparent that, even in antiquity, anomalism and nonnormative grammar were endangered species. The dictionary of Festus, the grammar of Charisius, Varro's *Latin Language,* the Bobbio scholia on Cicero, the longer version of Servius—these are among the most important texts that preserve for us the remains of the odd Latinities of the Roman republic, and they are all works the survival of which has been precarious at best. Some antiquarian and lexicographic repertories do survive more abundantly: Gellius's *Attic Nights* and Nonius Marcellus's *Shortcut to Higher Learning (De Compendiosa Doctrina).* But these are exceptions, and they are less obscurantist than the others. The most learned of the normative grammars, the vast and scholarly treatise of Priscian, the last of the classical grammarians, owes its learning to the fact that it was not part of the Western European mainstream but was written in Constantinople and is heavily indebted to Greek models.

The bulk of Latin grammatical writing after the fourth century is mind-numbingly dull, elementary, and repetitive. Even that mind-numbing exterior, however, conceals a basic doubleness within normative grammar itself. On the one hand Mistress Grammar insists that we speak and write correctly the Latin of today, and that the Latin of today is closely dependent on the *auctoritas* of the canonical classics. On the other hand her twin keeps reminding the students that there is more to it than that: that Virgil and Cicero are the source of examples *not* to follow just as much as models of what should be done. With Virgil and Cicero, we call it a figure of speech, or an archaism, or poetic license; we moderns, however, can get the frisson of license only through reading and commentary, not through doing it. Mistress Grammar makes us keep our hands to ourselves, while her sister makes us all voyeurs.

The Law and the Prophets

To follow the permutations of grammar and philology from late antiquity into the Middle Ages would require more space and more knowledge than I have. What is clear, however, is that while the audience for linguistic authority in Latin narrowed to its present constituents (barbarians), the sources for linguistic authority spread: not just the classical canon, but the religious one as well. And there, of course, Philology and her sister encountered a whole new set of problems. How is one to judge the Latinity of sacred texts or of theological works written by semiliterate fanatics? What is the proper authority for proper Latin? Jerome's dream is famous—the choice between Christian or Ciceronian was not an easy one. The grammar of the scriptures, and later of writers of such sterling Latinity as Benedict of Nursia and Gregory of Tours, puts the aspirant to sanctity in a bind: can you be a good Christian and write classical Latin? Is bad Latin a sign of good faith? And how, to turn to textual philology, is one to interpret or edit or even read the Bible?

According to Augustine—and he is not alone—even the errors are true; indeed, that is part of the tradition of Hebrew biblical philology that percolated through Origen and Eusebius to Jerome.[42] What, then, is Philology to do? In part, exactly what the non-Christian grammarian does: to recognize how bad theological Latin is (its language; never mind the content) and to dress it gauzily under the rubric of "figure of speech," "Hebraism," "the word of God." And we start to reshape our textbooks to include examples of bad Latin from the Bible instead of the *Aeneid.* Mistress Grammar the dominatrix has become Sister Grammar—gone to Britain in a missionary position.

In editing, the safest course is what it has always been in the classical tradition: do nothing. But this time, we don't ignore the mistakes or quietly correct them, we celebrate every piece of textual idiocy as a manifestation of the divine. "Credo quia impossibile est." There is a large theoretical leap from saying "it makes no difference which text is right" (as is found in Servius from time to time) to saying "even what is wrong is right" (as Augustine does), even if, in practice, the result is much the same.

We began from Sextus Aelius the lawyer and the disciples of Crates the Greek philologist, one side being strictly conservative on the surface and radical in its interpretations, the other being radical in its ideas but having nowhere much to employ them. Law and scripture—in this case, the *Carmina Saliaria* and other similar archaic hymns—are on one side, literature is on the other. In late antiquity, law and scripture are on opposite sides: where the religious tradition extends and enlarges the conservatism of the lawyers in dealing with scripture, the legal tradition changes its colors. No text is more radical, in fact, than the last great monument of Roman legal thought, Justinian's *Digest.* While it claims to cite with reverence the thousands of excerpts of classical law that make up its fifty vast books, it alters them wholesale and ruthlessly to make them conform to the law of Justinian's time. Indeed, the entire history of the development of classical law can be seen as a claim to preserve what is old while constantly making it new. Lady Philology has gone to court, asserting her age-old right, going back to her origins in the work of Sex. Aelius, to swear that what is old is new, what is wrong is right, and what inevitably involves duality, compromise, and conflict is in fact single, consistent, and harmonious.

Tossing the Bouquet

It's time to get back to the wedding. Which Philology did Mercury wed? When he fondles his bride in the night, does he pat Philology, or does he pat 'Pataphilology? Perhaps both: in the immortal words of Fred Ebb, "Twosies beats onesies, but nothing beats threes."

> How I wish I had a gun—a little gun.
> It would be fun to shoot the other two
> And be only one.

This quotation has the same source as the quotation in my first paragraph, a Dietz-Schwartz song entitled not "Twins," but "Triplets"—and perhaps it would have been entertaining to imagine a tripartite philology rather than a bipartite one.[43] But however many philologies we choose to define, they yearn, like the triplets in the Dietz-Schwartz song (or like the divided bodies in Aristophanes's speech in the *Symposium*), to be simple, to be one, to be uniform, to be coherent. But they are not. Philology and grammar alike are always stuck between the analogist and the anomalist, between the desire to explain the messy nature of language and its changes over time and the desire to claim that it is clear and simple and comprehensible, between the text as something to be respected and the text as something to be played with, between mistress and Mistress. We are all 'Pataphilologists.

Striving for Meaning

A Short History of Rabbinic Omnisignificance

YAAKOV ELMAN

ISRAEL ARRIVED relatively late on the ancient Near Eastern cultural and religious scene; writing had been practiced in Mesopotamia for a millennium and a half when Abraham left his birthplace. Thus, it is not surprising that surviving Jewish literature from its beginnings as a continuous tradition in the early second century B.C.E. manifests an already complex philological character, concentrating as it does on texts that either are commentaries on other texts, that is, intertexts, or rely on other texts. And those other texts frequently involve ancient Mesopotamian literature.

Such reliance on texts can be detected not only in the later layers of biblical literature, such as the books of Chronicles, but also in much earlier foundational texts, such as the book of the Covenant of Exodus 21–23, which is, in essence, a critical restatement of the cuneiform legal tradition that dates back to the middle of the third millennium. Likewise, Genesis 1 may be seen as a rejection of Enūma Eliš, the Babylonian creation epic, and similar myths.[1] The fact that the Pentateuch itself quotes an otherwise unknown "Book of the Wars of the Lord" may be taken as emblematic of the layered nature of Israelite religious literature. Thus, it is not simply that the basic belief in the divine inspiration of biblical texts encouraged this complex philological character; that complexity is a basic characteristic of biblical literature. However, once that approach to texts took hold, even far more mundane texts—such as *leshon hedyot,* "common speech" (Bava Metzia

104a)—were subjected to the same sort of careful legal analysis as Scripture.

The Hebrew Bible, aside from its complex textuality—it contains critiques, satires, and appropriations of ancient Near Eastern wisdom, such as parts of Proverbs, along with the ancient Mesopotamian tradition of *Listenwissenschaft* (an attempt to encompass a subject by naming its parts, as in the description of the Tabernacle in Exodus)—also represents a quantum leap forward in human moral and intellectual understanding. The latter is generally conceded, and the former was not appreciated until Karl Jaspers's suggestion that the civilized world—from China and India to the Fertile Crescent and Greece—underwent a watershed advance in its consciousness and intellectual understanding during the sixth century B.C.E., an "axial age."[2]

The Hebrew Bible, and in particular the Pentateuch, presents three aspects of this intellectual revolution that actually *preceded* the axial age posited by Jaspers: the creation of abstract categories that allowed for explicit reasoning by analogy (as in Deuteronomy 22:25–27), a logical operation that Sumero-Akkadian culture never managed, together with the ability to generalize from those analogies; and the use of self-referentiality, that is, the production of compositions that are conscious of their own identity, such as the collection of laws in Exodus 21–24 that is given the aforementioned name *sefer ha-berit* ("the Covenant Code") in Exodus 24:7, and the book of Deuteronomy, which is called *mishneh torah* ("the repetition of the Torah") in Deuteronomy 17:18. Likewise, Pentateuchal laws are categorized as laws, statutes, negative commandments, and so on.[3] This drive to abstraction and conceptualization came to exquisite expression in the rabbinic era of late antiquity and has worked to reshape Judaism up to the present day.

This essay concentrates on rabbinic literature, not only because it offers a rich, continuous tradition of engagement with texts but also because one rabbinic text, the Babylonian Talmud, became the preeminent Jewish text during the Gaonic period (600–1100 C.E.), and somewhat later, the central text of all Jewish education, a status it has held into modern times, at least in traditional circles. Indeed, we may venture to say that the earliest rabbinic legal text and the basis for all later rabbinic law, the Mishnah (c. 220 C.E.), gained importance only because it was the focus of the Babylonian Talmud (c. 530 C.E.) and the Talmud of the Land of Israel, the Yerushalmi (c. 370 C.E.). However, since the Mishnah is our earliest rabbinic text, tracing the *roots* of the rabbinic approach to texts requires a glimpse at earlier, nonrabbinic scribal activities, namely, inner-biblical exegesis and exegesis of the Qumran Dead Sea texts, which shed light on the development of biblical exegesis and, to some extent, on the sectarian controversies that involved the Pharisees, by all accounts the precursors of the rabbis.

However, the sheer size of what may be called "classic rabbinic literature" is such that we could hardly do full justice to it in less than an encyclopedic work. Thus, we will concentrate on legal interpretation, to the exclusion of *midrash aggadah,* or nonlegal exegesis, large portions of which were collected in late Roman Palestine during the fourth through the seventh centuries. This is due in part to lack of space, but also to the wide-ranging nature of midrash and the dearth of epistemological studies of its development. Midrash is so variegated that scholars usually define it in terms of what it is not: as Marc Hirshman has recently written, "generally, scholarship and tradition alike have found it expedient to define aggada as a catch-all term for those parts of rabbinic literature which do not relate strictly to law, i.e., halakha."[4] Many of the techniques described here are also used in midrash, but midrash is much freer and its techniques are more difficult to describe adequately.[5]

There is another problem, related more specifically to the issue of the prerabbinic period: rabbinic literature, even when ostensibly dealing with exegetical problems related to the Hebrew Bible, and more precisely with the Pentateuch, is primarily focused on an unsystematic building of rabbinic law and lore. In other words, once the rabbinic movement really got under way, it tended to its own concerns, and the exegesis of biblical literature was a relatively minor part of those unless the understanding of that literature as a basis for the rabbis' own activities was threatened by sectarian movements. As a consequence, for most of its history rabbinic literature has been primarily self-referential rather than Bible-centered. Still, enough rabbinic biblical exegesis remains for us to assess the scope, direction, and methods of that approach to the biblical text; below are some examples, and in addition we will assess the significant contribution the fourth-century Babylonian scholar Rava (d. 353) made to the rabbinic use of Scripture.

The essential fact is that the Hebrew Bible, although concerned with legal issues far more than is the Christian Bible or the Qur'ān, was still insufficiently "legal" for rabbinic needs, given that the legal sections of the Pentateuch take up less than half of its relatively small space and frequently do not go into the necessary detail, at least from a rabbinic point of view. Moreover, the Hebrew Bible presents a series of problems inherent in its style and text that made it much more difficult to parse than, say, the Epic of Gilgameš, and eventually aroused the attention of would-be biblical exegetes. First, there are the problems presented by any text that has been composed over a long span of time and within different cultural orbits, but this one was nevertheless viewed by the rabbis as a unit. Linguistic changes, stylistic incongruities, and, perhaps even more serious for texts of religious import, changes in cultural and moral outlook and style—all these are inevitable. However, the Hebrew Bible, and especially the Pentateuch, would have presented its early interpreters, as it does us, with yet another set of problems consequent on its nature as a compilation: repetitions and contradictions, concerns that come to the fore especially in regard to legal texts.

All of these problems—except repetition—were dealt with by late biblical writers, such as the author of Chronicles, when they studied earlier biblical texts. Another type of problem that eventually became a concern to medieval commentators relates to narratology, or mimesis, the "representation of reality," as Erich Auerbach put it.[6] Not only had customs changed, but the sense of *how* to tell a story or present an exposition had changed as well. The amount of detail necessary, the continuity of the action, the introduction of characters, the treatment of time and chronology, as well as more concrete matters such as linguistic style—all varied across and within biblical texts. What presented itself to later interpreters was thus a gapped text, full of contradictions, seemingly otiose repetitions, missing details, mysterious terms and incidents, and the like. In the case of texts of a historical nature, we must add to this a changing view of the past, or a changed political or theological outlook.

However, most of these questions, especially in regard to narratives, did not come to be examined systematically (if at all) until medieval times, though a number of exegetical matters are addressed sporadically throughout the biblical and rabbinic canons. The superscriptions attributing various psalms to David and others and describing the conditions in which they were composed, and the dates provided for Ezekiel's prophecies, all seem to be the result of later editorial interventions and the exercise of exegetical judgment. If we are to grasp the extent to which ancient Israelite scribes themselves (as opposed to later interpreters) were sensitive to these issues—the relationship of a biblical author to his sources—we need a relatively assured source. The book(s)[7] of Chronicles provides this. Thus, examples of inner biblical exegesis will be drawn from the exegetical efforts and editorial techniques by which the Chronicler utilized his sources for Pentateuchal law and Deuteronomi(st)ic history (nearly half of Chronicles is drawn from the books of Samuel-Kings),[8] which will serve as an apt preface to our history of Jewish/rabbinic philology, since Chronicles comes precisely at the intersection of ancient Israelite and subsequent Jewish exegetical practice.

Inner-Biblical Exegesis

A perusal of chapter headings in Isaac Kalimi's recent study provides an overview of the changes the Chronicles author made to his sources: "the creation of literary or chronological proximity between unconnected historical events," "the removal of internal contradictions," "removal of contradictions between contemporary reality and the earlier text," supplementing with narratives from other sources, "attribution of names to unnamed figures," "addition of the site of an event," omissions of all sorts, "harmonizations," and much else. Thus, Chronicles is in many respects a "proto-midrash," so these are not merely cosmetic changes, as in reconciling contradictions; rather, they reflect and produce a reworked Israelite history that expresses the Chronicler's theological and ideological agenda, and that of the Judaism that became normative. Thus, the author of Chronicles quite deliberately omits stories that reflect negatively on the founder of the Davidic dynasty and thus on the future Messiah, quite apart from reconciling contradictions in his sources or providing useful historical or philological notes.

Even without such a systematic reworking, we find historical and linguistic glosses in other biblical books; for example, Ruth 4:7 refers to earlier Israelite practice: "now in earlier times in Israel [lefanim be-Yisra'el], for the redemption and transfer of property to become final, one party took off his sandal and gave it to the other. This was the method of legalizing transactions in Israel" (NIV), or in I Samuel 9:9: "Formerly in Israel [*lefanim be-Yisra'el*], if someone went to inquire of God, they would say 'Come, let us go to the seer,' because the prophet of today [*la-navi' ha-yom*] used to be called a seer [*ha-ro'eh*]" (NIV). The Chronicler attempts to reconcile conflicting Pentateuchal texts in two noteworthy instances: Exodus 12:9 requires that the paschal sacrifice be eaten roasted *(na'),* not boiled in water *(baššel u-mevuššal ba-mayyim),* while Deuteronomy 16:7 *commands* boiling *(u-viššalta),* so the Chronicler in 2 Chronicles 35:12–13 brings the two texts together by main force: "Then they boiled the paschal offering in fire, according to the law" (v. 13: "*va-yevaššelu . . . ba-eš*"). Here two different ritual rules are exegetically harmonized, in the belief that the truth of the Pentateuch is indivisible.[9] "The Pentateuchal Torah of Moses is integral and indivisible. The antiquity of this perception is thus of considerable note in the overall growth of biblical exegesis."[10]

However, the Chronicler's conflation of boiling and roasting is linguistically unsupportable in light of its use in the Hebrew Bible, where the word is never used in that sense, but the need to reconcile conflicting texts was most important. It would seem that the Pentateuchal text had been stabilized enough so that the Chronicler had no other option but to reconcile these two verses, that is, there was no variant reading of Deuteronomy 16:7 available to him whereby he might obviate the contradiction. His text was identical to our text in this case.

Another case of exegetical harmonization occurs in the Chronicler's reconciliation of the requirement of Exodus 12:5 that the paschal offering be brought only from sheep and goats with that of Deuteronomy 16:2, which allows cattle as well. While the Chronicler has King Josiah bringing all of these species for his monumental Passover (2 Chronicles 35:7–9), thus conflating the two Pentateuchal texts, the rabbis interpret Deuteronomy 16:2 as referring to a "distinct 'festival' sacrifice," the *hagigah* offering.[11] This is the standard rabbinic interpretation of this verse, as Michael Fishbane amply documents, and it also shows the progress made in the interpretation of Deuteronomy 16:2 in the intervening six centuries.

Moreover, this sort of interpretation of conflicting biblical verses, or even of conflicting rabbinic texts, is typical of classical rabbinic sources, from the legal midrashim of the first three centuries on through the talmuds of the fourth and fifth centuries. If little of this type of interpretation appears in later texts, it is precisely because postbiblical and postmishnaic texts were not considered univocal; indeed, in many cases talmudic treatment of Mishnaic texts attributes conflicting texts to the differing opinions of second- and third-century authorities.

Second Temple Period

The Qumran texts (150 B.C.E.–70 C.E.) provide an invaluable prehistory of the rabbinic movement before written evidence for that movement becomes available.[12] Many of the sectarian controversies mentioned in them centered on questions of ritual impurity,[13] priestly gifts, and Temple service. The rise of such sectarianism in the wake of the Maccabean revolt may be connected with a rise in literacy and the consequent intense study of the Hebrew Scriptures.[14] One of its consequences, however, was that the adherents of what had previously been an inchoate "tradition" or "traditions" were forced to justify traditional practice on the basis of the only authority on which all could agree—Scripture. With this came the elaboration and development of scriptural exegesis—midrash.[15] As Aharon Shemesh put it recently, "the sages' efforts to make the biblical text coincide with their [nonbiblical(?) legal] traditions forced them to develop highly innovative exegetical techniques, which in turn influenced and changed [those legal traditions]."[16]

Those traditions also reflected popular practices, some of which were of great antiquity, represented by the Pharisees (despite their depiction in the New Testament).[17] They also represented a nonpriestly view of Judaism, which enabled it to survive the destruction of the Temple when other sects ceased to exist. But that view also constituted a change from ideas about the family and society that had been unquestioned in early biblical times, such as *patria potestas* (the power of the father) or the degree of severity with which ritual impurity was regarded.[18] At least in regard to the latter issue, the Qumran sect represents a conservative, biblicizing movement, but one whose biblical exegesis bears a certain resemblance to what we may assume was early rabbinic biblical exegesis.[19]

The Flourishing of the Rabbinic Tradition in the Postdestruction Period

With the destruction of the Second Temple in 70 C.E. and the subsequent victory of rabbinic Judaism,[20] these early controversies receded into the distance of ancient history, and classic rabbinic literature came to assume something resembling its current form and size. This huge accumulation of texts (comprising several million words, originally orally transmitted) began with the Mishnah (redacted c. 220 C.E.), the very earliest surviving collection of any significance. Traditionally, the motive for redacting such materials was considered to be the fear that, under the stresses of the time, they would be lost, so they were either reduced to writing or at least organized in oral form.[21] Modern scholars, especially of the post-Holocaust generations, have suggested that this editorial activity was a reaction to the destruction of the Second Temple,[22] but this has recently been called into question.[23] The Mishnah bears a certain resemblance to slightly earlier (written) works of Roman law, and the rabbis may simply have been responding to that aspect of the overlord's culture, though admittedly the relationship between the two legal cultures, if any, is hard to pin down.[24] There are also similarities in redactional technique between the fourth-century Talmud of the Land of Israel and the early sixth-century Code of Justinian, and again Roman influence cannot be ruled out, though the exact form this took is difficult to determine.[25]

The Mishnah was joined in relatively short order by a collection of pre- and postmishnaic teachings, redacted in the following three centuries as supplements or commentaries on the Mishnah. These included the *Tosefta,*[26] a collection of legal material now arranged as a parallel to the Mishnah, and the exegetical midrashim, or collections of exegetical and homiletical glosses, sometimes quite elaborate and including discussions and exchanges between second-century scholars *(midreshei halakhah),* and ultimately arranged as a series of "commentaries" to the Pentateuch[27] that to some extent served as a basis for the two major (and giant) talmuds, the Yerushalmi (produced in Roman Palestine in the 370s)[28] and the Babylonian Talmud, the Bavli, produced in Sasanian Babylonia by 530 C.E.).[29] Beyond that are a series of "homiletical midrashim" *(midreshei aggadah),* collections of primarily nonlegal comments on the Pentateuch that range from the fourth to the eighth century.[30]

The Rise of Omnisignificant Exegesis

These modes of interpretation lay in the future, when the later rabbis applied source-critical methodologies to texts that were clearly not univocal. However, the second-century rabbis introduced a concept that has held sway in rabbinic literature to this day, the idea of the "omnisignificance" of the biblical text, where "nothing . . . ought to be explained as the product of chance," according to James Kugel:

> The basic assumption underlying all of rabbinic exegesis is that the slightest details of the biblical text have a meaning that is both comprehensive and significant. Nothing in the Bible . . . ought to be explained as the product of chance, or, for that matter, as an emphatic or rhetorical form, or anything similar, nor ought its reasons to be assigned to the realm of Divine unknowables. Every detail is put there to teach something new and important, and is capable of being discovered by careful analysis.[31]

As I noted a decade later,

> If we equate Kugel's "something new and important" with aggadic [theological/ethical] or halakhic [legal/ritual] truths, his definition is a restatement of the rabbinic interpretation of Deut. 32:47: "For it is not an empty thing for you, it is your very life, and if [it appears] devoid [of moral or halakhic meaning], it is you [who have not worked out its moral or legal significance].[32]

Still, "integral and indivisible" is not quite "omnisignificant." Moreover, a text need not be divine to be "indivisible," that is, not self-contradictory. Ideally, law collections should be indivisible, and so should narratives. A doctrine of omnisignificance requires at least one other basic characteristic: it must deal (as the later rabbis were to do) with duplications and perceived redundancies, even when they are not contradictory. By its very nature, the Pentateuch is full of such duplications—but so are rabbinic texts, which were collective enterprises. It is thus hardly surprising that the Babylonian Talmud's redactors often inquire as to why an earlier teaching has been transmitted in more than one form; would one statement not have sufficed?[33]

To return to the Bible, let us examine a well-known example of such duplication: the prohibition of seething (that is, boiling, *baššel*) a kid in its mother's milk appears (in identical language) no fewer than three times in the Pentateuch (Exodus 23:19 and 34:26 and Deuteronomy 14:21). There are also two lists of animals prohibited for consumption (Leviticus 11 and Deuteronomy 14).

For the rabbis, the contradictions and duplications were challenges: how could an omnisignificant text tolerate either of these deviations from the precision posited of Scripture? If every letter were weighed, how could Scripture contradict itself, repeat itself, or deal with matters that seemed not terribly significant?

Generally, in legal passages, redundancies and duplications are assumed to apply to different cases. This method became the hallmark of rabbinic textual interpretation; thus, for the Tosafists, the twelfth- and thirteenth-century French and German commentators on the Babylonian Talmud, this was their preferred approach to similar problems in the text of the Babylonian Talmud (the Bavli); moreover, the Tosafists suggested that in regard to biblical texts, only when these dialectical methods fail should one fall back on the plain sense of the language (see Tosafot Sotah 3a, s.v. *lo*)![34]

We now turn to the ways the omnisignificant doctrine influenced rabbinic exegesis, noting a sea change in rabbinic intellectual thought: the role of individuals whose ideas and interpretations may be attributed to them. Thus, along with new cultural, economic, and political factors, there began for the first time to be influential rabbinic figures. Our sketch is "intellectual" in that it deals with things of the mind, and historical in that it acknowledges that ideas develop over time and are affected by the surroundings of those who hold them. That being said, intellectual history may be the last redoubt of "the great man/woman of history" approach, since ideas germinate, grow, mature, and reproduce in the minds of creative human beings. Indeed, we may say that intellectual history begins where we have real biographical information, or at least enough information to associate a point of view with a particular person or group.

Unfortunately, the origins of the doctrine of omnisignificance are shrouded in mystery; no Second Temple or post–Second Temple group seems to have developed such an approach to Scripture. By a curious parallel, in late fifth-century Zoroastrian texts we find the beginnings of such an approach to the Zoroastrian Avesta, but it is never carried as far as the rabbis went, nor applied to other, nonscriptural compositions, as in rabbinic tradition.[35] Indeed, in reading through the chapters of this book I am struck all the more by how rabbinic "philology" differs from the other interpretative traditions devised by the human mind, in particular those of what I like to call the "nomistic" (as opposed to "antinomian") religions, like rabbinic Judaism, Zoroastrianism, and Islam, that attempt to dictate the lifestyles of their adherents down to the smallest details of their lives. For the present, I must leave that question as a desideratum for further work, but I am grateful to the editors of this book for bringing home to me just how unusual that rabbinic approach is.

To continue the description of omnisignificant interpretation: in regard to the threefold repetition of the prohibition of seething a kid in its mother's milk, second-century sages are reported to have offered a variety of interpretations:

> Why is this law stated in three places? R. Ishmael says: To correspond to the three covenants which the Holy One, blessed be He, made with Israel: One at Horeb (Exodus 27:4–8), one in the plains of Moab (Deuteronomy 29:11) and one on Mount Gerizim and Mount Ebal (Deuteronomy 28:69). . . .
>
> R. Jonathan says: Why is this law stated in three places? Once to apply to domestic animals, once to apply to wild animals, and once to apply to fowl.
>
> Abba Hanin states in the name of R. Eliezer[36]: Why is this law stated in three places? Once to apply to large cattle, once to apply to goats, and once to apply to sheep.
>
> R. Shimon b. Eleazar says: Why is this law stated in three places? Once to apply to large cattle, once to apply to small cattle, and once to apply to wild animals.
>
> R. Shimon ben Yohai says: Why is this law stated in three places? One is a prohibition against eating it, one is a prohibition against deriving any benefit from it, and one is a prohibition against even the mere cooking of it. . . .
>
> R. Akiva says: Why is this law stated in three places? Once to exclude wild animals, once to exclude domestic animals, and once to exclude birds.[37]

Although each of these authorities reads the repetition in different ways, they all apply essentially the same methodology, but for R. Ishmael, who proffers a historical explanation. However, none of them asks why Scripture expresses the prohibition in such specific terms—seething a "kid in its mother's milk"—when the intent is all edible animals. Generally speaking, the rabbis took Scripture as they found it and did their best to make it meaningful in their own terms. However, one development of note took place in Babylonia in the fourth and fifth centuries. The omnisignificant doctrine never developed a full-scale commentary on the Pentateuch that met the requirements of this assumption regarding the character of a divine text. The Babylonian rabbi Rava and his disciples in the fourth century C.E. pointed out deficiencies in the received rabbinic corpus, that is, places where certain elements in the biblical text were not interpreted in omnisignificant fashion, or not interpreted consistently.[38] In the fifth century the Bavli's redactors produced long, involved discussions of these matters, which have no parallel in its sister talmud of Roman Palestine, the Yerushalmi.

Once this mode of providing different explanations for repeated passages in the Bible took hold, it was applied to rabbinic texts as well. Thus, the omnisignificant doctrine that the Pentateuch was formulated with a wondrous exactitude and could tolerate no superfluities became the key that fit all hallowed texts of the rabbinic canon—the Oral Law of the classic rabbinic period, and even later texts. Thus, a passage in Mishnah Shabbat (11:4) is interpreted in both talmuds (Bavli Shabbat 100b and Yerushalmi Shabbat 11:4 [13a]) just as in the case of Pentateuchal superfluity:

> If one throws [an object] four cubits into the sea, he is not liable [for transgressing the Sabbath law of transferring objects from one domain to another]. If there is a pool of water and a public road traverses it, and one throws [an object] four cubits therein, he is liable. And what depth constitutes a pool? Less than four handbreadths. If there is a pool of water and a public road traverses it, and one throws [an object] four cubits therein, he is liable.

On this the Bavli records the following discussion:

> One of the rabbis said to [the fourth-generation Babylonian authority] Rava: The duplication of "traversing" is fine—it informs us that "traversing with difficulty [that is, passing into territory forbidden for carrying objects when there is an impediment]" is [still] considered "traversing" [within the limits of the prohibition], while "use with difficulty" [as in utilizing a pit nine handbreadths deep for storing something, which is inconvenient] is not considered "use." [Thus the repetition "traversing" is explained.] But why [is there a] duplication of "pool"?[39]

The discussion concludes with three suggestions as to the cases covered by this duplication. One is that the Mishnah wishes to distinguish between summer and winter; the second, attributed to Abaye, Rava's contemporary, distinguishes between pools that are less than four cubits across, which people will wade through, and those that are four cubits across, which they prefer to go around; finally, the sixth-generation R. Ashi modifies Abaye's suggestion, proposing that people are wont to step across pools that are less than four cubits rather than wade through them. These interpretations are proferred in order to account for the repetition; no other burning issue is involved.

It is noteworthy that the Yerushalmi (which was apparently redacted in the 370s, a century and a half before the Bavli, which seems to have been redacted before 530), reports the interpretation of "one of the rabbis" in the name of R. Pinhas, a contemporary of Rava and Abaye in Roman Palestine. Aside from demonstrating that such interpretations are shared by both talmuds, this also indicates that the Babylonian sages built on the interpretations of their Palestinian colleagues.

The additional century of work of which the Babylonian Talmud gives evidence indicates that the lines laid down by the first- and second-century sages in regard to the Pentateuch and the postmishnaic sages of both Roman Palestine and Sasanian Babylonia of the third through the early fifth centuries were continued by the Bavli's redactors, who contributed more than half of its 1.86 million words. Thus, the redactors deal with the question of why the Mishnah should be interpreted as conveying three different ideas in its repetition.

> But why [state] "pool" twice?—One refers to summer, and the other refers to winter, and both are necessary. For if only one were stated, I would say: That is only in summer, when it is the practice of people to walk therein to cool themselves; but in winter [it is] not [so]. And if we were informed [this] of winter, [I would say that] because they are mud-stained they do not object [to wading through a pool]; but in summer [it is] not [so]. Abaye said, [The repetition is] necessary: I might argue, That [rule] applies only where it [the pool] is not four cubits [across]; but where it is four cubits [across], one goes around it [instead of wading through it; it is therefore not public ground]. R. Ashi said: They are necessary: I might argue, [That rule] applies only where it [the pool] is four [across]; but where it is not four, one steps over it [and thus avoids it]. Now, R. Ashi is consistent with his opinion. For R. Ashi said: If one throws [an object] and it lands on the junction of a landing bridge [perhaps where the bridge joins the quay], he is liable, since many pass across it.[40]

The late fifth-century redactors felt the need to justify each repetition as dealing with other possibilities, thereby providing a unified interpretation. Eventually this method was applied to repetitions (of ordinary phrases), duplications, and, according to some, any feature of the text that could be deemed not strictly necessary (including words such as the word *et,* the *nota accusativi,* or even individual letters such as the *waw* attached to words and meaning "and" or "but"); all were to be interpreted so as to impart some legal/ritual, moral/ethical, or theological meaning—or even some edifying teaching. In the Bavli this doctrine is associated with R. Akiva and his teacher, variously identified as Shimon ha-Amosni or Nehemiah ha-Amosni,[41] and became dominant in the Bavli and in all subsequent rabbinic literature. It may be doubted that R. Akiva would have endorsed some of the more extreme examples of this genre, but from the viewpoint of intellectual history it is important to realize that the Bavli's redactors clearly do, and, moreover, attribute such interpretations to him and other sages of the second century.

The Bavli's redactors follow those of the Yerushalmi in attributing these hermeneutic moves to adherents of one of two second-century schools, that of R. Akiva and that of R. Ishmael. The source for the passage on the prohibition of seething quoted above, the Mekilta deR. Ishmael, is supposedly a compilation of the Ishmaelian school,[42] but the passage itself betrays the hybrid nature of our collections. First, both R. Ishmael and R. Akiva are mentioned in a compilation supposedly belonging to the school of the former; R. Shimon b. Yohai, a prominent Akivan, is also mentioned. Moreover, all the other views, with the exception of R. Ishmael's, employ the supposedly Akivan technique of *ribbuy,* "inclusion," or *mi*^{c}*ut,* "exclusion." In this case, the repetitions are said to exist so as to include or exclude various classes of animal. Only R. Ishmael takes each to refer to a particular covenant made with Israel in the desert, but here too the division does not reflect the plain meaning of the text. The three covenants referred to are those of Horeb, that is, the Ten Commandments given at Sinai and the attendant legislation of the Book of the Covenant (Exodus 21–23), which would include the mention of a calf in its mother's milk from the first Exodus passage. The reference to the covenant made in the plains of Moab and on Mount Gerizim and Ebal refers to the book of Deuteronomy and the mother's milk prohibition. But then the middle verse, the second mention of the prohibition in Exodus 34, is not accounted for. The compiler merely wished to coordinate three verses with three eras of covenant making, we are told, and did not much care for the details; in other versions of R. Ishmael's view, the three covenants are those of Sinai, of the Tent of Meeting, and of the plains of Moab (Zevahim 115b).

Later rabbinic sources enumerate various lists of interpretative techniques; in particular, the list of the Thirteen Modes of R. Ishmael, which has been incorporated into the Siddur, the commonly used prayer book, was for some reason, early on, appended to the Akivan Sifra. Presumably this was done because there was no handy list of Akivan modes. But there is a list attributed to the first-century sage Hillel,[43] which includes other types of analogical exegesis, such as arguments *ad majoram,* or interpreting similar words in different contexts as implying the same legal principle.

However, neither the doctrine of omnisignificance nor the interpretative techniques themselves provide much guidance as to *how* they should be employed, that is, the religious or social policies that are reflected in the interpretations they produce. These reflected rabbinic values, which, of course, changed over time and place.

Omnisignificance in the Babylonian Talmud

Clearly, the line between exegesis and eisegesis—between reading out of a text and reading into it—had been obliterated. The word *peshat,* or *peshut* (as in the Aramaic expression *peshuteih di-qera',* "the *peshat* of a verse"), which in medieval times would be used to designate the "plain sense of a text," apparently meant merely the interpretation that would account for more features of the text than a competing one.[44] Nor was *peshat* discussed very often altogether. The question *peshateih di-qera' be-mai ketiv?* ("In regard to what is the *peshat* of the verse written?") appears only some dozen times in the Bavli. And several of those dozen cases have become a cause célèbre, since the talmudic explanation so clearly departs from what later exegetes considered the plain meaning of the verse. Thus, in Ketubot 111b, the Bavli proffers one non-plain-sense interpretation of Genesis 49:11–12, and when the redactorial voice asks "What is the plain sense of the verse?" provides yet another one, an even more (to our eyes) far-fetched interpretation. Thus, R. Dimi is quoted as interpreting Genesis 49:11 by means of a series of plays on words, such as the Hebrew words for "foal" and "city," which share the same spelling, and proceeding through several verses using the same technique. The redactors then raise the question of the verses' *peshut* and respond as follows:

> When R. Dimi came [from the land of Israel] he made the following statement: What is the implication in the Scriptural text, "Binding his foal unto the

> vine?" (Gen 49:11) [This means:] There is not a vine in the Land of Israel that does not require [all the inhabitants of] one city to harvest it. . . .
>
> In what [sense] is the plain meaning of the text (Gen 49:12) to be understood?—When R. Dimi came [from the land of Israel] he explained: The congregation of Israel said to the Holy One, blessed be He, "Lord of the Universe, wink to me with Thine eyes, which [to me will be] sweeter than wine, and show me Thy teeth, which will be sweeter than milk."[45]

The latter interpretation is based on a reading of the rare Hebrew word *hakhlili,* "red," as *hakh li li,* "laugh to me to me." The play on words in this case involves not only breaking up the biblical word but also taking part of it as Aramaic and not Hebrew.[46]

However, the very fact that the redactors saw fit to ask this question is significant, and I would attribute its rarity to the possibility that it reflects a very late intrusion into the Bavli's text—the major part of which was redacted by 530 C.E.—perhaps as late as the seventh or eighth century, under the influence of the burgeoning field of Arabic grammar.[47]

Although omnisignificant interpretation of authoritative texts is typical of rabbinic textual practice insofar as it distinguishes that practice from what we know of alternative streams of postbiblical Jewish hermeneutics, such as the Samaritan or that of the Qumran sect(s), the rabbis did recognize other aspects of the text that required elucidation. Thus, whatever the origin of the Aramaic translations of much of the Hebrew Bible, they were accepted as authoritative, including the one attributed to Onkelos, which generally hewed to a plain-sense interpretation of the Pentateuchal text. And, though *peshat* was not a particularly noticeable aspect of classical rabbinic biblical interpretation, neither was it nonexistent. Thus, we have rabbinic dicta such as "the biblical text does not depart from its plain meaning" (Shabbat 63a), or the query "What [then] is the plain meaning of the verse?" However, the true state of affairs is shown by the fact that the first principle appears only once in the Bavli, and on the lips of a rabbi who admits that although he is thoroughly conversant with rabbinic literature, he has not known of that principle, whereas the query appears only some dozen times in the entire Bavli.

Omnisignificance and the Law

As noted above, the earliest attempt at an authoritative collection of rabbinic law that has come down to us in complete form is the Mishnah, reportedly redacted under the authority and supervision of Rabbi Judah the Prince and completed around 220 C.E.

To get an idea of the difference between biblical and mishnaic law, let us examine a mishnaic text that seems ultimately to be based on the rabbinic exegesis of the biblical prohibition of seething a kid in its mother's milk, discussed above. Mishnaic law may be divided into two segments: that part for which there is substantial biblical precedent—this primarily concerns the Temple service (in the form of the Tabernacle) and the festivals; and that for which there is little or no biblical precedent, as for example commercial and real estate law (included in the tractates Bava Metzia and Bava Batra). The latter may stem from ancient Jewish customary law,[48] but even when we can trace the Mishnah's rule back to its biblical roots through rabbinic exegesis, and even when some details may be accounted for by the rabbinic principle of "erecting fences," that is, by ruling stringently in more remote instances that may lead to a violation of the biblical norm, other details reflect an inner-rabbinic development beyond this.

A good example is the mishnaic teachings that stem from the Mekilta passage regarding "seething a kid in its mother's milk." Here is the Mishnah at the beginning of Hulin, chapter 8:

> MISHNAH. Every kind of meat is forbidden to be cooked in milk, except the meat of fish and locusts; and it is also forbidden to place upon the table [meat] with cheese, except the meat of fish and locusts.
>
> If a person vowed to abstain from meat, he may partake of the flesh of fish and of locusts.[49]

Clearly, "every kind of meat" reflects the various debates regarding the status of domestic and wild animals, and birds, and so on, within the rabbinic system of dairy and milk dishes. Likewise, "milk" has been generalized from the goat milk of the biblical verse; fish and locusts are not mammals and so are excluded. Again, the prohibition against placing on the table cheese and meat (except that of fish and locusts) is to prevent their consumption together. But how do we understand the last clause regarding vows? Here another rabbinic innovation is at work: the language of vows is held to reflect ordinary usage (in mishnaic Hebrew), where "meat" apparently did not generally include (as it does not in modern English) fish and locusts. As the Babylonian rabbis worked their way through the text, quite a few of these subsidiary principles were required to explain the meaning of the mishnaic law.

Nevertheless, while the rabbis often drew on Scripture, they made it fit their own framework.[50] And these rabbinic themes were often more abstract than their scriptural sources.[51] For example, who would think that the Pentateuchal passage mandating that when a person dies in a "tent," the biblical rule that a tent and all its contents would become ritually polluted would be taken by the rabbis to apply to any object or person "overhanging" that corpse, or any person, vessel, or foodstuff that a corpse would overhang—that is, that the objects or corpse would themselves become "tents" in that abstract sense?

Constructing a Legal System

As a code of laws, the Mishnah presented later rabbis with several major drawbacks. First, by all accounts it circulated as an oral compilation, with alternate versions of various individual teachings arising either because the redactor(s) had changed their minds or from the fact that variation is an inevitable consequence of oral transmission.[52] Second, the Mishnah, perhaps because it is an oral compilation, does not provide reasons for its decisions.[53] Third, as a compilation of various views and schools, it contains many internal contradictions that had not been ironed out or reconciled by its redactors. This characteristic of the Mishnah is not unique to it, but is found in other legal collections of late antiquity, such as the Roman Code of Justinian and the Sasanian Book of a Thousand Decisions.

For these reasons and others, it is clear that the Mishnah was not accepted as the final authority even late into the third century, in either Roman Palestine or Sasanian Babylonia. However, later generations saw the promulgation of the Mishnah as a fundamental watershed in Jewish history, perhaps even more important than the destruction of the Second Temple in 70 C.E.; it marked the end of the tannaitic era—the era of *tannaim,* those rabbis mentioned in the Mishnah and related literature who were active centuries before the Mishnah, back to the time of Alexander the Great.

In Roman Palestine the decades after the completion of the Mishnah marked the "transition generation" between the tannaim and the amoraim,[54] who were formally considered bound by the Mishnah's decisions. Nevertheless, the premier authorities of the last half of the third century, R. Yohanan (d. 279 C.E.) in the west, who is among the most frequently cited authority in both talmuds, and first-generation Babylonian authorities (Rav, his colleague Samuel, and Rav's student R. Huna), were not loath to reject a mishnaic decision in favor of other traditions. One reason given is that its redactor ("Rabbi [Judah the Prince]") had adopted an individual opinion different from that of the majority of rabbis. R. Yohanan especially suggested that a particular authority had changed his mind, thus yielding alternate variants of his view; he also laid down rules for determining which opinion cited in mishnaic disputes is to be considered normative, thus beginning the process of undoing mishnaic indeterminacy.[55] As a consequence, these authorities/commentators (whose views were likewise transmitted orally) did not emend the text of the mishnaic teaching with which they disagreed.[56] For these generations, the task was to explain the Mishnah and decide what opinion represented the accepted legal norm. And by and large, that is how matters remained in the west.

In Babylonia, however, R. Judah, another influential early fourth-century authority and founder of the Pumbeditan school, began to *emend* the text of mishnaic teachings rather than reject them. Moreover, he and later Babylonian rabbis faced yet another problem: they had to adapt a law collection produced for Roman Palestine to Babylonian conditions. Thus, in regard to Mishnah Bava Metzia 9:8, concerning leasing a field, we have the following, from the Bavli, Bava Metzia 106b–107a:

> MISHNAH. If one leases a field from his neighbor to sow barley, he must not sow wheat [which exhausts the soil more quickly than barley] . . . ; [If rented to sow] wheat, he may sow barley. But Rabban Simeon b. Gamliel forbids it. [If rented for] cereals, he may not sow pulse, but if [for] pulse he may sow cereals. [The reasoning is the same as in the case of barley and wheat.] Rabban Simeon b. Gamliel forbids it.
>
> TALMUD . . . [107a] [If he rented a field for] cereals, he may not sow pulse, etc. R. Judah taught Rabin: [If he rented it for] cereals, he may sow pulse. Said he to him: But did we not learn, [If he rented for] cereals, he may not sow pulse?—
>
> He [R. Judah] replied: There is no difficulty; this [my ruling] refers to ourselves; the other [—that of the Mishnah—refers] to them [the inhabitants of Roman Palestine].[57]

The point is this: since Palestine was not as well watered as Babylonia, which can rely on irrigation, the impoverishment of the soil is a real danger; hence, if the field is rented for cereals, pulse must not be sown, as they are a greater drain on the soil. Since Babylonian soil is more marshy and humid, there is no such danger. For the same reason of geographically bounded practices, Hebrew words unfamiliar to Babylonians are glossed in Babylonian Aramaic, occasionally even more than once, since these terms changed with time and place even in Babylonia.

The Bavli eventually became the dominant Talmud, and its importance as a factor in later Jewish rabbinic intellectual history can scarcely be exaggerated. Though much of what characterizes the text—its orality, its dialectical and dialogical nature, its fraught relation to the Mishnah, its overall theology—was actually taken over from the sages of the Land of Israel, the Bavli made these features its own by developing them in its peculiar way, and these ways of thought and expression became typically "Jewish." Still, not every Babylonian cultural trait became normative; for example, oral transmission in Babylonia, probably under Zoroastrian influence, brooked no exception in legal matters, while "hidden scrolls" providing exceptions in legal matters existed in Roman Palestine, where the culture of the written scroll was pronounced.

The Yerushalmi is half the size of the Bavli (900,000 words versus 1.86 million), and this is due largely to two factors. First, the Bavli has an enormous redactional layer—about 55 percent—of anonymous discussion while that of the Yerushalmi runs to only about 10 percent. This redactional activity reflects developments of the fifth century, by which time active work on the Yerushalmi had ceased. The difference between the two is not merely a matter of quantity; the redactional layer in the Yerushalmi is merely a late addition, but the Bavli's redactional layer had become the framework of the rest, and thus the prism through which later generations understood the work of the preredactional Babylonian rabbis.[58] Moreover, the influence of the fourth-century authority Rava (d. 352/3) was dominant in Babylonia and all but insignificant in Palestine, and the redactors were promulgators and developers of Rava's work on conceptualization and consistent omnisignificance, so the Bavli took on a different and more developed exegetical aspect than its sister talmud. This, along with the usual cultural, economic, and political factors, had much to do with its later predominance.

About a third of the Bavli contains nonlegal material (much of it from Roman Palestine), while the Yerushalmi has only about a sixth of such material. The reason is that while the Yerushalmi was being compiled, the rabbis of Roman Palestine were also compiling collections of such aggadic (nonlegal) material (the early parts of Midrash Rabba, the Pesiqtas, etc.), while in Babylonia everything apparently went into its talmud, which thus became an oral encyclopedia of rabbinic learning.[59]

With the third-generation sages Rabbah of Pumbedita and R. Nahman of Mahoza there was an attempt at producing a more comprehensive legal system, especially in regard to tort law. However, once newly minted legal concepts took hold, the Babylonian rabbis faced the problem of *reinterpreting* traditional texts with the new conceptual system a-building. In the early fourth century Rabbah proposed a series of problems that investigate the role of intention in torts, which attempts to move away from a system of strict liability (i.e., the tortfeasor is liable whether or not there was an intent to do damage) to one in which degrees of negligence are assessed (Bava Qamma 26b–27a), and even created a new category: "criminal negligence" (Bava Qamma 32b). For his part, his older contemporary R. Nahman seems to have introduced the abstract term *peshi'uta* for the category of negligence, as opposed to the earlier use of the participle, *poshe'a,* "one who acts negligently," which we know from Roman law.[60]

However, this development seemingly contradicted the mishnaic ruling that "a person is always [considered] forewarned [and therefore liable even in cases of] inadvertent damages" (Mishnah Bava Qamma 2:6). In order to reconcile the mishnaic statement with the new development, the Talmud reinterprets that rule as not relating to the tortfeasor's responsibility for damages, which remains in place. In cases of inadvertent damages (such as having caused damage while asleep), the tortfeasor is not liable for pain, medical expenses, loss of time at work, and any degradation occasioned by the injury. Thus the rabbis tailored the liability to fit the intention, or lack thereof. They accomplished this by a hyperliteral reading of the text accompanied by an analogical analysis.

Since the Mishnah in question provides two examples of torts, one involving blinding a person and the other breaking a vessel, they analogize the two: just as one is liable for even inadvertent damage to a vessel, but not its pain, and so on, so too in cases involving humans. This of course would not apply in cases of criminal negligence. Nowadays, we have insurance companies to level the playing field, and there are authorities who argue for a restoration of the old rule in any case, but for its time it attempted to resolve the conundrum of responsibility for inadvertent damages.[61]

In the end, both the amoraim and the redactors were willing to emend traditional sources to make them conform to the views of recognized authorities such as Rava. In one noteworthy instance a tannaitic text (not part of the Mishnah) is emended from "below" to "above" and then reinterpreted to refer to a minimum height rather than a maximum one; as the Soncino edition comments, "the entire passage [is thus] in the nature of an elliptical note" (Eruvin 3a–b)!

However, the issue is not as outlandish as it may seem. It relates to a rabbinic enactment regarding virtual partitions to permit carrying objects beyond a certain weight on the Sabbath. In order to permit such carrying within an alleyway, a "virtual doorway" must be created, and the Mishnah (Mishnah Eruvin 1:1) mandates that the doorway so created must be less than twenty cubits in height. However, there is an ambiguity in its formulation:

does that height include the lintel or not? Rava rules permissively, that even though the lintel is higher than twenty cubits, the virtual partition is valid, since the rabbinic requirement of twenty cubits refers to the open space below, while Rabbah b. Ula rules stringently. Aside from the ambiguity mentioned above, there are also conflicting tannaitic (second- and early third-century) sources involved. In the end, the principles on which this question is decided are basically three: (1) rabbinic enactments are sometimes (but not always) treated as strictly as biblical ones; (2) requirements governing public ground are less strict than those governing private property (a booth) because in the former we may rely on someone calling attention to the deficiency; and (3) when there are two competing interpretations, it is the one by Rava, who is considered to be a greater authority than Rabbah b. Ula, that is preferred, despite the need for emendation of a tannaitic text.

There is also the hope (and goal) of reconciling conflicting anonymous (and therefore authoritative) texts by reinterpretation, if possible, or by emendation, or a combination of the two. In only five places in the Babylonian Talmud is the suggestion made that a tannaitic source was erroneously formulated,[62] and in only one case is the source ultimately rejected and the suggestion made to "follow logic" instead (Gittin 73a). Despite this reluctance, however, the reliance on logic, or that the texts "make sense"—rabbinically speaking—is powerful enough that a good logical argument *(sevara)* is deemed equivalent to a biblical verse *(qera)* in authority.[63]

Of the hundreds of rabbis mentioned in the Bavli, only about a dozen are major figures whose comments and views dominate the discussion (that is, those who are mentioned at least a thousand times). They are scattered through seven generations (from 220 to about 450 C.E.), not more than two or three per generation. No "school" remained active for more than two or three generations, but each did have its own character, in part based on geographic and cultural location. The Mahozan school mentioned above was located in a suburb of the Sasanian capital, Ctesiphon, and represented the more cosmopolitan, acculturated Babylonian elite.

Another fourth-century school, that of Pumbedita, was located in a much smaller town on the Euphrates, with a much more insular Jewish community, and its authorities, Rabbah, R. Joseph, and in part Abaye, continued the tradition of the first two generations (Rav of Sura, Samuel of Nehardea, and their successors, R. Judah, R. Huna, and R. Hisda) and concentrated on Mishnah exegesis and legal rulings. Typically, a talmudic passage will open with the comments of two of the first four authorities named, concentrating on difficult words in the text, identifying the Mishnah's anonymous authority, fleshing out the details of the cases presented, reconciling conflicting sources. These discussions are most often continued by the Pumbeditans; the Mahozans (Rabbah b. Avuha, R. Nahman, Rava), while not totally absent, are cited far less often; they also seem more interested in deriving legal principles from mishnaic teachings and often turn their attention to more general issues. However, regarding the limits of the authority of a court, the Pumbeditans continue the work of the scholars of Roman Palestine.[64]

These early Babylonian schools did not resemble their later Gaonic successors, but were rather made up of groups of students surrounding a charismatic master, without physical plant, with few faculty members and little continuity. Pumbedita, supposedly founded in 299 C.E. according to later Gaonic tradition, ceased operating with Abaye's death in 338; Mahoza flourished during the tenures of R. Nahman and Rava (and perhaps Rabbah b. Avuha, R. Nahman's teacher), but with Rava's death in 352/3, his students apparently returned to their hometowns (R. Nahman b. Yitzhak to Pumbedita and R. Papa to Naresh, for example), and established or reestablished schools there.[65]

During Rava's tenure, Mahoza made significant strides in systematizing earlier traditions of interpretation, presenting them in a more conceptually coherent way, and also engaging the world outside rabbinic circles. Among his nonlegal concerns, Rava dealt with theological issues (theodicy, the influence of astrology, resurrection, the authority of the rabbis as against the Pentateuch). Many of these issues were generated by the cosmopolitan nature of Mahozan Jewish society, and betray the openness of that society to Zoroastrianism, Manichaeism, and Christianity. Still, Pumbedita, despite its more insular population, was also open to some of these influences, as we see in the work of R. Joseph on theodicy and of Abaye on the *eschaton* (see Sanhedrin 97a).[66]

While R. Nahman contributed principally to the emerging area of rabbinic negligence law, civil law, and family law, the work of his disciple Rava displays a full-fledged effort to limn the contours of the role of intent in matters of both civil and ritual law and marks the beginning of an explicitly conceptualist approach to Jewish law, although he seems to have been joined, at least in part, by his Pumbeditan contemporary Abaye.[67]

The Conceptualist Revolution

A number of scholars in the last generation or two have pointed to the influence of Rava in turning Babylonian learning in a conceptualist direction,[68] but a monograph by Leib Moscovitz published a decade ago is the first systematic study of rabbinic conceptualization, and particularly in the Bavli. However, he employs the term in a more restricted sense than we will use it here. He is primarily concerned with "significant concepts and conceptualization," and prefers "metaphysical concepts such as causation and potentiality."[69] More precisely, "abstract concepts include three principal types of notions . . . : (1) psychological concepts, such as intention and desire; (2) legal concepts, such as rental, acquisition, and negligence; (3) metaphysical concepts, such as change, inevitability, causation and potentiality" (6–7). He dates the beginning of this process with the work of Rava, whose influence on the redactors, in this and other matters, was decisive.[70] He limits the scope of the term "conceptualization" at the insistence of the great Romanist David Daube, who required that in order to have "conceptualization" there must be an "action noun," "which facilitates application of the relevant concept, legal definition, or classificatory principle in different contexts and in connection with different legal domains."[71] The somewhat counterintuitive result is that conceptualization emerges only in the Bavli, even though Moscovitz must concede that earlier rabbinic documents like the Mishnah, Tosefta, and Yerushalmi have what he calls "implicit conceptualization."

Using looser criteria, that is, including concepts that are not necessarily "quasi-philosophical" but merely legal, and not requiring verbal nouns, we will date the process somewhat earlier, perhaps with the emergence of the sort of thinking evident in the abstract definition of a "tent" discussed above.[72] Moreover, Abaye may have been an even more enthusiastic conceptualizer than Rava, who seems to have been constrained by the practical concerns of a busy court calendar in the capital suburb of Mahoza. In any case, Moscovitz himself, while denying the label "conceptualization" to the principle of using ordinary speech to define the parameters of a vow, does term it "the discretionary application of broad, indeterminate, but readily inferable principles."[73] To illustrate how this conceptualist approach transformed rabbinic law, let us again take a brief look at the rabbinic use of Scripture's milk and meat prohibition, this time in Mishnah Hulin 8:3, the problem of what happens when a drop of milk falls into a pot of meat.

> MISHNAH. If a drop of milk fell on a piece of meat [boiling on the fire] and it imparted a flavor into that piece [that is, the piece was not sixty times as much in bulk as the drop of milk], it [the meat] is forbidden. If the pot was stirred [thus distributing the flavor within the pot], then it is forbidden only if [the drop of milk] imparted a flavor into [all that was in] the pot.

The abstract principle of "nullification" stands behind this casuistically formulated mishnaic text, even though the term does not appear: it had not yet been formulated. Nevertheless, it is undeniable that Rava and his successors (in particular, the redactors of the Babylonian Talmud) fostered the process of continued abstraction and conceptualization that came to typify "talmudic casuistry."

How do the rabbis bridge the gap between these rules and the biblical prohibition against "boiling a kid in its mother's milk"? The talmudic discussion on this mishnah takes up this theme (Hulin 108a).

> Abaye said: [Since the Mishnah insists that the flavor of the milk must be perceptible in the meat in order for the mixture to be forbidden, we must conclude that] in all cases wherever the flavor [of a forbidden substance is perceptible] but not the substance itself [because for example the forbidden substance had been removed from the mixture], [the mixture is forbidden] by the law of the Torah [because the biblical expression "meat in milk" implies that once they have been cooked together they are forbidden even if they have been separated]. For should you say that it is forbidden by rabbinic enactment only, and the reason we may not draw any conclusions from the case of [the biblical expression] "meat in milk" is that it is an anomaly [since each substance—the meat and the milk—is itself permitted, and it is only their mixture that is forbidden], then by reason of that anomaly [the mixture of meat and milk should be forbidden] even though the one does *not* impart a flavor in the other!
>
> Rava said to him: Since the Torah has expressed this prohibition by the term "cooking" [this expression implies that one substance has imparted its flavor to the other].[74]

In other words, according to Abaye, the rabbinic framework is assumed to lie behind the biblical formulation, and further rules are deduced from a very literal understanding of the text within that framework. The plain meaning of the biblical text (as opposed to its literal meaning) is thus all but irrelevant, but the text itself is highly malleable and very relevant within its rabbinic understanding. This then is the fruit of rabbinic omnisignificance. Rava, on the other hand, deduces this from the Pentateuch's use of the word "cooking," which inevitably results in one substance imparting its flavor to the other, a somewhat more naturalistic reading.

In any case, we have come a far distance from the plain sense of the biblical verse. Thus, while the Talmud may be seen as a commentary on the Mishnah and related tannaitic literature, its relation to Scripture is much more complex; there is no doubt that the rabbis saw themselves—and their tradition—as its divinely authorized interpreters. This permitted Rava to read his innovations into the existing rabbinic texts. In an astoundingly innovative ruling, he holds that one who has performed an idolatrous act out of fear or love of a person is nevertheless not guilty of a capital crime, though the act itself is prohibited, and this is because he had not accepted the idol as his god, that is, his intention was not idolatrous. Abaye, in contrast, sees the act itself as culpable, despite the person's intentions (Sanhedrin 61b–62a). Rava's ruling seems to stem from a hyperliteral reading of Mishnah Sanhedrin 7:6:

> MISHNAH. He who engages in idol worship [is executed]. It is all one whether he serve it, sacrifice, offer incense, make libations, prostrate himself, accept it as a god, or say to it, "You are my god." But he who embraces it, kisses it, sweeps or sprinkles the ground before it, washes it, anoints it, clothes it, or puts on its shoes, he transgresses a negative precept [but is not executed].[75]

Rava reads the list of forbidden acts (serving it, sacrificing, offering incense, making libations, prostration, and accepting it as a god) as exhaustive rather than typical. Moreover, "accepting [the idol] as [his] god" is taken as a *quality* that *affects* all the other acts in the list, so that one is only culpable for the sin of idolatry if one performs one of these acts while accepting the idol as a god.

Although this seems to be a relatively straightforward (though not inevitable) reading of this mishnaic text, it is not one that is actually proposed in the name of Rava in our talmudic passage; it reflects my own understanding of Rava's position. Even more remarkable, while the passage relates no fewer than three justifications for Abaye's ruling in his own name ("from where do I say this"), Rava appears only as a respondent to Abaye's arguments rather than taking the initiative and speaking in favor of his own ruling. And even more remarkably, in these cases it is not Rava's own words that we read, but those of the redactors speaking for him, and, in one case, referring to an interpretation given by the Babylonian-Palestinian R. Jeremiah a generation before, which does not so much support Rava's view as counter Abaye's. And finally, the three arguments that Abaye brings do not actually relate to the interpretation of the Mishnah. What accounts for this unwonted silence?

David Halivni Weiss concludes that this discussion is entirely the work of the redactors; presumably they did not have Rava's original arguments.[76] What I have suggested is an opportunistic reading of the Mishnah at hand; Rava's intentionalist reading of the text was so epistemically revolutionary that he almost spoke a different language. Here, as elsewhere, some of the redactors still attempted to forge a view of matters based on *texts* rather than *concepts*.[77] But Rava's view regarding the role of intention in assessing liability in ritual as in civil matters was a *novum* difficult for a traditional society to digest, though Rava's charisma and influence were such that his opinions almost always carried the day. Thus, in the following sketch of Babylonian rabbinic intellectual history we will concentrate on Rava's view of the world rather than his view of texts, because it was the former that drove him rather than the latter.

Generally speaking, it is the redactor(s)' voices that we hear in the talmudic discussions on these matters, often prefaced with the expression *amar lakh So-and-so,* "So-and-so *could* say to you." As I noted above, and Moscovitz has emphasized,[78] the sources on which the conceptualist model is erected often do not support it, philologically speaking. Here is a fairly straightforward case. The Mishnah (Sukkah 2:4) frees those who are ill from the commandment of eating in a booth for the seven days of Tabernacles. Rava adds another category to those free of the obligation, even though, as the talmudic discussion (hence the redactors) points out, a plain reading of the relevant Mishnah does not support this ruling (which nevertheless became authoritative).

> Rava permitted R. Aha b. Adda to sleep outside the booth on account of the odor of the clay [sprinkled on the floor of the booth]. Rava is here consistent, since Rava said, He who is in discomfort [due to conditions in the booth] is free from the obligation of *sukkah* (Sukkah 26a).
>
> But have we not learned: "invalids and their attendants are free from the obligation of *sukkah* [a booth on the festival of Tabernacles]," [from which it follows,] only an invalid [is exempt] but not one who is merely in discomfort?—
>
> I will explain: An invalid is free together with his attendants, whereas he who is in discomfort is himself free, but not his attendants.[79]

Note the redactional comment: "Rava is here consistent [lit., "Rava (is) according to his reason"]—despite what a plain-sense reading of the sources might imply. This comment recurs no fewer than forty-four times in the Bavli. Perhaps more revealing are the cases in which the redactors note that both Rava and Abaye interpret the sources in accordance with their own positions—sixteen cases.

Some of the disagreements between them may stem from the differences between the two communities in which they functioned. Rava was the rabbinic authority of a suburb of Ctesiphon, the Sasanian capital, one of the termini of the Silk Road and thus the metropolis of the empire, while Abaye was in Pumbedita, a middling town on the Euphrates that housed a much more insular Jewish community.[80] Moreover, while Abaye and his predecessor uncle were at loggerheads with the townspeople (Ketubbot 105a, Shabbat 153b), Rava apparently was able to walk a fine line in countering arguments hostile to rabbinic authority while maintaining the allegiance of most of his flock.[81]

Moscovitz himself refrains from attempting to explain the origins of this conceptualist departure of the Babylonian Talmud, and while some have suggested the influence of Graeco-Roman culture in fourth-century Babylonia,[82] the jury is still out on the matter. However, I would like to add two other considerations. First, Rava's usual disputant and older contemporary, Abaye, also makes use of a conceptual approach; indeed, in one of Moscovitz's own studies[83] he examines a talmudic passage in which Abaye takes the conceptualist side (Sanhedrin 47b), and there are others as well (Eruvin 15a, Sanhedrin 27a). It would seem that Abaye also adopted the conceptualist approach; the major difference seems to have been that the practical difficulties of carrying out such decisions did not deter him as they did Rava, who, as a Mahozan and a disciple of R. Nahman, was more attuned to practical rabbinics.[84] The other consideration is the increasing use of hypothetical problems by the first four generations of talmudic rabbis, in particular in Babylonia. This can be seen in the vast increase in the number of questions that end with the word *teyku,* "let it stand [over]," indicating that many of these questions, which stand on the boundaries of traditional categories, cannot be answered on the basis of traditional sources. R. Yannai, R. Hoshaya, Hezekiah, and R. Hananiah proposed two such questions in the first third of the third century; in the next generation, R. Yohanan and R. Simeon b. Laqish proposed two and three, respectively; but R. Zeira in the third generation proposed eleven, and his disciple R. Jeremiah proposed no fewer than thirty-two. The number of these puzzling hypotheticals reaches a height of forty-seven with Rava, who also introduced the new style of study, and his disciple, R. Papa, proposed thirty-three.[85] Note that the rabbis associated with the marked increase in such questions were all Babylonians, or Babylonian migrants to Roman Palestine.

Thus, we have the following problem regarding the definition of the category of "at rest" in regard to Sabbath laws.

> Rava set a problem: If a nut is in a container and the container floats on water, do we see it from the point of view of the nut and so it is at rest [in regard to the Sabbath laws regarding impermissible movement of objects from one Sabbath domain to another], or do we perhaps see it from the point of view of the container, which is not at rest but moving? Let [the question] stand. (Shabbat 5b)[86]

Or:

> Rava said: If a man said: "I take an oath that I will not eat" and he ate dust, he is exempt. Rava set a problem: If a man took an oath saying: "I take an oath that I will not eat dust," how much [dust must he eat to be liable to a flogging]? Since he said "I will not eat" he means an olive's bulk [the usual measure for "eating"] or perhaps since it is not something that people eat, he means even the smallest amount. Let [the question] stand. (Shavuot 22b)[87]

In essence, this is the same type of question as in one celebrated dispute between Rava and Abaye, about unconscious abandonment, where a person is unaware of having lost something but will eventually despair of its return when her or she realizes that it was lost: is it considered as legally abandoned from the time of loss or from the time of awareness (Bava Metzia 21b–22a)? This involves the question of intention and awareness and also of *bererah,* the retrospective determination of reality; both issues are typical of the concerns of Abaye and Rava and also of the redactors; and, incidentally, both fulfill Moscovitz's definition of conceptualization.

However, as decisively important as this aspect of Rava's work was, it is only one aspect of his influence on the redactors of the Bavli, and thus on rabbinic thought for the next millennium and a half. Indeed, his influence can scarcely be overestimated. He is mentioned over five thousand times in the Bavli, and is the most frequently cited Babylonian authority in it. R. Yohanan alone is mentioned almost as often (forty-five hundred times), though at times his name serves as a cipher for another Roman Palestinian authority whose name has been lost. In any case, the history of classic Babylonian rabbinic thought can quite legitimately be divided into three periods: the three generations before Rava, the three after him, plus the redactors, on whom his teachings had a decisive influence; Rava's work constitutes a watershed of rabbinic thought.

His influence is felt in several areas, all of which serve to define the work of the Bavli: in the systematization of rabbinic law; as a theoretician of rabbinic law by deriving or applying legal concepts and a depth of appreciation for human behavior to it, as well as a quality somewhat lacking in rabbinical circles, then as now: a historical sense and the role of experience as a datum;[88] and as a theoretician of rabbinic legal midrash, where his major accomplishment was to demand a consistent omnisignificant approach and to point out cases in which his predecessors had failed to interpret biblical gaps. His interest in matters of theodicy and the ideology of the Oral Torah also left their mark on the Talmud, though later generations reinterpreted his remarks in the light of later ideologies, chiefly medieval Jewish philosophy and Kabbalah.

Again, among the concepts regarding whose validity or application Rava raised questions we find several that involve the extent to which human intention is a legal factor. It is noteworthy that these include most of the cases in which later jurists decided matters in favor of Abaye, who is almost always on the side rejecting Rava's proposals. These six issues involve intent, retroactive conditions, and the psychology of malfeasance. We have already examined cases in which psychology and retrospective determination play a role. Abaye and Rava also disagree on whether certain types of false witness are retroactively invalidated when the witness is subsequently convicted of that false testimony (Sanhedrin 27a), whether intent is required for certain ritual actions when the actions exist without the required intent (Eruvin 15a), whether betrothal in cases in which the marriage cannot be consummated is valid (Qiddushin 51a), and whether a husband's change of mind between the time he issues a divorce and the time the wife receives it is effective (Gittin 34a).

In all these cases Rava takes the more nuanced and flexible position; for example, in the case of retrospective abandonment, a person's eventual despair at getting back his loss overcomes the lack of such despair or awareness of loss at the time of loss; on the other hand, in another celebrated dispute as to whether designation is effective immediately for certain religious purposes, such as shrouds for the dead (which are forbidden for any other use), it is Rava who rejects that view, while Abaye accepts it (Sanhedrin 47b). In the six cases enumerated above, later authorities ruled against Rava. Of course, no legal system can serve its society when established on inflexible conceptual principles, and so, in most other cases, Rava's decision does prevail.

With the closing of the Bavli around 530 C.E. the basic contours of subsequent rabbinic philology were set. Thereafter the ideal of an omnisignificant text continued to animate rabbinic thought and commentary down to the current day, often tempered by a sense for the plain meaning, especially of prescriptive legal texts such as *responsa* or codes, and periodically accompanied with the need for codification. However, as Jews moved beyond the Middle East and into other times and cultural situations, other canons of text interpretation that influenced their search for omnisignificance were channeled into the use of strict Aristotelian logic, or overriding adherence to the plain meaning or structural coherence of a text in favor of edificatory omnisignificant interpretations. In a sense, though, the continued study of rabbinic texts reflects the desire for an ideal world, far from the ambiguities, uncertainties, disorders, and injustices of the real one.

Early Arabic Philologists

Poetry's Friends or Foes?

BEATRICE GRUENDLER

Classical Arabic was nobody's native tongue. Its foundations were laid down by a group of scholars who intended to do precisely that. The rapidly expanding Islamic empire in the seventh and early eighth century C.E. required an administrative language and a uniform scripture and liturgy.[1] The influx of foreign converts likewise necessitated the codification of the language, as did the prevalent diglossia in Arabic, for the colloquial idiom of the city-dwelling Arabs differed from the intertribal literary tongue *(ʿarabiyya)* of the Bedouins.

The *ʿArabiyya:* Sources, Transmission, and Ideology

But where did this *ʿarabiyya* come from? Leaving aside incipient prose, the majority of Arabic texts that formed its basis fell into two categories. The first, the Qurʾān, or Islamic Scripture, was the verbatim address by God via the prophet Muhammad to his community in their own language, to wit, "clear Arabic speech" (*lisān ʿarabī mubīn;* Qurʾān 16:103 and 26:195).[2] To preserve this meant to protect the integrity of the divine word. According to the Muslim tradition, the Qurʾān was first memorized and written down in pieces by various Companions of the Prophet until an authoritative edition was commissioned by the fourth caliph, ʿUthmān (r. 644–656).[3] The Qurʾān constituted the longest document as well as the first substantial prose text in Arabic. Because many of its features (syntax, style, and a flexible rhyme that alternated between verse groups, as opposed to the stable rhyme of poetry) were essentially new and some of its vocabulary remote, another text group, archaic poetry (on which more below), was adduced to throw light onto the Qur'ān's obscure passages and explain their grammar and lexicon. Furthermore, the script was open to slightly varying readings that had appeared already in the earliest stages of the text, and which were later codified as accepted "readings" *(qirā'āt)* by Ibn Mujāhid (d. 936).[4]

Here the script posed less of a problem, for the Qur'ān existed both as a recitation, safeguarded by professionals who knew it by heart (*qurrā'*, s. *qāri'*),[5] and as a written text, copied by scribes who already specialized in this in the eighth century.[6] Citations from the Qur'ān were also fewer in number than those from poetry, for instance, in the earliest systematic grammar by the Persian Sībawayhi (d. c. 796).[7] Out of reverence for the Scripture, some pious scholars of language even refrained entirely from discussing it, as this might be construed as exegesis, which they considered beyond their pale, and left that to *qurrā'* and scholars of the prophetic tradition (*muḥaddithūn,* s. *muḥaddith*). The pioneering Abū ʿUbayda (d. c. 822–828) raised eyebrows with his strictly language-based approach to stylistic issues in the scripture. He argued that "God spoke to the Arabs according to their language," and it was therefore necessary to resort to the *ʿarabiyya* if one wanted to understand the Qur'ān correctly.[8] Colleagues criticized his *Explanatory Rewriting of the Qur'ān* and refused to teach it at first, until its popularity among the following generation of students drowned out the opposition.

The second primary source of eloquent Arabic was pagan *(Jāhilī)* Arabic poetry. This seemed at first an unlikely companion to the Scripture, but for lack of other reliable linguistic data, it came to supply the proof texts for the explication of the Qur'ān and the codification of classical Arabic. Ironically, the Scripture whose presence had marginalized pre-Islamic poetry now endowed it with new status as the linguistic evidence that would serve to elucidate the divine word. Poetry in turn was governed by a complex prosody of sixteen quantitative meters and a rhyme that did not change throughout an entire poem. This mnemotechnic framework protected the full vocalization and the case endings of this highly complex literature—as the Arabs would say, "shackled" it—while such linguistic detail could be left out in the script.

Beginning in the late eighth century, some scholars retrieved pagan poetry by traveling to the deserts and interviewing tribal poets or their transmitters. For instance, a young grammar student (the later leader of the Kufan school, al-Kisā'ī; d. 805), who had come to Basra to attend the circle of the lexicographer al-Khalīl (d. 791) and was criticized by a Bedouin for studying Arabic in a city, asked his teacher where he had found his material. On hearing that Khalīl had received it from Bedouins in the Ḥijaz, Najd, and Tihāma (regions of the Arabian Peninsula), the student betook himself there, equipped with fifteen ink flasks, to gather his own corpus; in his eyes, not even the best scholar matched the original sources.[9] Alternatively, Bedouins whom drought, epidemics, or search of fortune had driven to the cities could be consulted on site. A third venue for collecting verse was the fairs outside Kufa (Kunāsa) and Basra (Mirbad), where poets assembled to recite their new compositions.

Scholars of the Arabic language thus responded to urgent needs; they recovered from Bedouin informants poetry in the high language variant and preserved it in editions. Working on a poetic heritage that preceded them by up to two centuries and was created in a Bedouin oral culture, they pursued not only preservation and comparative analysis but also authentication. Regarding the first task, they collected poetry from those Bedouin tribes whose language they deemed pure *(faṣīḥ)* and also showed a surprisingly modern interest in dialectal variants, which they likewise recorded in their books. However, in order to build out of this copious and disparate material a uniform grammatical system that could serve to instruct future learners, they distinguished between features they determined to be model language (*ḥujja* "authoritative" or *muṭṭarid* "regular"), to be used for the formulation of rules, and other features they classified as correct but recondite (*shādhdh* "irregular, anomalous") and not to be imitated.[10] The study of language soon diversified into lexicon *(lugha),* syntax *(naḥw),* and morphology *(ṣarf),* with phonology *(aṣwāt)* playing a minor role. Regarding the second task, authentication, scholars tested native informants in their knowledge of the intertribal high language before recording their recitations.

This being said, poetry, which was composed and performed orally, was not free of variants or linguistic errors. Variants might originate with the poet himself, who adapted his poem to changing audiences. Further editing was accomplished by transmitters (*ruwāt,* s. *rāwī*), the poets' assistants, and sometimes apprentices, who preserved their master's oeuvre *(dīwān)* and tacitly corrected any slips that had occurred. Furthermore, passages of poems became parts of accounts (*akhbār,* s. *khabar*) and were transmitted within them with slight changes. The earliest oral versions of poems are therefore irretrievable, since it was via the transmitters that *dīwān*s eventually made it into writing. However, to spot mistakes became a scholarly endeavor and display of erudition, as is shown, for instance, by the many cases of ancient, early Islamic, and modern poets taken to task by scholars, listed in al-Marzubānī's (d. 994) *Embroidered* [*Book*] *on What Scholars Faulted in Poets (al-Muwashshaḥ fī ma'ākhidh al-'ulamā' 'alā l-shu'arā').*[11] In this way, the guardians of poetry's linguistic integrity and authenticity practiced the earliest form of poetic criticism.[12]

Even linguistically unimpeachable poetry might be forged and ascribed to individuals and tribes in order to bolster their genealogical claims and political clout. Here the philologists viewed themselves as "assayers" (*nuqqād,* s. *nāqid*) of poetry using factual clues and intuitive experience to distinguish the true from the "false poetic coin."[13]

The codification of Arabic coincided with the emergence of the Arabic book culture and formed an essential part of it. A large share of the earliest written works were dictionaries, grammar manuals, and desk references for scribes that permitted Arabs and non-Arabs alike to partake in educated life, government employment, and scholarship. The massive production of books was made possible by paper-making technology, introduced from Samarkand at the end of the eighth century.

Arabic writing preexisted the coming of Islam, but the consonantal alphabet *(abgad),* taken over from the Nabatean branch of late Aramaic, left some grammatical and lexical details open to interpretation or misreading.[14] The problems posed by the reductive script were addressed by combining oral and written modes. The transmission from native informant to scholar and from scholar to student occurred aurally *(samā'),* so the full and correct pronunciation of each word was taught by ear. But written notes, and subsequently books, came increasingly into use and soon formed the basis of transmission between generations of scholars.[15] Still, a book was preferably studied with a teacher by reading it aloud *(qirā'a)* and clarifying the unwritten short vowels and grammatical word endings. A genre that reflects in its very name the described teaching procedure was the *majālis* or "gatherings" (lit. "sessions," s. *majlis*). These consisted of discussions of select linguistic puzzles in no particular order, which were recorded and thus became books under the same title. Information that was not acquired in this interpersonal and complementary, oral and written process was deemed incomplete and unreliable and did not give the student the authority to pass it on.

Indeed, some less productive scholars specialized in simply transmitting in class the book(s) of their teachers.[16] Only during the ninth century did the idea arise that a book might replace its author,[17] but some authors still opposed this and guarded their books carefully from being copied, even though such scholarly "stinginess" might be frowned on.[18] In the course of the eighth century the script had also been optimized with newly invented additional signs *(ḥarakāt, tashkīl),* added above or beneath the letters to denote short vowels, case endings, and other unwritten phenomena. However, this system was used only selectively in most texts. For lexica, in which the complete and correct rendering was vital, scholars developed a way of indicating the pronunciation of difficult words by paraphrase, which did not rely on vowel markers that a copyist might misplace or omit.

Poetry thus belonged to the domain of grammarians and lexicographers. But by the same token, these scholars, who edited and corrected poets' collected works, compiled selections of odes, and gathered accounts about poets' lives into biographical dictionaries, also assumed the task of commenting on the poetry's content: its catalogue of ethics, historical and genealogical references, and even anthropological, zoological, and botanic data. As the sole authorities on everything pertaining to poetry, which was the repository of Arab pre-Islamic heritage, the philologists acted by default as cultural historians.

A further dimension of the philologists' project was ideological. In the young Islamic empire's energetic incorporation of the knowledge of prior civilizations, namely the translation of Greek science and Iranian statecraft, the one item upheld as native and unsurpassable was the Arabic literary heritage. Dictionaries and grammars displayed the richness and perfection of the Arabic language, however foreign the content it might be used to express. More than any other factor, language embodied the self-image of Arabic-Islamic civilization. Philologists thus controlled a type of knowledge of the highest prestige and formative of cultural identity.

By now it has become clear that the scholars who devoted themselves to the investigation of Arabic language in all its aspects—authenticating its sources, integrating these into a system according to a scientific method, and understanding the object of their study as a cultural monument of pre-Islamic Arabia and early Islam—deserve the title of philologists no less than their German counterparts in the nineteenth century. This of course presupposes a more universal conception of the activity of "making sense of texts," for which Sheldon Pollock has made a convincing case. Within this greater commonality, however, the Arabic philological project retains its sociohistorical specificity. For instance, Arabic philologists would not have understood the point of the Nietzsche-Wilamowitz debate[19] between treating a text as an artifact of the past and bringing it alive in the present; in their case the first was a necessary condition of the second. For all their veneration of the textual witnesses they gathered, their sharp-eyed testing of their authenticity, and their linguistic commentary on them,[20] the Arabic philologists were devoted to extracting from these sources a usable language for the present. Their subject was not a dead language but a timeless one. The result of their labor was threefold: a pliable idiom that served translation (from Greek, for example, or Middle Persian) and supported the evolution of many scientific terminologies, a language that held together a society divided among changing dynasties across a far-flung territory that reached from Europe via North Africa to west and central Asia and the Indian subcontinent, and a cultural code whose mastery conferred social capital on its speaker and writer.

The philological dominion over poetry lasted until the end of the eighth century C.E., when the study of language and poetry parted company. The classical Arabic language had been conceived of as a stable, uniform code, constructed to endure—as it has in essence done to this day.[21] The developments that grammar underwent, such as the reordering and diversification of its topics and the reasoning about its foundations *(uṣūl al-naḥw),* did not affect its subject: the language was not expected to change; whatever change occurred was ostracized as corruption or "bad innovation" *(bidʿa).* This found an echo in two genres of books that listed spoken "solecisms of the common people" *(laḥn al-ʿāmma)* and written errors in the diacritical markings of similar-looking letters, or homographs, in texts *(taṣḥīf),* and which were penned by the same individuals who participated in the codification of the language.

The poets, however, did not cease to be poets. Despite their close adherence to the literary tradition—they would return again and again to every theme, motif, and *concetto,* once it had been cast into words—the poets manipulated and expanded this tradition in the late eighth and early ninth century with increasing fluidity and rhetorical savvy. Their conscious verbal artistry was no doubt a reaction to the *esprit du temps* of the Abbasid period, in which appropriated Greek and Iranian heritage and the emerging sciences that built on it widened the cultural horizon, and society grew cosmopolitan in both its composition and outlook. This is the moment when the torch of literary criticism passed, or rather, was wrested, from the hands of the philologists.

In some respects the call for a discipline that dealt with this poetry *as* poetry and not as a manifestation of model language and a sum of linguistic rules parallels the nineteenth-century opposition of German *Sachphilologie,* taking a holistic view of the life of an epoch through its written remains, to *Wortphilologie,* limiting itself to the critique of the "words, syllables, and letters."[22] *Sachphilologie,* to be sure, aspired to a broader range, including history, while advocates of Arabic poetic criticism, such as al-Ṣūlī, separated the subjects of law, prophetic tradition, and royal etiquette from both the linguistic and the poetic-critical disciplines.

The Abbasid-era trend of placing poetic criticism on a par with the other disciplines, but emphasizing its own specificity, arose in great part from the fact that its subject matter, the new poetry, felt the pulse of its time and expressed a sensibility that resonated with its contemporaries, even if they were, at this stage, more often amateurs than scholars. Nonetheless, they understood the new poetry better than did any scholar of the established language disciplines.

Instead of the rule-based approach of philology, the new critics followed the contemporary poets in the ways they stretched or violated conventions of style and verisimilitude to reality and invented new ways to generate metaphors. While acknowledging their debt to earlier poets, their Abbasid successors were granted greater artistic freedom, released from the normative codes of language for which their predecessors had supplied the specimens.

The main thrust of the argument was to see contemporary poems as not examples of linguistic rules but innovative creations; they were taken as unique and unusual pieces and could not be understood based on the standards that had until then existed. This view resembles Peter Szondi's insistence that literary creation must be understood as the outcome of a process and cannot be judged based on criteria imported from another discipline.[23] Mutatis mutandis al-Ṣūlī's demand that the critic possess the "ability to distinguish the rare, the mediocre, and the inferior," not merely be able "to reject a linguistic error or a lexical slip,"[24] parallels Szondi's emphasis on the "critical activity of distinguishing and deciding" ("die kritische Tätigkeit des Scheidens und Entscheidens"), which has a "dynamic moment," versus a mere knowledge of facts.[25]

"Good" Poetry

To start from the beginning, early Arabic grammarians and lexicographers had a clear concept of what "good" poetry should be. It had to be ancient and authentic, deriving from before the advent of Islam or its early years up to the Umayyad period (661–750 C.E.). Poetry further had to be linguistically sound *(faṣīḥ)* to carry evidentiary value as a textual source for the *ʿarabiyya.* On the literary plane, great poets had to demonstrate their mastery over a set of well-known subjects, namely, boast *(fakhr),* praise *(madīḥ),* love lyric *(nasīb/ghazal),* and satire *(hijāʾ);*[26] and verbal ornament owed much to physical description *(waṣf)* and comparison *(tashbīh),* delving into the rich and arcane lexicon *(gharīb)* of the Arab Bedouin. However, no quality label persists without an institution to safeguard it. This role these philologists assumed, as arbiters and experts who also had the ear of the political leadership, entertaining them in erudite evening conversations and tutoring their offspring.[27] According to one account, al-Mufaḍḍal al-Ḍabbī (d. 780 or 786) was commissioned by Caliph al-Manṣūr (r. 754–775) to compose an anthology of lesser-known pre-Islamic verse to teach his son proper Arabic.[28] In another, the reputable scholar al-Aṣmaʿī (d. 828) gained the favor of al-Rashīd by shortening the caliph's sleepless night with poetry.[29]

Excursus: Why Did Poetry Matter?

Why did poetry matter? Tribal warfare and peacemaking had been accompanied by poetry, and Arab phylarchs had already been patronizing poets in pre-Islamic times. In the eighth century the profession of poetry became more lucrative than ever, serving the imperial aspirations and representational needs of the newly ascended dynasty of the Abbasids (750–1258 C.E.). Poetry also continued to be a way to redress injustice, for either the poets themselves or people who appealed for their services. The range of suffered ills that poetry was charged to remedy included excessive taxation, abusive tax collection, damage to or loss of property, exorbitant interest on personal debts, and retrieval of requisitioned funds.[30]

Poetry was even presented at law courts for the redress of injustices *(maẓālim)*[31] and dispatched by letter from prison to plead for freedom. Certainly poetry did not guarantee the desired result, but it offered a last resort when all else had failed. The success of poetic petitions depended of course on the recipient: did he understand and appreciate good poetry? Most likely he did—if not, he pretended to. For those who served at court or in government, knowledge of and familiarity with Arabic poetry was a mark of affiliation with the cultural elite, both the Arab political and military leaders and their non-Arab bureaucrats, courtiers, and entertainers. Literary education was a ladder for social climbing.

Ancient versus Contemporary Aesthetics

At the turn of the ninth century, the simple equation between poetry's normative quality and its social significance no longer held true: simply put, the "good" ancient poetry and the poetry that mattered had grown apart. An aesthetic rift had arisen between audiences who applauded the contemporary poets and others who ignored them in a *querelle des anciens et des modernes* that continued for over a century.[32] Poetry had evolved in step with the more urban and cosmopolitan society of the Abbasid era. The controversy was sparked in particular by a kind of loan metaphor (*istiʿāra* in the parlance of philologists) in which the aspect of comparison *(wajh)* between image and reality was no longer visible, and the metaphor became imaginary, as in "the cutting off of fate at its forearm."[33] The term *badīʿ*, which poets and critics earlier used for this same trope, soon broadened to include other figures and denote the new style as a whole.[34] (The word *badīʿ* derived from the same root as *bidʿa,* the aforementioned term for a bad innovation.) For some, "the new style" *(badīʿ),* also called "modern" *(muḥdath)* poetry, was so new as to be incomprehensible. This was expressed by the Basrian grammarian al-Tawwazī (d. 845 or later), who enjoyed fame for his extensive knowledge and memorization of archaic poetry.[35] When al-Tawwazī was consulted about an ode by his contemporary Abū Tammām (d. 845) dedicated to the governor Khālid b. Yazīd b. Mazyad,[36] and was asked, "Abū Aḥmad, what do you think about this poetry?" he answered with bewilderment: "Some of it I find beautiful, and some of it I do not know and have never heard the like of. This man is either the best poet of all people, or all people are better poets than him."[37]

Another account with the philologist and transmitter Ibn al-Aʿrābī (d. 839 or 844) features a more damning comment: "If this is poetry, then what the Arabs have composed is worthless [*bāṭil*]."[38] Others focused their criticism on Abū Tammām (d. 845), who best exemplified the "new style's" intellectual and rhetorical thrust.[39] The wider debates in assemblies and audiences—whose literary recordings partly survive today—generated a spectrum of comments on modern poetry that touch on many further imaginary aspects of it. This pronounced abstract dimension went beyond what philologists had encountered in earlier poetry, and they lacked the appropriate expertise in it. Courtiers, conversely, who met contemporary poets regularly, had more exposure to the modern style and had their fingertips on the pulse of the changing literary fashion. If most of them must be considered amateurs, it is also in this milieu that some of the earliest preserved works of poetic criticism were written (in essence apologies of the figurehead of the modern style, Abū Tammām), namely by the prince Ibn al-Muʿtazz (d. 908) and the courtier and tutor of caliphs al-Ṣūlī (d. 946).[40]

Sources for the Debate on Evolving Aesthetics

Before surveying the various positions adopted, one needs briefly to take stock of the society and the textual traces it bequeathed. The eighth century had marked a major shift in the geopolitical center, ethnic composition, and social culture of the Arabic-Islamic world. The Umayyad dynasty with its capital in Damascus under a purely Arab leadership (661–750) had been overthrown by the Abbasids, who relied on newly various ethnic and religious interest groups to ascend to power. The Abbasids founded Baghdad, a new capital farther east, and purported to represent a more equitable Islamic government. They relied on non-Arab converts *(mawālī)* as administrative clerks, many of them from Aramaic and Persian families who passed an office down among themselves over several generations. The legitimatory program of the caliphs to have Greek and Middle Persian sources translated (mostly by Christians) and thereby innovate in Arab science and culture enriched the universe of knowledge.[41] Aristotle and Galen came to be seen as intellectual forebears, as much as the Sasanian king Kisrā Anūshirvān (Chosroes) and the Brahmin Baydabāʾ (Vidyāpati). The new converts did not limit themselves to the evolving Arabic prose, which they applied in administrative documents and epistles, but also tried their hands at Arabic poetry, which had been considered an indigenous Arab art, and they were distinguished from their predecessors as both "hybrid" and "postclassical" *(muwallad).*[42]

The first resource for understanding the new poetry is poets' collected works (*dīwān*s), which indicated the *gharaḍ,* or "intent,"[43] of a given poem, the name of the addressee in the case of an encomium or satire, and occasionally bits of circumstantial information, all of which is, however, too sketchy to reconstruct the context in which a poem was received.

More fruitful are those early critical treatises that do not ignore or marginalize modern poets, as do the grammarian Thaʿlab (d. 904) in his *Foundations of Poetry (Qawāʿid al-shiʿr)* and the secretary Qudāma b. Jaʿfar (d. 948) in his *Assaying of Poetry (Naqd al-shiʿr).* Ibn Ṭabāṭabāʾ (d. 934) in his *Yardstick of Poetry (ʿIyār al-shiʿr)* cites moderns but barely comments on them beyond the introduction. One work, the *Book of the New Style (Kitāb al-Badīʿ),* by the princely critic Ibn al-Muʿtazz, openly defends modern poetry, but precisely by denying its novelty in kind, if not degree, in relation to the older poetry and Qurʾānic prose. Most significant is his lengthy section on the aforementioned loan metaphor *(istiʿāra).*

Other tropes also shocked, or thrilled, audiences and critics with their imaginary potential, such as extreme hyperbole *(ghuluww, ifrāṭ, ighrāq).*[44]

The imaginary was not yet isolated and identified with a technical term. It would be two centuries until it received concerted attention in a poetic treatise, the *Mysteries of Eloquence (Asrār al-balāgha),* by the ingenious ʿAbdalqāhir al-Jurjānī (d. 1078).[45] Al-Jurjānī identified the concept of *takhyīl* ("evocation of imagination") as the generative principle underlying endless variations of imaginary tropes and provided a working list of phenomena and their Arabic terms.[46]

To appreciate *takhyīl,* however, did not take as long as formally to codify it. The early Abbasid poets' increased and conscious application of novel tropes anticipated a receptive audience; poetry did not exist in a vacuum, and if there were detractors, there were also supporters. This leads to the third and most substantial textual source, biographies of poets, which contain accounts *(akhbār)* of how contemporary poetry was received, examples of which will be discussed below. The difficulty lies in making these texts speak: they contain only scattered comments by poets, literati, and critics made during specific situations when a poem was performed. Or worse, no comments are given and the opinions of editors are left implicit in their selection (and omission) of verses in long odes. However, the recurrence of cases and the repetition of similar standpoints adopted yield a meaningful sample.

Among the authors of poets' lives, there is again a division of opinion on the selection of the poets deemed worthy of inclusion.[47] Al-Aṣmaʿī and al-Jumaḥī (d. 846–847) completely ignored their contemporaries. The judge and man of letters Ibn Qutayba (d. 889) occupied a middle position; he paid lip service to the moderns but treated them gingerly nonetheless, keeping the number of poets from his own century to 16 from among a total of 206 (i.e., 8 percent). Other critics in turn regarded only contemporaries as worthy of attention, notably the undersecretary Ibn al-Jarrāḥ (d. 908) and the already mentioned Ibn al-Muʿtazz and al-Ṣūlī.[48]

The earliest books devoted to poets of the first Abbasid era are *The Book of the Sheet (al-Waraqa),* by Ibn al-Jarrāḥ,[49] *Classes of* [*Modern*] *Poets* (*Ṭabaqāt al-shuʿarāʾ* [*al-muḥdathīn*]), by Ibn al-Muʿtazz,[50] the *Accounts (Akhbār)* of the modern poets Abū Tammām and al-Buḥturī, and the two preserved sections on poets in *The Book of the Sheets (al-Awrāq),* by al-Ṣūlī.[51] Variants of their accounts are preserved in al-ʿAskarī's dictionary of poetic motifs, *Dīwān al-maʿānī.* They all contain accounts that capture events in poets' lives along with terse general remarks and selections of their verse.

Most of these poets composed the controversial modern verse, or "new style" *(badīʿ),* as distinct from pre-Islamic, early Islamic, and Umayyad poetry, subsumed under ancient *(qadīm, mutaqaddim)* poetry. The *akhbār* vary in size, content, and structure. Their length ranges between a few lines and several pages. As to substance, the usual combination of a chain of transmitters *(isnād)* and narration is often enlivened by dramatic scenes and/or poetry. In terms of structure, prose and poetry about an event may be integrated, juxtaposed, or haphazardly interposed. Other than in the historical accounts limited to prose, poetry constitutes a vital element, if not the keystone of the plot in literary accounts.[52] These late ninth- and early tenth-century authors were no longer direct contemporaries of the Abbasid poets they studied. But much of their work consisted of poetic quotations and collected accounts that were considerably older. The latter still preserved their customary oral format: a short, self-contained text preceded by a list of transmitters. An account could thus antedate by two to three generations the compilation within which it survived.

Supporters of Modern Poetry

Why were accounts of contemporary poets thought worth collecting? It is not enough of an explanation that the three author-compilers under investigation belonged to the elite, either by birth, like Ibn al-Muʿtazz, or through skill and generations of service, like Ibn al-Jarrāḥ and al-Ṣūlī, and moved in the circles in which this poetry found acclaim. Rather, all three authors considered the practitioners of the new Abbasid poetry as worthy of scholarly attention, and one way of establishing the status and pedigree of a scholarly or professional class was to devote a biographical dictionary to it.[53] Two of them, moreover, were poets themselves. They promoted the new style by devoting *akhbār* books exclusively to modern poets and recording their oeuvres—even of those deemed obscure. Al-Ṣūlī compiled *dīwān*s of nearly every great modern poet.[54] What is more, in his *Awrāq,* he salvaged the works of lesser representatives, as did Ibn al-Muʿtazz and Ibn al-Jarrāḥ.

To glean a more precise image of their books' agenda and intended audience, we can also turn to occasional direct remarks and comments on accounts, as well as to the long preface of al-Ṣūlī's *Akhbār Abī Tammām.*[55] Al-Ṣūlī argued there explicitly: "their [sc. the moderns'] poetry is also more like the times, and people employ it more in their sessions, writings, proverbial sayings and pursuits."[56] He upheld contemporary poetry as culturally more relevant. In a polemic, cameo-like statement—attributed via al-Zubayr b. Bakkār (d. 870) to Muṣʿab al-Muwaswis (fl. first half of the ninth century)—that seems to epitomize the purpose of his book, Ibn al-Muʿtazz makes the accounts and events *(ayyām)* of modern poets "erase" the (ancient) Arab poetry *(shiʿr),* among other disciplines.[57] The account appears in a variant where conversation, not modern poetry, carries the day.[58] Irrespective of whether Ibn al-Muʿtazz or his source performed the substitution, the resulting version expresses the opinion of the former as a literary manifesto for the modern poets *(muḥdathūn).* This reading is confirmed by Ibn al-Muʿtazz's concluding comments in the vita of the poet Abū al-Shīṣ (d. 812):

> His poems, anecdotes, and jests are extremely copious, but we do not abandon the [selective] method of the book, lest the reader be bored, with a single section growing lengthy, and [we also retain it] so he may remember these jokes, anecdotes, and jests and rest from the accounts and poems of the forebears, for this is something people have much related and grown bored with. It is said: delight is in everything new. *That which one rather employs in our time are the poems and accounts of the moderns;* from here we have taken the best of each *khabar* and the core of each timeless poem [*qilāda*].[59]

The selected *akhbār* and the comments of Ibn al-Muʿtazz and al-Ṣūlī lead me furthermore to suggest that, besides crediting their own circles with properly appreciating modern poetry, they also claimed intellectual authority over it. Such an ambition was liable to create tension with those traditionally thought of as poetic specialists, namely, the philologists, who had built their careers and reputations on ancient poetry and other early proof texts of the *ʿarabiyya* but treated it merely as a quarry for grammar and lexicon.

The debate about the new style has been investigated in numerous studies by Wolfhart Heinrichs from the perspective of literary criticism. Beyond its novel tropes and rhetorization, this style also gave rise to a new terminology, most famously its designation *badīʿ,* used by poets, critics, and transmitters who moved with the times,[60] but shunned and paraphrased by philologists.[61] When in 887 C.E. Ibn al-Muʿtazz composed his pioneering book-length definition of *badīʿ,* he admitted the novelty of the term—if not its substance—and the absence to date of any authority as to its definition.[62] Such a statement implies that those to whose province the evaluation of poetry belonged limited themselves to the ancient period and avoided scholarly engagement with the new style—even though they might enjoy it privately.[63] Ibn al-Muʿtazz still strove to vindicate modern poetry by trying to integrate its phenomena[64] with the older tradition.[65] But a generation later, al-Ṣūlī went further and called for literary criticism of modern verse as its own discipline. In his eyes, such expertise had to be acquired by study and could not be practiced by simply transferring extant philological standards:

> The poems of the ancients have been made docile to them; they transmitted them extensively and found authorities who had gone through the [ancient poems] for them and tamed their motifs. Thus they recite [these] and explain them, approving the good and faulting the bad in the footsteps of others. The words of the ancients, even if they vary in excellence, resemble each other and are interconnected.[66] [Scholars] therefore deduce what they do not know from what they know and overcome the difficult with the accessible.
>
> For the poetry of the moderns, since the age of Bashshār (d. 784), however, [these scholars] have not found authorities or transmitters as they had [for the poetry of the ancients], who combined those needed qualities. And they have not recognized what [Abū Tammām] was capable of and accomplished. They have not given him his due, ignored him, and then opposed him; as God (Mighty and Glorious) says, "No; but they have cried lies to that whereof they comprehend not the knowledge,"[67] and as it is said, "Man is the enemy of that which he ignores, for he who is ignorant of a thing opposes it." Scholars [of this group], when asked to teach the poetry of Bashshār, Abū Nuwās, Muslim, Abū Tammām, and others, have avoided saying, "I do not know this well," by insulting Abū Tammām in particular, because he is closest to their time and his poetry is the most difficult.[68]

Al-Ṣūlī held that at the root of denigration of the modern poets—when it was more than objective criticism—lay a lack of expertise in what he declared to be a new discipline. He condemned the unfounded animosity as intellectual inertia and conservatism:

> How could someone not resort to such an expedient [as insults] who says, "Study with me the poems of the ancients," and then, when he is asked about anything in the poems of [the moderns], ignores it. What shall he fall back on if not insulting that with which he is unfamiliar? If he were fair-minded, he would learn it from its experts [*ahl*], as he has learned other [poetry], and [then] be preeminent in knowledge of it, for learning is not barred to anyone, nor has anyone a special right to it.[69]

In contrast to such narrow-minded scholarship, al-Ṣūlī argued that the two most preeminent philologists, Thaʿlab (d. 904) and al-Mubarrad (d. 898), acknowledged modern literary criticism as beyond their purview and did not falsely arrogate its knowledge to themselves. They claimed no understanding of the "new style" *(badīʿ)* of contemporary verse and recused themselves from judgment.

> Nor did they claim preeminence in the discipline of modern poets and their pioneers, who coincided with the beginning of the Abbasid dynasty (God prolong and safeguard it). Nor [did they claim], when they undertook such poetry, that they could do so and could compose the like of it. Nor [did they claim] that they fully knew each and every word of it and were able to distinguish the rare, the mediocre, and the inferior, beyond rejecting a linguistic error or a lexical slip. Nor did they claim preeminence over others in prosody and rhyme theory, genealogy and the writing of memoranda, correspondence and rhetoric, and the recognition of poets' plagiarisms and mutual borrowings, who excelled in it and who floundered. Nor did anyone else claim this for them. Instead, they were prominent in [knowledge of] syntax and lexicon, and both knew something of these fields, and neither said, "I make no mistakes," or, when he ignored something, felt embarrassed to say, "I do not know."[70]

Al-Ṣūlī corroborates this with an account about Thaʿlab—whose aforementioned poetic treatise leaves modern poetry aside—candidly admitting his ignorance on the subject. Set to participate in the literary session of Abū l-ʿAbbās Aḥmad Ibn Thawāba,[71] in which Abū Tammām's poetry was the going fare, Thaʿlab dreaded embarrassment and begged the Banū Nawbakht[72] for assistance:

> The Banū Nawbakht related to me—and I never saw Abū l-ʿAbbās Aḥmad ibn Yaḥyā [Thaʿlab], with all the veneration he enjoyed among everyone, to be more revered than by [the Banū Nawbakht], each of them attributing his learning to him—that [Thaʿlab] said to them, "I spend much time with scribes, in particular Abū l-ʿAbbās Ibn Thawāba, and most of what goes on in their gatherings is [discussion of] the poetry of Abū Tammām, which I do not know. Select some of it for me!" So we made a selection for him and gave it to him. He took it to Ibn Thawāba, who approved it.
>
> "It is not something I selected," [Thaʿlab] said, "rather, the Banū Nawbakht selected it for me."
>
> [The Banū Nawbakht further] said:[73] [Thaʿlab] used to recite to us some verse of [Abū Tammām's] poetry and then ask "What did he mean by this?" So we explained it to him.
>
> "By God," [Thaʿlab] then said, "he has done well and excelled!"[74]

Lesser philologists who lacked Thaʿlab's integrity attracted the ire of al-Ṣūlī for their uninformed and inappropriate limitation to the correctness of language in their dealings with modern poetry. He challenged the scholars of the former field to acknowledge modern poetry as fundamentally different from the earlier verse they knew and requiring a separate, if learnable, critical discipline: "Those critics would first have to study before they speak and criticize."[75] Yet while al-Ṣūlī chastised some philologists' self-serving disregard for the intellectual demands of modern poetry, he similarly furthered his own cause of validating a knowledge he possessed and from which he profited to earn his livelihood.

Diverging Standards of Philology and Poetics

Accounts from poets' biographical dictionaries capture occasions of philologists responding to and commenting on modern verse. Philologists applied their strictures to poets who took liberties with the *ʿarabiyya,* criticizing them for two sets of infractions. Closer to their expertise lay errors of linguistic order, which they pointed out. Thus Bashshār, usually a paragon of linguistic flawlessness,[76] was criticized by a grammarian for using in two poems a noun formation *(faʿlā)* that existed but was unattested for the particular etyma to which the poet applied it. The grammarian censured the poet for having misused grammatical analogy *(qiyās):* "It is Bashshār who derived the [words] by analogy, but this is not something that can be derived."[77] This type of reasoning had been introduced by the grammarians to explain existing words but not to derive new ones. The story ends with poetic justice, likely a literary topos: the poet, a feared satirist, invited the grammarian to debate him, and the latter, afraid to fall prey to the poet's sharp tongue, disavowed his earlier words and used the poet's verse henceforth as linguistic evidence to appease him. Philologists understandably insisted on the rule of grammar, but erroneous or deviant language occurred alike in ancient and modern poetry, and their focus on the latter was perceived as disingenuous and prejudiced.

Another sort of criticism touched on poetic themes, tropes, and style. Out of the many objections against the verse of Abū Tammām, al-Ṣūlī selects in his preface the one against his famous victory ode on Caliph al-Muʿtaṣim's capture of the Byzantine border fortress of Amorium in 838.[78] Abū Tammām's mention of figs and grapes incurred blame, and al-Ṣūlī rejects the criticism on both general and specific levels. First, these fruits had been mentioned in two earlier verses, which al-Ṣūlī cites, and could therefore not be deemed inappropriate in principle. Second, Abū Tammām mentioned them to indicate the season in which the Byzantine astrologers had predicted their own victory over the besiegers—a prediction subsequently proven wrong by the Muslim conquest—and they served a purpose in the ode's historical narrative. Al-Ṣūlī supported this explanation by citing his own teacher, who had himself studied with Abū Tammām, and whose father had participated in the siege.

Another example of criticism concerned a lamentation of a general from the Nabhān clan of the tribe of Tamīm.[79] Al-Ṣūlī set the scene with another general's acclaim of the ode in public. Abū Tammām had described the deceased's clan as "stars of the sky from whose midst the full moon had fallen."[80] Critics opined that a better image to portray the tribe's standing would have been to say, as a younger contemporary had done, "when a moon among them fades or is eclipsed, another moon looms shining from the horizon." But this, al-Ṣūlī pointed out, missed the poet's intended nuance, for Abū Tammām wanted to distinguish greater from lesser patrons and bring out the lamented general's uniqueness.

While linguistic nitpicking was at the worst tendentious but justified, criticism of poetry's substance as shown above was conspicuously wrong and revealed a lack of understanding. In the two examples involving Abū Tammām, critics were contradicted by the compiler al-Ṣūlī, writing a century later as part of his argument to defend poetic criticism as a discipline separate and independent from grammar and lexicography. But already in Abū Tammām's lifetime, another group had begun to wrest the role of aesthetic arbiter from the philologists. The first person entitled to respond to a poem was obviously its official addressee, such as the ruler receiving a panegyric, an apology, or a poem of admonition or condolence, and his reaction would often take the form of material reward.[81] But the wider audience of fellow poets, literati, and critics were more forthright and specific in their comments. Unconcerned with poetry for the sake of self-portrayal, they were eager to defend new aesthetic tenets or display their expertise therein before the presiding host. Such advocates showed their appreciation implicitly (as the terminology was still in flux) by skillfully editing the odes they were defending and letting them speak for themselves, in trimmed, "optimized" form.[82]

One such debate is set in Marw (in modern Turkmenistan), between two members of the Yazīdī family of literati.[83] Ibrāhīm b. Abī Muḥammad (d. 840), a grammarian, found fault with a verse by Abū Nuwās for its being "neither natural nor good speech." His nephew Aḥmad (d. before 874),[84] who was close in age to his uncle and himself a poet, transmitter, and familiar of al-Maʾmūn, took the opposite view: "[Abū Nuwās] rendered the motif well and excelled." The modern poet Muslim b. al-Walīd (d. 823), who was a frequent guest at the house of Ibrāhīm's brother, had to be called to the scene to arbitrate, and he pronounced the verse acceptable, though in a backhanded way: he declared it preferable to a more far-fetched verse by a lesser poet. Irrespective of Muslim's sarcastic reservation (which a later gloss attributes to jealousy), the two Yazīdīs parted company over the verse's dominant feature of a causal hyperbole:

rasmu l-karā bayna l-jufūni muḥīlu
ʿaffā ʿalayhi bukan ʿalayki ṭawīlu

The trace of sleep between my lids is one year old,
long weeping about you has washed it away.[85]

At the propositional level, the lover's weeping about the beloved's absence leaves him sleepless, a topos of the Islamic love lyric *(ghazal).*[86] This is expressed, however, on the level of the image by the pre-Islamic motif of rain effacing the traces of the departed beloved's encampment. This motif likewise expresses a separation of lovers, but one that by literary convention is final and irreversible, whereas the separation in the Abbasid *ghazal* is not necessarily so. The choice of the pre-Islamic motif then acts as an amplification. The genius lies in Abū Nuwās's exact matching of most elements in the analogy to the propositional level: the departed beloved is figured as fleeting sleep, and the poet's tears become the figurative rain. In these elements, however, the generative analogy is no longer visible, which was probably awkward for the conservative taste of the grammarian Ibrāhīm. Moreover, the campsite trace itself has no counterpart in the actual situation of sleeplessness and is an imaginary metaphor.

The daring artistry of this causal hyperbole was the new territory of poets in the early ninth century. This is the gist of another *khabar* about the same verse combined with the one following it in Abū Nuwās's *Dīwān,* in which the poet naturalizes the metaphor of the beloved's killing glances:[87]

yā nāẓiran mā aqlaʿat laḥaẓātuhū
ḥattā tashaḥḥaṭa baynahunna qatīlu

Oh, what an eye whose glances do not swerve
until the victim rolls before them in his blood.

Here the audience consists of a group of dignitaries, most likely scribes (*kuttāb,* s. *kātib*), of the Syrian city of Qinnasrīn. The orator-poet al-ʿAttābī (d. c. 835), one of the early moderns, sits in their midst, examining a handwritten note for a long time. At length he speaks, assuring himself that everyone has seen the note, and thereupon comments, "the author [of these lines] has traveled a valley no one has crossed before." As opposed to the grammarian above, the scribes proved receptive to poetic imagination.

Besides this fantastic dimension, for philologists perhaps the most offensive, modern poetry contained many other aspects, such as the overuse of rhetorical ornament, recherché archaisms, and far-fetched variations and clusters of familiar motifs. The two preceding anecdotes show a spectrum of attitudes, critical, aloof, and favorable, the last stance being that of a courtier-poet, an orator-poet, and a group of scribes. In their circles the modern style was obviously welcome. Courtiers and educated administrators, also labeled literati (*udabāʾ*, s. *adīb*),[88] thus claimed the aesthetic authority formerly enjoyed by the philologists; in status they even overtook them, occupying salaried positions in the administration and acting as patrons themselves.

Enlightened Philologists as Witnesses for the Defense

The editors of *akhbār* were most persuasive when they made champions of archaic poetry *nolens volens* argue in favor of modern poets. This occurred, for example, when ʿUmāra b. ʿAqīl (d. c. 847–861) appeared in Baghdad. As the last epigone of the archaic style, he made a perfect umpire for Abū Tammām's verse, which was contested for, among other things, its archaisms yoked together unevenly with modern rhetorical figures. The illustrious visitor listened to an ode recited to him in its actual verse order, but in installments. Each time the reciter stopped, ʿUmāra approved and demanded: "Go on." At verses 5–6, he vaunted the poet's refreshing reinvention of the commonplace complaint of exile as something the poet actually desired.

> *wa-lākinnanī lam aḥwi wafran mujammaʿan*
> *fa-fuztu bihī illā bi-shamlin mubaddadi*
>
> *wa-lam tuʿṭinī l-ayyāmu nawman musakkanan*
> *aludhdhu bihī illā bi-nawmin musharradi*
>
> But I possess no collected wealth
> to call my own, save a scattered assemblage.
>
> Nor did the days grant me restful slumber
> to savor, except for slumber chased. . . .

Listening thereafter to verses 7–8, ʿUmāra found this theme brought to perfection.

wa-ṭūlu muqāmi l-marʾi fī l-ḥayyi mukhliqun
li-dībājatayhi fa-ghtarib tatajaddadi

fa-innī raʾaytu l-shamsa zīdat maḥabbatan
ilā l-nāsi idh laysat ʿalayhim bi-sarmadi.

A man's long lingering in his quarter wears out
the freshness of his face—travel to refresh it!

I found the sun to be dearer to people
for not shining upon them in perpetuity.[89]

This sample sufficed for ʿUmāra to proclaim Abū Tammām the best poet, based on criteria seldom conceded him, such as good wording, beautiful motifs, sustained intent, and balanced speech *(jawdat al-lafẓ, ḥusn al-maʿānī, iṭṭirād al-murād, ittisāq al-kalām).*[90] In this literary debate the ode *(qaṣīda)* was not recited in total. Rather, the critical approach required the highlighting of certain aspects and produced a trimmed text that stood in for the whole. ʿUmāra's treatment thus cuts the ode down to its strophe but observes the verse order of the excerpt, only interrupting each couplet with commentary. This shortening or "excision" is a strategy of practical criticism for optimizing the impact of the ode on a resisting audience.[91]

Al-Ṣūlī even quotes the paragon of philology, al-Mubarrad, in favor of the maligned modern style (after having described him elsewhere as claiming no expertise in it).[92] The visiting grammarian was hindered by Prince Ibn al-Muʿtazz from leaving his palace, when a man from the Banū Nuʿmān challenged him to suggest any poet who could have outdone a famous apology by Abū Tammām. To make the case, the Nuʿmānī recited it to al-Mubarrad, suppressing the strophe and carving out the poet's defense from the antistrophe to show off its construction. In the recomposed version, Abū Tammām first tells about learning of the false accusation, namely his having satirized his patron, the governor of Damascus, Abū l-Mughīth Mūsā b. Ibrāhīm al-Rāfiqī (24); then the poet dismisses such alleged ingratitude (25, 27–28) and demonstrates with two rhetorical questions and a fantastic causal hyperbole the absurdity of the charge from the standpoints of both poet (31) and public (32–33). An excuse for any unintended offense concludes the excerpt (38, also the ode's last verse). The logical, tightly argued defense created by the streamlining is further accentuated by a variant of verse 28: "I am to have *denied* [*jaḥadtu*] so many a favor of yours," which is stronger than the *Dīwān*'s "I am to have *forgotten* [*nasītu*]."[93]

The apology's effect on the listening grammarian was immediate and total. He admitted that people who slighted Abū Tammām were either ignorant of the "discipline of poetry and speech" (*ʿilm al-shiʿr wa-maʿrifat al-kalām*) or scholars who had not themselves heard and studied his poetry in depth *(tabaḥḥara).* Al-Mubarrad's recanting late in life his earlier criticism of Abū Tammām not only delighted the princely host but also proved how well a "trimmed" recitation made a poem's case. Al-Mubarrad concedes the obvious point that the editor al-Ṣūlī wishes to make: the existence of a "discipline of poetry and speech," which is distinct from the science of correct language and must be learned from different authorities. The grammarian is made to arrive at this realization upon the skillful recomposition of the ode by the reciter, who displays in this act of intervention the very knowledge al-Mubarrad lacks. The encounter could thus be understood as an allegory for the tryst between the two disciplines, language-centered philology being vanquished by poetics. Yet things were more complex.

The chosen sample of *akhbār* appears to advocate that modern poetry had become de facto the literary currency of the new Abbasid elite and a bone of contention between philology and poetics. It is plausible, moreover, that Ibn al-Muʿtazz and al-Ṣūlī sought to invest this new audience of scribes and monarchs de jure with intellectual authority over it, ascribing to them a critical discernment philologists allegedly lacked. The two authors' shifting the locus[94] of this expertise creates a tug-of-war with traditional linguists, whose concept of poetry as the bulwark of an unchanging language was diametrically opposed to their own view of it as a living art form.

As in the debate over the nature and scope of German philology in the nineteenth century, a broader and more dynamic view was advocated by the new Arabic critics. They treated poetry as more than a product of language: as an art that breathed the changing sensibility of its time and deserved a particular approach (still evolving toward becoming a discipline) that did justice to its new kind of creativity.

Meanwhile, despite their protestations, early Arabic philologists, though unfamiliar with the professional terminology of the new style and baffled by its abstract, rhetoricized imagery, often privately appreciated it as art. What is more, in contexts unrelated to linguistic argument, they faithfully transmitted select verses and their fledgling practical criticism by courtiers and fellow poets.[95] The philologists' public denigration of the modern style, and their elevation of chronology over quality, must partly be chalked up to professional self-preservation. But their silent, self-abnegating service in documenting the growing reception of modern poetry as literary historians, attested to only in the chains of transmission of the *akhbār,* is substantial and must also be acknowledged.

Outlook

The foregoing essay has focused on a transformational phase that was concluded in the mid-tenth century (although poetics preserved its dynamic even beyond this, responding to further new literary styles and genres that emerged). However, to do justice to Arabic philology, one must add that the emancipation of poetics, once completed, was soon followed by the synthesis of linguistic and literary knowledge into the "art of philology" *(ṣinā ʿat al-adab)* or "the literary arts" *(al-ʿulūm al-adabiyya),* the latter of which even included creative writing.[96] In the thirteenth century C.E., rhetoric (including poetics) was integrated into a standard theory of language, famously laid down in the *Key to the Sciences (Miftāḥ al-ʿulūm)* by al-Sakkākī (d. 1229) and revised by al-Qazwīnī (1338).[97] Grammar meanwhile never lost its prestige throughout the entire premodern period but continued to form the basis of (in particular religious) learning, and it remained an essential domain of intellectual distinction among the educated elite. This prevailed even under the non-Arab dynasties of the Mamluks and Ottomans,[98] whose reigns were marked by social inequality and political disruption, while Arab letters provided a protective social network and manifested a sustained productivity—only to be cut short by the onset of colonialism.[99]

What Was Philology in Sanskrit?

SHELDON POLLOCK

EVEN READERS who know little else about the history of traditional Indian learning, at least Sanskrit learning, are likely to know that grammar was the queen of the sciences, with Pāṇini (fourth century B.C.E.?) at the head of a very long and distinguished list of dramatis personae. Over the past two centuries, an impressive body of Western scholarship has been produced exploring the structure of this intricate and sophisticated system of language analysis. What is astonishing, however, even to specialists in the field, is how little scholarship we possess—at least scholarship that is historically deep, systematically ordered, and conceptually rich—on the other traditional Indian forms of language-and-text analysis, beyond the phonology and morphology constituting the sphere of traditional grammar, that take us into domains we would include under any reasonable definition of philology—one that demands, not a specific set of methodological or theoretical features invariable across all time and space, but the broader concern with *making sense of texts.*

Under such a definition, "philology" is certainly the appropriate designation for a range of textual practices and interpretive protocols in the Sanskrit tradition. What is puzzling is that such practices and protocols were never identified as a separate "knowledge form" *(vidyāsthāna)*[1]—indeed, that no covering term exists in Sanskrit that even approximates "philology." But it is not after all surprising that people can have a conception of the parts of a thing without a conception of a whole; recall Bruno Snell's old argument that in archaic Greece, although there were words for limbs and muscles and frame and skin, there was none for the body as an organic unit.[2] Or perhaps philology too thoroughly pervaded the Indian thought world even to be identified, for there can be little doubt that Sanskrit, as the language of the gods, was the most densely philologized language in the premodern world.

A comprehensive account of the history of Sanskrit philology in that broad sense would address not only grammar but also lexicography, metrics, rhetoric *(alaṅkāraśāstra),* and hermeneutics *(Mīmāṃsā),* among other things, all richly developed to a degree of complexity virtually unknown elsewhere in the ancient world. For no other language do we have, for example, a complete grammatical reconstruction of sound changes, verbal roots, primary and second derivates, and the like; nor, at the other end of the spectrum, so systematic an analysis of meaning as that offered by Sanskrit hermeneutics—the "science of sentences" *(vākyaśāstra)*—which, although developed for the exegesis of scriptural texts in the late centuries B.C.E., found new and wide application to secular literature from the ninth century onward,[3] while providing the exegetical logic of later jurisprudence. In lieu of that comprehensive account of Sanskrit philology, I propose to examine here its most representative subspecies, the commentary. Commentators concerned themselves with interpreting texts—and often with establishing and editing them—by so broad a range of criteria that commentary may fairly be taken as a part standing for the whole enterprise of making sense of texts in traditional India. The scholarship devoted to commentarial practices, however, stands in inverse proportion, in both quantity and quality, to the materials themselves. It has been estimated that commentaries constitute as much as 75 percent of the Sanskrit written tradition,[4] and they embody some of its most insightful thinking about texts. But we have as yet a poor grasp of what this thinking consisted of, or of how the various genres of commentary developed historically or differed among themselves.

I narrow this already limited object of Sanskrit philology yet further by restricting my study to commentary on two genres, secular poetry and Vedic scripture. Commentary on philosophical and other scientific works has a notably divergent history. The core *śāstra*s of grammar, hermeneutics, and logic, whose foundational texts took shape in the last centuries B.C.E., had received their initial written commentaries already in the early centuries C.E. But those were far more concerned with the ideas of the base text than with its realization as a form of language or text, since for many centuries commentary was the one genre in which doctrinal intervention and innovation could be offered, until the rise of the independent treatise *(prakaraṇagrantha)* in the early modern period.[5] By contrast, systematic exegetical attention to secular poetry and to the Vedas was in both cases a remarkably late phenomenon, appearing at the end of the first millennium and gaining broad cultural traction only in the following centuries. And while these commentaries often demonstrate remarkable intelligence, they obviously never sought to usurp the place of the primary text; unlike a philosophical commentary such as Kumārila's *Exegesis in Verse* (*Ślokavārttika,* c. 650 C.E.), literary and scriptural commentary was always a secondary, not a primary, form of thought.

I first try to characterize what it meant to establish, edit, and interpret a literary text (both epic and courtly), pausing also to consider a remarkable defense from the mid-seventeenth century of nonstandard (or, rather, "nonstandard") Sanskrit in literary and other texts that has important implications for text editing. I turn next to the history of scriptural commentary, and follow this with an account of the contextual arguments that the greatest Vedic commentator used to frame his works. These data, taken as a whole, increasingly incline me to the hypothesis that a transformation in Sanskrit culture occurred around the beginning of the second millennium that was epistemic, not simply technological. The rise of philological commentaries represented a new, or newly standardized, form of knowledge, and not simply a new desire to commit already existing oral knowledge to writing. Since my concerns throughout this overview are more than historical, I conclude with thoughts about the pertinence of this traditional philology to contemporary philology's own ongoing quest to make sense of texts.

Literary Commentary

The early history of *kāvya,* or secular Sanskrit literature—"secular" *(laukika)* being typically employed to distinguish such language use from that of the "supermundane" *(alaukika)* Veda—has long been a matter of dispute. Inscriptional evidence from the beginning of the Common Era should probably be taken as indicating only the date after which (*terminus post quem*) we can assume the existence of *kāvya*—and not, as long believed, the date before which *(terminus ante quem)* it must have existed in full flower. Moreover, *kāvya* is constitutively dependent on writing, but in India this did not become widespread before the end of the first millennium B.C.E.[6] Whether or not this dating is off by a century or even two or three, *kāvya* at some point clearly *began,* whereas written commentary on *kāvya* is separated from that beginning by what, even conservatively estimated, is a gulf of ten centuries.[7]

The first preserved commentaries on *kāvya,* those of Vallabhadeva of Kashmir, date from the first half of the tenth century.[8] While Vallabhadeva refers to some predecessors, they are mostly unnamed, and all their "works," quite possibly because they were oral rather than written, have vanished without trace.[9] As for immediate successors, Vallabhadeva had none we know of.[10] A work like Bhoja's literary-critical masterpiece, the *Śṛṅgāraprakāśa* (Light on passion, c. 1050), certainly breathes the air of intense literary analysis and actually refers to exegetes of the early poets Kālidāsa and Bhāravi (late fourth and sixth centuries, respectively),[11] but the real boom in literary commentary came only several centuries later. This seems to have started in the twelfth century among the Jains of western India, but they were quickly followed by Kerala scholars in the thirteenth century, who had clearly learned from the Kashmiris; the practice then moved eastward, to Andhra by the early fifteenth century, and then Bengal (though there were earlier commentators in Mithila).[12] A remarkably similar history is presented by commentary on the epics, texts likewise excluded from the realm of scripture. The first such work on the *Mahābhārata,* the *Jñānadīpikā* (Light of knowledge) of Devabodha, a Kashmiri, dates from the early eleventh century; in the thirteenth century Udāḷi Varadarāja inaugurated what was to become a dynamic *Rāmāyaṇa* exegetical tradition in south India; in the east, commentary on the epics appeared only in the late fifteenth century, with Arjunamiśra. (He was born into a family of professional epic expounders, but they seem to have been oral performers since he never refers to written works of theirs.) We have no evidence of commentaries on the epics antedating Devabodha and Varadarāja—and vast production after them.[13]

Whatever more systematic research may show to be the true history of the later development of the philological commentary, there is certainly no reason to think that anyone before Vallabhadeva, Devabodha, Varadarāja, and the rest had attempted to do what they did: provide rational recensions, a more or less comprehensive inventory of variant readings, verse-by-verse exegeses, and, sometimes, coherent interpretations of entire poems (and, later, dramas) and epics. And even if the early second millennium is thought to have marked not a moment of intellectual inauguration, when scholars first began to direct serious attention to philological commentary, but instead a new moment of textual conservation, when the tradition began preserving and reproducing such works, the status of such commentary had clearly still changed: it had acquired a new cultural salience by mediating textual understanding in a way now deemed worthy of recording and preserving, and its elevation as an intellectual practice would influence the entire future of Sanskrit learning.

Scholars who have examined the traditional definitions of types of commentary in general have pointed to their often quite divergent functions—as simple glosses, linguistic exegeses, substantive argument and polemical correction of false views, and the like—as well as to their various discursive formats.[14] But we know next to nothing about how their three most important tasks of philological commentary were executed: text constitution (commentators were often also editors); emendation (they were also text critics); and analysis (they were also interpreters). These matters have been unstudied largely because they are unthematized in the tradition itself; the data to understand them were never assembled in any work of systematic thought but only exist dispersed in the commentaries themselves. What is more, commentators rarely describe what they were doing when they redacted, edited, and interpreted, or how they did these things; we must infer their precepts from their practices.[15] Such silence in what presumably were matters of tacit understanding can be found elsewhere in Sanskrit culture—as for example in the case of translation[16]—and of course is not unique to that culture. But the absence of an organized discourse on commentarial protocols, however we explain it, presents a serious obstacle to writing the history of Sanskrit philology. With this caveat, I will try to characterize some editorial, text-critical, and reading practices, to give a sense of what Indians—exemplified by a seventeenth-century scholar in eastern Bengal, a tenth-century scholar in Kashmir, and a seventeenth-century scholar in Tamil country, respectively—were doing when they did philology.

Recension

Some of our best (among largely bad) data regarding practices of recension, or the examination of manuscripts in order to select the most reliable witness, come typically from commentaries not on court literature but on the Sanskrit epics, especially the *Mahābhārata*.[17] Early *kāvya* commentators were often editors as well, though not invariably; manuscripts of commentaries often circulated without the target text (as was the case in Greek antiquity), suggesting the absence of dedicated recension. While clearly aware of variant readings, they never mention collating manuscripts, though there is a lot of evidence, direct and indirect, that they compared them. Dakṣiṇāvartanātha, a twelfth-century commentator on the court epic *Raghuvaṃśa* (Lineage of Raghu), tells us that he "prepared his commentary after examining variants in manuscripts from various regions, adopting the correct readings and rejecting the others." Indirect evidence is offered by Mallinātha in his commentary on the *Meghadūta* (Cloud messenger), where he identifies a half dozen verses as interpolations, something he can only have done by comparison of manuscript traditions.[18] Epic commentators, by contrast, often offer clearer testimony, especially those who worked on the culturally foundational *Mahābhārata,* a work that was repeatedly edited and—by a process not yet clear to us—"published" in the early-modern era (1400–1700).

There is a tendency, especially among scholars who have contested the claims of the critical edition prepared in Pune, India (1933–1971), to think of "the vulgate" as some sort of natural formation, a kind of alluvial deposit at the mouth of a *Mahābhārata* river of tradition. It is nothing of the sort, but instead the conscious construction of Nīlakaṇṭha Caturdhara, a Maharashtrian Brahman who worked in north India in the last quarter of the seventeenth century.[19] In the introduction to his edition of and commentary on the *Mahābhārata* (repeated in its supplement, the *Harivaṃśa*), Nīlakaṇṭha writes that he gathered "many manuscripts from different regions" and "critically established the best readings."[20] He seems to have done a substantial amount of editing in the process, since he frequently discusses variation in the sequence of verses or in individual readings (rarely does he indicate where, let alone why, he has emended the text), and even once admits failure, exclaiming "only Vyāsa [the traditional author of the epic] himself knows the true reading here."[21] Moreover, the text he established differs markedly from that of Devabodha, the earliest known commentator, who, given his location in Kashmir, established a recension affiliated with the northwest tradition. The opening section of Devabodha's *Jñānadīpikā* (Light of knowledge) itself offers no clear account of its critical method, and it is not easy to infer what this may have been from the available portions of the work. But Nīlakaṇṭha's explicit acknowledgment of the transregional dissemination of manuscripts, and his tacit recognition that these are all versions of the same text and must be compared with each other to attain textual truth, are important markers of a theory of textuality in general as well as of an understanding of this particular text's mode of being. And these beliefs were shared by every editor who cared to explain his editorial procedures.

Consider one edition prepared in the eighteenth century by a scholar named Vidyāsāgara in what is today Bangladesh. In his introduction Vidyāsāgara intimates something about his editorial method and his conception of the *Mahābhārata* as a textual phenomenon. He describes the edition as being based on "the traditional text of Bengal," the "manuscripts of the Bangalore-region traditional text," and a version found in "manuscripts from the West." He identifies additional copies, presumably not constituting recensions (*saṃpradāya*s), from various places in Bengal, Assam, and north and south Bihar. He also made use of at least a dozen earlier commentaries, including Devabodha's by then ancient *Jñānadīpikā,* several of whose verses Vidyāsāgara borrows for his own introduction.[22]

The transregional search for materials, along with the new geocultural consciousness it attests to, following a long-term regionalization of recensions (largely owing to the growth of regional scripts) that is observable across the history of Sanskrit literature, was clearly an early modern phenomenon. So too was the popularity of epic commentary itself, which experienced a striking upsurge during this period. This is especially the case with *Rāmāyaṇa* commentaries, which began to appear in the thirteenth century in south India and attained encyclopedic amplitude by the eighteenth, when Tryambaka Makhin of Tanjore produced his mammoth works. Indeed, the first of these commentaries, authored by Uḍāḷi Varadarāja, already referred to the corruptions introduced by "scribes unskilled in the various regional scripts" and the resultant need to establish "the correct reading" *(samyakpāṭha)* by "examining multiple manuscripts from multiple regions."[23] Never before had works such as these been written in India, and never before had such thinking been voiced about texts and how they were to be established.

Emendation

With respect to the procedures to be followed in text editing—the criteria for determining the correct or the best reading—scholars then as now differed, but they differed, then as now, on the basis of principles and not whim, however tacit those principles may have been. That Indian scholars were fully aware that the textual condition required editorial principles is clear from one of the very few general discussions available. The religious reformer Madhva (d. 1317) argues that the meaning of texts such as the *Mahābhārata* "has to be determined by way of the sentences of the text themselves," that is, as his sixteenth-century commentator Vādirāja explains, "rather than by way of sentences invented by our own cheeky imagination." But people interpolate passages of their own making in the body of the text, suppress passages that are there if they find them objectionable, transfer them to elsewhere in the text (in such a way as to interrupt the story, according to Vādirāja), or misinterpret them through ignorance.[24] "Many thousands of manuscripts have disappeared, and those that are extant have become disordered. So confused can a text have become that even the gods themselves could not figure it out."[25]

Given the lack of programmatic statements on editorial principles, we can discover them only by sifting our commentators' texts.[26] Vallabhadeva, the tenth-century literary scholar, wrote basically word-for-word commentaries, which required him to address very closely the textual state of a work.[27] From his commentary on Kālidāsa's celebrated court epic, *Kumārasambhava* (Birth of the war god), for example, we have several dozen text-critical discussions on the various manuscripts he compared.[28] These show how multifarious his criteria were: readings (or passages) could be judged as grammatically or contextually "correct/reasonable/proper/right" or "more correct/more reasonable"; "authoritative," "false," "mistaken," "corrupt," "unmetrical," "ancient"; "what was intended by the author," "interpolated," in need of "emendation," "obscene"; and last but not least, "lovely," "beautiful," and "more beautiful."[29] At least once he adduces paleographical (or at least graphical) criteria, as when he notes that a variant "results from confusing two similar characters" and rejects it on the grounds that it would contradict the narrative.[30] When evaluating readings he would occasionally make use of the familiar principle of difficulty and the antiquity or authenticity it implies: "this must be the ancient reading precisely because it is unfamiliar." Sometimes principles of antiquity could be combined with those of aestheticism: "the old reading in this verse is more beautiful." But antiquity can be too ancient, as it were, if it produces a grammatical (or lexical or metrical or rhetorical) irregularity such as a Vedicism. Here and elsewhere, like other commentators, Vallabhadeva shows himself ready on occasion to suggest a revision in order to save his author from a supposed solecism, but he hesitates to actually alter the text and winds up transmitting the offending lection.[31] The tension manifest here will mark the whole long history of Sanskrit philology (and is not unknown elsewhere). On the one hand, as the manuscripts show, some scribes and editors were highly attuned to text-critical problems and fully prepared to alter the text, whether on the basis of grammatical deviation or supposed aesthetic or logical fault (this was a source of worry to poets, as one from twelfth-century Kashmir declares: "noble learning, however pure in itself, / should not be applied to emending the works of good poets. // Holy ash is not scattered, in hopes of purification, / on water one is about to drink").[32] On the other hand, some scholars explicitly rejected emendation. Mallinātha, a prolific fifteenth-century commentator from Andhra, took care to assure readers that he was transmitting exactly what he found in his manuscripts.[33] And generally, it seems, editor-commentators did seek to establish as coherent and authoritative a text as they could on the basis of manuscript tradition as received *(āgata)* rather than as conjectured *(kalpita)*. Yet even Mallinātha sometimes adopted a conjecture that his predecessors had only suggested while they themselves preserved the received text.[34]

The text-critical practices followed by Vallabhadeva are common among commentaries on all kinds of Sanskrit literature, both court literature and epic, and have something significant, if complicated, to tell us about the philological standards at work. Consider the question of interpolation. Arjunavarmadeva (fl. 1215), editor-commentator of a celebrated sequence of love lyrics from the seventh century called the *Amaruśataka* (A century of poems by Amaru), rejects a number of verses as insertions by a second-rate poet hungry for even the anonymous fame of having his work included in Amaru's collection. Editors clearly understood the idea of interpolation and its close twin, forgery (something well attested in the world of literature and not just epigraphy, as shown by the "completion" of the *Kumārasambhava* by a later poet), but the criteria employed are typically subjective. In Arjunavarma's case, his judgment rests entirely on personal taste; the interpolated poems are inferior, he says, the sort of thing that might be produced by second-rate logicians, metricians, and grammarians, in whose hands the *rasa*—or emotional impact—of the work disperses like so much quicksilver in the wind.[35] But like every other editor, Arjunavarmadeva continued to include the interpolations in his edition, however convinced he was of their inauthenticity.[36]

The evidence of Sanskrit text criticism as a whole, then, indicates a model of textuality at once historicist-intentionalist and purist-aestheticist—standards that, if obviously contradictory, are perhaps not fatally so. Texts were held to be intentional productions of authors and were not to be altered without reason; the original intentions could be recovered by a judicious assessment of manuscript variants, supplemented by subjective criteria, especially in identifying interpolation. At the same time, literary texts were *lakṣyagrantha*s—instantiations of the rule-boundedness *(lakṣaṇa)* of Sanskrit literary production in terms of grammar, lexicon, prosody, and the poetics of sound and sense—and when conflict arose, editors sometimes felt compelled to yield to the superior claims of the rules and correct, or even emend, the original.[37]

Aside from the fact that secular Sanskrit text criticism arose, or appears to have arisen, so dramatically around the beginning of the second millennium, we are far from being able to impose any kind of developmental narrative on its subsequent history. No one like Lorenzo Valla, for example, ever appeared in early modern India to transform the rules of the text-critical game. While archaism, for example, could be invoked to discriminate among readings, the sense clearly implicit in this principle that the language of the past was different was never developed into a science of historical glottology. But the absence of a sense of language change comparable to Valla's assessment of Latin can be easily explained: change in Sanskrit itself (after the Vedic period) was impossible according to Sanskrit language ideology, which to some degree wound up producing in fact what it appeared only to represent in theory.

That said, one seventeenth-century scholar did begin to pry open the doors of ahistorical language purity, which in principle could have fundamentally altered text-critical practices. Among the works of Melpputtūr Nārāyaṇa Bhaṭṭatīri (d. c. 1660), the most remarkable intellectual of seventeenth-century Kerala, is a small treatise, today almost wholly forgotten, called *Apāṇinīyaprāmāṇyasādhana* (A proof of the validity of nonstandard Sanskrit), which he published along with an open letter to the scholars of "the Chola country" (Tamilnadu), who were his intellectual opponents.[38] Far more fundamentally new thinking is contained or implicit in this little text than is obvious from the title. By the middle of the seventeenth century in various domains of Sanskrit thought a kind of neotraditionalism had begun to manifest itself, reasserting the absolute authority of the ancients in the face of challenges from those known as the "new" *(navya)* scholars.[39] Nowhere was this clearer than in grammar, where Nārāyaṇa's contemporary to the north, Bhaṭṭojī Dīkṣita, vigorously reaffirmed as incontrovertible the views of Pāṇini and two other ancient "sages," Kātyāyana and Patañjali. Nārāyaṇa may not have sought to overthrow those views, but he certainly sought to supplement them. As he put it, "We are perfectly willing to accept that the school of Pāṇini has unique merits; what we do not accept is that others have no authority whatever."[40] The upshot of his arguments goes beyond mere supplementation and is in fact radical, since what he is actually doing, however tacitly, is restoring to Sanskrit at once its historicity and its humanity.

Many scholars of the epoch had come to view the old authorities as *avatar*s of the deity; in the eyes of one eighteenth-century scholar, the eleventh-century poetician Mammaṭa was an incarnation of the goddess of speech herself.[41] For Nārāyaṇa, however, a core contention is that Pāṇini was not a mythic personage but lived in time. Prior to him, he argues, there must have been other sources of grammatical authority—Pāṇini may have improved grammar, but he did not invent it—and therefore those coming after him (such as Chandragomin in the fifth century, Śākaṭāyana in the ninth, or even Bhoja in the eleventh and Vopadeva in the thirteenth-fourteenth) can be counted authoritative, since the basis of authority is knowledge rather than location in a tradition.[42] Even if the grammatical tradition were to be held as authoritative per se, the basis of its authority ironically relativizes it, as when Nārāyaṇa contrasts the grammarian Patañjali and the legendary epic poet Vyāsa (in respect to a particular usage): "One might object that since Patañjali is a supreme authority, his statements cannot be negated. But by the same token, Vyāsa is a supreme authority too, and since we are not prepared to negate his statements either, alternative grammars should be possible."[43] All of this Nārāyaṇa establishes not just abstractly but through an empirical analysis of the practices of respected poets and commentators.

The text-critical implications of this treatise are significant. Much of the variation in Sanskrit literary manuscripts derives from judgments on the part of scribes and commentators about the cultural authority of works on grammar, metrics, and rhetoric.[44] Nārāyaṇa Bhaṭṭa reverses the long-standing authority principle of Sanskrit culture whereby theory dictates practice (poetry is rarely cited in grammar and never to justify a usage—grammar alone can do that—but only to illustrate it); here practice can dictate theory.[45] He cites from the classical poets Murāri, Bhavabhūti, and Śrīharṣa, along with grammarians and philosophers, to establish this point. As he puts it in a verse cited from his grammar, "We reject the notion that [the forms cited] are a solecism as claimed by [*Kāikā*]*Vṛtti* [an eighth- or ninth-century Paninian grammar].[46] Who would dare to assert that the poets Murāri, Bhavabhūti and the like are not themselves authorities?"[47] Or as he proclaims more generally near the end of the work: "It is by relying on established usage and previous grammars but also by reasoning that intelligent people establish authority."[48] The implications here for text criticism are clearly substantial; whether they were put into practice by later commentators remains, like so much else, to be determined.[49]

Reading

What it actually meant to read and interpret Sanskrit literature—another, indeed a key, component of "making sense of texts"—is no less underthematized in the Sanskrit tradition and thus no less dependent on the extraction of data from actual practices. This can be especially laborious in the case of interpretation, where it is rare to find the fuller demonstration of expert reading of the sort offered by Aruṇagirinātha (also known as Śivadāsa), a fourteenth-century Kālidāsa commentator from Kerala.

At the end of his commentary on the *Kumārasambhava,* Aruṇagirinātha notes that his work is intended for three types of readers: those who have pedagogical needs (who "have difficulty understanding the meaning of the sentences"); those who have aesthetic needs (who "are addicted to bathing in the deep waters of aesthetic emotion [*rasa*]"); and those who have religious needs (who are "devotees of Śiva and the goddess").[50] And he seeks to provide for all three throughout his work. The sort of purely grammatical and rhetorical exegesis on offer here—glossing individual words, analyzing complex grammatical forms, establishing the correct syntax, citing sources, adducing parallel passages to establish meaning or usage, identifying and explaining figures of speech, in all of which vast learning, remarkable intelligence, and highly sensitive appreciation are in evidence—is standard in Sanskrit commentaries, and has been described elsewhere.[51] More relevant to our purposes here are Aruṇagirinātha's interpretive concerns. Unlike most commentators, whose attention is restricted to the individual stanza, the building block of Sanskrit versified literature, and who leave us in the dark about their understanding of any greater part of the work, let alone the work as a whole,[52] Aruṇagirinātha now and then offers a glimpse into the larger interpretive aims of Indian philologists.

Consider his exposition of chapter 1 of the *Kumārasambhava.* The poem narrates the union of the great god Śiva and Pārvatī, daughter of Mount Himalaya, to produce a son capable of destroying the cosmic demon Tāraka. It begins with a sixteen-verse section, construing (with the opening verse) as a single syntactic whole and therefore meant to be understood as a whole, that contains a eulogistic description of the mountain. To a contemporary philologist, whose first task would be to understand the unitness, so to speak, of this unit, its purpose appears to be double, replicating the double character of Himalaya in the poem. On the one hand "he" is a theophanic figure, father of the goddess heroine of the poem, and thus a subordinate hero *(patākānāyaka)* of the story, who must accordingly be described in a way commensurate with her grandeur. On the other hand "it" is also the location of the action of the poem, and in this aspect the mountain is, in the technical terms of Sanskrit literary theory, the "stimulant factor" to the creation of the character's basic affective state—that is, what we would think of as the scenery. It is thus the place arousing the erotic desire with which the story is concerned. But this too must be a stimulant commensurate with the nature of the erotic at issue: desire of the most transcendent sort, between the mother and father of the world. From this double perspective, we perceive how the section begins and ends with the enlivened aspect of Himalaya—the divinity on which the opening verse lays stress ("a deity in essence," v. 1) and to whom a share of the sacrifice has been assigned by the creator god (v. 17)—whereas the intervening verses emphasize the magical erotic qualities of the mountain in its stony aspect. Every sense organ is fully satisfied—by the scented breeze, the whistling reeds, the brilliant minerals that serve as makeup, and the magic plants that glow at night and do service as lamps. And every other accoutrement for romance is made available without effort and in abundance, from heaps of pearls to birch bark for love letters to the puffy clouds descending to act as screens during lovemaking. It is the perfect place—the only place, in fact—where the divine couple can join in union to beget the god who will counter the cosmic threat.[53]

While the traditional Indian reader was not insensitive to this sort of thinking—Aruṇagirinātha does observe how the verses sequentially describe the mountain's various virtues, including its beauty, which furnishes the various requisites for the erotic *rasa*—the poet's choice to produce a single textual structure and, associated with it, a single large-scale argument is of less concern to him. Even the logic of *rasa* aesthetics that shapes the narrative—a good part of the meaning of larger text structures was thought to lie in their emotional construction and (for later theorists) their impact on the reader[54]—holds surprisingly little interest.[55] What concerns Aruṇagīrinātha is the larger narrative argument of the chapter as a whole. Here is how he presents it:

> In this chapter the great poet has alluded to the section on attracting a husband in the *Kāmasūtra* chapter on an unmarried girl's marital relationship. . . . The first scholium[56] is as follows: "An adolescent girl if (a) she is slow at learning though otherwise virtuous; or (b) impoverished or orphaned and living with relatives; and/or (c) has received no marital propositions from suitable partners, should seek to bring about her marriage herself." The defining condition for a girl's "seeking to bring about her marriage herself" is failure to receive a suitable proposition when she reaches adolescence; and the usual reasons for this are, as the sutras tell us, a girl's dimness, poverty, or orphaned state, which is what we typically find to be the case in everyday life. The reason in our case, accordingly, has to be something different, namely the nature of the supreme lord, which has no parallel in worldly life. The absence of a proposi-

> tion is mentioned in v. 51 of the poem, and the absence of any other suitable groom is mentioned in v. 50. The goddess's "seeking to bring about [a union with Śiva]" is expressed in v. 20, where her innate desire for him is shown to be dimly awakened by her youthfulness, then to be more fully awakened by the explicit prophecy of the demigod Nārada. The *Kāmasūtra* is corroborated by the law books, which permit a "self-choice" for a mature girl. . . . The fourth scholium on the *Kāmasūtra* is that the girl's mother should have her approach the potential groom in the company of her friends and nurses. Here the friends are for assuaging her embarrassment, and "mother" stands for "elders" including father, and thus the service that her father has the goddess do for Śiva mentioned in v. 57 fully conforms to the sutra's prescription. The fifth scholium concerns her bringing fragrances, flowers, and betel nut and serving the groom in a private place at the appropriate time, and this is expressed in v. 59 of the poem.[57]

Making sense of Kālidāsa's text for Aruṇagirinātha, thus, meant above all embedding it in a set of intertexts, a body of ancillary knowledges, that preexist the poem. Philological reading was an exercise in reconstituting this intertextual network. The traditional reader could accordingly be said to have made sense of the first chapter of *Kumārasambhava* when he understood the paradigms—in grammar, rhetoric, the moral sciences, logic, erotics, law, and the like—the poet was striving at once to suggest and thereby to reaffirm, all in service of the reader's *Bildung*.[58]

Scriptural Commentary

With commentary on the Vedas we enter a domain of philology that, while differing to some degree from literary commentary in its methods and objectives, is surprisingly and unexpectedly similar in its historical shape. Although textual variation assuredly exists in the works included in the Vedic canon, and the texts themselves show traces of substantial editorial efforts in the early period,[59] they also exhibit an invariance in transmission that is virtually unique in world cultural history. The doctrine first argued out in *Mīmāṃsā* in the last centuries B.C.E., that Vedic texts are forever unchanging, clearly had some real basis; and it just as clearly militated against text-critical intervention. Moreover, given that the language of the Vedas was held to be at once archaic and unique, it is hard to see by what possible criteria variants even if recognized could be assessed.[60] This editorial difference aside, the historical parallelism between scriptural and secular commentary and their conceptual symmetry—why commentary came to be deemed necessary at all, what purposes it was intended to serve, and what methods it developed to serve them—are striking, and offer additional evidence for the literary-cultural innovation posited here for the early centuries of the second millennium.

The lateness of Vedic commentary appears all the more curious when we consider the long-standing interest among Buddhists and Jains in scriptural exegesis. Even leaving aside those kinds of scripture in both traditions that are themselves exegetical, we find commentaries from a very early period. Exegeses of "the words of the Buddha" *(buddhavacana)* are in evidence in the oldest part of the Pali canon, and Pali exegetical handbooks date from the beginning of the Common Era.[61] While full-scale Pali commentaries are known only from the fifth century, they are translations of earlier Sinhala texts, which were themselves supposedly translated from Pali works from the third century B.C.E. With the rise of Mahāyāna Buddhism, commentarial activity became even more intense. Many major scholars of the second through fifth centuries contributed commentaries on the (newly) canonized sutras, including thinkers of the stature of Nāgārjuna, Asaṅga, and Vasubandhu. In Jainism, the tenet was long held that scripture without commentary remained "asleep." Commentary in Prakrit, which occasionally was also elevated into scripture, dates to the first century, if not earlier (the works of Bhadrabāhu), and came into real prominence by the sixth, with full-blown treatises in Sanskrit being produced from the middle of the eighth century onward.[62]

With few exceptions, virtually all of this exegetical literature is concerned with the authority or authenticity of scripture, and is entirely indifferent to (if even aware of) its philology.[63] But it is the very precedent of scriptural commentary I want to emphasize here. No doubt much of this exegetical fervor derives from the fact that both Buddhists and Jains from an early date confronted disputes about what counted as the word of the founder—given the fact that there was a historical founder to have a word—and these disputes grew even sharper when Mahāyāna proposed a whole new class of texts as *buddhavacana.* To all this, and no doubt in reaction to it, the Vedic tradition as represented in *Mīmāṃsā* offers a very sharp contrast: not only was the Vedic tradition theorized as founderless but its texts were viewed, uniquely, as authorless. This ideological difference, however, seems inadequate to explain why Vedic scriptural commentary, like its literary twin, should be largely an early second-millennium phenomenon, which, given the date of the primary texts (c. 1400–800 B.C.E.), is breathtakingly late.[64]

"Editing" the Vedas

Although exegetical procedures for the Vedas were discussed already in the fourth century B.C.E. in the *Nirukta,* a work on etymology (it begins "Vedic tradition is to be interpreted [*samāmnāyaḥ . . . sa vyākhyātavyaḥ*]"), and narrower philological problems were addressed in the early grammatical tradition and of course in *Mīmāṃsā,* commentary more strictly construed on the Vedic corpus more strictly construed (that is, *mantrasaṃhitā*s, the collections of liturgical formulae, and *brāhmaṇa*s, the compendia of ritual prescriptions) was exceedingly rare before the beginning of the second millennium. Prior to the mid-seventh century no commentary on any Vedic text is known, leading more than one scholar to puzzle over this millennium-long exegetical "break" after the end of the so-called Vedāṅga period, around 300 B.C.E., when exegeses of core Vedic knowledges such as grammar were produced.[65] The sudden appearance in the seventh century of several scholiasts all in one place (Valabhī in Gujarat) and all connected with each other[66] seems to have been not the tip of an iceberg but an anomalous snowflake, for it was followed by four centuries of philological silence. Only at the beginning of the second millennium, precisely as in the case of literary commentary, did a historically meaningful density of exegesis appear that, like literary commentary, built to a critical mass in the thirteenth or fourteenth century.[67] The acme of this scholarly development, and a philological initiative without precedent in India for its ambition and scope, lies in the commentarial gigantism of Sāyaṇa (d. 1387).[68]

The absence of written commentary in the early period—if nothing else, the absence of a perceived need to commit oral exegesis to written form and to circulate it widely—and its sudden efflorescence in the late medieval period are questions as puzzling in the case of the Vedic corpus as they are for secular literature, and no easier solutions are available. One could easily point toward the philanthropic aspirations of regional kings, and their patronage (though by no means exclusive patronage) of Vedic learning. South Indian inscriptions provide substantial evidence to support this connection, and it is precisely the context in which Sāyaṇa achieved his success.[69] But this does little to clarify why such patronage manifested itself first when and where it did.

Whatever the true social-historical or intellectual-historical explanation, Sāyaṇa's achievement is staggering. First, he established or at least collected editions of a very large segment of the Vedic corpus—all four *saṃhitā*s, or collections of liturgical formulae; the *brāhmaṇa*s, their attendant ritual explanations; and the *araṇyaka*s, or "forest books," in all eighteen very sizable texts—an act of *recensio* comparable to but far exceeding what Nīlakaṇṭha and Vidyāsāgara were to achieve some three centuries later for the *Mahābhārata*.[70] To these texts were added extensive commentaries, making use of such earlier commentators as were available, as well as a very broad range of traditional learning.[71] The whole corpus in its printed form is to be measured, like carpet, in running yards.

Scriptural Philology

What Sāyaṇa attempted to achieve philologically in his work is no less complex a question than the sociocultural reasons motivating it. As already noted, textual criticism as such was largely irrelevant: the putatively changeless text needed in theory only one manuscript—or indeed, one living reciter—for each Vedic work. (Acknowledgment of variation appears, so far as I can see, only in Sāyaṇa's commentary on the, comparatively speaking, late *Mahānārāyaṇa Upaniṣad*.)[72] But the range of commentarial purposes beyond the text-critical was very broad, as a wider glance at Vedic commentaries shows. In the first rank stood the precise determination of grammar, syntax, and semantics, given the archaic register of the works. The genial twelfth-century commentator Ṣaḍguruśiṣya puts it this way:

> Do desire and anger and greed cease just because the *śāstra*s prohibit them? Does the ocean grow sweet just because a man is thirsty? How impossibly difficult it is to describe the meaning of the *brāhamaṇa* text. No more quickly comes the desired meaning of the Veda than the moon comes to a child who cries for it from his mother's lap.[73]

Hardly less pressing were the etymological, ritual, and mythological aspects of the text, which were exegetical concerns from the oldest period of reflection on Vedic meaning in the *Nirukta*. Finally, beginning with the religious proselytizer Madhva in the thirteenth century and intensifying in the partial commentaries of Ātmānanda, Rāvaṇa, and others into the sixteenth century, the spiritual ends of Vedic commentary were newly formulated for adaptation to the ever more powerful theistic religious movements of the early modern period.[74]

The history of this last development can be briskly suggested by reference to two examples, from the two ends of the historical spectrum. For the seventh-century scholar Skandasvāmin, the purpose of commentary was straightforward enough: "The meaning of the *Ṛgveda* must be grasped to ensure that the proper ritual application for all the different mantras is achieved."[75] Contrast with this the *Ṛgbhāṣya* of Ānandatīrtha (Madhva), whose purposes his subcommentator Jayatīrtha (late fourteenth century) explains as follows:

> The Vedas are meant to provide knowledge of Viṣṇu's grace, without which it is impossible for those who seek that grace in order to reach the ocean of transmigration's farther shore to do so. But the Vedas cannot achieve that efficacy if there is miscomprehension, let alone incomprehension. It is for this reason that the teacher decided to produce a commentary on some Vedic verses in order to demonstrate the variety of the ways they express the supremacy of Viṣṇu.

It is the purpose of Rāghavendratīrtha, a sixteenth-century sub-subcommentator, to show how, within the interpretive horizon of *Mīmāṃsā* (which seeks to constrain the proliferation of meaning), it is possible that all the verses in the Vedas should have Madhva's sectarian reference.[76] And though it is impossible to say for certain, since Sāyaṇa seems nowhere to mention the name of Ānandatīrtha/Madhva, it might have been precisely this sort of philological excess—or what appears to positivist philology as excess—that his own commentaries were meant to arrest.

As important as these purposes is the basic conceptual framework Sāyaṇa erected to house the vast exegesis he set out to provide. That this framework was central to Sāyaṇa's goal is indicated by the fact that he reproduced it, to varying degrees, in the introduction to every one of his commentaries on individual Vedic texts. Here is how he starts the *Aitareya Brāhmaṇa,* working his way through the four prerequisites *(anubandhas)* for inaugurating study of a particular *śāstra* (declaration of its subject matter, its purpose, its authorized reader, and its connection with an antecedent knowledge or preparatory activity):

> How do we define this thing we call "Veda"? What is its subject matter, its purpose, who is authorized to study it, and what relationship does the work bear to the person? And what kind of epistemic validity does it lay claim to? Absent answers to any of these questions, the Veda cannot be a fit object of commentarial attention.

The Veda is defined as a supermundane text *(grantha)* that provides the means of attaining the good and avoiding the bad, themselves supermundane phenomena for which only such a text is suited, and not mundane perception or inference. So much for the propriety of its definition and the nature of its content. Its purpose is the awareness of this content; the person authorized to study it is the person who desires that awareness; the work's relationship to him is one of benefactor to beneficiary.

While desire may be a primary qualification authorizing study, it is not the only one, and Sāyaṇa proceeds to argue out a restriction on women and people of lower castes: only someone properly inducted into Vedic study may study the Veda, and thereby actualize his desire for awareness. As for epistemic validity (picking up the problem of "supermundane means"), the Veda, as eternal, changeless, and unauthored, is subject to none of the epistemic failures of everyday discourse: its validity is accordingly intrinsic. One last question, which will be remarkable to contemporary readers, concerns the very propriety of commentary on mantras, or ritual formulae, whose actual meaning, according to one ancient school of Vedic thought, it was entirely unnecessary to know in order for them to be efficacious; it was sufficient that their wording be exactly enunciated in the course of the ritual. Sāyaṇa offers an elaborate account of why understanding the Veda—hence having a commentary on it—is not only necessary but commanded by the Veda itself.

Despite the novelty of Sāyaṇa's commentarial framework in which they are contained, all the topics he addresses reach back to the oldest levels of organized reflection on the nature of the Vedas at the start of the hermeneutical tradition in the *Mīmāṃsāsūtra*s. The exclusion of women and low castes is an old problem in the sutras and in the dharma texts coeval with or perhaps even earlier than them; the intrinsic validity of the Veda is a received postulate of the hermeneutical tradition, going back again to the sutras; doubts about the efficacy of the Veda being contingent on its comprehension are found as early as the *Nirukta,* and, as Sāyaṇa himself states, were decisively settled by Kumārila a thousand years before him.[77]

What is worth registering, however, is how these old values were being insistently reasserted in the fourteenth century, a paradoxical return of the archaic in the early modern, unparalleled in any of the older commentaries. And these values were to be restated in various ways after Sāyaṇa, especially from 1550 onward, as Vedic hermeneutics experienced its greatest flowering in half a millennium—until the whole thought structure began to crumble, of its own accord, at the end of the eighteenth century.

Envoi: For a Critical Philology

Sanskrit philologists were concerned with a wide range of problems entirely familiar to philologists today. They wanted to survey the distribution of manuscripts and determine how the text as a whole was to be constituted. They were keen to collate their sources and to frame principles by which they could decide among variants. They thought about what it means to read, usually at the level of the given utterance, but sometimes over larger textual structures, including the work as a whole. They were interested in the contexts within which texts were read, and the kinds of pedagogies suitable for those contexts. And like members of any discipline worthy of the name, they recognized that they were part of a tradition, cultivated that tradition (which sometimes stretched back, like that of the epic commentaries before Vidyāsāgara, nearly a millennium), and built on the work of their predecessors.

We are only beginning to understand any of these concerns in a general way, and their particulars, a fortiori, await serious attention, viewed both synchronically (what precisely were the stable norms?) and diachronically (what changed over time?). And even when these matters are better understood, a range of additional questions awaits us. Are we right, for example, to posit a commentarial revolution at the beginning of the early modern era? The sudden appearance of commentaries on both secular literary and Vedic religious texts, the remarkable synchrony of the two developments, and the ensuing routinization of a commentarial habit across South Asia certainly seem to be no mere artifact of preservation (the fact, namely, that, generally speaking, manuscripts from before the twelfth century have disappeared). We have quite a good understanding of the antecedent cultural practices, and neither literary nor Vedic commentary is prominent among them. The appearance of these new forms in the early second millennium would, therefore, seem to mark an actual intellectual-historical transformation. More than ever before, and in some ways as never before, two genres of text, *kāvya* and Veda, both culturally central, came to be mediated by a philological apparatus that with growing sophistication emphasized the need for careful recension, the dynamic changeability of transmission (at least for secular texts), the requirement of purification, and the systematicity of reading, an apparatus whose growing density and broad distribution bespeak new pedagogical needs and possibly new reading publics.

To the degree one is prepared to make something of it, the Indian date for this transformation broadly correlates with early modernity in western and eastern Eurasia, if that epoch is taken to start with the twelfth-century Renaissance in Europe and the Song dynasty in China, rather than with the beginning of global modernization (something quite different) around 1500.[78] Then again, another stage of early modernity certainly seems to have commenced in the seventeenth century. This is exemplified in India by Nārāyaṇa Bhaṭṭa's new and disruptive understanding of grammatical authority, and he was not alone. Recent work on the intellectual history of seventeenth-century south India has identified an array of new philological concerns, such as the textual instability of sectarian scriptures or standards of interpretation, and similar tendencies have been discerned in the north as well.[79] These concerns may never have included the critique of authority or of metaphysical foundations that marked early modern philology in Europe, but they were new concerns for India.

Hardly less consequential than questions of Indian periodization (let alone global synchronization) are the broader intellectual-historical issues. How far if at all did the epistemological model of Sanskrit philology have effects beyond its own domain, as was the case for the early modern European sciences? Did the *ars critica* of someone like Vallabhadeva in any way share in, let alone shape, other kinds of scientific practice, or come to be shaped by them? How far do Sanskrit philological practices parallel those of other high traditions like the Greek and Latin, whether in small matters, like the place of the lemma/*pratīka* and the *quaestio*/*śaṅkā* style of exposition, or in large ones, like the adducing of authorities, the analysis of rhetoric, concepts of interpretation, modes of reading, or rhythms of historical change?

Beyond such historical and comparative matters, little understood at present but important for a global history of philology, there is a discipline-theoretical problem that needs attention. Why should the practicing philologist, and not just the intellectual historian, want to know any of this past? What place, if any, should philology's past occupy in philology's future? Does it resemble that of mathematics or chemistry—have Vallabhadeva and Sāyaṇa become history for modern philologists, the way Laplace or Lavoisier have become history for modern scientists, and thus have no further role to play in the truth seeking of the discipline? And what, after all, is the truth of the discipline? Does past philology have value only in a Whiggish-historical way, as a record of the stages of progress that have brought us to our present moment of textual mastery, of once-useful but now permanently superseded ways of making sense of texts? Or, on the contrary, do the reading practices of a Vallabhadeva and a Sāyaṇa continue to affect our own? Should they?

These last questions at least, on disciplinary theory, have been raised before in Indology, especially in the late nineteenth-century controversy over the interpretation of the Vedas. Whereas some scholars (Otto Boehtlingk, A. B. Keith, Hermann Oldenberg, Richard Pischel, and Rudolf von Roth, among others) sought to recuperate a portion of the tradition's philology in a positivist spirit, the dominant view was that of W. D. Whitney, the pioneering American Sanskritist. For Whitney, a fourteenth-century C.E. reader like Sāyaṇa of a fourteenth-century B.C.E. text like the *Ṛgveda* had nothing of any possible philological importance to tell the modern scholar: "There are, in fact, in my opinion, few figures more absurd than that of 'Sāyaṇa' posing as one who comprehends, and can teach others to comprehend, a difficult Vedic passage—perhaps among the few exceptions is to be reckoned that of the Occidental scholar who professes to listen to him with admiring reverence." He refers to the commentator's "false etymologies and false constructions," "philological monstrosities," and "suggestions which . . . simply outrage universal human sense."[80] Whitney's view was not only dominant, it was also triumphant.

The judgment on how the practice of philology should relate to the history of philology that finds expression in Whitney's scholarship was the outgrowth of a particular history of Enlightenment views on textual truth that we can reconstruct. The conceptual transformation of crucial importance begins not, as usually supposed, with the distinction drawn by Giambettista Vico (c. 1725) between *certum* and *verum*—between the certitudes that people, such as commentators, accept in everyday life and the ultimate verities of the philosophers and scientists—but with the distinction between philological truth and commentators' truths introduced by Benedict de Spinoza (1670). Whereas for Vico *certum* and *verum* were two separate, if equally valid, domains of human consciousness, with *certum* the preserve of a hermeneutical philology,[81] for Spinoza—most pointedly, if not for the first time—philological truth was made distinct from and transcendent of not only the reader's own subjective response to the text but also the entire foregoing history of understanding.[82]

In line with the pluralism, discussed in the introduction, that should form part of a new philology for a new disciplinary order, I want to suggest that both positions, Vico's and Spinoza's, are at once true and false. There is no doubt always a deeper, ever truer textual truth to be obtained for historicists like Whitney, and contemporary philologists cannot but continue to strive toward it along that scientific path. But that is only one of the text's truths: what the text says to us (as philosophical hermeneutics teaches us) and what it has said to readers of the past (as philological history teaches us) are truths too. The "real meaning of the text" can only reside in the sum total of meanings that have been accorded it in history at all three levels, authorial, traditionalist, and presentist.

In the particular case of Sāyaṇa or Vallabhadeva or Nārāyaṇa Bhaṭṭa, we encounter in even more direct a fashion than earlier how a new philology might function—why we should care not only whether one or the other commentator is right according to some transcendent truth, or *verum* (what Whitney called "the true Veda" with its "true meaning, which must have been one, and not many") but also why the commentators thought what they thought was true, their *certum,* and what that would mean for a history of making sense of texts.[83] This method seems to me conceptually compelling, even a potential candidate for inclusion among the foundational principles of the twenty-first-century human sciences. And the premier site for its exposition and demonstration is critical philology, with its global history, its conceptual pluralism, and the massive, kaleidoscopic archive of methods and interpretations in the making sense of texts to which it gives access. But if the rich materials from traditional India are ever to be included in this new philological discipline, we Indologists have our work cut out for us.[84]

Reconciling the Classics

Two Case Studies in Song-Yuan Exegetical Approaches

MICHAEL LACKNER

WHAT DOES it mean to attempt to reconstruct intellectual and aesthetic processes of understanding the Chinese Classics during the period from the eleventh to the fourteenth centuries in China? The often evoked "rationality" as the pervasive characteristic of this period may be an exaggeration;[1] however, when analyzing the philological approaches of the Confucian literati during the Song and Yuan dynasties, one has to acknowledge that there was a decisive breakthrough in terms of textual analysis. The effort to dissect and dissolve into individual elements important texts of the Confucian tradition surpassed the analytical potential of all previous commentarial traditions. Instructions for "correct reading" of the Classics (Dushufa) multiplied. They contained not only indications concerning the progression of the study program but also concrete methods for isolating propositions and sentences.

The vital task of the student seemed to consist in elucidating the text and putting it in order by means of textual analysis. In Chen Kui's (1128–1203) *Wenze* (Rules of written texts), we find features of a pragmatic approach (emphasis, rhetorical question, etc.) as well as tentative ideas regarding the distinction between clauses and subclauses. Following several hints contained in the works of Zhu Xi (1130–1200) and Zhu's son-in-law Huang Gan (1152–1221), Cheng Duanli (1271–1345) composed the most elaborate system of punctuation China had ever seen. Four colors, four forms, and two positions of different circles were designed to highlight the ends of clauses and subclauses, proper names, book titles, geographical designations, and other text elements.[2]

"Understanding" is a term that might encompass philological, exegetical, and hermeneutical approaches. The early endeavors to make sense of the Chinese Classics were characterized by a large amount of "word philology"—by establishing glosses, semantic fields, and etymological observations, the Han commentators tried to bridge the linguistic gap that separated them from the language of the canonical texts.[3] The emergence of commentarial glosses like the *Cangjie pian* (The Cangjie wordbook) (compiled by Li Si, third century B.C.E.), the *Jijiu pian* (Dictionary for urgent use) (compiled by Shi You around 40 B.C.E.), and many other character manuals and dictionaries bears witness to the establishment of a "linguistic philology" during the Han period.[4] Milestones of this *Wortphilologie* are the *Shuowen jiezi* (Comments on the two types of characters) (compiled by Xu Shen, 100 C.E.) and the *Qieyun* (601 C.E.). The first derives its character classification system from cosmological views developed during the Han and constitutes more an attempt at ordering the world with the help of words than a method to enable a reader to find a character in a dictionary. The second is a dictionary of the pronunciations of characters that was meant to standardize existing differences between northern and southern Chinese variants.[5]

There is also no doubt that we are entitled to call many commentaries "exegetical," since they can be compared to the theological project of exegesis of the holy scripture in the West. In both cases, making sense of a passage in a text considered authoritative was inspired by exegetic methodologies. Although the four types of biblical exegesis (literal, typological, tropological, and anagogical) never acquired the status of explicit concepts in China, they can nevertheless be identified as implicit methodological devices for the exegetical purpose. John Makeham lists five commentarial strategies for the earliest extant commentary of the *Lunyu* (Analects) by Zheng Xuan (127–200): one based on a "reading off" the *Lunyu* in terms of the Classics; a second one of "modal distinction," pointing to the possibility of the same word having been used in more than one sense; a third, didactic strategy, which "accommodates" itself to different levels of understanding; emendation (although Makeham concedes that this is more a textual than a commentarial strategy); and historical grounding.[6] In contrast, the Song philological approach presented here admittedly is familiar with the practice of "reading off," but is highly reluctant as far as modal distinctions are concerned; it is characterized by a radically different didactic strategy that denies the existence of different levels of understanding; it uses the principles of emendation (albeit in ways different from previous periods) but very rarely uses historical grounding in textual analysis.

Definitions become somewhat more complicated when it comes to the term "hermeneutics." True, a metaphysical order in which the text is embedded, and to which the interpreter possesses privileged access, is one of the basic assumptions of many Chinese commentators (in the sense that meaning exists before the text), and it is precisely this fact that may justify the term "philosophical hermeneutics."

However, the self-reflective dimension of modern hermeneutics, which critically inquires into the aims and motifs of an interpretation, is a phenomenon hard to find in the Chinese tradition. Skepticism about the notion of "Chinese philosophical hermeneutics"[7] is thus advisable, but this should not prevent us from appreciating the philological seriousness of commentarial efforts in textual analysis.

On the other hand, reconstructing difficulties underlying historical interpretations of the Song/Yuan commentators is of course a part of world philology. Not only is my own approach a reaction to the difficulties of Chinese exegesis in the past but also their own difficulties were justified by problems inherent in the text they wanted to interpret. With Emilio Betti, I assume that a multiregional approach to the question of global hermeneutics—mine to the Song scholars, and the Song scholars to their own past—is legitimate.[8] The moment has come for a systematic consideration of non-Western literati practices against the framework of what was previously a predominantly Western definition of humanities. In fact, one can only wonder why this focus on world philology comes so relatively late, since comparative studies of other similarly universal practices, such as medicine, have long been cultivated. To a large extent, this is due to the shift from history of science to a history of knowledge, which encourages an increasing awareness of the historical dimensions of the various fields of humanities.

However, when it comes to the definition of the very essence of philology, we soon face some difficulties: if defined in the narrow sense of an academic discipline with its institutional background, philology might remain restricted to the West. If we accept a larger definition—the universal endeavor to deal with problems arising from codified texts—even civilizations without a writing culture must have had some kind of philological knowledge. We know the Aztecs had schools for their noblemen where, among other disciplines, "the rules of correct and beautiful speech" were part of the curriculum.[9] However, because of the almost entire destruction of Mexican civilization, we know about the existence of these schools and rules without, alas, knowing anything about their content. So the inquiry into philological practices of civilizations without writing is a field that may be left to social anthropologists for further study.

With Peter Szondi, I think that we have to develop a genre-specific hermeneutics.[10] However, we have to deal with the fact that there are only a few overlaps in literary genres in traditional China and the West. Rather than ruminating on the respective qualities inherent to both civilizations, I prefer an approach based on the performative power of textual analysis. This power goes far beyond "philology" as a mere descriptive procedure (which often remains deprived of any far-reaching significance) and, even more important, shows that a truly productive interpretation has to depart from any kind of mimetic prerequisites, at least the ones Hans-Georg Gadamer had in mind. As a matter of course, there must be something prior to interpretation, that is, the text. Texts are frequently contradictory; they offer an intrinsic resistance that has to be taken into account for any analysis and reconstruction of how previous interpreters struggled with their *interpretaments.*

China embodies writing culture and offers many parallels to other civilizations that deal not only with language but more specifically with texts. Philological efforts in the broadest sense are a vital part of the learned practices of traditional China. In this essay, my intention is not so much to describe the evident parallels of Chinese philology with Western practices in its lexicographical and phonological achievements; rather, I want to shed some light on the more neglected sides of the Chinese exegetical project: the use of techniques that, according to ancient and modern standards, can be understood as philological and textual analysis, in the service of a higher-ranking project. My claim is that it is preferable to compare this project with Western medieval theology as a "concern for texts." In this respect, we are entitled to say that Chinese philology from the eleventh to the fourteenth centuries suggests numerous common traits with early philological biblical exegesis in Europe. If we concede that Christian philology started with Augustine's *De doctrina Christiana,* where he tried to reconcile the Hebrew Bible with the Gospels by dissecting passages from the former in order to prove that they pointed to the history of salvation described in the latter,[11] we will also have to acknowledge that very similar formal principles of textual analysis were constitutive of the approaches presented in the following reflections.

Two case studies will illustrate this claim. First, I want to show how the exegetical techniques used by Zhang Zai (1020–1078),[12] one of the founding fathers of what later came to be known as *daoxue,* the "Study of the Way," and, much later, as "neo-Confucianism," created an entirely new body of canonical writings.[13] The second case study is meant to show that Xu Qian (1270–1337) put into practice some of the guiding principles of the method developed by Zhang Zai by using visual tools for his demonstration. In Zhang Zai's work, the philological technique of dissecting and isolating individual passages led to the establishment of a universal coherence of all classical writings (not unlike the idea of the "Scripture"), which, in turn, prepared the ground for a *summa* of them all; in the works of Xu Qian and some other scholars, who relied on diagrams, the same method of dissection was used for a more profound understanding of the isolated passages. The second way may seem more pedestrian, but it was nonetheless inspired by a methodological approach that had started more than two centuries before.

A Fifth Gospel

Generations of historians of ideas (including historians of Chinese philosophy) have treated Zhang Zai as a philosopher.[14] However, since all of them were looking for philosophical ideas and argumentation according to the Western concept of philosophy, only two or three of the sixteen chapters of his *Discipline for Beginners (Zhengmeng)* have ever been taken into consideration. The Marxist approach has been obsessed with an alleged "materialism" in Zhang Zai's first chapter, which deals with cosmology. Modern Confucianism has based itself on a couple of sentences in chapter 6 to prove that, in contrast to Immanuel Kant, who reserved the idea of the so-called intellectual intuition for a Supreme Being, Chinese philosophy was able to contend that intellectual intuition was within the realm of human beings.[15] I will not go into the details of all these arguments; suffice it to say that practically no modern historian of ideas has made an effort to analyze the *Discipline for Beginners* by means of modern philological inquiries, which, in itself, is a nice footnote to the history of philology.

However, Zhang Zai's project cannot be described by terms like "philosophy" or "cosmology." Imagine you are a European medieval scholar who thinks that the four Gospels are much too complicated to be understood by a novice, and you are sufficiently self-assured to think that your interpretation is the only valid one, which implies that you have a privileged access to the meaning of the texts. This assumption is in accordance with "philosophical hermeneutics" insofar as it takes the metaphysical embedding of the text for granted. In order to demonstrate the essentials of the four Gospels for "beginners," you basically have two choices: one is to write a kind of *summa* (or rather a summary) in your own words, and the other is to write a fifth Gospel, using a maximum of sentences and expressions, and sometimes allusions, stemming from the other four. This is precisely what Zhang Zai did, and later scholars qualified this attempt as an "exaggeration."[16] One could ask whether there was an element of self-assertion in this attempt, and I am inclined to answer in the affirmative: the respect for the Scripture was deeply rooted and the rise of a new prophet rather inconceivable—but a mere commentary was not what Zhang Zai had in mind. The question remains, however, to what degree he identified himself with Confucius, at least during the last period of his life.

Let me give an example of what I have called the creation of a fifth Gospel. Chapter 11 of the *Discipline for Beginners* deals with the life of Confucius,[17] and I propose a close reading of the first paragraph, which is a kind of orchestration of a few sentences Confucius is believed to have uttered about the different periods of his life.

The original text in the *Lunyu* (Analects) 2:4 reads as follows:

> At fifteen, I set my will on learning.
> At thirty, I took a firm stand.
> At forty, I no longer suffered from doubts.
> At fifty, I knew the call of Heaven.
> At sixty, my ears were docile.
> At seventy, I followed the desires of my heart, and no longer overstepped the boundaries.

At thirty, we read in the chapter of the *Discipline for Beginners* with the title "At Thirty,"[18] "he was a vessel for the Ritual." The expression "vessel for the Ritual" is taken from the *Record of Ritual* (*Liji,* chapter 10), where it is immediately followed by the explanation: "a vessel for the ritual means to be fully prepared, it means abundant magnificence, it means virtue." In Zhang Zai's reformulation of the passage from the *Analects,* this part of the sentence is followed by the words "not that he had to force his standing firmly" (*qiang li,* e.g., with respect to the world of morality). This is another allusion to the *Record of Ritual,* or more specifically to the term *qiang li* (from *Liji* 18 *Xueji* 2), according to which "after nine years a firm stance has been reached, and there is no turning back, which means the same as 'grand completion.' " This first orchestrating of "At thirty" implies that the text accompanying the "At thirty" observation should be read to mean that Confucius, at thirty, had already reached the "grand completion."[19]

"At forty," we read, "his awareness was nascent and he entered into the spirit, employing it to achieve the greatest effect" ("jing yi [ru shen yi] zhi yong"), and "he brought about the [proper] measures" ("shi cuo"). The first of these textual modules appears in the "Great Commentary or Appended Judgments" to the *Classic of Changes* (*Yijing, Xicizhuan* B3), containing a statement about how the "changes" *(yi)* act or work. The second derives from the "Practice of the Mean" *(Zhongyong),* a mystical piece (originally a part of the *Classic of Ritual*) that only gained greater recognition again in Zhang Zai's lifetime, and in this context had to do with a more precise determination of "truth" or "truthfulness" *(cheng)* (see *Zhongyong* 25).[20] The full text there reads: "the virtue of nature [xing] is the way of bringing together what is without with what is within; therefore it is also what is appropriate in bringing about [the proper] measures."[21] In phonetic and ideographic senses the homonymous pronunciation of *cheng,* as well as the ideographic proximity of the characters for "completion" and "truthfulness," combined with the aforementioned determination through *Zhongyong* 25, all resonate in the explication of what "at forty" means. But to put it more starkly, "truth or truthfulness," which is the goal of the Confucian ideal type as applied to people, is thereby attributed to Confucius already at the age of forty!

"At fifty," the text continues, "he had exhausted the pattern, completely laid out nature *(xing),* and reached for the call of Heaven" *(qiong li, jinxing, zhi tian zhi ming).* This paraphrases a sentence from the *Classic of Changes* (*Yijing, Shuogua* 1) about the activities of the Holy Sage *(shengren).* In another passage *(Yulu A),* Zhang Zai had described the expression "receiving the call" as a precondition for holiness *(shengzhe);* in this context, he alters this "call" into a "call of Heaven." (Recall that the passage from the *Analects* had simply stated: "I knew the call of Heaven.") In one of the few comments he adds to the usually completely mosaic structure in the entire work, Zhang Zai continues: "yet he himself could not call it 'arriving at,'" and thus instead said: "I knew the call of Heaven." We may suppose that this was to signal that in Confucius's case it was not the individual "call," often considered as coeval with fate, that is inherent to every human being, but the call issued to the Son of Heaven at the time of the Zhou (eleventh century B.C.E.). Thus, here for the first time we find Zhang Zai reading Confucius against the grain or against his overt intention, explicating what he considers to have been the true meaning in Confucius's assertion.

Following *Zhongyong* 22, "only the most truthful under heaven can explain their nature fully," and with this, "the nature of humans and things." Thereby, the original *Zhongyong* text continues, "he may support the changes and nourishment of heaven and earth, and may become a trinity together with heaven and earth." It is for this reason that Zhang Zai's paragraph referring to the passage "At Sixty" says that Confucius "completely explained and laid out the nature of humans and things," which, in Zhang Zai's reading, is what Confucius himself (in *Lunyu* 2:4) meant by "docile (or attuned) ears." Zhang Zai continues: "The sound entered, and his mind understood." Thus, for this stage of life as well, a formulation was chosen describing Confucius as the apotheosis of humankind. In this case, it occurs through the connotation, established by the context of the *Zhongyong,* of Confucius being the embodiment of the "three powers" *(san cai),* the unity of heaven, earth, and humankind, without which the world would be inconceivable. Zhang Zai's only additional explanation that does not rely on a passage from the Classics, "sound entered, and his mind understood," has become a *chengyu,* one of the frequent tetrasyllabic idiomatic expressions that characterize the Chinese language.

"At seventy," finally, "he had the same virtue as Heaven, did not strive or make an effort; he was instead finding the middle way of composure." If one follows Zhang Zai, the phrase "having the same virtue as heaven and earth" is the same as the one applied to the first hexagram of the *Classic of Changes, Yijing,* at least in the *Wenyan* commentary. That hexagram, *Qian,* is equated with the holy Sage. As for "not striving, making an effort, finding the middle way of composure," these are applied (in *Zhongyong* 20) to those who "make everything true/authentic" *(cheng zhi)* and thereby correspond to a heaven that "is truthful and authentic" *(cheng zhe).*

In following the extremely complex introductory passage, we have thus come upon quite a coherent pattern, which allows for a tentative conclusion. Zhang Zai's intent or goal was less to elucidate the individual ages of Confucius than to present, using these ages themselves, something having little to do with the diachronic process of Confucius as a historical figure, namely the quality of "the sacred or holy Sage." From the outset, I would argue, this quality was identical with (1) "grand completion"; (2) the manner in which the "Changes" functioned; and (3) "truthfulness" or "truth/authenticity."

Zhang Zai uses this dual diachronic/synchronic perspective throughout to explain the two moments of the sage, which one can also see as standing in permanent dynamic tension. Actually, this is an impossible task, not unlike the squaring of a circle, at least at the level of the text, for a written text by definition provides a linear temporality, and not simultaneity. A linear and diachronic text can only render synchronicity by—as Zhang Zai does—using quotes that come from the synchronous realm (thereby also alluding to "completeness"), making references that are temporally bound or limited, or substitution within the temporal level itself.

Here one should pause to examine how Zhang Zai proceeds, for that helps in better understanding the goal of his argument. The entire text of the *Zhengmeng* is indeed a mosaic: a passage from a canonical work is illuminated with the aid of another passage from a different canonical work, in a manner well known to early biblical exegesis in the West. However, this procedure is only made explicit and highlighted in the few places where his reading goes too strongly against the received wisdom. A case in point is the replacement of the original "knowing" (or recognizing the call of Heaven) by "arriving at": here a justification was necessary. Otherwise, Zhang Zai relies on the implicit power of the way he intersperses texts. In contrast to the mainstream of Chinese commentarial literature, he seldom speaks in an explicit manner about philological problems, but rather enacts their solution. The performative dimension of this procedure opens into a symphonic orchestration, in which both written and deliberately omitted passages, both verbalizations and silence, play their respective roles. In very few cases (as for instance in the chapter on the sacrifices), he uses wording different from the original text in order to reconcile inconsistencies of the original.

In philological terms, the frequent use of ellipses has its desired effect or is an important tool—though only because it is used under the assumption that the texts themselves are known by heart and readers could fill in the missing elements themselves. This could more generally be regarded as "resonance," or a form of intertextuality existing prior to widespread literacy, inasmuch as a word or a turn of phrase would evoke an entire quote. When combining passages apt to "resonate" with selected—or omitted—parts of the original passage that is being "commented" on, or the added commentaries (in themselves no longer commentaries but passages in their own right), one in the end creates a new canon that exists exclusively by virtue of that resonance. Long before Julia Kristeva's theories of intertextuality or Genette's "Palimpsest"[22] with its different layers of paratext, hypertext, and hypotext, Zhang Zai's unique work put into practice some of the main tenets of these theories. Resonance is meant to "prove" the unity of the Classics. As a matter of course, the modular character of Classical Chinese facilitates the embedding of entire sentences from the Classics into his new "Gospel," a reminder of Lothar Ledderose's study on the modular character of Chinese art.[23]

Just as significant are changes made to the original, for example when one word replaces another. In this manner, Zhang Zai created a main connecting thread out of bits and pieces of canonical works, binding on all the areas of his encyclopedic worldview: nothing was to remain unexplained. The technique is that of the Socratic method, based on a questioning of passages that is intended to bring hidden insights to light. The long scholarly tradition in China, whose educational goal in principle was enlightenment to be reached through meditating on the hidden meanings of texts, reached its high point with Zhang Zai's *Zhengmeng.* Individual works of the Classical canon had been commented on in China both before and after Zhang Zai; his singular contribution was to create a new canon out of passages of other canonical works, whose meanings could be extrapolated. The resonance, which in itself is a carefully crafted product of philological knowledge, is meant to give evidence for the unity of the canonical scriptures, a corpus that is believed to have been inspired by one voice. The original texts of the Holy Scriptures may have been scattered into fragments—but who cares, once a new Scripture is there, which, on the surface, is not new at all.

Weavers at Work

By the twelfth century, "Neo-Confucian" ways of exegesis had been firmly established, and, beginning with Zhu Xi (1130–1200), visual tools were introduced alongside the linear text of written commentaries.[24] Several schools (whose origins can mostly be traced back to Zhu Xi) recurred to diagrams to illustrate passages of the ancient Classics and some of the already canonized works of the Neo-Confucians. Some of these diagrams were devoted to the analysis of sentences and laid the foundations for a visual approach to issues of syntax that otherwise could not be addressed, since traditional China had no explicit grammar and hence no terms for syntactic relations. Once again, the majority of the diagrams dealing with the structure of sentences, passages, or entire works served as proof of the unity of the Classics, demonstrating that apparent contradictions in the originals could be reconciled by textual analysis. As we have seen through the analysis of how Zhang Zai proceeded, the focus of this kind of exegesis was definitely more on "reconciling" contradictions than on merely tracking down their existence. Moreover, it had taken over the "modular character" of Zhang Zai's treatment of sentences and words by dissecting these elements into a nonlinear arrangement.

Let us have a look at an example of "competing" diagrammatic interpretations, where we can find confirmation of the interest the authors of the diagrams took in a strict parallel organization and eventual remodeling of a passage.[25]

The diagrams I present have been drawn by Wang Bo (1197–1274)[26] and Xu Qian (1270–1337),[27] respectively. They both deal with sections 8–10 of paragraph 20 of the *Zhongyong,* which seem to defy a strict parallel order.[28] The sections read as follows:

> 8) The Ways of fullest attainment in the universe are five, and [the qualities required for] putting them into practice are three. [These are the cardinal relations between] ruler and subject, between father and son, between husband and wife, between elder and younger siblings, and between friends. These five constitute the ways of fullest attainment in the universe. Knowledge, human kindness (benevolence), and courage, these are the three virtues of fullest attainment in the universe, yet there is but one (single quality) for putting them into practice.
>
> 9) There are those who possess knowledge from birth (i.e., inborn knowledge); there are those who acquire knowledge by learning; and there are those who gain this knowledge by adversity (painfully acquired knowledge). Yet, once one has reached this knowledge, then it is all one. There are those who put it into practice with equanimity (lit., "in peace"); there are those who put it into practice for personal advantage (lit., "for profit"); and there are those who put it into practice with concerted effort ("under pressure"). Yet, once success has been achieved, then it is all one.
>
> 10) The master said: Love of learning is close to knowledge; putting into practice is close to human kindness; and a sense of shame (knowing shame) is close to courage.

A close look at the three sections of this paragraph clearly shows that problems of interpretation can arise on account of the search for a strict parallelism. First of all, there is no evident connection between the Five Ways and the Three Virtues (knowledge, human kindness, courage). This is probably why, as we will see, Xu Qian didn't even bother to illustrate this relationship in his diagram. Section 9 seems to be incomplete when compared to the Three Virtues mentioned in sections 8 and 10. In the first part of that section, we find a statement about a "knowledge" (to be acquired from birth, through learning or painfully); however, the second part, whose principal concern is the way of "putting into practice," does not include any reference to the two remaining virtues, human kindness and courage. Instead, it reiterates the "putting into practice," although it is not clear what is to be "put into practice": the Five Ways or the Three Virtues. The text is not explicit as to whether we are dealing with the latter, and if "putting into practice" refers to them. (Zhu Xi solved this problem by referring to "authenticity" [*cheng*], the key concept of the *Zhongyong.*)[29]

Moreover, the second part of section 9 does not reiterate an already mentioned element (as was the case for the three ways of "knowledge") that pointed to "knowledge" as a conclusion, but finishes with a new element: "achieved success." In the framework of a rigorous parallel order that would demand a predicate for each of the Three Virtues, part of a sentence is clearly missing. Most diagrams increase the tendency to observe a parallelism even stricter than the one of the text. Let us have a look at the solutions provided by two different diagrams.

First of all, we observe that in Figure 6.1 there is only a very loose link relating the Five Ways to the Three Virtues. But we have already noticed that this is not the real problem of the passage in question. Second, in the view of the author of the first diagram, section 10, which contains the Master's statements about attitudes that are "close" to the Three Virtues, seems insufficient. In adding the names of three disciples supposed to embody each of the different virtues, this diagram is in accordance with the great lines of

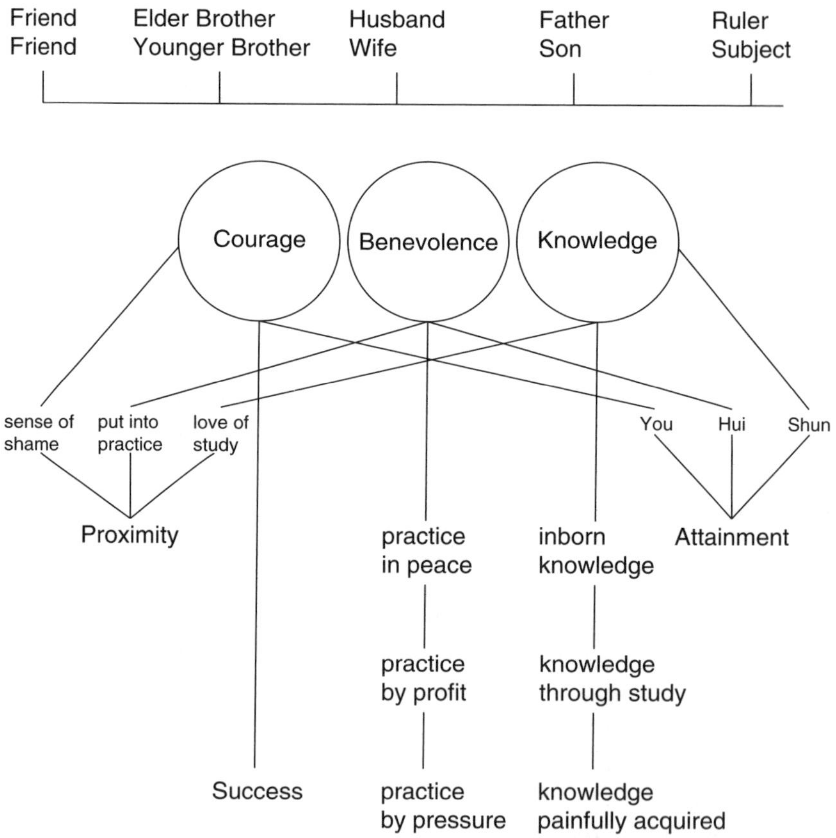

Figure 6.1. Diagram on the "Universal Ways and Virtues."

behavioral typology found in earlier and later passages of the *Zhongyong* (equating Emperor Shun with "knowledge," para. 6; the *Zhongyong* itself with the disciple Yan Hui, para. 8; "courage" with the disciple Zilu, para. 10). Thus, the right side of the central part of the diagram expands on the virtues by extrapolating from other passages. This is exactly the way Zhang Zai rearranged his "fifth Gospel." However, the vertical order of the center of the diagram is most important for our purpose. The first part of section 9 is not problematic, since the three forms of "knowledge" are subsumed under the word "knowledge," which acts as a main clause (a "topic"). Following the order of enunciations concerning the Three Virtues in sections 8 and 10, the author attributes some elements of the second part of section 9 to "human kindness," that is, the three ways of "putting into practice"—with equanimity, for "profit," with effort.

Now a parallel juxtaposition is achieved: "from birth" matches "equanimity," "learning" matches "profit," and so forth. "Knowledge" and "putting into practice" are in a perfectly balanced relationship. However, only one element remains for the third virtue: "achieved success," that is, the concluding statement of that part. If reading in linear order, a reader may assume that "achieved success" refers to "putting into practice" rather than to "courage," as in the diagram. Although the chart is "imbalanced" to a certain extent (because of two missing elements), an at least superficially parallel order is achieved. This is in accordance with Zhu Xi's commentary on the passage: "the things known by those who know something, the things put into practice by those who put something into practice, are the (Five) Ways. If one explains this according to the individual elements, the parts (of the linear discourse of the sentence), then, the reason for which they know something is knowledge; the reason for which they put something into practice is human kindness; and the reason for which they manage to know something and to achieve success [in putting something into practice], success which is only one in kind, is courage."[30] The attribution of "human kindness" to "putting into practice" and the invention of the expression "success of knowledge" all derive from Zhu Xi, who has, in a most arbitrary way, established a connection between "knowledge" and "courage," leaving apart "human kindness." The diagram represents this interpretation by a bar that connects "knowledge" to "courage."

Xu Qian's solution of the puzzling problem of the "missing link" is far more complex, although he attempts to be faithful to Zhu Xi's interpretation. Xu proposed a multidimensional solution with a series of intertwined diagrams.[31]

The title of the first diagram in that series, "explanation with regard to the individual parts" is still in accordance with Zhu Xi's interpretation (linking the expression "success of knowledge" to "courage") mentioned above. Contrary to the diagram by Wang Bo, Xu Qian does not refer to the Five Ways but rather focuses on the central textual problem. Moreover, he places the Three Virtues at the bottom of the diagram, at the very end of the series of propositions of section 9, as though they were the result of those propositions, not their point of departure.

These positions do not correspond to the text; they represent an inversion of the "topic and comment order" of the original. Parallelism is saved, albeit at the expense of the original balance of the elements constituting the sentence. While essentially modeling his diagram in accordance with the basic pattern of Wang Bo's *Yanjitu* (inserting "courage" by introducing "success" or the "success of knowledge"), Xu Qian recurs to a graphic tool that did not occur in Wang Bo's *Yanjitu:* connecting, by a horizontal line, "knowledge," "human kindness," and "success of knowledge=courage," he creates the image of a loom whose warp is constituted by the series of vertical propositions,

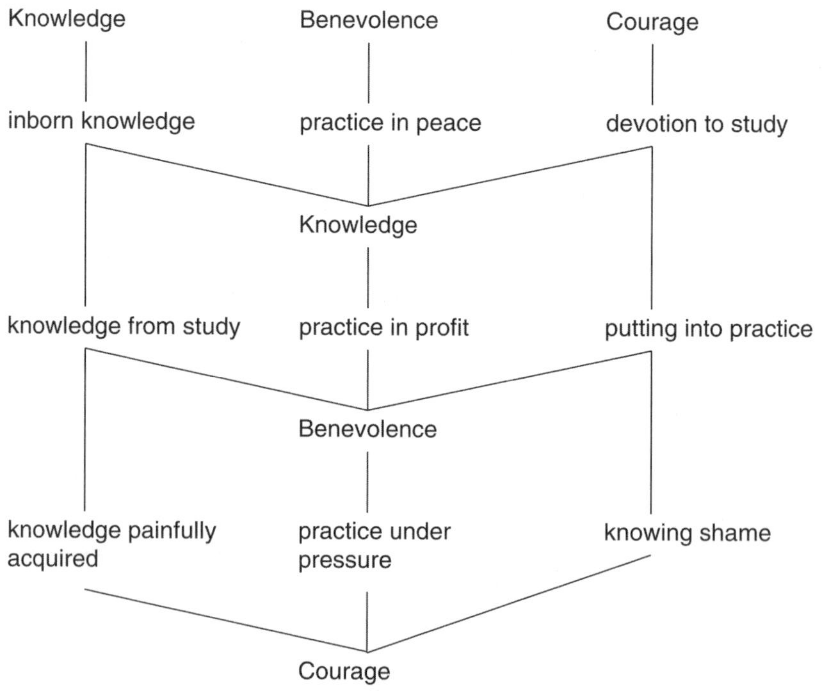

Figure 6.2. Synoptic Explanation of the 3 Passages B: Vertical Order.

which are connected, in turn, by the weft of the Three Virtues in a horizontal line. This system of warp and weft, as we will see, is capable of illustrating the multiple transformations of the positions of the basic elements.

In the following diagrams, "success" will not be mentioned anymore, because Xu Qian has resolved the problem by isolating it and linking it to "courage." The remaining problem for the three sections, however, consists in transforming the two parts of section 9 into three propositions that can be attributed to the Three Virtues. First operation: subordinate the six propositions of section 9 (knowledge from birth; from learning; painfully acquired; putting into practice with equanimity; for profit; under pressure) to the Three Virtues. Next step: these six propositions have to be completed by the three propositions of section 10 (love of learning; putting into practice; sense of shame) so that finally, a total of nine propositions will have to match the Three Virtues. Thus, the problematic issue of a missing sentence or the uncertainty where to insert "success" into this system has been spirited away.[32]

The second part of the diagram, titled "Explanation According to the Hierarchy of the Sections," illustrates this commentary: each of the Three Virtues is connected, in the framework of a triangle, to two propositions of section 9. The diagram simulates the absence of any problem related to parallelism, and, from an arithmetic point of view, all the attributions seem to be successfully carried out. Moreover, the very position of the propositions on the diagram has not been subject to change: the different forms of "knowledge" remain, in vertical order, on the right side, and the respective forms of "putting into practice" on the left. But two-thirds of the attributes possess a different point of reference, because they are connected to different virtues. It is the virtues that have changed places. They act as weft in the warp of propositions. The innovative configuration of the first diagram, which has been taken over in the second one, seems to have facilitated the task of "repairing" any offense to the laws of parallelism. In the transition from the first to the second diagram, the Three Virtues are being treated like mobile and flexible modules so that the equation leaves no remainder.

But Xu Qian goes further. He proposes an ever more complex collage, a synthesis titled "Synoptic Explanation of the Three Sections" (Figure 6.2). The two arrangements of this synopsis are designated as "horizontal" and "vertical" "deductions" or "extrapolations" *(heng tui, shu tui)*. In order to find a representation that does justice to the entirety of possible relationships among all the elements of all three sections (apart from "success"), Xu Qian first faces the problem of inserting the three propositions of section 10, which had been left apart so far. The arrangement he calls "horizontal" is in fact to be understood as vertical, since the reading direction follows vertical columns. In this first arrangement, the enunciations attributed to the Virtues follow a sequence that is already familiar from the second diagram. Thus, "knowledge from birth" and "putting into practice with equanimity" refer to "knowledge," and so on. However, Xu Qian has added the enouncements of section 10, "love of learning," and so on. Now, each of the Three Virtues possesses three propositions from section 9 and 10.

This statement not only provides the formal pattern of the diagrammatic procedure (i.e., the choice of positions related to the system of variable correspondences) but also justifies the insertion of section 10 into the diagram. Only by introducing a third "sentence" can one manage to unify the propositions of the three sections. So Xu Qian associates semantic elements (the quest for authenticity, successfully achieved only by those who exert themselves indefatigably and strive for Oneness; this was Zhu Xi's clue to the passage) with purely analytic elements derived from the imperative of parallelism.

The vertical and horizontal arrangements in Xu Qian's diagram resemble the image of a loom, whose system of coordinates allows for multiple connections in both longitudinal and transversal directions. In the diagram from the *Yanjitu,* the position of words was relatively stable and did not allow for more than one reading of the passage. However, although it solves the passage's most important problem (the lack of strict parallelism), this model corresponds to only one of the layers of interpretation provided by Zhu Xi. To do justice to the multiplicity of layers, Xu Qian invented an ingenious multilayered system of reciprocity, where horizontal and vertical arrangements of the terms (propositions and virtues) intertwine. This system constitutes a performative transformation that reminds us of the principle of metamorphosis underlying the trigrams and hexagrams of the *Classic of Changes.* This principle is based on numerological devices, and we are perhaps entitled to say that Xu Qian deals with sentences as if they were numbers.

This diagram certainly reveals an intellectual process. Its purpose does not seem to be memorizing a given interpretation of a passage in the Classics; it rather enacts the endeavor of interpretation itself. The diagram—as an operation of the mind—is a tool to enable its author to understand, in an unexpected, nonlinear way, the different steps leading to the final result. Although instead of doing justice to the original, it quite violently introduces the pervasive rules of parallelism, the diagram displays a creative process of invention. It seems that Xu Qian's goal of a least common denominator, a conclusion for each passage, can only be reached by applying the strictest rules of parallelism, if necessary, even through doing violence to the original.

The proof that the Scriptures were but one, and that their true meaning sometimes had to be deciphered against their apparent wording, has been undertaken on a "macro level" by Zhang Zai, and we have seen the same spirit at work in the diagrams on the "micro level." If we leave aside the often futile speculations about the philosophical character of Confucianism (and, in particular, of "neo-Confucianism"), we certainly will come to some fresh insights on literati practices and exegesis, and perhaps we will see more parallels between East and West than any approach in comparative philosophy has perceived so far.[33]

The *daoxue* or "Neo-Confucian" approach to the Classics was not shared by all the literati of the Song period. On the contrary, it began as a minoritarian movement and gained momentum only after Zhu Xi's death. During the eleventh century, it was still possible to take different paths of interpretation, less guided by a holistic view of the canonical writings than by the one embodied by the *daoxue* scholars. Ouyang Xiu (1007–1072) argued that the *Xici* commentary to the *Classic of Changes* (a text that, as we have seen, was crucial for Zhang Zai's thought) could not have been written by Confucius. In Ouyang's view, it was a confused mass of sayings that could not even be traced back to one and the same author.[34] Although Ouyang's skepticism was not yet fed by the methodology of classical empiricism that characterized eighteenth-century philological discourses (see Benjamin A. Elman's chapter in this volume), the very fact that it was possible to question Confucius's authorship of such a vital text shows the potential of a critical differentiation of textual sources that would later become the base of "precise scholarship" described by Elman. However, it was centuries until the *daoxue* philological approach was abandoned in favor of radically novel forms of philological inquiry.

Humanist Philologies

Texts, Antiquities, and Their Scholarly Transformations in the Early Modern West

ANTHONY GRAFTON

EARLY IN THE nineteenth century, an Oxford undergraduate read aloud passages from his diary of a trip to Venice. "Painted Beauty 2£," he noted, presumably with a smirk, recalling his visit to a prostitute. One of his hearers, Edward Harrison, immediately rose, said, *"Philokaloumen met'euteleias,"* and left the room, to general applause. None of his friends ever forgot the event. None of them needed an explanation, either. For they knew at once that Harrison had condemned his college mate's vulgar words in the most crushing possible way. He had quoted a supremely apposite classical text: a slightly abridged phrase from Pericles's funeral oration for the Athenian dead in the first year of the Peloponnesian War, recorded by the Greek historian Thucydides. The statement forms part of Pericles's description of the Athenian character. It reads, in its original wording: "Philokaloumen te gar met'euteleias kai philosophoumen aneu malakias": "For we are lovers of beauty without extravagance and lovers of wisdom without effeminacy" (2.40.1).[1] As the witness to this confrontation recalled, "the audience were all men to whom the second book of Thucydides was familiar and the speech of Pericles like household words."[2]

Harrison remembered this particular sentence because it was a lovely example of the early Greek rhetorician's art, just asymmetrical enough to be musical, with partial anaphoras and near-rhymes to emphasize its beauty and enhance its force. More important, it formed part of a canon: a set of texts that upper-class English boys studied, first at school and then at university, with extraordinary dedication (one estimate, based on the notes of a teacher at Eton, is that a student at the midpoint in his schooling spent twenty-one hours a week on Latin and Greek—as opposed to three hours on writing and arithmetic and three in church).[3] Ancient Athens, all members of the British elite learned while still in their teens, was the preeminent model for modern Britain: a maritime empire whose fearsome navy terrified all opponents, and whose cosmopolitan, spectacular capital city amazed all visitors.[4]

This general lesson was reinforced by the practices embedded in the curriculum. Students not only construed their way through the tragedies of Aeschylus, Sophocles, and Euripides, the histories of Thucydides and Xenophon, and the philosophical works of Plato and Aristotle but also did their best to imitate them.[5] Boys and young men wrote exercises in classical Greek prose and verse, and mature professors continued to practice the art. Gilbert Murray, for example, served as professor of Greek at Oxford for many years. He translated an article from the London *Times* into classical Greek every day before breakfast. J. D. Beazley, who became the world's greatest expert on Athenian ceramics, achieved fame in Britain for a brilliant essay in which he described, in the language of the Greek historian Herodotus, a visit to the London Zoo.[6] No wonder then that a memorable phrase from Thucydides stuck in a gifted student's mind, or that his friends knew what he meant. They shared a training that formed them to rule and had an impact far outside the universities: its results were manifest everywhere from the House of Commons, where the clerk had to keep classical reference books handy in order to settle bets between MPs who accused each other of misquotations, to the world of literature.[7]

The classical curriculum that still flourished in nineteenth-century Britain originated centuries before, in the transformation of the canon that took place in Europe between 1350 and 1650. In this period, Western intellectuals radically enlarged the corpus of works from ancient Greece and Rome, dramatically revised the methods of exegesis that were applied to them, and began to study the Bible not only in the Latin translation used through the Middle Ages but also in its original Hebrew (for the Old Testament) and Greek (for the New). They did this, moreover, in a literary world transformed first by the creation of an active urban trade in manuscript books, many of them secular, and then, to even more radical effect, by the introduction of printing. The results were far-reaching. Self-consciously modern approaches to ancient texts, which set out to make them useful for a modern, Christian society, were flanked by historical approaches, designed to set ancient texts back into their original contexts. Traditional Christian forms of exegesis were not replaced, but enriched by pagan and Jewish methods. The humanists did not create or practice the modern discipline of philology that took shape in the universities of the eighteenth and nineteenth centuries. Nonetheless, they reconfigured the canon in ways that reshaped religion, education, and much more.

Ancient texts have played a central role in every period of Western cultural history, down to the present, when they continue to inspire everything from movies about Greece and Rome to evangelical politics. But they have taken many different shapes and been read in many different ways. In the European high Middle Ages—the twelfth through fourteenth centuries—ancient texts and modern commentaries and treatises based on them formed the core of higher education. But they did so in forms that their own creators would have found hard to recognize. At universities, for example, the arts course—the basic course that taught young men the skills of reasoning and prepared some of them for higher studies—centered on formal dialectic, an ancient discipline taught, in large part, from ancient textbooks and commentaries. The systematic works of Aristotle and other ancients, like Porphyry, were studied not in the original but in Latin versions, some ancient but most rendered, word for word, from earlier Arabic translations, themselves derived from Syriac. Students learned the forms of argument, as Aristotle and his commentators had framed them. But they learned them as sets of abstract rules, out of time and space, couched in a technical Latin designed to teach formal logic—a language in which even ancient names were systematically deformed. Socrates, the subject of many sample propositions, usually appears as "Sortes."[8]

In the three higher faculties—law, medicine, and theology—courses also rested on ancient authorities, but they too were highly mediated. Roman lawyers studied the *Corpus iuris,* a systematic collection of Roman legislation and legal opinion, much of it quite ancient, which had been compiled at the command of the emperor Justinian early in the sixth century. But these texts were embedded in a mass of commentary designed to make them serve up-to-date purposes. The commentators explained the bundle of six "fasces," or rods, carried by Roman officials called lictors, as months: the fact that the bundle contained six rods meant that a modern official's term should last no longer than six months.[9] Medical men read the biological works of Aristotle and the medical treatises of Hippocrates and Galen in

Latin translations, doing their best to reconcile their opinions and choosing critically when they could not. They found guidance in the twelfth-century Canon of Avicenna.[10] Theologians, though they had their own textbooks, took the Bible as the one absolutely valid authority, propositions from which should serve as the basis of all arguments. Normally, they read one of the endlessly varied Latin versions that had taken shape from the fourth and fifth centuries onward.[11] When engaged in serious inquiry they read the Scriptures, as the jurists and medical men read their canonical texts, not in isolation but embedded in commentary.[12] The numerous fifteenth- and sixteenth-century theologians who wrote treatises on the spread of witchcraft, for example, based their chains of argument on Exodus 22:18, "maleficos non patieris vivere" ("thou shalt not suffer a witch to live"). They simply assumed that the "malefici" mentioned in the text were the witches who supposedly had been detected in their own day, having intercourse with devils, stirring up storms, and killing babies. The university teachers and students of the later Middle Ages, in short, copied, collected, lectured on, and studied ancient texts intensively. But they concentrated on those that played well-defined roles in the curriculum and in the professional life of their time, and treated them as ahistorical authorities, sources of powerful, pithy statements to be used in the here and now, rather than as the works of historical individuals. Even the format of these canonical texts highlighted the way they were meant to be read. Large manuscripts in which small islands of text floated on vast oceans of commentary in much smaller script, they often occupied stately positions in libraries and individuals' studies, propped up on massive reading stands, as if awaiting reverent readers who would spend long periods on every page or set up to impress clients who came to consult a learned lawyer.

Monastic libraries had never ceased to copy, or all scholars to read, a wide range of other texts. Mendicant friars, the Franciscans and Dominicans, who devoted themselves to preaching in the cities, read widely, often in search of anecdotes to improve their sermons. Their search for materials sometimes took them into what were, from a Christian standpoint, potentially deep waters: the Roman histories of Livy, which Augustine had denounced as a record of illegal and destructive conquests, and the mythologies of Ovid, with their witty celebrations of sensuality. In these circles, interpretative methods drawn from Christian tradition rendered what might have been dangerous texts harmless. Prefaces defined the purposes of ancient literary texts in terms of a scholastic system of causes and ends. Allegorical exegesis folded passages that seemed at variance with Christianity back into orthodox sense. When the poet Orpheus descended into the underworld in the hope of bringing his wife, Eurydice, back to life, he stood for Christ, who would harrow Hell and bring forth the saints; when Pandora disobeyed the gods and let loose a flock of evils on humanity, she stood for Eve, who had done exactly that in the Garden of Eden.[13]

But in fourteenth-century Italy, a new approach to the same texts took shape. Individuals began to treat the ancients less as disembodied texts, more as individuals. Through the Middle Ages, librarians and readers normally assumed that the Pliny who wrote the vast *Natural History* and the Pliny who wrote a set of letters were the same man. Giovanni de Matociis, a cathedral official in Verona, noticed that the second Pliny described the death of the first Pliny, who was his uncle, and wrote up a short critical essay about it.[14] The very fact that he thought it worthwhile to make the point reveals the change in his attitude. Collectors of florilegia—anthologies of Latin poems—began to differentiate the works of ancient Roman writers, whom they called "poets," from their medieval imitators, whom they called "versifiers."[15] Many of the north Italian scholars who began to read their texts in this way were notaries or lawyers: official handlers and readers of texts, but in secular contexts.

Francesco Petrarca (1304–1374) transformed these new ways of appreciating texts into a cultural program. From early in his life, he felt profound dissatisfaction with existing approaches to the ancients. Sent, like so many others, by his father to study law, he hated the legal discipline but found the Roman histories to which the legal texts alluded compulsively fascinating. Becoming famous as a Latin and Italian poet and a writer of moral and historical essays in Latin, he gained access to a wider range of texts than anyone before him had had in centuries.[16] Of the work of Livy, originally 142 books long, only 35 books survived the Middle Ages; these circulated, for the most part, in isolated groups of 10. Petrarca brought thirty of them together in one manuscript, thus gaining access to the most detailed account available in Latin of Rome's origins and the city's wars with Carthage. He also wove dense webs of annotation across the margins of this and other books, collating the information they provided and coming to see the ancients in radically new ways.[17]

Through much of the Middle Ages, Cicero had been read and remembered chiefly as a philosopher, a moralist who had written wisely about the divine order of the cosmos, the duties of a good man, and the best way of coping with old age. Petrarca read the letters to Atticus, in which Cicero described his active political career in the last decades of the Roman republic, and realized that a man he had imagined as a sage, living in retirement, had actually been an engaged politician, a discovery that filled him with horror. By the middle of the fourteenth century, Petrarca was writing letters to Cicero and other ancients in which he underlined both his love and respect for their accomplishments and the vast distance that separated him, as a Christian, from them and their world. "How much better," he reproached Cicero, "had it been never to have held office, never to have longed for triumphs, never to have vaunted of crushing such men as Catiline." The very way Petrarca dated the latter underlined its point: "Written in the land of the living . . . in the thirteen hundred and forty-fifth year from the birth of that God whom thou never knewest."[18]

In the course of the next century and a half, Petrarca's admirers and followers transformed the world of the book and its uses in education. Coluccio Salutati, the humanist chancellor of Florence, and his younger associate Poggio Bracciolini devised a new form for the book, based on models from the Carolingian period. Instead of swamping ancient texts with modern commentary, the humanists produced books in a rounded, open script, with broad, clean margins and little or no commentary: an invitation to direct study and collation.[19] The urban patriciate in Florence and Venice and patrons like the Este in Ferrara, the Medici in Florence, and the Sforza in Milan hired humanists to write their official letters and histories in classical Latin. Humanist teachers, first in advanced cities like Florence and courts like those of Ferrara and Mantua, began to offer young boys, and a much smaller number of girls, a classical curriculum centered on the reading and imitation of ancient literary works—a curriculum like that portrayed in ancient manuals of rhetoric.[20] Like Petrarca, these men read the works of Cicero in the context of his career—but unlike Petrarca, Leonardo Bruni, who succeeded Salutati as chancellor of Florence, saw Cicero as exemplary for his ability to combine the active with the contemplative life. The classics could now be understood, in other words, as directly relevant to the active life. Teachers supported by Renaissance princes, like Guarino of Verona, who worked at the court of the Este of Ferrara, could offer Julius Caesar as a model in place of the republican Cicero.[21]

By the middle of the fifteenth century, schoolboys were already attacking tasks that their nineteenth-century counterparts would have recognized. They worked their way through a newly defined set of texts: humanist grammars, textbooks on rhetoric by Cicero and others, and selected works of Latin historiography, poetry, and moral philosophy, which their teachers explained for them orally, working word by word and emphasizing the literal meaning and classical syntax and grammar. They compiled systematic commonplace books in which they noted exemplary statements and anecdotes. And they deployed these in compositions of their own, doing their best to write as the ancients would have when addressing the same subject.

Erasmus exaggerated in his satirical work *The Ciceronian* in which he portrayed one imitator of Cicero who confined himself when writing Latin not only to the words that Cicero had used but also to the particular grammatical forms that appeared in his works—and wrote only at night, in a darkened, absolutely silent room, after pursuing an ascetic regime in preparation for the task of imitating the greatest of the classics. But all agreed that anyone who wanted to prepare for a significant career as a king's counselor or a high cleric needed to master the classics. Language itself—at least the official written language of documents—reflected the new classical tastes. The pope's own secretaries, in fact, were the purest of the purists, and wrote official documents in which they described the pope as "pontifex maximus" and the Christian God as "Jupiter optimus maximus."[22]

Perhaps the most radical change begun by Salutati was the teaching of Greek. Thanks to his official support, an erudite Byzantine Greek, Manuel Chrysoloras, taught Greek in Florence from 1397 to 1400. His pupils, who included Poggio and the influential young Aretine humanist Leonardo Bruni, began translating previously unknown Greek texts into Latin. Others went to Constantinople to learn the language, or stayed home and used the new textbook Chrysoloras devised for his Italian pupils to learn the language on their own. From the middle of the fifteenth century, when the erudite Pope Nicholas V invested heavily in a systematic translation program, even those who knew only Latin could read the histories of Herodotus and Thucydides, the geographical work of Ptolemy and Strabo, and the essays and biographies of Plutarch.[23] Though Greek was never studied so thoroughly, or written so fluently and correctly, as Latin, schoolboys and their elders and betters could now draw on an even wider range of sources.

A system of manuscript publication, urban and secular, enabled the most skillful Latinists to reach a wide public. *Cartolai* or stationers in the major cities compiled stocks of ancient and modern texts, which they reproduced, in the fashionable style, for a very broad public—including not only professional scholars and teachers but also bankers and merchants, clerics and well-off women. The Milanese humanist Angelo Decembrio described the situation in the middle of the fifteenth century: "the most handsomely made books are generally bought in the Tuscan city of Florence, and they say that there is one Vespasiano there, a superb bookseller who takes great pains with books and scribes alike. Everyone who wants the best-looking books—all Italians, and men from distant nations as well—flocks to him."[24]

From the 1460s onward, printing transformed the situation in multiple ways. It consolidated the aesthetic transformation of the book, since printers soon adopted the new humanistic format. It also consolidated the position of the classical literary and philosophical texts that had not been read in the Middle Ages. The numbers of classical texts on the market multiplied, lowering prices in Rome, for example, by half or more—a process that bankrupted the German printers, Conrad Sweynheym and Arnold Pannartz, who had started printing classical texts there.[25] But even as first mover advantage evaporated, others persisted. By the early sixteenth century, Aldus Manutius, a Roman scholar based in Venice, had created a great program for preserving and fostering the new classicism. Big folio editions of the works of the ancient Greek writers, in the original language, ensured that they would never vanish, even though Constantinople itself had fallen to the Turks in 1453. Smaller-format octavo editions of the Latin classics, printed in italics, enabled the well-educated young to take their favorite books with them everywhere—not only to the classroom but also to court, where, as satisfied customers told Aldo, they could read a Latin poem or history in the intervals between bouts of official business.[26]

In the second half of the fifteenth century and the first half of the sixteenth, finally, the humanists turned their attention not only to literary classics but also to the texts that had long formed the basis of the higher faculties. Medieval scholars knew perfectly well that the Old Testament had originally been written not in the Latin of the Vulgate but in Hebrew, and the New Testament in Greek, and they collated and debated about the different Latin versions. Where the Vulgate diverged from the original, they noted, it might well be necessary to correct it—even though the original texts had been preserved and studied, through the Middle Ages, by Jews and Greeks rather than by orthodox Catholics, while the Latin text had gained—as Augustine influentially put it—the authority of being "custom." Fifteenth-century humanists like Lorenzo Valla drew heavily on their medieval predecessors when working on the biblical text: the general idea that old manuscripts are preferable to new ones, for example, was well established in the medieval scholarly tradition.[27] But they argued with a new sharpness and precision for the need to correct the Latin against the original languages and to reconsider the status of dubious texts like the story of Bel and the dragon. In the first two decades of the sixteenth century, a series of editions—a massive polyglot Bible sponsored by Archbishop Ximenes at

Alcala in Spain and a much more modest Greek-Latin edition of the New Testament carried out by Erasmus in Basel—fundamentally challenged the preeminence of the Latin Bible, even though Ximenes compared the Vulgate Old Testament, which appeared between the Hebrew and the Greek in his edition, to Christ, crucified between the two thieves. Once the Protestant Reformation began in 1517, the Vulgate would never again be the sole source in which Christians read the Bible—much less the basis for all scholarly argument.[28] Meanwhile Valla, Guillaume Budé, and others noted that the legal texts on which both Roman lawyers and the church's canon lawyers depended for their authority were marred by errors and anachronisms, and another group of scholars based in Florence and Ferrara argued about whether the newly available texts challenged the authority of Greek medical works in their traditional, clunky Latin form. By the 1520s, when a Latin translation and then, a year later, the Greek originals of the medical texts ascribed to Hippocrates appeared, Galen and Aristotle seemed to be wobbling on their pedestals.

For the next century and more, debate on all these texts and their status would continue. But by now a course had been set—for compromise, rather than revolution. In schools, universities, and publishing, the humanists and their new canon joined the scholastics and their older one. The new literary studies did not replace, but flourished alongside faculties where logic, law, medicine, and theology were still taught in the scholastic way. In Italian universities, scholastic theology was a relatively novel import from the north, and it spread alongside the methods of the humanists. Gradually, traditional and novel methods intersected. Young men who wanted to study law or theology mastered the humanist curriculum first—especially after Protestant towns and the Jesuit order created networks of classical schools that stretched across Europe, and both had their best students master first classical rhetoric and then the more rigorous studies that the first humanists had shunned. Professors of law and theology accepted the need to know history, Hebrew, and Greek as well as the areas their disciplines had traditionally embraced. Humanists, for their part, learned to love the commentary—though theirs concentrated on grammatical, rhetorical, and historical, rather than logical, questions—and buried classics like Virgil and Caesar under variorum commentaries. On any given page, six or seven different individuals, ancient and modern, might appear discussing a single line of the ancient text. Humanism had become institutionalized, and its practitioners went in for every sort of interpretation, from allegorical to political.[29] Changes would take place, of course, in many areas of the curriculum and its wider context. But by 1650 scholars, teachers, and publishers had laid the foundations on which the classical teachers of the British elite were still building, two centuries later.

This narrative established, the big question remains: what sort of philology, if any, did the humanists practice? What methods did they apply, what methods did they devise as they prepared texts for consumption by readers, isolated and solved individual scholarly problems, and challenged the authority of Europe's licensed intellectuals? Long ago, Erwin Panofsky argued that Renaissance intellectuals developed a historical as well as a spatial sense of perspective. They came to see the ancient past not as a continuous part of their own world, as medieval scholars did, but as a different realm that existed at a fixed distance from their own, and which they could see in all its colors and dimensions.[30] If such transformations took place anywhere, they should have done so in the realm of philology—and generations of historians have argued that they did, and there was a "historical revolution" in the early modern period.[31] Two case studies in philologists' practice will pose—if not answer—the question whether such radical changes happened. Two major conclusions will emerge. First, the humanists did not devise their practices de novo, as a whole, but worked them out on the fly; second, they derived substantial elements of their methodology from the ancient texts they read and taught, which were themselves, after all, the products of a textual and scholarly tradition.

From the fifteenth through the seventeenth centuries, Western humanists prepared hundreds of ancient texts for readers: first as manuscripts and then, after the 1460s, as printed books. Their methods evolved surprisingly little. For the most part, a scholar chose a base text—sometimes the only one to be found, sometimes one especially old or valuable. Then he copied it, correcting evident errors as he went—or entered corrections and passed the manuscript to a professional scribe for copying. The corrections made by a scholar like Poggio Bracciolini or Lorenzo Valla often revealed expert command of grammar, idiom, and historical fact. But the reader of the second, corrected text could appreciate these qualities only in the most general way, since the process was documented only in the original manuscript. Most humanists made little effort to record the details of their textual labors. Even the most precious new sources tended either to disappear completely—for example, the first known full manuscript of Cicero's *De oratore,* a central text for the rhetorical tradition—or to fall out of circulation, for example, the Carolingian manuscript of Cicero's letters *Ad familiares,* another text considered vitally important, from which all later Italian manuscripts are descended.[32] Commentaries dealt, for the most part, not with textual criticism but with questions of grammatical, rhetorical, and historical analysis. Even Valla—who had studied the causes of scribal error with great care and applied what he had learned to correcting the text of Livy—left his methods stated implicitly, though brilliantly, in one segment of a polemic against his literary foes at Naples.[33]

The advent of printing changed the conditions of reproduction dramatically, as scholars who worked in both regimes clearly recognized. Giannantonio Campano, who served as an editor for manuscripts and then as a corrector for Roman printers, stated the point clearly. In 1470, Campano oversaw an edition of Livy for the Viennese printer Ulrich Han. In his preface, he celebrated the powers of printing. From now on, he exulted, texts would no longer be riddled with errors. Previously, every scribe had felt free to make—or ruin—his copy of a given text in his own way. The printers, by contrast, "produce as many copies as they want, all uniform, from a single exemplar that has been scrutinized and corrected."[34]

That was the ideal. Yet as Campano admitted, reality did not live up to it. For copyists continually intervened in and altered the texts they were employed to reproduce: "they think what they do not understand is superfluous, or what they do not grasp is obscure, or what the author deliberately inverted is corrupt. Turning themselves from scribes into correctors, they apply their own judgment most stringently where they understand the least." Printing amplified their errors: now the scribes' arbitrary changes were reproduced hundreds of times. Campano insisted that he had set himself to produce a critical text by choosing an entirely different method. He had "relied on many exemplars" and refrained from making unnecessary changes: "I was never," Campano insisted, "a curious interpreter or diviner." Instead of being clever at the expense of his author, he had tried not to change the text but to stabilize it, "to remove the errors of the scribes."[35] Yet even Campano's Livy offers the curious reader no specific information about the particular manuscripts he used or the individual variant readings he drew from them. In other editions—notably one of Plutarch's *Lives,* in which he assembled existing Latin translations and corrected them pretty much at random—Campano made less effort to clarify the nature of his texts.

Giovanni Andrea Bussi, bishop and future librarian of the Vatican, edited a series of Latin texts in Rome for the German publishers Swyenheym and Pannartz between 1467 and 1472. They printed between eleven and twelve thousand volumes, an accomplishment that fired their first customers with enthusiasm. Another bishop, the curial insider Leonardo Dati, bought a copy of their edition of Augustine's *City of God* in November 1467. He noted in it that he had received the book "from the Germans who are presently in Rome, and who do not write, but form innumerable books like this one." And this purchase may well have inspired Dati's close friend Leon Battista Alberti to began his late work *On Ciphers* with an eloquent passage in which he and Dati strolled in the gardens of the Vatican, discussing printing, and marveled at the device that enabled "no more than three men to turn out more than two hundred copies of a book, from a given exemplar, in a hundred days."[36]

But soon the enthusiasm turned to horror. As early as 1470, Niccolò Perotti, another Roman scholar, complained in a public pamphlet that the printers and their humanist collaborators were actually defacing classical texts by adding prefaces to them. Worse still, they were introducing changes arbitrarily. "It would be better," he argued, "to do without these [printed] books than to have them copied a thousand times and sent out through all the provinces of the entire world." Perotti proceeded to subject Bussi's edition of Pliny to a paralyzingly painful, word-by-word dissection, rather like the public anatomies that were popular spectacles in this period. He claimed to have exposed twenty-one major errors just in the preface.[37] It should not come as a surprise that scrutiny revealed so many flaws in these first editions. Editors were, in the end, content providers, who not only provided and polished texts but also wrote the equivalent of blurbs. Francesco Rolandello prepared the first edition of the dialogues of Hermes Trismegistus, supposedly an Egyptian sage and contemporary of Moses. He added no preface to explain what changes, if any, he had made in Marsilio Ficino's Latin translation. But he did compose a charming little piece of front matter, printed on the title page, in which the author addressed potential buyers directly: "whoever you are who read this, whether you are a grammarian or an orator or a philosopher or a theologian, be it known to you: I am Mercurius Trismegistus, whom first the Egyptians and barbarians, and soon after the ancient Christian theologians admired, thunderstruck by my remarkable learning and theology. Hence if you buy and read me, you will gain something splendid: bought at a low price, I will enrich you as you read with pleasure and profit."[38] Such men worked under high pressure, often taking only a couple of weeks to prepare an edition. No wonder, then, that they often made errors that slower work would have prevented (as when the corrector of Aldus Manutius's edition of the Greek Anthology, a collection of ancient lyric poetry, changed the line "Drink to me only with thine eyes" to read "Drink to me only with thy lips").

Accordingly, few changes took place in the editorial practices of humanists who prepared texts for print. For the next century and more, even scholars such as Pier Vettori, Joseph Scaliger, and Isaac Casaubon, who specialized in textual criticism and gained fame for their ability to find reliable manuscripts, identify corrupt passages, and correct them by conjecture, prepared their editions in the same way. They laid out a text—often one copied from the last edition or a single, randomly chosen manuscript—and emended with pen in hand. The printer set this in type. Only then did the scholar prepare his commentary and offer his most detailed proposals for emending the text. The sequence is clear from a simple fact: in almost all cases, the textual notes in commentaries were keyed to page and line numbers in the printed text—which, accordingly, already existed before the commentary was written. In circumstances like these, critics could propose in their commentaries brilliant theses about the state of the texts they studied—as Scaliger did when he argued, from the existence of common errors, that all the manuscripts of the Latin poet Catullus must have descended from a single archetype written in a script in which *a* and *u,* tall *I* and *l,* and other letters could easily be confused. But they could not insert all, or most, of the changes they thought necessary into the text, since it had already taken stable form.[39] Even in the later sixteenth century, when commentaries on textual points were commonly written, texts rarely matched their editors' stated principles.

True, some humanists looked for better methods, and the manuscripts they worked with seemingly offered ancient models of philological work. The humanists knew that ancient predecessors had created large collections of manuscripts, especially in the fourth and fifth centuries: subscriptions, notes preserved for the most part in later copies, recorded that members of the Nicomachi and the Symmachi—two great Roman families—had "corrected" the text of Livy.[40] Salutati, who called for the creation of public libraries in which texts could be first corrected and then preserved, as a basis for later copies, noted that many manuscripts of the Latin poet Terence contained an ancient subscription reading "Calliopius recensui" (I, Calliopius, corrected this text).[41] Guarino of Verona, one of the most influential humanist scholars and teachers, deliberately emulated these subscriptions when he corrected manuscripts of Caesar and Pliny.[42] After Perotti denounced Bussi and his ilk for meddling with the ancient texts and advertising what they had done in prefaces, another Roman scholar, Pomponio Leto, had subscriptions clearly modeled on the ancient ones added to his editions: "Finis Pompei Festi quem Pomponius correxit: Vale qui legeris. H. G." (End of Pompeius Festus, whom Pomponio corrected. Farewell, reader. H. G. [probably the initials of the printer and proof corrector, Hans Glim]).[43]

Unfortunately, the ancient model did not repair the defects of fifteenth-century practice. Ancient emenders, like their Renaissance imitators, did not state exactly what they did to the manuscripts they corrected—a gap that has given rise to considerable scholarly debate in recent decades.[44] Accordingly, even those who tried to follow their example ended up, as Pomponio did, saying too little to make clear exactly what they had done to their texts: "Vbi librarii litteras mutauerunt correxi: In his que inscitia penitus corrupit non ausus sum manum imponere ne forte magis deprauarem" (Where the scribes changed the text, I corrected it; but I did not dare even touch those points that their ignorance had completely corrupted, since I was afraid I would make them worse)[45]—an impressive profession of faith unsupported by precise notes identifying the changes Pomponio did make. The printers, of course, did not help—not only were they unwilling to add marginal notes that identified textual changes, but they also added random errors of their own. Leto tried to say that the dedicatee of his edition of Varro, Bartolomeo Platina, stood out among the shitty men of his own day ("in hac fece hominum"). But his printer turned *fece* into the meaningless *sece,* which had to be corrected in pen.

Occasionally, a scholar prepared a manuscript in such a way that posterity could see what he had done to it. As Gemma Donati has shown, the fifteenth-century Roman humanist Pietro Odo of Montopoli corrected a number of manuscripts destined for the Vatican Library of Nicholas V. Surviving codices reflect his efforts to produce attractive, textually reliable versions of the classics for the pope and "the court of Rome." Odo collated his manuscripts with others: "This verse," he remarks at one point in the margins of his Claudian, "I didn't find in the other codices in which I went over the text, nor do I think it belongs there, because it is above the line and does not fit."[46] He distinguished between the manuscripts he used, describing one as "really really old" *(antiquissimus)* and according it special authority.[47]

In the late fifteenth century, moreover, scholars in Rome and elsewhere realized that the corrupt editions they despised offered one advantage: they provided their texts in a uniform state that readers could discuss and criticize. Soon clouds of debate hung around prominent passages that appeared in varied forms. As the Roman scholar Martino Filetico wrote of the beginning of Virgil's great epic, the *Aeneid,*

> It is hard to say how hard they have worked to corrupt the following passage in Virgil, among innumerable others:

> *Italiam fato profugus Lavinaque venit*
>
> *littora* [*Aeneid* 1.2–3: he who, forced into exile by fate, came to Italy and the Lavine shores]
>
> For that is what the poet wrote, that is what we have always read in the most correct codices and always heard, indeed, you will not find a variant in all the MSS of Virgil to be found everywhere, and this is how we have always taught that it should be read. But they, who are ignorant of both Latin and the shit of the Roman language, bark continually that *lavina* must be deleted and that *lavinia* should be set in place of that particle [-que]. In fact, they have done this so loudly that the benches and walls of the Roman Academy, torn and broken by their barking, seem to bark back. Sometimes they correct the boys with words, sometimes they frighten them with threats, and they ask many others to delete that passage, and with such success, I hear, that many books have now been corrupted.[48]

Domizio Calderini, Angelo Poliziano, and others began to ransack the Vatican and other libraries for manuscripts that offered new readings or confirmed old ones.[49] Poliziano, imitating the ancient Roman grammarian Aulus Gellius, published in 1489 a work entitled *Miscellanea*—despite its nonchalant title, a sharp methodological manifesto. Gellius had lambasted the grammarians of his own day for the poor education and judgment displayed in their texts of the Latin classics. He offered readings from older manuscripts that he claimed went back to Virgil and Cicero themselves. Emulating Gellius, Poliziano pointed out not only that the printed editions rested on poorly chosen base texts but also that in some cases, the manuscripts themselves all descended from a single original, which should serve as the basis of a critical text. Thus, he noted that parts of the text in Italian manuscripts and printed editions of Cicero's letters *Ad familiares* were out of order. In the oldest manuscript, the pages in question had been transposed—a physical error that not only explained the textual ones in later codices but also showed that they had no independent value.

Poliziano thus suggested that the study and editing of texts should begin from, or at least involve, the identification of the earliest stage of the manuscript tradition. Some of his readers took his ideas further. In 1521 Pierio Valeriano, after collating many manuscripts of Virgil, printed not a text but a critical apparatus: a collection of variant readings drawn from the manuscripts in the Vatican, some of which were literally ancient, and destined to be used by future editors. Thirty-three years later Florentine scholars published a facsimile, line by line, word for word, of the great manuscript of the *Digest,* a Roman law text, preserved in the Palazzo della Signoria. But these efforts remained outliers—richly historical exceptions to a rule of editing that was very different.[50]

The conditions of editorial work go far to explain the way the humanists prepared their texts. But so does the larger situation in which they operated, as suppliers of texts for young men and women who planned to write in classical Latin themselves. Writing Latin was dangerous: a single slip into medieval habits, such as referring to oneself in the plural, not the singular, when writing a letter, could expose to the world the limits of one's mastery of literary art and its refinements. In order to reveal the inadequacy of Poggio's Latin, Lorenzo Valla published a dialogue in which the cook and stable boy of another humanist read one of Poggio's books aloud and identify error after error.

The only way to write Latin without suffering public humiliation was to turn for editorial guidance to an acknowledged expert—a social equal or superior, often of older age, who was known to have a skilled editorial hand. The Florentine scholar Niccolò Niccoli, for example, refused to write anything of his own, since he believed himself inferior in ability to the ancients, eight hundred manuscripts of whose work he collected. He dismissed most modern Latin as fit for use only in the lavatory, not the library. But for close friends—like Poggio—he provided detailed, unsparing criticism, and the manuscript traditions show that his suggestions were put into effect when they revised their texts.[51] It became fashionable for scholars to begin their works with prefaces in which they thanked colleagues for their corrections, or asked them for help—as Leon Battista Alberti did in his famous books *On the Family* and *On Painting,* as well as a number of his Latin works. Campano, whom we have already encountered correcting Livy for the press, began life as a corrector of contemporary Latinists. He received the contract, for example, to correct the magnificently wry autobiographical work of the humanist Pope Pius II. Though he discreetly claimed to have changed nothing, in fact he did a good bit of editing, even introducing some of his own poems into Pius's text. Many of the changes are hard to detect in the manuscript he edited, and even harder to find in the versions that went into circulation.[52]

The similarities between the ways humanists produced their own Latin and corrected that of the ancients are clear—even down to the provision of brief prefaces, not found in the oldest manuscripts, to explain how a text had reached its present form. Evidently, the standard methods of text handling took shape not in the course of editing texts, but in composing them—a process more social and collaborative than composition in our world, now that copyediting has become rare. Scholars then transposed these methods into the scriptorium and the printing house. Humanist philology was not historical, in Panofsky's sense: it did not treat ancient texts as having come into existence at a fixed cultural and temporal distance from the present. For what mattered, in the end, was not making texts perfect but making them useful. The whole weight of a system of schools and literary patronage bore against the historical transformation of editing of which a few scholars dreamed.

If the production of texts remained relatively static—a domain of custom, ruled more by the needs of education than by the demands of radical analysts—historical criticism became a battleground early on, where new methods asserted themselves more powerfully. The humanists, as we have seen, emphasized rhetoric: the production of texts that seemed convincingly classical. And the formidable skills needed to do this had direct applications to the analysis, as well as the creation, of texts. The humanist who wrote an oration, as many did, in the character of Catiline, the aristocratic Roman rebel whom Cicero first denounced in a series of speeches and then defeated, had to produce a text appropriate to its supposed author—a text whose style, content, and flavor were unmarred by slips or anachronisms. The ancient textbooks of rhetoric contained detailed instructions. At the same time, they provided detailed ways of showing that the textual evidence cited by an adversary did not deserve credence: instructions on how to look for factual errors and contradictions. Both sets of techniques were revived in the Renaissance, and they proved more fruitful than those of the ancient textual critics.

When Lorenzo Valla wrote his commentary on the ancient treatise on rhetoric by Quintilian, he showed that he saw these two approaches as intimately connected: "To narratives," Quintilian wrote, "is annexed the task of refuting and confirming them. This may be done not merely in connection with fiction and stories transmitted by the poets, but with the actual records of history as well."[53] Valla began by noting, with excitement, that the orator could also call into question the authenticity of ancient and later texts—for example, the biblical apocrypha (texts transmitted not in the Hebrew Bible, but only in its ancient Greek version) and medieval saints' lives, which swarmed with incongruous details: "this question can also be raised in ecclesiastical matters, as about Susanna, about Tobias, about Judith. Also about more recent histories, like that of Saint George, where we have many arguments to use in refutation." He then gave examples of the best way to do this, showing that even Livy, the Roman historian whose work he cherished and glossed, had committed a gross error in dealing with the genealogy of Tarquinius and his descendants. By detecting internal inconsistencies in Livy's account and comparing it with that of another ancient writer, the Greek historian Dionysius of Halicarnassus, Valla made the point that all traditions needed scrutiny, and that the forensic skills supplied by classical rhetoric were essential to the task: "it is sheer heedlessness and indolence that has led these historians to publish that account of them without first examining any of the impossibilities and absurdities that are fatal to it. Each of these absurdities I will endeavor to point out in a few words."[54]

Valla's most celebrated scholarly work, his demolition of the Donation of Constantine, showed at length and in pulverizingly precise detail that this text, which the Roman church used to claim that the Emperor Constantine had given it control of the western Roman empire in the early fourth century C.E., could not be genuine. Playing with the rhetorical canon of decorum, Valla composed the speeches that the pope, the Roman senators, and the sons of Constantine would actually have given if the emperor had offered to give up his empire. By creating what were in effect forgeries more skillful than the original, Valla showed that the latter document did not fit its supposed context—a time when, in his view, the church had not yet become corrupt and would have rejected an offer of wordly wealth and political power. At the same time, by revealing contradictions between the Donation and other historical accounts and showing that the Latin of the Donation included many terms not used in the fourth century, only in much later writing, Valla made clear that the text could not in fact have been written when it claimed.[55] The methods that he unleashed against this Latin text would later be refined and applied to Greek ones—for example, by Isaac Casaubon, who showed, in a work published in 1614, that the dialogues ascribed to the ancient Greek thinker Hermes Trismegistus, long taken as the source from which Plato had drawn his ideas, were written in a late Greek that did not fit their supposed time of origin—a violation of decorum—and referred to Greeks who lived centuries after the supposed dates of Hermes's lifetime: a clear contradiction of historical plausibility.[56]

Consideration of context and decorum, close scrutiny for consistency with other documents for internal coherence: these methods—the central ones applied in historical criticism—were themselves ancient. By contrast, the use of material remains and other nontextual evidence in the early modern period departed dramatically from ancient precedents.[57] Stimulated by the vast and relatively well-preserved ruins of Rome, both the Byzantine scholar Chrysoloras and the Latin humanist Cyriac of Ancona declared that—as Cyriac put it—"the stones themselves afforded to modern spectators much more trustworthy information about their splendid history than was to be found in books."[58] Cyriac devoted much of his life to recording everything from the Parthenon's friezes to the obelisks of Egypt, as well as dozens of ancient inscriptions. In the next generation, antiquaries like Leon Battista Alberti and Flavio Biondo scrutinized ancient monuments and relics in minute detail. Examining the Egyptian obelisk that stood by the old Basilica of Saint Peter (and now stands before the new one), Alberti measured its height, studied the effects of wind and weather on the metal globe that crowned it, deciphered the Roman inscriptions on its sides, and made ruthless fun of the traditional legends that held that the great stone shaft had been made by magic—or at least moved, by magic, from the Temple of Solomon to Rome. It was clearly a single, human artifact, quarried in one piece and still showing, in its one substantial flaw and repair, the clear signs that it was the work of human artisans.[59]

Alberti and Biondo even tried to raise one of the two Roman pleasure barges that fisherman discovered on the bottom of Lake Nemi in the Alban Hills. Their Genoese divers, "more like fish than men," failed, managing only to tear off one fragment and bring it to the surface. But they analyzed the materials that went into that fragment with the same minute care and the same eye for differences between past and present with which Valla had analyzed the language of the Donation of Constantine: "the ship [they explained in a joint report] was entirely made of larchwood, braced by beams three inches thick and caulked on the outside with pitch. The pitch was covered and protected by a coating of yellow or red material, as can be seen even now, and the entire surface was clad with sheets of lead to protect the ship and the caulking from the waves and rain. A mass of bronze nails (not iron as we use now) was driven into the sheets of lead to seal them."[60] The up-to-date antiquary not only knew that ruins offered information texts did not, he also knew how to read them.

As new ruins came to light and notebooks filled up with information about them, scholars argued, far more specifically than Cyriac had, that nontextual evidence, properly applied, could actually transform the understanding of the ancient world. The Romans had dated events, for the most part, not from a single early date—such as that of the founding of their city—but by reference to the pair of magistrates, or consuls, who led the city each year. This system gave rise to many baffling apparent contradictions. In the middle of the sixteenth century, Roman antiquaries discovered in the Forum the fragments of a list of the consuls and other magistrates, carved in stone. Michelangelo was chosen to restore it, in the Palace of the Conservators on the Capitoline Hill, and erudite scholars like Carlo Sigonio and Onofrio Panvinio wrote elaborate commentaries on it.[61] At exactly the same time, the astronomer Petrus Apianus realized that he could compute the dates and times of eclipses mentioned in historical sources—and did so for the lunar eclipse that accompanied the defeat of Darius of Persia by Alexander the Greek in 331 B.C.E., one of the defining events of ancient history.[62] Meanwhile, Gian Maria Tolosani, Copernicus, and others identified the ancient king of Babylon, Nabonassar, whose accession date Mesopotamian, Greek, Roman, and Islamic astronomers had used as the baseline for their tables and computations, with Salmanassar, the Assyrian king who sacked Jerusalem. Suddenly it seemed possible to bring Greek, Roman, and biblical history into alignment on a single chronological grid, defined by the movements of the stars.[63] Ancient history took on a new definition and precision, as sharply and rapidly as if the records in question had somehow been placed under a more powerful lens.

To be sure, the techniques that uncovered forgeries and supplemented the biblical record could also be deployed to the opposite effect. Many traditional intellectuals—notably members of the mendicant orders, Franciscans and Dominicans, a large number of whom did not share their colleagues' taste for the classics—found the new humanism, with its passion for ancient gods and goddesses, distasteful. "How many false stories," argued the Dominican Giovanni Dominici, "are told by the historians, when one tells a story this way, and the other in another! The great Livy himself bears witness to this. In this case the devil had only one thing in mind: to make the reader, while he sees celebrated writers appear as liars, feel similar doubts about the saints."[64] Late in the fifteenth century, another Dominican theologian, Giovanni Nanni, or Annius, of Viterbo, set out to wipe the cultural slate clean. In 1498 he published a set of twenty-four texts, ascribed to such ancient authorities as the Chaldean priest Berosus, the Egyptian priest Manetho, and the Persian priest Metasthenes. These told a comprehensive story about the ancient world. It was packed with details, many of them thrilling and all of them in contradiction to the Greek and Roman accounts of the past. Noah, it turned out, had used astrology to predict the Flood, and brought his ark to rest in Rome, on the hill known as the Gianicolo or hill of Janus (Noah invented wine; the Hebrew word for wine was *yayin,* which gave rise to Janus; the Roman myth of Janus, accordingly, was actually a corrupt recollection of biblical history. Even better, Osiris turned out to be the ancestor of Nanni's patron, the Borgia pope Alexander VI.)[65]

In support of his general account, Nanni produced an inscription that he claimed was a record, in Egyptian hieroglyphs, of the adventures of Osiris. Actually, he himself had manufactured this and the other inscriptions, including some in an impressively esoteric version of Etruscan letters. To give his texts credibility, he larded them with cross-references and embedded them in a rich commentary, which argued that the principle of decorum proved his writers more credible than the Greeks. For as priests, they had written official records that could not possibly distort the truth, while the Greeks had written arbitrarily, as individuals. "But," says the supposed Persian Metasthenes, "we must not accept everyone who writes about these kings, but only the priests of the kingdom, whose annals have public and incontrovertible authority, like Berosus. For that Chaldean set out the entire Assyrian history on the basis of the ancients' annals, and we Persians now follow him alone, or above all."[66] "Metasthenes," Annius explains, "gives rules for chronology, which will enable us to determine which authors should be accepted and which rejected. The first rule is: we should accept without reluctance all who wrote with publicly approved authority. And he declares that the priests were formerly the public recorders of events."[67] The new antiquarian scholarship thus helped give rise to a massive forgery—which sold out in many editions and provided the basic structure of world history textbooks, especially in the Protestant world, for the next century and more. In the middle of the sixteenth century, when lawyers and historians started to write manuals of historical method, they liberally quoted not only Annius's texts, which most of them took as genuine, but also his instructions on how to decide which historians to trust.[68]

Humanistic scholarship eventually proved equal to this test. Rightly applied, the principle of decorum revealed severe problems in Annius's work. Almost all of his twenty-four writers, supposedly Chaldean, Persian, Greek, and Roman, wrote in the same Latin style: that of Annius's own commentary. The implausibility of this was clear at once to humanists schooled in trying to produce compositions that seemed genuine. Beatus Rhenanus, friend of Erasmus and editor of many Latin texts, found a pithy Erasmian way to say that the authors and the commentator were really all the same person: "one of them milks the he-goat, while the other holds out the sieve to catch the milk."[69] Others pointed out that Nanni's authors often contradicted the very ancient texts that had mentioned their works and inspired their production. In the end, Nanni's falsifications proved productive. Real ancient priests from Mesopotamia and Egypt, Berosus and Manetho had written their accounts of their nations in Greek for the rulers who succeeded Alexander the Great. In 1598, Joseph Scaliger collected the genuine fragments of their writings, in Greek, and commented on them at length—an effort to recover everything that could be known about lost texts, rather than canonical ones, that again has no counterpart in ancient Western scholarship and continues, down to the present, as a core enterprise of classical scholarship.[70]

Seen anachronistically from the present, the scholarship of the antiquarians strikingly resembles that of the French Annales school of the twentieth century, founded by Marc Bloch and Lucien Febvre. Renaissance antiquaries used the most up-to-date methods of natural science to illuminate historical areas that texts did not cover; like the French too, they concentrated more on recreating customs, institutions, and practices than on crafting the narratives that had previously been the central concern of historians. As Francesco Patrizi wrote in a work on historiography that he published in 1560, "some historians have not so much described events as customs, ways of life, and laws. . . . And there is another sort, those who, especially in our day, write in another way about the clothing of the Romans and the Greeks, the forms of armament they used, their ways of making camp, and their ships, their buildings, and other things of this sort, which are necessary for life."[71] Patrizi knew whereof he wrote. It was he and a Flemish antiquarian, Justus Lipsius, who first recreated in detail the Roman way of waging war. Their work interested generals as well as scholars. Maurice of Nassau, the military leader of the late sixteenth-century Dutch revolt against Spain, went so far as to equip two troops of soldiers, one with contemporary Spanish and one with ancient Roman arms and armor, in order to see which outdid the other. Lipsius gently explained that the superiority of Roman technique had to do not with their short swords and shields, but with their use of uniforms, set words of command, and precise military discipline—all of which Maurice emphasized as he reformed the Dutch armies to the point where they could meet the Spanish, the dominant soldiers of the sixteenth century, with some chance of success. From their own standpoint, however, the antiquaries' success lay at least as much in their ability to lay firm foundations for the history of ancient and medieval times.[72]

Yet the use of nontextual evidence had its limits. Much of this evidence never reached print, remaining the property of small, local groups of intellectuals, and the monuments and inscriptions that were printed were normally far less accurate copies of the originals than Cyriac and others had made by hand in their notebooks.[73] More serious than these problems of execution were those gradually revealed by continued use of the new methods.

Scholars, as we have seen, wanted to forge a single chronological system that embraced the Bible as well as Greek and Roman history. But the Greek and Hebrew versions of the Old Testament contradicted each other on the length of the period between the Creation and the coming of Jesus, and the Gospels gave inconsistent information on details of Jesus's life and career. By the early seventeenth century, Joseph Scaliger—whose prowess as a chronologer had won him a full-time research post at the University of Leiden—was deeply worried about the fact that the history of Egypt, as he reconstructed it, began before the world did, and that the Old and New Testaments did not supply full, consistent records. Astronomy offered little help, since the earliest precisely dated eclipses came only from the eighth century B.C.E.—far too late to date the biblical Flood or the fall of Jerusalem, or to clarify the relation of early Jewish history to that of Greece and Rome. In despair, he told the students who lodged with him that he did not dare publish these conclusions: "it's a strange thing: it would be different with a pagan author."[74] Protestants wanted to have an absolutely authoritative Bible, but the best evidence on the history of Hebrew writing, another favorite subject for antiquaries, suggested that the Old Testament had not taken on its current form until after 500 C.E. Scaliger was not the only one who realized the import of this uncomfortable fact. The leading Protestant Hebraist Johann Buxtorf, who taught at Basel, admitted that he could not prove that the Bible, as traditionally written, went back to Moses. Indeed, the evidence that he knew seemed to prove the contrary. He found himself reduced to begging those who disagreed with his published arguments for the inerrancy of the Hebrew text not to publish their findings, not because they were wrong but because they were dangerous. The stage was already set, fifty years in advance, for the entrance of Martino Martini, who drew from the Chinese annals, their dates confirmed in his view by astronomical evidence unknown to Europe, the evidence that made many learned Europeans lose their belief in biblical history. Historical criticism thus combined the ancient tools of rhetoric with newer ones actually forged in the early modern period. But the new methods of philological and antiquarian research, systematically applied, could end up destroying the very structures they had been created to support.[75]

Such was premodern philology in the early modern West: sometimes severely practical, sometimes systematic and theoretical; sometimes based on ancient methods derived from the same canonical texts that philologists had to correct and explicate, sometimes based on novel methods of great sophistication; always shaped and constrained by the conditions of publication and the needs and desires of patrons. Sometimes, the philologists did, as Panofsky argued so brilliantly, historicize the ancient world, making clear its distance from their own time and the sheer difficulty and range of methods needed to study it; more often, they did their best to close these gaps and keep ancient texts relevant to modern needs. Always, philology existed not in a void, as a matter of purely abstract argument, but in the lively, hard-pressed worlds of active teaching and publication—worlds that offered both nourishing resources and rigid constraints. Nothing mattered more, after all, to most humanists than training young men when in a tight spot to quote an apposite line from the classics—an enterprise that did not require a historical revolution.

Mughal Philology and Rūmī's *Mathnavī*

MUZAFFAR ALAM

UNDER THE Mughal emperor Akbar (r. 1556–1605), the *Mathnavī* of Jalal al-Din Rūmī (d. 1273) acquired a particular social and political resonance in India. It was recited for the emperor and recommended for the edification of his officials.[1] Abū l-Faḍl, the noted Mughal ideologue and historian, in a note on the *Mathnavī,* invokes the expression *ṣulḥ-i kull* (peace with all), the oft-cited Mughal policy, recommending the work because with its help, one could reach the height of universality, far above the world of particularities. Writing while traveling in the imperial retinue, Abū l-Faḍl also mentions ruefully the difficulty of finding complete texts of the work. He was forced to make do with an extract from it and expressed his personal desire to make a selection of his own.[2] Given the demand for and eager readership of the text in this period, it is not surprising that a Mughal Indian scholar of Persian, ʿAbd al-Laṭīf ʿAbdallāh ʿAbbāsī Gujarātī, who lived during the time of Jahāngīr (1605–1627) and the early years of Shāh Jahān (1628–1658), resolved to edit and study Rūmī's *Mathnavī,* because of its literary value as well as its special position in the Muslim mystical tradition.

ʿAbd al-Laṭīf's desire was thwarted since, like Abū l-Faḍl, he could find no carefully copied manuscript of the *Mathnavī* in India, let alone one prepared with the rigor and meticulousness the work deserved. He then embarked on a project of preparing his own edition of the text, which he finally produced after about a decade of travel and tribulations. Later, he found that to conduct a comprehensive study of the *Mathnavī,* he would need to also study Sanāʾī's *Ḥadīqa,* to which Rūmī himself acknowledged his debt. This too he accomplished.[3] The manuscripts that formed the basis of this project hailed from Afghanistan, outside the formal boundaries of Hindustan. However, the work of producing a "perfect" edition of them was done within Hindustan, in a peculiarly Mughal context. The trajectory of ʿAbd al-Laṭīf's venture—and adventure—has a very close bearing on the history of Mughal Indian Persian scholarship and philology, as well as literary and religious culture. ʿAbd al-Laṭīf was himself in Mughal state service, and in the preparation of these texts, a number of important Mughal figures played key facilitating roles.

While ʿAbd al-Laṭīf is by no means unknown to Persian specialists, his work has received limited attention in modern scholarship.[4] I will consider here his unprecedented attempt to produce a critical edition of the *Mathnavī*—which ʿAbd al-Laṭīf himself described as *muqābala* (comparison, collation), *taṣḥīḥ* (correction), *tanqīḥ* (purging, inquiry). I will examine his process through the sometimes hyperbolic words of ʿAbd al-Laṭīf himself, paying attention in particular to the Mughal context in which this work was accomplished, and then briefly review the reception of this critical edition, including the summarily dismissive criticisms of it in some modern Western writings.

ʿAbd al-Laṭīf's Life and Works

ʿAbd al-Laṭīf was born in Ahmadabad, Gujarat, in the late sixteenth century to a family noted for their interest and involvement in learning, literature, and Mughal service. He received his early education and training in this city, before entering service himself. While still in Ahmadabad as a young scholar, he benefited from the presence of Muḥammad Ṣūfī Māzandarānī (d. 1625), who visited the city at that time.[5] While in Ahmadabad, Ṣūfī Māzandarānī compiled an anthology including over forty-five thousand verses selected from the *dīvāns* of thirty-six Persian poets, called *Butkhāna* (Idol house), completed in 1601.[6] The anthology also contains verses from ninety other poets who did not have their own *dīvāns*. ʿAbd al-Laṭīf assisted Ṣūfī Māzandarānī, with whom he enjoyed a close relationship, in compiling it. Ṣūfī Māzandarānī is generally known to us as a poet par excellence. To ʿAbd al-Laṭīf, however, he was important not simply because of his poetic accomplishments but because he combined literary excellence with Sufic gnosis. These two interests, literary and religious, evident from his youth, converged perfectly in his endeavors to read and comprehend the *Mathnavī*.

Later, during his stay in Bengal and Orissa in the department of accountancy in the service of a Mughal official named Muʿtaqid Khān, ʿAbd al-Laṭīf added an introduction to *But-khāna* and wrote biographical notices of the poets included in the anthology, calling this account *Khulāṣa-i Aḥvāl al-Shuʿarā* (Brief accounts of the poets). He also edited the work afresh in several places. Thus, perhaps it was here in Orissa, while completing his labors on the *But-khāna,* that he first found the yearning to work on the *Mathnavī.*

From Orissa, ʿAbd al-Laṭīf left for Afghanistan and the northwest frontier in search of copies of the *Mathnavī* about which he had heard and which he wanted to make the base for his own edition. During the years 1616–1617, when his former employer Muʿtaqid Khān was leading the Mughal campaigns against a frontier uprising by a group known as the Raushniyas, ʿAbd al-Laṭīf was able to muster the resources for his travels in the regions of Kabul, Tirah, and Yulam. In 1616, while in Tirah, he came across a remarkable copy of the *Mathnavī* that had been prepared by several scholars over a period of thirty-five years, the fruit of several attempts at collation and examination ("muqābil karda baʿd az jarḥ va taʿdīl") of sixty different manuscripts.[7]

From this time, ʿAbd al-Laṭīf was engaged in the preparation of his own edition of the *Mathnavī,* which he completed in 1622.[8] During these years, he also appears to have maintained his close relationship with Lashkar Khān Mashhadī. It was with him that ʿAbd al-Laṭīf was associated in the period 1628–1632, when he was engaged in researching Sanāʾī Ghaznavī's *Ḥadīqat al-Ḥaqīqa.* Finally, in 1632, he succeeded in bringing the second and last of his major works to fruition, an edition and detailed commentary of Sanāʾī's *Ḥadīqa.*

ʿAbd al-Laṭīf was then at the court of Shāh Jahān; he is included in the list of important *manṣabdārs* with high positions. ʿAbd al-Ḥamīd Lāhawrī writes that in 1632 ʿAbd al-Laṭīf was appointed minister of salaries with a high personal rank of 7,000 and an armed contingent of 150 horsemen in consideration of his expertise in accountancy and draftsmanship. In 1633, he led a diplomatic mission to the court of the Qutbshahi ruler of Golconda, but he was taken ill and replaced by Diyānat Rāy. We do not know exactly when ʿAbd al-Laṭīf died, although some have cited the twelfth regnal year of Shāh Jahān (1638–1639) as the probable date.[9]

Among ʿAbd al-Laṭīf's writings that have survived are *Muqaddama* (Introduction) to the *But-khāna* and the *Khulāṣa-i Aḥvāl al-Shuʿarā; Nuskha-i Nāsikha,* a corrected edition of Rūmī's *Mathnavī;* and two other works related to it, *Laṭāyif al-Lughāt* (Subtleties of the words) and *Laṭāyif al-Maʿnavī min Ḥaqāyiq al-Mathnavī* (Sublime spiritualities of the truths in the

Mathnavī), the former a lexicon to explain the difficult words in the *Mathnavī,* the latter a commentary;[10] the *Sharḥ-i Ḥadīqat al-Ḥaqīqa* (Commentary on the garden of truth), a recension of Sanā'ī's *Ḥadīqat al-Ḥaqīqa* (The garden of truth); and the *Laṭāyif al-Ḥaqāyiq min Nafāyis al-Daqāyiq* (Sublime truths of the refined subtleties), a detailed commentary on the *Ḥaqīqa.* Aside from these scholarly writings, there is also a collection of his letters, *Ruq'āt-i 'Abd al-Laṭīf.*[11] 'Abd al-Laṭīf, as a great traveler of his time, also wrote a notable travel narrative, the *Risāla-i Sayr-i Manāzil va Bilād va Amṣār* (Treatise on a journey through the caravanserais/places, cities, and countries), which received some attention in the twentieth century, and which described his travels in Hindustan, Punjab, Bihar, and Bengal, though not the trips in connection with the preparation of the edition of the *Mathnavī.*[12] The chronicler Muḥammad Ṣāliḥ Kambūh also mentions that 'Abd al-Laṭīf was given the responsibility of writing a history of Shāh Jahān, but since several of the courtiers did not approve of it, the work was stymied.[13]

The Manuscripts of Rūmī's *Mathnavī* and the Preparation of *Nuskha-i Nāsikha*

'Abd al-Laṭīf considered his critical edition of the *Mathnavī* his most important work. He not only produced an accurate text but also compiled several critical and scholarly aids, including a lexicon specific to the vocabulary of the *Mathnavī.* He wrote an extensive introduction *(dībācha)* to this edition, entitled *Mir'āt al-Mathnavī* (Mirror of the *Mathnavī*).[14] In this, he describes the editing process, his reasons for publishing a commentary and lexicon alongside the text, the format of his footnoting, and the need for specifying and correcting the headings of each section of the text. Above all, 'Abd al-Laṭīf defends the importance, both religious and literary, of the *Mathnavī* and offers his work in response to what he perceived to be an inadequate appreciation of its value.

'Abd al-Laṭīf was aware of how the *Mathnavī* had been received in the Perso-Islamic tradition, as he cites other works in this tradition, notably 'Abd al-Raḥmān Jāmī's *Nafaḥāt al-Uns* (Fragrant breezes of the meadows of love) and some earlier commentaries on portions of the *Mathnavī,* in demonstrating the prime importance of Rūmī and his work.[15] However, it was from Rūmī that he drew the greatest support in making his case for the *Mathnavī* because, as he is careful to highlight, the poet Rūmī himself understood the significance of his work. 'Abd al-Laṭīf explains that, in Rūmī's terms, the *Mathnavī* represents the axioms of the very foundations of faith and belief, and is both divine jurisprudence *(fiqh)* and luminous divine commentary. He notes that most of its stories and anecdotes correspond to authoritative passages of the Qur'ān, the *ḥadīth* of the Prophet, issues of jurisprudence, principles of theological doctrine, and the utterances and spiritual states of saints and pious figures. Thus, ʿAbd al-Laṭīf explains that Rūmī, in order to sharpen the minds of readers, clothed the gnosis of divinity in the garb of stories and anecdotes in Persian. By composing a poem in this manner, he not only specified the true creed in detail and extensively, he also in fact repudiated the falsity of a variety of sectarian partisans, like the Muʿtazilites, the fatalists *(jabarī),* the believers in free will *(qadarī),* and the Grecophile philosophers.[16] In ʿAbd al-Laṭīf's eyes, therefore, Rūmī's achievement was unmatched by scholars and theologians in their learned tomes. Indeed, there was no book better than the *Mathnavī* to stimulate the soul for the love of God. ʿAbd al-Laṭīf even appropriates Sanā'ī's epithet for his own *Ḥadīqa* in crowning the *Mathnavī,* and not the *Ḥadīqa,* the Persian Qur'ān. As he put it, what was present in potentiality in the *Ḥadīqa* appeared to full effect in the *Mathnavī.* Like the eternal speech of the Qur'ān itself, the *Mathnavī,* ʿAbd al-Laṭīf argues, possessed a depth that accommodated each person, so that he could approach its core and partake in it in accordance with his own inner state and faith. To him it was like the Qur'ān in Persian, in meaning/reality itself the Persian Qur'ān. He notes that Rūmī himself understood his text for what it was, and quotes the following verse from the *Mathnavī* in his support: "Even if the entire woods turned into a pen and the sea into ink / the [meanings of] the *Mathnavī* cannot be brought to an end" (i.e., like the Qur'ān, the *Mathnavī* is infinite in meaning and could never have been completely committed to writing).[17] It appears as if the substance of the famous verse "The *Mathnavī* of Rūmī is the Qur'ān in Persian," attributed to Jāmī (d. 1492), already formed part of common parlance at least among a certain section of the Mughal Persian literati.[18]

Despite its lack of pedantry, however, the *Mathnavī* was not transparent: it was believed that unless one was acquainted with Sufi ideas and practice, one could not comprehend its inner meaning, one's external or worldly knowledge notwithstanding. As ʿAbd al-Laṭīf puts it,

> until the theme and the subject of the narrative, the prequels and sequels of the story, the subject and predicate of the anecdote, the thread between the beginning and the end of the discourse is not in one's grasp, it is not possible to comprehend the *Mathnavī* simply with a proclivity and disposition for poetic understanding and with the conventional way of comprehension and common sense, which people designate as *sukhan-rasī* (poetic understanding).[19]

'Abd al-Laṭīf thus recognized both the literary and religious significance of the *Mathnavī* and the understanding thereof among the Mughal literati. And yet, as he noted with astonishment, there was no reliable and accurate copy of the text available to this readership, at least not to his satisfaction, even if others of his acquaintance believed that the existing editions were reasonably reliable and authentic.[20] 'Abd al-Laṭīf thus undertook the project of producing such an authentic *(ṣaḥīḥ, mustaqīm)* edition, which he described as "a copy that abrogates the infirm/inauthentic copies of the *Mathnavī (nuskha-i nāsikha-i Mathnaviyyāt-i saqīma),* and confirms and validates the correct and authentic ones *(muthbiṭ va muravvij-i nusakh-i ṣaḥīḥa-i mustaqīma).*" He also called it "a book that is outstanding *(kitābīst mustaṭāb),* and a discourse that distinguishes the truth from falsehood *(kalāmīst faṣl al-khiṭāb).*" As he later wrote in the introduction to *Laṭāyif al-Ma'navī min Ḥaqāyiq al-Mathnavī,* this edition came to be known as *Nuskha-i Nāsikha* (a copy that abrogates, i.e., a definitive copy), very likely because this is the phrase *(īn nuskha-i nāsikha)* with which he begins his introduction to this edition. Leaving aside the hyperbole of his language, 'Abd al-Laṭīf himself never intended it to be the name of his edition.

The preparation of this edition was a long and arduous process, requiring repeated attempts over many years to collate the text. The first attempt, in 1616, involved preparation of a copy, collating *(muqābala)* the Afghanistan text that, as already noted, was based on sixty manuscripts of the *Mathnavī* and prepared after much critical examination by previous scholars. The second attempt at collation occurred later in the same year in Yulam Pass and in other places in the district of Peshawar, where he checked *(muḥādhāt)* his copy against four or five other copies of the *Mathnavī.* The third time, he discussed and reexamined *(munāẓara)* the copy with a friend and traveling companion during a journey toward the Deccan in 1620. For the sake of verifying the meanings *(taḥqīq-i ma'ānī)* in the *Mathnavī,* 'Abd al-Laṭīf consulted yet another set of four or five copies of the *Mathnavī* in 1621 in Burhanpur, where he also conferred *(mudhākara)* with some of the learned scholars of the time who, engaged in studying the *Mathnavī,* not only possessed a high level of literary knowledge but also had sought *sanad* (verification) from Sufi masters.

Still, his work was far from over. He found that in the course of research and investigation *(taḥqīqāt va tanqīḥāt),* his master copy had undergone so much editing and reediting *(jarḥ va ta'dīl)*—including marginal explanatory notes, Qur'ānic verses, *ḥadīth*s, glosses of words, and the variant readings among different copies *(ikhtilāf-i nusakh)*—that it had become illegible. He therefore gave the copy to a scribe, who had also been his colleague in collating and discussing the manuscripts, to copy it neatly. For the fifth time, he collated this copy with three or four other manuscripts and had it recopied. Then, for the sixth and last time, he compared this copy with still another set of manuscripts, and the work was, in his own eyes, finally accomplished. In all, thus far, ʿAbd al-Laṭīf's copy had been collated, directly and indirectly, with a total of about twenty manuscripts, and these were in addition to the Afghanistan text with which he began his work. Even after this, however, he continued to work on the *Mathnavī,* correcting, polishing, commenting on, and refining his edition, sometimes at the behest of his respectable mentors.

The six iterations of text collation had a symbolic dimension. ʿAbd al-Laṭīf writes at length regarding the spiritual symbolism of the number 6 with regard to the *Mathnavī,* itself divided into six volumes, for which ʿAbd al-Laṭīf, displaying his erudition for his discerning readership in Mughal India, provides again six reasons.[21]

The first of these was the creation of the world in six days, for which he cites the Qur'ānic verse.[22] Rūmī, according to ʿAbd al-Laṭīf, composed the *Mathnavī* in six volumes to correspond to each day of creation. Second, according to the Qur'ān, the human body, which is a *ʿālam-i saghīr* (microcosm) of the *ʿālam-i kabīr* (cosmos), is composed of six parts.[23] Following the practice of God, Rūmī composed the *Mathnavī* in six parts. Third, as ʿAbd al-Laṭīf explicates at length, in the Sufi understanding of cosmology, all existence comprises six levels of reality: *Aḥadiyyat* (Unity), *Vaḥdat* (Wholeness), *Vāḥidiyyat* (Oneness), *Arvāḥ-i Mujarrada* (Incorporeal Souls), *Malakūt* (the Angelic Realm), and *ʿĀlam-i Mulk* (the World of Dominion). Since in the World of the Perfect Man *(ʿĀlam-i Insān-i Kāmil)* all these are manifested, ʿAbd al-Laṭīf deduces that Rūmī wrote his august book so that each volume focuses on one of the six levels of existence and further explains the secrets and realities thereof.[24] Fourth, ʿAbd al-Laṭīf writes, each volume of the *Mathnavī* corresponds to the six directions in the world—up, down, front, back, right, left—and contains the secrets of each direction.[25] The fifth reason stems from a Sufi belief that there are six stages to be traversed in order to reach the highest level of spirituality: the carnal soul, the heart, the spirit, the secret, the hidden, the most hidden. Every stage in this journey can be negotiated using the six books of the *Mathnavī,* which guides the seeker as he ascends from one level to the next. However, there are only six volumes, and the very highest stage is the seventh one, the most hidden station in this spiritual journey. ʿAbd al-Laṭīf resolves this apparent dilemma by appealing to the Naqshbandi Sufi tradition, which by the early seventeenth century had achieved a prominent place in the Mughal religious landscape.[26]

The sixth and last reason ʿAbd al-Laṭīf cites is based on the axiom that true science is divided into two, the science of religion and the science of bodies, and the science of religion depends on the healthiness of bodies. Therefore, ʿAbd al-Laṭīf argues, guarding the body is obligatory, and it requires the observation of the six factors on which health depends, as they had been laid down in the books of medicine. These factors are of six categories: (1) the air that surrounds the body; (2) what one eats and drinks; (3) physical movement and rest; (4) the movement and rest of souls; (5) sleep and wakefulness; (6) excretion and retention. In an analogous manner, the six volumes of the *Mathnavī* are concerned with the six factors necessary in the science of religion. Again, ʿAbd al-Laṭīf draws on the prevailing medical knowledge in Mughal India.[27]

This symbolic schema even determines the binding of ʿAbd al-Laṭīf's edition in six volumes, for which he provides yet again six reasons, mundane but pragmatic. First, such a manner of binding the book would facilitate group study, where several individuals could read the *Mathnavī* simultaneously. Second, if one wished to acquire a copy of this manuscript, six different copyists could be employed to finish the task more speedily, thus saving the reader "from the trouble of prolonged waiting, which in the case of beloved books is more severe than death." The third reason is that if a borrower wishes to steal the book, he can take only one and not all six volumes at a time, thus limiting the owner's risk of being deprived of his book. In providing six volumes, ʿAbd al-Laṭīf also ensured that the heft of the *Mathnavī* would not prevent readers from being in its company, as one could always carry at least one of the six volumes in all circumstances.[28] The fifth reason ʿAbd al-Laṭīf gives is that he was following Rūmī's own practice of dividing the *Mathnavī* into six volumes, with a separate introduction to each. Finally, ʿAbd al-Laṭīf states that since his edition is exceptional in its authenticity, purity, and distinctiveness, it should be novel and distinct even with regard to its binding, the means for the preservation and protection of a book. This too would be the reason, in ʿAbd al-Laṭīf's opinion, for the publicity and circulation of his edition in the six directions of the world, and why he titles his edition alternatively the *Sixfold Mathnavī (Mathnavī-yi musaddas)*.

ʿAbd al-Laṭīf's confidence in his edition is as grand as the effort he made to produce it. He contends that, if one were to survey the libraries of the grandees of the time on the basis of the criteria of textual quality and authenticity, it would be improbable that any other copy of the text, however valuable with regard to calligraphy, gilding, size, and antiquity, would compare to his own. He further claims that from the time of Rūmī himself, no one has exerted himself in verifying, editing, and revising this copy from beginning to end in this manner, and no one has done it in so assiduous and disciplined a manner *(ta'kīd va taqyīd).*[29] Although ʿAbd al-Laṭīf's labors were evidently heroic, he benefited at every stage of this project from a lively and informed scholarly community, many members of which were at work on the *Mathnavī,* as well as from generous patronage. He is acutely aware of this readership in intellectual terms and is also careful to consider the pragmatic aspects of book making and reading in Mughal India. In the reasons for binding the work in six volumes, he explicitly addresses all the logistical problems associated with the lack of a tradition of printed books, the difficulties of traveling with hefty and rare volumes, producing texts despite scribal error, and the perennial dangers of outright theft of books and the surreptitious theft of permanent borrowing. Yet, despite these obstacles in the path of disseminating his beloved work, ʿAbd al-Laṭīf was confident that its qualities would make it renowned. What precisely were these much-vaunted qualities of his edition?

Collation and Comparison

There were many discrepancies among the various copies regarding the number of verses and the wording of the story titles in the *Mathnavī.* ʿAbd al-Laṭīf therefore had to decide on criteria by which to judge which verses deserved to be included in his edition. He specifically mentions the following criteria: the smoothness of the poem *(salāsat-i kalām),* the aptness of the words *(tanāsub-i alfāẓ),* the force of meaning *(jazālat-i maʿnī),* and the correspondence with the style and usage *(ṭarz va iṣṭilāḥ)* of the *Mathnavī.* In light of these principles, those verses he found completely incongruous and altered by scribes he discarded, and he retained lines in the book that he identified as consistent with the style and usage of the *Mathnavī.* He ensured that no verse that deserved, even remotely, to be included in the text on the basis of his criteria was left out. Making a special effort to include two thousand additional verses, which were scattered throughout the text and often written in the margins of several other copies, he marked them with the letter *zā* above the line, meaning *zāyida* (addition).

ʿAbd al-Laṭīf acknowledged that some readers would wonder if these additional verses were interpolations *(ilḥāqī),* perhaps from the poetry of

Rūmī's son, Sulṭān Valad. ʿAbd al-Laṭīf was adamant, however, that all of these additional lines, derived from the margins of other copies in the course of repeated study and then inserted in the text of this edition, were entirely part of the original. Here, he was also sensitive to the Persian medieval literary tradition. Whereas there was a long-standing practice in Persian poetry of attempting to imitate and best the style of great masters, such as Amīr Khusraw (d. 1325) with regard to Niẓāmī of Ganja (d. 1209), no such attempt was recorded with regard to Rūmī in Persian literary history until ʿAbd al-Laṭīf's time.[30] This tradition of imitation *(istiqbāl)* and response *(javāb),* however, depended on the *possibility* of imitating these great masters.[31] ʿAbd al-Laṭīf argues that no individual could compose poetry like Rūmī and that even if some attempted to imitate and respond to *(javāb gufta-and)* the *Mathnavī,* their replies would be immediately obvious as interpolations to scholars like himself who, through years of research and experience, had understood the specific usage and style of the work.[32] ʿAbd al-Laṭīf thus reminds his reader that the additions in his edition, far from being interpolations, were based on certain criteria and were the result of the discernment of an extraordinary master of poetry, including that of Rūmī. One can infer his confidence in his judgment when he reminds readers of the Qurʾānic verse "Suspicion in some cases is a sin" (49:12) and quotes the following verse of the *Mathnavī* itself as well:

> In my eyes, the denier of this word
> is like the [sinner] upside down in hell.
> O Husamuddin, you have seen his state. Did you see his fate?
> God has shown you what destroyed his status.[33]

Despite his injunctions against the doubting reader, ʿAbd al-Laṭīf was careful to guard his edition against the vagaries of time and scribal error. Therefore, he counted and numbered the verses and titles of each volume and wrote the total at the end of each, and then provided the grand total at the end of the *Mathnavī.* Moreover, he also provided at the end of each story or anecdote a total of the number of lines in that story, so that the scribe could not skip even a single one. In this way, ʿAbd al-Laṭīf placed his stamp repeatedly on the text, with the hope of clearly establishing, once and for all, the authentic verses in the *Mathnavī* for knowledgeable researchers and investigators of the time.

ʿAbd al-Laṭīf also corrected the six prefaces written by Rūmī, mostly in Arabic, as they were of doubtful accuracy in existing manuscripts due to the negligent transcriptions of scribes. In addition, he corrected the titles of chapters and anecdotes in which the wording was not in accordance with familiar usage or was wrong. He also provided a table of contents for each of the six volumes, intended to guide the reader through the different themes and anecdotes of the *Mathnavī,* a text whose vastness he compared to "an overflowing ocean and a shoreless sea," which thus defied the memory of any reader to remember the exact location of each story and anecdote. The copyists, however, as we can guess from the available manuscripts of *Nuskha-i Nāsikha,* rarely did the job as meticulously as ʿAbd al-Laṭīf intended.

Annotation and Commentary

ʿAbd al-Laṭīf provided several scholarly aids to his discerning readers. He annotated the *Mathnavī* with the precise chapter and part of the Qurʾānic verses to which Rūmī alluded. Here again, he was aware of the realities of book making, noting that if scribes committed an oversight or error with the passage of time in copying the edition, they could always refer to the marginal notations to find the correct Qurʾānic words and diacritical marks. Moreover, ʿAbd al-Laṭīf also referred to commentaries on the Qurʾān, noting down verses that correspond to stories in the *Mathnavī.* In a similar manner, he verified and noted the *ḥadīth* of the Prophet and the sayings of the saints alluded to in the *Mathnavī,* providing the translation and sense of the verses in question through his own research and writing.

Next, ʿAbd al-Laṭīf verified rare and difficult Arabic and Persian words and technical phrases composed of terms in various tongues. He used Arabic dictionaries, *Qāmūs* (The ocean), *Ṣurāḥ* (Open speech), *Kanz al-Lugha* (Treasure of the words), *Nihāya-i Jazarī* (The exquisite [book] of Jazari), and Persian lexicons, *Farhang-i Jahāngīrī* (The lexicon dedicated to Jahāngīr) of Mīr Jamāl al-Dīn Ḥusayn Injū Shīrāzī, *Kashf al-Lughat* (Disclosure of the words), *Madār al-Afāḍil* (The pivot for the learned) of Shaykh Ilāhdād Sirhindī, *Muʾayyid al-Fuḍalā* (Support to the learned) of Shaykh Lād Dihlavī, *Sharḥ-i Iṣṭilāḥāt-i Ṣūfiyya* (Explanation of the Sufi terms) of Shaykh Ibn ʿAṭṭār and Shaykh ʿAbd al-Razzāq Kāshī.[34] He also drew on his knowledge of the use of these words by learned and pious authorities of the time. He then collected these glosses separately in a dictionary and titled it *Laṭāyif al-Lughat* (Subtleties of words). Under the words in question in the *Mathnavī* itself, he wrote *lām-tā-alif,* to refer the reader to the dictionary. He wrote the letter *ʿain* below a word to indicate that the word was Arabic, while the letter *fā* indicated that it was Farsi. To indicate *maṣdar* or verbal noun, he wrote *mīm-ṣād.*

ʿAbd al-Laṭīf was insistent that his work should not be compared to dictionaries compiled on the basis of speculations and guesswork; in sharing his sources, he emphasized that it was the result of meticulous research and identification of each and every word *(taḥqīq va tanqīḥ va tashkhīṣ).*[35] Again, this edition benefited from the intellectual climate of the time—ʿAbd al-Laṭīf recognized the contributions of one Ibrāhīm Dihlavī, a noted teacher of the *Mathnavī,* in the compilation of the dictionary. He notes that his friend listened to the words, read them, and aided him in finding their meanings. Moreover, the draft of the work remained in Ibrāhīm's hands for many days when he was engaged in teaching the *Mathnavī.*

In keeping with this scholarly orientation, the dictionary is scientifically organized, with the words arranged in alphabetic order using the first letter of the word and then each section further subdivided on the basis of the last letter of the word.[36] The main division according to the initial letter he termed *bāb* (chapter), and the second subdivision he termed *faṣl* (section). In the dictionary too, after each word he indicated with the letter *ʿain* for Arabic, *fā* for Persian, *tā* for Turkish, and *sīn* for Syriac, and combinations thereof which words were commonly claimed to have originated in more than one of these languages. Notably, ʿAbd al-Laṭīf wrote the combination of letters *fā hā* to indicate the combination of Persian and Hindi, showing again the Mughal context of his work. He was careful throughout his dictionary to transcribe words only in the manner of the *Mathnavī,* regardless of other common variations that may have existed in their orthography, in order not to confuse the reader. Nevertheless, he noted that one might find words in the dictionary that did not appear in the *Nuskha-i Nāsikha,* including words that were present in older and relatively good-quality manuscripts used by earlier scholars, because he had decided that it would be inappropriate to ignore them. Moreover, for words with multiple meanings recorded in other dictionaries, he was careful to include not only the meaning he considered to have been implied by the word's use in the *Mathnavī* but also the other meanings that may or may not have been relevant in the text itself. Thus, ʿAbd al-Laṭīf would make available to the student of the *Mathnavī* all the meanings of the relevant words and even allow him to decide which was most appropriate in reading the text, not foisting his own judgment on the reader. This was far ahead of whatever little had been attempted to explain the difficult words in some earlier commentaries on portions of the *Mathnavī.*[37]

Everywhere he thought it necessary, ʿAbd al-Laṭīf also provided marginal notes in every volume on convoluted Persian verses, which in his opinion were in need of clarification, and Arabic verses, which required translation or explanations of verbal obscurity. Moreover, on the request of some "sincere brothers and faithful friends," he collected all the marginal notes indicating his explications of difficult Persian couplets, the translations of Arabic verses, relevant Qur'ānic verses, *ḥadīth*s, and saintly utterances.[38] He then compiled them, with significant additional research, in separate volumes, arranged in accordance with each volume of the *Mathnavī.* He named these volumes *Laṭāyif al-Maʿnavī min Ḥaqāyiq al-Mathnavī* (Sublime spiritualities of the truths in the *Mathnavī*). ʿAbd al-Laṭīf was not unaware of the immensity of his accomplishment, comparing his condition to that of the seemingly lowly hare in an anecdote from the *Mathnavī,* whose intelligence, despite his small stature, is finally universally recognized.[39] A commentarial tradition on the *Mathnavī* existed, but the earlier commentaries that are known are incomplete—on a volume or two or just on some selected verses.[40]

However, as ʿAbd al-Laṭīf makes clear, his decision to publish separately the volumes of his commentaries and lexicon was not only in response to the positive demands of his scholarly community but also to prevent spurious textual interpolations by imitators. By consulting these volumes alongside the *Mathnavī,* ʿAbd al-Laṭīf believed that even if a later author added incorrect commentaries or lexicographic information to the text, the reader would know immediately that they did not derive from ʿAbd al-Laṭīf's own research. Thus, in the text itself, under the marginal notes, he wrote the words *min Laṭāyif al-Maʿnavī* (from the sublime spiritualities) to refer to his research on the *Mathnavī,* or indicated other useful notes in this guide with the letters *lām-tā.*

Although ʿAbd al-Laṭīf bound the book in a portable set of six volumes, he did not approve of making a selection of the verses, contrary to existing practice. To him it was difficult, if not impossible, to deem certain verses good or bad, the way one could with the works of other poets. Moreover, Rūmī himself had disapproved of making extracts from his work. ʿAbd al-Laṭīf also heard from reliable authorities that separate volumes of essential verses *(lubb-i lubāb)* or of other selections from the *Mathnavī* had not been accepted or gained popularity. Here again, Abū l-Faḍl's experience is instructive. Nevertheless, since previous scholars had not dared to provide such selections and since ʿAbd al-Laṭīf, through his long years of research, had acquired "a kind of expertise and practice and the recognition of styles," he identified for the reader those verses that were the essence of the stories or provided the basic moral of the anecdotes, the conclusive verse *(shāh-bayt)* that spoke the truth. His spiritual nature "involuntarily" liked these verses but, given his earlier trepidations, he put dots over them *(nuqṭa-i intikhāb rīkhta)* without making an extract. These dots not only "decorated and beautified the pages of the *Mathnavī*" like "the mole on the face of the beloved" but also allowed those readers who sought a brief anthology from the lengthy stories of the *Mathnavī* to either extract them and make an abridged copy for themselves or read the selected dotted lines of this edition separately. Here too the copyists were not so meticulous.

Apart from discussing his own editorial work, ʿAbd al-Laṭīf also responded to certain critiques of the *Mathnavī* that were presumably current in scholarly circles of the time. As he repeatedly insisted in extolling the spiritual virtues of the text, the *Mathnavī,* despite its form, could not be understood solely on the basis of literary knowledge. Attempting to do so, he warns, may lead to the misconceptions shared by those "unbalanced and unprincipled people who claim to understand poetry," namely that Rūmī "did not care to observe the rules of rhyme [*qāfiya*] and that in many places he deviated from and transgressed the formal rules of poetry."[41] To those quarters in Mughal literary society who criticized the *Mathnavī* on formal poetic grounds, ʿAbd al-Laṭīf was quick to reply that such criticism was a reflection of their own folly in bringing only the tools of external, literary knowledge to what was also a spiritual text.

Specifically, ʿAbd al-Laṭīf responded to critiques of Rūmī's rhyme-making abilities, citing a verse that critics often pointed to in making their case about the poet's literary deficiencies. This verse, ʿAbd al-Laṭīf is careful to point out, is one that Rūmī, "out of his sober mind and immersed in his love for God, uttered at the time of intoxication, at the peak of ecstasy":

> I am looking for rhymes, but my beloved says:
> don't think of anything but of seeing me!
> Where could I come upon order and rhyme
> after I am deprived of nobler principles?[42]

ʿAbd al-Laṭīf insists that, during the repeated collation and study of the text, even with the sharpest eye of scrutiny aimed at the rhyme, nowhere in the whole *Mathnavī* could he find any fault of rhyme or violation of any other rule. Indeed, he continues, nowhere could a reader notice any instance of straying or deviation from soundness *(salāmat),* purity of language *(faṣāḥat),* eloquence *(balāghat),* aptness of words *(tanāsub-i alfāẓ),* and the established rules of poetry. If any such weakness is found in the inauthentic copies, ʿAbd al-Laṭīf avers, it is because of the errors and alterations committed by the scribes, the mixing up of similar words *(tajnīs)* and the changing of diacritical points *(taṣḥīf),* and because of lack of comprehension on the part of the reader.[43]

As an example, ʿAbd al-Laṭīf cites this verse, which figures in book 2, at the end of the story of God's consultation with the angels concerning the creation of mankind:

> Yak zamān big'dhār ay hamrah malāl
> Tā bigūyam vaṣf-i khāl[i] zān jamāl
> dar bayān nāyad jamāl-i khāl-i ū
> har dū ʿālam chīst ʿaks-i khāl-i ū
>
> Oh traveling companion, put aside weariness for a while,
> so that I can describe a mole of that beauty.
> The beauty of that mole cannot be described—
> what are the two worlds? A reflection of his mole.[44]

If the word *khāl* is used in the same meaning in the last two lines, it is against the established norms, and "those critics of poetry whose knowledge is based on the formal rules of poetry would call it a faulty application of rhyme." But, ʿAbd al-Laṭīf argues, if one of them is read with the letter *khā* and the other with the letter *ḥā,* one obtains in the second case the word *ḥāl* (condition), which, taken from the word *taḥavvul* (change), denotes God, the Changer of Conditions *(muḥavvil al-aḥvāl).* To date, however, ʿAbd al-Laṭīf claims, no one has read the word in this way. Moreover, if in both cases the word is read with the letter *kh,* then, as ʿAbd al-Laṭīf notes, these homonyms will have a separate meaning, for *khāl* in Sufi terminology is a level of certainty of the truth, an inference he supports by citing Shams al-Dīn Maghribī. Thus, ʿAbd al-Laṭīf continues, the first *khāl* in Rūmī's verse means existence *(kawn),* which refers to the aspect *(iʿtibār)* of the beauty of existence, while the second *khāl* means the certainty of truth. As the difference between the meanings of the two instances of *khāl* is proven, ʿAbd al-Laṭīf proclaims, the rhyme is correct. Further, if the word in the second case is read with the letter *ḥā* and is taken in the sense of *sha'n* (affair, nature, dignity), then the problem becomes simpler and there is no need, in his eyes, to undergo the trouble of such interpretation.[45]

Following this detailed critical response to literary critiques of the *Mathnavī,* ʿAbd al-Laṭīf concludes that the person who sees only the surface/appearance, who does not know the subtleties of vocabulary or usage and does not understand the difference in the meanings of two words and considers these verses faulty, proves only his own "lack of rhyme" *(bī-qāfiyagī),* not that of the *Mathnavī.*

Here again, despite answering literary critics in the terms of their own craft, ʿAbd al-Laṭīf insists on the inadequacy of a conventional evaluation of the text, citing his support from the *Mathnavī* itself: "Call this the Water of Life—don't call it poetry; / See a new soul in the body of old word."[46]

In his view, debasing such verses by bringing them down to the superfluous level *(majāz)* of the appreciation of poetry and of rhymes, and thus ignoring behind the appearance of those words all the nuances and the psychic states they invoke *(ighlāq-i ḥālī va qālī),* betrays nothing except the weakness of intellect and ignorance of the critic. To understand the *Mathnavī* and partake of its sweetness depends ultimately on the *dhawq* (taste) and *shawq* (love/earnestness) of the reader and the listener. Indeed, ʿAbd al-Laṭīf promises, the work will reveal all the pleasures of its "picture gallery of divine realities" to dedicated readers who recite and discuss it, no matter how worldly they may be, citing the following verse: "The poem has so much fresh pleasure / that it has passed beyond a reckonable measure."[47]

Nonetheless, ʿAbd al-Laṭīf was not blindly dismissive of the value of literary knowledge in understanding the poem. Moreover, in order that a student of the *Mathnavī* need not resort to any other handbook of prosody to know about the meter and the scanning *(baḥr va taqṭīʿ)* of the verses, ʿAbd al-Laṭīf provided a discussion of prosody *(ʿarūḍ)* in the text, "on which depends the detailed knowledge of a poem." The *Mathnavī* was composed in the meter *ramal,* which, he affirms, is the best of all meters, according to the authors of the handbooks, and which explains in part the popularity of the poem with both elite and common readers. He then goes on to demonstrate, with examples, how the meter works, elucidating the difference between *ramal-i musaddas-i maqṣūr* and *ramal-i musaddas-i makhdhūf.*

ʿAbd al-Laṭīf concludes his review of the *Mathnavī* and his own work on it with twenty-six verses, beginning with:

> I have not brought to you an ordinary thing with this book
> I have put my life and heart in it

and ending with:

Nobody has composed anything like this in this world,
and if there is anyone, then bring him and read his work before me.
Nobody will compose better than this speech
until the last day of judgment—and here I conclude.[48]

It takes nothing away from the indefatigable energy and painstaking effort ʿAbd al-Laṭīf poured into his work to mention not only the wider scholarly community of Mughal India that facilitated such endeavors but also and especially the network of elite patrons. As he himself noted in the introduction to his edition of Sanāʾī's *Ḥadīqa,* he was not a scholar by profession but was rather impelled by financial need to earn his living through courtly service. Although he devoted his free time to scholarly pursuits, this work was not possible without noble patronage. In this regard, ʿAbd al-Laṭīf acknowledged Mīr ʿImād al-Dīn Maḥmūd al-Hamadānī, a noble with a special interest in the *Ḥadīqa* who used the pen name "Ilāhī," invoking the *Ḥadīqa* itself since the poem was alternatively known as the *Ilāhī-nāma.*[49] This noble also composed three chronograms for ʿAbd al-Laṭīf's work, with which he closed his introduction. ʿAbd al-Laṭīf also thanked the Mughal emperor Shāh Jahān, as well as his most immediate patron and benefactor, Lashkar Khān, whom he describes as "master of the sword as well as of the pen, patron of Persian and Arabic genres *(aṣnāf),* and every work by [ʿAbd al-Laṭīf]." The series of acknowledgments is short, but they permit us to perceive the climate of patronage among political elites that allowed the scholarly community of which ʿAbd al-Laṭīf was a part to flourish.

Conclusion: The Reception of ʿAbd al-Laṭīf's Work

While there is no doubt that ʿAbd al-Laṭīf was fully aware of his edition's value, it remains to be seen whether his work was recognized by the contemporary scholarly community with the respect that he claims for it. One indication of the popularity and acknowledgment the work garnered in ʿAbd al-Laṭīf's own day and after his death is the profusion of manuscript copies of his edition, many of which remain extant. Indeed, ʿAbd al-Laṭīf himself took this as confirmation of the popularity of the work; he writes: "one of the signs of the acceptability of these researches is that today thirty-five beautiful copies of the *Mathnavī,* the lexicon [*Farhang*] and the commentary [*Sharḥ*] that this humble man had compiled are spread in different directions of the world."[50]

More interesting, however, are the practices of reading and transmission that seem to have developed around the *Nuskha-i Nāsikha* and are evident from a perusal of some of these manuscripts. The particular manner and milieu in which they were transmitted can also be discerned from a manuscript housed in the Rampur collection, which deserves special attention for the details of the copyist that it preserves and also for the distinction of the people who possessed it. The manuscript was originally of the *Mathnavī* only, copied in Ahmadabad by an eminent scholar and poet, Sulaymān Kurd. Later folios from volume 5 of the *Nuskha-i Nāsikha* were bound with it. Except for a brief period when it was owned by one Ḥaydar ibn ʿAbdallāh ibn Vajīh al-Dīn ʿAlavī, it remained in the possession of Sulaymān Kurd's descendants, beginning with his son Aḥmad ibn Sulaymān and then passing to his great-grandson Muḥammad Riḍā ibn Ghulām Muḥammad ibn Aḥmad ibn Sulaymān. After that, it came into the possession of a relative, Shaykh ʿImād al-Dīn ibn Shaykh Valī Allāh ibn Shaykh Muḥammad.[51]

This genealogy allows us a brief glimpse of the caliber of scholars who collected, read, and carefully transmitted the work after its composition. From a brief statement written by Muḥammad Riḍā about Sulaymān Kurd, we learn that the latter was an important scholar of *Ḥadīth* and Qur'ān. He was a disciple of one of the best known scholars of the seventeenth century, Shaykh ʿAbd al-Ḥaqq Muḥaddith Dihlavī, who was reported to have made his own extract of the *Mathnavī* before ʿAbd al-Laṭīf's time. Sulaymān Kurd was also a noted literary figure, a poet who composed about four hundred thousand verses in Arabic and Persian. Sulaymān's son Aḥmad, who reacquired the copy from Ḥaydar ʿAlavī sometime before 1674, was also a noted scholar of his day. Ḥaydar ʿAlavī himself came from a very important family of seventeenth-century Sufis. His grandfather, Shaykh Vajīh al-Dīn ʿAlavī (d. 1589), was a *khalīfa* of Shaykh Muḥammad Ghawth Gvāliyārī (d. 1562), a well-known saint of the Shattari order in the sixteenth century.[52]

If in Abū l-Faḍl's writings we can see the expressed need for an authoritative text of the *Mathnavī* in Mughal India, from the lines of transmission evident in the Rampur manuscript we can discern the reception of such an authoritative text. The act of copying and recopying was not a passive activity but rather demonstrated the value that that the text acquired in the contemporary scholarly climate. In particular, the distinction of the copyists and the care with which the lines of transmission were preserved indicates both the value of the work and something of the structure of the Mughal scholarly environment.

However, modern scholars have not been as kind to ʿAbd al-Laṭīf's edition. The noted scholar of Persian R. A. Nicholson, who produced in the 1920s the first complete edition and English translation of the *Mathnavī,* dismissed the work out of hand. In his introduction, Nicholson evaluated the efforts of his predecessor thus:

> [ʿAbd al-Laṭīf] states that his recension of the poem was based on more than eighty MSS. Unfortunately the abundance of his sources has only increased the depravation of his text; the portion covering Books I and II includes about 800 verses over and above those comprised in the text of this volume, so that, roughly speaking, one verse in every ten is interpolated. My present acquaintance with the *Nuskha-i nasikha* does not encourage belief that the time needed in order to examine it thoroughly would be well spent. What has been said will, I hope, convince the reader that this new edition of the *Mathnawi* is justified by the result.[53]

Although Nicholson's edition is undoubtedly of prime importance even today, his opinion needs reconsideration. For example, his remark that ʿAbd al-Laṭīf used eighty separate manuscripts shows inattention both to the author's own words and to the cataloguers of the British Library and the Bodleian, who indicate that ʿAbd al-Laṭīf used an earlier collation done on the basis of sixty manuscripts in Afghanistan, in conjunction with other manuscripts that he consulted individually.[54] His inattention to ʿAbd al-Laṭīf's own explanation of his work can also be gauged in that he mistook ʿAbd al-Laṭīf's *Mirʾāt al-Mathnavī,* his introduction to *Nuskha-i Nāsikha,* for an independent commentary on the *Mathnavī.*[55] However, Nicholson's opinion has continued to hold sway in the Western academy.

Such an oversight is strange from a scholar who must have gone through one complete manuscript of the *Nuskha,* at least, which included a combined introduction for all the six volumes. ʿAbd al-Laṭīf calls it *Mirʾāt al-Mathnavī* and says that in it he intends to tell his readers the details of his research for the *Mathnavī* ("tafṣīl-i ān tadqīqāt va taḥqīqāt az Dībācha-i Kull ki musammá ba-Mirʾāt al-Mathnavī ast vāḍiḥ va lāyiḥ mī gardad"). Elsewhere in the same introduction he uses the expression "tasṭīr-i īn Dībācha ki musammá ba-Mirʾāt al-Mathnavīst [writing of this introduction which is called Mirʾāt al-Mathnavī]." He repeats it in the summarized preface for each of the six volumes of the *Mathnavī* as well as in the introduction to his *Laṭāyif al-Maʿnavī.* Nicholson relied on Hermann Ethe's cataloguing of this "fragment" under the folios of the commentary on the *Mathnavī (awrāq-i sharḥ-i Mathnavī).* Ethé is not correct, clearly. His inference regarding the title as *Mir'āt al-Mathnavī* is based on it having figured somewhere in the middle of the folios only; nowhere at either the beginning or the end of these fragmented pages does this title appear.[56]

Nicholson's dismissive criticism of ʿAbd al-Laṭīf seems to be based on a rather simplistic critical tradition in which the criteria of textual authority are chronologically ranked—the older the (necessarily) better. ʿAbd al-Laṭīf operated on a different set of assumptions. His notion of authenticity was based first on the quality and excellence of the genealogy of transmission. One indication of this may be found in a small section in the Tehran manuscript pertaining to the reception of ʿAbd al-Laṭīf's work in Mughal India, written by one Jalāl al-Dīn Muḥammad around 1648. He boasts of having learned of the *Mathnavī* from the disciples of ʿAbd al-Laṭīf, indicating the latter's standing as a teacher of renown. Muḥammad also provides some details of the genealogy, beginning with Rūmī himself and including noted Sufis and saints, such as Khwāja Zayn al-Dīn Muḥammad Qavvās and Mīr Fatḥallāh, to highlight the significance of the lines of transmission through which ʿAbd al-Laṭīf learned about the *Mathnavī* and showing how his knowledge was then passed on to the next generation. Muḥammad then claims these personalities, including ʿAbd al-Laṭīf, for his own genealogy.[57] Specifically mentioning ʿAbd al-Laṭīf's commentary and researches on the *Mathnavī,* this genealogy indicates both ʿAbd al-Laṭīf's legitimacy and his authority to write on the *Mathnavī,* as well as the popularity and the continuity in the readership of his work. Thus, texts used by and belonging to renowned teachers, known through genealogies of transmission, would be considered more authoritative; mere chronological antiquity of the manuscript was never enough to establish its authenticity. In the ethos of learning of seventeenth-century Mughal India, every Tom, Dick, and Harry was not qualified to teach, let alone pass down, authentic texts of the *Mathnavī.*

The second criterion ʿAbd al-Laṭīf applied was aesthetic, as described above. For him, as a master of the text, the work of authors of Rūmī's stature necessarily showed clear evidence of genius, high literary ability, and personal style, allowing one to discriminate between authentic lines and spurious interpolations.[58] Again, this ability to discriminate bore the deep impress of the Mughal ethos of learning. As ʿAbd al-Laṭīf writes:

> the scholars who possessed insight spent their precious time for years in researching and specifying the usage and style of this reality-containing book, learned and earned authority [*sanad*] from the great masters of this art, and in fact offered the best years of their life in learning and cultivating speech and [a taste for] poetry, and acquiring the ability to differentiate the good from the

bad in poetry. Thus, any spurious verse or interpolation in the *Mathnavī* looks to these masters like a worn-out and ugly patch on a piece of brocade.[59]

Following this, ʿAbd al-Laṭīf describes his years of literary study on the *Butkhāna* and his training from spiritual masters, thus establishing his credentials to undertake such a task.[60] Moreover, as Muḥammad's encomium shows, ʿAbd al-Laṭīf's reputation and authority were well accepted even after his death. Thus, even if these criteria are judged arbitrary by modern editorial standards, it is important to recognize that ʿAbd al-Laṭīf applied these "early modern" standards rigorously to his work.[61]

Aside from the specific question of the value of ʿAbd al-Laṭīf's editions as a resource for contemporary textual scholarship, it is worth exploring why ʿAbd al-Laṭīf's work deserves mention in the history of Indo-Persian scholarship. The tradition of editorial concern with "correct words" has a long history in the Islamic world, beginning with early Islamic Arabic texts and continuing into the Abbasid period, when one can discern, for example, the translator's concern with variation in words in the original text in preparing Arabic translations of Greco-Hellenic works.[62] Although others have noted that this concern seems to have informed the early reception of the *Mathnavī* too, they rarely discuss the scholarly techniques employed in ensuring textual integrity, and particularly what evidence there may be for the continuity of this tradition in the medieval Perso-Turkic world.[63]

The Arab editorial technique seems to have continued in the Perso-Turkic world, albeit on a smaller scale. Ḥamdallāh Mustawfī's *Shāhnāma,* published as *Ẓafarnāma,* and Baysunghar's *Shāhnāma* are the two major examples of this tradition.[64] By the sixteenth century, the kind of philological activity we have seen in ʿAbd al-Laṭīf can be documented in the Ottoman capital as well. For example, in a discussion of the preparation of a translation of the *Miftāḥ al-Jafr* in 1597–1598 for Sultan Mehmed III, the translator Şerif b. Seyyid Mehmed b. Şeyh Burhan describes the lack of manuscripts available in the country, his efforts to find copies, which were often marred by scribal errors, and how he applied the logic of context and reason in order to reconstruct the correct text. Only after this editorial activity did he undertake his translation.[65] The Afghanistan edition of the *Mathnavī,* prepared by a group of scholars, comes close to ʿAbd al-Laṭīf's *Nuskha-i Nāsikha.* Unfortunately, we know nothing about this text. One can certainly hear echoes of ʿAbd al-Laṭīf's own descriptions of his editorial techniques, but his efforts were on a different scale altogether, in terms of both the number of manuscripts he consulted and the systematic way he went about editing the text. He developed a technique for flagging lines he thought were authentic but insufficiently attested in his manuscript sources; produced indices to enable the reader to navigate through the vast text; produced a commentary identifying scriptural references; provided lexicographical aids, combined with etymological reflection across a half-dozen languages; and refrained from making an anthology of "Rūmī's greatest hits" but provided all the materials necessary for the reader to do so himself. He created a total philological toolbox.

I must, however, note here that I did not find all the features of the edition that ʿAbd al-Laṭīf mentions so boastfully in any one of the manuscripts that I saw. Preparation of a copy of his edition must have been very cumbersome. It is interesting that his friends advised him to publish his notes and comments separately, some of which are cited with appreciation as well as with criticisms by later Mughal editors and commentators like Muḥammad Riḍā Lāhawrī and Valī Muḥammad Akbarābādī.[66] ʿAbd al-Laṭīf's edition was perhaps ahead of his time. He therefore had to write a long introduction to highlight its significance. Still he did not earn full appreciation for his editorial work from the copyists and their patrons. Unfortunately, a copy of the *Nuskha* prepared under the care of ʿAbd al-Laṭīf himself is yet to be located. In addition, ʿAbd al-Laṭīf's claim of a distinction between addition *(zāyida)* and interpolation *(ilḥāqī)* does not simply remain ambiguous; it is also discretionary, as he focuses on the mystical dimensions of Rūmī's poetry, and in that context his aesthetic criteria for judging the authenticity and inner meaning of the *Mathnavī* trumped "mere" research.

Still, it would not be fair to call his edition a mere "compendium of lines attributed to Rūmī in a wide variety of faulty exemplars of the text."[67] It *is* a proto-critical edition. Moreover, ʿAbd al-Laṭīf was not merely an editor; he also mounted a spirited and extremely erudite defense of the *Mathnavī* as a literary text. Rūmī's unconcern with the technical aspects of prosody and formal elements of poetry was generally recognized.[68] Yet ʿAbd al-Laṭīf, basing his argument in careful research on the rules of prosody, took pains to show how even by these narrow standards of literary excellence, any criticisms of the *Mathnavī* could be legitimately dismissed. Thus, in a very technical discussion of the *ramal* meter, he showed the various ways that even what appeared in the *Mathnavī* to be a clear violation of this meter can be reread so that the literary defects disappear.

ʿAbd al-Laṭīf's work also stands out in the context of the wider practices of lexicography, philology, and literary ctiricism in the early modern Indo-Persian world. He is a link in a chain that took a new turn in Mughal India in the late sixteenth century, beginning perhaps with the compilation of Injū's *Farhang-i Jahāangīrī,* continuing through the debates carried on in other philological works like *Burhān-i Qāti'* and *Farhang-i Rashīdī,* and culminating in the works of Siraj al-Dīn 'Alī Khan Arzū in the eighteenth century. These philological debates and practices preceded the intervention of British colonial scholars.[69] Whether or not his work meets the standards by which literary criticism is practiced today, these standards would never have been developed without the philological explorations in which 'Abd al-Laṭīf was a remarkable pioneer.

The Rise of "Deep Reading" in Early Modern Ottoman Scholarly Culture

KHALED EL-ROUAYHEB

PREMODERN ISLAMIC education has often been characterized as personal rather than institutional, and as fundamentally oral rather than textual. A student would ideally seek out a respected teacher, become part of his entourage, attend his classes, and "hear" knowledge from him. From cultivating this personal, oral-aural relationship with one or more teachers, rather than from any institutional affiliation, a student would hope eventually to get recognition as a scholar in his own right and be sought out by a new generation—in effect becoming a link in a chain of transmitters of knowledge extending back to early Islamic times.

In this pedagogic model, listening, discussing, repeating, memorizing, and reciting were of paramount importance. The private reading of texts, by contrast, played a subordinate and auxiliary role, and was sometimes even the source of anxiety and censure. This model is of course an ideal type, and the actual process of acquiring knowledge would only have approximated it. There is abundant evidence for the existence in various times and places of students who were intractable or who, by virtue of their intelligence and private reading, came to surpass their teachers in scholarly accomplishment. Nevertheless, as a depiction of a widely held cultural ideal, the model does arguably do justice to considerable stretches of Islamic history.[1]

In what follows, I will present evidence for the emergence of a more impersonal and textual model of the transmission of knowledge in the central Ottoman lands in the seventeenth and eighteenth centuries. It is not just that the time-honored, oral-aural ideal did not fully correspond to actual educational realities; the ideal itself appears to have been modified. This development may, I suggest, have been related to the far-reaching reforms that the Ottoman learned hierarchy underwent in the sixteenth century.

I

On January 4, 1691, a prominent Ottoman scholar residing in Mecca completed a treatise in Arabic on a topic that, as far as he knew, had never before received sustained attention: the proper manner *(ādāb)* of perusing books *(muṭālaʿah).* The scholar's name was Aḥmed ibn Lütfullāh el-Mevlevī, also known as Müneccimbāşī.[2] He was born in Salonica in 1631 or 1632, and began his education in his hometown, where he was also initiated into the Mevlevī Sufi order. He pursued his advanced education in the Ottoman capital, Istanbul, studying with some of the leading scholars of his day. He appears to have had a particular aptitude for mathematics, astronomy, and astrology, and in the year 1668 he was appointed to the post of court astronomer-astrologer to Sultan Meḥmed IV (r. 1648–1687). When Meḥmed IV was deposed in 1687, Müneccimbāşī fell from grace and was exiled to Cairo. In 1690 he went to Mecca, performed the pilgrimage, and took up a position as head of the local Mevlevī lodge. He died in the city twelve years later, in 1702. Though possibly best known today for his universal chronicle *Jāmiʿ al-duwal* (written in Arabic but later abridged and translated into Turkish), he also wrote a number of other works, some of which appear—from the number of extant manuscripts—to have been widely copied and read in later times. One of these was his innovative treatise on the "proper manner of perusing books," which he completed just a few months after having arrived in Mecca from Cairo.[3]

Müneccimbāşī wrote in his introduction that he had hesitated before venturing to write on a topic that no one had treated before. When he decided to write nonetheless, he entitled the treatise "The Inspiration of the Sanctuary" *(Fayḍ al-ḥaram).* Without the guidance of previous authors, he would have to rely entirely on the divine inspiration and munificence *(al-fayḍ wa l-inʿām)* that one could hope was forthcoming in the presence of the Sanctuary in Mecca.

Müneccimbāşī's remark about the absence of any previous extended treatment of the "techniques of studying books" appears to be quite true. Since the ninth century, there had been a tradition of Arabic works partly or entirely devoted to the proper ways of teaching and acquiring knowledge, but these had said very little about studying and perusing books on one's own.[4] Their focus was invariably on the proprieties of student-teacher interaction, and the proper demeanor and conduct expected of student and teacher inside and outside of class. This can be seen in two typical and influential educational treatises from earlier centuries: *Taʿlīm al-mutaʿallim ṭuruq al-taʿallum,* by the central Asian jurist Burhān al-Dīn al-Zarnūjī (fl. 1203), and *Tadhkirat al-sāmiʿ wa l-mutakallim fī adab al-ʿālim wa l-mutaʿallim,* by the Syrian scholar and judge Badr al-Dīn Ibn Jamāʿah (d. 1333).[5] A brief overview of these two works will be helpful for bringing out the novel emphasis of Müneccimbāşī's treatment.

The title of Zarnūjī's treatise can be translated as "Instructing the Student in the Pathways of Learning." It begins by praising the importance of knowledge, both of religious law and of ethics, adducing to this effect a number of quotations from the Qurʾān as well as from the Prophet and venerable figures and scholars of the past.[6] It goes on to emphasize the importance of acquiring knowledge with the right intentions—not to win worldly fame and glory but to obey God and maintain the religion of Islam.[7] The student should choose his teacher carefully, and having made the choice, he should submit to the authority of that teacher and venerate him.[8] He should not walk in front of his teacher, speak to him without permission, or seek him out at inopportune times, and he should show respect to the teacher's children.[9] The student should be careful to avoid idle chatter and too much eating and drinking, which may induce laziness and forgetfulness.[10] Instead he should devote himself to the task of learning with single-mindedness and diligence, and should in general lead an upright, modest, and pious life. Classes should preferably start on Wednesdays, for a number of religious traditions state that that day of the week is particularly auspicious.[11]

At the early stages of education, a teaching session should cover as much material as is amenable to "apprehension" *(ḍabt)* by repeating twice. A sixteenth-century commentator on Zarnūjī's treatise glossed the word "apprehension" with "memorization and learning."[12] The gloss seems very much in the spirit of Zarnūjī's work. On the one hand the centrality of "memorization" *(ḥifẓ)* for the learning process as described by Zarnūjī is undeniable. The work is full of practical advice on how to improve one's memory and exhortations to avoid activities that may have an adverse effect on it. On the other hand Zarnūjī clearly believed that there is more to "learning" *(taʿallum)* than mere memorization. He emphasized the importance of understanding *(fahm),* considering *(taʾammul),* and thinking things over *(tafakkur).*[13] Especially at a more advanced stage of studies, a student should make a habit of "considering" the more intricate problems of individual disciplines and of "considering" before venturing to speak about scholarly matters.[14] To aid the process of "understanding," Zarnūjī urged the student to "repeat" *(tikrār)* his lessons after class and to engage in discussion *(mudhākarah),* disputation *(munāẓarah),* and exchanges *(muṭāraḥah)* with his fellow students.[15]

By contrast, the private reading and studying of books does not feature as an aid to "understanding," and in general plays a very marginal role in Zarnūjī's work. The term *muṭālaʿah* (perusal of texts) occurs only once in passing: books should be square in format, since that was the shape preferred by the venerable Abū Ḥanīfah (d. 767), founder of the Ḥanafī school of law, to which Zarnūjī belonged, and because it was the shape most conducive to lifting, placing, and *muṭālaʿah.*[16] Zarnūjī considered books and writing to be a normal part of the educational process. Students must, he wrote, show respect for books, only touching them in a state of ritual purity and not extending the soles of their feet toward them.[17] He also urged the student not to "write anything down" without understanding it first, clearly considering the taking of notes or dictation by students to be perfectly normal.[18] However, the solitary reading and study of books was not something he emphasized. Tellingly, he advised the student to always have ink on hand so that he could write down what he "hears" *(yasmaʿu)* of unfamiliar scholarly points, and to leave generous margins in his own copies of handbooks so that he could write down what he "has heard" *(samiʿa)* of helpful comments and elucidations.[19] Knowledge, Zarnūjī explicitly declares, is something that is obtained "from the mouths of men" ("al-ʿilm mā yuʾkhadh min afwāh al-rijāl").[20]

The treatise by Ibn Jamāʿah, completed in 1273, evinces the same indifference to the private reading of books. The view that imparting knowledge is primarily an aural and oral matter is revealed already in the title, which translates as "The Memento to the Listener and Speaker of the Manner of the Scholar and the Student." The work is divided into five chapters. The first adduces a number of quotations from the Qurʾān and traditions from the Prophet in praise of knowledge.[21] The second presents the manners proper to the scholar.[22] He should be pious and God-fearing and not use his knowledge for the sake of worldly gains. He should be clean and ritually pure when he comes to class, start by reciting some verses from the Qurʾān, and invoke blessings on the students and all Muslims. He should lecture clearly and pause to allow questions. He should not be afraid to admit it when he does not know an answer. He should behave in a kind and fatherly manner to his students and avoid undue favoritism. He may occasionally test his student's grasp or "apprehension" *(ḍabt)* by posing questions relating to material covered.

The third chapter deals with the manners proper to the student.[23] He should seek knowledge with the proper motives, and live a diligent and pious life centered on his studies. He should eat and sleep moderately. He should seek out a pious and reputable teacher and show him respect and veneration at all times. For instance, he should be clean and neatly dressed before entering the presence of the teacher, avoid addressing the teacher in the second person singular, and be courteous in his manner of posing questions. He should keep his eyes focused on the teacher during class, sit still and upright, and avoid fiddling with his hands, stroking his beard, picking his nose, leaning against a pillar or wall, or presenting his back to the teacher. The student should begin his studies by memorizing the Qur'ān and learning its meaning, and then move on to the study of hadith (reports about the sayings and doings of the Prophet Muḥammad), creedal theology, jurisprudence, and grammar.

In each field he should memorize a short introductory manual and then attend the classes of a reputed teacher to hear the manual explained and commented on. Before memorizing, however, he should make sure his copy of a manual is correct. He should therefore read out his own copy in the presence of the teacher or the teacher's assistant and incorporate corrections. He should behave to his fellow students in a mild and brotherly fashion, and should not get into acrimonious debates or bicker over seating order. Like Zarnūjī, Ibn Jamāʿah stressed the importance of *mudhākarah:* after class, the students should discuss among themselves the points that have been covered. Should the student find no one to discuss with, he should discuss with himself, repeating the meaning *(maʿnā)* and the wording *(lafẓ)* of "what he has heard" *(mā samiʿahu)* so that both are taken to heart.

The fourth chapter concerns a student's proper behavior with books.[24] He should treat books with respect, for example not placing them on the floor, nor using them to fan himself or to squash bedbugs. When copying a book, he should be in a state of ritual purity and face in the direction of the Kaʿbah in Mecca. His copy should start with the standard pious formulae, and every time the copied text mentions God, prophets, or respected predecessors, standard expressions of respect and veneration should be added in full by the copyist—even if these are not to be found in the text of the exemplar. He should collate his copy carefully, and introduce needed corrections and disambiguations in the text or in the margins. The fifth and final chapter concerns the behavior proper to those residing in a college *(madrasah).*[25] For example, they should not be idle or engage in frivolous chatter. Noise levels should be kept to a minimum, as should unnecessary visits to and from the outside world.

As is clear from the preceding overview, the role of private study and reading is also marginal in Ibn Jamāʿah's presentation. There are a dozen passing references to *muṭālaʿah* in the work, but most of these place the activity *outside* the context of a student's acquisition of knowledge. For instance, Ibn Jamāʿah writes in his preamble that he gathered the material included in the book from what he had heard from his teachers and from what he had come across in his readings *(muṭālaʿāt).* He also notes that he aimed to be succinct so that the work would not be deemed too long or boring to its reader *(muṭāliʿ).*[26] *Muṭālaʿah* is also presented as one of the things expected of an established and advanced scholar: a teacher-scholar should not rest content with his level of knowledge but seek to develop it by means of thinking, discussion, memorization, writing, and *muṭālaʿah.*[27]

Writing scholarly works requires the *muṭālaʿah* of numerous texts.[28] A student should not interrupt his teacher if he finds him engaged in prayer or writing or *muṭālaʿah.*[29] A copyist should disambiguate a word in the margin if it is of a sort that may be perplexing to the *muṭāliʿ.*[30] Only a handful of occurrences of *muṭālaʿah* relate it specifically to the process of a student's acquisition of knowledge. Nights are especially suitable for peer discussion *(mudhākarah)* and *muṭālaʿah.*[31] After having memorized and mastered the introductory manuals, a student should move on to longer and more advanced works, and regularly engage in *muṭālaʿah.*[32] A student should not omit the introductory pious formulae, whether he is engaged in *muṭālaʿah* or in recitation *(qirāʾah).*[33] A teacher at a college should make himself available at set periods of the day for students who are preoccupied with the task of *muṭālaʿah* in their own copies of the handbook studied.[34]

Ibn Jamāʿah was well aware that students engaged in *muṭālaʿah,* just as they engaged in peer discussions outside of class. Nevertheless, he gave only passing attention to the activity, highlighting instead the teacher-student relationship in the process of the acquisition of knowledge. Like Zarnūjī, he stressed that knowledge should be taken from scholars, not from books. A student should seek out recognized and pious scholars who themselves had studied with recognized and pious scholars. He should avoid those teachers who "take knowledge from the insides of folios" ("man akhadha min buṭūni l-awrāq").[35] "Knowledge should not," he writes, "be taken from books, for this is one of the most harmful of vices" ("inna l-ʿilma lā yuʾkhadhu min al-kutubi faʾinnahu min aḍarri l-mafāsid").[36] Following a tradition that was already centuries old in his time, Ibn Jamāʿah presented the transmission and acquisition of knowledge as taking place primarily in the presence of a teacher, and as being brought about by the activities of listening, reciting, memorizing, posing questions, and grasping orally delivered answers and explanations.

This emphasis on student-teacher interaction and on the oral-aural aspects of learning seems to reflect the character of education in most parts of the medieval Islamic world. A number of modern historical studies have emphasized the highly personal and noninstitutional character of the educational process in Baghdad, Damascus, and Cairo from the eleventh to the fifteenth centuries.[37] It was from teachers, not from any institution, that a student obtained recognition as well as a certificate *(ijāzah)* to teach a work. Contemporary biographers regularly felt it important to indicate with whom a scholar had studied, and almost never in which institutions he had done so. The madrasah functioned as a college that often provided accommodations and food for students and kept one or more teachers on its payroll. But it did not issue degrees, nor was it a necessary part of the educational process, for some teachers conducted classes in mosques or Sufi lodges, or at home.

The transmission of knowledge and authority from teacher to student was basically face-to-face, with private reading and study playing an unofficial and complementary role. This model also seems applicable to the remnants of traditional Islamic education studied by anthropologists in the twentieth century.[38] For example, Brinkley Messick has distinguished between various ways twentieth-century Yemeni students at traditional madrasahs interacted with texts: memorization *(ḥifẓ),* recitation *(qirāʾah),* listening *(samāʿ),* and private reading *(muṭālaʿah).*[39] He notes, however, that *muṭālaʿah* was commonly used to describe interaction with books on topics not formally studied at the madrasah, such as history and poetry.[40] The other three modes of textual interaction, by comparison, were central to the pedagogic process, or at least to the ideal-typical representation of that process.

II

The works of Zarnūjī and Ibn Jamāʿah were paradigmatic for a number of later treatments of education. For example, the discussions of the topic by the Damascene scholar Badr al-Dīn al-Ghazzī (d. 1577), the Syrian Shīʿī scholar Zayn al-Dīn al-ʿĀmilī (d. 1558), and the Ottoman scholar and judge Aḥmed Ṭāşköprüzāde (d. 1561) are clearly in the same tradition.[41] There are some differences between these later authors that might be worth pursuing in a different context, but they all shared with Zarnūjī and Ibn Jamāʿah the emphasis on teacher-student interaction at the expense of activities such as peer learning and private reading. It is precisely the shift in emphasis toward the latter two activities that is so conspicuous in Müneccimbāşī's work.

Müneccimbāşī, after the aforementioned preamble in which he expressed his hesitation about writing the treatise at all, introduces his book with a proposed working definition of *muṭālaʿah*. Lexically the verbal noun means "examination" or "perusal." In its technical sense, however, it refers specifically to the examination or perusal of texts, or as Müneccimbāşī proposed, "perceiving writing so as to obtain an understood meaning," and more expressly, "perceiving written utterances whose conventional meaning is familiar to arrive thereby at the intention behind their use."[42] The ability to engage in *muṭālaʿah* is not, he wrote, present in the beginner: "a student in the earliest stages of seeking knowledge is not in a position to engage in *muṭālaʿah* and derive meanings from written expressions; rather his concern is to take what he seeks from the mouths of men."[43]

Müneccimbāşī is not referring in this passage to a lack of literacy. The ability to "derive" meanings and authorial intentions from a written text is, he wrote, dependent on "learning the principles of the instrumental sciences and being able to call their most important parts to mind" ("bi-itqāni l-uṣūli min al-ʿulūmi l-āliyyati wa bi-istiḥḍāri l-muhimmāti minhā").[44] In other words, the inability to engage in *muṭālaʿah* is not due to sheer illiterate incomprehension of the writing. It is rather because, without a grounding in a range of "instrumental disciplines"—syntax, logic, dialectic, semantics-rhetoric *(ʿilm al-maʿānī wa l-bayān)*—a beginning student would not go beyond a reading that Müneccimbāşī characterized as "superficial" *(saṭḥī),* "literalist" *(ẓāhirī),* and "simple-minded" *(ḥashwī).*[45]

The terms *ẓāhirī* and *ḥashwī* were often used by Muslim scholars who were open to logic and the rational sciences to disparage more literalist and fideist currents associated with the defunct Ẓāhirī school of law (which rejected analogy in jurisprudence) and the minority Ḥanbalī school of law (which rejected rational theology and figurative interpretations of anthropomorphisms in the Qurʾān and Ḥadīth). The idea that *ḥashwī* groups are led to crudely literalist and anthropomorphic readings of scriptural texts due to ignorance of the rational and instrumental sciences was an old accusation, made for example by the influential North African Ashʿarī theologian Sanūsī (d. 1490), whose works were known in Ottoman scholarly circles.[46] However, the terms *ḥashwī* and *ẓāhirī* were often used in a broader and less determinate sense, and Müneccimbāşī need not have had any particular religious groupings in mind.[47] He may simply have thought that a reader equipped with nothing more than literacy in classical Arabic was unlikely to make much headway with the highly technical handbooks on theology, jurisprudence, and Qur'ān commentary that would have been studied by more advanced Ottoman students.

After having gained a familiarity with the basics of the instrumental and rational sciences, a student develops "the ability to engage in derivation" *(malakat al-istikhrāj)* of meanings from written scholarly handbooks, that is, the ability to do *muṭālaʿah.* The intermediate and advanced student who engages in this manner with a scholarly text is seeking one of four things: (1) to obtain knowledge that he does not have but for which he is prepared; (2) to move beyond knowledge taken on trust and uncover the evidential basis for scholarly propositions; (3) to deepen his evidentiary knowledge by repeated perusal, thus obtaining a thorough familiarity with the evidence and "the ability to call to mind at will" *(malakat al-istiḥḍār);* (4) to deepen his evidentiary and consolidated knowledge by strengthening it through reviewing familiar texts or exposure to new texts and alternative presentations and proofs.[48]

In the first chapter Müneccimbāşī presents the proprieties that are relevant to all four categories of readers.[49] Before commencing, a reader should mention the name of God and invoke blessings on His Prophet, followed by some choice prayers asking for divine inspiration and guidance. If he is reading a handbook on a scholarly discipline, he should have some initial conception of this discipline: its definition, its subject matter, and its aim. The reader may also be consulting the discussion of a particular issue *(mabḥath)* in a work, in which case he should have a clear initial conception of this issue. Should he, for example, wish to read a section on the proof for the existence of prime matter *(hayūlī),* he should know from the start that philosophers *(ḥukamā')* believe that there is an externally existing substance called "matter," which, along with "form" *(ṣūrah),* is a constituent of every body *(jism).* He should then consult the relevant section of books on philosophy. On encountering a passage, he should start by focusing on its language: lexically, morphologically, syntactically, semantically, and rhetorically. He should then turn to the level of "second intentions" *(al-maʿqūlāt al-thāniyah),* that is, second-order concepts, which are the province of logic. He should pay attention to what kind of definitions are being adduced, what kinds of propositions, and the logical structure of any arguments. In general, Müneccimbāşī wrote, a student would find the disciplines of logic and syntax to be especially helpful in his efforts to understand demanding scholarly texts. He wrote: "the truth is that these two disciplines are like the parents of the student with regard to his education and his reaching perfection. So every student should strive to obtain a thorough ability in these two fields by heeding them in all his perusals."[50] It is telling that Müneccimbaşī should compare two *disciplines* to a student's parents. In the older educational literature it was typically the *teacher* who was cast in a paternal role.

Muṭālaʿah for Müneccimbāşī is obviously more than just reading. It is rather a close examination of a scholarly text that starts with noting its syntactic, semantic, rhetorical, and logical features. Having done this, the reader should sum up the relevant issue by conceiving in his mind the claim *(mabdaʾ),* the argument *(wasaṭ),* and the principles on which the argument rests *(maqṭaʿ).* A sign that he has achieved this is that he is able to express the issue briefly and in his own words ("an yaqtadira ʿalā l-taʿbīri ʿanhu bi-ayyi ʿibāratin shāʾa wa bi-awjazi l-ʿibārāt"). In his endeavors to thus unlock a scholarly handbook, a reader should heed and follow the example of an acknowledged commentary *(sharḥ)* on the relevant work and of an acknowledged gloss *(ḥāshiyah)* on that commentary. Müneccimbāşī made clear, however, that one should not get into the habit of consulting such commentaries and glosses before trying to understand the handbook oneself.[51]

The second chapter presents the techniques of reading that are relevant to readers of the aforementioned category (1), that is, those who examine the text with the aim of acquiring *(taḥṣīl)* new knowledge.[52] Such a reader should keep in mind whether the text affords "imitative" *(taqlīdī)* knowledge devoid of proof or "verified" *(taḥqīqī)* knowledge in which proofs are supplied. If he is reading a text on an instrumental science such as grammar or logic, then he may be content in the first instance with "imitative" knowledge—though he should at some point return to the discipline and become familiar with the evidence underlying its claims. If the text belongs to a discipline that is sought for its own sake, like theology *(kalām)* and philosophy *(ḥikmah),* then he should have a distinct idea of claims, proofs, and basic principles and consider these carefully. He should turn these over in his mind without remaining bound to the particular linguistic utterances used to express them. A way to accomplish this is to express to oneself the basic points in different ways or in different languages.

The third chapter deals with the techniques relevant to the reader who falls into category (2): the one who seeks to obtain knowledge of the evidential basis of scholarly propositions.[53] In fact, much of the introduction and the second chapter already dealt with this task. At this stage, Müneccimbāşī adds that the reader should heed the different natures of various disciplines with respect to proofs. In linguistic sciences proofs will take the form of attestations in works by canonical authors and poets, and analogies will be made on the basis of this. In the sciences of Qurʾān commentary and hadith a "proof" would be to adduce a report with an acceptable chain of transmitters. Some disciplines do not admit of "proof" at all, such as literary anecdotes *(muḥāḍarāt),* poetry, and belles lettres, and—curiously—history *(taʾrīkh).* The mention of the last three subjects is somewhat puzzling. The first chapter, dealing with general techniques for engaging in *muṭālaʿah,* emphasized the pivotal importance of the instrumental and rational sciences. It may well have been Müneccimbāşī's view that one needed morphology, syntax, and semantics-rhetoric for a proper reading of poetry and history, but did he really believe that logic is relevant in that context too? Does it make sense to say that one should carefully separate claim, argument, and axioms while reading poetry, or that a criterion for understanding a poem is that one can express the point succinctly and in one's own words, or that before starting to read a poem or chronicle one should have an initial conception of the issue discussed? It is clear that the focus of Müneccimbāşī's treatise is on the perusal of the technical and tightly argued handbooks studied intensively by Ottoman students, and that works on poetry, belles lettres, and history are mentioned in this particular context merely for the sake of comprehensiveness. This is in marked contrast to the situation in the traditional Yemeni colleges described by Messick. There the object of *muṭālaʿah* tended to be precisely works belonging to such fields, which were not normally subjects of formal instruction in colleges.

Chapter 4 presents the techniques appropriate to readers of category (3): those who seek to develop "the ability to call to mind at will."[54] Such a reader has already been exposed to and understood the evidential bases for particular scholarly propositions, but is not yet familiar with them to the point of being able to expound them independently and at will. This ability results from repeated *muṭālaʿah.* If the ability relates to an "instrumental" science like grammar or logic, then one can also deepen one's knowledge by regularly "making use" *(istiʿmāl)* of it when reading texts that belong to other fields, for instance, noticing the grammar or logic of a text on jurisprudence or theology. This consolidated knowledge of all the issues of a discipline does not yet amount to consolidated knowledge of the discipline. A person who has the former but not the latter is not able to give a summary as well as a comprehensive account. The reader who thinks he has a consolidated knowledge of all the issues must consider whether he also has a consolidated knowledge of the discipline as such. If not, he must reexamine his supposed knowledge of issues or consider whether the proper ordering principle that governs them is still unclear to him.

The fifth and last chapter presents the proper manner of reading for the student who seeks to strengthen his consolidated and evidentiary knowledge.[55] Such a reader should strive to approach an issue in a number of different ways and from a number of different sources. He should also carefully consider whether the thesis advanced in a text admits of an objection, and what an answer to that objection would be. He should ask himself, preferably aloud, "If an objector were to say such and such, what would the answer be?" In effect, he should consider himself a participant in an organized disputation. Müneccimbāşī counseled this type of reader not to rely entirely on his own *muṭālaʿah* but to listen to what his teachers and fellow students have to say about the texts in question.

In the conclusion, Müneccimbāşī discusses various sources of error relating to language.[56] These can be errors with respect to individual words, for example, confusion between homonyms or between figurative and literal meaning. They can also be errors relating to single propositions, both on the level of utterance, such as a preposition whose referent is not clear, or on the level of meaning, such as confusing various forms of predication (for example, asserting that a phoenix exists when it only does so possibly). They can be errors relating to a complex of propositions, such as fallacious or circular arguments, or mistaking, for example, "Only men are rational" for a single proposition whereas it is in fact two. Müneccimbāşī's account of various types of error seems to be indebted to the commentary of Naṣīr al-Dīn al-Ṭūsī (d. 1274) on *Pointers and Reminders (al-Ishārāt wa l-tanbīhāt),* an epitome of logic and philosophy by Avicenna (d. 1037)—which he cited earlier in his treatise.[57]

As an appendix, Müneccimbāşī discusses the proprieties of discussion *(mudhākarah)* with one's fellow students.[58] *Mudhākarah,* he wrote, is distinguished from "disputation" *(munāẓarah)* by the fact that there may be more than two parties involved, and the roles of claimant and questioner are not fixed and may shift in the course of the exchange. One should be modest and friendly with the interlocutors, and as much as possible avoid being in the position of claimant, "for all difficulty and hardship lie in that role." If he cannot get out of assuming the role, then he should express himself cautiously, emphasizing that he is merely expounding the author's views and drawing in his fellow students by means of such questions as "What do my brothers think?" and "What is your opinion?"

III

The differences between the work of Müneccimbāşi and those of Zarnūjī and Ibn Jamā'ah are conspicuous. In Müneccimbāşī's treatise, *muṭāla'ah* especially but also *mudhākarah* are at the center of attention. The student-teacher relationship is acknowledged as important, but otherwise plays a subordinate role in a discussion of the proper means of "extracting" meanings from texts. In the works of Zarnūjī and Ibn Jamā'ah, it is the other way around: the existence of *muṭāla'ah* and *mudhākarah* is acknowledged, but the authors' focus is on the teacher-student relation and the oral-aural transmission of knowledge. Also noteworthy in Müneccimbāşī's work is the emphasis on logic, dialectic, semantics, and rhetoric, as well as the prominent and positive references to "philosophy." These disciplines are not mentioned in the works of Zarnūjī and Ibn Jamā'ah, who clearly assume that a student would focus on the core religious disciplines: Qur'ān recitation and interpretation, hadith and law, supplemented with Arabic grammar.

The emphasis on the student-text relation and on the rational and instrumental sciences does not seem to be mere idiosyncrasy on the part of Müneccimbāşī. Both emphases are also found in an educational work by Müneccimbāşī's younger contemporary Meḥmed Sāçaḳlīzāde (d. 1732). Sāçaḳlīzāde was one of the prominent Ottoman scholars of his age, despite being active far from the imperial capital, Istanbul, in or near his hometown of Maraş in southeastern Anatolia.[59] In his *Tartīb al-'ulūm* (The ordering of the sciences), a fair copy of which he completed in 1716, he criticized what he considered the wrongheaded ways the students of his time went about their work. The proliferation of sometimes demanding commentaries and glosses on scholarly handbooks meant, he wrote, that students often got lost in a maze of subtleties and failed to get an initial overview of a discipline.

Another evil Sāçaḳlīzāde bewailed was the related tendency to spend too much time on a particular work and its commentaries, glosses, and superglosses while neglecting more important fields of learning. He gave as an example a treatise by the Persian philosopher and theologian Jalāl al-Dīn al-Dawānī (d. 1502) that discusses proofs for the existence of a Necessary Being *(ithbāt al-wājib).* Sāçaḳlīzāde wrote that students "waste" up to a year studying this work and its commentaries and glosses even though they are apt, with their dense web of arguments and counterarguments, to do nothing but weaken faith.[60] The intensive study of philosophy by Ottoman students is a recurrent complaint in Sāçaḳlīzāde's work. Having declared that the classical Islamic philosophers like Fārābī (d. 950) and Avicenna (d. 1037) "and their likes" were infidels, he wrote:

> If you say: "Who are their likes?" We say: Those who are fond of philosophy and indulge in it and call it "wisdom" *(ḥikmah)* by way of extolling it . . . and are proud of what they have learned of philosophy, and who consider as ignorant those who are innocent of it. By the Lord of the Heavens and the Earth! These are the unbelieving philosophizers! One encountered their likes in the time of [the jurist] Āḫī Çelebī [d. 1495 or 1496] and he said about them. . . . "the desire to study jurisprudence is slight among the philosophizers, whose lot in the afterworld is nothing but fire. Verily they will reach hell, and what an end!" Perhaps the philosophizers in our time are more than they were in his time.[61]

Sāçaḳlīzāde, however, was no fideist. He went out of his way to declare astronomy, mathematics, and medicine to be commendable sciences.[62] He also considered the study of logic and dialectic to be commendable and indeed a *farḍ kifāyah,* that is, a collective duty incumbent on the Muslim community (but not on each and every Muslim). Knowledge of logic, and in particular of the conditions and varieties of proofs *(adillah),* was, he wrote, particularly useful in the science of jurisprudence.[63] As for dialectic, "he who has no share of this science will hardly be able to understand scholarly discussions [in any field]."[64] He himself contributed to the discipline, writing an esteemed summa, *Taqrīr al-qawānīn al-mutadāwalah fī ʿilm al-munāẓarah* (Presenting the common principles of the science of disputation), and an epitome of it dedicated to his own son, *al-Risālah al-Waladiyyah* (The son epistle), which became a standard handbook that was in use until the early twentieth century. Sāçaḳlīzāde's hostility to philosophy was also modified by his repeated stress on the importance of studying classical handbooks of rational theology such as *al-Mawāqif,* by Ījī (d. 1355), and *al-Maqāṣid,* by Taftāzānī (d. 1390). These devoted considerable space to epistemological and metaphysical preliminaries, including rebuttals of skepticism, the nature of modality, the relation between essence and existence, the soul and its relation to the body, and the Aristotelian categories of substance and nine types of attribute.

Like Müneccimbāşī, Sāçaḳlīzāde considered a working knowledge of the instrumental and rational sciences to be a necessary condition for engaging in *muṭalaʿah.* He wrote:

> The student is not prepared for *muṭālaʿah* after just gaining knowledge of lexicography, morphology, and syntax; only after also gaining knowledge of logic, dialectic, rational theology, semantics, and the principles of jurisprudence. . . . And I do not mean by "rational theology" the creedal issues alone, but rather the discussions of substances and attributes, as included in works like *al-Maqāṣid* and *al-Mawāqif*.[65]

Sāçaḳlīzāde recommended that the student, after learning Arabic, the Qurʾān, and the basics of the faith, should study the sciences in the following order: morphology, syntax, basic positive law *(al-aḥkām),* logic, dialectic, theology, semantics-rhetoric, jurisprudence. Again he specified that by "theology" he did not mean basic creedal works, but the aforementioned summae of philosophical theology with their extensive epistemological and metaphysical preliminaries. Only then should the student venture to study hadith and Qurʾān exegesis.[66] This order tallies well with what we know of the curriculum of Ottoman education, in which instrumental and rational sciences were typically studied at basic and intermediate levels, and jurisprudence, *ḥadīth,* and Qurʾān exegesis would be reserved for the most advanced levels.[67] But it is very different from the order envisaged by Zarnūjī and Ibn Jamāʿah, who, like the venerable Ghazālī (d. 1111), assume that the student will focus on the core religious disciplines and study them in the order of their importance.[68] It is particularly striking that in Ghazālī's *Iḥyāʾ ʿulūm al-dīn*—which is cited on a number of occasions in Sāçaḳlīzāde's work—the student is advised to begin by studying the Qurʾān, then Ḥadīth, then the Qurʾānic sciences (including Qurʾān exegesis), then the hadith sciences, then positive law, then jurisprudence, and only then other sciences.[69] Ghazālī elsewhere explicitly rejected the suggestion that one should study rational theology before jurisprudence.[70]

The increased importance of the rational and instrumental sciences in Ottoman education was part of a more general trend in the Islamic world. After the twelfth century, and helped by the endorsement of prominent religious scholars such as Ghazālī and Fakhr al-Dīn al-Rāzī (d. 1210), logic started to feature regularly in the education of Muslim students.[71] This was reinforced by the immensely influential Timurid scholars Taftāzānī (d. 1390) and Jurjānī (d. 1413), whose works in a number of fields—including logic—were standard fare in Ottoman education. A number of Ottoman grand muftis in the seventeenth century explicitly traced their intellectual lineage to these two, often via later Sunnī Persian scholars who themselves contributed to the fields of logic, semantics-rhetoric, and philosophical theology, such as the previously mentioned Dawānī (d. 1502) and ʿIṣām al-Dīn al-Isfarāʾīnī (d. 1537).[72]

Not only was logic widely studied by Ottoman students, but a familiarity with the discipline was assumed by later authors writing on other fields. Jurists, theologians, and grammarians increasingly made conscious use of Greek logical concepts and argument forms in their writings.[73] Sāçaḳlīzāde noted, for example, that the standard commentary by Jāmī (d. 1492) on the popular handbook of syntax *al-Kāfiyah* could only be mastered by a student familiar with logic and dialectic.[74] A standard work on creedal theology for Ottoman students, Taftāzānī's commentary on the Creed *(ʿAqāʾid)* of Nasafī (d. 1142) assumes as a matter of course that the reader would—in a discussion on the problem of divine foreknowledge and universal fatalism—understand the statement that "the impossibility of the consequent implies the impossibility of the antecedent" ("inna istiḥālata l-lāzimi tūjibu istiḥālata l-malzūm").[75] A reader who has not been exposed to logic might think, like the English translator E. E. Elder, that *malzūm* in Taftāzānī's statement refers to the consequent and *lāzim* to the antecedent, thus imputing a plain fallacy to Taftāzānī and mistaking the sense of the passage as a whole.[76]

The science of semantics-rhetoric, in which the writings of Taftāzānī and Jurjānī played a central role, also became increasingly important in later centuries. Ghazālī, Zarnūjī, and Ibn Jamāʿah had not felt the need to mention this discipline, but for a scholar like Sāçaḳlīzāde it was a precondition for the mastery of jurisprudence and Qurʾān commentary.[77] The most widely studied Qurʾān commentaries in Ottoman scholarly circles were those by Zamakhsharī (d. 1144) and Bayḍāwī (d. 1316), and both works—as well as their standard glosses by later scholars—are indeed practically incomprehensible to a reader who has had no exposure to semantics-rhetoric.[78]

The other basic point on which Müneccimbāşī differed conspicuously from previous authors was his focus on the student-text relation as opposed to the teacher-student relation. Saçaḳlīzāde's work betrays the same novel emphasis. He regularly exhorts the student to study particular works, to avoid others, and to read works in a particular order. At one point, he recommends his own handbook on Qurʾān recitation *(tajwīd)*, *Juhd al-muqill*, together with his own commentary, stating: "he who has perused *(iṭṭalaʿa ʿalā)* these two works [i.e., the handbook and its commentary] will not be in need of most other works on this topic, and will become a recognized authority in this discipline."[79] This would seem to be a fairly straightforward exhortation to take knowledge "from the insides of folios." Sāçaḳlīzāde repeatedly singled out particular works as especially useful and advised the budding scholar to have a copy of them.[80] He followed Ghazālī in distinguishing among three levels of proficiency in a discipline, basic *(iqtiṣār)*, intermediate *(iqtiṣād)*, and advanced *(istiqsā')*, and recommended works appropriate to each level. He then added that one need not memorize these handbooks; the aim should rather be to correct one's own manuscript copies and examine their contents, either by formal instruction *(ta'allum)* or—tellingly—by looking over and reading *(muṭāla'ah)* them so that one could look up whatever issue one needed.[81]

It may well have been Sāçaḳlīzāde's assumption that the student, particularly in his younger years, would study such works with a teacher. The point is not that Sāçaḳlīzāde (or Müneccimbāşī) thought good teachers unimportant or dispensable. However, the emphasis of Sāçaḳlīzāde's work is conspicuously on the student choosing the right texts, not the right teacher. He had few kind words to say about the teachers of his day: they often imposed advanced issues and discussions on students who were not prepared for them, and in their eagerness to have a large number of students they often did not put them in their place when they wanted to study works above their level.[82] Many teachers were also, he claims, woefully ignorant of core religious sciences, while vaunting their grasp of issues like "species and genus, matter and form, and circularity and infinite regress."[83] In light of Sāçaḳlīzāde's low opinion of his colleagues' manner of teaching, it is perhaps not surprising that he appears to have been less troubled than Zarnūjī and Ibn Jamā'ah by students learning from books rather than "from the mouths of men."

IV

The two Ottoman works on education by Müneccimbāşī and Sāçaḳlīzāde, written independently of each other between 1691 and 1716, are markedly different from the classical Arabic-Islamic pedagogic literature. They both evince a distinct shift of emphasis away from the student-teacher relationship and the oral-aural transmission of knowledge and focus instead on the proper and "deep" reading of texts. This change may conceivably have been related to the increased importance of the rational sciences. The oral-aural model of education was developed in early Islamic times, when "knowledge" *('ilm)* paradigmatically consisted of reports (about the sayings and doings of the Prophet and other venerable figures or about Qur'ānic readings and exegesis) whose acceptability was largely a function of the personal reputations of their transmitters. It is perhaps not surprising that the hold of this model weakened when the greater part of students' education was spent poring over dense scholastic handbooks on syntax, semantics, rhetoric, logic, dialectic, rational theology, and jurisprudence. However, the increased importance of the rational sciences in Islamic education was a trend that started well before the early modern period, and it was evident throughout the Islamic world. This makes it unsatisfying as the sole explanation of a development that appears to have occurred specifically in the core Ottoman lands in the seventeenth and eighteenth centuries.[84]

It may be more plausible to relate the shift in focus to the peculiar situation (from an Islamicate perspective) of Ottoman students after the sixteenth century. Starting with a series of measures instituted by the famed Ottoman grand mufti Ebū l-Suʿūd Efendī (d. 1574), the character of Ottoman education was transformed in significant ways.[85] One aspect of these reforms that is particularly relevant is that access to higher teaching or judiciary posts came to depend on the obtaining of a certificate *(mülāzemet).* Significantly, relatively few scholars occupying the higher echelons of the judicial and educational apparatus were entitled to grant these, and only at specific times. It is generally recognized in modern scholarship that this led to a "bottleneck" in which the number of certificates granted was small in proportion to the number of students seeking them.

This must have meant that for many students, the person who taught them and the person who granted them a formal certificate were no longer the same.[86] The most coveted *mülāzemet*s were those granted by the highest-ranking authorities in the learned hierarchy, the grand mufti and the military judges of Rumelia and Anatolia, learned scholars, to be sure, but usually no longer directly involved in teaching. Ambitious Ottoman students would usually seek to become part of the entourage of such high-ranking dignitaries, serving as clerks, scribes, or teaching assistants. Obtaining such connections certainly involved a great deal of networking, ingratiation, and sometimes outright bribery, but it is unlikely that assessments of academic abilities were entirely irrelevant in this sharpened competition for certificates.

In fact, it was not unknown in the seventeenth century for the granter of a *mülāzemet* to ask an applicant to take an examination *(imtiḥān).* After having received a *mülāzemet,* a young scholar would start teaching at lower-ranking colleges and usually get promoted to higher-ranking colleges according to a fixed and graded pattern. Before obtaining a teaching position at higher colleges paying more than 40 akçe per day, he would often be examined again. There is scattered evidence for such examinations in the seventeenth century,[87] and after an imperial edict of 1703 they became the rule. One in 1754, for which we have vivid evidence in the form of an extant diary by one of the examinees, was administered at the office of the grand muftī, and only twenty-six of ninety-nine applicants passed.[88] Ottoman social historians have given some attention to these educational reforms and the extent to which they may have made it easier for the higher echelons of the learned hierarchy to consolidate their control and perpetuate "dynasties" of scholarly families.[89] For present purposes, however, what is striking is just how different the resulting educational system was from that which had prevailed in previous centuries, and still prevailed in Islamic regions beyond the central Ottoman lands. The reforms meant that an ambitious student's academic abilities would at crucial stages be evaluated by a scholar who was not his own teacher, sometimes even by means of the "modern" and impersonal institution of the centrally administered examination. In such a situation, the older literature that set forth the proprieties of student-teacher relationships may have appeared less timely and relevant, particularly for more advanced Ottoman students, than literature that focused on how to peruse demanding works and gave advice on what texts to study and in what order.

V

One other noteworthy feature of the treatises of Müneccimbāşī and Sāçaḳlīzāde deserves some consideration: their almost exclusive focus on understanding and evaluating the contents of works. By contrast, the aforementioned works of Zarnūjī and Ibn Jamāʿah offered the budding student advice on how to interact not only with teachers and fellow students but also with manuscripts, as physical objects and scribal artifacts. In the sixteenth-century educational manual of Badr al-Dīn al-Ghazzī, such earlier discussions are expanded into a fairly lengthy treatment of what one might call "philological" tools, a passage that underlies the presentation in Franz Rosenthal's classic *The Technique and Approach of Muslim Scholarship* (1947).[90]

Ghazzī underlines the importance of the collation *(muqābalah)* of one's manuscript with others, especially with an autograph, or a copy that has been collated with the autograph, or at least a copy owned by one's teacher. He then describes in some detail how to proceed with the results. Potentially unclear words should be disambiguated by, for example, vocalizing the word fully and adding the relevant diacritical points, or indicating by means of a number of conventional signs that a letter should be read without diacritical points (for example, adding three points under the Arabic letter *s* to indicate that it should not be read as a *sh*). A potentially problematic word that has been ascertained to be correct should be marked with a small *ṣḥ*. A mistake in the manuscript that seems to be original should be marked with a small *kadhā*. If the scribe/student finds a reading in the manuscript possibly correct but not certainly so, he may indicate this by marking it with *ṣ*. Passages in the main text that are erroneous additions should be marked by, for example, crossing out the passage or drawing a line over it, or adding a small *lā* or *min* over the word that begins the passage that should be deleted and an *ilā* over the last word.

An omission *(saqṭ)* should be indicated in the main text by a vertical line whose top is angled toward the margin where the missing word or passage *(al-laḥaq)* should be supplied, with a clear indication that it is a correction *(ṣḥ),* as opposed to a marginal comment or explication. Ghazzī also introduced some of the more important scribal abbreviations with which the student should be familiar. In the science of Prophetic traditions it was, for example, common to abbreviate the phrase "he related to us" *(ḥaddathanā)* to *nā,* or the title of an authoritative collection such as that of Muslim b. al-Ḥajjāj (d. 875) to *m.* In works on the rational sciences, it was common to abbreviate, for example, "absurd" *(muḥāl)* to *mḥ,* or "in that case" *(ḥīna'idhin)* to *ḥ,* or "the proposition to be proved" *(al-maṭlūb)* to *almṭ.*

It is conspicuous that there is no analogous discussion in the treatises of Müneccimbāşī and Sāçaḳlīzāde. This might appear particularly puzzling given their marked (and novel) emphasis on private reading, as opposed to "hearing" knowledge from a teacher. The reason is, I would suggest, that Müneccimbāşī and Sāçaḳlīzāde were addressing a more advanced type of student—one who was presumed to know how to read manuscripts and to be familiar with the conventional signs and abbreviations used by scribes. There is no reason to believe that Ottoman scholars in their time had ceased to pay attention to manuscript variants or to scribal conventions, and it is difficult to see how—in a manuscript culture—they could have afforded to do so. Rather, it seems that they considered familiarity with such matters to be something a student would acquire in the earlier phases of his education, and that more advanced students would focus on the task of interpreting and discussing the contents of scholarly works, already having a thorough grounding in the auxiliary disciplines of grammar, semantics-rhetoric, logic, and dialectic. Sāçaḳlīzāde did in fact counsel the reader to collate his manuscript copy, but in passing, noting that he might waste time trying to make sense of a corrupt text unless care was taken to make sure that the manuscript copy was free from scribal misreadings and omissions. This, however, was clearly a preliminary step before the student/reader moved on to other, more advanced tasks: "Then," Sāçaḳlīzāde wrote, "he [the student] can proceed with deep reading [al-muṭālaʿah al-ʿamīqah] and exploring subtle aspects [al-istiṭlāʿ ʿalā l-wujūh al-daqīqah] and raising questions and suggesting answers [wa-ithārat al-asʾilah wa l-ajwibah]."[91]

The assumption that attention to manuscript variants belongs to the preliminary stages of scholarship is illustrated by an influential scholarly work by an Ottoman contemporary of Müneccimbāşī and Sāçaḳlīzāde, Ḳara Ḫalīl Tīrevī (d. 1711). Completed in May 1694, it is an extensive set of glosses *(ḥāshiyah)* on a treatise by the Azeri scholar Meḥmed Emīn Ṣadrüddīnzāde (d. 1627) on what makes the numerous inquiries of logic into one discipline.[92] Ḳara Ḫalīl's glosses illustrate the kind of scholarly work that resulted from the reading strategy described and commended by Müneccimbāşī, with its emphasis on attentiveness to grammar, semantics-rhetoric, logic, and dialectic.

Few aspects of the glossed text were considered unworthy of attention, from the semantic and rhetorical aspects of the florid preamble in rhymed prose to intricate metaphysical discussions of "second intentions." Ḳara Ḫalīl also sometimes cast the author's argument into explicit syllogistic form or gave the dialectical structure of a certain extended piece of reasoning. There are also sophisticated discussions of the philosophical contents of the work, and Ḳara Ḫalīl, though in general charitable, not infrequently expressed reservations about or criticism of the author's substantive views. Ḳara Ḫalīl obviously felt it to be his task to cover any issue that might arise in the reading of the work: grammatical, semantic, rhetorical, logical, philosophical, or theological. In this respect, his glosses are typical of the Islamic scholastic genres of commentary *(sharḥ)* and gloss *(ḥāshiyah)* after the fourteenth-century Timurid scholars Taftāzānī and Jurjānī. Indeed, the very consolidation of the genre of the gloss *(ḥāshiyah)* as a standard vehicle for scholarly writing in Islamic civilization seems to date from the fourteenth century.[93]

What makes Ḳara Ḫalīl's work particularly relevant to the present context is that he was aware of significant variations among the manuscripts of the treatise of Ṣadrüddīnzāde. In the introduction to his glosses, he mentions that the "most correct" *(aṣaḥḥ)* manuscript, in terms of both sense and transmission *(dirāyatan wa riwāyatan),* was the one in the possession of the author's grandson Meḥmed Ṣādiḳ b. Feyżullāh b. Meḥmed Emīn Ṣadrüddīnzāde (d. 1708)—himself a prominent Ottoman scholar and judge.[94] What did Ḳara

Ḫalīl mean by "most correct in terms of transmission"? He apparently faced a situation in which numerous and significant variants in available manuscripts resulted from the fact that the author had revised the work. Finding a single autograph would therefore not resolve the problem of adjudicating among these variants.

The manuscript in question apparently stood out not by being an autograph, but by indicating which revisions represented the author's final and considered version. This is clear from the fact that Ḳara Ḫalīl twice argued that a particular passage should be removed from the text on the grounds that it was crossed out in the manuscript "that is relied on" ("al-muʿawwal ʿalayhā").[95] To this extent, his approach seems similar to the "best-text" theory of textual criticism associated in modern times with Joseph Bédier. However, there are important differences. Ḳara Ḫalīl frequently indicated that he preferred—on the grounds of sense or grammar—a reading present in other manuscripts and not in the manuscript "that is relied upon."[96] He also on a number of occasions adjudged a word or phrase to be a result of scribal error, even when it was attested by all available manuscripts.[97]

Most important, Ḳara Ḫalīl's interest in manuscript variants was part of an enterprise whose main aim was not establishing a text but assimilating and critically assessing the content of a work. Knowledge of manuscript variations played an ancillary role, whereas an intimate knowledge of grammar, logic, and philosophy was absolutely central. The emphasis on careful collation of manuscripts and special attention to early or autograph copies, evinced in the earlier works of Ibn Jamāʿah and Ghazzī, had not disappeared. Rather, it had been supplemented with an increasing emphasis on the use of "instrumental sciences" like logic, syntax, semantics, and rhetoric for achieving "deep reading."[98] Though that ideal was not novel—its roots can be traced back to the Timurid age—it appears that it first began to be consciously articulated in educational manuals in the seventeenth- and eighteenth-century Ottoman Empire. As was suggested in the previous section, this development may well have been related to the specific character of the early modern Ottoman educational system.

VI

The philological techniques and aims of European humanists, as well as seventeenth- and eighteenth-century Chinese "evidentiary" scholars, described in this volume were intimately linked to the rejection of the immediate past and the attempted recovery of the texts of an earlier and preferred age.[99] There is little evidence for such a concern among Ottoman scholars of the seventeenth and eighteenth centuries. On the contrary, most were keen on presenting themselves as standing in an unbroken intellectual tradition going back to the fourteenth-century Timurid scholars Taftāzānī and Jurjānī.

It is not difficult to find bibliophiles like the prominent judge and scholar Veliyüddīn Cārullāh (d. 1738)—a student of the aforementioned glossator Ḳara Ḫalīl—who displayed an interest in collecting old and out-of-the-way manuscripts.[100] However, such individual antiquarian interests must be distinguished from a broad and sustained intellectual and cultural movement that discards the immediate past in the name of an older and partly lost intellectual heritage. Failure to heed this distinction leads to what historians of science have aptly called "the virus of the precursor": any interest in old or autograph manuscripts or in manuscript variants is termed "humanist" and seen as continuous in aim and approach with early modern or contemporary European philology.[101] It was in the nineteenth and twentieth centuries that full-fledged movements analogous to European humanism and Chinese evidentiary scholarship appeared in the Middle East, leading to a systematic interest in recovering works that had not been regularly read or studied for centuries.[102]

One such movement was that of modernizing and/or nationalist literary scholars, who held that the belles lettres of the immediate past constituted a period of "decadence" *(inḥiṭāṭ)* or weakening of the "national spirit" and accordingly sought to recover, edit, and study the poets and authors of an earlier age. Another movement was that of self-styled Islamic "reformers" and "revivers," including both those who sought to recover the more "rationalist" heritage of the early Arabic Aristotelian philosophers and the early theologians of the Muʿtazilī school and those who sought to recover an earlier, more purely "Islamic" intellectual tradition unadulterated by mysticism, Greek logic, and Aristotelian metaphysics. These modern movements have been largely successful, and scholars like Müneccimbāşī, Ḳara Ḫalīl, and Sāçaḳlīzāde are now obscure figures—even to specialists in Islamic and Ottoman studies—belonging to an intellectual tradition whose details are little known and whose general features are often disparaged. For this very reason, the fact that their works attest to and are reflective of a novel development within Islamic education and scholarly culture appears to have been entirely overlooked.

It is widely assumed that the "Islamic" model for the transmission of knowledge remained largely personal, informal, and oral-aural until the modern period, and it has recently even been suggested that this might have been one of the reasons for the "failure" of Islamic civilization to develop modern science and modern scientific institutions.[103] The fact of the matter is that, after the sixteenth century, a more formal and text-centered model for the transmission of knowledge emerged in the core areas of the Ottoman Empire, resulting in centralized examinations and certification as well as a marked shift in educational manuals from the proprieties of teacher-student interaction to strategies for "deep reading."

Early Modern or Late Imperial?

The Crisis of Classical Philology in Eighteenth-Century China

BENJAMIN A. ELMAN

MOST HISTORIANS treat late imperial China, 1400–1900, as a time of fading and decay. Viewed backward from the Opium War (1838–1842) and Taiping Rebellion (1850–1864), events before 1800 appear at first to have left China unprepared for modernity. In this essay, however, the seventeenth and eighteenth centuries will be considered not only as a "late imperial" prelude to the end of traditional China but also as an "early modern" harbinger of things to come. Indeed, what we now consider as "early modern" in European terms may have originated in the trading and textual world of East and South Asia.

By undoing the earlier globalized "rise of the West" narrative about the era from 1500 to 1800, we can begin to see things in East Asia regionally as they were dynamically developing from the inside, rather than just passively from the outside and in hindsight. That is, by shedding new light on the global "beginnings" of the early modern period it is possible to shift perspective regarding the history of East Asia as a region and global history and world philology as a whole. Rather than the "me toos" of the early modern world, China, Japan, and India were by 1600 among its essential motors and the engines that made Europeans rethink their own political, economic, social, and cultural values.[1] The ideological rationalization of wealth occurred first during the "silver age" in Ming China (1368–1644), for instance, which included the long-term transformation of the god of wealth from a malevolent devil wreaking havoc among the people to a Weber-like charitable deity who would answer the prayers of educated commoners for economic prosperity.[2]

The philological discourses of Chinese classical scholars during the eighteenth century reinforced a shift from Song-Ming rationalism (see Michael Lackner's earlier essay in this volume) to a more skeptical and secular classical empiricism, what I have elsewhere called an "epistemological revolution." By making precise scholarship rather than pure reason the source of acceptable knowledge, Qing classicists, unlike their Song predecessors described by Lackner, contended that the legitimate reach of ancient ideals should be reevaluated impartially through comparative delineation of the textual sources from which all such knowledge derived. This turn to empirically based classical inquiry meant that abstract ideas, metaphysical diagrams, and rational argumentation gave way as the primary objects of elite discussion to concrete facts, verifiable institutions, ancient natural studies, and historical events.[3]

In general, Qing classicists regarded Song and Ming "Learning of the Way" as an obstacle to verifiable truth because it discouraged further inquiry along empirical lines. The empirical approach to knowledge they advocated placed proof and verification at the heart of analysis of the classical tradition. During this time, scholars and critics also applied historical analysis to the official Classics. Classical commentary, although not yet historicist, yielded to textual criticism and a "search for evidence" to refortify the ancient canon. In intellectual terms, China's evidential scholars and their epistemological revolution represented the last great imperial movement in Confucian letters before 1900.[4]

Classical Studies in Imperial China

After the formation of imperially sanctioned New Text classicism *(jinwen jingxue)* during the Former Han dynasty (202 B.C.E.–8 C.E.) and admixtures of Old Text philology *(guwen jingxue)* during the Later Han (25–220), political, social, and cultural discourses in succeeding dynasties usually were expressed by elites through the archaic language of the Classics or Dynastic Histories. Idealistic scholar-statesmen, cynical political opportunists, and even autocratic rulers were forced to articulate their political views through the controlled medium of dynastic ritual, classical sanctions, and historical precedents such as the *Rituals of Zhou.*

The millennial connection between the Five Classics *(Change, Documents, Poetry, Rituals,* and *Annals)* of antiquity and premodern Chinese political discourse, whether reactionary, moderate, or radical, suggests the power these texts had in channeling political behavior and expression in imperial China. Because the cultural legitimacy of the imperium in China was articulated through classical political discourse, political reformism and classical iconoclasm often went hand in hand. The New Text versus Old Text forms of writing the Classics in ancient times, for example, became embroiled in classical-*cum*-political debates in which philology, especially paleography *(wenzi xue),* was necessary both to legitimate imperial policy classically and to gainsay it by charging that certain classical texts were forgeries.

A set of abstruse texts written in ancient forms of classical Chinese, the Five Classics preserved the orthodox teachings, natural philosophy, and political institutions of the sage-kings. Generation after generation, century after century, the Classics and histories were the core curriculum for all those who would participate actively in the political arena. Replaced in relative importance by the more readable Four Books *(Analects, Mencius, Great Learning, Doctrine of the Mean)* after the Song dynasties (960–1279), the Classics nonetheless remained keys to advancement, fame, and power in the political arena of late imperial China. The past had to be studied and cherished if the ideals of the sage-kings were to be realized. Students gained a rich fund of human experience from the Classics: descriptions of mistakes that should be avoided and successes that should be emulated. The Classics contained paradigms for social order and had an absolute claim to transhistorical truth.

Manipulation of the machinery established for political control was justified through the classical ideals on which the imperial dynasty was based. Classical erudition provided officials, scholars, and students with a set of general assumptions about good and evil in government and society. The raison d'être of public institutions and explanations of natural phenomena were enshrined in the Classics. The civil examinations instituted in medieval times tested knowledge of this content for millions of people. Accordingly, the centrality of classical studies for political discourse in imperial China was a prerequisite for the important role of philological studies in literati learning.

Because of the diversity of Chinese ancient scripts, paleography in imperial China was a key philological tool to unravel the Classics, which predated by centuries anything comparable in medieval or Renaissance Europe. For example, the paleographical dictionary *Analysis of Characters as an Explanation of Writing (Shuowen jiezi),* compiled by Xu Shen (58–147) during the Later Han dynasty (25–220), contained 9,373 different characters arranged according to 530 radicals *(bushou),* a framework that despite modification remained the basic organization in most premodern classical dictionaries.[5] Dom Bernard de Montfaucon's (1655–1741) pioneering *Paleographica graeca,* published in 1708, which looked closely at the writing in Greek manuscripts and invented the word "paleography," was the first work in Europe to understand that the history of writing was an important key to classifying manuscripts systematically. Later Scipione Maffei (1675–1755) realized that the diversity of Latin scripts in the early Middle Ages was due to the existence in antiquity of certain basic written types, variations of which were continued independently in Europe after the breakup of the Roman Empire. Classical scholars in imperial China had been debating such textual issues since the first century C.E.[6]

To control the interpretation of the Classics in imperial China was to control the articulation and justification of dynastic power. Literati scholars and officials were indispensable partners of the imperial court. Setting a precedent that lasted from 1313 until 1905, Mongol rulers during the Yuan dynasty (1280–1368) were prevailed on by their literati advisors to install the interpretations of the great Song philosophers Cheng Yi (1033–1107) and Zhu Xi (1130–1200) as the orthodox "Cheng-Zhu" guidelines for the civil examination system. Ming and Qing (1644–1911) emperors followed suit, similarly persuaded that the Cheng-Zhu school of Daoxue (Learning of the Way, i.e., "Neo-Confucianism") provided the most acceptable justification for their rule. In effect, the Cheng-Zhu persuasion had captured the "voice of imperial politics" since the early Ming state.[7]

Song Confucians had been concerned with building symbolic structures of meaning in which all human experience would be related. This approach was perfectly respectable and gave relatively little importance to philology. Learning of the Way symbols of correspondence and political allegories, like their Han dynasty predecessors, did not require, and thus did not encourage, the development of critical thought. The charts *(tu)* of such symbolic correspondences, called "cosmograms," had to be questioned before the historical foundations of the Cheng-Zhu orthodoxy could be reevaluated.

The Cheng-Zhu moral persuasion was increasingly challenged, however, beginning in the sixteenth century. Criticism accelerated during the seventeenth and eighteenth centuries. A tug-of-war developed among scholars and officials over how the Classics and Four Books should properly be evaluated. The locus for the legitimation of political power remained the Classics, but the textual provenance of parts of the canon was called into question. The Classics were still inviolate, but they were read and interpreted with new eyes and with new strategies. In part due to the Jesuit impact, literati in the seventeenth century began to reevaluate the classical canon in light of both natural philosophy and astronomy.

The Intellectual and Social Context in Eighteenth-Century China

During the seventeenth century a unified academic field of empirically based classical knowledge emerged among Qing literati scholars in the Yangzi delta provinces of Jiangsu, Zhejiang, and Anhui and eventually informed the orthodox curriculum authorized in Beijing. This philological grid for classical learning represented a fundamental shift in the common codes of elite knowledge about the past. The textual vocabulary of classical scholars during the eighteenth century in turn reinforced a shift from Song-Ming rationalism, typified by the moral philosophy of Zhu Xi, to a more skeptical and secular classical empiricism. The empirical approach to knowledge advocated by Qing classicists, "to search truth from facts" *(shishi qiushi),* placed proof and verification at the heart of organization and analysis of the classical tradition. During this time, scholars and critics also began to apply historical analysis to the official Classics. Classical commentary by now had yielded to textual criticism and evidential learning (*kaozheng,* lit. "search for evidence") to refortify the ancient canon.[8]

A scholarly position stressing that valid knowledge should be corroborated by external facts and impartial observations in turn added impetus to the study of what eighteenth-century literati called the "natural world" *(ziran xue).* A full-blown scientific revolution, as in Europe, did not ensue,[9] but evidential scholars made astronomy, mathematics, medicine, and geography high priorities in their research programs. Animated by a concern to restore native traditions in the precise sciences to their proper place of eminence after less overt attention during the Ming dynasty until the coming of the Jesuits in the sixteenth century,[10] evidential scholars such as Dai Zhen (1723–77), Qian Daxin (1728–1804), and Ruan Yuan (1764–1849) successfully incorporated technical aspects of Western astronomy and mathematics into the literati framework for classical learning. Qian, in particular, acknowledged this broadening of literati traditions, which he thought reversed centuries of focus on moral and philosophic problems: "in ancient times, no one could be a literatus [*Ru*] who did not know mathematics. Chinese methods [now] lag behind Europe's because *Ru* do not know mathematics."[11]

Qing scholars were also determined to pierce the thick veil of Song and Ming metaphysical and cosmological systems of thought known popularly as "Learning of the Way." During the early Qing, when Cheng-Zhu learning revived, scholars such as Yan Ruoju (1636–1704) dramatically demonstrated that the Old Text chapters of the *Documents Classic* were a later forgery. Although Yan's discovery was passed around only in manuscript form until 1745, it helped to gainsay certain Learning of the Way doctrines concerning the "human mind and the mind of the Way" that had been based on one of the Old Text chapters.[12] Without great fanfare, Hu Wei (1633–1714), Yan's colleague, exposed the heterodox origins of Song cosmograms known as the "Luo River Inscription" *(Luoshu)* and the "He [Yellow River] Map" *(Hetu)*. Their findings later were corroborated in the mid-eighteenth century by the Suzhou scholar Hui Dong (1697–1758), whose followers revived ancient "Han Learning" (Hanxue) and criticized Cheng-Zhu Song Learning more forcefully than Yan Roju or Hu Wei.

Language became an object of investigation in the Qianlong (1736–1795) and Jiaqing (1796–1820) reigns. Dai Zhen, from Anhui, described such investigation as follows: "the Classics provide the route to the Way. What illuminates the Way are the words [of the Classics]. How words are formed can be grasped only through [a knowledge of] philology and paleography. From [the study of] primary and derived characters we can master the language. Through language, we can penetrate the mind and will of the ancient sages and worthies." The distinguished classicist and historian Wang Mingsheng (1722–1798) echoed Dai's words: "The Classics are used to understand the Way. But those who seek the Way should not cling vacuously to meanings and principles in order to find it. If only they correct primary and derived characters, discern their pronunciation, read the explanations and glosses, and master the commentaries and notes, the meanings and principles will appear on their own, and the Way within them."[13]

The philologists' research program was taken literally by thousands of literati trained in evidential methods during the eighteenth and nineteenth centuries. They hoped to recapture the pristine meaning formulated by the sage-kings of antiquity in the ancient Classics. Thus the Qing classicists in effect called into question the dominant classical tradition, which Manchu rulers had enshrined as the norm in imperial examinations and official ideology.

Toward the end of the eighteenth century, the prestige of the Classics, though politically unchanged, had diminished vis-à-vis historical studies.[14] Using the phrase "the Six Classics are all Histories," Zhang Xuecheng (1738–1801) placed the timeless Classics within the framework of the endless flux of history, but even in the eighteenth century his appraisal was not unique. Philosophical concepts were not immune to empirical analysis. Though most evidential scholars preferred an empirical program for research, a few, led by Dai Zhen, saw in linguistic analysis, historical phonology, and glossing of terms a new and more precise textual approach to traditional philosophical questions. As a result of Dai's influence, important classical concepts and ideals were subjected to philological study. A methodology that had proven fruitful in textual criticism, it was hoped, would prove equally productive in moral philosophy.[15]

The Rise of "Han Learning"

Changes in Qing classical traditions closely followed changes in the political, social, and economic circumstances to which they referred. The classical ordering of reality, like all traditions, was subject to the inherent tensions between reality and the literati's conceptions of it, including perennial moral and political issues that called for a variety of responses. These responses, while governed by the politics of the imperial dynasty, were not static. Classical concepts, interpretations, verbalizations, and the actions based on them changed over time. The same terms drawn from the Classics could mean different things to literati faced with different problems. For the followers of Learning of the Way, the orthodox repossession of the Way *(daotong)* represented the transmission of the mind of the sages. Increasingly for Qing scholars, however, it represented a Song literati version of sagehood, which drew its inspiration from the individual transmission of Buddhist enlightenment by Chan monks "from mind to mind."[16]

Philological studies evolved during the eighteenth and nineteenth centuries because technical works were published and became part of a dynamic classical research enterprise. Scholarly goals were not "scientific" or "objective" per se; instead, classicists now advocated an impartial program that would resume the interrupted conversation with antiquity. Moving back in time, Qing literati first sought out Tang and then Later Han dynasty sources to overcome limitations they found in Song and Ming dynasty commentaries. Because Later Han dynasty classical sources and commentaries were relatively unaffected by Daoist and Buddhist notions that had influenced Tang, Song, and Ming literati, Han dynasty literati increasingly received respect and attention from purists during the seventeenth and eighteenth centuries.

The debate between those who favored Later Han dynasty classical scholarship, "Han Learning," and those who favored the Cheng-Zhu school, the "Song Learning" (Songxue) of Cheng Yi and Zhu Xi, represented more than an antiquarian quest. Han Learning advocates cast doubt on the orthodoxy that Manchu rulers had enshrined in their official legitimation of imperial power. Reconstruction of Han Learning during the eighteenth century brought with it the discovery that Later Han dynasty classicism, when the Old Text school (see below) became the most influential intellectual force, was very different from that of the Former Han, when the New Text tradition had been in vogue.

Strictly speaking, Han Learning denoted a school of scholarship that came into fashion in Suzhou with Hui Dong in the mid-eighteenth century. Because Hui and his sizable Yangzi delta following actively opposed Song Learning, they turned instead to reconstruction and study of Later Han classical commentaries, especially those of Zheng Xuan (127–200), who had successfully synthesized earlier New and Old Text doctrines. Because such interpretations were closer to the time the Classics were compiled, they were thought more likely to reveal authentic meanings.

The Poetry Revival and Classicism in the Eighteenth Century

Along with the rise of Han Learning, the late Qianlong era also witnessed the revival of the Five Classics and Tang poetry among literati. This represented one of the great reversals away from the Learning of the Way classical regime stressing the moral philosophy of the Four Books and the eight-legged essay. Revival of ancient learning, particularly pre-Song forms of literati writing and scholia, brought an increased awareness among Qing literati of the role of poetry and belles lettres in Tang and Song civil examinations and intellectual life. The epochal shift toward the examination essay, which began in the Song, had continued in the Yuan and climaxed in the early Ming, when poetry was finally eliminated from civil examinations, had run its course in the mid-eighteenth century. Despite some misgivings, the Qianlong emperor called in the 1750s for the increased use of poetry in the examinations, and in 1760 he commanded that rhymed poetry should become part of the dynastic school curriculum and tested monthly.[17]

Slowly but surely, the Qing court rolled back key elements in the Yuan-Ming examination curriculum.[18] First the discourse, documentary, and legal judgments questions were challenged by reform-minded officials. Then poetry was reconsidered as a proper measure of literati talent for officialdom. Many Qing traditionalists who favored Cheng-Zhu orthodoxy over Han Learning, such as Zhang Xuecheng, looked back to the 1756–1757 reforms favoring poetry as the beginning of a forty-year process that turned the civil examinations into a trendy contest of literary taste where the most recent fads in classical prose and poetry held sway. The earlier stress on "solid learning" *(shixue)* in the civil examinations, according to Zhang, had been displaced.[19]

Poetry had been the key to the Tang selection process for palace graduates *(jinshi),* which privileged it as a genre among literati. After the Tang, both ancient-style poetry *(gushi)* and regulated verse *(lüshi)* lost their high positions in civil examinations and somewhat in literati life, although poetry remained a pervasive genre in cultural life. For Qing literati, however, it was precisely its comedown in the Yuan-Ming age of Cheng-Zhu Learning of the Way that, in Pauline Yu's words, guaranteed its "aesthetic incorruptibility" from an era that was closer to antiquity and unaffected by the Buddhist infiltration of literati thought in Song times.[20]

In 1756, regulated verse in five words (=syllables, i.e., "pentasyllabic") and eight rhymes *(wuyan bayun)* was formally reintroduced as a required literary form; this took effect in the 1757 metropolitan examination and was then extended to the 1759 provincial examinations.[21] Initially the poetry question was added to the second session of examinations, fittingly replacing the documentary and legal judgments questions that had four centuries earlier replaced poetry during the high tide of Learning of the Way. In 1758 the requirement that literati be examined in regulated verse was extended to local qualifying examinations, and then to the renewal and licensing examinations in 1760.

To facilitate the transition to the new emphasis on form and the rules of prosody, books of rhymes were increasingly printed and distributed. Young boys (and girls) learned how to balance five- or seven-word lines in regulated verse by referring to several poetry primers, which consisted of lessons for matching characters and phrases of varying lengths. Such developments were a clear marker of revival of interest in Tang-Song poetry as a

Table 10.1 Reformed Format of Provincial and Metropolitan Civil Service Examinations during the Mid-Qing, 1757–1787

Session no.	No. of questions
One	
1. Four Books	3 quotations
2. Discourse	1 quotation
Two	
1. Change	4 quotations
2. Documents	4 quotations
3. Poetry	4 quotations
4. Annals	4 quotations
5. Rites	4 quotations
6. Poetry question	1 poetic model
Three	
1. Policy questions	5 essays

testable measure of cultural attainment. Within ten years, publication and republication of Tang and Song poetry anthologies increased. Other anthologies of "poetry discussions" *(shihua)* from the Ming were reprinted, and Qing scholars compiled several new ones.[22] The early anthology *Poems by a Thousand Authors (Qianjia shi)* became one of the key collections students and candidates used to learn regulated verse.[23]

Subsequently, examination reformers began to square off between those who favored upgrading the new poetry question, which had vanquished the documentary and legal judgments questions in session 2, and those who favored continuing the emphasis on the discourse question, which had been moved to session 1 after 1756. In this struggle, the discourse question became a Song Learning cause. Han Learning scholars favored highlighting Tang regulated verse because of its pre-Song ties to ancient learning, and they sought first to diminish and ultimately to eliminate the discourse question entirely.

Fueling the popularity of the revival of poetry in the examinations was the close tie between the rules for rhyming in regulated verse and the field of phonology, which became the queen of philology *(xiaoxue)* in evidential research during the eighteenth century. Qing dynasty evidential scholars framed a systematic research agenda that built on paleography and phonology to reconstruct the meaning of Chinese words. One by-product of these philological trends was the full realization of how important poetry, particularly regulated verse, was for the reconstruction of antiquity via phonology, paleography, and etymology.[24]

Abrogating Classical Specializations on Examinations

Despite the addition of a poetry question after 1756, Qing classical scholars remained unhappy that examination candidates still mastered mainly the *Poetry* and *Change* Classics, leaving the others, particularly the *Annals* and *Rituals,* unstudied. In 1765, for example, the Manchu governor-general in Sichuan described in a memorial the distribution of specialization for the sixty candidates on the Classics in the Sichuan provincial examination: fourteen (23 percent) specialized in the *Change;* thirteen (22 percent) in the *Documents;* twenty-one (35 percent) in the *Poetry;* nine (15 percent) in the *Rites* and *Annals;* three (5 percent) on the Five Classics as a whole. The memorial and attached materials indicated that the problem of encouraging students to specialize in the less popular Classics remained, despite the 1756 reforms, which had moved the Five Classics to session 2.[25]

The final step in changing the specialization requirement began in 1792, after the last of the Five Classics, the *Annals,* had been tested on a revolving basis between 1787 and 1792. This dramatic increase in classical requirements paralleled the increase in competition on Qing examinations. China's demographic realities, to which the reform of examination requirements was in part addressed, meant that as the civil examinations became more difficult, the odds against passing them because of the increasing number of competing candidates became prohibitive. Not until after the Taiping Rebellion (1850–1864) did the court consider increasing civil quotas. The late Qing curriculum is outlined below.[26]

Beginning in 1793, for both the provincial and metropolitan examinations, examiners chose a single quotation from each of the Five Classics, which all candidates had to analyze and answer in the second session. The authorities accepted the Han Learning slant of the new stress on the Five Classics and documented how Later Han scholars had mastered all the Classics and not simply specialized in one. By 1787, sentiments favoring Song Learning in civil examinations were often controverted.[27]

Han Learning advocates were still not completely satisfied. Qian Daxin recommended in his private writings that the Four Books—not the Five Classics—should be moved back to session 2, giving the Five Classics priority in session 1. After four centuries of use, Qian contended, there were essays on every possible quotation in the Four Books an examiner might choose.[28] Consequently, candidates could read such essays, which were widely circulated by printers, and avoid reading the Four Books themselves.

Table 10.2 Reformed Format of Provincial and Metropolitan Civil Service Examinations during the Late Qing, 1793–1898

Session no.	No. of questions
One	
1. Four Books	3 quotations
2. Poetry question	1 poetic model
Two	
1. Change	1 quotation
2. Documents	1 quotation
3. Poetry	1 quotation
4. Annals	1 quotation
5. Rites	1 quotation
Three	
1. Policy questions	5 essays

The Five Classics were too extensive and difficult for the same thing to happen to them, Qian maintained. Similarly, in a memorial to the emperor, Sun Xingyan (1753–1818) called for reinstating Han classical commentaries and Tang subcommentaries to the Qing examination curriculum to supplement the Song commentaries included in the early Ming trilogy of orthodox scholia. Neither request was acted on.[29]

In one area, the Han Learning group in Beijing was able to shape the examination curriculum with surprising ease. In 1792, Ji Yun (1724–1805), then a minister of rites, requested deleting Hu Anguo's (1074–1138) Song Learning commentary on the *Spring and Autumn Annals* from the examination curriculum. This commentary had enunciated Learning of the Way themes that Han Learning scholars such as Ji thought were anachronistic. He contended that Hu Anguo had used the *Annals* as a foil to express his own opinions about the fall of the Northern Song and the move of the dynastic court to the south. Hu also attacked the barbarians in his commentary, which focused on the Jin Jurchen precursors of the current Manchus. His commentary thus was very much out of touch with contemporary concerns of the Qing dynasty. The Qianlong emperor rejected all such interpretations of the *Annals* because of their possibly deleterious effects on Manchu-Chinese relations. For his part, Ji preferred the three Han commentaries to the *Annals* that had duly informed the Kangxi era *Qinding chunqiu zhuanshuo huizuan* (Imperially prescribed commentaries and explications of the *Annals*) and had on many points refuted the Hu version. The Qianlong emperor responded by immediately ordering that beginning in 1793 the Hu commentary would no longer be used in the civil examinations.[30]

Ji Yun's victory was incomplete, however. The Han Learning challenge to the Four Books had been successful in authorizing the Five Classics for all candidates, but the Four Books monopoly on the highest ranks in the local, provincial, and metropolitan civil examinations was maintained. Indeed, the examiners' tendency to grade each of the candidate's five essays on the Classics uniformly undermined the essays' significance individually in the rankings. Nevertheless, the court's penchant for compromise had enabled the Qianlong reforms to take hold successfully within the bureaucracy and mollify its Song versus Han Learning advocates.

New Text versus Old Text Classical Scholarship

The philological and philosophical rebellions spawned by evidential studies as an impartial "search for evidence" also set the stage for the social and political conclusions that New Text scholars drew from their research and scholarship. Because most New Text sources were from the Former Han dynasty, and therefore were unaffected by Daoist and Buddhist accretions in Later Han and post-Han writings, the New Text version of Confucius's role vis-á-vis the Classics slowly received new respect and attention. New Text classicism did not arise in the Qing period as a rationalization for Westernization, but as respectable Han Learning scholarship in mainstream centers of learning, before being linked to problems of reform in the nineteenth century. Moreover, New Text scholars promoted traditional types of Confucian reform before they initiated a radical call for Westernization.

By 1800, more radical philologists hoped to establish as normative their new and iconoclastic views of the Classics. The stakes were high, and in the course of these intellectual changes, the content and form of political discourse legitimating state power in late imperial China also evolved in new directions. Rediscovery of the Old Text versus New Text debate in the late eighteenth century led some Qing scholars to a new perspective on the classical tradition. Scholars from the Zhuang and Liu lineages in Changzhou prefecture were the first Qing literati to stress the New Text tradition of the Former Han. Deep and irreconcilable differences among competing orthodoxies had emerged in the Han Learning agenda for classical studies. By returning to what they considered a purer form of Han Learning, New Text scholars in Changzhou touched off, from within its ranks, the breakup of Han Learning itself. New Text scholars began to argue that much of what had once been considered orthodox by Song and Ming Cheng-Zhu followers and even early Qing evidential scholars was in fact based on Old Text sources allegedly fabricated by imperially sponsored scholars during the reign of the so-called Han usurper Wang Mang (r. 9–23). New Text iconoclasm peaked in the late nineteenth century with Kang Youwei (1858–1927; see below), but the Han Learning philology on which such views were based is no longer normative.

The Zhuang and Liu lineages' early nineteenth-century association with new trends in Han Learning also documents how scholarly groups, family, and lineage played important roles in the evolution of evidential research in the eighteenth century. The complex machinery of lineages was clearly at work among the Zhuang and Liu families in the construction of a literati "school of learning" such as the New Text group. New Text advocates turned to the *Gongyang Commentary (Gongyang zhuan)* for Confucius's *Spring and Autumn Annals,* one of the Five Classics, because it was the only New Text commentary on the Classics that had survived intact from the Former Han dynasty. Recorded in "contemporary-style script," hence called "New Text" (*jinwen;* i.e., the forms of ancient "small seal" calligraphy that evolved into "clerical" and then "regular script"), the *Gongyang Commentary* provided textual support for the Former Han New Text school's portrayal of Confucius as a visionary of institutional change, an "uncrowned king."[31]

Among the texts in the Former Han dynasty archives, however, was another commentary on the *Spring and Autumn Annals,* which later became known as the *Zuo Commentary (Zuozhuan).* It provided textual support for the Later Han Old Text (*guwen,* lit. "ancient-style script," i.e., more ancient "large seal" forms of calligraphy) school's portrayal of Confucius as a respected teacher and transmitter of classical learning rather than the charismatic visionary New Text scholars had earlier painted. After the demise of the Later Han dynasty in 220 C.E., however, the classical canon was not reconstituted officially until the seventh century under the Tang. Thereafter, the *Zuo Commentary* remained the orthodox commentary to the *Annals* until the middle of the eighteenth century, when Changzhou Han Learning scholars called it into question.

Classical texts and their interpretation had been the basis for political loyalties in a "schools system" *(jiafa)* for Han classical studies. When they reopened the New Text versus Old Text controversy, eighteenth-century Changzhou scholars reconstructed the fortunes of an academic and, by implication, a political movement that had been replaced. Han Learning and New Text studies played an important role in the steady drift of gentry-officials toward new forms of political discourse to replace what they considered outmoded Song political values, which since the Yuan-Ming transition had legitimated authoritarian government.

Standing for new forms of belief in a time of political, social, and economic turmoil, New Text studies and Han Learning championed pragmatism and the imperative of change. Recasting the literati tradition in Changzhou also marked an initial step toward emancipation from the encumbrance of accumulated imperial norms and ideals handed down since the Later Han dynasty. Like their late Ming predecessors, evidential research scholars opposed the Cheng-Zhu "voice" of the state. Like their Song and Ming predecessors, evidential scholars drew on ancient sources to express their political aspirations, a long-standing classical tendency that would climax in the 1898 reform movement.[32]

In the late nineteenth century, first Liao Ping (1852–1932) and then Kang Youwei drew on the New Text scholarship of the Changzhou school and its various followers. A Cantonese scholar, Kang developed his ingenious and politically perilous interpretation of Confucius in his influential *Study of Confucius as Institutional Reformer (Kongzi gaizhi kao),* which was published in 1897 but banned for political reasons in 1898 and again in 1900. Confucius, according to Kang, was a visionary of institutional change and had enunciated a concept of progress that Old Text scholars had covered up by allegedly forging several of the Classics that had been rediscovered during the Han. This provocative reinterpretation invested Kang's ideal of "institutional reform" *(gaizhi)* with all the modern trappings of institutional reform. Kang's alternative expressions of legitimate classical learning challenged the Cheng-Zhu orthodoxy.

Qing Philology and Natural Studies

The impact of evidential research was also felt in the increased attention *kaozheng* scholars gave to mathematics and astronomy as introduced by the Jesuits in the seventeenth century. In addition, for Ming-Qing literati-physicians, textual mastery of the medical classics was more than an auxiliary tool. Classical learning was required to recover medical principles and practice from ancient writings and their commentaries. The formation of evidential scholarship and the return to antiquity *(fugu)* in medicine thus reinforced each other. Reemphasis on ancient texts such as the *Treatise on Cold Damage Disorders (Shanghan lun)* in the seventeenth and eighteenth centuries stimulated the reexamination of pre-Song therapies for cold and heat factor illnesses. Instead of using warming medicines, physicians increasingly prescribed cooling drugs and methods for infectious illnesses. The diseases of the south, with its richer variety of climates, infections, and infestations, led to new medical frameworks in Jin, Yuan, and Ming China, which challenged confidence in standard approaches to acute fevers derived from the canonical cold damage therapies.

Qing debates between antiquarians and modernists concerning early medicine paralleled those between Han Learning and Song Learning classical scholars. Evidential scholars of the Five Classics, for example, focused on the distant past to overcome the failures of the recent Cheng-Zhu tradition. The rhetoric entered the discussion of medical texts. Like Han Learning scholars, for example, Qing scholar-physicians began their studies with Han dynasty medical texts such as the *Treatise on Cold Damage Disorders* and the earliest classical interpretations, because the latter were closer in time to the composition of the Classics and thereby more likely to reveal their authentic meaning. They rejected Song dynasty sources, on which Song Learning scholar-physicians had relied, because of their questionable authority and great separation from antiquity.

In contrast, Qing mathematical and astronomical interest grew directly out of the Jesuit studies and the mid-Qing findings of Mei Wending (1633–1721) and others. Mei had contended that the study of physical nature gave scholars access to the "principles" *(li)* undergirding nature. In essence, Mei saw Jesuit learning as a way to enhance the mathematizing of the Learning of the Way notion of moral and metaphysical principles.[33] However, he continued to believe in the native Chinese origins of Western natural studies, which made it imperative, Mei and his highly placed patrons in the early Qing court thought, to rehabilitate native traditions in the mathematical sciences to their former glory. Under imperial patronage during the Kangxi reign, mathematical studies, including mathematical harmonics, were upgraded from an insignificant skill to an important domain of knowledge for literati that complemented classical studies.[34]

During the Kangxi revival of interest in mathematics, Mei Wending's grandson Mei Juecheng (d. 1763) and others could not find many of the works originally included in the medieval *Ten Computational Classics (Shibu suanjing).* Moreover, in addition to Li Ye's (1192–1279) *Sea Mirror of Circular Measurement* (*Ceyuan haijing,* 1248), the seminal works of Qin Jiushao (1202–61) and Zhu Shijie (fl. c. 1270–1330) on polynomial algebra and other important topics were not widely available and perhaps lost during the Manchu conquest of the Ming.

After 1750, a large-scale effort to recover and collate the treasures of ancient Chinese mathematics became an important part of the late eighteenth- and early nineteenth-century upsurge in evidential studies. Many mathematical texts were collated under imperial auspices during the last years of the Kangxi reign, when the encyclopedia *Synthesis of Books and Illustrations Past and Present* was also completed. When published in 1726, it included some European texts from the late Ming and early Qing *Mathematical Astronomy of the Chongzhen Reign.* Five works on Chinese mathematics were also included in the astronomy section:

1. *The Gnomon of the Zhou Dynasty and Classic of Computations (Zhoubi suanjing)*
2. *Notes on the Mathematical Heritage (Shushu jiyi)*
3. *Mathematical Manual of Xie Chawei (Xie Chawei suanjing)*

4. The mathematics part of the *Brush Talks from the Dream Book (Mengxi bitan)*
5. *Systematic Treatise on Computational Methods (Suanfa tongzong)*

When the first set of the Qianlong Imperial Library collection was completed between 1773 and 1781, its compilers included several collators well versed in classical mathematics, such as Dai Zhen, Kong Jihan (1739–84), and others. The Astronomy and Mathematics *(Tianwen suanfa)* category incorporated fifty-eight works into the collection (see below). Several older, lost mathematical texts were recopied from the early Ming *Great Compendium of the Yongle Reign (Yongle dadian),* which had survived in the imperial court relatively intact. The general catalog of the Qianlong Imperial Library, for example, included twenty-five notices on mathematics. Of these, nine were on Tang classics, three were for Song-Yuan works, four were on works from the Ming period, including the Matteo Ricci (1552–1610) and Xu Guangqi (1562–1633) translation of Euclid's *Elements of Geometry (Jihe yuanben),* and nine were on works from the Qing, most importantly the *Collected Basic Principles of Mathematics (Shuli jingyun)* and several works by Mei Wending.

The role of Korea and Japan in preserving lost Chinese works is not generally well known. Worthy of special mention, however, is Ruan Yuan's recovery of the lost *Primer of Mathematics (Suanxue qimeng)* by Zhu Shijie from a 1660 Korean edition that had been reprinted as a textbook in 1433. When transmitted to Japan, the *Primer* and its single unknown (*tianyuan shu; tengenjutsu* in Japanese) algebraic notations also played a significant role in the seventeenth century.[35]

Overall, Ruan Yuan's compilation of the *Biographies of Astronomers and Mathematicians (Chouren zhuan),* completed while he served as governor of Zhejiang province in Hangzhou, reprinted in 1849 and later enlarged, marked the crucial period in the celebration of natural studies by Yangzi delta literati in the eighteenth century. Containing biographies and summaries of the works of 280 mathematical astronomers, including thirty-seven Europeans, this work was followed by four supplements in the nineteenth century. The mathematical sciences had begun to grow in importance among literati beyond the reach of the imperial court in the late eighteenth century. Because Ruan Yuan was a well-placed literati patron of natural studies in the provincial and court bureaucracy, especially at the Imperial College *(Guozi jian),* his influential *Biographies* represented the integration of the mathematical sciences with evidential studies. Mathematical study was no longer independent of classical studies.[36] Literati scholars had incorporated mathematical study into evidential research and made natural studies a part of classical studies.

Philology and natural studies were wedded when Mei Wending and Mei Juecheng evaluated early modern European findings in astronomy and searched through the classical canon for evidence that this new information was likely based on ancient Chinese knowledge that had been transmitted to the Western regions in antiquity. Mei Juecheng contended, for instance, that the Song-Yuan "single unknown" (*tianyuan,* lit. "heavenly origins") method for representing algebraic equations was the equivalent of the algebraic formulas *(jiegen fang)* later introduced by the Jesuits. This "Chinese origins" argument legitimated renewed Qing literati interest in the sciences, and philology became one of the key tools that later evidential research scholars employed.[37]

The mathematics associated with evidential research in the eighteenth century had been algorithmic, that is, focusing on getting the right results, and thus less concerned to justify methods and formulas. Wang Lai (1768–1813) and Jiao Xun (1763–1820), for example, each tried to build on traditional Chinese algebraic equations *(tianyuan shu)* rather than just automatically accepting the Indic-Arabic forms of algebra *(daishu)* that the Jesuits and later the Protestants taught when they came to China. Wang in particular derived more than one positive root for a *tianyuan* equation, which contributed something new to the traditional focus on a single, positive solution for any algebraic equation by following Western views of positive and negative roots.[38]

Wang Lai, who was appointed to the dynastic observatory in Beijing, employed Western methods accepted in the calendrical office since the Kangxi reign in his calculations of *tianyuan.* As a result of his professional ties to the Jesuit "new studies" harbored in the observatory, Wang was criticized by more conservative evidential scholars interested in traditional mathematics for going too far in his emulation of Western methods. Because he was a literatus outside the court and thus part of the Yangzi delta academic community, Li Rui (1765–1814), who devised a theory of "single unknown" equations strictly in terms of Song mathematics, received more support from literati, many of whom still revered Yang Guangxian (1597–1669) for his prosecutions of the Jesuits in the Kangxi court in the 1660s. Before 1850, then, classical learning still took precedence over Western learning, and the antiquarian interests of evidential scholars stimulated them to study the textual history of native mathematics rather than build on the findings of Western mathematics, as Wang Lai had.[39]

This "Chinese origins" argument legitimated renewed Qing literati interest in the sciences, and philology became one of the key tools later evidential research scholars such as Xu Shou (1818–1882) and Li Shanlan (1810–1882) employed in the nineteenth century to build conceptual bridges between Western learning and the traditional Chinese sciences. In the process, modern Western science was initially introduced in the nineteenth century as compatible with native classical learning.

The legacy of Qing evidential research in the nineteenth century was important but not unique. Certainly Han Learning and New Text studies played an important role in the steady drift of scholar-officials toward new forms of political discourse to replace outmoded imperial political values, which since the Ming dynasty had legitimated authoritarian government. Social and economic pressures, coupled with population growth, placed demands on Qing China that rulers and officials had never before faced. By 1800, over three hundred million people lived in China. Ancient ideals drawn from feudal times were already deemed unsatisfactory. Many literati realized that the institutions enshrined in the imperial system were not inviolate: unprecedented conditions required unprecedented solutions. To "accord with the times" became the slogan of a generation of statecraft *(jingshi)* scholars who during the early nineteenth century sought pragmatic solutions to the myriad organizational and logistical breakdowns that seemed to come all at once and were exacerbated by the Opium War (1839–1842) and Taiping Rebellion.

Literati faith in the past as a guideline for the present remained intact. Increasingly, however, the past represented conflicting ideals of moral and political commitment. Established institutions, whether defended in Song or Han Learning terms, were undergoing a crisis of confidence from which the imperial system would never recover. The turn to evidential research revealed that the crisis had extended from the institutions of the imperial system to the very nature of the intellectual values literati had favored since the Ming. Neither marginal literati nor disgruntled petty officials, Han Learning scholars disclosed in their search for new truths in ancient and unorthodox classical texts that they no longer had confidence in answers provided in the Learning of the Way lexicon, which they had mastered as youths and defended as scholar-officials.[40]

With hindsight, we know that Qing China was on the eve of a confrontation with Western imperialism and a rising Japan, which would unleash revolutionary forces at all levels of Chinese society. Literati by 1800 comprehended that if the Chinese Empire hoped to cope with its problems, fundamental changes were required. Tragically, appeals to alternative forms of classical learning to revamp the imperial system never succeeded. Reemergence of New Text classicism coincided with the end of imperial China. Reformism, however, survived the debacle of the Sino-Japanese War in 1894–1895 and the failure of the 1898 Reform Movement.

Han Learning was never revolutionary. Although evidential scholars proposed changes in the classical agenda, they reaffirmed the role of classical ideals in the present. For them, classical learning was the starting point and unquestioned constituent for new beliefs and patterns of political behavior. New Text classicists appealed to a radical reconstruction of the past to authorize the present and prepare for the future. They had not yet reached a concept of political revolution or demonstrated a full understanding of social progress, but evidential styles of empirical research and New Text notions of historical change and advocacy for practical adjustment of institutions to changing times were important "early modern" stepping-stones to a modernist vision of political and cultural transformation. It is impossible to think of Gu Jiegang (1893–1980) and China's "New History" in a "modernist" vacuum. Many of his building blocks came from Qing evidential research, and with them he and others in the May Fourth era after 1919 unraveled the lies posing as truths in "late imperial" history.

The historical and philological consequences of evidential research thus contributed to the emergence in the decades of the late Qing and early Republic, 1890–1930, of a virulent form of cultural iconoclasm, in part via philology, and political revolution that found its roots, hence its legitimacy, in such studies. But in the end, the scholarly intentions and cultural consequences of Qing dynasty evidential research are analytically distinct. Too often we have read the twentieth-century consequences of evidential research anachronistically into the intentions of classical scholars writing during the seventeenth and eighteenth centuries.

Such a procedure has incorrectly turned classical scholars such as Dai Zhen and Qian Daxin into a sort of radically modern intellectual that they never were. As literati they remained committed to classicist *(Ru)* ideals. They sought to restore the classical visions of state and society, not replace them. The early modern consequences of their cutting-edge philology, however, yielded to a corrosive modern decanonization and delegitimation that went beyond the intellectual limits they had imposed in their own writings.

The Politics of Philology in Japan

Ancient Texts, Language, and Japanese Identity

SUSAN L. BURNS

IN 1989, YI YONG-HUI, a child of Korean parents who was born and educated in prewar Japan, published a study of the *Man'yōshū* (Ten thousand leaves) that immediately caused a sensation in both Japan and Korea, attracting the attention of the mass media and scholars alike. The *Man'yōshū* is Japan's oldest extant collection of poetry and dates to the eighth century, although it incorporates poems believed to be much older. In the eighteenth century, this anthology, together with another eighth-century text, the *Kojiki* (Record of ancient matters), came to be at the center of what is now known as Japanese nativism (*kokugaku,* lit. "our country's learning"), a scholarly movement organized around the philological study of Japan's earliest texts. Written entirely in Chinese characters, in a form of inscription that was discarded with the emergence of the Japanese syllabaries in the ninth century, much of the *Kojiki* and the *Man'yōshū* had become unreadable in the thousand years since their compilation, until nativist scholars in the eighteenth century succeeded in deciphering this script and reconstructing the vocabulary and grammar of ancient Japanese. As a result of their efforts, the *Man'yōshū* and the *Kojiki* were transformed into canonical texts and are now known to every Japanese.

Yi's work, titled *Mō hitotsu no Man'yōshū* (Another *Man'yōshū*), made a bold claim: the poems of the anthology, she argued, were not really "Japanese" at all.[1] Rather, they were written in a combination of "Korean" and

"Japanese," by migrants who moved from the Korean peninsula to the Japanese archipelago, and who used Chinese characters to inscribe the poems. In Yi's rereading of select *Man'yōshū* poems based on this principle, gentle lyrics of love and longing became instead descriptions of political and sexual intrigue. A case in point is the very first poem, traditionally believed to describe an early emperor's romantic encounter with a young woman who is gathering herbs. In Yi's rendering, the poem instead relates the words of a man from the Korean kingdom of Koguryŏ who announces his intention to take control of the land where he stands and to establish himself as its ruler.[2]

Japanese scholars of language, literature, and history were quick to attack Yi's interpretations, arguing that her choice of which words to read as "Japanese" and as "Korean" was entirely arbitrary, and that she had only a rudimentary knowledge of ancient Korean and Japanese.[3] She was, in other words, a poor philologist. Such critiques notwithstanding, Yi clearly captured the popular imagination. *Another Man'yōshū* became a best seller in Japan and inspired the organization of a group known as the Society for the Study of *Another Man'yōshū (Mō hitotsu no Man'yōshū* wo yomu kai*),* which is said to have had more than two thousand members at its height.[4] Yi went on to publish seven more books that popularized her theory of the influence of Korea on early Japan, but by the end of the 1990s, interest in her project had largely waned. Her books are now long out of print, and a website created to promote her work has not been updated since 2001.[5]

The *Another Man'yōshū* craze might seem nothing more than a manifestation of the political and cultural tensions that have defined postcolonial relations between Japan and Korea. But what the journalistic, scholarly, and popular responses to Yi's work ignored was that what were posed as the "orthodox" and "correct" readings of the *Man'yōshū*'s poems were themselves the product of a long process of etymological, semantic, and grammatical analysis that involved contentious debates about language and culture. The intellectual historian Koyasu Nobukuni has noted that the central claim of the nativist philologists—that is, that the *Man'yōshū* and *Kojiki* were written in a pure Japanese untainted by Chinese influence—was "Japan's *imago,*" the source of the modern ideology of Japanese identity.[6] This essay aims to explore the philological work of the nativist scholars whose work rendered the *Man'yōshū* and *Kojiki* not only readable but also powerful expressions of Japanese cultural identity. As we shall see, when Yi Yong-hui called into question the "Japaneseness" of the ancient texts, she was confronting, perhaps unknowingly, a powerful philological tradition that stretched back to the eighteenth century and also profoundly shaped the formation of the modern academic disciplines of national literature *(kokubungaku)* and national language *(kokugogaku).*

The Prehistory of Nativist Philology

Nativist philology emerged within an intellectual and cultural milieu dominated by the study of Chinese Confucian texts. Decades of political turmoil in the late sixteenth century, which included the invasion of the Korean peninsula by the warlord Toyotomi Hideyoshi (1537–1598), were accompanied by movement of people, books, and ideas from the continent to Japan. In the aftermath of the founding of the Tokugawa shogunate in 1603, professional scholars, many of whom enjoyed the patronage of the new samurai rulers, focused on producing commentaries on the work of Song Confucianists, the most influential of whom was Zhu Xi (1130–1200). As Benjamin A. Elman and Michael Lackner note in their essays in this volume, the scholarly work of the Song Confucianists was organized around the identification of patterns of correspondence that were said to bind together the cosmological, natural, social, and even bodily aspects of existence. Not surprisingly, given this paradigm, when Japanese Confucianists of the seventeenth century first turned from Chinese classics to Japan's earliest texts, it was with the aim of reconciling them with the metaphysics of Song Confucianism in order to confirm its universalist paradigm. They began, then, with a body of a priori knowledge and turned to the Japanese texts for verification. A key figure in this era was the scholar Yamazaki Ansai (1619–1682), whose work on the *Nihon shoki* (The chronicles of Japan, 720) inspired new interest in the early Japanese texts. The *Nihon shoki* and the *Kojiki* were Japan-centric mytho-histories produced within the early imperial court as a means of legitimation: both works describe the formation of heaven and earth and the appearance of a group of primordial deities who produce the Japanese islands and an elaborate pantheon of deities. The central event of the so-called divine age sections of these texts was the descent of the second-generation descendant of the sun deity, who left heaven to found the imperial lineage in the Japanese islands below. The "age of men" chapters that follow describe the exploits of the legendary first emperor, Jimmu, the fourth-generation descendant of the sun deity, and his successors.

There was a long tradition of court-centered scholarship on the *Nihon shoki* dating back to antiquity, but in Yamazaki's hands the work assumed new meaning. He argued that the *Nihon shoki* was analogous to the Chinese classic the *Yijing* (The book of changes) in that both revealed the workings of *li,* the fundamental moral principle that permeated the cosmos, and *qi,* the ethereal substance of existence that gave form to *li.*[7] Yamazaki and his followers believed that the events recorded in the *Nihon shoki* were metaphorical representations of the interaction of these two principles and the other key concepts of Confucian metaphysics such as yin and yang and the five elements. Their aim was to find textual evidence of these ideas in the *Nihon shoki,* and to that end they employed a number of interpretive strategies. These included the construction of new (and often entirely speculative) etymologies, the forging of metonymical links between words extracted from the *Nihon shoki* and Confucian concepts, and the assertion that events in the plot were in fact allegorical representations of metaphysical processes.[8]

Yamazaki's attempt to read the *Nihon shoki* in light of the conceptual system of Song Confucianism attracted the attention not only of Japanese Confucianists but also of members of the hereditary priesthood associated with major shrines where Japan's indigenous deities were worshiped. For the former, it confirmed the relevance of Confucianism for Japan, while for the latter it invested the deities they revered with a new and sophisticated set of ethical and metaphysical meanings. But if enthusiasts were many, so too were critics. The second half of the seventeenth century saw the emergence in Japan Confucian circles of a new skepticism toward Song Confucianism and a new concern for historical understanding based on empirical research. The philological shift that Benjamin A. Elman describes in seventeenth-century China, in which scholars turned to new strategies of textual criticism and historical analysis, influenced Japanese Confucianists as well, evidence of the ongoing process of intellectual exchange, even though the policies of the shogunate made direct contact between Chinese and Japanese scholars impossible. While Song Confucianism, institutionalized within the academies sponsored by the shogunate and some domainal lords, continued to enjoy official support, new networks of scholars formed and began to deploy methods of analysis that departed from the "verification" strategies used by Yamazaki and his students.

Emblematic of this new empiricism was the project undertaken by Tokugawa Mitsukuni (1628–1700), the lord of the powerful domain of Mito and the grandson of the founder of the Tokugawa dynasty. In 1657 Mitsukuni ordered the compilation of a comprehensive history of Japan, with the aim of illuminating Confucian virtues, particularly as they pertained to issues of governance. Mitsukuni himself had been educated in Song Confucianism, but both he and the scholars he employed were committed to the positivist historical method employed by the Han dynasty historian Sima Qian (145/135–86 B.C.E.), which began with the assemblage, comparison, and evaluation of evidence. In preparation for writing his "History of Great Japan," Mitsukuni authorized the editing, in many cases for the first time, of some of the earliest texts produced in Japan, the *Kojiki* and the *Man'yōshū,* as well as later histories and early ritual texts.[9]

For scholars of this period, the *Kojiki* and the *Man'yōshū,* which like the *Nihon shoki* dated from the period before the phonetic scripts had developed, were something akin to a linguistic labyrinth. Although both were inscribed entirely in Chinese characters, they utilized different forms of inscription. In the case of the *Kojiki,* some sections were easily understood according to the rules of Chinese syntax, but others were oddly irregular. Elsewhere it was clear that characters were used as phonetic symbols to "spell out" the names of actors and place names. Most confusing were the characters that seemed to signify syntactical elements of an unknown grammar. To most Japanese readers, the *Kojiki* appeared to be inscribed primarily in Chinese, albeit a peculiar and seemingly corrupt Chinese. The *Man'yōshū* was even more puzzling: while some poems were inscribed using Chinese characters purely as phonetic symbols, others were written in what David Lurie has termed a "logographic" style in which Chinese characters were used to represent Japanese words of equivalent meaning and arranged according to the order of Japanese syntax.[10]

Because the *Kojiki* seemed to be written in "Chinese," it became subject to a linguistic operation known as *kundoku* (reading in Japanese). A method of reading routinely utilized by Japanese consumers of Chinese texts, "reading in Japanese" involved several different strategies, including the rearrangement of word order, the pronunciation of Chinese characters as Japanese words, and the addition of new grammatical elements. All of this was accomplished by the insertion of diacritical markers, pronunciation glosses, and particles into the original text. Although *kundoku* has long been regarded as a Japanese innovation, recently Kin Bunkyō has argued that similar reading strategies developed elsewhere in ancient East Asia, including in the kingdom of Silla on the Korean peninsula and among the Qidan and Uyghur people, as a means of reading Chinese texts.[11]

In its Japanese form, *kundoku* ostensibly preserved the original Chinese text, but it was nonetheless both a translation and an interpretation. The author of the diacritical markers had to make a series of choices. Should meaningful differences that existed in Japanese be introduced into the

Chinese text even though they were not elements of the original work? Should characters grammatically necessary in Chinese but not in Japanese be pronounced, even if the result was stilted or unnatural-sounding Japanese? When the first print version of the *Kojiki* was produced in 1644, the editor inserted all three of the devices outlined above into the text, even though the medieval manuscripts from which he must have been working contained only rudimentary markers. But the result was a strangely unstable mix of verbal registers: for example, while the editor attached honorifics to verbs describing the actions of deities, he often refrained from attaching them to nouns. More strikingly, pronunciation glosses were used to indicate readings of characters that departed from their literal meanings. In one instance, characters that literally meant "like floating oil"—presumably a description of the unstable landmass that resulted with the separation of heaven and earth—were rendered "as within the womb."[12]

The first sustained effort to grapple with the language of the ancient Japanese texts came from a scholar who was involved in Mitsukuni's history writing project. Keichū (1640–1701), a Buddhist monk, was assigned the task of editing the *Man'yōshū.* A gifted linguist, Keichū soon grasped what others seem not to have fully recognized—that language changes and evolves over time. On the basis of this insight, he undertook a rigorous comparative study of various early texts in order to understand the process of euphonic change, which he regarded as a necessary first step toward understanding the system of inscription used in the *Man'yōshū.* By 1690, he had completed his work *Man'yō daishōki* (A substitute's analysis of the *Man'yōshū*), the first exegetical work on the anthology in four hundred years. Whereas the author of this earlier work had been unable to make sense of many poems, rendering them incomprehensible or even nonsensical, Keichū succeeded in making every poem readable, and his extensive annotations carefully explained the textual basis for his readings, a method that later scholars would emulate.[13]

Keichū's concern for language was part of what might aptly be termed Japan's first "linguistic turn." In eighteenth-century Japan the historical analysis of language assumed a new primacy for both Japanese Confucianists and the nascent nativists. The central figure in the Confucian school known as *kogaku* or "ancient learning" was Ogyū Sorai. Railing against the scholarship of Yamazaki and other students of Song Confucianism, Ogyū accused them of misreading the Confucian classics by using what he called "today's words." He was particularly critical of the practice of reading Chinese texts via *kundoku.* Famously describing this as akin to "trying to scratch one's itchy feet while wearing shoes," Ogyū called on students of Confucianism to master the language of ancient China and to read the texts with the aim of recovering their original meaning.[14] He was renowned for his mastery of both vernacular and classical Chinese and advocated writing poetry in classical Chinese *(kanshi).* Poetic composition, he suggested, would not only allow Japanese to participate in a Confucian cultural world, it would also allow for emotional insight and thereby promote social order.[15]

The work of both Ogyū and Keichū reveals the contours of an important intellectual transition that began in the late seventeenth century, as the transculturalism and transhistoricism that had been the intellectual orthodoxy for some decades came under new scrutiny. As we have seen, the examination of the early Japanese texts had begun within the context of first Confucian metaphysics and then Confucian empiricism, but in the second half of the eighteenth century, the scholars we now term "nativists" began to reject the idea that Japan shared a cultural, intellectual, or moral affinity with China. They turned to the early Japanese texts with the explicit aim of discovering the distinctiveness of Japanese culture, which they sought in the language of the early textual record.

The work of the scholar Kamo no Mabuchi is revealing of the new cultural politics that shaped nativist philology. In his study of the *Man'yōshū, Man'yō kō* (A theory of the *Man'yōshū,* 1758), as well as in a series of essays on grammatical and other linguistic issues written in the 1760s, Kamo argued for the fundamental difference—and superiority—of the Japanese language over Chinese. Decrying the influence of the Chinese language on Japan, Kamo argued that in the ancient period, the fifty sounds of the Japanese syllabary had been sufficient to speak of the myriad events and objects of the world. Moreover, these sounds were "natural" and allowed the Japanese people to experience the world directly and to relate to each other "directly," "forthrightly," and "sincerely." With contact with the continent, however, came the introduction of thousands of Chinese characters that altered the seamless relationship between language and the world. As people began to communicate using language now characterized by artifice, abstraction, and empty rhetoric, social relations came to be characterized by divisiveness and turmoil.

Kamo's advocacy of a "return to the *Man'yōshū*" was a scholarly project, but it also revealed his anxiety about his own society, which was shared by many in this period as Japan experienced a commercial revolution that began to undermine the political system based on status that had endured for almost two centuries. Ironically, given his antipathy toward Confucianism,

Kamo echoed the philological methods advocated by Ogyū Sorai: he urged his students to master the vocabulary and grammar of the *Man'yōshū* and to write prose and compose poems using the archaic language in order to recover the "spirit" of the ancient Japanese.[16] As a result of this kind of advocacy, a host of manuals began to appear that aimed to instruct eighteenth-century writers in the vocabulary and style of what is now termed "imitation ancient Japanese" *(gikobun).*

Motoori Norinaga: Ancient Language and the Divine Age

In 1764, Motoori Norinaga, a physician of (again ironically) Chinese medicine and a part-time teacher of poetry and poetics in a provincial town, took up the study of the *Kojiki.* For the next thirty years, he labored over the exegesis of this work, producing an annotated version of the text he called the *Kojikiden* (Commentaries on the *Kojiki*). The modern print version consists of four hefty volumes, more than two thousand pages total, the bulk of which are devoted to Motoori's notes on the text. For example, his analysis of the opening two lines of the work, which describe the formation of heaven and earth and the appearance of the heavenly deities, stretches over twelve pages of tiny print.[17] The *Kojikiden* sent shock waves through the intellectual circles of the day, impressing critics and fans alike with its scholarly virtuosity and its radical claims. The latter included Motoori's assertion that this work, not the *Nihon shoki,* should be the central object of analysis and that it alone accurately recorded the true transmissions from the "divine age" in the pure language of that time. Motoori argued that when read correctly, the *Kojiki* revealed that "the imperial land," as he termed Japan, had once been a natural community in which subjects and ruler lived in perfect harmony with each other and the deities, with no need for laws or institutions. Like Kamo, Motoori believed that this idyllic situation had prevailed until contact with China led to the introduction of the Chinese language and Chinese texts. With them came new ethical ideas and political doctrines that fundamentally altered the natural community of the original Japan. Motoori termed the effect of Chinese influence on the Japanese people *karagokoro* ("Chinese mind"), and he believed that it led to discord and conflict as social relations came to be shaped by coercion, violence, and oppression.[18]

This description of ancient Japan is, to be sure, utter fiction. Contemporary historians and archeologists are in agreement that the early inhabitants of the Japanese archipelago were in close and continual contact with the cultures of the continent throughout the ancient period. However, Motoori insisted that the Japanese lived in splendid isolation until the seventh century, when Japan's rulers began to actively embrace Chinese ideas, practices, and institutions. It was not long, however, until members of the court became alarmed at the unintended consequences of this stance: the oral transmissions from the "divine age" were being forgotten or altered as the Japanese internalized Chinese concepts. Recognizing that crucial knowledge was endangered, the emperor decided to act: he ordered a member of his court to seek out and memorize the ancient oral traditions before they were lost. According to Motoori, decades later these ancient transmissions, safely preserved in oral form, were recorded in the *Kojiki*. In sharp contrast to the *Nihon shoki,* which was meant to be a Chinese-style chronicle and accordingly used highly sinicized language, the *Kojiki* was written in pure Japanese.[19]

To produce what was later described as the "ancient language *Kojiki*" *(kokun Kojiki),* Motoori expanded on the earlier philological work of Keichū and Kamo. He recognized that Chinese characters were used in the *Kojiki* in three distinct ways: as purely phonetic symbols *(kana),* as ideographs that represented meaning but were meant to be vocalized in Japanese *(masaji),* and as "borrowed characters" *(ateji)* to which a new reading was attached without reference to the meaning of the characters. But discerning how to read a particular phrase or character compound was merely a preliminary step. According to Motoori, "all of the ancient texts are written in Chinese [characters], so when one tries to vocalize them, then even if one changes the words one by one into the ancient language, the way of connecting them together is still in the style of Chinese."[20] As this suggests, the explication of the grammar of ancient Japanese was a crucial part of the *Kojikiden,* and while Motoori acknowledged the scholarship of Keichū and Kamo, he felt that neither had completed the task of syntactic reconstruction. He was aghast at the efforts of many of his contemporaries, who were attempting to write poetry in the style of the *Man'yōshū* but in fact did little more than insert an ancient vocabulary into contemporary syntax.

Although much of the *Kojiki* was readable as Chinese, Motoori was particularly interested in those sections that did not reflect the grammar of Chinese. There were, for example, passages that made use of what he called the *senmyō* style, a term that refers to the imperial edicts recorded in later texts. In these instances, the verb root was indicated by a Chinese character used logographically, while the inflection of the verb was written in Chinese characters used phonetically. Motoori carefully analyzed the latter in order to understand the conjugation of verbs, auxiliary verbs, and adjectives. Elsewhere, there were passages that seemed to follow Chinese syntax but contained irregularities in the word order. Motoori did not believe that these were simply mistakes on the part of an author writing in a new and unfamiliar language and script. Rather, he insisted that such deviations from Chinese syntax signaled the true intent of the author, the recording of the transmissions from the "divine age" in pure Japanese. In other words, these were indications of the need to think beyond the written text.[21]

In the end, the project of linguistic reconstruction necessarily required Motoori to turn to later texts: he argued that traces of the ancient language could be found in the imperial edicts recorded in the *Shoku Nihongi* (Chronicles of Japan, continued, 797), in ritual prayers recorded in the *Engi shiki* (Rites of the Engi era, 927), and in poems recorded in the *Man'yōshū* and *Nihon shoki.* But using these texts to reconstruct pure Japanese was not as unproblematic as Motoori would have it. The Japanese linguist Kojima Noriyuki has argued that Motoori's conception of the ancient language was deeply influenced by the form of ritual prayers, which were characterized by lengthy, sonorous passages. Thus, while the *Kojiki* contains many passages that took the form of a series of paired four-character sentences that have a similar structure, a symmetry typical of Chinese prose style, Motoori inserted conjunctive particles to join them together to make up the lengthy sentences he believed were typical of the ancient language.[22] Another critic of Motoori's "reconstruction" has described the "ancient language *Kojiki*" as "a free translation," arguing that Motoori ignored much of the linguistic complexity of the original text in order to produce a new version that *seemed* authentically ancient and Japanese but actually drew on later prose styles.[23]

These criticisms notwithstanding, it is undeniable that Motoori's "ancient language *Kojiki*" is a masterpiece. Parallel to the Chinese characters that made up the original *Kojiki,* he inscribed line after line of *hiragana,* the Japanese syllabary, rewriting the work in the ancient language as he imagined it and rejecting entirely the conventions of the *kundoku* operation. It is possible to read Motoori's new *Kojiki* while completely ignoring the original text that lies to its left, and by the early nineteenth century it had fundamentally transformed how the *Kojiki* was read. No longer did readers rely on diacritical markers and the other *kundoku* techniques. And this approach to the *Kojiki* endures. Even a cursory examination of any modern version of the *Kojiki* reveals the influence of Motoori's work. Take, for example, the version of the *Kojiki* in *Nihon koten bungaku taikei* (The compendium of Japanese literary classics), a collection of canonical versions of classic works, edited by renowned scholars.[24] In the volume on the *Kojiki,* the phonetic rendering of the text (which derives from the *Kojikiden*) appears first and on a page of its own, while the original "Chinese" text is treated as secondary.

The rewriting of the *Kojiki* was Motoori's greatest achievement, but the lengthy annotations that follow each section are a crucial part of the *Kojikiden.* Motoori would repeatedly stress that he did not interpret the text—"interpretation," he implied, meant the addition of some meaning not already present. Instead, he insisted that he merely "read" the text, and that this was sufficient to reveal its meaning. The vast majority of the notes are devoted to issues of language and deal with etymological, morphological, and syntactical issues. The result is a complex web of intertextual relations that validates Motoori's conception of pure Japanese by referencing later texts, in spite of the fact that Motoori elsewhere rejected many of these same works as the products of what he called the "Chinese mind." But another category of notes establishes links between the world of the text and the world of the early modern reader: objects, places, names, and words are explained by referencing contemporary knowledge. In gathering information, Motoori utilized his expanding network of disciples, whom he queried about local dialects, customs, and other matters, aiming to provide empirical verification for his claim that even a millennium after the onslaught of Chinese influence, traces of Japan's original culture could still be found.

The *Kojiki* after the *Kojikiden*

Chapters of the *Kojikiden* began to circulate in manuscript form in the 1780s, first among Motoori's disciples and from them to other scholars. By the time publication began in 1790, the *Kojikiden* was already well known in intellectual circles, and it quickly inspired a new and intense interest in the *Kojiki,* which became the primary text in the intellectual movement that some had already begun to call *kokugaku,* a term coined to distinguish it from *kangaku* or "Chinese studies." Motoori quickly became the target of considerable criticism—not only from Confucianists but also from those who considered themselves practitioners of *kokugaku.* Motoori's central claim—that the *Kojiki* recorded oral transmissions from the "divine age" in a pure form of Japanese—came under intense scrutiny by other self-identified nativist scholars such as Ueda Akinari (1734–1809) and Tachibana Moribe (1781–1849), and even from Motoori's best known, although self-proclaimed, disciple, Hirata Atsutane (1776–1843). Read against each other and as a response to Motoori's work, their works reveal the complexity of nativist philology in the early nineteenth century.

The initial attack on Motoori's understanding of the *Kojiki* came from Ueda Akinari, now better known as a writer of fiction than for his nativist scholarship. In the 1760s and 1770s, when Motoori was living quietly in his provincial town, Ueda was an active participant in the intellectual life of the cultural centers of Kyoto and Osaka. Sometime in the mid-1760s, he became interested in the work of Kamo no Mabuchi and began to study it with one of his students. Early in the 1780s, having gained access to some chapters of Motoori's work, he began to voice a powerful critique of the *Kojikiden.* The traces of their dispute survive in a text known as *Ashikari yoshi* (Cutting through the weeds, c. 1790), which takes the form of a series of exchanges between the two men.[25] This work was edited by Motoori and not surprisingly portrays him as the winner on every point. Even so, the comments attributed to Ueda reveal that he was an insightful reader of the *Kojikiden.*

The dispute between Ueda and Motoori was apparently sparked by a disagreement over orthography, but it expanded into an intense debate about the impact of inscription and textuality on oral transmissions. Keichū's work on the *Man'yōshū* had begun with the recognition of euphonic change over time, an insight that allowed him to decipher how Chinese characters were used phonetically in the *Man'yōshū.* However, in the work of both Kamo and Motoori, euphonic change was not regarded as a natural or inevitable process. Because the "original" sounds of the ancient language were judged to be authentically "Japanese," change was understood as "decline," "corruption," and "loss," and thus the goal of philology became "recovery." In contrast, Ueda argued that euphonic change was a naturally occurring process, and he ridiculed the efforts of his contemporaries to write in the style and vocabulary of eighth-century texts. Moreover, he insisted that writing was never simply an act of recording: the intentions and skills of the scribe were always potentially mediating factors, making it impossible to discern the relationship between the text and the oral transmissions.[26] In making these assertions, Ueda was, of course, questioning the very foundation of the *Kojikiden*—the idea that pure Japanese was recoverable from the *Kojiki.*

In his heated response, Motoori put forth a highly detailed and technical discussion of the orthography deployed by the *Kojiki,* one that modern linguists suggest reveals his superior knowledge of the ancient language. But to evaluate the debate in this way is to miss Ueda's point: he was not trying to provide an alternative reading of the *Kojiki.* His aim was to expose the problematic foundation of Motoori's work. It is not surprising, given his critique of Motoori, that Ueda never attempted an exegetical study of the *Kojiki.* Instead, he used the ancient texts as inspiration for the writing of narrative fiction *(monogatari),* and in a series of stories and essays he explored the contradictions and silences of the *Kojiki, Man'yōshū,* and other early texts.

Unlike Ueda, who encountered the *Kojikiden* while Motoori was clearly the dominant figure in the nativist movement, Tachibana Moribe and Hirata Atsutane turned to the exegesis of the *Kojiki* at a moment when the nativism movement had splintered into competing "schools," organized around personalities as much as ideas. In terms of social and political influence, Hirata Atsutane was the most prominent figure, building a network of more than five hundred students and angering the shogunate with his outspoken advocacy of imperial rule. However, in works such as his cosmological treatise *Tama no mihashira* (The pillars of the spirit, published 1813) and *Koshiseibun* (The true text of ancient history, published 1818), Hirata showed little interest in the philological work that had been central to Motoori's *Kojikiden.* He rejected Motoori's assertion that the truth of the "divine age" was to be found only in the *Kojiki* and argued that elements of the oral transmissions were in fact dispersed among the early texts. His *Koshiseibun* takes the form of a "reconstruction" of the "true text." By weaving together elements of the *Kojiki, Nihon shoki,* and other works, Atsutane constructed a new cosmology that, as Harry Harootunian has demonstrated, offered an affirmation of the life, work, and beliefs of Japanese villagers in particular by asserting the sacredness of agricultural and reproductive labor.[27]

Tachibana took up the study of the early Japanese texts in the 1820s, as Hirata's work was becoming well known, but unlike Hirata, he was intensely concerned with the issues of language that had been at the center of nativist practice. The son of a villager, he was, like many of those attracted to nativism in this period, largely self-educated, but as a young man he gained something of a reputation, at least in the Kantō region around Edo, for his skill in composing poems in the archaic style of the *Man'yōshū.* In the 1830s, he took up the analysis of the ancient language when he published *Yamabiko zōshi* (Book of the mountain god, 1831).[28] Subtitled "Thoughts on Difficult Words," at first glance, this work appears to be an exercise in what Michael Lackner describes as "word philology." Each of the 225 entries is devoted to the examination of a "difficult word" selected from the ancient texts. But Tachibana sought not only to explain the "original" meaning of the word but also to explore how it was transformed over time and how new expressions took form. This approach is at odds with that of Motoori, who explicitly criticized any attempt to understand the ancient language primarily through etymological analysis, arguing in essence that context mattered. In contrast, Tachibana, by discerning semantic content and lexical relations, tried to trace the diachronic development of the Japanese language, approaching it as a semantic chain that evolved from the past to the present.[29]

The concern for historicizing language that characterized this early work was at the heart of Tachibana's exegetical work on the ancient texts, including *Nan-Kojikiden* (A critique of the *Kojikiden,* c. 1842) and *Itsu no chiwake* (Distinguishing the ancient way, 1844). In the *Nan-Kojikiden* Tachibana contrasted passages from the *Kojiki* with those from the *Kojikiden* in order to criticize Motoori's work, while *Itsu no chiwake* was an exegesis of the *Nihon shoki.*[30] In contrast to Motoori, who had insisted that the *Kojiki* was a transparent inscription of the oral transmissions from the "divine age," Tachibana argued that the long process of oral transmission and reception over many generations had altered the knowledge of the age of the deities that was passed down in this way. As evidence of this he pointed to the term *katari kotoba* (lit. "narrating words"), which he discovered in the *Kojiki.* According to Tachibana, in relating the events of the "divine age," storytellers in the period before writing had relied on a number of narrative techniques. "Narrating words" referred to these verbal strategies, which with the passing of time had come to adhere to the story to such a degree that at some point the original meaning of the oral transmissions was obscured and then forgotten. These included the use of not only metaphor and allegory but also childish language to attract the attention of children, and the insertion of extraneous folktales to enliven the story. Tachibana's work aimed to identify the "narrating words" in order to uncover the essential cultural knowledge that was hidden beneath them.[31]

As the work of Ueda, Hirata, and Tachibana reveals, nativist scholars after Motoori struggled to reconcile the scholarly and ideological objectives of his practice. While Motoori's philological expertise was generally acknowledged, his claims about the ancient Japanese language, the "divine age," and the meaning of the *Kojiki* were called into question by new attempts to historicize the text and its language. Rather than viewing philological reconstruction as the end of the exegetical project, Ueda and the others made it a starting point and began to ask who had written the *Kojiki* and the other texts and with what intentions. Rather than viewing the reconstructed pure Japanese of the *Kojiki* as transparently meaningful, they regarded it as a complicated linguistic artifact that required interrogation and interpretation.

The intertwined nature of the philological and political aspects of nativist philology are perhaps best exemplified by attempts to use it to challenge forms of "Chinese" knowledge that were deeply embedded in everyday life. A case in point is the attempts by nativist doctors in the nineteenth century to define an "imperial medicine" *(kōchō idō)* that could challenge medical knowledge derived from Chinese texts. Unlike Motoori Norinaga, who seems never to have addressed the Chinese origin of the medicine he practiced, Hirata Atsutane was deeply concerned with accounting for the assumed foreign origins of medical knowledge. Although educated in Chinese medicine, like other Japanese physicians of his day, by 1810 Hirata was deriding Chinese medicine as defective and corrupt and advocating the use of healing rituals that invoked the aid of indigenous deities. A little more than a decade later, however, Hirata had rethought his position and acknowledged the efficacy of Chinese medicinal compounds, but this reversal required him, in the words of Wilburn Hansen, to "ideologically domesticate" Chinese medicine by explaining its true Japanese origins.[32] Citing an elaborate array of sources, both Japanese and Chinese, Hirata attempted to demonstrate that the medical knowledge of the eminent Han dynasty physician Zhang Zhongjing had in fact originated with two Japanese deities who had spread knowledge of healing techniques to China, where it was preserved and passed down until reintroduced to Japan as "Chinese medicine."[33]

Another approach was taken by Gonda Naosuke, the most famous nativist physician of the mid-nineteenth century. Born into a family of village doctors in 1809, Gonda was trained as a physician under the shogunal physician in Edo, but after becoming a student of Hirata in the late 1830s, he made it his mission to reform medical practice in Japan by restoring its indigenous roots. The central object of his work was called the *Daidō rui ju hō* (Classified formulae of the Daidō period), an early ninth-century medical text mentioned in an 840 C.E. chronicle that was assumed to have been lost until it mysteriously reappeared in the late eighteenth century. The work was enthusiastically received by some students of nativism, but Motoori Norinaga quickly labeled it a forgery, as did others who argued that its language and textual form were evidence of much later origin. Gonda, in contrast, embraced the text and over the next two decades produced not only a series of exegetical works that aimed to demonstrate its authenticity but also an array of popular works that sought to transform medical practice.[34]

Modern Japan and "Japanese Philology"

As the foregoing discussion reveals, although the nativist movement gave rise to new and rigorous forms of scholarly practice that illuminated previously unreadable texts and produced a new understanding of the early Japanese language, it was always entangled in the ideological project of demonstrating the authenticity and superiority of a distinctive "Japanese" culture. Throughout much of the nineteenth century, nativism was only one aspect of a lively market in ideas: it competed with multiple schools of Confucianism, various forms of Western learning, and new attempts at nativist-Confucian syncretism. However, in the aftermath of the establishment of the modern Japanese state, as the modern academic disciplines of national history and national literature were established within the new national university, Motoori Norinaga's work in particular acquired new meaning. It was valorized not only as the crowning achievement of nativist scholarship but also as a model form of philological practice for modern scholars. In his essay on Academia Sinica's Institute of History and Philology in this volume, Ku-ming Kevin Chang traces the rethinking of Chinese textual practices in relation to Western philology in the early twentieth century. In Japan too, this encounter profoundly influenced the emergence of modern academic disciplines.

A central figure in this process was Haga Ya'ichi (1867–1927), professor of national literature at Tokyo Imperial University from 1902 to 1917 and an influential member of several government committees that dealt with issues of language and literature, including the National Language Research Committee and the Investigative Committee for Kana Orthography. As a member of the Committee for the Selection of School Textbooks and himself the editor of many textbooks, Haga played an important role in defining the content of "national literature" for several generations of Japanese schoolchildren. Born into a family with strong ties to the early modern nativist movement, Haga entered Tokyo University, Japan's first modern university, in 1889 as a student of the newly established National Literature Department. In 1900, after graduation, Haga was selected for further study in Europe and was dispatched to Germany at government expense to research "methods for studying the history of literature." During his eighteen months at Berlin University, Haga encountered the work of German philologists such as Wilhelm von Humboldt, August Böckh, and Herman Paul, and by the time he returned to Japan, he had reinterpreted the task he had been given. Rather than discovering in Europe a method for studying national literature, Haga had concluded that Japan's own nativist tradition offered a method as modern as that being deployed by European scholars.

Back in Japan, Haga quickly began to popularize his view that nativism, which he now preferred to call *kotengaku* ("classical studies") and *bunkengaku* ("textual studies"), provided the foundation for the modern discipline of national literature. In a seminal speech in 1904 that was later published and widely cited, Haga evoked von Humboldt's description of philology as "Wissenschaft der Nationalität," which Haga translated as "science of the nation," and he described early modern nativism as a "science" that studied the "special character" of the Japanese people.[35] Citing the achievements of European philology, Haga declared: "their method is precisely like the method employed by the nativist scholars of our country. . . . In other words, taking the national language and national literature as a foundation, they tried to explain the country."[36] But when Haga spoke of nativism as a "science of the nation" he meant in particular the work of Motoori Norinaga, whom he praised as a scholar "who held the nationalist view that the way of the nation must be clarified." It was Motoori who had recognized the significance of the *Kojiki* and established the principle that "the way of the nation must be based on Japanese texts."[37] In contrast, Haga cast a critical eye on Motoori's critics. While he admired Ueda's prose fiction, he dismissed his nativist work, describing him as someone who lacked the nationalism necessary to qualify as a true practitioner of "the learning of our country," a criticism he applied to Tachibana as well.[38] Haga was far more sympathetic to Hirata, whom he praised for reading Chinese and Western texts from the perspective of Japan's cultural centrality.[39]

As these comments reveal, like many of Japan's new intellectual elite, Haga was a committed nationalist, and he was critical of the pursuit of Westernization that had followed the establishment of the modern Japanese state after 1868, based on the presumption that Japan's progress toward civilization lagged behind that of Europe. The discovery of an indigenous scholarly tradition that seemingly paralleled developments in contemporary Europe offered him evidence that Japan's modernity did not rely upon the imitation of the West. But if the impetus behind Haga's analogical logic is clear, it should be evident that his attempt to recast early modern nativism in this way was problematic. While Haga described the texts that were the object of nativist practice as examples of "national language and literature,"

Motoori never conceived of the *Kojiki* as a literary work. It was the "divine text." Ironic as well was Haga's description of Motoori as a scholar of "textual studies," when it might be said that the *Kojikiden* was founded on the suppression of textual issues and the claim that the *Kojiki* recorded the reality of the "divine age" directly, objectively, and transparently.

Such issues notwithstanding, in the early decades of the twentieth century, modern scholars such as Haga Ya'ichi and his successors succeeded in establishing Motoori's scholarly reputation. As a result, Motoori's problematic claims about the *Kojiki*—that it was written in pure Japanese, that it transcribed ancient oral transmissions, that it revealed important truths about Japanese identity—continue to be widely regarded as "facts," the product of objective, rigorous, even scientific study. And this understanding of Motoori's work endured well into the postwar era. A powerful expression of the enduring legacy of his "ancient language *Kojiki*" comes from Kobayashi Hideo, one of the most influential literary scholars in Japan from the 1930s until his death in 1983. In 1977, Kobayashi published a six-hundred-page biography of Motoori that became a best seller, a development that sparked much journalistic comment. Describing his subject's work on the *Kojiki,* Kobayashi wrote: "within the act of annotation that required selflessness and reticence, he encountered something unknown, the oral transmissions. . . . What Motoori touched directly was the body of the narrative, what he heard directly were the words it expressed, its naked heavy voice."[40] Kobayashi's evocation of the "naked heavy voice" of the *Kojiki* almost two hundred years after Motoori began his philological work reveals the powerful influence of nativist philology in shaping modern discussions of Japanese culture and identity.

Conclusion

This essay has explored the historical context within which nativist philology took form. As we saw, the turn toward the ancient Japanese texts was part of a larger intellectual shift in which transcultural and transhistorical conceptions of culture came under scrutiny. However, while the nativist philologists Keichū, Kamo no Mabuchi, and Motoori Norinaga rendered texts such as the *Man'yōshū* and the *Kojiki* accessible to early modern readers, they also advanced problematic conceptions of the special nature of the Japanese language and the Japanese people. Most significantly, in the hands of Motoori, the *Kojiki* was transformed from an obscure text known to only a few scholars into a work of primary cultural significance. Motoori's philological work made the *Kojiki* the object of intense debate and discussion for two generations of nativist scholars who pursued how to read the work and what it meant. However, it was not until the early twentieth century that his *Kojiki* came to have canonical status within the new disciplines of national literature and national history, a development that required the dismissal of the work of Motoori's early modern critics. Haga Ya'ichi was an important figure in this process: he found in Motoori's work an indigenous scholarly tradition that could serve the interests of the modern Japanese nation.

Yet if Motoori Norinaga's work shaped both scholarly and popular efforts well into the twentieth century, the popularity of Yi Yong-hui's work in the 1990s seems to signal that the understandings of "Japan" and "Japanese" that took form within nativist philology are now finally open to question and scrutiny. Although nationalist sentiments clearly prompted Yi's engagement with the *Man'yōshū,* the willingness of so many Japanese readers to embrace her ideas suggests the rise of a new vision of a "multicultural Japan" that challenges the long prevalent discourse on Japanese language and identity. However, we still await a new generation of scholars with the linguistic and philological skills to push beyond the nationalist framing of the ancient texts that has so long ordered their study.

"Enthusiasm Dwells Only in Specialization"

Classical Philology and Disciplinarity in Nineteenth-Century Germany

CONSTANZE GÜTHENKE

IN LATE 1896, Basil Gildersleeve traveled to Greece on a trip sponsored by the *Atlantic Monthly,* to cover the first modern Olympic Games for the American public.[1] Gildersleeve was an experienced and willing writer for a broader audience, but mostly he was the inaugural holder of the chair of Greek philology at Johns Hopkins University, which itself had been founded only twenty years earlier on the model of the German research university. Gildersleeve was an early mover and shaker of the new American Philological Association (founded in 1869), the founding editor in 1880 of the *American Journal of Philology,* and as a card-carrying philologist of the German persuasion (with a Ph.D. from Göttingen), an ardent defender of specialized research, which in late nineteenth-century America was a contested strategy whose value was not self-evident.

The Olympic Games themselves had happened, with considerable American support and participation of an American team, in April 1896. The belatedness of his reporting does not seem to worry Gildersleeve, but issues of modernization and progress appear throughout the piece with some regularity. While Gildersleeve tries to identify positive commonalities between contemporary Greece and America, he does, for all his journalistic jauntiness, acknowledge the complicated relationship that both shared with Old Europe, with a latent sense of belatedness that is maybe most manifest in the long description of a visit to the local lyceum, the pride of the town of Sparta. There he found a "room [that] was a facsimile of the one in which I myself had sat some forty years before in Göttingen," school grammars "constructed on the basis of Curtius, Meyer and other German authorities," whose content was "nothing but German done into conventional modern Greek," and Greek academic journals, summarizing (German) philological work, that were more up-to-date in this respect than American ones.[2]

And yet, while he professes great admiration for the standards of learning already achieved, he describes the emulation of the Germanic model with a note of disappointment. Earlier, a highly technical lecture by his German archaeological guide had prompted a "perverse interest in the prickly pears, which were just then full of blooms, and pushing their purple and yellow flowers from the edge of the barbed disks with an insulting opulence like so many ficos to the universe. No one would expect such insolent, not to say indecent beauty of a plant that is all made up of greenness and prickles,—a plant that might well serve to embody the popular conception of the philological guild."[3] Gildersleeve's philologist is precariously positioned between disciplinary tedium and unexpected, creative flourishes (not unlike those of his own prose), a tension contemplated against the backdrop of the Greek landscape. A little further on, Gildersleeve returns to such institutional preoccupations when he compares the open, expansive site of Olympia to a great exposition and the stern, vertical location of Delphi to a great university, and makes clear his preferences: "the life of earth and sky, the life of ancient Greece, and the life of modern Greece,—one sees life whole who sees it at Olympia."[4]

On his last stop, in Constantinople, Gildersleeve lectured before the graduating class of the American College for Girls, recycling a lecture he had given two years earlier to the female students of Bryn Mawr: "The Spiritual Rights of Minute Research."[5] It is clear that Gildersleeve's satirizing attitude toward philology and the model philologist of a scientific, "German" mold could coexist with genuine appreciation and a respectful defense of specialized research. What is more, this tension between science and its other—whether the self, the persona of the scholar, art, the nature and immediacy of the ancient world, or an enlarged sense of antiquity—is as characteristic of Gildersleeve as it is of nineteenth-century philology itself, and of its historiography. Many of the tensions that reverberate through Gildersleeve's reports from Greece are those that he took away with him from Göttingen as a student—and that marked German scholarship throughout the nineteenth century.

This is not only the tension between an inward and outward focus, between the concentration of "minute research" in the university and the image of the "world exposition" conjured up by Gildersleeve apropos Olympia. The tension between concentration and diffusion was literally mapped onto a relationship between Germany, with its dominant scientific system, and other national cultures, which would increasingly define the standards of their own academic research on the export model of German institutionalized science.[6] But this tension also characterizes, by extension, a relationship between classical philology and modern philologies, which could be just as easily represented in a geography of power. The German classical philologist and archaeologist Friedrich Welcker (1784–1868), in a lecture on "The Significance of Philology," which he gave in 1841 at the fourth Meeting of German Philologists and Teachers, speaks of the "newly cultivated areas of all languages, literatures and histories, which we ought to consider our colonies"—colonies that might reduce the population of the motherland, but will inevitably have a positive feedback effect.[7] Welcker's lecture suggests the confidence of classical philology as much as its mutual relationship not only with other philologies but also with the scientific approach to natural history, including the history of languages and cultures. Thus, he hints at the challenges to philology as a freestanding field and at its constant need to reflect on its self-definition and limits.

On the face of it, nineteenth-century philology is a practice that deals with units conceived as individual-national. That means it is based on the assumption that the national is best understood as an extension of the individual, which enables the discipline of philology to coincide with Romantic nationalism as both a cultural and political discourse.[8] At the same time, this discourse of modernity, for all its national and individual focus, involved an awareness of and a good deal of anxiety about being seen, being compared, the sense of a self studying an other and of an other seeing the self.[9] This simultaneous inward and outward view is thus not so far from the central paradox of philology that Sheldon Pollock identifies in the introduction: philology's simultaneous tendency toward the extremes of hypercanonicity and hyperinclusiveness, of hyperconcentration and hyperdiffusion.

This paradox is not accidental but is structurally constitutive of philology as it was imagined and theorized especially in the programmatic writings of German classical philologists themselves. Through the establishment of disciplinary institutions and the founding of academic "schools," they contributed greatly to the centrality of philology as a privileged way of knowing.[10] The programmatic writings of such towering figures as Friedrich August Wolf and August Boeckh, which will be treated in detail here, show well how tensions such as limitation and expansion, canonicity and inclusiveness, impersonal specialization and care of the self, rationality and inspiration were acknowledged as a challenge, but for the most part still considered compatible within the reach of science.

In Gildersleeve's Bryn Mawr lecture on the spiritual rights of minute research, he quotes Friedrich Ritschl, the philologist now best remembered as the teacher of Friedrich Nietzsche and whom Gildersleeve had met and admired on his educational grand tour to various German universities.[11] Ritschl is in many ways considered the founder of a "Bonner Schule," marked by an unusual strength of Latinists (as opposed to Hellenists, even though Friedrich Gottlob Welcker, with Ritschl, shaped the University of Bonn) and by an open-minded focus on historical-critical philology. This approach in the tradition of Wilhelm von Humboldt and Wolf insisted on the importance of method in textual work, but did not restrict itself to textual criticism.[12]

In his defense of specialized research, Gildersleeve repeats Ritschl's pronouncement, from a set of notes on the method of philological study, that "Enthusiasmus liegt nur in der Einseitigkeit; das Enzyklopädische kann nicht begeistern" ("enthusiasm lies only in one-sidedness; the encyclopedic cannot enthrall").[13] Gildersleeve's translation as "enthusiasm dwells only in specialization" recognizes the force of the statement, but does not fully capture the ambivalent tone Ritschl himself introduces. *Einseitigkeit* is not a positive or even neutral term, and it is provocatively twinned here with "enthusiasm" and "enthrallment," which itself sits uneasily with the demands of scientific method. Wolf himself, in his *Darstellung der Alterthumswissenschaft* (1807), had acknowledged a *mürrische Einseitigkeit* (sullen one-sidedness) for which the philologist is often blamed, as well as a *dornige Gelehrsamkeit* (prickly learnedness—not so far from Gildersleeve's prickly pears) that might actually hinder rather than help a fuller understanding of human nature and culture such as he thought was the overall aim of classical study (on which more below).[14] In other words, when Nietzsche, a generation after Ritschl and several after Wolf, indulged in now much better known invective against a professional and professorial caste of what he calls *engherzige, froschblütige Mikrologen* ("narrow-hearted, frog-blooded micrologists"), he was not voicing a new concern (though he did it with considerable gusto).[15]

Einseitigkeit and *Bildung*

In his provocative aphorism Ritschl is pitting focused and creative *Einseitigkeit* against superficial encyclopedism as its own end in a mistaken pedagogy, and he advocates the profile of an independent professionalized researcher over that of the trained teacher with limited practical knowledge, who will not make the "wise detour of scientific insight."[16] At the same time, he worries about a specialization that leads to a drifting apart of areas of expertise and of the individuals who practice them. In a lecture given in front of the *Philomathische Gesellschaft* in Breslau in 1833, "On the Most Recent Developments of Philology," Ritschl calls for a "Verknüpfung der Einseitigkeiten" ("linking up of specializations") as *the* task of modern philology, a need "to bring together in objective unity what had been spread variously as individual manifestations; as well as the true revitalization and reanimation of the dead bulk of material through a pervasive idea, material which had previously been categorized only by way of rational criticism [sondernde Verstandeskritik]."[17]

In this passage the nuance of the "bisher in individueller Gestaltung zerstreuten Manigfaltigen" is ambiguous: is Ritschl talking about the individual manifestations, texts, works of art of and in an ancient past, or about the individual, specialized approaches and insights of modern scholars, both of which need the unifying perspective of a science of antiquity? Such an ambiguity is not accidental, since it points to the stereoscopy of ancient and modern individuality that under the terminology of *Bildung* (education, development, cultivation, or formation of the self) gave the study of antiquity much of its conceptual traction in the academic and cultural landscape of the late eighteenth century to begin with.

Bildung structured the terms of interpretation operative in classical scholarship, both to explain its subject matter and to justify itself. In the logic of a new educational model, inflected by developing historicism, charting the history of humankind meant charting *Bildung* as it manifested itself in individual epochs, under the relevant geographical and climatic influences and with regard to individual nations and societies. Ancient Greece, in particular, had a history that seemed to exemplify the momentous balance of human reason and beautiful self-realization—maybe this more than anything else was the take-away point of Johann Joachim Winckelmann's influential account of Greek art for the cultural importance of Hellenism as a cultural ideal and a field of academic inquiry. The ancients, in sum, exemplified the effect they should have on the moderns. *Bildung,* therefore, as a program of self-transformation or self-direction, aligned itself smoothly with the study or understanding of antiquity, becoming its content as much as its end result. Friedrich Ast's *Grundriss der Philologie* (1808), a university textbook and in that sense a representative example of a standard approach to classical philology, shows how philology, *Bildung,* and an operative use of images of life, liveliness, and individual personality coalesced. Philology is the study of the spirit *(Geist)* suffusing the inner and outer life of the classical world and its textual sources, and true philology harmonizes the study of material, or essence, and form: "in this unity Being and Form are sublimated into a true Essence; the latter comes alive, and the former takes [human] shape, both together become an intricately formed and cultivated life, as an expression of spirit [ein gestaltetes und gebildetes Leben, als Ausdruck des Geistes]."[18] Given the balance of those elements in the ancient world, Ast concludes that the true objective of philology, as opposed to a dead learnedness and mechanical knowledge, is "to reach a true and lifelike intuition and understanding of classical antiquity, since this is, as the ancient world, the paradigm of genuine *Bildung.*"[19] In that context, Greece in particular could be singled out as one of the prime examples of a culture or nation containing in its history the entire circle of *Bildung,* its growth, maturity, and decline, enabling the reader to comprehend and thus advance the progress of history.

With a definition of *Bildung* as the development of the individual, antiquity in turn became personified; to describe the character of antiquity was to recount its life story and to understand its *Wesen* (essence, character, or being). Humboldt (tasked in 1809 with developing the plan for the new research university at Berlin that would one day bear his name) made this understanding of antiquity as a form of *Bildung* quite literally the goal of classical study in his programmatic essay *On the Study of Antiquity, and of Greek Antiquity in Particular* (1793): "the study of a nation offers all the advantages which history has in general, namely to increase our knowledge of human beings by examples of actions and events, to sharpen our power of judgment, and to improve and raise our character. Yet it does more. In trying not only to unravel the thread of successive events, but rather to explore the condition and the state of the nation altogether, this kind of study gives us a *biography,* as it were."[20] Humboldt's mirroring of *Bildung* and biography and of nation and individual was symptomatic of a wider and lasting tendency to establish a developmental, narrative model both for use in scholarly discourse and for articulating the discipline's own self-understanding.[21]

The standard narrative of the rise of philology in the nineteenth century posits an increasingly professionalized, institutionalized discipline within the secular university, where philology is separated from theology. In addition, the traditional historiography of the discipline sees a shift from the "ideal" neohumanist university, exemplified by Humboldt's program for the newly founded Friedrich Wilhelm University in Berlin and marked by a top-down administrative endorsement of *Bildung,* and toward the highly successful and tyrannical academic machine of the latter part of the century. That machine is said to have favored increasing specialization and to have become increasingly bound by the stranglehold of a fraying empirical-positivist historicism; to have at once cultivated projects of the micro scale (philological overspecialization) and the macro scale (big-science projects such as the ambitious collections of Latin and Greek inscriptions, made up of a multitude of microprojects); and to have paid only lip service to the notion of a comprehensive individual *Bildung*—with a brief flourishing of a new Third Humanism and reexamination of the classical in the 1920s, before World War II changed things for good.[22]

Such a narrative, however, underestimates the tensions *within* philology as a privileged scholarly method of approaching past or otherwise foreign cultures and the question of how to understand them, constitutive tensions that were visible from the late eighteenth century onward and cannot simply be mapped onto a detached idealist superstructure increasingly lagging behind philological practice. We should therefore not reduce this narrative to the story of a failed idealism deteriorating into hyperspecialization.

The rise of philology as an independent discipline is still often linked (though in an increasingly disputed way) to Wolf's self-styled foundational act of matriculating in 1777 at Georgia Augusta in Göttingen as a *philologiae studiosus.* If conferring centrality on his figure misrepresents the beginnings of philological independence, it serves to reveal the self-perception of the discipline and its search for heroic exempla.[23] The first philological seminar was in fact founded in Göttingen, in 1738, by Johann Mattias Gesner, and was continued and expanded by Christian Gottlob Heyne, with whom Wolf studied and from whom he sought to distinguish himself.[24] Not only was Wolf not the first signed-up philologist, his best known work, the *Prolegomena ad Homerum* (1795), shows significant continuities and dialogue not only with the traditions of early modern textual criticism (especially in Holland and England) but also with developments in biblical criticism.[25]

Wolf's contribution to a growing cultural and scholarly debate about the history of Homeric epic was the skeptical text-critical claim that any original text of an epic poem that began as oral poetry was beyond recovery, and that any textual account could only begin at the earliest in the Hellenistic period, in the world of Alexandrian scholarship and its source texts. In other words, Wolf paved the way for *Textgeschichte* as it was conceptualized later by, for example, Otto Jahn and Ulrich von Wilamowitz-Moellendorff, and the establishment of a "history of a text," a subdiscipline already in antiquity.[26] This minimalist philological attitude, however, did not stop Wolf from speculating maximally about the cultural environment of early oral epic, and his promotion and defense of his work shows most importantly the confidence with which he claimed rigorous philological analysis was an approach that participated fully, and with conclusive answers, in a much wider literary and cultural debate.[27]

Such confidence in the authority of philological criticism was part of the persona of the critic—or at least this is suggested by the works and personality of Richard Bentley (1662–1742), whom Wolf gladly included in his genealogy of philological dignitaries.[28] Bentley, too, tried to negotiate his standing as a textual critic within the context of the rising class of literary critics in London and their cultural clout. Although his insertion into that group may have been shaped by slightly different priorities than Wolf's, it is the rise of the critic himself, as a new kind of active reader and writer no longer defined by reference to the imitation of models, that looms large here; without it, the role and definition of the professional philologist might have looked very different. The emergence of the critic was one effect of the so-called *querelle des anciens et des modernes,* the debate over the relative authority of ancient models in all branches of knowledge that so exercised thinkers and artists at the turn of the seventeenth century, radiating from the center of the debate in France to the rest of Europe.[29] If nothing else, the memory of the *querelle* should be a good indicator that the genesis of modern philology makes it difficult to distinguish the role of the philologist from those of the historian, the cultural critic, and the critic of cultural normativity and value.[30]

Raising Philology to a Comprehensive Science: Wolf's Program

In the introduction, Sheldon Pollock comments on the relative dearth of theory in a good deal of philological practice as we know it. In the long nineteenth century, though, especially in the German-speaking world, there was certainly no shortage of programmatic writing about philology and its status as a form of criticism.[31] A good and far-reaching example is

Wolf's *Darstellung der Alterthums-Wissenschaft,* originally published in 1807 in the inaugural volume of the short-lived journal *Museum der Alterthums-Wissenschaft,* which Wolf edited with Philipp Buttman in Berlin.[32]

Even if Ritschl thought that Wolf, whom he considered one of the earliest visionaries of a *Verknüpfung der Einseitigkeiten,* offered only a rather random juxtaposition of features in his *Darstellung,* the treatise is not without methodological traction or interest.[33] In it, we can see reflected all of the topics and questions that will reappear in theoretical or programmatic writings on philology in the course of the nineteenth century: the task of a broadly conceived philology that lays claim to the status of a professional discipline with its own canon of materials, techniques, and qualifications; the need for limitations and the kinds required; the definition of the scholar, and the boundaries between academic and nonacademic knowledge; and the relation between rationality and a nonrational element in the practices of philology.

Off the starting block, Wolf subtly but authoritatively slides from offering "an introduction to a revision or an encyclopedia of the knowledge usually known as *philological*" to declaring his project an ambitious attempt to combine the individual opinions expressed at German universities in the past, present, and future into an organic whole, so as "to raise everything that belongs to the complete knowledge of learned antiquity to the status of a well-ordered *philosophical-historical science.*"[34] This is the *Altertumswissenschaft* of his title—a comprehensive science of antiquity that combines various branches of knowledge but still gives pride of place to textual sources and to a philological way of reading even nontextual sources: an approach that is analytic and critical as well as synthetic, seeking to identify a larger idea that counters dispersion.[35] Wolf's organic project aims to remedy fragmentation, and magnifies the scope and range of philology at the same time. He is equally aware from the start that philology will need strategies of limitation. Introducing a distinction between *Zivilisation* and *Geisteskultur,* he preempts the question of how broadly to conceive of antiquity by claiming that while Oriental civilizations may have existed earlier, true "spiritual culture" only began with the Greeks.[36] Wolf here (and throughout) engages explicitly and implicitly with earlier scholarship on the ancients (such as that by Joseph Scaliger) and with other philosophical histories of the eighteenth century whose more cosmopolitan outlook, including acknowledgment of Near Eastern and Asian civilizations, he has to work hard to curtail, or to fit around the strong Hellenism that takes its place.

Limitation may go—or have to go—even further than Wolf suggests here: toward the end of the essay he comments on the paradigmatic quality of Greek culture (in essence, Winckelmann's Periclean Athens) as the confluence of free and beneficial conditions in political, artistic, and natural terms. Compared to this high point of humanity, though, and even within the already limited frame of the Greco-Roman world that for Wolf is the standard of value, Roman culture already raises a problematic counterpoint: the Romans cannot provide a fully desirable subject matter, since from the beginning they displayed some of the one-sidedness *(einseitige Richtungen)* that has also "in the last centuries bedeviled some of most highly respected nations."[37] This is undoubtedly meant as a stab against neighboring France and its Roman tradition, but Wolf is not the only philologist or historiographer of philology who represent Greece and Rome as grossly unequal, a view very much created and magnified through the increasingly strong differentiation between the two in exactly this period. Although the Hellenism of German scholarship and culture has been well studied, there regrettably exists as yet no separate and comprehensive treatment of the history of Latin studies and Latin philology in the German academy.[38]

There are additional strategies of limitation, of which Wolf is aware, concerning the range of philology and of its method that have to be addressed in relation to the amount of materials available—and growing. In defining more precisely the scope of subject matter, he estimates that some sixteen hundred writings in Greek and Latin are available in his time, explicitly discounting for the moment all Christian writings and thus creating another category of limitation.[39] For Wolf and his contemporaries, being able to give a precise figure may still suggest an optimistic belief in the synoptic view that is possible. We may want to compare Hegel, who in his *Lectures on Aesthetics* suggests, in passing and in the context of his more famous pronouncement on Sophocles's *Antigone,* that "among the fine creations of the ancient and modern world—*and I am acquainted with nearly everything in such a class, and one ought to know it and it is quite possible*—the Antigone of Sophokles is from this point of view in my judgment the most excellent and satisfying work of art."[40] Here we get a glimpse of the confidence, still possible, of knowing and mastering all of classical antiquity—a belief in control that would become increasingly difficult to maintain, and that is already fraying at the edges in Wolf's *Darstellung:* quite aside from ancillary knowledge of other ancient and modern languages, the proper territory of *Altertumswissenschaft,* as he has it, "has already become impossible to traverse in every direction even for the most diligent and optimistic."[41] Thus he concedes that the philological scholar will have to negotiate constantly between "drawing modest boundaries" and being able to engage extraneous materials fully when they present themselves, even if he has reduced the scope considerably.[42] Anthony Grafton has commented on the shifting balance between the polyhistor of the early modern period and the *philologus* of the world of professionalizing scholarship, as two ends of a spectrum; Wolf seems to suggest that the task of the modern scholar is to be the philologist who knows enough about polyhistory to control it with his new-found skills, when needed.[43] In fact, this is not so different from the usage of the term "encyclopedia" established from Wolf onward and throughout the nineteenth century (see below in detail for Boeckh) as an introduction to the philological method. Turning an earlier pyramid of knowledge on its head, the encyclopedic is the foundation that specialization both builds on and tempers (an expectation that did not come to an end, certainly in the Germanic academic system, with the age of grand cumulative projects in the late nineteenth century).

If there were limits to be drawn on what any given philologist could know, there were fewer on the monopoly claimed by philological knowledge compared to other forms of knowing antiquity, though tellingly some ambivalence remains. Wolf himself offers a little embedded history of the uses of antiquity, and he acknowledges the different use of ancient materials for contemporary ends in humanist practice, which looked to add content to new developing disciplines, but also to maintain a sense of the artistic or historical exemplarity of antiquity and of the classical languages as a medium of literary expression. Wolf is clear that he considers the latter a need now superseded: in the modern world, "our knowledge has taken such patriotic shape" that there are neither judges nor venues any longer for such a unifying use of the ancient languages.[44] But using them to dig out any last remaining nugget of practical wisdom now, to try to find exemplarity in antiquity, would lack all proportionality: "even gold can be purchased at too high a price."[45]

Still, in his survey of justifications put forward for the engagement with antiquity, Wolf concedes that there exist amateurs, like those who have good historical knowledge without being historians proper, who can through a natural affinity with antiquity hit the mark more effectively in their understanding and in their thinking and doing than those who have devoted a lifetime to specialization and offered their services as mere translators *(Dollmetscher)*.[46] While Wolf here mentions explicitly "one of our kings, the pride of all Prussians and Germans," he is also indirectly referring back to the already authoritative figure of Goethe, to whom the *Darstellung* is dedicated in an encomiastic preface.[47] This is a preview of the enormous admiration for Goethe that would be shared and articulated by many later philologists (many, but certainly not all, German), always aware that he embodies the comprehensively talented artist and scholar in perfect union, whose range lies beyond the expectations and possibilities of the trained philologist and whose extraordinary character helps to articulate the boundaries of the ordinary practitioner.[48]

The scholar is confronted with different expectations, among them that he ought to enable others both to gain access to antiquity (i.e., pedagogy) and to fulfill the aims of science, which, as Wolf lays out in a long but significant footnote, can and should also stretch to moral improvement—he quotes a letter from Gronov to Heinsius stating that the purpose of reading the classics lies in emending one's character rather than the text's punctuation.[49] *Emendatio,* in other words, should not be considered synonymous with the work of "trockene Kritiker" but should by extension be demanded of all branches of science.[50] As for scientific standards, the *Altertumswissenschaftler* is obliged to examine everything for himself and to be ready for his work to be reexamined in turn with a view to "the knowledge of sources and their correct use."[51] Wolf's exposition of a new scientific accountability comes exactly at the place in the text where he has pointed out the need for or tendency toward specialization that characterizes the modern world, where the fundamental condition of knowledge is the "sure command of the *organon,*" meaning in the first place the assured knowledge of the languages that he has just expounded.

Wolf's essay, which is both a systematic survey of the branches of *Altertumswissenschaft* in their hierarchical and pedagogical relation and a historical and programmatic account of the value of studying antiquity, works itself up to the articulation of the highest aim of such study, the quasi-mystical *Epoptie* of the sacred, comparable to that experienced by the initiates at Eleusis: "this goal is *nothing other than the knowledge of the humankind of antiquity itself, a knowledge that is based on the study of its remains and emerges from observation of an organically grown meaningful national Bildung.*"[52] This "national *Bildung*" is, as in Humboldt's (and Winckelmann's) writings, exemplified by the Greek world (up to the period of Philip and Alexander) of "peoples and states which had by nature most of those features on which a character's perfection of true humanity is based."[53] Leaving aside the ostensibly objectivist tone in which highly subjectivist knowledge is turned into authoritative knowledge of human subjectivity, the Humboldtian tone of an anthropological mission of classical study is not accidental, and recent study has shown how deeply implicated with Humboldt's own writings Wolf is at this juncture.[54] How much, then, is Wolf getting sidetracked by a language of humanistic *Bildung* that is mostly grafted onto his own interests? The end of his essay suggests that he is aware of the dangers of such an approach: "and yet, the science I have suggested here is as little going to be helped by such humanist knowledge as philosophy is by popular writings on practical wisdom, or any other science by having its most useful results become part of public education. For this can be rather more a disadvantage to scholarly and detailed treatment, and broad dissemination can lead to superficiality. Our own branch of science knows similar worrying phenomena already, even in the writings of respected scholars."[55] And yet, Wolf is more worried about a superficiality due less to a lack of specialization and more to a lack of coherence: an *Einseitigkeit* that fails to see the overall, organic idea that gives coherence to the study of a national (ancient) culture: "the worst such phenomenon is the constant attempt to heap up isolated material especially in the field of history and the languages of antiquity, without taking charge of first principles, without even trying to grasp a sense of the intellectual component that forms everything individual into a harmonious whole."[56]

It is this form of limitation that makes for bad science, for confusion between unconnected knowledge and scientific standards. At this moment of the highest *Epoptie* about the aim of classical philology Wolf also recoils from giving his insight about its dangers further rational analysis: "but to argue properly against this form of error and others like it, which has damaged the dignity of philological study and the scholarship of antiquity for a long time now, such argument belongs to the treatment of the best kinds of scholarship and its rules, a topic that lies outside our present scope."[57] Disconnected one-sidedness, isolated philological findings that do not add up to a larger organic picture, are presented as a long-standing threat to philology proper, but the treatment of this history and a programmatic suggestion of best practices to counteract such diffusion is deflected in this strangely muted and inconclusive conclusion to Wolf's *Darstellung*. The treatise at this point ends, below Wolf's signature, with a numbered list of the constituent parts and materials of such a comprehensive *Altertumswissenschaft*, a format that has made it (all too) easy to conclude that what we find in Wolf is more compilation and less a programmatic account of philology.

Boeckh's Capital-P Philology and the *Erkenntnis des Erkannten*

The credit for articulating the program for a comprehensive *Altertumswissenschaft* that relies on philology as the royal road to any form of interpretation in the study of culture is usually given to August Boeckh, who was appointed as one of the first professors at the newly founded University of Berlin in 1810, after Humboldt failed to move an increasingly intractable and peevish Wolf to accept the same position. In Berlin, where he founded the seminar for philology in 1814, Boeckh left his mark on a discipline that he taught until his death in 1867 and represented as a high-ranking administrator at both the university and the Prussian Academy of Sciences, where he shaped and oversaw such big projects as the *Corpus Inscriptionum Graecarum* (from 1815).[58] His series of introductory lectures, which he gave over thirty years and which shaped generations of students and professional scholars across the German-speaking world, was posthumously edited in 1877 as the *Encyclopädie und Methodologie der Philologischen Wissenschaften.*

Where Wolf's *Darstellung* opens with a daring slide from a piecemeal reservoir of philological knowledge toward a holistic science of antiquity, Boeckh imitates and emulates it: a definition of philology cannot be tantamount to a list of its component parts, nor does it exhaust itself in a science of antiquity: "ancient times are not comprehensible without the complement of the modern ones; no one can fathom antiquity without intuition of the more modern."[59] Philology is a general method of scientific interpretation in which, as will become clear, antiquity holds only a privileged place. Science *(Wissenschaft)* as such is a whole, a philosophy or science of ideas, whose disciplinary differentiation is a reflection of the emphasis we give to the material or ideal aspects of the world, to physics or to ethics (broadly speaking). Philology, in a way, contains that entire spectrum yet does not belong to either category only.[60] Philology offers a way into an understanding of all previous thought covered by *Wissenschaft,* thus making it the meta-*Wissenschaft* par excellence, and of necessity historical in its outlook too. Boeckh's prime example through which he introduces this thought is the writings of Plato, as a thinker whose range comprised all branches of knowledge, from the physical world to the ethical and spiritual, and whom we seek to understand rather than imitate:

> As philologists, our task is not to philosophize like Plato, but to understand Plato's writings not only as works of art with respect to their form, but also in terms of their content. Explanation, which is fundamentally philological in nature, has predominantly to do with understanding content. . . . Thus the proper task of philology is to recognize and understand the products of the human mind, and what it has understood [das Erkennen des vom menschlichen Geist Producirten, d.h. des Erkannten]. Philology presupposes a given knowledge, which it sets out to recognize. The history of all sciences is thus philological.[61]

Philology, as an *Erkenntnis des Erkannten,* an understanding of what has once been understood before, or, as he glosses it a little further on, a "reconstruction of the constructions of the human mind," is a fundamental historical method; at the same time, since it examines the articulation and communication *(Mittheilung)* of knowledge and of anything intellectual or conceptual *(geistig),* it can cover as its subject matter also all historical events, which are nothing other than *Geistiges* changed into action. The advantage of making antiquity the body of material for such philological inquiry is its self-sufficiency and completeness—it is linguistically, culturally, historically distinct as a classical period, and recognizable as such from a later vantage point.

Whether and how antiquity is a complete entity is a different and arguable question, of course, but Boeckh is able to reinforce this argument by relying not only on the limitations seen already in Wolf (the relatively greater availability of Greek and Roman sources, their quality, their canonicity) but also on a subtle but consistent use of Plato throughout his *Encyclopädie* as a foil for the content and the method of philological, hermeneutic inquiry, for a way of knowing. With Boeckh, who was a pupil of Friedrich Schleiermacher and, among other things, a reviewer of his translations of Plato, we are in a period when Plato as a systematic thinker, the author of a complete body of works and the creator of a body of coherent, finished, organically grown thought, had gained new traction.[62] And just as Schleiermacher's theoretical reflections on (literary and cultural) translation were very much shaped around the example of Plato, Boeckh here profits from an underlying seamless extension he suggests from Plato's works to a culture made coherent by ideas, the proper and exemplary subject of philology as a method of interpretation.[63] The exact relationship between Schleiermacher's hermeneutics, or philosophy of interpretation, and that of Boeckh is a matter of scholarly debate.[64] What Boeckh could undoubtedly have taken from Schleiermacher is his basic structure of interpretation of something nonself by a self, of a "you" by an "I," of a foreign individuality by an individual.

This Platonic foil allows for the difficult and rare possibility of what Boeckh considers deep and genuine insight. At the same time, historical distance and the loss incurred through it make antiquity paradoxically all the more exemplary and fruitful as the subject of philological reflection and reconstruction: "antiquity is more remote, more alien, more incomprehensible and fragmentary and thus in need of reconstruction to a far higher degree."[65] Even if Boeckh does not say this explicitly, antiquity's paradigmatic closeness through foreignness exemplifies the constitutive paradox and tensions of philology if and as soon as it is understood as practice or method of reflection, reconstruction, recovery, or representation: it contains within itself, constitutively, the tendency toward both concentration (and its extremes of hyperspecialization or hypercanonicity) and expansion (and its extreme of hyperinclusiveness or diffusion). Especially in the Romantic period, which valued reflection and its cognates as one of its favorite operations, philology could thus be essential. Whichever end of the spectrum any given philology gravitates toward, it is, in Boeckh's words, by necessity incomplete: "philology, like every other science, is an infinite task of approximation. In philology, we will always be one-sided [einseitig] collectors and never bring to fruition a total union with speculation; for speculation too is always one-sided. And yet, incompleteness is no mistake; the only true deficiency is not to acknowledge it."[66] At the same time, like Wolf and Humboldt before him, Boeckh gestures toward the need for a unifying viewpoint to save philology from a fragmentation that goes beyond the present conditions of its materials (but note the need for the assumption that such fragmentation is a phenomenon of its present state, not its original one). Philology, here too always threatened by *Einseitigkeit,* is realized only in the sum of its practitioners, "in a thousand heads, partial, dismembered, broken, not to mention strange and in a broken tongue; but the great love alone, with which so many have embraced [philology], guarantees the reality of the idea, which is nothing other than the reconstruction of the constructions of the human mind in their totality."[67]

This language of *Gesamtheit,* of totality and wholeness, is repeated in Boeckh's assessment of how any insight is possible into what he significantly glosses as a "fremde Individualität"—a body of texts or cultural materials that represent an "alien individuality," a formulation that makes clear how inseparable the language of philology is from the imagining of its subject matter as reflecting coherent human agency.

Such approximation or convergence *(Annäherung)* relies on skill, technical knowledge, and expertise, but it needs to be complemented by an intuitive disposition:

> In certain cases, feeling can reach a complete form of understanding, and the hermeneutic artist will be all the more perfectly accomplished the more he is in possession of such a feeling, which can cut through a knot but cannot otherwise offer justification. It is this feeling by which we can suddenly recognize what someone else once already understood, and without it there would indeed be no ability to communicate at all. Even though individuals are different from

> each other, they also harmonize in respect to many things; one can understand another individuality up to a point by way of calculation, but one can grasp completely certain of its expressions in a vivid intuition [lebendige Anschauung], which rests in feeling.[68]

This intuition as a sudden, unpredictable recognition that lacks any justification beyond itself suggests again the Platonic, or at any rate Platonizing, language of vision and insight.[69] With the mention of the "hermeneutic artist" *(hermeneutischer Künstler)* it also hints at the uncertainly defined interplay between the spheres of science and art. Earlier in the *Encyclopädie,* Boeckh had quoted Schelling's opinion that the philologist "stands at the highest level together with the artist and the philosopher, or rather they merge in him. His task is the historical construction of works of art and science, the history of which he must grasp and represent in vivid intuition [in lebendiger Anschauung]."[70] Boeckh quotes Schelling apropos his own definition of the characteristics required of the philologist, among them "a pure heart and mind, open to everything that is good and beautiful, equally receptive to the most transcendental and to the smallest thing below, feeling and imagination combined with a sharp rational mind, a harmonious integration of feeling and thought, of life and knowledge, which, aside from unstinting industry, are the fundamentals of philology, as they are for any other science."[71] This is in some ways a familiar trope, glossed from Cicero's description of the ideal orator and not exclusive to Boeckh.[72] In conjunction with Schelling's comment on the philologist as mediator between philosopher and artist, though, Boeckh's statement here seems closer to Friedrich Schlegel than to Cicero, and more daring in his reach.

In the collaborative set of aphorisms published in the journal *Athenäum,* which Schlegel coedited, Schlegel states that the poet, "if he wants to be an expert [Kenner] and understand his fellow citizens in the realm of art, has to be a philologist as well."[73] Schlegel highlighted what was otherwise latent: that the boundaries between poetry, philosophy, and philology (as the skill and method of reading and interpreting texts and linguistic sources) were more porous than the self-image of a discipline coming into focus suggested. His radical program may not have reflected common or comfortable beliefs of institutionalized scholarship, busy at that moment building its disciplinary framework.[74] But his own prominence (as a writer, a translator and, not least, a promoter of the study of language and its origins, including especially the study of Sanskrit) and his indirect influence suggest that Boeckh's reflections on an artistic, intuitive element of philological insight were part of an ongoing negotiation of the demarcation of philology.

Philology in Theory and Practice

Where does this leave Boeckh the practicing philologist, and how removed from the actual task of philology are such programmatic writings? Boeckh contributed significant studies to fields as varied as Platonic geometry, the public economy of Athens, and Pindaric meter, aside from his involvement with the newly established Academy project of a complete edition of all Greek inscriptions. It was the latter, and the publication of its first volume, that from 1825 accelerated a heated review exchange between him and Gottfried Hermann that has often been taken to exemplify a breaking apart of German philology into two incompatible methodological camps: *Sachphilologie,* an inclusive understanding of antiquity based on a wide range of materials and approaches and aimed at interpretation, and *Wortphilologie,* which limits the task of the philologist to textual knowledge, textual criticism, and the establishing of text editions that treats interpretation as only secondary.

The slightly older Hermann (1772–1848), who dominated philology at the University of Leipzig and was well known especially for his critical work on the Greek tragedians and on meter, did not hesitate to call Boeckh out on text-critical and linguistic weaknesses or to claim pride of place for text constitution rather than contextual speculation, and both participants certainly contributed to the appraisal of this particular controversy as one between two incompatible methods. At the same time, neither of them fit this narrative particularly neatly.[75] Thomas Poiss has shown convincingly that the sharpness of the debate likely owes more to the narcissism of small differences (both scholars established a profile in metrical analysis, at the time considered a privileged way to appreciate the individual character of a literary text) and that in many ways the controversy boils down to differing opinions about the relative transparency and possibility of interpretation: Boeckh, as shown above, believed in a structurally inevitable approximation and incompleteness that characterizes interpretation, in short, in the Romantic hermeneutic circle. Hermann, especially in his essay "The Task of the Interpreter" *(De officio interpreti)* of 1834, formulates interpretation as a challenge that within its given limits, which are considerably narrower than those set by Boeckh, is solvable with reference to rational techniques and criteria.

In other words, their "quarrel" is not over philology and an unspecified alternative, two incompatible methods, but over the relative scope and scale of philology and its focus. Boeckh is a good reminder that, in its claims, Romantic, organic, idealistic thought is not necessarily unsystematic; Hermann is a reminder that textual criticism is not self-evidently systematic: Sebastiano Timpanaro has drawn attention to Hermann's lack of interest in the systematic collation and study of manuscripts and his overemphasis on intuition of style and conjecture, a skill that, to Hermann and to many of his contemporaries, had as much to do with individual talent and nonrational insight as with teachable technique.[76]

Timpanaro makes his comments on Hermann in the context of his own historicizing study of the genesis of "Lachmann's method"—named after the philologist Karl Lachmann (1793–1851), whose name is connected to the rise of the "stemmatic method," in short, the establishing of the relationships among manuscripts in the form of a family tree, a technique for arriving at preferred authentic readings that form the basis for text editions and that, to stay with the genealogical image, keep the relatives at bay. This implied a systematic, standardized, mechanical collation of manuscripts as the royal road, a demand for a full *recensio* (a practice going back to antiquity), then followed by selection and, if necessary, emendation.[77] Lachmann, who neither invented the method nor always consistently applied it,[78] helped to turn it into a model approach that could extend beyond classical philology (though he was a trained classicist), as for example in his edition of the German medieval *Nibelungenlied.* Its appeal was strengthened by its successful application to other textual traditions, national literatures, and language families, especially in the developing study of Indo-European linguistics.[79]

Timpanaro mentions Hermann in this context less as a predecessor to Lachmann than to show that Hermann's pronounced attention to style, conjecture, and intuitive insight, although in the name of discipline, should be read as a regression from the achievements of textual criticism of the eighteenth century, exemplified by the advances of biblical criticism and the works of figures such as Johann August Ernesti and Wolf. Does this suggest that we can sidestep Hermann and his arguments with Boeckh, and simply make a distinction between the idealist-Romantic programs of philology on the one hand and a rigorous, concrete, widely applicable method of textual criticism and edition on the other, saving philology from ideology?

Maybe not, because the rigor of this rigorous method itself emerged from a specific ideological and historical context, with its own organizing metaphors. The language of family trees, of relationships between manuscripts, remains indebted to an imagery that searches for ostensible organic coherence, for identifiable individual character, for comprehensive, self-contained integrity. It is an approach that readily acknowledges fragmentation, contamination, and stratification, but in an attempt to postulate an original underlying cohesion, to identify and to arrive at a hypothetical original that expresses through language that can and should be reconstructed the selfsame individuality of an author or culture.

We see this already in Wolf. Here, systematic *recensio* aims at restoring authenticity, whether we like what we see as a result or not:

> True, continuous, and systematic recension differs greatly from this frivolous and desultory method [i.e., only looking up a manuscript when the vulgate is not satisfactory; this lets lots of minor issues slip through]. In the latter we want only to cure indiscriminately the wounds that are conspicuous or are revealed by some manuscript or other. We pass over more [readings] which are good and passable as regards sense, but no better than the worst as regards authority. But true recension, attended by the full complement of useful instruments, seeks out *the author's true handiwork* at every point. It examines in order the witnesses for every reading, not only for those that are suspect. It changes, only for the most serious reasons, readings that all of these approve. It accepts, only when they are supported by witnesses, others that are worthy in themselves of the author and accurate and elegant in their form. Not uncommonly, then, when the witnesses require it, true recension replaces attractive readings with less attractive ones. It takes off bandages and lays bare the sores. Finally, it cures not only manifest ills, as bad doctors do, but hidden ones, too.[80]

The assumption that there is an "author's true handiwork" that should be the ideally recovered object makes clear once more the impetus of *modern* philology (in its ideological dimension): it wants not simply to replace a mimetic energy, which sought artistic and stylistic models in ancient texts, with a historical investigation; instead, it *transforms* this energy into critical analysis, making the critic the true judge of interpretation, authorship, and the origins of cultural expressions through language. Whether practiced by Wolf's careful doctor, Boeckh's Platonic seeker of knowledge, Hermann's conjectural hero, or Lachmann's judge of genealogy, philology, however broadly or narrowly conceived, has become the approach that is demanded by the sources themselves and that in turn exemplifies and furthers the critic's authority. In addition, this authority was held in place by the sheltering walls of an institutionalized and hence recognizable discipline, with its own set of practices, qualifications, and conventions.

Does the philology of the second half of the nineteenth century really simply jettison neohumanist intentions, replacing them with a narrow-minded historicism, the quasi-industrial production of historical fact and detail? The overspecialized, dust-blind "micrologist" satirized by Nietzsche and the antlike but somehow still spiritually beneficial condition of Ritschl's scholar who feels his own significance in "participating in building the cathedral of science" ("sich zu wissen als Mitarbeiter am Dombau der Wissenschaft")[81]—these describe figures of the scholar who continue to be defined through their own ability (or inability) to create a vision of a foreign or ancient individuality (a body of texts and cultural artifacts) that stimulates reflection on themselves. The aim continues to be to see an overall, whole picture, whether of a text, an author, a culture, or a nation. If the scope of individual works narrows down (as for example in the increasingly smaller and more specific projects that make up such collaborative mammoths as the epigraphic collections), the belief persists that there is an overall understanding of a larger whole that will emerge at a point in the future. The limited vision of the small-scale philological project depends structurally on the expectation that there is a larger whole that will emerge as a matter of fact.

Christoph König makes reference to the need for "insistent reading": a reflective, theoretically astute, and nonnaïve way of philological practice that takes account of the cognitive conflicts inherent in such pairs as objectivity versus values and history versus aesthetics, that tries to take account of more than one side without prejudice.[82] This is also a form of reading that constantly recalibrates its scale without assuming that there is a self-evidently and naturally right-sized image of the thing we try to interpret. It is a call for philological practice that takes inspiration from the language of a highly reflexive nineteenth-century philology, but does not content itself with one perspective only. Instead, it encourages the cognitively challenging stereoscopy and constant renegotiation of different kinds of *Einseitigkeit* (and even the resulting enthusiasm) in one and the same philological process and practitioner, embracing the object of philology as a moving target.

This conclusion is latent in the programmatic writings of nineteenth-century philology, which could be remarkably aware of its own history and historicity, acknowledging the need for making reflection on philology and its history a part of philological practice itself—a philological practice, in turn, that in order to continue to be productive ought to embrace its unsettling cognitive dissonances as fully and explicitly as possible.

The Intelligence of Philological Practice

On the Interpretation of Rilke's Sonnet "O komm und geh"

CHRISTOPH KÖNIG

A Classic Problem of Interpretation

IN THE BRIEFEST SPAN of time—within only a few days in February 1922—Rainer Maria Rilke (1875–1926) penned a twin cycle of fifty-five poems and gave them the title "The Sonnets to Orpheus." The title is a dedication. The sonnets are directed "to" Orpheus, the focus of the ancient, orphic, mystical poetic tradition. Ovid's *Metamorphoses* constituted Rilke's source for the three tales that surface again and again in these poems: first, Ovid's account of the singer Orpheus, whom the Maenads kill and whose head and lyre, intact and continuing to sing, float down the river Hebros and into the sea; second, the story of how the animals and trees themselves flocked around the singer; and finally, the story of Orpheus's journey into the underworld to win back his wife, Eurydice.[1] Yet Rilke also adds a second dedication. The sonnets bear the subtitle "Geschrieben als ein Grab-Mal / für Wera Ouckama Knoop" ("Written as a monument / to Wera Ouckama Knoop"). Rilke's friend Wera Ouckama Knoop was a young dancer who died at the age of nineteen.[2] These two figures, the dancer and Orpheus, meet in the penultimate sonnet, on which I shall focus:

XXVIII

O komm und geh. Du, fast noch Kind, ergänze
für einen Augenblick die Tanzfigur
zum reinen Sternbild einer jener Tänze,
darin wir die dumpf ordnende Natur

vergänglich übertreffen. Denn sie regte
sich völlig hörend nur, da Orpheus sang.
Du warst noch die von damals her Bewegte
und leicht befremdet, wenn ein Baum sich lang

besann, mit dir nach dem Gehör zu gehn.
Du wußtest noch die Stelle, wo die Leier
sich tönend hob—; die unerhörte Mitte.

Für sie versuchtest du die schönen Schritte
und hofftest, einmal zu der heilen Feier
des Freundes Gang und Antlitz hinzudrehn.[3]

XXVIII

O come and go. You, still half a child,
fill out the dance figure for a moment
to the pure constellation of one of those
dances in which we fleetingly transcend

dumbly ordering Nature. For she roused
to full hearing only when Orpheus sang.
You were the one still moved from that earlier time,
and a little surprised if a tree took long to consider

whether to go along with you by ear.
You still knew the place where the lyre
lifted sounding—: the unheard-of center.

For this you tried the lovely steps and hoped
one day towards the perfect celebration
to turn the pace and countenance of your friend.[4]

Translations can be helpful for revealing potentially important idiosyncrasies. The syntax of the original allows the word "Freund" to be read either forward or backward in the original German: "zu der heilen Feier / des Freundes Gang und Antlitz"—a classical interpretive problem created by means of the rhetorical figure of the *apo koinu.* Yet the question whether the poem refers to the friend's celebration ("Feier") or to the friend's pace and countenance ("Gang und Antlitz") is summarily decided in the English version: "pace and countenance of your friend." The ascription involved in this English translation determines the interpretation of "friend." Is it Orpheus, or is it Wera's mourner, Rilke himself (who has disguised himself as a poet in the poem, attending Orpheus's celebration)? We are not yet in a position to settle or even to properly understand this issue. For now, let us simply preface our investigation with Rilke's warning to Margot Sizzo in a letter of March 17, 1922: "not a single word in a poem (and this holds of every "and," "the," "it," or "this") corresponds to any one of the identical-sounding words as they appear in everyday conversation and usage."[5]

This essay chiefly addresses the philologist's difficulties in understanding the meaning of difficult texts and the means by which such interpretative questions can be settled. It will develop a few approaches toward a solution in five sections. First I lay out the epistemological conflicts that confront philology conceived as a praxis and then, in the second section, present hermeneutics as the theory of such a philological praxis. The third section concerns the relation of nondiscursive understanding and the philological history of interpretations. This enables me to propose an interpretation of Rilke's sonnet within a critique of philological praxis. And finally, I demonstrate a way to derive methodological guidance from the history of this poem's interpretations.

Philological Praxis

Philology is an activity.[6] Friedrich Nietzsche underscores the aspect of craftmanship in this activity in a famous sentence from *Daybreak (Morgenröte):* "it is not for nothing that I have been a philologist, perhaps I am a philologist still, that is to say, a teacher of slow reading. . . . For philology is that venerable art which demands of its votaries one thing above all: to go aside, to take time, to become still, to become slow—it is a goldsmith's art and a connoisseurship of the *word* which has nothing but delicate, cautious work to do and which achieves nothing if it does not achieve it *lento.*"[7] It is to praxis that one must look in elaborating the fundamental features of an epistemology of philology.

The foundations of the subject matter and method of philological disciplines become apparent not through theoretical deduction but by reflection on acts of philology. Grounding philology within the framework of a theory of philological praxis may result in a critically reflected discipline, but one that will inevitably appear to many today as doubly alien—first in relation to literary studies, and second in relation to a philological tradition that has eschewed methodological reflection. Literary studies in the German sense of "Literaturwissenschaft" understands itself, on the strength of its (rapidly changing) theories, as a science: it aims to fix its topic and its methods for analysis theoretically.[8]

Historically, literary studies is a young discipline, which has developed within and in contrast to philologies since the end of the nineteenth century.[9] And rightly so, for the naïveté of philologists has devolved into a sort of adage,[10] and the naïveté of philology is unwittingly paired with political functions that pervade even the exercise of the craft. The sort of philology I am interested in here—the sort that investigates the conditions of the possibility of philological praxis—has little in common with naïve philology, yet neither is it a form of literary studies.

Philological practice consists of an open series of operations: collecting, editing, annotating, commentary and elucidation, interpretation, translation, literary history, judgments of taste, aesthetic criticism, canon formation, and the application of culture and erudition *(Bildung)*. These activities manifest both technical acuity and a generally unacknowledged critical rationality. To invoke a Kantian notion on which we will later dwell at some length, one might speak of a nondiscursive intelligence in the practice.[11] Technical applications are entirely rule-governed, but no particular application of these rules can itself be determined by rules. In this respect, practical facility is a question of phronesis and not of theory. (Of course, the activities of editing, annotating, etc. are, in large part, discursively constituted. The point here is that the ability to engage in such activities on any particular occasion cannot itself be a purely discursive capacity.) The implicit capacity of the praxis enables one, in principle, to enrich the exploration of contemporary questions through older investigations. By referring to a praxis that has the power to emancipate one from historical dependencies, one can legitimately invoke and discuss past philological insights and results, regardless of the circumstances surrounding their origin. This considerably extends the possibilities of the discipline: one can make a claim for the truth or validity of a view within and despite the sociological (Pierre Bourdieu), epistemic (Michel Foucault), or systemic (Niklas Luhmann) entanglement of knowledge.

The fatalism that marks such modern theories of knowledge and scholarship comes across as outdated. Instead of giving up on past knowledge with a gesture at its conditioned nature, philology is capable of distinguishing genuine insight from misunderstanding. To do so presupposes a commitment to translating the language in which those insights were formulated—a language that can often appear rather curious. The governing principle is that the ingenuity immanent in a practice manages to preserve itself in philologies despite the external, historical conditions of that practice.

The praxis of *understanding* plays an immensely important role. Indeed, it pervades all other philological practices (namely, editing, annotating, and interpreting). And the theory of the praxis of understanding was developed quite early, though without yet being recognized within the disciplines of philology themselves. I am referring to Friedrich Schleiermacher's hermeneutics and criticism, which continued the tradition of Kant's third *Critique* in formulating the preconditions of "the art of understanding particularly the written discourse of another person correctly."[12]

To the extent that philology dealt with individual linguistic evidence, it was deemed an "art." "Exegesis is an art,"[13] said Schleiermacher in his lectures on hermeneutics (1805–1832). Philological praxis is artful, according to Schleiermacher, because it *reconstructs* its object and thus, in "reconstructing," creates it anew. Yet it does so without being able to specify rules for the application of rules. The practice therefore falls back on Kant's "power of judgment." The reader thus confronts every literary work anew, as an absolute beginner. In this way, the work expresses its claim to be "monarchical" (Paul Valéry).[14] Now, if exegesis is an art, then only once a theory of this activity is available will philology be in a position to explicitly articulate its conflicts (and develop a discipline Schleiermacher calls "dialectic," the essence of which consists in the exchange of opinions). With the aim of contributing to a theory of philological praxis, I will examine, in what follows, philologies' hermeneutic foundations as part of their epistemology.

At root, philological praxis is everywhere shaped by two cognitive oppositions: the tension between scientific objectivity and cultural values and interests, and the tension between historical and aesthetic aims.

Conflict 1: Objectivity versus Value Judgments As a discipline, philology faces both outward and inward; it is shaped by a dual function: facing outward, philology is supposed to satisfy the demands of culture and erudition; facing inward, it simultaneously undermines these demands, in keeping with good scientific practice. Both functions are essential to philology. One praises Homer in panegyrics and then disputes the unitary authorship of the *Iliad* and the *Odyssey* in seminar (Ulrich von Wilamowitz-Moellendorff).[15] The values propagated in such a practice do not lie outside of philology but are rather conceived of as "theories." In Germany, they form a historical sequence from "Nation" to "Life," "Spirit," and "Culture."[16]

Conflict 2: Historical versus Aesthetic Interests The *historical* approach aims at a diagnosis of cultural-historical situations (with which texts are then identified), while the *aesthetic* approach focuses on the particularity of every great text. Here too, philological research is not going to resolve this tension, or eliminate it, or otherwise pacify it. Hence, a number of questions arise. What role does (aesthetic) interpretation play in a (historical) scholarly commentary? Conversely, what significance do tradition and the historical epistemic context have for interpretation?[17] And not least of all: to what extent are readings bound up with antecedent aesthetic or theoretical reflections by philologists? The history of the discipline evinces the formative influence of this pair of historical and aesthetic interests.

As a matter of fact, one cannot have the one without the other. With regard to the second conflict this implies that, in order to prevent contemporary aesthetic theories from predetermining one's understanding of foreign works, one must radically *historicize* the genesis of a work so that the implicit reflections that accompany the process of creation lead, as a theory of the praxis, to a philosophical (and now, historical, individual) aesthetic.[18] Conversely, a commentary can, as a genuinely historical exercise, be delimited and kept in check by the text and an understanding of it. The history of a text's interpretations offers the same options (and here the text's history is itself significant for the history of scholarship). The history of scholarship is the area where the effects of the first cognitive conflict within philologies (objectivity versus values) are predominantly felt. And finally, both options provide valid ways of combining interpretation and the history of interpretation: an interpretation must be measured against suggestions from the history of such interpretations (in Schleiermacher's sense of "dialectic").

Readings that can live up to the creative potential offered by cognitive conflicts in philologies, I will call "insistent" readings.[19] Their peculiar sort of tenacity distinguishes them from methods of close reading (like *Werkimmanenz* in Germany, or *explication de texte* in France). *I call those readings "insistent" because they not only pursue two distinct paths tenaciously, practically, and without direct recourse to any theory but also seek to merge these two paths.* On the one hand there is the path of philological, historical-aesthetic *reading* (conflict 2), which carefully and patiently reconstructs the genesis of the literary work while attending to both its *individuality* and its literary *necessity.* On the other hand hypotheses regarding the sense of the work are assessed through constant dialogue with scholarly, cultural, and literary interpretive traditions (conflict 1). The interpretation binds itself—insistently—to an analysis of interpretive conflicts.

Hermeneutics as the Theory of Philological Praxis

Hermeneutics can be conceived as the theory of philological praxis inasmuch as it takes its starting point to be *insistent* readings and the transcendental primacy of *understanding* with respect to both conflicts. Recent insights into the nature of this praxis and the conflicts peculiar to it demand a new conception of hermeneutic theory. The epistemic approach to philology as a praxis is new as well. Hermeneutics has quite a history, and the concept is employed today with the most diverse—indeed sometimes mutually incompatible—meanings. Thus it is useful to take the orientation of the text itself as the measure of a historical critique. Two aspects, already mentioned briefly, deserve particular attention: "individuality" and "necessity." In this connection, the rationality that pervades literary works is revealed to be a precondition of understanding.

Individuality and Necessity

Understanding is, in the first instance, connected with the individual. As we have seen, Schleiermacher defines hermeneutics as the "art of understanding particularly the written discourse of another person correctly." He does not have in mind any and all discourse of others, but only such discourse as presents difficulties for understanding, insofar as it creates something novel and is individual for this reason. Discourse that merely repeats things that have already been said—here Schleiermacher refers contemptuously to "Wettergespräche," or "conversations about the weather"—is not the proper object of exegesis.[20] The sort of discourse that *is* of exegetical value is individual, in Schleiermacher's sense. The difficulties such discourse presents demand understanding.

How does individuality arise in discourse? Two strands of Schleiermacher's theory converge here. They are distinguished in accordance with the whole to which the individuality in question is referred. In the first case, that whole is *language* (the underlying general basis of which Schleiermacher terms "grammar"); in the other case, the whole is *thought,* understood as a form of knowledge that goes beyond the content expressed in a person's discourse. These two modes of creating individuality correspond to two hermeneutic methods—the grammatical and the psychological—that are so contraposed that they condition each other. Subjectivity—understood as any maneuver toward sense on the part of the subject—remains bound to language: "but no one can think without words. Without words the thought is not yet completed and clear."[21]

In order to do justice to a work of art (and its individuality), however, one must also consider its necessity alongside its individuality. Now hermeneutics focuses on production of individual discourse—out of language or out of the spectrum of possible thoughts. Here, understanding is not a decoding of the work but rather a repetition of its production. Hence, one can only understand the creative process and the individuality it generates by grasping its *necessity.* One can only repeat a discourse or comprehend it in thought when its internal sequence is compelling. What it is to understand is bound up with what it is to compel. "I understand nothing that I cannot recognize and construe as necessary."[22] Language does not produce such compulsion out of itself, and the psychological aspect too is initially a free stream of thought; only once a compositional and stylizing will asserts itself (within thought, as bound to language) can something become compelling. *Henceforth, whenever I use the term "individual," what I have in mind is this sort of necessary individuality.*

Types of Hermeneutics

One can, as I have done here, start with Schleiermacher and compare the answers offered throughout the history of hermeneutics to the question: How might we understand individuality that is linguistically constituted? And: How does a text emerge from the general preconditions of a language and particular historical occurrences (as might be documented in a commentary)? Within this conversation with Schleiermacher, we can distinguish three types of hermeneutics.

Schleiermacher himself advances a *descriptive, explanatory* hermeneutics insofar as the universal and the discourse strike a balance, mutually conditioning each other. In 1970, Peter Szondi renewed Schleiermacher's theory as a *literary* hermeneutics.[23] Historical commentary as an erudite compendium is *alien* to such a hermeneutics, which equally refuses to conceive of the *individual* as anything other than linguistic. The unutterable whole and the inarticulable particular (insofar as these are non- or extralinguistic matters) are *none of its business.*[24]

A second possibility is offered by a style of hermeneutics that I call *Tiefenhermeneutik,* or "depth hermeneutics," since it privileges the universal and can only interpret the individual as an expression of the universal—from a "depth" inaccessible to the individual. The foundations of this hermeneutical approach, which reached its height in "classical modernism," are rooted in a philosophical construal of history. It no longer conceives of the universal in linguistic terms. Wilhelm Dilthey's analysis of the individual—in keeping with his critique of historical reason[25]—conceives of the individual as an *intersection* of historical forces. Martin Heidegger introduced the notion of language as the "Haus des Seins," the "House of Being" (with poetry as its privileged form of expression). Hans-Georg Gadamer, the last great descendant of the historical, depth hermeneutics line, seizes on homogeneous cultural tradition in order to explain how the "conversation" between the text and the reader and between past readers and contemporary readers can become fruitful in a "fusion of horizons." The *written* text only hinders one's approach to it; the work is hardly more than a poorly conceived crutch.[26]

With a renewed focus on Schleiermacher and in an effort to oppose Gadamer, Jean Bollack and his "Ecole de Lille" have, since the 1960s, developed a *critical* hermeneutics that is *hermeneutic* inasmuch as it, like Schleiermacher's, once more places a great deal of value on the linguistic—though it parts company with him in eschewing the extralinguistic universal ("psychology," or the stream of the thinkable per se) and replacing it with a universal developed by the works themselves. Bollack's hermeneutics is "critical" in the sense that the works reflect their own preconditions and are thereby joint creators of themselves.[27] On this view, then, the work formulates both a universal claim and its actual individual realization. The claim to be meaningful that an individual discourse makes is now to be measured against its own achievements. But what role does the history of the discipline, which I have identified as essential to the practice of insistent reading, play here?

Nondiscursive Understanding and the Role of the History of the Discipline

The singularity and strength of *critical* hermeneutics become evident in connection with a central question that has preoccupied hermeneutics ever since Schleiermacher: How can we conceive of understanding in such a way that it finds its confirmation and legitimation in the object itself? What are the conditions of a relationship between object and method? The phenomenon of individuality lends the latter question a particular form and significance, for understanding is fundamentally bound to universal rules.

Although all literary works are, to a greater or lesser extent, particular, the individuality of a poem does not prevent us from understanding it. According to critical hermeneutics, a poem can be understood, despite its particularity, because it constructs itself and is thus self-reflective. The activity of the interpreter converges with a binding reflexive activity of the text itself. The slogan "Textus interpres sui" suggests itself here, deriving as it does from the principle of Protestant exegesis, "scriptura sui ipsius interpres" ("Holy Scripture interprets itself"). The interpreter thus confronts an *activity of thought,* which is capable of explaining why we can today understand various works despite their foreignness to us—whether that foreignness be aesthetic, historical, or spatial.

The work does something and reflects on it; and in both instances an intelligence is present—the one practical and the other explicit. This opposition shapes the work itself. Self-reflection can be ascribed to a theoretical history of hermeneutics, while the praxis itself creates the novel and individual—even if it does so by addressing the theory put forth in the work itself. The work, then, by talking about itself, engages in a commentary about the various theoretical, normative, cultural, or literary claims it has come to be associated with within its particular, radically historicized situation. Often, these claims are generalizations or prejudices the work cites in taking a stance on them.

If both the interpreter and the work itself are striving toward understanding—the interpreter to understand the work, the work to make itself understood—then hermeneutics, as the theory of understanding individual discourse, can be applied to both the work *and* the interpreter. But the immediacy of such understanding is opposed by what Peter Szondi has called the historicity of knowledge.[28] Because a work's own thoughts participate in a tradition of interpretation (namely, a tradition of understanding texts), problems of understanding arise between the work and readers who do not inhabit the same historical, cultural, or geographical context. The historicity of knowledge is, in this disciplinary context, above all a historicity of philological understanding.

The assessment of philological readings therefore requires a historically informed critique of the discipline, which resists the presupposition that philology, to take August Boeckh's famous formulation, concerns the "recognition of the cognized" ("Erkenntnis des Erkannten")[29] and rather allows that the genesis of "the cognized" is subject to certain normative, strategic, and disciplinary constraints,[30] so that philology, resisting this trend, must become a technique for recognizing the "unrecognized"—that is, for appreciating how the history of the discipline has led readers to insufficient understanding, to *nonunderstanding*.[31] This leads precisely to the question: How can one acknowledge the historicity of misunderstanding without simultaneously surrendering oneself to a historicity of reason altogether—a historicity that insinuates that there is, in principle, no such thing as a correct interpretation of a text?

Once all reference to the texts is neglected, interpreters no longer pay any attention to whether or not their readings correspond with an object. If this conception of "interpretation" were correct (which is precisely what the concept of hermeneutics I have advanced here denies) then there would be no such thing as an incorrect interpretation. All interpretations would just be forms of human consciousness—and forms of consciousness cannot be correct or incorrect. This conception, which seeks to dissolve the appearance of textual individuality by revealing the work to be merely an expression of the dominant mode of cultural or ontological consciousness, is based on Gadamer's reception of Heidegger's views in the tradition of philosophical hermeneutics.

My suggestion is that we avail ourselves of the distinction between a praxis and the theory of that praxis. If one develops hermeneutics as a theory of readings, then one can utilize the historicity of philological readings. This is the task of a (tertiary) disciplinary critique of hermeneutics. And mistaken readings are thereby made intelligible. As a theory, hermeneutics is historical and normative—it is also shaped culturally and by its disciplinary history. The standpoint from which mistaken readings can now be judged is located in the literary praxis of the object itself, not in the dominant theory of that time, whose reconstruction sometimes even takes place within an explicit commentary integrated into the work itself—though such reconstruction is more often performed by philosophers and philologists in the course of their own readings.

Such reconstructions are subject to historical intellectual traditions. They are part of a historical, aesthetic context and continue to be confronted with the problem of overcoming the historicity of knowledge. Yet there is an alternative. For what prefigures later theoretical work—namely, implicit reflection—is precisely what enables understanding that can transcend historical epochs. Implicit reflection is the authority that *endorses* particular readings. It falls to the philologist to search for possibilities of doing justice to the nondiscursive (though subsequently articulable) reflection embedded in the praxis.

It is not hermeneutical theory that enables understanding, but the praxis that subsequently receives explicit reflection. This opposition underwrites a constitutive misunderstanding in every reading: namely, mistaking the intelligence that guides our understanding for a theory and institutionalization of such intelligence. Institutions see to it that readings trace distinct paths, literary or philological—and these paths are not always separate. What one might term "philological content" occupies, over the course of history, different genres (in antiquity it is to be sought in the works themselves) and different institutional frameworks or disciplinary purviews (e.g., "German philology" in the nineteenth century or "literary studies" in the twentieth). Intuitive and, in this sense, "naïve" reading comes to understand itself and its relation to the hermeneutical theory in the text through hermeneutical reflection. Yet an insistent reading must—to be practical once again—forget the theory in order to be "naïve" again at a second level. In referring to Schiller's distinction in his treatise "On Naïve and Sentimental Poetry" I would like to speak of a *sentimental practice of philology.*

Finally, the history of interpretation becomes a component of the interpretation itself, and extends beyond the critique of nonunderstanding. Jean Bollack's argument that an interpretation is improved through critical engagement with the history of such interpretations (see, for example, his *magnum opus, L'Oedipe Roi*) might be formulated as follows: "Every interpretation is subject to historical factors. Historical influence comes on the scene as the corrupting influence of values and institutional interests. Such historical interests are nourished by suspicion. Only he who uncovers the corruption is capable of understanding the interpretation and grasping why it interferes with one's own reading." This argument combines a critique of ideology with the question of truth. It principally introduces a new critical attention to the scholarly tradition that we implicitly (and sometimes unwittingly) adhere to. But it also introduces an aspect of the discipline's psychology, since a polemical will is capable of unleashing new cognitive forces.

I would like to propose a further argument that forges a historical-*aesthetic* link between a work's interpretive history and the interpreted work itself.[32] The advantage of this new argument is that it absolves us from having to explain the conflicts that crop up throughout a work's interpretive history solely by reference to the malevolent will of the people involved, enabling us to recognize these conflicts, if need be, as an expression of the work itself.

My argument runs: A history of conflicting interpretations reveals difficulties engendered, negotiated, executed, and reflected by the work itself. The term "critical hermeneutics" must be expanded: the work generates its own universal, which then unfolds itself in textual difficulties and solutions difficult to understand. It is in this that its praxis consists. These movements of thought are later dealt with in the interpretive tradition. To the extent that the praxis is resolved into a reflected form, the work engages—in a way the philologist can track—in a commentary about its own interpretive history, which mostly follows the universal, frequently misrepresented as an explicit idea.

Let us now turn to the interpretation of sonnet II.28 and an analysis of some of the current philosophical readings of it. What follows must not be an instance of philosophical ratiocination, for it is the object itself that should speak. This is not an emphatic demand for some sort of immediacy, as though we were abandoning the critical standpoint. Rather, it expresses the requirement that we "allow the poem itself to speak," that our interpretation be restricted to attempting to understand the poem and relinquish all methodological aspirations. The only decision that confronts us is ethical in nature—one must decide to stand in solidarity with the literary work and be poised to give it an attentive hearing.

To what extent a "theory of philological praxis" may manifest itself in the concrete reading is difficult to say. One must have mastered philological methodology, but such methods do not provide any rules for concrete engagement with the sense of a work. This even holds true for the injunction concerning spontaneity itself, that it should not be restricted. Even that rule cannot be the guide of when it is to be applied. The nondiscursive thought awakened in engaging with the text is not a disruptive incursion of (antecedently elaborated) theoretical commitments so long as it issues from the reading of the text itself. In other words, the poem to which we gain access in a reading is capable, under certain circumstances, of vindicating (or "endorsing") theoretical remarks (like those made in the first three sections of this essay), but our method for reading the poem is not to be derived from such remarks.

Toward an Interpretation of Sonnet II.28

The poem begins with an address, a call to "komm und geh" ("come and go"), which immediately establishes a pronominal relationship: a "we" (or an "I" who turns out to be the spokesperson for the group) addresses a "you." Up to this point in the poem cycle we have encountered a group of singers similar to the chorus in a Greek tragedy. They emulate Orpheus.[33] In sonnet I.26, we read: "sind wir . . . ein Mund der Natur" ("are we . . . a mouth of Nature") (line 14). Yet now they have shifted the emphasis in their metier. The singers in Orpheus's tradition want to explore the new medium of dance or pantomime. A metamorphosis has taken place. The poem gives individual shape to a general principle crystallized in the poems—namely, that the speakers are poets and the addressee is Orpheus and/or his media. Now, the speaker and the addressee are both dancers.

As before, the poets lack Orpheus's poetic facility, and so their hope rests on "Du" ("you"). This is therefore a privileged "you"—the characterization "still half a child" ("fast noch Kind," line 1) legitimates the "you." The child is opposed to the girls in the earlier sonnets. For as a "young woman" ("Mädchen"), the dancer has a prehistory within the sonnet cycle. Earlier in the cycle, "young women" are identified as the protagonists of art (art having been recovered from and in opposition to women [Frauen]). Inasmuch as this gets explained in the course of the poem itself, we have the requisite poetical endorsement to invoke the context of the cycle as a whole.

The first stanza introduces a hierarchy: only "you" can create the constellation (a kind of cosmic intensification) of the dances. The "constellation" ("Sternbild") serves as an abstraction of the dancer's "dance figure" ("Tanzfigur"), and while the "we" group is incapable of such activity, they can nevertheless profit from it. The "you" creates a foundation for their dances.

Her dancing is a form of thought—a *form* in which (unlike in thought) the moment of ecstasy is accessible ("bewegt" / "moved," line 7). It is through an error that our reading runs across this connection between dancing and thought. The genitive construction "einer jener Tänze" ("one of those dances") in the sentence "Du . . . ergänze . . . die Tanzfigur zum reinen Sternbild einer jener Tänze, darin" ("You . . . fill out the dance figure . . . of one of those dances in which") is grammatically incorrect. The indefinite article "einer" is (and must be) genitive here, but it has a *feminine* (singular, genitive) ending and so demands a feminine noun, not a masculine one like "der Tanz." (The correct form of the article here would be "eines [Tanzes] jener Tänze.")

The literature on the poem and editors of it do not know what to make of this—the best of them diplomatically and faithfully reprint the "error." And in point of fact, there are no poetic strategies that possess greater authority than syntax: the passage remains bothersome. But this grammatical error, if retained, allows for its own interpretation. For the error reveals an unexpected set of poetic principles. Rilke's feminine genitive "einer (jener Tänze)" refers, in my view, to the French word *danse* (which Rilke surely had in mind), and this influence of his French usage—which informs all of the *Sonnets to Orpheus*—restores the regularity of the phrase.[34] To this extent, one can very well take Ernst Zinn, who edited Rilke's complete works, at his word when he speaks of not a "written" but a "linguistic lapse" ("Sprachversehen"; the word denotes errors in language as well as in speech—not only a slip of the tongue but a slip between tongues).[35]

Nor was it Rilke's general fluency in French that exerted such a formative influence, but rather the prose and poetry of Paul Valéry, in which Rilke had steeped himself immediately before the *Sonnets to Orpheus* as in no other literature during that period. Rilke regards Valéry as the incarnation of the French Symbolist tradition. In Valéry's dialogue *L'Âme et la Danse,* which Rilke translated,[36] the dance becomes a movement of thought that enables an unconscious spiral of thoughts. Applying these reflections to the sonnet *O komm und geh,* this means that the orphic dancing thinker is supposed to represent the paradigm for all dancers.

Why orphic? And what form does such dancing take? These questions can be answered together: the address to the dancer, which invokes the tradition of addressing the muses, determines from the outset what is involved—namely, a combination of coming and going: "Oh come and go" (line 1). These are forms of movement—performed and practiced in the cycle of poems—that Orpheus, the muses' model, is said to engage in, for example, in sonnet I.5, where "Er kommt und geht" ("He comes and goes") (line 6).

This is the preeminent series of steps, contained in the movement of reversal, which privileges the *moment* of directional change. The instant can now become central. The coming and going is oriented around the moment or instant. By employing the common colloquial "für einen Augenblick" ("for a moment")—"komm' doch für einen Augenblick vorbei" ("do drop in for a moment")—Rilke distills and deploys both the goal-oriented ("to the benefit of") and the explanatory ("on the strength of") senses of the preposition "für" ("for"). It is all about the moment: the word itself, "Augenblick," makes available to the poem's implicit "I" a concept for the potentially decisive contribution that the "you" can make in coming and going. The moment is the mode of salvation. It is for the moment—as a telos—that thought *dances*.

In the phrase "ergänze / für einen Augenblick" (lines 1–2), the verb "ergänzen" ("fill out," "complete") generates the very sense of the moment per se, which is joined with the verb as a prepositional object. This sense is revealed by the absence of a second prepositional object, which one would expect according to the model "fill out . . . *with*. . . ." Thus, the dancer herself enters into the roundelay, completing the dance figure: "Du . . . ergänze . . . die Tanzfigur" ("You . . . fill out the dance figure"). The aim is to attain a whole (Ganzes), or rather an entirety (Gänze)—for in Rilke's willful idiom the prefix *er-* (e.g., in "ergänzen") is accorded a peculiar, and peculiarly *productive* meaning. This productivity bears on the second element of the verb. The syllabic separation executed throughout the cycle anticipates this process.

For example, Rilke elsewhere analyzes the verb "erinnern" ("remember") (I.25) into "er-innern," which has something like the sense of "at just the moment that one remembers something, it becomes a part of one's *inner* self, internalized." "Er-gänzen" would then mean that, in supplementing a particular thing in some way, one creates a *Gänze* (an *entirety*), the thing becomes an *entirety*. This is an intensification in which the poem's speakers wish to participate in order to influence the relationship among "dance figure," "constellation," and "dances." To summarize the first few lines, one could say they articulate the wish of the dancers: that the dancers use the self-generative moment to transform the reflective dance figure, whose motor elements are coming and going, into a whole. It is for this reason, in virtue of this ability, that the "you" is called on like a muse.[37] (The traditional notion of muses is criticized herewith, since the dancer does not address herself to the muse but instead becomes a muse for the poets representing Orpheus.)

If the first four lines of the sonnet concern the yearned-for epiphany of the dancer, the rest of the poem sheds light on the *conditions* of this occurring. For this critique the sonnet regresses temporally to a time when the dancer was close to Orpheus (lines 5–6) and then (lines 7–14) moves forward to her attempt (still situated in the past) to recover and repeat that historical event. The first event was characterized by a specific relation of Nature to Orpheus and by the power of their comprehension: "Denn sie [die Natur] regte / sich völlig hörend nur, da Orpheus sang" ("For she [Nature] roused / to full hearing only when Orpheus sang," lines 5–6). Nature could understand Orpheus in virtue of its (her) form of movement.

The dancer was at "that earlier time" ("damals," line 7) part of the movement. Thus, the second stanza begins with a reflection on the relationship of the arts to one another—of dance ("regte"/"roused"), listening, and speaking/singing. This is a hermeneutic reflection made explicit; the poem itself reflects on what it is to understand a linguistic expression. How so? To understand, we must start from the concentration of a past moment, when the later dancer experienced Orpheus. This concentration involves the coincidence of movement and hearing. Dancing listens (and understands, one must add). Rilke invokes a modern poetic argumentative figure, inherent in the conception of the *Gesamtkunstwerk:* in light of their speechlessness, poets employ other arts—opera, theater, stagecraft, or pantomime.

This is to explain why—in precisely this historical moment—dance will replace the word. In Rilke's sonnet vocabulary, "listening" encompasses production as well; his poetics is: *He who listens, speaks,* or: speaking (namely, singing) itself enables the *exegesis* of what is heard, a hermeneutical means immanent to original usage. To listen is to interpret. Dance consummates this exegesis here, yet orphic song remains the foundation, which the other auditory arts analyze. Thus, the poem is about creativity (listening, dancing creation) as the possibility of understanding. *The question is how Orpheus can be heard, and the answer is: through creativity.* By creating Orpheus. Listening to Orpheus is an act of creation. The sentence "Denn sie [Natur] regte / sich völlig hörend nur, da Orpheus sang" ("For she [nature] roused / to full hearing only when Orpheus sang") contains our model: the song can be heard, but it is only through hearing (read: understanding) that a complete and perfect movement (compare "regte/sich" ["roused/moved herself"]) can be achieved, by nature and—with nature—by the dancer. The meaning of the word "hören" ("listen" or "hear") has changed. It is in this way, both here and elsewhere in his poetry, that Rilke creates an idiolect, a consistent private use of language, that goes beyond Schleiermacher's hermeneutics, positioning itself somewhere between discourse and grammar.

In the further process of the poem, dance is analyzed as a postorphic form. Dance is all that is available in the time of the poem. So far in the poem, a hierarchical systematic has been developed within the dance itself. It leads from Nature to the poet-dancers and from them to the dancer. That is the topic of the first stanza. Nature still contains the reminiscence of an orphic order (compare "völlig" ["full"] in line 6) to which the poets connect in their dances. Nature cannot anymore live up to the needs of the dancer ("befremdet"/"surprised," line 8). The characterization of the poet's movement as "fleeting" ("vergänglich") (line 5) already contains a (dancing) gait (Gang)—"ver-gäng-lich/Gang"—of minimal temporal duration. This realization dovetails with the whole sentence, which expresses the fact that everything the group is capable of is nevertheless not identical with the "Sternbild" ("constellation") and is therefore insufficient.

Thus, the specific "dance figure ("Tanzfigur," line 2) is contrasted with the indefinite plurality of "dances" ("Tänze," line 3), while only the dance figure can be "filled out" into a "constellation." The "dance figure" is an idea, which distinguishes the dancer as superior to Nature and her poets to the extent that she succeeds in participating in orphic understanding. The "constellation" is then the *perfect* image for the figure of a young, female, childlike dancer. Once the dance has perfected itself in listening to Orpheus, its constellation would be valid for everyone. Thus the dancer construes a basis for the "dancers" to act on.

As the second part of the poem analyzes the art of dance, the third part articulates the historical conditions for the initial invocation to make sense. By way of dancing, Orpheus's song—never understood ("unheard-of," line 12) by poets in history—shall be created. Orphism as a poetic tradition in the wake of Orpheus presupposes Orpheus, who, however, can only come into being by that tradition of singing. This paradox is solved by the conclusion that in the end Orpheus rests—by way of creation—untouchable. The paradox comes into being within this poem itself. What ensues is a tale of the lyrical subject (lines 7–9): "Du warst noch . . ." ("You were the one still . . ."). This section connects up with the first two parts in which the idea of production as a process of understanding is conjoined with a history of the deterioration of Nature. The poem recounts the first attempts of the dancer, about whom the speaker reminisces, to revive that primordial scene. His "Du warst" ("You were," line 7) picks out a point in time that both is historical and marks the beginning of the history of the cult. It comes *after* the original natural event. For, at its root, the poem is driven by its reflection on the history of an inadequate cult of understanding. Three phases of this exegetical history of a cult are distinguished: the dancer's original experience, her attempts to recover and repeat that experience from memory, and the group's hope for her success in the future.

Silence is the precondition for productive reception—dancers know this. They know it as "master singers," which is to say, as if out of a textbook, the textbook being the cycle of sonnets itself. Silence is part of their craft.

Everything was, as their speaker reports, silent. With deliberate calculation, Rilke inserts a dash, meaningless in spoken language, in line 11: what was to be heard was what cannot be heard. And thus even the meaning of the word "unerhört" ("unheard-of") changes in the course of this thoughtful recollection, as it takes on a threefold significance: a common reaction to something peculiar ("Das ist ja unerhört!"/"That's just unheard of!"), the poetic-hermeneutic use ("not heard"), and the theological usage ("not accepted by God"). This threefold significance represents a rupture in the tradition: Orpheus, with his extraordinary song, finds no salvation among his followers, who fail to hear him.

The final word in the German original, "hinzudrehen" ("to turn toward," lines 13–14), is syntactically connected to "die unerhörte Mitte" ("the unheard-of center") (line 11): the phrase "Für sie" ("For this," line 12) refers to this center and is followed by two verbs—"versuchtest" and "hofftest" ("tried" and "hoped"). Thus, "to turn toward" is the object of the hope that, after the rupture in the tradition, is directed toward the center, which we must connect with the earlier "Augenblick" ("moment"). What we still need to explain is *how* the "unheard-of center" (line 11) can be attained. And the answer emerges in clarifying how we need to read the coreference of the genitive "des Freundes."

The lines "und hofftest, einmal zu der heilen Feier / des Freundes Gang und Antlitz hinzudrehn" (lines 13–14) formulate two incompatible hypotheses in true *apo koinu* form, concerning either a mythical or a historical event Orpheus is embedded in. The double reference cannot be rendered in the translation—as I have shown in the beginning of this essay—yet it serves as a precondition of the meaning of the inherent paradox. If the topic is (1) the "heilen Feier des Freundes" ("the perfect celebration of your friend"), then the event the speaker hopes for is one of *veneration.* The vision is of a celebration or a ritual *in memoriam.* If on the other hand the topic is (2) "des Freundes Gang und Antlitz" ("your friend's pace and countenance"), then the event hoped for is an *evocation* of the friend that transcends the historical dimension to which the veneration (and the story of the rites) remains bound. These are the options toward which the poem moves. Are they mutually exclusive, or can they be brought into some kind of relation to each other? How is the rhetorical form that generates the ambivalence related to their potential resolution in an interpretation? In the end we are confronted with a problem of understanding. It arises as soon as one has read the poem and shapes one's whole reading of it. Clarifying the sense of this *apo koinu* is important, for it is in precisely these lines that the thought experiment prescribed by the poem in its formulation of the incipient wish "O komm und geh" finds its culmination. The experiment seeks to uncover the conditions under which that wish might intelligibly be fulfilled.

Only the coreference itself can lead to an interpretation that eliminates the ambivalence. That is its function. The ambivalence is generated by a syntactic inversion, and the interpretation of that inversion involves a decision. In German, the sentence would normally read "und hofftest, einmal Gang und Antlitz zu der heilen Feier hinzudrehen" ("and hoped one day to turn pace and countenance toward the perfect celebration"). Had Rilke chosen this formulation, he would have had to decide whether "des Freundes" pertained to the direct object "Gang und Antlitz" ("pace and countenance") or the prepositional phrase "zu der heilen Feier" ("toward the perfect celebration").

But the syntactic inversion requires that "des Freundes" appears between the two objects (he surely could not have said "zu der heilen Feier des Freundes Gang und Antlitz des Freundes hinzudrehen"). Such inversion consequently raises the following question: Are the "pace and countenance" those of the friend, or are we rather talking about a *celebration* of the friend ("der heilen Feier des Freundes")? And as the poem unfolds, we do indeed observe the (friendly) closeness of the dancer to Orpheus. In addition, the cyclical movement of the *Sonnets to Orpheus* suggests that Orpheus is the friend. Indeed, the next sonnet, II.29, characterizes the divine singer, who sings breathily: "Stiller Freund der vielen Fernen, fühle, / wie dein Atem noch den Raum vermehrt" ("Silent friend of many distances, / feel how your breath is still increasing space," lines 1–2).

We can now link Orpheus to the *celebration,* for the attributes of "pace" and "countenance" are certainly alien to him: gait and visage are embodiments of pantomimes and dancers (and thus also our dancer here), whereas the instrument of the divine singer is the lyre (line 10). It is therefore Orpheus who does not dance, to whom the "center" belongs; that is, the place where his lyre sounds. His is the celebration; it is in his honor. He is to be understood.

In this way, the movement of "turning toward" takes on a precise sense. The dancer, while she still lived, turned toward the dead Orpheus—she *went* away, as one might put it. This performance does not take place within the poem, but is presupposed by it. For in the interim, she has since followed him into the shadow of death, which is why the poets desire her return, her "coming," so that she can then "go" (in the twofold sense of dancing and disappearing, line 1). It is as if she were meant to undertake Eurydice's project of following Orpheus into the world of the living.

The dancer, as the magical medium of her "friend," only fulfills her task when Orpheus reveals himself in her (pantomimic) art of memory (hypothesis 1), when her "pace and countenance" are also those of her friend (hypothesis 2). This vision is anticipated by the syntax itself: the second syntactic option in the *apo koinu* points to a future, contended, and long hoped-for time, when the rupture in the tradition, in which the dancer took part, has been overcome. The relation between the two initial hypotheses of "veneration" and "evocation" is thereby resolved: *the evocation is precisely achieved through veneration*—although this presupposes the death of the dancer, without which there would be no invocation of the muses at the beginning.

This interpretation finally leads us to recognize how this sonnet segues into the next in the cycle. The word "einmal" ("one day," "one time") is connected to both the hope of the dancer for the future and the hope—reserved for the "moment"—of "you" for the past: "und hofftest, einmal . . ." ("and hoped / one day," lines 12–13). The hope of the dancer is directed toward the "center," which transcends any poetry or art. Therefore Wera's death and perfection coincide. This is the poem's conclusion. The poem longed for a solution to the paradox—the perfection in her dance will be possible only once. Perfection implies her death. The poets' future differs from the dancer's; they do not intend to equal her (see the first stanza). Their future can now, in the very moment of the sonnet's articulation, after the dancer's death, be fulfilled—a fulfillment that emerges precisely *from* her death itself. This is what the priest-poets yearn for. The reality they hope for in the dancer's coming and going is thus anticipated by the history of the orphic cult. It is this reality that they invoke, the reality of the cult. The last sonnet, II.29, is testimony to this.

Conflicts of Interpretations

An insistent reading seeks to assert itself within the agon of interpretations in its full historical expanse. Its strength lies in the praxis, on whose intelligence it relies. The praxis is intelligent because it can—without any theoretical or institutional aspirations—seek the endorsement of the poem. In other words: it seeks to understand the poem without any methodological motives. Analysis of other interpretations is part of this process. Others' interpretations are by no means indispensable premises, for even new works lacking a history of readings can, of course, be understood. But this agon does contribute to objectivity, not only in the sense that the discipline is conceived as a dialogic ("dialectical") activity in pursuit of truth, but also in the sense of a process of objectification that culminates in an *objectité*

(Denis Thouard) of the poem.[38] The conflict between interpretations (once the culturally alien elements have been removed) is rooted in conflicts, paradoxes, or difficulties within the work itself, which—in this case—manifest themselves and find articulation.

If the conflict reveals itself, it should already be understood within the poem. The tumult in the mind of the interpreter can be retrospectively disentangled, yet the reading itself is not an organized process in which pure interpretation is followed by a democratic survey of others' opinions, in light of which the interpretation might be retroactively corrected. Quite the contrary—one's own reading, whose authority resides in the work itself, seeks to assert itself within the agon. The work performs the task of critique: it provides the conditions for the possibility of understanding the conflict. If an interpretation is truly critical, then it is capable of elucidating opposed interpretations on its own terms. It thereby advocates for the work; the relevant conflicts can be systematized from the standpoint of the work (namely, its interpretation). In this way, one arrives at a "theory" of philological-disciplinary praxis that is custom suited to the poem under consideration.

The sonnet "O come and go" has generated a twofold wake of interpretations, all of which focus on its opening. But opinions have been divided throughout the poem's interpretive history: some favor a formal-poetological sense of the initial invocation, others an existential-philosophical sense. Neither group, however, sees the invocation as having a *critical* meaning. If we take this neglected third option into consideration, we have three respective possibilities for interpreting the opening "O come and go." It can be interpreted (1) as "O enter and dance," where "go" takes on the sense of "dance," as it does in Valéry's dialogue, which Rilke translated; (2) as "O enter and exit," where this is taken to be a metaphor for the opposition of life and death, both understood as "Dasein"; or, finally, (3) as the movements of approach and withdrawal in the act of dancing, whereby dance itself becomes a code for similar movements within Rilke's work.

The third possibility lies at the root of Annette Gerok-Reiter's formal analyses in *Wink und Wandlung* (*Hint and Transformation,* 1996),[39] for which the poem in question furnishes an example. Analogy provides the favored modus operandi here: "coming and going embodies countermotion [Gegenläufigkeit] in its simplest form. From here, this form can be extended to other figures such as the rose (blooming—wilting), the mirror (collecting—reflecting), or the constellation (illumining—extinguishing)."[40] Gerok-Reiter illustrates a form of movement and seeks its variations within poems throughout the cycle—movements of a ball as much as those of a dance. In doing so, she refrains from tracing the figure (which she rightly emphasizes) through the movements of the poem itself.

This formal and structuralistic analysis understands itself as poetological because, according to Gerok-Reiter's view of Rilke, Rilke believed that art alone was capable of creating a mythos, whose process itself presupposed the death of Orpheus, whose historically authenticated teaching has not filtered down to the poem itself. Now Hans Blumenberg is the authority here for Gerok-Reiter, but her poetological turn consciously severs the reference of the mythos to nature—a nature that the mythos, on Blumenberg's theory of metaphor, is supposed to poetically master, as it were. Orpheus then becomes the name for Rilke's "poetological," omniprevalent principle—not an instance that forces epistemic questions on the poems. The formal parallels thus automatically enable the "leap into a qualitatively different mode of being [Daseinsweise],"[41] that is—within the system articulated above—the transition from interpretation 3 to 2. "Poetological" therefore signifies an existential confidence in formal structures that purportedly realize themselves outside the concrete, critical thought process of the poem.

Gerok-Reiter's arguments thereby approach a much older book, *Rilkes Sonette an Orpheus,* by Hermann Mörchen (1958).[42] In the Heideggerian tradition, Mörchen recognizes an ontological difference that Rilke's critical reflections do in fact elicit. Yet Mörchen assesses the coming and going as the "form" of Dasein (compare option 1) without registering that Rilke treats the beyond (das Jenseitige) from an epistemic distance, which casts the poem into a utopian structure. May what was once, "damals" (line 7), possible come again.

Following his thought that Being pulses in accordance with this form, Mörchen refrains from granting Rilke's specific poetical procedure and themes their own status. At best, they serve to make the real issue "evident" ("sinnfällig"). Mörchen writes: "a Dasein that in this manner is given over to decay [death], that of its own accord transpires into the 'whole' ['Ganze'], thus 'completes' itself 'to perfection, to entirety, to the real, perfect [heil], and full sphere and globe of *being*' (Rilke to Countess Sizzo, Jan. 6, 1923), as it is here viewed as 'pure constellation.' . . . In her [Wera's] dance, the 'coming and going' of Dasein as a unified whole becomes evident [sinnfällig]."[43]

The specific form is unnecessary for this reading, since the beyond determines all the action. Hence, Mörchen understands the chapters of his book devoted to each of the poems as a *commentary* and as *expositions*

[*Erläuterungen*] and divides them accordingly.[44] This philosophical certainty, indefensible though it may be, gives Mörchen a freedom in his individual observations, which constitute the value of his study to this day. In the word "ergänzen" ("complete"), Mörchen reads the concept "Ganzes" ("whole") yielded by Rilke's syllabic analysis and derives from this the abstracting sense of the dance figure of coming and going. Yet he does not trace his nondiscursive reading back to Rilke's idiolecticizing procedure.

Instead of taking Rilke at his word, Mörchen understands "Tanzfigur" ("dance figure") not reflexively, but rather metaphysically, as making reference to a Being ("Sein") he had put in place from the outset: "the imperative 'ergänze' is no instruction to act, but rather, like 'come and go' a pure invocation of Being. What, as an isolated artistic act, would be a mere individual and a 'patchwork' ['Stückwerk'], blazes forth 'as if it were the whole [Ganze]' (I 16) that 'is meant' in it. The dance becomes a 'constellation' (I 8, I 11), a primordial symbol of Being within the relations of the whole."[45]

The proximity of Gerok-Reiter and Mörchen is due to their confidence (whether poetological or ontological) that these forms immediately express a "higher" meaning. Paradoxically, the diametrically opposed principles that structure their books serve the same end. Gerok-Reiter provides no interpretations of single poems, but rather draws on them in order to illustrate poetological structures that are common to the sonnets throughout the cycle. Likewise, Mörchen's commentaries refrain from reading single poems as *individual* commentaries on a large philosophical assumption.

Only the first possibility of interpreting "O come and go" (1) combines the form of dance with the aspiration to a higher meaning. The dancing gait (the approaching and departing) reveals itself in the course of the poem to be an epistemic form of encounter in death—a death presupposed by the dance itself. From this perspective, the two other—in themselves blind—options can be integrated. Both Gerok-Reiter's and Mörchen's interpretations, neither of which can explain the apparent rationale of the other, are directed at the poem that provoked them and that rejects them as one-sided. The interpretation I have presented in this essay concentrates on the conditions that make these readings possible in the first place. To this extent, my interpretation understands itself as *critical.*

It is within the history of its own interpretations—at least those that participate in the agon of readings—that the poem reveals its capacity for refutation, and, in so doing, itself. Such productive engagement with prior "insight" (namely, with the manifest lack of understanding contained therein) is alien to Germanic studies (to the extent that it is preoccupied with Rilke) today. For not only is the history of the discipline held to lack any interest in the discipline's genuine object (it studies the discipline itself as an internally functional structure, which formulates no truth claims), but even research into a literary work's reception views the work itself as a mere screen for free projections of meaning, whose multitude and variety purportedly constitute the best measure of the work's quality. Contemporary research into the reception of literary works (particularly in the form of reader-response criticism) has so put its object in its place—in keeping with its "dogma of openness" (Jean Bollack)—that the text is incapable of generating any appreciable resistance at all.

Genuine recognition is mixed with nonunderstanding. How are errors to be treated? Generally, one should proceed on the understanding that, in every interpretation, there is a nondiscursive praxis at work, whose voice can be set free on the strength of insight into the core conflicts of the poem. Instead of assuming the typical cynical attitude toward previous interpretations, one does them some justice, which benefits one's own interpretation.

Sentimental Naïveté—a Summary

"The proof of the pudding is in the eating." The praxis itself calls out for readings. After taking account of the several conditions of insistent reading I have adumbrated here, the reader must return to Rilke's sonnet with renewed intensity. Facing the poem as an utter beginner, the reader may achieve a second sentimental naïveté. But the return to praxis is inevitable. My topic in this essay has been what the reader is obliged to "forget" in order to achieve this:

1. Philological praxis—which alone leads the reader to his object—affords a twofold reconstruction. First, its contours trace the epistemological conflicts between the historical and the aesthetic as well as between truth claims and cultural values. Second, philological praxis can be viewed in accordance with the respective operations of understanding that play a primary role in such conflicts.

2. The dissolution of such conflicts is attained by reading a literary work insistently. The conflicts enrich the result and provide for their own conceptual supersession. Hermeneutics, as the theory of this practice of understanding, must be expanded in order to account for the nondiscursive aspects of the praxis. This nondiscursivity represents a helpful corrective of the hasty, theoretical stipulations that can inform a reading. Rather than a reading being subjected to methodical considerations, its sole aim becomes

understanding the work. Whoever pursues this goal will grant the nondiscursive praxis the requisite space.

3. The foundation of this praxis consists in the rationality and precision of the literary work. By following a work's necessary progression—in a critical vein—a reading discloses the conditions of literary compulsion, that is, what the text forces us to understand. This compulsion replaces what many today dogmatically tout as the openness of literature. The interpretation that retraces a work's poetical thought process receives a stylistic inflection far removed from any aspiration to set a theoretical example.

4. By incorporating the interpretations of others, in their historical expanse, into one's own activities of reading, one further increases the potential of the praxis already present in the readings of particular readers. Yet genuine disputes can only be set in motion when one engages with past interpretations with a certain kind of fidelity and fairness. That means lending them our tongue, instead of being contemptuous and conniving in our reception of seemingly antiquated forms of expression.

5. This agon imbues its object with a higher degree of visibility, which enables it to serve as a standard for critique. One might say: the work itself can thereby take up a certain stance—not only on its own historical situation but also on later readings. This power of critique that the work thus possesses gives meaning to the interpretations that accumulate over the history of the work's reception. The reader achieves his aim when his interpretation becomes a critique of others within transcendental understanding. For then, the swath of interpretations that follow the work prove to be a manifestation of the interpretational questions raised by the work itself.

6. Of course, such manifestations are generally deficient in various ways. The deficiencies themselves can be diagnosed through the critique of readings, yet *explaining* them is the task of historical disciplinary research, which traces nonunderstanding back to the conflicts that shape philological praxis: the isolation of a historical interest, disciplinary boundaries, scholarly biases, or adherence to a particular academic school. For ultimately, the praxis corrupts when it remains praxis alone.

Philology or Linguistics?

Transcontinental Responses

KU-MING KEVIN CHANG

AT THE TURN of the twentieth century, philology was already a mature, prominent discipline well established in the faculty of philosophy (or the arts) in European academia. Starting in Germany, chairs in classical philology, philology of modern European languages, and comparative (or "Indo-Germanic") philology were established in universities across Europe in the nineteenth century.[1] At what was perhaps its peak, philology was undergoing at least two important developments. First, it continued to be widely disseminated, now outside Europe. In East Asia its formal arrival was marked by the appointment of Ueda Kazutoshi (or Mannen) (1867–1937) to the chair of philology at the University of Tokyo in 1894. Ueda had studied philology in Berlin, Leipzig, and Paris from 1890 to 1894. Once back home, he repeated in Japan what his European predecessors had done in the nineteenth century, launching a movement to study Japanese as a national language and compiling a critical and comprehensive Japanese dictionary.[2]

The arrival of European philology in China, though later than in Japan, is no less significant. The first institutionalization of philology brought with it the other development that was just taking place in Europe and the United States: the emergence of linguistics as a science independent of philology. Philology and linguistics were welcomed by Chinese intellectuals with relatively little resistance, as both of them were integrated into a renewal of evidential learning (*kaozheng,* lit. "search for evidence") and traditional phonological work, which had been prominent in Qing and early Republican scholarship. The arrival of philology in China thus embodied important developments of scholarly traditions in both the West and China.

The growing divergence of philology and linguistics generated a paradox in a different continent when both fields received their institutional base with the foundation of the Institute of History and Philology at the Academia Sinica in 1928. The Chinese name of this institution is Lishi yuyan yanjiusuo (歷史語言研究所), literally Institute for Studies in History and Languages. This would lead today's Chinese speaker to read it as an institute for history and linguistics, and indeed its faculty's publications in the first few decades made it increasingly clear that their work on languages was linguistics. However, "The Institute of History and Philology" was selected as its English name.[3] Philology and linguistics, it appears to us, are not the same. Did its founders misunderstand philology? Or what else created this paradox?

The answer lies in the disciplinary identities of philology and the then emerging linguistics, and the intellectual orientations of two founding members of that institute. The first is Ssu-nien Fu (or Fu Sinian, 1896–1950), the director from its foundation in 1928 to 1950, when the Academia Sinica had relocated to Taiwan. He was entrusted with the creation of a new institute for humanist studies shortly after his return to China from Germany. Essentially, he alone determined both the Chinese and English names of his institute. The other was Yuen Ren Chao (or Zhao Yuanren, 1892–1982), a Harvard Ph.D. in philosophy who went through an atypical training in linguistics before he was invited to lead the language division of Fu's new institute.

The difference between Fu and Zhao was not just personal. It in fact reflected the divorce of linguistics from philology that was occurring in the West. This divorce was signaled in the statement in Ferdinand de Saussure's *Cours de linguistique générale,* "[Philology] is neatly distinct from linguistics, in spite of the points of contact of the two sciences, and the mutual services that they make."[4]

Though focusing on the early years of Fu and Chao's institute, this study is far from a local history. Instead its objective is to demonstrate that the founding of the institute marked a very important page of the global history of scholarship, where accomplished German philology, emerging Anglo-French linguistics, traditional Chinese evidential learning and phonological studies came together to shape a successful humanist institution in East

Asia. In this essay I will first review the traits of German philology that Fu embraced, and will examine the emergence in the 1910s and 1920s of an Anglo-French identity of linguistics that wanted to claim independence from German-dominated philology. Thereafter I will trace the formation of Chao's professional outlook, and finally analyze the conjunction of European and Chinese schools of learning at the institute that Fu and Chao created. This conjunction in China, together with the divorce of philology and linguistics in the West, I suggest, constituted an important moment in the worldwide development of philology.

Fu and Philology in Germany

The urge to modernize Chinese society and learning dominated Fu's student years at Peking (Beijing) University. Fu studied there in the late 1910s, when the recent political revolution that had toppled the Qing dynasty failed to deliver a healthy, working democracy, even though repeated aggressions by foreign powers from the nineteenth century generated ever greater urgency for reform. He was a prodigy of humanist studies, showing a level of proficiency in traditional Chinese scholarship that amazed his teachers and friends. Not confined to traditional subjects, he published with friends a popular student magazine, the *New Youth,* that advocated thorough Westernization of China. For them, the success of Western civilization was characterized by two institutions: democracy and science.

To learn Western democracy and science firsthand, Fu left for England to study science after his graduation from Peking. From 1919 to 1922 he did serious course work in chemistry, physics, mathematics, and medicine at the University of London, followed closely the works of Sigmund Freud and William James, and entered a laboratory to study experimental psychology. At last, however, he was disappointed that the laboratory psychology he did on animals could not be applied to humans. He thought it better to study science in the home country of Max Planck and Albert Einstein. So he moved to Berlin.[5]

During Fu's stay in Berlin, the concern about the status of Chinese studies that had been in his mind germinated into interest in philology. While continuing to do course work in natural sciences, he read the latest works in European history and took courses in philology and languages.[6] He lamented that the center of Sinology was not in China but in Paris. The esteemed Sinologists in Paris then were Henri Maspero (1882–1945), Marcel Granet (1884–1940), and especially Paul Pelliot (1878–1945), the person known for taking to Paris thousands of medieval manuscripts from caves in Dunhuang. Relying on philological analyses of Dunhuang manuscripts, written in medieval Chinese and various Central Asian languages, Pelliot emerged as the leading authority in Chinese studies. He was justly credited with making Dunhuang studies known to the world. Fu's awareness of the works by Pelliot and his colleagues in Paris seems to have gradually convinced him that instead of reforming his country with a specialty in natural science, he could contribute more by reforming Chinese scholarship with his humanist training in Germany.

Germany doubtless was an excellent place for Western learning, especially in philology. William Dwight Whitney (1827–1894), a pioneer American scholar of language, judged that "to Germany belongs nearly the whole credit of the development of comparative philology; the contributions made to it from other countries are of only subordinate value."[7] Berlin was, moreover, the epicenter of German philological scholarship. Even though philology had passed its heroic age at Fu's time in the city,[8] the Chinese student continued to hold it in high regard.

As Constanze Güthenke's chapter in this book has reviewed the practice of philology in nineteenth- and early twentieth-century Europe, this chapter will just indicate the three trends that characterized the previous development of philology that influenced Fu's scholarly outlook. The first was the expansion of philology-based *Altertumswissenschaft,* or science of antiquity. *Altertumswissenschaft* had already taken shape at the hands of the philologist Friedrich August Wolf (1759–1824) at the turn of the nineteenth century. For Wolf, this science consisted of three fundamental parts: grammar or language study *(Sprachstudium),* hermeneutics, and textual criticism *(Wortkritik).* It further included a number of major parts *(Haupttheile):* studies of ancient geography, political history, mythology, literature, science, and art.[9] These areas were essentially historical knowledge attained by applying philological analysis to almost all dimensions of ancient life.

An early twentieth-century introduction to *Altertumswissenschaft* that Fu bought in Berlin basically followed Wolf in drawing the terrain of the science of antiquity.[10] Wolf had already embraced as the objects of *Altertumswissenschaft* nontextual materials such as monuments, archeological finds, coins, architecture, and artworks from antiquity. This orientation only intensified in the next century. Ulrich von Wilamowitz-Moellendorff (1848–1931), for example, in his acclaimed *Geschichte der Philologie,* highlighted the contribution of the excavations of Greek Olympia, Crete, and Egyptian

Menes.[11] Fu therefore studied in Berlin at a time when history, philology, and archeology had become integral parts of classical studies. Presumably unaware of, or at least unconcerned about, the independence war that archeologists were waging against philology,[12] Fu would materialize this integration in the institute he founded in China.

The second trend of philological development emerged from comparative studies of Sanskrit, Greek, Latin, and other Indo-European languages, which went beyond texts to study the historical and familial relationships of languages. It was inspired by European scholars' discovery of Sanskrit, which seemed to be older than all European languages then known. That language appeared to preserve a grammar more rigid and well-formulated than any in the West, astounding learned European scholars who were proud of their training in grammar as part of their liberal arts education.[13] Although at first the principles of classical philology were applied to the study of Sanskrit,[14] comparative philology eventually moved beyond the terrains of *Altertumswissenschaft,* Rome and Greece. Its new track of study started with Franz Bopp's 1816 classic *Über das Conjugationssystem der Sanskritsprache in Vergleichung mit Jenem der griechischen, lateinischen, persischen und germanischen Sprache.*[15]

Bopp's work laid the foundation for further monumental works in comparative philology by August Friedrich Pott, *Etymologische Forschungen auf dem Gebiete der Indogermanischen Sprachen* (1833–36), August Schleicher, *Compendium der vergleichenden Gramatik der indogermanischen Sprachen* (1861), and Karl Brugmann and Georg Curtius, *Grundriss der vergleichenden Grammatik der indogermanischen Sprachen* (1886–1900). Their original intent was to compare the grammars of the Indo-European languages, and yet in the process their attention was drawn to phonetics. To take one of Bopp's examples, the verb "I may be" appears in Sanskrit in the form of *syām, siem* in Latin (as in Plautus), and *siyau* in Gothic.[16] Their common stem strongly suggests a shared prototype or root among these languages, and their syllabic variations, exhibited in phonetic differences, give information about their transformations from the shared root. By systematically comparing the patterns of the phonetic differences of verbal inflections across languages, Bopp maintains, one can identify very scientifically the familial and historical relationship of languages and establish regularities or laws of their development.

Alongside this trend a sense of the science of language emerged. To reconstruct a historical language, some scholars conceived of differences between natural language and literary language. Natural, spoken language was considered the language in its purity, whereas literary language was "contaminated" by words borrowed from foreign languages. Literary or written language became the inferior form, though it was indispensable for historical studies. In contrast, spoken or oral language was primary.[17] Giving primacy to spoken languages, such philological studies transcended written words and textual criticisms to examine the language as a system of grammar and sounds. Beyond making sense of texts, comparative philology introduced the consciousness of a *Sprachwissenschaft,* a science of language.

The third development was the growth of German national literature, or *Germanistik,* as knowledge and skills in classical philology were applied not only to Sanskrit study but also to German language and literature. The starting point of German philology was rather different from that of classical philology, as there were no holy scriptures or philosophical canons written originally in ancient German. Practitioners of German philology such as the Grimm brothers instead went out to collect folktales, sagas, and epics. The collections led them to the study of dialects when they were confronted by different versions of the folk literature, and to the study of German etymology and grammar and the compilation of a German dictionary. Despite the fact that the Bible was not first written in German, Luther's translation of the Bible was for Protestant Germans a text as holy as the Hebrew and Greek original. At a time when the absolute truth of the Bible was contested by foreign chronological records such as those from China, geological findings, and philological analyses of the scriptures, its holiness might be somewhat tarnished. The literary status of Luther's translation, however, was celebrated as monumental.[18] The formation of German philology thus incorporated folklore, dictionary compilation, religious writings, and literary productions into the whole of national literature.

Philology, *Sprachwissenschaft,* and Linguistics

While Germany dominated philology, scholars of language in other countries gradually reacted. The passage quoted above from Saussure illustrates their reactions in the 1910s and 1920s.[19] Saussure acknowledged that linguistics and philology had shared roots, while emphasizing that linguistics studied more than just the historical relationship of languages. For Saussure, these disciplines' common ancestry was the Greek learning in grammar, one of the seven liberal arts. The second and third stages of their common past were represented by Wolf and Bopp. The objective of Wolfian philology, however, was above all to fix, interpret, and comment on texts. Bopp's comparative philology was closer to linguistics, yet had not reached the true status of linguistic science, for it was not mainly concerned with the elucidation of the nature of individual languages. Saussure placed more emphasis on sounds and speech than written words and texts, and, as is well known, granted much importance to the studies of signs or semiology, "a science that studies the life of signs within social life."[20]

Though a champion for an independent linguistics, Saussure was not the first to differentiate the science of language from philology. Whitney, the American scholar of language mentioned above, had already called in the 1870s for a science of language that would be superior to philology. For him, "linguistic science" and philology are two sides of a science. Philology is the working phase, while linguistic science is "the regulative, critical and teaching phase of the science." Yet unless Germany as the superpower of studies of language should accept it, Whitney judged, this science would not succeed.[21]

Henry Sweet (1845–1942), the eminent English phonetician, proposed in 1899 to distinguish between what he called living philology and antiquarian philology. Living philology makes accurate observations of spoken languages by means of phonetics and forms the basis of all studies of language, while antiquarian philology, that is regular philology, subordinates living to dead languages. By calling his favorite science "living" philology, Sweet still recognized the primacy of philology, although he replaced its content with spoken languages and phonetics.[22] The independence of linguistics was first declared, it seems, in the 1910s and early 1920s by Saussure and Otto Jespersen (1860–1943), a Danish linguist very influential for his works on English grammar and phonetics. Jespersen wrote:

> In breaking away from philology and claiming for linguistics the rank of a new and independence science, the partisans of the new doctrine were apt to think that not only had they discovered a new method, but that the object of their study was different from that of the philologists, even when they were both concerned with language. While the philologist looked upon language as a part of the culture of some nation [as in *Altertumswissenschaft*], the linguist looked upon it as a natural object.[23]

Phonetics and the study of natural, spoken languages, rather than the study of written words and texts, characterizes the true science of linguistics.

To be fair, in Germany advocates of *Sprachstudium* or *Sprachwissenschaft* (the study or science of language) had appeared since the early nineteenth century. Wolf mentioned the terms *Linguistik* and *Sprachkunde* in his *Lectures on Altertumswissenschaft,* although he took them to be interchangeable with philology.[24] F. Max Müller, a distinguished German philologist who had a career at Oxford, understood in the 1860s the "science of language" precisely as comparative philology; so did Berthold Delbrück in the 1880s.[25] On the other hand some important German philologists granted *Sprachwissenschaft* its own room. A rather early work, August Ferdinand Bernhardi's *Anfangsgründe der Sprachwissenschaft,* saw the object of his science as the absolute *(unbedingt)* form of language that transcended individual empirical languages. Language for him was the whole of articulated sounds *(artikulirten Lauten).*[26]

Theodor Benfey considered the science of language to be a theoretical study of languages that deserved a life outside philology, though its importance is largely defined by its contribution to that field.[27] Brugmann, having read Whitney, agreed to give *Sprachwissenschaft* its own nature and goal. Notwithstanding, he would rather regard it and philology as complementary to each other.[28] Georg von der Gabelentz was one of the very few German authors on *Sprachwissenschaft* who viewed it as superior to philology. His idea of the science of language, however, seems to have never become the mainstream in Germany.[29]

Nineteenth- and early twentieth-century German proponents of *Sprachwissenschaft* thus accepted one of four views. The first view was that philology subsumed all works on languages, including linguistics. The second was that philology *was Sprachwissenschaft.* The third was that while *Sprachwissenschaft* had its own life, it was connected to philology as two sides of the same coin. The fourth, a minority view, took *Sprachwissenschaft* to be different from and superior to philology. Those who still retained allegiance to philology, such as Fu, must have found it easier to regard *Sprachwissenschaft* as the same as or part of philology.

The reign of German philology in the nineteenth and early twentieth centuries in studies of language cannot be neglected. It is remarkable that the pioneers of modern linguistics, Whitney, Sweet, Saussure, and Jespersen, for example, were all trained as philologists in Germany and belonged to philological organizations early in their careers. When they recounted the prehistory of their linguistic science, they, like their German colleagues, accepted comparative Indo-European philology as their own past. Also remarkable is that, even though philology was losing ground to linguistics in countries where the new independent science was emerging, it retained its grip on literary and historical studies, which still heavily depended on learning antiquarian languages and textual criticism of manuscripts and printed works.

Half of the paradox described at the beginning of this essay is solved by understanding what Fu meant by the science of language. In the 1920s, there was no native concept of the linguistic science in Chinese and no standard translation for either "philology" or "linguistics." Fu translated "philology" as *yanyu xue, yu xue,* or *yuyan xue* at different times and places.[30] Despite the slight variations, they all meant literally a learning or science of language in Chinese. A reading list in his *Nachlasse, Yanyu xue beijian,* included titles in Indo-Germanic philology and a category of phonetics and general linguistics.[31] Obviously it was the contemporary German conception of philology that worked behind Fu's translation of philology as a science of language (*Sprachwissenschaft,* that is) and behind his incorporation of studies on languages (phonetics and general linguistics) as a part of philology. For Fu, there was no conflict between the Chinese and English names of the institute he created.

This is not to suggest that Fu was completely unaware of developments outside Germany. He had in his personal library a copy of the 1922 edition of Saussure's *Cours* and a remarkable number of Jespersen's works.[32] The titles in phonetics and general linguistics on his reading list include Whitney's *Life and Growth of Language* and works by Sweet and the American linguist Edward Sapir.[33] Fu's decision to use philology to name his institute just shows his allegiance to the scholarly mainstream in Germany.

Chao and Linguistics in the 1920s

Although Fu's conception of the science of language makes sense in its German context, his institute's work on the study of language became linguistics rather than philology. This is because the Anglo-French sense of linguistics took root on the institute's foundation, and then thrived as a prominent part of its program. The introduction of Anglo-French linguistics was first and foremost Chao's contribution.

Chao was never trained as a linguist or philologist in school. After high school in China he went to study at Cornell in 1910, on a scholarship that drew from the Boxer Indemnity Fund. His first exposure to language studies was a course in phonetics with Hermann Davidsen (1880–n.d.),[34] who translated Jespersen's *Textbook on Phonetics* from Danish into German. This course sowed the seed of Chao's interest in language studies and introduced him to the International Phonetic Alphabet and the international language Esperanto. However, it constituted only one course credit of the eighteen that he took in the spring term of 1912.[35] Chao finished his undergraduate studies as a mathematics major who also took many courses in physics. He went to graduate school at Harvard in 1916, and in 1918 took an introductory course in linguistics with Charles H. Grandgent (1862–1939),[36] a scholar of Italian. These two courses very likely were the sum of his course work in linguistics in school. He went on to work on mathematical philosophy, finished a thesis entitled "Continuity, a Study in Methodology," and received his Ph.D. in philosophy at Harvard in 1918.

Though not a professional linguist or philologist, Chao published his first ideas on language in 1916 in a three-part serial article, "The Problem of the Chinese Language," in a periodical organized by and circulated among Chinese students who were studying in the United States. The objective of the article, Chao stated, was "to discuss the general problem of the scientific study of Chinese philology." He wrote of the study of Chinese language as philology, obviously because linguistics was not yet the fixed name for language studies, even in the United States. He divided this study under four headings: phonetics; grammar and idiom of the dialects; etymology, including the study of characters; and grammar and idiom of the literary language.[37] The article was the first indication of Chao's interest and reading in language studies. He wrote that he had had ideas about his subject, only to realize that much work had already been done in the West, especially in the field of phonetics.[38] He proposed that foreign scholarship be applied to the study of the Chinese language. On this application he showed his knowledge of phonetics and the traditional Chinese scholarship on rhymes, essentially interpreting Chinese traditional phonology in terms of Western phonetics. He also drew analogies with the studies of English, French, and German when appropriate. For example, on the necessity of standardization of modern Chinese, he brought up the case of High German, which was accepted while dialects continued to exist.[39]

Chao's early interest in languages derived in part from his early conviction, shared with many of his reform-minded contemporaries in China, like Fu, that his country needed an alphabetical language for its modernization. Half of the 1916 article was dedicated to the reform of the Chinese language, and much of that to the alphabetization or romanization of Chinese. Chao provided fourteen arguments for romanization, proposed methods, and provided rebuttals to sixteen objections.[40] For Chao, written Chinese in the form of ideograms was unintelligible to the hundreds of millions of illiterate Chinese who spoke the language. Romanized writing, on the other hand, advanced auditory intelligibility; facilitated standardization of the modern national language; avoided the difficult process of learning thousands of individual characters; enhanced the assimilation of the foreign concepts, proper nouns, and technical terms spelled in alphabetical languages; eased movable-type printing; and simplified the organization of dictionaries, indices, catalogues, and references that were necessary for the modernization of China.[41]

After receiving his Ph.D., Chao wandered for a few years without settling on a career choice. Since childhood he had been aware of his good ear for different Chinese dialects.[42] It was aided by his enthusiasm for music, which trained him in sounds and tones. Shortly after the publication of his article on Chinese language, he wrote in his diary: "I think that I am essentially a born linguist, mathematician, and musician." A month later he wrote: "I might as well be a philologist as anything else."[43] Here "philologist" meant essentially one who studies languages, as the distinction between philology and linguistics was just about to emerge. Chao spent a semester at the University of Chicago and another at the University of California at Berkeley on a travel fellowship. Thereafter he taught as a lecturer in physics at Cornell. Then came an appointment as a lecturer in philosophy and mathematics at Tsing Hua College in Beijing, for which he returned to China in 1920. Apart from his university appointment he also served as the Chinese interpreter for Bertrand Russell, who was teaching and lecturing in the country for a year.

Chao was able to realize his vision for language reform when he was appointed in 1920 as a member of the Committee for the Unification of the National Language (Guoyu tongyi choubeihui), an organization commissioned by the Ministry of Education of the Republican government. He was offered the position no doubt thanks to his 1916 essay on the Chinese language, and to his gift for learning a great diversity of dialects quickly and correctly, which greatly impressed his contemporaries, like Hu Shi.[44] The position compelled him to work seriously on the ideal national language in part by recollecting the phonetic knowledge he had learned at Cornell and Harvard. His input was crucial to the final version that was adopted.

As the committee was to unify different dialects, the final version was a compromise that was identical to no actual dialect in China, although on Chao's suggestion its basis was the one spoken in Beijing. This final version was thus an artificial language that no person had spoken. Chao was considered by many the only person able to speak it correctly and fluently, as he knew this version from its making, had modern knowledge of pronunciation, and was knowledgeable about a great number of Chinese dialects and gifted in speaking them.[45] He was thus invited to prepare a textbook and make a set of phonograph records for learning this language. In that capacity he became the preceptor of the modern Chinese language.

Chao decided to pursue language studies while he was in China in 1920–1921. His participation in the national language committee and his linguistic gift first convinced his friends and his new wife that he would be a great person to carry out a linguistic survey and to consolidate the unification of the national language.[46] They then persuaded Chao that language studies could be his career. He returned to Harvard in the fall of 1921 and began to teach Chinese in 1922, thus given another opportunity to reflect on the nature of Chinese as a language. From 1921 to 1924, he audited courses on linguistic subjects "almost full-time," as if doing a second graduate degree.[47] From 1922 on he published quite a number of articles on the romanization, intonation, and phonetic alphabet of the Chinese language.

The figures in language studies Chao looked up to or associated with show his identification with what can be considered the Anglo-French school. In 1921 he wrote about a plan to visit noted language scholars in Europe.[48] In 1924–1925, when he finally made the trip, he took courses with Arthur Lloyd James (1884–1943), Daniel Jones (1881–1967), and Stephen Jones (1871–1941), all phoneticians who were then teaching at University College London (UCL). He also learned to use kymographs at Stephen Jones's Phonetics Laboratory at UCL and often saw Edward Wheeler Scripture (1864–1945), a phonetician and a speech clinician.[49]

In Paris Chao met two masters in phonetics, the experimentalist Jean-Pierre Rousselot (1846–1924)[50] and the comparatist Paul Passy (1859–1940), and took classes with Antoine Meillet (1866–1936) and Joseph Vendreyes (1875–1960), both leading scholars of languages in France, at the Sorbonne and the Collège de France.[51] Though he also went across Germany, he never wrote about visits with philologists there. Instead he only called on a phonetician at the University of Hamburg, Wilhelm Heinitz (1883–1963), then still a junior scholar, who shared Chao's interest in both phonetics and music.[52] Thus before he took up a career in linguistics, Chao had visited or studied with all the leading British and French scholars, with a conspicuous focus on phonetics and a disinterest in philology.

In the meantime Chao's interest in language and phonetics progressed with the editing of a rhyme book, *Guoyu xin shiyun* (The new book of rhymes [based on the national language]).[53] The rhyme book received a prominent place in traditional Chinese learning, as pronunciations in an ideogramic language created problems that were considerably greater than those in alphabetical languages. There is often little clue to pronunciation in an ideogramic character. In addition, as there is often no inherent tie between a character and its pronunciation, a character could develop very different pronunciations in different dialects over time. These complexities gave rise to the rhyme book, which Chao believed the arrival of the new national language required.

Rhyming in poetry has a long history in China, and especially after the Tang dynasty (618–907 C.E.) the prominent genre of regulated verse made it imperative that poets rhyme their verses or poems exactly. They relied on rhyme manuals that registered characters by the rhymes to which they belonged in the Mandarin of the time. The Mandarin pronunciation was accepted not because it was officially the national language but because, instead of each following the pronunciation in his own dialect, all speakers of different dialects must follow one common pronunciation to be able to appreciate the rhymed verses. In this sense, the manuals turned from practical references into a norm that regulated pronunciation. As Chinese Mandarin evolved through the centuries, books of rhymes were often updated. Recording information about earlier pronunciations, historical rhyme books therefore became indispensible for Qing scholars of phonology, then considered the queen of philology (see Benjamin A. Elman's chapter in this book), in their reconstruction of ancient sounds of Chinese characters. When working to create a new rhyme book for modern China, Chao familiarized himself with the traditional phonological works.

Beginning to prepare for his own empirical linguistic research, Chao turned to Bernhard Karlgren (1889–1978), a pioneer in Chinese phonology, then teaching at Göterborg, Sweden. This Swedish scholar's dissertation of 1915 at Uppsala, "Études sur la phonologie chinoise,"[54] easily became the paradigm for the work on Chinese phonology of the next generation. He surveyed a considerable number of dialects in China, transcribed them with phonetic symbols, and compared the pronunciations of selected characters in those dialects and in historical rhyme books. On the basis of that comparison, Karlgren reconstructed the phonology of medieval Chinese, or Middle Chinese, by tracing the shared root of each character. He went beyond traditional Chinese phonologists in not only relying on the rhyme manuals but also conducting surveys of modern dialects. Chao was introduced to Karlgren's "Études" in 1921.[55] When in Europe, Chao took the opportunity to visit his Swedish colleague at Göterborg in 1924, and from then until 1927 carried out intensive correspondence with him. On January

18, 1925, for example, on Chao's request, Karlgren suggested that for dialectal studies Chao learn general phonetics and that he practice by working out the phonetic system of his own dialect. In addition, he offered to prepare a "compendium of Chinese historical phonetics and a dialect type-word list" for Chao's proposed research in China.[56] Even after Chao had begun linguistic research and teaching in China, he continued his correspondence with Karlgren and planned to translate his "Études."[57]

Karlgren had received training in dialect studies pioneered by his mentor at Uppsala, Johan August Lundell (1851–1940), a professor of Slavonic languages for whom phonetics and dialectology were his career-long interest. In 1877 Lundell proposed a phonetic alphabet of 120 signs to be used for the investigation of Swedish dialects.[58] His dialect studies attracted Karlgren, who was not yet fifteen, to participate as a junior investigator and transcriber. The junior participant later entered Uppsala, studying dialects and Russian with Lundell while also excelling in the historical grammar of Greek.[59] Tempted by Lundell's suggestion that the lack of Sinologists would provide the best career opportunity in Sweden, Karlgren turned to Chinese studies. He first studied with the Russian Sinologist Aleksei Ivanoich Ivanov (1878–1937) at St. Petersburg in 1909–1910, and then went on a scholarship to China, where he began to study Chinese phonology and carried out a dialect survey.

While in China Karlgren had the idea of applying European comparative philology to Chinese and even connecting Chinese with Indo-European languages.[60] He left in late 1911 and studied in London briefly in 1912 before going to what Fu considered the capital of Sinology, Paris, where he immersed himself in the Sinological works of Éduoard Chavannes (1865–1918), Henri Maspero (1882–1945), and Pelliot. In Paris, the direction and framework of Karlgren's doctoral thesis took shape. He also had a chance to work in Rousselot's phonetic laboratory. There Karlgren considered himself and his mentor, Lundell, outdated, as they were of the old school that "relies on the ear and classifies sounds according to how the tongue works." The other school, which Rousselot represented, "deals with experimental phonetics, a new science which only relies on instruments."[61] Nonetheless, Karlgren was aware that the Sinology he had done so far was linguistics oriented, different from mainstream Sinology that had begun in Europe in the nineteenth century. Yet he never called for a divorce of linguistics and philology. Instead he contended that "philology without linguistics is impossible. . . . Linguistics, and especially historical phonetics, has proved to be an incomparably more indispensable aid to philology in the field of Sinology than in most other linguistic areas."[62]

Chao's career was far more detached from philology than Karlgren's. Though he was also gifted in modern European languages, he never did work on classical or comparative philology. His practical involvement in the unification of modern Chinese, course work at Cornell and Harvard, and studies in London and Paris all concerned phonetics and phonology. It was sounds rather than texts that occupied him. On his path to professionalization, Chao received Anglo-French training in linguistics, which became his identity. In contrast, his future colleague Fu, exposed to both philology and linguistics, embraced the German philological profile. Their different training dictated their understanding of the science of language.

The Conjunction of European and Chinese Schools of Learning

A complete solution to the paradox of the names of the Institute of History and Philology needs to answer why "history" and "philology" were selected for its English name. These choices illustrate the way Western and Chinese learning came together on the institution's founding.

Chao and Fu returned to China to begin their scholarly careers in 1925 and 1926, respectively. Chao first taught at the new graduate program of Tsing Hua College in Beijing, and Fu at Sun Yat-sen University in Canton. In 1928 Fu was entrusted with the creation of a humanist institute in the Academia Sinica, to be based in Canton. He invited Chao to chair the division on the studies of language. Before Chao's arrival, however, his mind was set on the name of his institute.

In his essay introducing the institute's journal, *Bulletin of the Institute of History and Philology,* "Objectives of the Work at the Institute of History and Philology" *(Lishi yuyan yanjiusuo gongzuo zhi zhiqu),* Fu elaborated a vision for history and philology that explains his selection of these two subjects for the institute. He begins with a brief survey of history and philology in Europe. Historical science in Europe is able to use everything from geology to newspapers as material for its analysis, so much that Darwinism can be seen as applied history. Modern philology, he continues, began after the discovery of Sanskrit had reshaped Greek and Latin philology at the turn of the nineteenth century. Indo-Germanic philology especially is one of the most glorious modern disciplines, while the studies of Finno-Ugrian, Semitic, and African languages, and experimental phonetics are also admirable.[63] This review praises the success of history and philology in Europe and confirms that Fu comfortably saw phonetics and field studies of languages as part of philology.

For Fu, the greatest strength of traditional Chinese scholarship lay in historical and philological studies. He had written a year earlier, in the essay introducing the *Weekly of the Institute of Philology and History of Sun Yat-sen University:* "philology and history started very early in China, and their accomplishments were," compared with other areas of Chinese learning, "the richest."[64] His accounts of the development of Chinese history and philology were not always consistent. In his "Objectives" he judged that Chinese history and philology culminated with Gu Yenwu (1613–1682) and Yan Ruoju (1636–1704) in the seventeenth century and thereafter declined, despite exceptions such as Duan Yucai (1735–1815).[65] Elsewhere Fu once opined that the textual criticism of Chinese scholars throughout the Qing was more sophisticated than that of their European counterparts, although the Chinese had a serious weakness in relying only on printed texts.[66]

One theme was nevertheless consistent in all of Fu's writings. Philological work had nearly exhausted all the laudable Chinese scholarship from the previous three centuries, and had produced good works in traditional phonology and *xungu*, that is, glosses of ancient texts based on the study of the forms, sounds, and meanings of Chinese characters.[67] Despite those good works, Chinese scholarship eventually degenerated. Even Zhang Binglin (1869–1936), whom Fu had once thought to be the greatest of the last generation of traditional Chinese scholars, was inferior to his predecessors in the Qing dynasty in evidential philology and phonological studies.[68] The conclusion was clear: in comparison with the West, China already lagged far behind in the early twentieth century.

Fu wanted to realize the promise of modern history and philology in his new institute. On the one hand he thought that Chinese scholarship had made progress in Republican China thanks to the input of new visions and methodology. For example, his college friend Gu Jiegang (1893–1980) had surpassed traditional learning with his critical analyses of ancient Chinese texts. Gu applied modern historical methodology to his scrutiny of the authenticity of historical accounts of Chinese antiquity, even though he had never studied overseas. Significantly, Gu was also one of the three members of the preparatory committee for the Institute of History and Philology.[69] On the other hand Fu stressed the Chinese weakness in relying on printed texts alone. He vowed to expand the primary sources for Chinese history to all the types of material of which professional European historians had taken advantage: archeological finds, inscriptions, manuscripts, archives, and ethnographical fieldwork.[70] He accordingly set up four divisions in his institute: history, language (which for him was philology), archeology, and anthropology *(renlei xue)*. He secured resources for the excavation of the Shang capital in Anyang and sent colleagues to do fieldwork in western and southwestern China.

Fu formulated the studies on language for his new institute in four areas. The first was Chinese dialects. Karlgren had demonstrated that surveys of dialects served as the foundation for historical phonology. The second was the study of non-Chinese languages spoken southwest of China, including Tibetan, Burmese, Thai, and their related languages within Chinese borders. The third was the scripts circulated in historical Central Asia, which included Sanskrit, Turkish, Mongolian, Manchu, and different branches of the Tocharian languages of the Indo-European family. Studies of these languages, based on extant historical documents, were the specialties of Paris scholars such as Pelliot. Fu entrusted work on these languages to Chen Yinke (1890–1969), who had also received philological training in Germany and was invited to head the history division. The last area was linguistics. Although Fu figured that Chinese scholars were not yet able to make contributions to general linguistics, the construction of a phonetic laboratory in his institute could help train fieldwork recorders of dialects.[71]

The execution of the actual study of languages was largely left to Fu's colleagues in the language division, directed by Chao. Having just published his first survey of Wu dialects,[72] Chao moved from Tsinghua to lead his division in carrying out dialect surveys, historical phonology, and phonetic studies that Fu assigned. Work on southwestern languages in particular was pursued by his colleague Fang-Kuei Li (or Li Fanggui, 1902–1987), who joined the institute in 1929 after receiving his Ph.D. from the University of Chicago. Li was one of the first in the world to receive formal training in linguistics. He studied with two leading American linguists, Leonard Bloomfield (1887–1949) and Edward Sapir (1884–1939), in what was then known as the Department of Comparative Philology, General Linguistics and Indo-Iranian Philology at Chicago, and would become the first department of linguistics ever in 1934. Li's dissertation was a study on Mattole,[73] an American Indian language that had no written form. It was obvious that Chao, Li, and their colleagues in the division of language studies had little interest in philology. Chao's and Li's Anglo-French training and outlook guided the development of their division even after they both had left for teaching positions in the United States. The work of the language division was squarely linguistics, no longer philology.

In his own research Fu endeavored to apply his knowledge of European philology to Chinese materials. This effort is particularly visible in his "Lecture Notes on Ancient Literary History," prepared for his course at Sun Yat-sen University shortly after his return from Germany. He studied the Confucian classics, such as the *Books of Documents,* the *Analects,* and the *Spring and Autumn Annals,* which had long been considered to represent infallible truths, as sources of literary history. These works had been somewhat desacralized by the Qing scholars, who regarded them as historical documents (see Benjamin A. Elman's chapter in this book). His friend Gu Jiegang moved further to cast doubt on many historical accounts in these documents. In spite of the precedents, Fu seems to have been one of the first to view the Confusion classics as literary materials. In the theoretical discourse of this work, he addressed the difference between spoken and written languages, a theme elaborated in European philology. He further differentiated in ancient literature five layers of language: dialect (or colloquial language), class language (languages spoken by different social classes), Mandarin, literary language, and antiquarian language (dead languages such as Latin that could only be read, no longer spoken).[74]

Fu's attention to linguistic difference also connected to his concern with the ethnic diversity in Chinese antiquity. His knowledge of ancient Greek and Roman states must have played a role in his doubt about the long-held presumption of the ethnic homogeneity of ancient peoples who had lived in the place now known as China. That perspective led him to produce works that redrew the ethnic and geopolitical picture of Chinese antiquity.[75] Concern with linguistic diversity also motivated him to set for his new institute the goal of collecting in large scale myths, ballads, and tales, materials he found especially meager in China.[76] His model was the Vedas in India, Homeric epics in Greece, and especially the *Songs of the Nibelungs* in Germanic and Nordic countries.[77]

The affinity of European philology with traditional Chinese scholarship explains why the former was met with little resistance, and why the scope of the institute's work was limited. The inaugural essay Fu wrote for the institute journal went undisputed, and the institute's early publications were warmly received. Fu in particular inherited the tendency of Qing evidential scholars to despise theoretical speculation in favor of straightforward discoveries and compilations of primary materials (see Benjamin A. Elman's chapter in this book). Although he published works on Chinese antiquity that were highly speculative in nature, he often proclaimed that primary sources told everything, so that there was no need, and indeed no room, for interpretations, which he considered dangerous. Many of the publications from Fu's institute studied glosses of words, place names, or institutions in a style that resembled Qing evidential learning more than European philology.

Although the institute's contribution to the studies of non-Chinese languages is significant, its greatest strength has been in Chinese phonology, an area where Qing scholars had laid formidable groundwork. In comparison, grammar played little part in the work of the language division of the institute. That is a curious lacuna, considering that the best nineteenth-century philologists or historical linguists in Europe were the so-called Young Grammarians, *Junggrammatiker,* such as Brugmann and Delbrück. This lack of interest in grammar can only be ascribed to the void of grammatical work in Chinese scholarly tradition.[78] Chao finally completed a monumental work on Chinese grammar in the 1960s, when he was teaching at Berkeley.[79] He may have been inspired to do so less by the Chinese tradition than by the mood of the linguistic community at a time when Noam Chomsky had just published groundbreaking studies on grammar and structural linguistics.

Conclusion

The opening paradox of this essay is thus the result of two competing, if not directly conflicting, viewpoints. From Fu's point of view, there was no discrepancy between the Chinese and English names of his institute. Philology was *Sprachwissenschaft,* and the Institute of History and Philology indeed meant one for studies in history and language. From the Anglo-French perspective that Chao acquired, philology was not linguistics. So an institute for the study of history and language was not equal to one for history and philology. There a discrepancy between the Chinese and English names arises.

At a time when linguistics was emerging as a science independent of philology in the West, Fu and Chao's institute gave a home to both in China. European philology as Fu understood it was shaped by at least three previous developments: (1) the expansion of the *Altertumswissenschaft,* at first based on classical philology, to incorporate textual studies, archeology, and history for studies on almost all dimensions of antiquity; (2) the growth of comparative philology beyond written documents to study the historical and familial relations of languages as systems of grammar and sounds; and (3) the formation of national philology that integrated folklore, dictionary compilations, religious writings, and literary productions into the whole of national literature. Fu set up his new institute according to his knowledge of modern historical and philological scholarship, which he applied to his work on Chinese antiquity. His introduction of European philology was received without much resistance in China, for it appealed to an academic community that found a close affinity between European philology and Chinese evidential learning. Chao, a mathematical philosopher turned linguist, embraced the Anglo-French profile of language studies and finally led his division to carry out dialect surveys, historical phonology, and phonetic studies.

The implementation of Fu's and Chao's visions of philology and linguistics helped their institute, which relocated to Taiwan in 1949, rise as one of the most productive humanist institutions in East Asia in the first half of the twentieth century. Four examples should suffice to illustrate its significant contribution to the global history of knowledge in archeology, philology, history, and linguistics. First, the institute's archeological excavation in Anyang that unearthed the Shang civilization established the history of the Shang as part of authentic human history, an accomplishment that amazed even Pelliot.[80] Second, from the excavation came an amazingly large number of oracle bones and tortoise shells. Despite previous works on the oracle script since the early twentieth century, Fu's colleagues started the first large-scale, systematic studies of the inscribed language. They periodized the scripts on the bones and shells, then produced a rigorous chronology of the Shang kings by studying the inscriptions.

Third, Fu's work on Chinese antiquity has been very influential, for it awakened Chinese historians' awareness of ethnic diversity and geopolitical complexity in the ancient world. Last and not least, Chao's division conducted studies of Chinese dialects and non-Chinese languages that were unprecedented in quality and scale, and pushed the reconstruction of Chinese phonology back to antiquity.[81] With his accomplishments in Chinese linguistics, Chao was elected president of the Linguistic Society of America in 1945, a very early date for an Asian scholar to receive such an honor.

The discrepancy in Fu's institute's names is apparent to us today for two more reasons. First, there were too few scholars in Fu's institute and country who understood, let alone practiced, the European model of philology. Although Chen, to whom Fu entrusted the philology of historical Central Asian languages, published works of a philological nature in the first few years of the institute's history, he soon shifted his interest to the political history of the Tang dynasty. Neither Chen nor Fu trained junior scholars in

Western philology. Almost no one with German training joined the faculty of the institute later. Western philology, therefore, was never reproduced to a significant degree at the institute or in China at large.

Second, today's scholars and students in the West and in East Asia have all accepted the definition of linguistics proposed by Saussure and internalized by Chao. Over the twentieth century linguistics indeed grew independent of philology to become a successful science. Philology as a discipline on the other hand has declined. Few college students in the United States, or perhaps anywhere, even know what philology is. In American academia, there is perhaps no formal vestige of this once glorious science except in the name of the organization for classical studies, the American Philological Association, and its journal, the *American Journal of Philology.* And even that is no longer true, as the association voted in 2013 to rename itself the "Society for Classical Studies." Philology has declined so much that it needs a redefinition—Sheldon Pollock's definition, "making sense of texts," is one of the best known.[82] Only when people no longer interpret the science of language as philology does the discrepancy between the Chinese and English names of Fu's institute become conspicuous.

Notes

Introduction

1. Pollock 2009.
2. See Tenorth 2010.
3. Clark 2006; Schwindt 2009.
4. Leventhal 1994: 255.
5. See Berman and Gold 2007: 4.
6. Grafton 1991: 3; Burton 2001: 309.
7. Holquist 2000: 1975.
8. Pollock 2011.
9. Auerbach 1969: 5.
10. Ziolkowski 1990; O'Donnell n.d.
11. Brownlee et al. 1990.
12. De Man 1986 (1982); Patterson 1994; Said 2004. "Philology in a new key" was recently announced (McGann 2013; see also McGann 2009, 2011), but this seems to be basically old-fashioned text editing with new-fashioned technology.
13. For example, König 2009; Hummel 2009; Most 1997–2002; Lerer 1996, and Barck and Treml 2007; Alt 2007; Gumbrecht 2002, 2003; Gurd 2010.
14. *Diogenes* 1999, no. 2 (see especially the programmatic essay of Jacob); König et al. 2009. (*Geschichte der Germanistik* has in fact recently enlarged its editorial board to acknowledge the ferment in the field outside of German literary studies.)
15. Bollack 2000; König and Thouard 2010 (especially the essay by Judet de La Combe on Lille).
16. Gumbrecht in Schwindt 2009: 275.
17. See further in Pollock 2009.
18. Dainat 2010: 321, who refers to Johann Matthias Gesner's 1737 seminar; see also Leventhal 1994: 88–89, 237, 250–252. On Wolf see Grafton 1981; Most 1997: 752; on Heyne, Vöhler 2002.
19. Zini 2013: 68, and more generally, Canfora 2008.
20. Schestag 2007: 36, and more generally, Leventhal 1994.
21. Vico 2001: 79, 5 (though see Zini 2013 for Vico's "philology without philology"). So essentially Dilthey, "the fundamental historical science, therefore, is philology"

(2002: 280); compare his remarks on Nieburh and Mommsen as "philologists in that [large] sense" from whose "rigorous concept [of philology] "an infinite blessing for the sciences of history issued" (118).

22. Schlegel 1959–90, 16:42, and see Leventhal 1994: 283 and 287.
23. "Das Erkennen [des vom menschlichen Geist Producirten, d. h.] des Erkannten," Boeckh 1877: 11, and Horstmann 1992. Compare the gloss "the reconstruction of the constructions of the human mind" cited by Güthenke in her essay in this volume.
24. Nietzsche 1980a: para. 5 (trans. Kennedy); 1980b: para. 52 (trans. Menken).
25. See for example Szondi's 1967 essay on "philologische Erkenntnis" (translated, tellingly, as "On Textual Understanding" in Szondi 1986).
26. Whitney 1911: 414. It is only in this narrow sense—the default sense in French thought; see note 29 here—that Foucault understood the term, leading him to locate the origins of "philology" as such in Bopp's comparative historical linguistics in early nineteenth-century Berlin (see Pollock 2009: 936–937).
27. The history of the differentiation of linguistics from philology in the United States (especially after 1925, with the founding of the Linguistic Society of America), and the growing marginalization of the latter as nonscience in contrast to the former, is charted in Winters and Nathan 1992. See also Chang in this volume.
28. See for example Olender 1992 and Pollock 1993. On the politics of philology—Franco-German and Germano-British—see Bloch 1990 and Utz 2009, respectively, and more generally Canfora 1995.
29. On the outsiders' view, see Pollock 2009: 934. For their 1992 article Winters and Nathan surveyed (literally) philologists to chart the confusions over the "multiply polysemous" term "philology" in the United States. Note that in France "philology" before Bollack connoted historical (essentially Indo-European) grammar (see note 26), and the recoding of the term by Bollack and his colleagues was meant as a deliberate "provocation" (Judet de la Combe in König and Thouard 2010: 365). In 2013 the board of the American Philological Association voted to change its name to "Society for Classical Studies," apparently untroubled by the fact that "classical" is not the exclusive preserve of Greek and Latin.
30. Here the scholarship of V. S. Sukthankar, general editor of the critical edition of the *Mahābhārata,* is representative (Sukthankar 1944). Pace Alphonse Dain, "the rules developed by classical philologists" are unfortunately not "just as valid" in "the realm of the East" (cited in Jacob 1999: 4).
31. The phrase "Wissenschaft der Nationalität" is von Humboldt's, but it is usually forgotten that he used it in reference not to the Germany of his own time but to ancient Greece. (It is found in his essay "Eine Skizze der Griechen.") The so-called Madras School of Orientalism (see Trautmann 2009) may have played a mediating role.
32. This was introduced into India in the late 1950s through Rockefeller Foundation–sponsored institutes. The story of how the rise of linguistics was shadowed by a decline, swift and dramatic, in the number of people who read and edited old texts remains to be told.
33. I thank Islam Dayeh and Khaled El-Rouayheb for comments on this paragraph.

34. See for example Tu 2005, Chang 2001, Yu 2003.
35. See Nippel 1997.
36. See further in Pollock 2009.
37. Though this is an aspect of modern philology. The study of foreign philologies, whether in Asia or Europe, was nonexistent before the nineteenth century (aside from Chinese or Tibetan study of Indic languages, or Korean or Japanese study of Chinese). Hebrew philologists of late antiquity were as indifferent to the relationship between Hebrew and Aramaic, Greek, or Middle Persian as the Sanskrit grammarians were to the philological study of any of the regional languages they actually spoke. Premodern philology was, thus, always the study not only of one's own world but of that world long lost.
38. The quote is from Calhoun 2010: 229.
39. See Frahm 2011.

1. From Book to Edition

English translation by Rachel Barritt Costa. I would like to thank Fausto Montana, Lara Pagani, and Alessia Ferreccio for their valuable help.

1. For a survey of the history of classical scholarship see Pfeiffer 1968; Montanari 1993, 1994; Montana 2012; Matthaios, Montanari, and Rengakos 2011; Matthaios, Montanari, and Rengakos (forthcoming); LGGA is a specific lexicon of the figures of the ancient scholars. Dickey 2007 provides an overview of the materials of ancient scholarship. For an outline of the ideas and concepts of literary criticism present in these materials, see Meijering 1987; Nünlist 2009 (with the review by L. Pagani, *Rivista di Filologia e di Istruzione Classica* 137: 201–211).
2. Broggiato 2001.
3. Pfeiffer 1968: 232.
4. *P.Amh.* 12: B. P. Grenfell and A. S. Hunt, *P.Amh.* II (London 1901), 3–4 and pl. 3; A. H. R. E. Paap, *De Herodoti reliquiis in papyris et membranis Aegyptiis servatis* (Leiden, 1948), 37–40; cf. Pfeiffer 1968: 224–225.
5. This problem is connected to a number of aspects, which cannot be addressed here. Cf. Montanari 1998, 2000b, 2002a, 2004, 2009a, 2009b, 2011; Rengakos 2012.
6. Rizzo 1973: 209–215.
7. Pfeiffer 1968: 102.
8. On the role of Aristotle and of the Peripatos see Montanari 2012 with the bibliography, and in particular Montanari 1994; Montanari 2000a.
9. Suidas, *Zenodotos Ephesios* (*zeta* 74 Adler).
10. Tzetzes, *Prolegomena de comoedia, Prooem. I* 1–12, *Prooem. II* 1–4, 33.22–39 Koster; Alexander Aetolus TrGF 1, 100 T 6=T 7 Magnelli; Lycophron TrGF 1, 101 T 7; cf. Pfeiffer 1968: 101, 105–106.
11. Pfeiffer 1968: 110.
12. Nickau 1972: 30–31; cf. Nickau 1977.
13. Thiel 1991: IX–XIII; Thiel 1996, 2010^2: V–VI; Thiel 1992, discussed by Schmidt 1997, with a reply in Thiel 1997.

14. West 2001b: 39; cf. Montanari 2002a: 123.
15. Montanari 1998, 2000b, 2002a, 2004, 2009a, 2009b, 2011, and forthcoming, with extensive bibliography.
16. Turner and Parsons 1987, 92; text in Kouremenos, Parássoglou, and Tsantsanoglou 2006.
17. Montanari 2009a: 146–147; 2011: 3–4.
18. *P.Heid.Lit.* 2 (inv. 1262–1266)+*P.Hib.* 1.22 *(Bodl.Libr. inv. Ms.Gr.Class. b3(P)/2)*+*P.Grenf.* 2.4 *(Bodl.Libr. inv. Ms.Gr.class.b.3(P))*=MP[3] 979; cf. S. West 1967: 136–191; Sforza 2000.
19. It is well known that the witnesses (both direct and indirect) of the Homeric text that date from the early Hellenistic age (roughly up to the second century B.C.E.) show the presence of numerous additional lines as compared to the *numerus versuum* fixed at a later stage, which corresponds to that of the modern editions; cf. Haslam 1997 for an effective overview.
20. *P.Sorbonne inv.* 2245 A=MP[3] 1081; cf. S. West 1967: 223–224.
21. Cf. Haslam 1997: 64–66; Rengakos 2012: 241–242.
22. Haslam 1997: 64–66; on the references to the *ekdoseis* of Homer in the papyri, see Pagani and Perrone 2012.
23. *P.Univ.Milan.* 309: see Bastianini and Gallazzi 2001: 15, 76–77; Montanari 2009a: 147; Montanari 2011: 4–5.
24. Montanari 2009a, 2009b, 2011; also Montanari forthcoming.
25. Detailed analysis in Montanari 2009b with bibliography; on related problems, see above all Turner 1980: 92–93.
26. Other useful material can be found by using S. West 1967 and Haslam 1997: 63–69.
27. Turner and Parsons 1987: 15–16, with reference to examples in plates; see also Turner 1980: 93 and pl. 8; Bastianini 2001.
28. Turner and Parsons 1987: 15–16; Turner 1980: 93 and pl. 8.
29. Cf. Nickau 1977: 10–11.
30. Conte 2013: 63 mentions in general terms a basic principle of good philology: "it should not be forgotten that the cases of athetesis proposed . . . should not fill us with terror almost as if they were irreparable death sentences. The athetized text survives, thank goodness, it remains readable, it can always come back from momentary exile." This intellectual breakthrough was achieved by Zenodotus with his little *obelos*.
31. Montanari 2011.
32. This is the most plausible explanation for the different terminology used in the scholia for Zenodotus's text alterations of *athetesis* by the *obelos* on one side and line deletion on the other side. For cases of deletion, one finds the expressions *ou graphein* (do not write: the most frequent), *ouk einai* (is not there), *ou pheresthai* (is not handed down) and a few others (cf. Ludwich 1884–85, 2:132–135; Nickau 1977: 1–30). In Montanari 1998, 2000b, 2002a, 2002b, I discuss some possible objections to this reconstruction; Rengakos 2012 expresses some reservations with regard to this vision: reply in Montanari, forthcoming.

33. Perhaps *ou graphein* (do not write: see previous note), which is the most frequent expression for elimination, may go back to Zenodotus himself and may have been an indication to whoever transcribed his *ekdosis* that the element in question was not to be copied.
34. Helpful confirmation comes from a testimony by Galen, mentioned further on.
35. Montanari 2002a: 123–125; West 2001b: 36: "clearly Aristophanes and Aristarchus were not dependent on Zenodotus' text but followed another source or sources more similar to the vulgate"; cf. West 2002: 138.
36. Haslam 1997; West 2001b: 40; cf. previous note.
37. Or else, if genuine deletions were still carried out, they were of such minor relevance that all knowledge of them was lost; cf. notes 32 and 33 here.
38. Haslam 1997: 85; West 1998–2000, vol. 1: VII; Führer and Schmidt 2001: 7.
39. It is sometimes stated, instead, that they were "recovered" or "reintroduced": this would have involved far more complicated operations.
40. As regards Aristarchus's Homeric *ekdos(e)is* here I will restrict myself to referring the reader to the arguments put forward in Montanari 1998, 2000b, and 2002a, of which approval has been expressed by Nagy 2003 and 2010: 21–37; Rengakos 2012: 252 (cf. West 2001b: 61–67).
41. They could also be repeated in the *hypomnema* beside the lemmas, as was the case for instance in *P.Oxy.* 1086 (pap. II Erbse).
42. Manetti and Roselli 1994; Manetti 2006, 2012a, 2012b, forthcoming; Roselli 2010, 2012.
43. Editions: Boudon Millot and Jouanna 2010, Kotzia and Sotiroudis 2010, Garofalo and Lami 2012.
44. Cf. Roselli 2010, 2012; Stramaglia 2011; Manetti 2012b: 14–16; forthcoming.
45. *Paragraphoi* and *coronides* are mentioned.
46. Cf. Boudon Millot and Jouanna 2010, xxxiii–xxxiv; Manetti 2012a; Roselli 2012; Manetti forthcoming, with bibliography; on lectional signs, punctuation, and accentuation, cf. Pfeiffer 1968: 178–179.
47. Cf. Manetti and Roselli 1994: 1625–1633; Manetti 2012a, forthcoming; Roselli 2012.
48. Roselli 2012: 64–67.
49. Pfeiffer 1968: 110.
50. Pfeiffer 1968: 114.
51. First of all, M. van der Valk (Valk 1949, 1963–64), whose line of interpretation was also adopted (naturally with individually differentiated stances) by H. van Thiel and by M. L. West (West 2001a, 2001b, 2002, cf. 1998–2000, Praef. VI–VIII: discussion in Montanari 2002a, 2004, forthcoming). Sharp criticism of van der Valk's ideas has been put forward: for example, Rengakos 1993: 17–48; Haslam 1997 (see 70 n. 31); Rengakos 2002a: 146–148. H. van Thiel 1992 and 1997 (see also 1991, *Einleit.;* 1996, 2010^2, *Einleit.*) has argued that the readings attributed to the Alexandrian grammarians were actually exegetic glosses or mere indirect references or reminiscences of parallel passages, written in a "Rand- und Interlinearapparat," which Didymus, Aristonicus, and others then wrongly interpreted as textual variants: as far as I know, no one has accepted this rather idiosyncratic vision (discussed in

Montanari 1998: 4–6). West 2001b: 36 and West 2002: 140: "in fact, the first scholars known to have cited manuscript authority for variant readings are Aristarchus' contemporaries Callistratus and Crates. Didymus is the first author known to have compiled anything in the nature of a 'critical apparatus.' It is entirely unjustified to project his methods back onto Aristarchus or Zenodotus."

52. Haslam 1997; Schmidt 1997; Führer and Schmidt 2001: 6–7; Nagy 2000, 2003, 2004: 3–24, 2010: 1–72; Nardelli 2001 (especially 52–70) in direct opposition to West's theories; Rengakos 2002a, 2002b, and 2012; Montanari 2002a, 2004, forthcoming; Conte 2013: 44–50.
53. Lately Rengakos 2012 (on "Konjekturalkritik": 247).
54. Rengakos 2002a: 149; cf. Rengakos 1993, 2001, 2002b, 2012; an interesting case pertaining to Zenodotus is highlighted by Fantuzzi 2005.
55. Lately Rengakos 2012.
56. Pfeiffer 1968: 110–114: the citation is on 114; the three examples adduced by Pfeiffer concern *Il.* 1.5, *Il.* 1.225–233, and *Il.* 16.432–458, *Il.* 4.88. Pfeiffer normally attributed the collation of copies to the great philologists who succeeded Zenodotus: cf. for example 173. Pfeiffer's arguments should have been awarded greater consideration.
57. Cf. Rengakos 2012: 244–248, with bibliography. The abovementioned evidence of Didymus in sch. *Il.* 9.222 *b* is rightly underlined by various scholars (Nagy, Janko, Rengakos, and myself) and cannot be dismissed out of hand, as does West (2001b: 37 n. 19). On Aristarchus's second thoughts, see Montanari 1998 and 2000b.
58. I believe that it is simply begging the question to claim that Didymus's method is "projected back onto Aristarchus" or Zenodotus (see note 51 here): in actual fact there is absolutely no evidence that Didymus was the first to apply this method rather than having inherited it from his predecessors. West's "Didymean" hypothesis is rejected by Nagy 2000; Nardelli 2001: 61–64; Janko 2002; Rengakos 2012.
59. West 2001b: 34; West 2002: 138.
60. West 2001b: 38; West 2002: 140. The idea of the possible use of signs for material deletion placed on the base copy was clearly put forward already in Montanari 1998: 6, but West does not seem to be concerned with the distinction between *athetein* and *ou graphein* in the terminology on the textual interventions of Zenodotus (see above, notes 32 and 33).
61. Whatever idea of a critical edition of Homer, whatever idea of spurious and authentic lines one has in mind: G. Nagy and M. L. West have two very different conceptions, but it would be beyond the scope of this essay to address the issue here (but see Montanari 2004; Conte 2013: 38–78).
62. Janko renders this concept rather more clearly. He believes that the majority of the readings of the Alexandrian philologists are indeed arbitrary conjectures, but he does not go so far as to deny recourse to manuscripts and comparison among copies as part of their work (Janko 1992: 23 and 27; 2002). On the one hand, Janko argues, there stands the problem of the origin of their proposed text choices (subjective emendation, documentary sources) and therefore of their working procedures; on the other, he points out, "my own concern, as a Homerist, has always been whether such readings are authentic." Cassio 2002: 132 offers an extremely

apt remark, on the issue of pre-Alexandrian criticism but perfectly applicable to Alexandrian philology as well: "the earliest scholarly approach to the Homeric text is totally foreign to us . . . we do right to think along very different lines, but we should never forget that it was the commonest approach to the Homeric text in the times of Socrates, Plato and Aristotle. As a consequence, we ought to be wary of looking at it with a superior smile, and ought to try to understand its motives in more depth instead."

63. My italics: the phrase is insidiously reductive, given the hundreds of cases preserved by a very incomplete tradition.
64. West 2001b: 37: at least the case of *Il.* 9.222 clearly contradicts this; cf. above.
65. West 2001b: 38: "No doubt it would have been easy for him [*scil.* Zenodotus] to collect several copies if he had taken the trouble": a somewhat lazy philologist?
66. Rengakos 2012 provides highly cogent arguments in this regard.
67. Montanari 1998: 2; Rengakos 2002a: 146.
68. Naturally Homer comes to mind, but also the texts of the tragic and comic poets.
69. Pasquali 1920 (citation from the reprint of 1998: 26): "a costituire un testo . . . occorre la stessa preparazione che a interpretare . . . ; costituire un testo e interpretarlo sono, in fondo, tutt'uno" ("constituting a text . . . requires the same learning and knowledge as interpreting . . . ; constituting a text and interpreting it are, ultimately, one and the same thing").
70. Cf. now Conte 2013: 44–50.

2. The Bride of Mercury

I am grateful to Sheldon Pollock, Gareth Williams, and John Henderson for suggestions and comments on an earlier draft of this essay. My manifold debt to Henderson's writings will be apparent throughout. I am, as always, grateful to Bruce Frier, jurisconsult extraordinary, for his responses to my questions, and to Christopher Jones for alerting me to the important discovery of Galen, *On Not Feeling Grief* (note 35 here). I am currently working on a book that will offer a fuller version of the argument advanced here. All translations are my own.

1. John Henderson offers another apt image, the tale in Phaedrus (2.2) of a man with older and younger women in love with him. The older woman plucks out his dark hairs, the younger his white ones, leaving him bald. Sexual criticism with a vengeance.
2. *Ad Quintum fratrem* 3.5.6: "De Latinis vero [sc. libris] quo me vertam nescio; ita mendose et scribuntur et veneunt."
3. Fr. 236 Funaioli, from Diomedes 426.21–31K: "Grammaticae officia . . . constant in partibus quattuor, lectione enarratione emendatione iudicio. . . . Emendatio est . . . recorrectio errorum qui per scripturam dictionemve fiunt." A broader definition of grammar (of which the *officia* form a part) is given, among others, by Quintilian (1.9.1) as "ratio loquendi et enarratio auctorum"—correct speech and the explanation of texts—but it is fairly clear that in Varro's time it was conceived as purely the study of texts, e.g., fr. 234, that the *ars grammatica* is "knowledge of

the normal usage of poets, historians, and orators." In this he is translating the definition of Dionysius Thrax.

4. *Philologus* in antiquity is never a professional title; cf. Kaster 1995: 142. Traditionally it was Friedrich August Wolf who first inscribed himself as a student of philology at Göttingen in 1777. In classical Latin, neither *philologus* nor *philologia* is common, and they are generally used in the broad sense of "student/study of literature." The modern definitions of philology as either the study of classics or the study of linguistics are indeed modern, and I will shift unscrupulously between "philology" and "grammar" as needed. For a recent (unsuccessful) attempt to deal with the subject, see Hummel 2009.
5. See Henderson 2004: 101–102. It might be observed that Martianus, by making the liberal arts, including grammar, the servants of Philology, seems to make much the same point; see now Chin 2008: 119–123.
6. The standard treatment of Crates as a philologist is that of Broggiato 2001; see also Mette 1952 and Pfeiffer 1968: 234–251.
7. Suetonius, *De Grammaticis et rhetoribus,* c. 2.
8. See the detailed discussion of Kaster 1995: 42–68.
9. Although one still finds sweepingly false interpretations, e.g., Robins 1995: 18–19, who connects the Stoic element in Roman linguistic theory with the presence of Crates. In addition to Kaster 1995, see also Zetzel 1981: 10–14, with further references.
10. On Sextus Aelius and his version of the Twelve Tables, see Schulz 1946: 35–36; Wieacker 1988: 289–295 and 535–538; and Herzog and Schmidt 2002: 78, for recent bibliography. The (four) fragments are collected in Lenel 1889: 1.1–2. A good, brief explanation of his importance in the development of the civil law (and its interpretation) is in Harries 2006: 41–45.
11. For the fragments of the Twelve Tables, see Crawford et al. 1996: 555–721. Note for example the discussion of the meaning of various terms in XII 1.2–3 in Festus 408–410 and Gellius 20.1.9–29; Gellius's insertion of *civi* into XII 1.4 at 16.10.5 (with Crawford 1996: 589); and the gradual transformation of the amount of the fine at XII 1.15 from *uigintiquinque* to *vigintiquinque assium* to (in *Collatio* 2.5.5) *quinque et viginti sestertiorum.* On this see Crawford 1996: 606. There is no sign of awareness of textual problems in any of the other twenty-five laws known through quotations (in Crawford 1996: 723–812). On spelling, note the variation between *pagunt* and *pacunt* in the quotations of XII 1.6–7 (Crawford 1996: 592–596): a separate letter *g* did not exist in Latin in the fifth century B.C.E. On changes in the text see also Wieacker 1988: 291–293. I could not find a single acknowledgment of textual difficulties or variants in any quotation of any Roman law in Crawford's collection, nor are there any in the fragments of the Republican and Augustan jurists collected by Lenel.
12. A lucid and convenient discussion of the Lex Aquilia, its meaning and changing interpretation, is in Frier 1989.
13. Note in particular in the third chapter of the Aquilian Law the interpretation of the original *ruptum* "broken, rent" to mean *corruptum* "spoiled" or "made less valuable"; see Gaius, *Inst.* 3.217.

14. On the eighty-three books of Ulpian's commentary on the Edict, see Schulz 1946: 196–201. The 1,628 fragments are collected in Lenel, 2.421–898.
15. On the commentary as the dominant form of legal scholarship in the classical period, see Schulz 1946: 183–186. On legal fiction, it is still worth reading the classic account of Maine 1931: 17–36 (originally published 1861).
16. On these works, see Zetzel 1981: 12–14; Kaster 1995: 61–68.
17. The best general assessment of the goals of Alexandrian scholarship remains that of Pfeiffer 1968.
18. For fuller discussion of this problem, see Zetzel 1981: 27–54, which does not, however, include discussion of the problems of legal texts. The obvious caveat here is that some Alexandrianizing poets of the late first century B.C.E., notably Helvius Cinna, deliberately wrote poetry so difficult that it required commentary within a generation. Even Virgil is said to have said of a riddle in the *Eclogues* that he had placed a *crux* for the grammarians. Of course a grammarian preserves the anecdote.
19. Testimonia to the activities of Aelius Stilo and the seventy-eight surviving fragments of his grammatical work may be found in Funaioli 1969: 51–76. Only two fragments (18, 44) concern the explanation of words in Plautus; two more (50, 51) suggest a broader interest in the interpretation of Plautus and Ennius. The texts most frequently mentioned in the fragments are the Twelve Tables and the *Carmina Saliaria.*
20. A great deal, much of it speculative, has been written about the early transmission of Plautus; still remarkable for its good sense is the account by Pasquali 1962: 331–354; see a brief summary in English by R. J. Tarrant in Reynolds 1983: 302–303. The most recent major discussion is that of Deufert 2002; for an assessment, see Ferri 2003.
21. For this interpretation, see Zetzel 1981: 240–246.
22. On the modern theory of textual criticism and its origins, see Timpanaro 2005; for a critique of the method, see Zetzel 2005.
23. The commentator's craft has been a topic of great interest recently; see, for instance, Most 1999, Goulet-Cazé 2000, and Gibson and Kraus 2002. See also my review of the last of these, Zetzel 2004.
24. It should be noted that the design of the ancient book, both scroll and codex, discouraged placing more than occasional notes next to the text. Commentary and text were not adjacent, and very frequently not in the same volume.
25. I discussed the evidence in grim detail in Zetzel 1981; my argument has been criticized, at times rightly, by (in particular) Timpanaro 1986 and 2001. A response is in Zetzel 2002.
26. For a text, see Zetzel 1980.
27. There are a few exceptions, notably when Asconius (76C) says that the scribes were wrong to write *restituerent* in a passage of *Pro Cornelio,* but should instead have written *constituerent* (cf. Zetzel 1981: 17) and in a few passages of Servius. On Servius as a textual critic, see Zetzel 1981: 81–147.
28. On Statilius, see Zetzel 1973 and Pecere 1982.
29. On Caecilius and Fronto, see Zetzel 1980.

30. See Timpanaro 2005.
31. There is a huge and polemical literature on Probus. For a judicious review, see Kaster 1995: 242–269; of the large literature on his textual criticism, the most useful starting point is Delvigo 1987. See also Timpanaro 1986: 77–127, and Timpanaro 2001: 37–105.
32. Paris Lat. 7530 has been extensively studied for its contents and for its script; for a partial bibliography, see Passalacqua 1978: 231–232. The fullest discussion is by Holtz 1975. On the significance of the fragment, see Zetzel 1981: 14–16, with reference to earlier studies. The text is available in Keil 1961, 7: 533–536.
33. Preserved by DS on *Aen.* 1.21: "In Probi adpuncti sunt et adnotatum 'hi duo si eximantur, nihilominus sensus integer erit.'" See Zetzel 1981: 48–49; Timpanaro 2001: 95–97.
34. Preserved by DS: "Probus sic adnotavit: 'neotericum erat flavos ergo bene floros.'" On this passage see Zetzel 1981: 49–50 (on the meaning of *neotericum*); Timpanaro 2001: 77–93; most recently Tarrant 2012: 244, describing it as "a difficult but not particularly interesting textual crux."
35. The recent discovery of Galen's treatise *On Not Feeling Grief* makes it clear that books from respected sources were valued, at least by scholars, but it does not mean that the texts in question were scholarly in a modern sense. Discussing the loss of books in the great fire of Rome in 192 C.E., he refers to the value of (destroyed) copies taken from books prepared by, or under the direction of, Cicero's friends Atticus and Sextus Peducaeus, both scholars, as well as by Aristarchus, and similarly of copies that he had had made from texts in the imperial libraries on the Palatine and at Antium. See Jones 2009: 390–397.
36. To cite Dillon's memorable phrase, "to delight the other half-dozen demented pedants in the universe to whom the data herein contained could be of any interest whatever."
37. Scorn for "mere" grammarians is apparent not only in Aulus Gellius, where the *grammaticus* is always shown up by the learned amateurs, but in Macrobius's *Saturnalia,* with its sneer at the ignorance of the *grammaticorum cohors* (5.18.3), and in Martianus Capella, where the gods hurry the technical disciplines to finish up their narratives and go away. On the hostility between "higher" and "lower" philology (nothing unfamiliar there)—the successor, in later antiquity, to the hostility between philosophy and rhetoric—see, e.g., Chin 2008: 118–123, and Henderson 2009.
38. Kaster 1988 is the fundamental treatment of the social position of the grammarian; on Servius, see particularly 169–197. On the normative nature of grammar, see also now Chin 2008. Kaster (175 n. 17) usefully quotes Augustine: "If a boy is criticized for a barbarism and tries to defend himself by claiming Virgilian 'metaplasm,' he will get whipped." Mistress Grammar enjoys beating little boys. . . .
39. On Donatus, see Holtz 1981.
40. See Chin 2008, particularly 11–38. Adams 2013 is a vast and valuable repertory of material on the social variations of Latin; on the role of grammarians, see particularly his summary, 864–866.
41. Cf. Law 1982.

42. Cf. Chin 2008: 72–109.
43. Howard Dietz, "Triplets"; music by Arthur Schwartz not included here (for which see http://www.youtube.com/watch?v=UjW_yvrC0cE). Lyrics taken from http://www.songlyrics.com/danny-kaye/triplets-lyrics/, accessed May 6, 2014. The lyrics are widely available, with varying punctuation.

3. Striving for Meaning

1. Walton 2006.
2. Jaspers 1965.
3. Elman forthcoming.
4. Hirshman 2006: 113.
5. For an interesting recent attempt, see Boyarin 1990.
6. Auerbach 1948.
7. While the division of Chronicles into two books dates back to the Septuagint, it was not adopted by Hebrew scribes (or printers) until 1448 (Kalimi 2005: 313).
8. Kalimi 2005: 1.
9. Fishbane 1985: 36.
10. Ibid.
11. Fishbane 1985: 136–137 n. 80.
12. Schiffman 1994, Shemesh 2009.
13. Noam 2010.
14. Baumgarten 2005.
15. Urbach 1984, Schremer 2001, Shemesh 2009.
16. Shemesh 2009: 96.
17. Shemesh 2009, Knohl 2003.
18. Halbertal 1997: 42–69, Noam 2010: 240–41.
19. See Bernstein and Koyfman 2005.
20. Cohen 1984.
21. Abramson 1989.
22. Neusner 1982, Bokser 1983.
23. Klawans 2012.
24. Boaz Cohen 1966, Elman 2004b.
25. Hezser 2007: 159–60.
26. See Neusner 1992.
27. The two Mekiltas to Exodus, Sifra on Leviticus, Sifre and Sifre Zuta on Numbers and Deuteronomy, the remnants of a Mekilta on Deuteronomy; see Kahana 2006.
28. Sussman 1990.
29. Elman 2003.
30. Hirshman 2006.
31. Kugel 1981: 103–104.
32. Elman 1993: 2–3.
33. The question is asked some ninety-one times in various contexts, but in regard to the third-century legal collection, the Mishnah, it is asked some sixteen times.
34. On the tosafists' methods, see Soloveitchik 2008: 116.

35. See Elman 1993: 2.
36. Rabbinic texts consider it an important theological point to quote statements along with at least part of the list of tradents who have passed it along; see Mishnah Avot 6:6.
37. Mekilta deR. Ishamael, ed. Horovitz-Rabin, 335–336. For translation, see Lauterbach 1965: 195–96.
38. Elman 2004c.
39. Epstein Mo'ed I, 1938: 480–81.
40. Idem.
41. See Pesahim 22a, Qiddushin 57a, Bava Qamma 41b, and Bekorot 6b.
42. Hoffmann 1970: 39–41, Melamed 1957: 521–536, Kahana 2006: 17–40.
43. Strack & Stemberger 1991, Harris 1995.
44. See for example Yevamot 11a, and Halivni 1991: 52–88.
45. Translation reproduced from that of the Soncino Press, condensed and with minor changes. See Epstein, Nashim II, 1936: 722–23.
46. See Halivni 1991: 63–65.
47. Elman 2005.
48. See most recently Milgram 2012.
49. All translations of the Bavli and the Mishnah follow *The Babylonian Talmud* published by the Soncino Press, 1935–1948, with modifications by the author. See Epstein, Kodashin II, 1948: 576.
50. Neusner 1982: 268.
51. Ibid., 244.
52. Elman 1994: 71–85.
53. Elman 2006b: 40.
54. That is, talmudic authorities of the third through the fifth centuries in Babylonia, and the third and fourth centuries in Roman Palestine.
55. See Urbach 1984: 202–203.
56. Epstein 1965: 349–351.
57. See Epstein, Nezikin I, 1935: 609–10.
58. Friedman 2010, Halivni 1982: 5–27; 1986: 76–92.
59. See Havelock 1963.
60. Daube 1992, Elman 2010, Strauch-Schick 2011.
61. See Haut 1989–90.
62. See Shabbat 121b, Pesahim 100a, Gittin 73a, Qiddushin 47b, and Hulin 141b.
63. See Pesahim 21b, Yevamot 35b, inter alia.
64. Pumbedita on the Euphrates was often a host of visiting scholars from the West, more so than Mahoza on the Tigris to the east.
65. Rubenstein 2002.
66. Elman 2004c, 2006, 2007c, Boyarin 2007, Gafni 2007.
67. Moscovitz 2002, Rubenstein 1997.
68. See Moscovitz 2002: 14 n. 54 for a listing.
69. Ibid., 5.
70. Ibin., 247.

71. Ibid., 126.
72. See Rubenstein 1997.
73. Moscovitz 2002: 48.
74. See Epstein, Kodashin III: 597–98.
75. See Epstein 1935, Nezikin III: 410.
76. See Halivni 2012: 113–114. Needless to say, this dispute sparked a tremendous discussion among medieval commentators, for whom this was literally a life-and-death issue.
77. As Moscovitz has shown, other redactors were enthusiastic conceptualizers; see Moscovitz 2002, 2003.
78. See especially Moscovitz 2003.
79. See Epstein 1938, Mo'ed III: 113.
80. Elman 2007d.
81. Elman 2007c, 2007d.
82. Kalmin 2006, Boyarin 2007, 2009.
83. Moscovitz 2003, Rubenstein 1993.
84. See Pesahim 30b-31a, Sanhedrin 27a, and Elman 2012 in regard to Bava Metzia 21a–b; see also Hulin 77a, where Abaye's disinclination to render practical decisions is made manifest, and see Urbach 1984: 209 and endnotes.
85. Jacobs 1981: 296–297.
86. See Epstein 1938, Mo'ed I: 14–5.
87. Ibid, 1935, Nezikin IV: 17.
88. Novak 1990.

4. Early Arabic Philologists

This chapter grew out of an earlier article published in *Geschichte der Germanistik* 39/40 (2011): 6–20. I thank the editors, Christoph König and Marcel Lepper, for their permission to reuse parts of it here. All translations in the essay are my own unless otherwise indicated.

1. Arabic became the caliphate's official tongue under Caliph ʿAbdalmalik (r. 685–705), replacing Greek in the western parts of the empire. Pahlavi was replaced in the eastern parts under his son Hishām (r. 724–743).
2. See, e.g., Neuwirth 1987: 101–104, Gilliot and Larcher 2004: 109–110, and Gilliot 2011: 110–112.
3. This process is much debated. Motzki (2001) discusses the various positions regarding it and, based on his method of *isnād-cum-matn* analysis, dates the earliest circulation of the Muslim accounts into the first quarter of the second century A.H. (eighth century C.E.).
4. Neuwirth 1987: 106–110 and Leemhuis 2004, IV: 356–358. On the interaction between memorization and redaction of the text during its evolution, see Neuwirth 1996. On the nature of Qur'ānic variants in the readings, see the recent study by Nasser 2011.

5. The meaning is literally "reader/reciter." The verb *qara'a* stands both for "reciting" and "reading," and is thus ambiguous, unless the act of reading is made explicit, as in "He read the Qur'ān off the page" (*qara'a al-Qur'āna naẓaran;* al-Lughawī, *Marātib,* 44) or "He looked into a book" *(naẓara fī kitāb).*
6. Among the first who copied Qur'āns for a living was the preacher Mālik b. Dīnār (d. 748); Pellat 1987.
7. Carter (2004: 43–44) counts 1,056 poetic versus, 421 Qur'ānic passages. Antedating the canonical theory of grammar, Sībawayhi still evinced a more pragmatic approach to language, and the bulk of his evidence was the spoken language of those desert tribes that were least contaminated by Islamic urbanization (39–42). Given that the *'arabiyya* was an artificial tongue everyone had to learn, non-Arabs, especially Persians, contributed a significant share of the books written in Arabic.
8. For the account, see al-Khaṭīb al-Baghdādī, *Ta'rīkh Baghdād,* XV: 341–342 and Abū 'Ubayda, *Majāz al-Qur'ān,* I: 29, translated and discussed in Gruendler 2011: 16–17 and 27–28.
9. Ibn al-Anbārī, *Nuzhat al-alibbā',* 68–67.
10. Bohas et al. 2006: 17–22.
11. Al-Marzubānī includes beyond linguistic errors others of prosodic, stylistic, logical, and semantic order.
12. See Ouyang 1997: 94–102.
13. Bad forgeries were quickly discarded (for an example, see al-Jumaḥī, *Ṭabaqāt,* I: 46–48). However, in cases where a skilled transmitter was himself the forger, detection became even for experts extremely difficult.
14. See Gruendler 1993 and 2006 and bibliography cited in the latter.
15. On this process, see Schoeler 1992 and 2009. For the changed situation in the Ottoman period, see the chapter by El-Rouayheb in this volume.
16. One example is al-Athram (d. 846), from whom the grammarian Tha'lab received the works of Abū 'Ubayda; al-Lughawī, *Marātib,* 96.
17. This is Caliph al-Ma'mūn's comment about the books of al-Jāḥiẓ (d. 868), reported by this author; Ibn al-Nadīm, *Fihrist* I, 2:580.
18. Cited for not sharing their dictionaries are, for instance, Abū 'Amr al-Shaybānī (d. 820 or later; al-Lughawī, *Marātib,* 91–92) and Abū 'Amr al-Harawī (d. 866; Ibn al-Anbārī, *Nuzhat al-alibbā',* 196–197).
19. See Pollock 2009: 931–933.
20. Still to come was the time when commentaries would grow into sizable collections of manifold genres supposedly bearing on a basic text but in reality often overwriting it; al-Sharīshī's (d. 1222) commentary on al-Ḥarīrī's (d. 1122) humorous and stylistically intricate *Maqāmāt* may serve as an early example of this type. For an Indo-Persian commentary on the *Mathnavī* in this broader fashion, see the chapter by Alam in this volume.
21. Modern Standard Arabic differs only in style and vocabulary, not grammar, from Classical Arabic. The typical Arab reader can thus access texts spanning fifteen centuries.
22. Nippel 1997.

23. Szondi 1967: 30.
24. Al-Ṣūlī, *Akhbār Abī Tammām,* 9.
25. Szondi 1967: 11–12.
26. Al-Jumaḥī, *Ṭabaqāt,* I: 389–390. These terms stand for either genres or their core themes, which could be combined with secondary themes. The exact makeup of this basic list varies with the different sources. Lament *(marthiya)* is a further requirement for al-Aṣmaʿī, *Suʾālāt* [*Fuḥūlat al-shuʿarāʾ*]: 48,1 and 53,8. See also Ibn Rashīq, *al-ʿUmda* (and for an English translation, van Gelder 2013: 277–280), where more detailed and comprehensive classifications are given. In the basic fourfold classifications that Ibn Rashīq cites, "boast" is replaced variously with "lament" (*rithāʾ; al-ʿUmda,* I, 120: 11–12) or apology (*iʿtidhār;* ibid., I, 120: 13–16), or the list is augmented to five by adding description (*waṣf,* subsuming comparison [*tashbīh*] and metaphor [*istiʿāra*]; ibid., I, 120: 17–19), or six (counting *waṣf* and *tashbīh* as separate entities; see Qudāma b. Jaʿfar, *Naqd al-shiʿr,* 91). For comprehensive discussions of poetic themes, see Schoeler 1973, 2010–11; Heinrichs 1973: 38–43; and Hussein 2004.
27. See for example the Kufan grammarians al-Kisāʾī (d. 805), employed as tutor by al-Rashīd; al-Farrāʾ (d. 822), by al-Maʾmūn; and Thaʿlab (d. 904), by the Ṭāhirid governor of Baghdad Muḥammad b. ʿAbdallāh; see Troupeau 1962.
28. See Schoeler 1992: 15, and Jacobi 1991.
29. See Ibn ʿAbdrabbih, *al-ʿIqd al-farīd,* V: 309–317.
30. For further detail, see Gruendler 2005b.
31. See Gruendler 2009.
32. See van Gelder 2004 and literature given there, Stetkevych 1991: 5–37, and Gruendler 2005a. Thereafter the arena of the debate shifted from philologists versus poets and *udabāʾ* to literary critics arguing for (or against) individual *muḥdath* poets; see Ouyang 1997: 132.
33. Heinrichs 1984.
34. For the description of this style as mannerism, see Heinrichs 1974 and Sperl 1989, with different underlying concepts. The "new style" *(badīʿ)* appeared with the beginning of the Abbasid dynasty, its earliest forerunners being considered Ibn Harma (d. c. 792) and Bashshār (d. 784). In the *akhbār, badīʿ* appears most often as an adjective for the style as a whole.
35. His expertise in semantically intricate Umayyad and earlier poetry is attested in al-Ushnāndānī, *Maʿānī al-shiʿr,* for which al-Tawwazī was a major source. See also al-Sīrāfī, *Akhbār al-naḥwiyyīn al-baṣriyyīn,* 65–66.
36. Abū Tammām, *Dīwān,* I, no. 40.
37. Al-Ṣūlī, *Akhbār Abī Tammām,* 245.
38. Al-Marzubānī, *Muwashshaḥ,* 343.
39. On Abū Tammām, see Larkin 2005 and Gruendler 2010 and literature cited there; for a survey of his adversaries, see Ouyang 1997: 131–146. His entry in al-Marzubānī's *Muwashshaḥ* on poets' errors is one of the two longest (Ouyang 1997: 343–369), the other one being devoted to Abū Nuwās (303–329).
40. Their works are discussed in the following two sections. On further formative impulses of poetics, among them philology, see Heinrichs 1987.

41. See Gutas 1998: 136–141.
42. The term was even extended to Arabs who were not true Bedouins; see Heinrichs 1992.
43. Here *gharaḍ* could also be translated as "genre," since *dīwān*s usually classify whole poems. Elsewhere the term refers to (sub)themes within poems, or to a poet's emotional stances that prompt his or her compositions; see literature cited at the end of note 26.
44. The positions on hyperbole differed among early Abbasid critics. Qudāma b. Jaʿfar freed the hyperbole from its problematic relation to truth by explaining it as an analogue *(mathal);* Ibn Rashīq condemned its extreme form; see Jacobi 1970: 92 and 94 and Bürgel 1974: 59–62, 64–66. See further Heinrichs 1991 and literature cited there.
45. For practical criticism of this poetry before its theoretical formulation, see Gruendler 2008. For its development in poetics, see the introduction by Wolfhart Heinrichs (with bibliography) in Hammond and van Gelder 2008: 1–14, and on al-Jurjānī, the chapter by van Gelder, ibid., 221–237. Portions of al-Jurjānī are translated by van Gelder ibid., 29–69, and a revised section thereof in van Gelder 2013: 281–296. The meaning of *takhyīl* differs in philosophical poetics. Al-Fārābī (d. 950) and Ibn Sīnā (d. 1037) understood it as a concept applying not to certain features but underlying all poetry, because it engaged the human "power of imagination" (*al-quwwa al-mutakhayyila).* This philosophical discussion had little impact on poetics proper before Ḥāzim al-Qarṭājannī (d. 1285) integrated both.
46. For a list of tropes, see Reinert 1990, and for a definition of *takhyīl,* Heinrichs 1998.
47. For a detailed assessment of biographies of modern poets, see Gruendler 2005b: 86–88.
48. Copious *akhbār* on modern poets are further preserved by two scholars who studied with al-Ṣūlī, Abū l-Faraj al-Iṣbahānī (d. 967) and al-Marzubānī (d. 994); others are found scattered throughout most *adab* works from the tenth century onward.
49. A member of the Banū Jarrāḥ of Iranian origin, skilled administrator, and esteemed man of letters, he headed different offices under al-Muʿtaḍid and al-Muktafī and was connected with their viziers; Sezgin 1967, I: 374–375 and Sourdel 1968.
50. An Abbasid prince, he abandoned political ambitions for most of his life, aside from a short spell at the court of al-Muʿtamid befriending his viziers and a failed quest to unseat the young al-Muqtadir, which ended with his execution. He was one of the earliest critics and a talented practitioner of *muḥdath* poetry; Sezgin 1975, II: 569–571 and Lewin 1968.
51. These were edited by J. Heyworth Dunne under the titles *Ashʿār awlād al-khulafāʾ wa-akhbāruhum* and *Akhbār al-shuʿarāʾ al-muḥdathīn.* Al-Ṣūlī served al-Muktafī as *nadīm* and al-Rāḍī as tutor and *nadīm,* while he enjoyed the support of both caliphs' viziers. He was a prolific author and edited numerous *dīwān*s of *muḥdath* poets (see n. 54); Sezgin 1967, 1:330–331 and Leder 1997. A new edition with translation of the *Akhbār Abī Tammām* under the title *The Life and Times of Abū Tammām* by this author is forthcoming.
52. Cf. Leder 1987: 8.
53. See Cooperson 2000: 9–13.

54. Preserved wholly or partly are those of Abū Nuwās (d. 815), Muslim b. al-Walīd (d. 823), Abū Tammām, Ibrāhīm b. al-ʿAbbās al-Ṣūlī (d. 857), and Ibn al-Muʿtazz. Others of al-ʿAbbās b. al-Aḥnaf (d. 804 or after 808), Diʿbil (d. 859 or 860), ʿAlī b. al-Jahm (d. 863), Khālid b. Yazīd al-Kātib (d. 867 or 883), Ibn al-Rūmī (d. 896), al-Ṣanawbarī (d. 945), and Abū Shurāʿa al-Qaysī (d. 893) are lost, not to mention numerous collections of *akhbār* with selections of poetry in addition to those contained in his *Awrāq;* Sezgin 1975, 2: 331, Leder 1997: 848. Moreover, al-Ṣūlī compiled the *akhbār* of al-Farazdaq; al-Ṣūlī, *Akhbār Abī Tammām,* 12–13.
55. All other works lack their original prefaces.
56. Al-Ṣūlī, *Akhbār Abī Tammām,* 17. This statement completes a distinction of the ancients' artistic goal of naturalistic description from that of the moderns, who refined and developed the ancients' motifs.
57. *Wa-ammā lladhī ʿaffā ʿani l-jamīʿi fa-akhbāru l-muḥdathīna wa-ayyāmuhum;* Ibn al-Muʿtazz, *Ṭabaqāt,* 386: 8. For *ʿaffā ʿalā* as synonymous with the first form, "to efface, to forgive," see Ibn Manẓūr, *Lisān al-ʿarab,* XV: 78a: 8–9.
58. Al-Ḥuṣrī, *Zahr al-Ādāb,* I: 155 and Najjār 1997, I: 345. It is related by al-Ḥasan b. Sahl (d. 850), secretary and vizier of al-Maʾmūn, and ends less apodicticly: "the one [art] that surpasses [*arbā ʿalā*] them [sc. all other arts] are snippets of speech, nocturnal conversation, and what people in sessions take from each other." Other differences concern the composition of the fields and their designation as "arts" *(ādāb)* rather than "disciplines" *(ʿulūm).*
59. Ibn al-Muʿtazz, *Ṭabaqāt,* 86: 7–12. Author's emphasis.
60. Heinrichs 1984: 188 and 201–202.
61. E.g., as "sophisticated poetic ideas" *(al-maʿānī al-ẓarīfa);* see Heinrichs 1994: 215–216.
62. Ibn al-Muʿtazz, *Kitāb al-Badīʿ,* 2–4 and 57–58, translated and discussed by Heinrichs 1984: 214–216. For a different interpretation, see Stetkevych 1991.
63. Heinrichs points out, however, that the term after its first application to *muḥdath* poetry was adopted by fashion-conscious transmitters and secondarily applied by al-Jāḥiẓ to ancient poetry as well. All remaining occurrences gleaned from early literary criticism refer to modern poets; Heinrichs 1984: 192–199.
64. Without insisting on the exact number, he counts five constitutive of speech (loan metaphor, antithesis, paronomasia, anticipation of the rhyme word, dialectic jargon—the last four often combined with the first) and twelve additional ornaments *(maḥāsin)* of speech.
65. Stetkevych 1991: 19–37 deems the attempt unsuccessful. Ibn al-Muʿtazz also represents his other book, *Ṭabaqāt al-shuʿarāʾ* [*al-muḥdathīn*], as a collection of not commonly known masterpieces to be learned by heart for entertainment purposes (ibid., 80 and 86).
66. Lit., "take each other by the neck."
67. Qurʾān 10: 39, translated by Arberry 1955: 229.
68. Al-Ṣūlī, *Akhbār Abī Tammām,* 14–15; cf. also the translation by Stetkevych 1991: 40–41.
69. Al-Ṣūlī, *Akhbār Abī Tammām,* 15.
70. Ibid., 9.

71. From a family of officials of Christian origin, he assisted from 869 the viziers Sulaymān b. Wahb and Ismāʿīl b. Bulbul under the reigns of al-Muhtadī, al-Muʿtamid, and partly al-Muʿtaḍid; Boustany 1969.
72. The Banū Nawbakht (or Naybakht) were a Persian family highly instrumental in the advancement of scholarship, literary patronage, and the legitimation of the Imāmī Shīʿa during the early Abbasid era; Massignon 1992.
73. The *inquit* formula *(qāla)* does not take account of the plural subject.
74. Al-Ṣūlī, *Akhbār Abī Tammām,* 15–16.
75. Ibid., 31.
76. See for example, al-Iṣbahānī, *al-Aghānī* III: 143.
77. Al-Iṣbahānī, *al-Aghānī* III: 204–205 (where the grammarian is identified as either al-Akhfash al-Awsaṭ [d. 830] or Sībawayhi) and al-Marzubānī, *Muwashshaḥ,* 286–287 (as two separate accounts with either grammarian).
78. Al-Ṣūlī, *Akhbār Abī Tammām,* 29–32 and Abū Tammām, *Dīwān,* I, no. 3: 1 and 59.
79. Al-Ṣūlī, *Akhbār Abī Tammām,* 121–125 (account), 125–138 (commentary).
80. Ibid., 125–132, and Abū Tammām, *Dīwān,* IV, no. 192: 14.
81. For examples, see Gruendler 2007: 330–333.
82. For examples, see Gruendler 2007: 371–373; 2008: 213–219.
83. For the following account, see Ibn al-Jarrāḥ, *al-Waraqa,* 4: 13–5: 11.
84. See Sezgin 1975: 610 on both.
85. For the poem, see Abū Nuwās, *Dīwān,* IV: 93. The verse opens a *ghazal* of five verses, describing his beloved Janān in the *Dīwān* but a slave girl by the name of Narjis in a *khabar;* see Abū Hiffān, *Akhbār Abī Nuwās,* 40–43, and Ibn Manẓūr, *Akhbār Abī Nuwās,* 111–114 (with only the first four verses and the variant *bukan ʿalayhi*).
86. See Bauer 1998: 377–381.
87. Ibn Rashīq, *ʿUmda,* II: 120. See also a slightly longer variant with the entire five verses of the poem describing here Janān; Ibn Manẓūr, *Akhbār Abī Nuwās,* 66. The initial couplet also figures in a *khabar* in which the already mentioned grammarian and transmitter Ibn al-Aʿrābī (d. 839 or 844; see page 100) is moved by it but dismisses the verses on learning of their modern provenance; Abū Hiffān, *Akhbār Abī Nuwās,* 141–142 (after al-Ḥuṣrī, *Zahr al-ādāb*). The couplet had become a classic by the time of Ibn Rashīq, who lists it among his exemplary specimens of *nasīb.*
88. For a later meaning of *adīb* as an individual commanding a body of linguistic and literary scholarship, see note 96.
89. For the poem, see Abū Tammām, *Dīwān,* II, no. 46: 5–8.
90. For the account, see al-Ṣūlī, *Akhbār Abī Tammām,* 59–61. Cf. Abū Tammām, *Dīwān,* II, no. 46 in fifty-five verses, praising Muḥammad b. Yūsuf al-Ṭāʾī. The *khabar* cites verses 1–4, 5–6, and 7–8.
91. The term is adopted as a synonym for Genette's *excision* (1982, chap. 47), i.e., the reduction of a text by "scissor cuts and crossouts" as opposed to *concision* (chap. 48), in which the reduced version of a text is entirely reformulated. In the case of Abbasid odes, the great majority of editing is done by excision, whether of a single large chunk (Genette's *excision, suppression*) or numerous smaller pas-

sages throughout the work (Genette's *élagage, émondage:* "trimming, pruning"). For further detail, see Gruendler 2007: 371–373; 2008: 213–220.

92. See pages 105–106.
93. Al-Ṣūlī, *Akhbār Abī Tammām,* 202–206. Cf. Abū Tammām, *Dīwān,* II, no. 56 in thirty-eight verses. The *khabar* cites verses 1–2 (incipit), 24–25 (24 var. *ẓanantuhū*), 27–28 (28 var. *jaḥadtu*), and 31–33 (32 var. *usarbalu*), and 38.
94. My understanding of critical expertise as ascribed to a social class is broader than its definition as a profession, proposed by Ouyang 1997: 166–175.
95. See, e.g., the numerous philologists in *isnād*s of entries on modern poets in Fleischhammer 2004 and Zolondek 1961.
96. The trends toward the establishment of this body of knowledge (*ṣināʿat al-adab,* translated as "philology") surfaced since the tenth century C.E., but it was conclusively formulated only by al-Zamakhsharī (d. 1144; see Heinrichs 1995: 121 and 133–139).
97. See Heinrichs 1987: 184 and Bauer 2005: 291–298.
98. See the chapter on Ottoman scholarly culture by El-Rouayheb in this volume.
99. Gully (2006: 86–87 and 94), for instance, sees parallels in how both the critic and stylist Ibn al-Athīr (d. 1239) and the grammarian and exegete Ibn Hishām al-Anṣārī (d. 1369) treat grammar as more than a set of rules but (in the words of Martin Irvine coined for the medieval Latin *artes grammaticae*) as a "point of access" to a textual community and "discursive procedures for establishing meaning in the texts central to a culture based on texts." In a broader way, Musawi (in press) describes the "learned and the common reading publics" of the Mamluk age as a textual community. For the close web of intertextuality displayed in the genre of anthology writing during the Mamluk period, see Bauer 2003: 72 and 110.

5. What Was Philology in Sanskrit?

I thank Andrew Ollett and Christopher Minkowski for comments on this essay. All translations in the essay are my own unless otherwise indicated.

1. The division of traditional knowledge is sketched in Pollock 1989.
2. On the absence in Homeric Greek of a conception of the body as a totality, something more than "a mere construct of independent parts variously put together," see Snell 1960: 6.
3. In Ānandavardhana, ninth century (like the Veda, secular literature is teleological); Bhaṭṭa Nāyaka, tenth century (*bhāvanā,* or meaning as hermeneutical "reproduction," is applicable in both); Bhoja, eleventh century (the two sets of six *pramāṇa*s, or textual diagnostics, that are used to make sense of Vedic commandments can be used for poetry). For the first see McCrea 2009; for the second, Pollock 2010; the last remains unstudied (see for example *Śṛṅgāraprakāśa* 481–485; also 318–322; 397–399; 1212–1218). *Mīmāṃsā*'s understanding of vernacular languages is discussed in Pollock 2011.
4. According to Ashok Aklujkar (cited in von Hinüber 2007: 99).

5. For an account of the history of commentaries on logic, see Preisendanz 2008; for an analysis of commentarial practice in hermeneutics, Slaje 2007. The rise and rationale of the *prakaraṇagrantha* awaits special treatment.
6. On the history of Sanskrit literature see Pollock 2003.
7. The oral commentarial habit itself is of course far older. Aside from pedagogy, poets themselves typically were expected to offer exegeses of their poems in the course of recitation; see Pollock 2006: 87 and n. 33, and 166 n. 4 for such early anomalies as a sixth-century "commentary" on *Kirātārjunīya* 15.
8. Goodall and Isaacson 2003: xv–xx. His teacher Prakāśavarṣa wrote a commentary on the *Kirātārjunīya* of Bhāravi, but it is not clear to me that the extant manuscripts (now published; see Jaddipal 2008) actually preserve the tenth-century scholar's work.
9. For example, Vallabhadeva ad *Śisupālavadha* 1.61, 75; 2.9, 19, 93; 3.6, 8; 4.57; 5.2, 3.7. As Goodall and Isaacson point out, Vallabhadeva's was almost certainly the first commentary on the culturally central *Raghuvaṃśa,* which suggests very strongly that written commentary was a novelty.
10. A recently discovered Sanskrit commentary on the Prakrit *Setubandha* is dated to the middle of the eleventh century, but the published portion suggests this was more a transposition into Sanskrit (the commentary uses the word *anuvāda* itself) than a full-scale philological exegesis. See Acharya 2006.
11. *Śṛṅgāraprakāśa,* 618 (the solution noted there to the putative Kālidāsa solecism in *Raghuvaṃśa* 1.71c is known to Aruṇagirinātha; Vallabhadeva ignores it). A Kannada inscription of Govinda IV Rāṣṭrakūṭa of Śaka 851 = 929 C.E. refers in v. 30 to the teaching of commentary *(ṭīkā)* composition, though it is not clear this is in reference to literature (*Epigraphia Indica* 13.326 ff., v. 30).
12. Western India: Āsaḍa, Janārdana, Caritravardhana, possibly Sthiradeva; Kerala/Chola country: Dakṣiṇāvārtanātha, Aruṇagirinātha; Andhra: Mallinātha (though Sarasvatitīrtha may well belong to the thirteenth century); Bengal: Govindānanda Kavikaṅkaṇa; Mithila: Divākara. (Some of these data come from the rich tradition of *Meghadūta* commentary—more than fifty works are known—discussed in De 1955; for a later dating of the commentator Vidyāmādhava, see now Bronner and McCrea 2012: 441). But then, further research may well show that this arc of dissemination of commentarial energy was far more disjointed than it now appears.
13. Corroborative evidence of this historical development in Sanskrit is offered by the Tamil tradition, whose sometimes very ancient literary texts receive commentarial attention precisely in this period. For example, the first (securely attested) commentaries on the (fifth century?) *Tirukkuṟaḷ* and the (seventh- to eighth-century?) hymns of the Āḻvārs date from the thirteenth century; no commentaries on belles lettres more narrowly construed (e.g., *Tirukkōvaiyār, Cilappatikāram,* and the others among the "five great poems," seventh- to ninth-century?) are found before the twelfth or thirteenth century (see also Cutler 2003, 308 n. 96; I thank Blake Wentworth for additional information).
14. With some exceptions, terms for genres of commentary—*bhāṣya, vārttika, vṛtti, ṭīkā,* and so on—are generally more normative than historically descriptive (rightly

Griffiths 1999: 112–113), and sometimes not even normative. Discursive formats include the *khaṇḍānvaya* or *kathaṃbhūtinī,* or analytical style, descending from the hermeneutic tradition, and the *daṇḍānvaya* or *anvayamukhī,* or synthetic style, descending from that of logic.

15. Note that many commentarial or editorial practices exist solely at the scribal level (marks that identify syntactical structures, for example, or that signal variants rather than corrections) and are lost in modern printed editions (Colas 2011).
16. While Sanskrit was a target language for translations from Greek, Tamil, Persian, and other languages, and a source language for translations, often in massive quantity, into Chinese, Tibetan, and Javanese, as well as many Indian vernaculars, translators into Sanskrit say not a word about translation, and translators out of Sanskrit hardly more. See further on this in the introduction.
17. The following two paragraphs are adapted from Pollock 2006: 230–231.
18. Dakṣiṇāvarta's unpublished commentary is cited in Unni 1987: 42 (*vaideśikeṣu kośeṣu pāṭhabhedān nirīkṣitān / sādhūn ihārpayann anyāṃs tyajan vyākhyātum ārabhe //*). For Mallinātha see *Meghadūta* 17, 26, 52 (omitting, however, the grounds for his athetization).
19. An account of this work and its early modern character is given in Minkowski 2005.
20. "*Viniścitya ca pāṭham agryam.*"
21. On *Harivaṃśa* 1.37.30 ("true reading," *pāṭhatattvam*); cited in Bhattacharya 1990: 220 n. (see also 224 n. on transpositions). Bhattacharya also collects references regarding the evaluation of manuscripts, according to age (old, recent, damaged, "good") and region of origin (Bengal, Kashmir, "the west," "the north"), and of readings, especially by their frequency (common, occasional, rare).
22. Not only were older commentators systematically studied (Nīlakaṇṭha follows "the explanations of early teachers" *(prācāṃ gurūṇām anusṛtya vācām),* v. 6 of his introduction), but the chronology of their succession was preserved in memory and understood to represent a meaningful order.
23. Whitney Cox reminded me of this passage (cited in Raghavan 1942), and traced back to Uḍāḷi the reference to recension made by the somewhat later poet-philosopher Vedantadeśika, who in defense of his sectarian scriptures (see further below) writes of "consulting the readings of multiple independent [or: unconfused] manuscripts" *(asaṃkīrṇabahukośapāṭhāvalokanād)* (Cox forthcoming). Few editors other than Uḍāḷi ever discuss issues of script, let alone paleography, though we know transcription mistakes often occurred, in particular from early Brāhmī and later Śāradā manuscripts.
24. *Svakapolakalpitavacanaiḥ; prakṣipanti; antaritān kuryuḥ; vyatyāsaṃ kuryuḥ; anyathā* sc. *kuryuḥ.*
25. *Mahābhāratatātparyanirṇaya* 2.2–5; see also Gode 1940. (This paragraph is adapted from Pollock 2003: 113 n. 162, where the Gode reference was inadvertently omitted.)
26. For a pioneering survey see Colas 1999.
27. The genre is called *pañc[j]ikā,* and may have been something of an innovation of Vallabhadeva's, given that the work of his teacher Prakāśavarṣa (if again his

recently published commentary on Bhāravi has any claim to authenticity) shows no interest in textual criticism.

28. Vallabhadeva's terminology alone indicates comparison of exemplars, but he elsewhere also implies something like *recensio* when noting that a given verse is "only infrequently transmitted" in manuscripts (*viralo 'sya ślokasya pāṭhaḥ,* on *Raghuvaṃśa* ad 18:17; cited by Goodall and Isaacson 2003: xxxi).
29. The Sanskrit terms are, respectively, *sādhu/yukta/samīcīna/samyak, sādhiyān/yuktatara; prāmāṇika; ayukta* or *apapāṭha; prāmādika; duṣṭa; asaṃbaddha; ārṣa/prācīna/jarat* (all modifying *pāṭha*); *prakṣipta śloka; śodhana; asabhya* (once, *Kumārasambhava* 3.41); *sundara/ramya/ramyatara pāṭha.* Also (on *Meghadūta* 72) *anārya,* "meritless, inferior" (from the point of view of grammatical correctness). See also Colas 1999: 35–36. The sources of such readings are rarely indicated, and then only vaguely ("an old manuscript," "an eastern manuscript," etc.).
30. *Lipisārūpyamohāt* (see his commentary on *Meghadūta* 2). The variant in question is *prathama* for *praśama.*
31. Commentary on *Kumārasambhava* 3.44 ("we should read . . ." while preserving the solecism; cf. 3.28); see also Goodall 2001. For Vallabhadeva's first principle see *Kumārasambhava* 1.46, *aprasiddhatvād ārṣaḥ pāṭhaḥ,* the Sanskrit version of the familiar maxim *lectio difficilior melior/potior est;* for the second, 2.26, cf. 2.37, *jaratpāṭho 'tra ramyataraḥ.*
32. Pollock 2003: 112.
33. "I transmit nothing that is not found in the source" *(nāmūlaṃ likhyate kiṃcit),* a statement repeated in the introductions to his commentaries on all the major *kāvya*s (others have understood this as a more general statement, "without evidence," which, however, would be unusual with the verb *likh*).
34. Thus Mallinātha on *Meghadūta* 2.39 reads *pratanu* for *tanu ca*—which Vallabhadeva on v. 99 had suggested since "*ca* is meaningless here"—making no mention of the old variant. Mallinātha read Vallabhadeva and thus must have *chosen* to accept the conjecture. For Mallinātha's characteristic conservatism see McCrea 2010.
35. *Amaruśataka* 46–47. We elsewhere hear of scholars who believed certain verses were interpolated *(upakṣipta)* into Prakrit court poems to satisfy certain (later) genre rules (*Śṛṅgāraprakāśa* 679–680). On forgery in epigraphs see Salomon 2009.
36. Very frequent in the *Rāmāyaṇa* (see for example my notes on 2.89.19; 3.45.27, 47.30). A well-known instance from *dharmaśāstra* is Medhātithi on *Manu* 9.93. After editing book 2 of the *Mahābhārata,* Franklin Edgerton could find no evidence that any scribe "ever *deliberately or intentionally* omitted a single line of the text" (Edgerton 1944: xxxiv). The same conservatism can be noticed among Alexandrian scholars.
37. Some of the preceding two paragraphs is adapted from Pollock 2003: 112–113.
38. Two (otherwise unknown to me) are named, Someśvara Dīkṣita and Yajñanārāyaṇa Dīkṣita.

39. See Pollock 2005. There are noteworthy parallels with the *Querelle des anciens et des modernes*—save for the outcome.
40. *Apāṇinīyaprāmāṇyasādhana* para. 18.
41. Pollock 2005: 39.
42. *Apāṇinīyaprāmāṇyasādhana* paras. 27, 19, 35 (citing the grammarians mentioned).
43. Ibid., para. 13.
44. For the last see Goodall 2009.
45. This is perhaps something he learned from south Indian vernacular grammars. In Kannada grammatical theory, for example, from at least the mid-thirteenth century, the relationship of grammatical rule and literary example was reversed: example establishes norm (see Pollock 2004b, especially 407, 411–412).
46. See *Kāśikāvṛtti* ad 7.3.34 (it calls the forms *anyāya,* deviant). One of the words, *viśrāma* (for *viśrama*) is used by Kālidāsa and called a mistake *(pramādaja)* by Vallabhadeva (on *Meghadūta* 25).
47. Sarma 1968: 15.
48. *Apāṇinīyaprāmāṇyasādhana* para. 33.2–3.
49. A more thorough review of the works of Nārāyaṇa Bhaṭṭa's student, the commentator Nārāyaṇapaṇḍita (who wrote on Kālidāsa and Bhavabhūti, among others), may turn up evidence I have missed.
50. *Kumārasambhava* 3: 327.
51. See for example Tubb and Boose 2007.
52. The same is true in the Tamil world (see Cutler 1992: 553; the article actually explores how a larger "text" could be generated out of the independent verses of the *Tirukkuṟaḷ;* a good Sanskrit parallel is offered by the commentary of Rāmacandra Budhendra on the *śataka*s of Bhartṛhari); it is true too in classical Rome ("Even less than their modern counterpart did ancient commentators lift their eyes from the lemma immediately before them to contemplate the text as a whole," Kaster 2010: 496). Only once in his half-dozen commentaries does Mallinātha summarize a whole work (see *Kirātārjunīya* 1.46: he identifies the protagonist [the middle Pāṇḍava, a partial incarnation of Nārāyaṇa] and antagonist [the heavenly Kirāta], the dominant and subordinate *rasa*s [the heroic and the erotic], the narrative elements [descriptions of mountains the like], and the goal [the acquisition of heavenly weapons].
53. A similar logic applies to the (once again sixteen-verse) *kulaka* (1.32–47) describing the body of the goddess.
54. A full account will be available in Pollock forthcoming b.
55. Thus, one important "meaning" of chapter 3, the love god's attack on Śiva, is the martial rasa *(vīra),* just as that of chapter 4, the lament of Rati after the fiery death of her husband, is the tragic *(karuṇa).* Also crucial for many theorists (such as Abhinavagupta at the end of the eleventh century) is the sequence and relationship between such *rasa*s.
56. This refers to the *Jayamaṅgalabhāṣya* on *Kāmasūtra* 3.4.36.
57. *Kumārasambhava* v. 1, 108.

58. See also McCrea 2010. At the end of his commentary Aruṇagirinātha discusses the narrative and moral logic of a range of episodes (the absence of the death of Tāraka and even the birth of Skanda from the poem; the attack on Kāmadeva; his death; Śiva's acceptance of marriage) in order to show that "a wide range of moral instruction [*puruṣārthavyutpatti*] is offered in this text" v. 3, p. 327.
59. In the case of the oldest text, the *Ṛgveda,* the sole surviving oral recension, that of Śākalya (500 B.C.E.?), did effectively arrest textual drift in the work itself, though variants abound when its hymns are found in other contexts. While there are multiple recensions of the other *saṃhitā*s, to what degree commentators ever attended to textual variation has never been systematically studied, so far as I know. In other scriptural traditions, such as the Jain, commentators recorded variants but did not typically adjudicate among them (see Balbir 2009).
60. Thus Kumārila (seventh century): "Where have words such as *īḍe* [*Ṛgveda* 1.1.1] ever been used in the sense of 'praise'?" etc.; "the form itself of the Veda" shows it to be a transcendent text (*Tantravārttika* ad 1.3.12, in *Mīmāṃsādarśana,* vol. 1, 165–166).
61. For the former, the *vibhaṅga,* or explanation, found in the *Madhyamanikāya* itself; for the latter, *Nettippakaraṇa* and *Peṭakopadesa.*
62. Von Hinüber 2007; Nance 2011, especially chapter 1; Schoening 1996. According to Griffiths's rough estimation, nearly one-quarter of first-millennium Mahāyāna Buddhist texts were commentaries (1999: 110). For the Jain tradition, see Dundas 1996, especially n. 19 (and p. 78 for the date of Bhadrabāhu, who is traditionally placed as early as the fourth century B.C.E.), and Balbir 2009.
63. I must reserve for another occasion a more detailed discussion, only noting here the one exception among the Buddhists, Vasubandu's *Vyākhyāyukti,* or "Rationale of Exegesis" (on which see Skilling 2001, especially 319). But his insights were never developed, and later writers such as Śāntideva (eighth century) are concerned only with the truth, not the form, of the text. This remained true of apologists of sectarian scriptures (Yāmuna in his tenth-century *Āgamaprāmāṇya* is exemplary) until the early modern period. For Jain commentators see note 60 here.
64. There seems to exist no systematic scholarly study of the commentaries on the Vedas, aside from Dandekar 1990 (thin and mechanical is Gonda 1975: 39–44). What follows here should be taken as a very preliminary sketch.
65. Dandekar 1990: 157.
66. Skandasvāmin, a commentator on the *Ṛgvedasaṃhitā,* and his coauthors Udgītha and Nārāyaṇa; Skandasvāmin's student Harisvāmin commented on the *Śatapathabrāhmaṇa* in 639 C.E. (on Skandasvāmin, in particular, his division of mantras; see now D'Intino 2008); so too one Mādhava, a commentator on the *Sāmaveda.* None even hints at predecessors. Note that Valabhī, besides being at this period a center of intellectual innovation (other scholars included Bhāskara I, the Āryabhaṭa commentator who completed his work in 629 C.E.; very possibly, "Bhaṭṭi," the author of the *Bhaṭṭikāvya;* and in the previous generation, the great Mahāyāna Buddhist scholar Sthiramati, fl. 570), was the site of the first redaction of the Jain canon by Devarddhigaṇi a century earlier, as a response to the threatened disappearance of the oral tradition after a famine killed many

monks (Balbir 2009: 44). If there is any truth to this tradition, one may well wonder if the Valabhī Vedists were prompted by a similar motive, or at least by the model.

67. Mādhava, son of Śrīveṅkaṭārya, often dated to the tenth century (Gonda 1975: 41) but possibly belonging to the twelfth (*Ṛgvedabhāṣya* ed. Sastri, 6; for his other works, Kunhan Raja 1930: 240); Uvaṭa *(Vājasaneyīsaṃhitā),* eleventh century; Mahīdhara *(Śuklayajurveda),* early twelfth century; Ṣaḍguruśiṣya's commentary on the *Aitareyabrāhmaṇa* is dated to 1173 (he does refer to one predecessor, Govindasvāmin); Bhaṭṭabhāskaramiśra *(Taittirīyasaṃhitā),* 1200; Guṇaviṣṇu (*Chāndogyabrahāmaṇa,* Sāmaveda), 1200; Halāyudha *(Brāhmaṇasarvasva),* 1200 (in his commentary on at least one mantra he claims that no earlier commentary was available, ed. Bhattacharya xxxi); Bhaṭṭa Govinda (*Śrutivikāśa* on the eighth book of the *Ṛgveda*) available in what I believe is an autograph manuscript dated Saṃvat 1367/1310 C.E. (National Museum of India 1964: 10).
68. As a matter of convenience I refer to "Sāyaṇa" alone, ignoring the division of labor with his brother Mādhava and undoubtedly others (see, e.g., Gune 1927).
69. All of Sāyaṇa's prefaces contain references to Vijayanagara patronage, and inscriptions attest to the rich gifts given to the commentator and his collaborators. For a new sociohistorical analysis, see Galewicz 2009.
70. See the list in Galewicz 2009: 292–294.
71. His use of Bhaṭṭa Bhāskara has been known since Müller's time; for his references to Veṅkatamādhava, see Sarup 1946; for his borrowings from Guṇaviṣṇu, Bhattacharya's ed., xxvii ff.
72. "The tradition of its textual transmission *(tadīyapāṭhasaṃpradāya)* is widely dispersed across regions. The Draviḍas transmit sixty-four sections; the Āndhras eighty; some among the Karṇātakas seventy-four; others, eighty-nine. I shall comment on the eighty-section transmission by and large, while intimating variant readings to the degree possible" (cited in Colas 2009: 232).
73. *Aitareyabrāhmaṇa,* last verses of introduction.
74. Dandekar 1990: 162–163. Grammatical commentaries continued at least into the seventeenth century; one is the (fragmentary) *Vedabhāṣyasāra* from the grammarian Bhaṭṭojī Dīkṣita.
75. *Ṛgbhāṣya* of Skandasvāmin, 1.
76. *Ṛgbhāṣya* of Ānandatīrtha, 1–2.
77. Authorlessness of the Veda, *Mīmāṃsāsūtra* 1.1.5; its intrinsic validity, 1.1.2; exclusion of women and low castes, 6.1.1 ff.; the meaningfulness of mantras, 1.2.31 ff. (this last also figures centrally in the introduction to Skandasvāmin's commentary seven centuries earlier; for some different emphases see D'Intino 2008: 161–165). Earlier studies of Sāyaṇa's *Ṛgveda* preface include Peterson 1890 (translation) and Oertel 1930 (translation and analysis of the argument).
78. For some parallels to the European case, and counterarguments or at least cautions about a supposed symmetry, see Pollock 2004a; for Song modernity, Woodside 2006; for current rethinking of the European twelfth century, see Bynum 1984. Modernization, not modernity, is what people like John Richards are describing in the post-Columbian era (Richards 1997).

79. For the former, see Cox 2014 and Fisher 2013, for the latter, Minkowski 2010. For Europe see for example Canfora 2008.
80. Whitney 1893: 93–96 (the "Occidental scholar" attacked here is Theodor Goldstücker). He maintained this view over his entire career, having written two decades earlier, "we are fully of the opinion, therefore, that the help of the commentaries was dispensable to us. We shall not finally know appreciably more of the Veda than we should know if such works had never been compiled" (1874: 113). For a brief recent summary of the controversy see Dodson 2007 (which, however, curiously ignores Whitney).
81. A good discussion is Auerbach 1967, especially 238.
82. Israel 2007: xi–xii. See, e.g., *Tractatus* 7.2 (7.8–9).
83. For the one "true Veda" see Whitney 1874: 125. Whitney could find a restricted place for tradition ("He who is curious as to the history of Hindu learning may pay what heed he please to them; he who strives simply to know what the Veda means can only look at them with curiosity" [1874: 126]); what he could not see was that the "history of Hindu learning" is *an essential part* of "what the Veda means."
84. For elaboration on these methodological reflections see Pollock 2009 (from which some of this paragraph is adopted), and Pollock forthcoming.

6. Reconciling the Classics

I am indebted to an assignment at the Freiburg Institute for Advanced Studies that provided ideal working conditions, and I greatly benefited from the suggestions of Benjamin A. Elman and Sheldon Pollock, who offered constructive criticism of this article.

1. For a critical discussion of this term, see Hargett 2009.
2. For bibliographical references to these works, see Lackner 2011.
3. Makeham 2003.
4. Cf. Bottéro 1996.
5. For more detailed information about the evolution of linguistic philology in China, see Bottéro 2004.
6. Makeham 1997.
7. As defended, for instance, by Huang 2001.
8. Betti 1980.
9. León-Portilla 1990: 140.
10. Szondi 1995.
11. Cf. Steinfeld 2009.
12. Zhang Zai died on January 9, 1078, shortly before the end of the Chinese lunar year. Cf. Friedrich et al. 1996.
13. This is not the place to deal with the difference between the two terms, and the question of whether this term really applies to Zhang Zai. Hoyt Tillman has devoted a series of publications to this question; cf. Tillman 1992.
14. Besides the standard histories by Ren Jiyu, Feng Youlan, and Hou Wailu, see the more detailed study by Chen (1986); but the emphasis on a "philosopher" is also

present in Ommerborn 1996 and Feuillas 1996. All of these authors focus on a small selection of chapters of Zhang Zai's works, and all of them reiterate the mistaken death data.

15. The best example is Mou 1971.
16. Cf. the remarks by Zhu Xi (1130–1200) in *Zhuzi yulei* (Master Zhu's collected sayings), where he qualifies parts of the *Zhengmeng* as "exaggerations," especially in chapters 98–99.
17. Zhang 1978: 40–43.
18. Ibid., 40.
19. *Lunyu* 8.8 is also paraphrased here: "Elevation in song; Fulfillment in ethics; Mastery of music."
20. Here, and in what follows, I am not relying on the *Zhongyong* order found in the *Liji,* but instead on the version handed down from Zhu Xi. It can be found in Zhu 1983: 33–34.
21. Zhu 1983: 34.
22. Kristeva 1980; Genette 1982.
23. In this book, the author relates the modular character of the Chinese writing system ("its fifty thousand characters are all composed by choosing and combining a few modules taken from a relatively small repertoire of some two hundred parts") to the creation and mass production of works of art by assembling objects from standardized parts. Ledderose 2001: 1.
24. Lackner 2007.
25. In the following, I try to provide a new interpretation of materials I have dealt with in Lackner 1996.
26. Wang 1965–68: 8–9.
27. Xu 1965–68: 79.
28. My translation follows Plaks 2004: 38, with modifications.
29. Zhu 1983: 29.
30. Ibid.
31. In his preface to Xu's work on the Four Books, Xu Qian's friend, Wu Shidao (1283–1344), mentions his six commentarial strategies; the fifth one is "drawing diagrams to give form to the subtleties of the text and separating the paragraphs to make its meaning manifest." Cf. Zhou 2007.
32. Zhu Xi's commentary to our passage continues as follows: "if one explains the sentence according to hierarchy (as different from the 'isolated elements'), then 'knowledge from birth' and 'putting into practice with equanimity/peace' both refer to 'knowledge.' 'Knowledge by learning' and 'putting into practice for personal advantage/profit' both refer to 'human kindness.' 'Knowledge painfully acquired' and 'putting into practice under pressure' both refer to 'courage.'" Zhu 1983: 30.
33. I have drawn some preliminary parallels in Lackner 2000; even more promising would be a comparison between the Chinese materials and the evidence provided by Hamburger 2009.
34. Smith et al. 1990.

7. Humanist Philologies

All translations in the essay are my own unless otherwise indicated.

1. Ogilvie 1964: 102–103.
2. Ibid., 103. The witness was A. J. Ashton, who took care to point out that the Venetian diarist was Jewish.
3. Wallbank 1979: 5; Coltman 2006: 13.
4. Quoted by Ogilvie 1964: 103.
5. See Stray 2007.
6. Beazley 1907; see also the wonderful parody in Shewan 1911, which includes not only a Greek epyllium but also a Greek commentary on it.
7. For the very different experience of women, who began to study the classics formally in the later nineteenth century, see, e.g., Prins, forthcoming.
8. See Kretzmann et al. 1982.
9. Kantorowicz 1957.
10. Siraisi 1981, 1987, 1990.
11. See Linde 2012: 7–48.
12. Schwarz 1955.
13. Smalley 1960; Friedman 1970; Minnis 1988; Minnis et al. 1991.
14. Merrill 1910: 175–188. The text appears at 186–188.
15. Ullman 1955: 81–115.
16. See in general Quillen 1998.
17. See in general Reynolds and Wilson 1991: 128–134; for specimens of his annotation see the classic work of de Nolhac 1907. Full editions of his notes have begun to appear: e.g., Refe 2004.
18. Cosenza 1910: 4.
19. See Ullman 1960, 1963.
20. See Kallendorf 2002.
21. Baron 1988, vol. 1; Canfora 2001.
22. See McLaughlin 1995; Rowland 1998.
23. See Reynolds and Wilson 1991: 146–154.
24. Decembrio 2002: 459.
25. See Bussi 1978; Miglio and Rossini 1997; Hall 1991.
26. Lowry 1979; Davies 1999.
27. See Linde 2010, 2011.
28. Schwarz 1955; Bentley 1983; Botley 2004. On the polyglot Bibles, Dunkelgrun 2012 has rendered earlier studies obsolete.
29. For case studies see Allen 1970; Gaissr 1993, 2008; Kallendorf 2007.
30. Panofsky 1960. The core of this argument first appeared in *Kenyon Review,* 6 (1944): 201–236.
31. Fussner 1962; Gilmore 1963; Franklin 1963; Kelley 1970; Levine 1999.
32. Reynolds and Wilson 1991; Rizzo 1973.
33. Linde 2010: 191–224.
34. Campano 1502: LXIII verso–LXIIII recto.

35. Ibid.
36. Leon Battista Alberti, *Dello scrivere in cifra* (Turin: Galimberti, 1994), 27. See in general Miglio and Rossini 1997.
37. See the classic study and edition by Monfasani 1988: 1–31. On Bussi's edition of Pliny, the object of Perotti's invective, see the fine study by Casciano 1980: 383–394.
38. F. Rolandello, blurb, printed on the verso of the first leaf of the first edition of Ficino's translation of the Hermetic corpus (Treviso, 1471): "Tu quicunque es qui haec legis, sive grammaticus sive orator seu philosophus aut theologus, scito: Mercurius Trismegistus sum, quem singulari mea doctrina et theologia [ed.: theological] Aegyptii prius et barbari, mox Christiani antiqui theologi, ingenti stupore attoniti, admirati sunt. Quare si me emes et leges, hoc tibi erit commodi, quod See Garin 1988: 8.
39. See Kenney 1974.
40. Reynolds and Wilson 1991: 39–43.
41. Ullman 1963; Rizzo 1973.
42. In the Caesar that Guarino prepared, now in the Biblioteca Estense (MS V C 2), he wrote: "Emendavit Guarinus Veronensis adiuvante Io. Lamola cive bononiensi anno Christi MCCCCXXXII. IIII nonas iulias Ferrariae" (I, Guarino of Verona, emended this, with the help of Giovanni Lamola, citizen of Bologna, on 2 July 1432). Similar notes appear elsewhere in his work. In a Pliny, now in Milan (Biblioteca Ambrosiana MS D 531 inf.), he wrote: "that eminent gentleman Guarino of Verona corrected this with the help of Guglielmo Capella, that learned and eminent gentleman, in the prince's palace at Ferrara" (Emendavit c.v. Guarinus Veronensis adiuvante Guglielmo Capello viro praestanti atque eruditissimo Ferrariae in aula principis anno incarnati verbi MCCCCXXXXIII. VI. kalendas septembres). Both texts quoted and discussed in Remigio Sabbadini, *La scuola e gli studi di Guarino Guarini Veronese* (Catania: Galati, 1896), 115–123.
43. Festus c. 1472: fol. 83 verso.
44. See the article by J. E. G. Zetzel in this volume.
45. Varro 1471–72: 2 recto.
46. Vat. lat. 1660, fol. 55 vo.: "Hunc versum non inveni in aliis in quibus revidi opus nec puto esse debere quia supra est. nec quadrat."
47. Vat. lat. 1595, fol. 287 vo. on *Fasti* 3.567–568. See the excellent work of Donati (2000).
48. Filetico 2000: 3–4.
49. Campanelli 2001.
50. Grafton 1983–93: vol. 1, chaps. 1–3.
51. Harth 1967: 29–53.
52. See Bianca 1995: 5–16.
53. Quintilian *Institutio oratoria* 2.4.18.
54. Martinelli and Perosa 1996, on 2.4.18; cf. Ginzburg 1999 and Linde 2011: 35–63.
55. Valla 2007.
56. See Mulsow 2002.
57. See in general Momigliano 1950; Weiss 1988; Brown 1996; Miller 2007.

58. Scalamonti 1996: 117; cf. Smith 1992.
59. Grafton and Curran 1995.
60. Biondo 2005: 191.
61. Mandowsky and Mitchell 1963; McCuaig 1989; Stenhouse 2005.
62. Apianus 1540: I iiii recto.
63. Grafton 1983–93: II (vol. 2).
64. Giovanni Dominici, *Lucula noctis,* ed. Edmund Hunt (Notre Dame, 1940), 412, cited in Frazier 2005: 19.
65. See Rowland 1998; Curran 2007.
66. Berosus 1545: 218 verso.
67. Ibid., 219 recto.
68. Grafton 2007.
69. Rhenanus 1551.
70. Scaliger 1598; Grafton 1983–93: II (vol. 2): 434–436.
71. Patrizi 1560: 11 recto.
72. Momigliano 1973; De Landtsheer 2001: 101–122.
73. See Stenhouse 2005; Haskell 1993.
74. Grafton 1983–93: II (vol. 2): 739–740.
75. Rossi 1984; Jorink 2006; Weststeijn 2007: 537–561.

8. Mughal Philology and Rūmī's *Mathnavī*

Sheldon Pollock inspired and encouraged me to write this article. Hajnalka Kovacs and Ananya Chakrabarti gave me so much of their valuable time in preparing and finalizing it. Cornell Fleischer, Thibaut d'Hubert, Rajeev Kinra, Frank Lewis, and Mohamed Tavakoli-Targhi were kind enough to suggest some important references, and Sanjay Subrahmanyam was always available for discussions and advice. I acknowledge their help with gratitude. All translations in the essay are my own unless otherwise indicated.

1. Abū l-Faḍl 2002: 520. See also Abū l-Faḍl 1896: 57–58.
2. Abū l-Faḍl 1920: 55. The noted religious scholar ʿAbd al-Ḥaqq Muḥaddith Dihlavī (d. 1642) too was reported to have made an *intikhāb* (selection) of the *Mathnavī.* See Nizami 1964: 184; Khan 2001: 99.
3. See ʿAbd al-Laṭīf's introduction to his commentary and edition of Sanāʾī's *Ḥadīqa,* published as *Laṭāyif al-Haqāyiq min Nafāyis al-Daqāyiq* (ʿAbd al-Laṭīf [1876] 1905). See also Stephenson 1911: x–xxvii. Stephenson relied heavily on ʿAbd al-Laṭīf's edition in the preparation of his text.
4. ʿAbd al-Laṭīf has recently received scholarly attention in Persian and Urdu, but this has largely ignored the Mughal context in which he worked. See Akber 1970; Ahmad and Jayasi 2004; Khatoon 2007. For a survey in English, see Ali 1957: 39–54. For references in early English scholarship to him, see Blochmann 1868: 32; Beale 1894: 9.
5. On Ṣūfī Māzandarānī's life and work, see Gulchīn-i Maʿānī 1990: 1233–1242; Haravī 1979: 39. See also the short entry in Hadi 1995: 419–420.

6. The book remains unpublished. An important manuscript is housed in the Bodleian Library; cf. Sachau and Ethe 1889; another exists in what has been mentioned as the personal library of Qāḍī Ṣāḥib of Ahmadabad, cf. Ali 1957: 45; yet another in the Central Library of Bhopal, cf. Ahmad 2002: 95–120. The Bhopal manuscript does not contain ʿAbd al-Laṭīf's introduction or *Khulāṣa-i Ahvāl al-Shuʿarā.*
7. ʿAbd al-Laṭīf. *Dībācha/Mir'āt al-Mathnavī/Mathnavī–i Mawlavī,* f. 8a. For Raushniyas' revolts, see Ahmed 1982. For a contemporary account of these events in Persian, see Kambūh 1967–72, 3: 301–302 and 313–317.
8. This remains unpublished, although several manuscripts exist. Among the oldest manuscripts that I have consulted are Bodleian Library, Oxford, Elliot 264, Sachau and Ethe 1889: 663; Maulana Azad Library, Aligarh Muslim University, Subhanallah Collection, No. 5514–54/891. For a description of the latter and also the other copies of the manuscript available in Aligarh, see Khatoon 2007. Another important manuscript copied in 1660 was in the personal collection of Professor Kabir Ahmad Jayasi, and is now available in Raza Library, Rampur, India. See Ahmad and Jayasi 2004: 44–62. Yet another old manuscript, illuminated, illustrated, and written in extremely beautiful Nastaliq in 1674, is available in the Library of the Majlis-i Shūrā-yi Islāmī, Tehran. For a description see Afshār et al. 1989: 85. References to ʿAbd al-Laṭīf's *Dībācha,* his preface to *Laṭāyif al-Mathnavī,* and my preliminary notes for this essay are from this manuscript. I am grateful to Janāb Khwāja Pīrī, Director of Noor Microfilms, Iran Cultural House, New Delhi, for a digital copy of it. In addition, I saw a number of other late seventeenth-/early eighteenth-century manuscripts, complete or in fragments, available in the British Library, London; the Bodleian Library, Oxford; the Asiatic Society of Bengal, Kolkata; the Khuda Bakhsh Oriental Public Library, Patna; and the Nawwab Muzzammilullah Khan Sherwani Collection, Aligarh.
9. On his rank, see Lāhawrī 1865–72: 2, 442. Kambūh also mentions a rank of 1000 *dhāt*/400 *savār* for ʿAbd al-Laṭīf, but it is not clear when exactly he received this rank. Lāhawrī adds that in 1647, ʿAbd al-Laṭīf was honored with the title ʿAqīdat Khān. Kambūh 1967. See Lāhawrī 1865–72, 2:92; Kambūh 1967–72, 3:339. On the diplomatic mission, see Lāhawrī 1865–72, 2:135; Khān 1868–74, 535. On Diyānat Rāy replacing ʿAbd al-Laṭīf, see Lāhawrī 1865–72, 2:92. For Diyānat Rāy, see Ali 1985: 111, 149, 158, 166, 181, 219, 232, 236, 260, and 302. On ʿAbd al-Laṭīf's death, see Storey 1953: 807; Rieu 1966: 588–589; Stephenson 1911: xxiv. For *dīvān-i tan* and *manṣab*s, see Habib 1999: 299, 308n, and 330n; Ali 1985: 37–68.
10. Both these texts were published in the nineteenth century, the first in 1887 by Naval Kishore, Lucknow, the second in 1876 by Naval Kishore, Kanpur, and then again in 1886 by Naval Kishore, Lucknow. ʿAbd al-Laṭīf completed them, as he tells us in *Dībācha,* f. 16b, in 1032/1622, much before 1038/1628, the year that Sayyid Akbar Ali guesses; cf. Ali 1957: 48–49. According to the preface of one India Office Library manuscript, *Laṭāyif al-Maʿnavī,* copied in Jumada II, 1080 AH/1669, in Amethi near Lucknow, ʿAbd al-Laṭīf dedicated all his *Mathnavī*-related works to the Mughal emperor Shāh Jahān (r. 1628–1658). He projects his works as a manifestation of the high spiritual stature of the emperor, describing him as a "mujaddid" of

the eleventh Hijra century. Cf. *Laṭāyif al-Maʿnavī,* Ethe, *Catalogue,* 1101/I.O. Islamic 382, ff., which means 1a and 1b.

11. For a description of this unpublished collection, see Ivanow 1924, 159. See also Desai 1999: 188–197.
12. See Sarkar 1919: 597–603; 1928: 143–146; Ahuja 1967: 93–98; 1973: 147–172.
13. Kambūh 1967–72, 3:339–340.
14. Cf. *Dībācha,* f. 16b; preface of *Laṭāyif* reproduced in *Mathnavī–i Mawlavī,* Majlis Ms, f. 4b. See also Lucknow (1886) and Kanpur (1876) editions. Kambūh seems to be particularly impressed by its prose: "Bar Mathnavī–i Mawlavī-i Rūm sharḥ-i matīn navishta va Dībācha-i rangīn ba-qalam āvurda." Kambūh 1967: 340.
15. *Dībācha,* f. 12b. See also the British Museum manuscript of *Laṭāyif al-Maʿnavī,* Ms. Add. 16770, f. 4b. Rieu 1966: 590.
16. For early Muslim philosophers and Islamic sects, see Shahrastānī 1984: 41–76; Watt 1985, and Groff and Leaman 2007.
17. *Dībācha,* 12a and 12b. 12. The verse is from book 6; l. 2248 in Nicholson's edition (Rūmī 1925–40), l. 2255 in Istiʿlāmī's (Rūmī 1990). In both editions the last words of the two *miṣra*ʿs rhyme imperfectly: "gar shavad bīshah qalam daryā midād / mathnavī rā nīst pāyānī umīd": "(even) if (all) the forest should become pens and (all) the ocean ink, (yet) there is no hope of bringing the *Mathnaví* to an end" (Nicholson's translation).
18. ʿAbd al-Laṭīf mentions only an anecdote from Jāmī's *Nafaḥāt al-Uns,* highlighting the sublime spiritual quality of the *Mathnavī.* There may also possibly be a sort of allusion to the oft-cited verse, which Valī Muḥammad Akbarābādī attributes to Jāmī. See Akbarābādī 2004: 4–5. Akbarābādī wrote this commentary in India in 1728. I am grateful to Professor Mohamad Tavakoli-Targhi for this reference.
19. *Dībācha,* f. 11b.
20. ʿAbd al-Laṭīf writes: "there have been many copies that friends trusted completely as authentic and correct, but none of them appeared to have even 1 percent of the features that I have mentioned above [which the *Nuskha-i Nāsikha* possessed]." *Dībācha,* f. 8b.
21. *Dībācha,* 13a and 13b.
22. Qurʾān 32:4.
23. *Dībācha,* f. 13a. ʿAbd al-Laṭīf mentiones the following Qurʾānic verses: "then We made the sperm into a clot of congealed blood; then of that clot We made a (foetus) lump; then we made out of that lump bones and clothed the bones with flesh; then we developed out of it another creature. So blessed be Allah, the Best to create!" (Qurʾān 23:14; Yusuf Ali's translation (1957); and "it is He Who has created you from dust then from a sperm-drop, then from a leech-like clot; then does He get you out (into the light) as a child: then lets you (grow and) reach your age of full strength" (Qurʾān 40:67; Yusuf Ali's translation).
24. In this connection, it is worth noting here that ʿAbd al-Laṭīf also invokes ʿAbd al-Raḥmān Jāmī, who commented on the collectivity of these six levels of existence in his *Rubāʿī. Dībācha,* f. 13b.

25. Here, ʿAbd al-Laṭīf draws support from the poet himself, quoting from the beginning of book 6 of the *Mathnavī:*

> Oh life of my heart, Husamuddin,
> The desire for a sixth part is boiling in me.
> The six directions get light from these six books
> so that the one who has not circumambulated it could do so.

These are ll. 1 and 4 of book 6 in both Nicholson's and Istiʿlāmī's editions (Rūmī 1925–40; 1990).

26. ʿAbd al-Laṭīf, according to a report, was associated with the Naqshbandi order, though it is unclear whether he had any connection with the Mujaddidi branch of it. Hamadānī 1988: 41. Notable in this connection is also the evaluation of the *Mathnavī,* as we saw above, by Jāmī, who belonged to the Naqshbandi order. For an account of the Naqshbandi shaykhs, see Rizvi 1978–83, 2: 174–263.
27. For a discussion of the state of medical knowledge in Mughal India, see Alavi 2008.
28. In this regard, one may remember that Abū l-Faḍl was deprived of the text precisely for this reason during his travels with the imperial army, and was forced to reconcile himself to a selection by Abū Bakr Shāshī. Abū l-Faḍl 1920: 55.
29. *Dībācha,* ff. 8b and 16b–17b.
30. Though there are exceptions, like a manuscript titled *Sharḥ-i Mathnavī maʿ Dībācha az ʿAbd al-Laṭīf,* Nawwab Muzammilullah Khan Collection, Aligarh, *Fārsiya* 1785, copied in 1702 in Kashmir, with an additional volume 7 comprising over twenty-one hundred verses, and the Bombay publication of volume 7 attributed to Rūmī. But in general such verses have rarely been accepted as a genuine part of the *Mathnavī.*
31. Losensky 1998: 100–114, for instance.
32. ʿAbd al-Laṭīf here refers to the traditions of *imitatio (istiqbāl, javāb),* and how several poets wrote such responses to Niẓāmī of Ganja's *Khamsa* or *Panj-Ganj* in this regard. For such a response by Amīr Khusraw, see Shekhar 1989: 64–238; Gabbay 2010: 41–65; Kinra 2011b.
33. *Dībācha,* f. 16b. The verses are from book 4; ll. 34–35 in both Nicholson's and Istiʿlāmī's edition and are slightly different from ʿAbd al-Laṭīf's text: "Dushman-i īn ḥarf īn dam dar naẓar / shud mumaththal sarnigūn andar saqar / Ay Ḍiyā al-Ḥaq tū dīdī ḥāl-i ū / Ḥaq numūd-at pāsukh-i afʿāl-i ū." "At this moment the enemy of these words (the *Mathnaví*) is pictured in (thy) sight (falling) headlong into Hell-fire. O Ẓiyá'u 'l-Ḥaqq (Radiance of God), thou hast seen his (evil) state: God hath shown unto thee the answer to his (evil) actions" (Nicholson's translation, 2248).
34. *Dībācha,* ff. 9b–10a; Khatoon 2007.
35. Khatoon 2007, quoting from ʿAbd al-Laṭīf's preface to the *Laṭāyif al-Lughāt.*
36. The weakness of this system in comparison with later dictionaries in Mughal India, which considered the alphabetical order of every letter of the word rather than just the first and last letters, is obvious. See Ansari 1985: 32–45.

37. Compare, for instance, with *Kashf-i Asrār-i Maʿnavī dar Sharḥ-i Abyāt-i Mathnavī* (Unraveling of the sublime mysteries in the commentary on the verses of the *Mathnavī*), by ʿAbd al-Ḥamīd Rifāʿī Tabrīzī. Rieu 1966: 588–589. In Tabrīzī's commentary, which does not go beyond the first two volumes, we have just straight and simple meanings of the words.
38. *Dībācha,* f. 10b.
39. *Dībācha,* f. 5a. For this story see Rūmī 1974, 1: 124–163.
40. For two such earlier commentaries, one by Aḥmad Ghazālī, the other by Ḥusayn Khwārazmī, see Lewis 2000: 476. See also Sachau and Ethé 1889–1954, 1: 646. Rieu mentions a third such commentary titled *Kashf al-Asrār* (Unraveling of the mysteries) or *Kashf-i Asrār-i Maʿnavī dar Sharḥ-i Abyāt-i Mathnavī* (Unraveling of the sublime mysteries in the commentary on the verses of the *Mathnavī*) by ʿAbd al-Ḥamīd Rifāʿī Tabrīzī (Rieu 1966: 588–589). ʿAbd al-Laṭīf also alludes to several earlier commentators and mentions Khwārazmī as one of them ("yaki az shurrāḥ-i Mathnavī"). See his *Laṭāyif al-Maʿnavī,* British Museum Ms. Add. 16770, f. 4b. Rieu 1966: 590.
41. *Dībācha,* f. 14b.
42. *Dībācha,* f. 14b. The two verses actually are taken from two different places of the Mathnavī: the first one is from book 1 (l. 1727 in Nicholson's edition and l. 1737 in Istiʿlāmī's); the second one is from book 5 (l. 1893 in Nicholson's edition and l. 1895 in Istiʿlāmī's). Mojaddedi's translation of the first one: "I think of rhymes, but the Beloved says: / 'Just for my face reserve your constant gaze!'" (Rūmī 2004: 107, l. 1737). Nicholson's translation: "I am thinking of rhymes, and my Sweetheart says to me, 'Do not think of aught except vision of Me.'" In the second verse both Nicholson's and Istiʿlāmī's editions have "uṣūl al-ʿāfiya" instead of "uṣūl al-ʿāliya": "kayfa ya'tī l-naẓmu lī wa-l-qāfiya / baʿda mā ḍāʿat uṣūl al-ʿāfiya." "How should poesy and rhyme come to me after the foundations of sanity are destroyed?" (Nicholson's translation).
43. *Dībācha,* f. 14b.
44. *Dībācha,* ff. 14b–15a. Book 2, ll. 190–191 in both Nicholson's and Istiʿlāmī's editions. The substory does not have a separate chapter title in either edition, but in the online text of the *Mathnavī* (based on the DVD edition of A. Surūsh, Rūmī n.d., which is based on the Konya manuscript) it is given the title *Ḥikāyat-i mashvarat kardan-i khudā-yi taʿālā dar ījād-i khalq.* Both Nicholson's and Istiʿlāmī's editions have *ḥāl* instead of *khāl* in the third *miṣraʿ*. "O my comrade on the way, dismiss thy weariness for a moment, / that I may describe a single mole (grain) of that Beauty. / The Beauty of His state cannot be set forth: / what are both the worlds (temporal and spiritual)? The reflection of His mole." (Nicholson's translation).
45. *Dībācha,* ff. 14b–15a.
46. *Dībācha,* f. 15b. The verse is from book 1; l. 2596 in Nicholson's edition and l. 2608 in Istiʿlāmī's.
47. *Dībācha,* f. 15b. "Ladhdhatī dārad īn sukhan tāza / ki birūn shud hamī zi andāza."
48. *Dībācha,* ff. 18b–19a.
49. For this alternative title, see De Bruijn 1983: 10, 124, and 128. Notable here is also that Muḥammad Riḍā Lāhawrī of *Mukāshafāt-i Riḍavī dar Sharḥ-i Mathnavī-i Maʿnavī,* a second major commentary compiled in Mughal India in 1084/1674, also

held a Mughal state office *(khidmat-i Sulṭānī).* Cf. Lāhawrī 2002: 3; Khalīlallāh ibn Fatḥallāh Ḥārithī Yamanī Lāhawrī, *Safīna-i Baḥr al-Muḥīṭ,* Staatbibliothek, Berlin, Ms. Orient. Fol. 248 f. 189b; Pertsch 1888: 38.

50. *Dībācha,* preliminary notes, f. 26a.
51. For a description of this manuscript, see Ahmad and Jayasi 2004: 167. My reading of this manuscript is different from Ahmad and Jayasi's, who evaluate it as a complete copy of the *Nuskha-i Nāsikha.* Riḍā cites several lines to illustrate the quality of Kurd's poetry. For Sulaymān Kurd, see Desai 1985: 11–20.
52. For Vajīh al-Dīn ʿAlavī and Muḥammad Ghawth Gvāliyūrī, see Rizvi 1978: 166–167, 156–163. For Shattari saints, see Nizami 1950: 56–70.
53. Rūmī 1925–40, 1: 18. ʿAbd al-Laṭīf's work on Sanāʾī's *Ḥadīqat al-Ḥaqīqa* has, however, been judged more favorably. See Stephenson 1911; de Bruijn 1983: 119–139. Mudarris Raḍavī, an eminent Iranian specialist in Sanāʾī's poetry, relies heavily on ʿAbd al-Laṭīf's efforts in his recent commentary on Sanāʾī's work. Introduction to Mudarris Raḍavī 1965: 156, 275, 357, 385, 392, 489, 509, 551–552, 554.
54. Sachau and Ethé 1889: 517; Rieu 1966: 588–589. It is not clear if Nicholson considered of any worth the difference that ʿAbd al-Laṭīf maintains between the *zāyid* (additions) verses and the *ilḥāqī* (interpolation), in making his overall judgment.
55. Rūmī 1925–40, 1: 18.
56. See Ethé 1937: 647. On the contrary, Charles Rieu mentions *Mirʾāt al-Mathnavī* as the title of the *dībācha* of the *Nuskha-i Nāsikha,* for which he also notes the chronogram, "inṣirām yāfta Dībācha-i laṭīf (the fine introduction completed)," that ʿAbd al-Laṭīf mentions as having been composed by a friend of his, and the value of which comes to 1032. Rieu 1966: 589. See also *Dībācha,* f. 19a.
57. *Dibacha,*Preliminary notes, f. 25a.
58. For a discussion of the relevant premodern criteria of aesthetic evaluation of poetry in the Persian tradition, see Schimmel 1992, in particular, 37–52; Bürgel 1988: 53–88.
59. *Dībācha,* f. 16a.
60. *Dībācha,* f. 16b.
61. This was evidently much more than what William Hanaway suggests with reference to the preparation of *Bāysonghorī Shāh-nāma* in fifteenth-century Herat. That edition then meant "to include all the verses that the taste of the times considered appropriate." Hanaway 1988: 551.
62. See Rosenthal 1947: 26. See also Beatrice Gruendler's article in this volume.
63. Lewis 2000: 307.
64. Mustawfī 2001: 15–17 ("sabab-i naẓm-i kitāb"), and the editor's introduction, where he discusses the reasons Ḥamdallāh wrote *Ẓafarnāma* in verse. See also Pūrjavādī and Rastgār's introduction to the facsimile edition of the British Library manuscript Melville 1998. For Baysunghar's *Shāhnāma,* see Motlagh and Lentz 1989.
65. Şerif 1961: 638. I thank Cornell Fleischer for this reference and Abdurrahman Atçil for translating the relevant portion of the text. For an analysis of the development of early modern Ottoman techniques of "deep reading," see Khaled el-Rouayheb's article in this volume.

66. See, for instance, Lāhawrī 2002: 3, 12, 341, 393, 397, 499, 580, 669, 676, 677, 704, 866; Akbarābādī 2004: 761, 853, and 932.
67. Lewis 2000: 306.
68. For a discussion of this issue with reference to Rūmī's *ghazal* poetry, see Bürgel 1994: 44–69.
69. On these debates, see for instance Kinra.

9. The Rise of "Deep Reading" in Early Modern Ottoman Scholarly Culture

I would like to thank Michael Cook, Benjamin A. Elman, Sheldon Pollock, and Beatrice Gruendler for their helpful comments on earlier drafts of this article. All translations in the essay are my own unless otherwise indicated.

1. For a description of this process in an earlier period, see the chapter by Gruendler in this volume.
2. On his life, see Şeyḫī [1724] 1989, 4:206–207; Kramers 1993.
3. In the colophon of Müneccimbāşī 1691a it is stated that a draft of the work was completed in Mecca "on the third of the third of the fourth of the third of the second of the second." I take this to mean "on the third hour of the third day of the fourth month of the third year of the second century of the second millennium," i.e., the 3rd of Rabīʿ II, 1102, corresponding to January 4, 1691.
4. This is of course primarily true of the study and reading of religious and scholarly works in a pedagogic setting, not for the transmission of written works in general. For an eighth-century mirror of princes that is concerned to formulate explicitly the way it should be read, see Gruendler 2013: 385–416.
5. For the centrality of these two works, see Rosenthal 1970: 294–298.
6. Zarnūjī 1203: 4–9; Grunebaum and Abel 1947: 21–24.
7. Zarnūjī 1203: 10–13; Grunebaum and Abel 1947: 25–27.
8. Zarnūjī 1203: 13–15; Grunebaum and Abel 1947: 28–29.
9. Zarnūjī 1203: 17; Grunebaum and Abel 1947: 32–33.
10. Zarnūjī 1203: 27; Grunebaum and Abel 1947: 44.
11. Zarnūjī 1203: 28; Grunebaum and Abel 1947: 46.
12. Zarnūjī 1203: 28. The commentator wrote during the reign of the Ottoman sultan Murad III (r. 1574–1595). The English translators have "retained in his memory" (Grunebaum and Abel 1947: 46).
13. Zarnūjī 1203: 29; Grunebaum and Abel 1947: 47.
14. Zarnūjī 1203: 30; Grunebaum and Abel 1947: 49.
15. Zarnūjī 1203: 30; Grunebaum and Abel 1947: 48
16. Zarnūjī 1203: 19; Grunebaum and Abel 1947: 35–36. Incidentally, the translators' reference to "silent reading" of the Qur'ān (Grunebaum and Abel 1947: 67) is based on a misunderstanding of the Arabic "qirā'at al-Qur'ān naẓaran," which means "reciting the Qur'ān while looking at the page" as opposed to reciting it from memory *(min ẓahri l-qalb)*—as explained by the sixteenth-century commentator; see Zarnūjī 1203: 41.

17. Zarnūjī 1203: 18; Grunebaum and Abel 1947: 34–35. The translators assume that the "book" *(kitāb)* is the Qur'ān, but the thrust of Zarnūjī's point is clearly general.
18. Zarnūjī 1203: 29; Grunebaum and Abel 1947: 47.
19. Zarnūjī 1203: 38, 41; Grunebaum and Abel 1947: 63, 66.
20. Zarnūjī 1203: 38; Grunebaum and Abel 1947: 63.
21. Ibn Jamāʿah [1273] 2008: 33–39.
22. Ibn Jamāʿah [1273] 2008: 44–78.
23. Ibn Jamāʿah [1273] 2008: 80–114.
24. Ibn Jamāʿah [1273] 2008: 116–124.
25. Ibn Jamāʿah [1273] 2008: 126–134.
26. Ibn Jamāʿah [1273] 2008: 29.
27. Ibn Jamāʿah [1273] 2008: 52.
28. Ibn Jamāʿah [1273] 2008: 54.
29. Ibn Jamāʿah [1273] 2008: 94.
30. Ibn Jamāʿah [1273] 2008: 122.
31. Ibn Jamāʿah [1273] 2008: 83.
32. Ibn Jamāʿah [1273] 2008: 106.
33. Ibn Jamāʿah [1273] 2008: 113.
34. Ibn Jamāʿah [1273] 2008: 127.
35. Ibn Jamāʿah [1273] 2008: 90.
36. Ibn Jamāʿah [1273] 2008: 105.
37. Ephrat 2000: ch. 3; Chamberlain 1994: ch. 2; Berkey 1988: ch. 2. There is also work on early reading practices by Touati 2007 and Musawi 2007. Especially on the history of reading in the Islamic middle period (twelfth to thirteenth centuries), see Hirschler 2012.
38. Classic studies are Eickelman 1985: chs. 3–4; and Messick 1993: chs. 4–6.
39. Messick 1993: 84–92.
40. Messick 1993: 90–91.
41. Ghazzī [1526] 2006; ʿĀmilī [1547] 2006; Ṭāşköprüzāde [1542] 1968, 1:6–70.
42. Müneccimbāşī 1691b, 2b; Müneccimbāşī 1691a, 162a.
43. Müneccimbāşī 1691b, 3a; Müneccimbāşī 1691a, 162b–163a.
44. Müneccimbāşī 1691b, 3b; Müneccimbāşī 1691a, 163a–163b.
45. Müneccimbāşī 1691b, 19b; Müneccimbāşī 1691a, 184b.
46. Sanūsī [1490] 1899: 140. See the reference to Sanūsī in Sāçaḳlīzāde [1716] 1988: 233.
47. The only example he gave of *ḥashwīs* and *ẓāhirīs* are the *qussāsīn* [*sic*], i.e., popular storytellers (Müneccimbāşī 1691b, 19b; Müneccimbāşī 1691a, 184b).
48. Müneccimbāşī 1691b, 3a; Müneccimbāşī 1691a, 162b.
49. Müneccimbāşī 1691b, 5b–10b; Müneccimbāşī 1691a, 166a–173a.
50. Müneccimbāşī 1691b, 8b; Müneccimbāşī 1691a, 170a.
51. Müneccimbāşī 1691b, 20a; Müneccimbāşī 1691a, 185a.
52. Müneccimbāşī 1691b, 10b–12a; Müneccimbāşī 1691a, 173a–174b.
53. Müneccimbāşī 1691b, 12a–13b; Müneccimbāşī 1691a, 174b–176b.
54. Müneccimbāşī 1691b, 13b–15a; Müneccimbāşī 1691a, 176b–179a.
55. Müneccimbāşī 1691b, 15a–17b; Müneccimbāşī 1691a, 179a–182a.
56. Müneccimbāşī 1691b, 17b–20b; Müneccimbāşī 1691a, 182a–186a.

57. Ṭūsī [1274] 1957–58: 225–227, 313–321.
58. Müneccimbāşī 1691a, 20b–22a; Müneccimbāşī 1691b, 186a–188b.
59. On Sāçaḳlīzāde, see Būrsalī 1914–28, 1:325–328. His work *Tartīb al-ʿulūm* has been discussed from a somewhat different perspective in Reichmuth 2004 and El-Rouayheb 2008.
60. Sāçaḳlīzāde [1716] 1988: 150.
61. Sāçaḳlīzāde [1716] 1988: 229.
62. Sāçaḳlīzāde [1716] 1988: 180–185.
63. Sāçaḳlīzāde [1716] 1988: 139–140.
64. Sāçaḳlīzāde [1716] 1988: 141.
65. Sāçaḳlīzāde [1716] 1988: 205.
66. Sāçaḳlīzāde [1716] 1988: 210. A similar ordering is recommended by Zayn al-Dīn al-ʿĀmilī (d. 1558), see ʿĀmilī [1547] 2006: 385–389.
67. Ahmed and Filipovic 2004: 191–193.
68. Ibn Jamāʿah [1273] 2008: 103–106. Zarnūjī's narrowly religious conception of what a student should study is noted in Grunebaum and Abel 1947: 3–4 and 15–16.
69. Ghazālī [1111] 1967, 1:58.
70. Ghazālī [1111] 1937, 1:5.
71. El-Rouayheb 2004; Spevack 2010.
72. See the lineage cited in the certificate issued by the grand mufti Yaḥyā Minḳārīzāde (d. 1677) in Khiyārī [1672] 1969, 1:310–311. See also the lineage given by the grand muftī ʿAbd ül-Raḥīm Efendī (d. 1656) in Efendī 1656, 18b.
73. This has been shown in the case of Islamic jurisprudence in Hallaq 1990.
74. Sāçaḳlīzāde [1716] 1988: 127.
75. Taftazānī [1390] 1974: 96.
76. Elder 1950: 92.
77. Sāçaḳlīzāde [1716] 1988: 161. Sāçaḳlīzāde at this point merely stated that studying semantics should precede the study of law and jurisprudence, but he elsewhere (163) made it clear that studying law and jurisprudence should precede the study of Qur'ān commentary.
78. For the popularity of these two Qur'ān interpretations, see Sāçaḳlīzāde [1716] 1988: 165–166; Ahmed and Filipovic 2004: 196–198.
79. Sāçaḳlīzāde [1716] 1988: 130.
80. See for example Sāçaḳlīzāde [1716] 1988: 102, 120, 121, 167.
81. Sāçaḳlīzāde [1716] 1988: 216.
82. Sāçaḳlīzāde [1716] 1988: 196.
83. Sāçaḳlīzāde [1716] 1988: 162; see also 138.
84. The force of this point obviously depends on whether there were parallel developments in other parts of the Islamic world. There is evidence for an increased prominence in the early modern period of particular institutions of learning such as al-Azhar in Cairo and Farangi Mahall in Lucknow. However, this development does not by itself imply a shift from an oral-aural model of the transmission of knowledge to a more textual model. The traditional personal and informal style of education appears to have been prevalent in Farangi Mahall in the eighteenth and nineteenth centuries (Metcalf 1978: 112).

85. On the sixteenth-century reforms, see especially Repp 1986 and Zilfi 1993. On the Ottoman learned hierarchy in the seventeenth century, see Uğur 1986 and Klein 2007. For what follows I have relied mainly on Klein 2007: 45–63.
86. An edict of 1715, designed to curb abuses, stipulated that seekers of a *mülāzemet* should be required to state how old they were and with whom they had studied (Repp 1986: 54–55), the assumption clearly being that an applicant's teacher was not normally the same as the person from whom a *mülāzemet* was sought.
87. For example in 1658, the scholar and judge Yaḥyā Minḳārīzāde (d. 1677)—later to be grand muftī—was appointed to the position of "examiner of the *ulema*" *(mümeyyiz-i ʿulemāʾ);* see Uğur 1986: 451.
88. Zilfi 1977: 169.
89. See especially Zilfi 1983a, 1983b, 1988.
90. What follows is based on Ghazzī [1526] 2006: 421–466. Rosenthal (1947: 7–18) used an epitome of Ghazzī's work by ʿAbd al-Bāsīṭ al-ʿAlmāwī (d. 1573) published in 1930.
91. Sāçaḳlīzāde [1716] 1988: 204.
92. Ḳara Ḫalīl [1694] 1871.
93. The genre of commentary *(sharḥ)* is of course older, but again the fourteenth century seems to have witnessed a substantial transformation of the genre. Pre-fourteenth-century commentators tended to confine their interventions to the subject matter of the main text, whereas later commentators tended increasingly to disregard disciplinary boundaries and, for example, engage in discussions of grammatical, semantic, rhetorical, philosophical, and theological issues raised by a text on logic. For an Andalusian (Spanish Muslim) example of a fourteenth-century commentary that transcends disciplinary boundaries, see Beatrice Gruendler's essay in this volume.
94. Ḳara Ḫalīl [1694] 1871: 3–4.
95. Ḳara Ḫalīl [1694] 1871: 62, 116.
96. Ḳara Ḫalīl [1694] 1871: 16, 33, 56, 57, 64, 66.
97. Ḳara Ḫalīl [1694] 1871: 52, 130, 146.
98. I am grateful to Sheldon Pollock for helping me clarify my thoughts on this point.
99. See Nauert 2006; Elman 2001.
100. The library collection of Cārullāh now forms an important part of the unrivaled manuscript collection of the Süleymaniye Library in Istanbul.
101. For an example of this tendency, see the otherwise informative study of the Cairo-based scholar Muḥammad Murtaḍā al-Zabīdī (d. 1791) by Reichmuth 2009, esp. xiv–xviii. In my view, Reichmuth does not provide any reason to believe that Zabīdī's attitude to old or autograph manuscripts or to manuscript variants was in any way different from what one can find in earlier centuries (as described in, for example, Rosenthal 1947: 18–20, 26–27).
102. As noted in Lowry and Stewart 2009, there has been little scholarly work on the "reinvention" of tradition in the modern Arabic and Islamic world resulting from the ascendancy of modernist and revivalist currents. This is surely—at least in part—because most historians have until recently simply accepted the self-presentation of self-styled "revivers" and their denigration of the premodern

scholastic tradition, thus making the recovery of older texts a simple matter of the "revival" of an earlier "golden age." A still unsurpassed overview of intellectual currents in the Arab Middle East in the nineteenth and early twentieth centuries is provided in Hourani 1962 and Hourani 1981. On the Turkish side, the still informative classic studies of Lewis 1961 and Berkes 1964 display an almost complete identification with the modernist/nationalist current.

103. Huff 1993: 155–156, 163–169, 220–222.

10. Early Modern or Late Imperial?

The writing of this article was supported and finalized by two grants from the Chiang Ching Kuo Foundation, Taibei, Taiwan, summer 2008 and 2009, and a Mellon Foundation Career Achievement Award in the summer of 2013. All translations in the essay are my own unless otherwise indicated.

1. Schwab 1984.
2. Von Glahn 2004.
3. Elman 2001: 72–102.
4. Elman 2001: 101–144.
5. Elman 2001: ch. 6.
6. Reynolds and Wilson 1968: 167–173.
7. For discussion, see James T. C. Liu 1973: 483–505, and Schirokauer 1977: 163–198.
8. See Henderson 1991, passim.
9. See Sivin 1995.
10. But see Peterson 1986: 45–61.
11. Qian Daxin 1968: 3.94–95.
12. See Elman 1983: 175–222.
13. Dai Zhen 1974: 146, and Wang Mingsheng 1960: 2a.
14. See Elman 1992: 265–319.
15. Elman 1985: 165–198.
16. See Elman 1983: 211–212.
17. *Qinding Da-Qing huidian shili* 1968: 382.6b.
18. See Elman 2000b: 23–69.
19. See Zhang Xuecheng 1936: 29.54a.
20. See Kondo 1967: 9–35, and Wang Zhenyuan 1991. Cf. Yu 1997: 83–104.
21. *Li Tiaoyuan* 1881: 14.11b–12b. See also James J. Y. Liu 1962: 26–29.
22. Guo Shaoyu 1963. See also Guo Shaoyu 1983: 1.
23. The authorship of the *Qianjia shi* itself is disputed.
24. For example, Liang Zhangju 1976, in which he outlined the study of poetry and the rules of regulated verse. See also Liang 1963: 1949–1997.
25. See *Libu tiben* 1765, ninth month, fifth day, for the memorial in this Sichuan case. The 1765 Sichuan figures were roughly the same as those for the distribution of the classical specialization before 1750. See Elman 2000a: chap. 5.
26. See Li Tiaoyuan 1881: 16.10a–12a.

27. *Guangdong xiangshi lu* 1794: 9a–10b, 36a–39b.
28. Qian Daxin 1804: 18.15b–16a.
29. See Sun Xingyan 1990: 3, 278–279.
30. See *Qingchao xu wenxian tongkao* 1936: 84.8429–8430. See also Xu Liwang 2010: 132–140.
31. See Elman 1979: 1–44.
32. See Tang and Elman 1987: 205–213.
33. See Henderson 1986: 121–148.
34. On medicine, see *Siku quanshu zongmu* 1974: 103.1a, 104.51a–55b. See also Chao Yuan-ling 1995: 72–80, 113–123, and Hanson 2002: 112–147. On mathematics, see Jami 1994: 223–256.
35. See *Siku quanshu zongmu* 1974: chs. (juan) 106–107. See also Martzloff 1996: 20, 32–33, and Li and Du 1987: 223–224. Compare Mingjie Hu 1998: 288.
36. Hummel et al. 1942: 402.
37. Henderson 1986: 121–148.
38. Horng 1993: 167–208.
39. Huang Yinong 1993: 47–69.
40. See Ying-shih Yü 1975: 125. On late Ming debates concerning the authenticity of new versions of the *Great Learning,* see Lin Qingzhang 1990: 369–386.

11. The Politics of Philology in Japan

All translations in the essay are my own unless otherwise indicated.

1. Yi 1989.
2. Yi 1989: 21–40.
3. Ono et al. 1990; Yasumoto 1991; Nishihata 1990.
4. Mō hitotsu no Man'yōshū wo yomu kai, http://manyousyu.cocolog-nifty.com/blog/2010/11/post-91df.html, accessed February 10, 2013.
5. I Yon-hi goenkai (The Society to Support I Yon-hi), http://manaho.sarashi.com/ankoen.html, accessed 8 May 2014.
6. Koyasu 2000.
7. Ooms 1985: ch. 6.
8. Burns 2003: 42–43.
9. Bitō 1977.
10. Lurie 2011: 271–277.
11. Kin 2010.
12. Burns 2003: 41.
13. Keichū 1977.
14. Nakai 1988; Sakai 1991.
15. Flueckiger 2011: ch. 3.
16. Harootunian 1998: 50–56.
17. Motoori 1968a.
18. Burns 2003: 72–73.
19. Burns 2003: 74.

20. Motoori 1968b: 20.
21. Burns 2003: 79–80.
22. Kojima 1968.
23. Nishimiya 1988.
24. Kurano and Takeda 1958.
25. Ueda 1990.
26. Burns 2003: 106–108.
27. Harootunian 1988.
28. Tachibana 1967c.
29. Burns 2003: 160–161.
30. Tachibana 1967a, 1967b.
31. Burns 2003: 171.
32. Hansen 2008: 92.
33. Hirata 1981.
34. Moroyama-machi machi-shi henshū iinkai 1975: 1–8.
35. Haga 1982b: 159.
36. Haga 1982b: 152.
37. Haga 1982a: 21, 35–36.
38. Haga 1982a: 24–25.
39. Haga 1982a: 35–36.
40. Kobayashi 1977: 555–556.

12. "Enthusiasm Dwells Only in Specialization"

All translations in the essay are my own unless otherwise indicated.

1. Gildersleeve 1897, published as "My Sixty Days in Greece" in installments in three issues of the magazine.
2. Gildersleeve 1897: 310.
3. Gildersleeve 1897: 304. What he chooses to omit is that his guide was Wilhelm Dörpfeld, then director of the ambitious grand-scale excavations at Olympia overseen by the German Archaeological Institute and funded in large part by the Prussian state and the kaiser himself. On Olympia's significance for German science, see Marchand 1996.
4. Gildersleeve 1897: 638–640.
5. Gildersleeve 1987: 209. The trip to Constantinople is not part of the route mentioned in the *Atlantic Monthly.*
6. There is as yet no synoptic account of the impact of the German university model on other national institutions, and its means of transmission. For some individual case studies, see Stephens and Vasunia 2010; Feuerhahn and Rabault-Feuerhahn 2010.
7. Welcker 1861: 2–3. On the claim to professional status and social authority implied by such an association in the first place, see Grafton 1983: 174.
8. A good outline is in Leersen 2006.

9. Goethe, whose references to "world literature" are frequently cited and just as frequently read extremely loosely, considers world literature a new way of thinking and knowing the self through the detour of others, prompted by confrontations as varied as warfare (the Napoleonic wars) or the (to him) somewhat uncanny experience of being read and reviewed abroad. Hoesl-Uhlig 2004 is excellent on Goethe's subtle and complex use of the term and its ramifications for the self-definitions of comparative literature from the end of the nineteenth century.
10. On the processes of institutionalization and the establishment of classical scholarship as foundational, see, for example, Paulsen 1885; Grafton 1983; Leventhal 1986; Marchand 1996; Clark 2006.
11. Gildersleeve devoted the 1883 presidential lecture to the American Philological Association to a memorial of Ritschl, published in the *American Journal of Philology* in 1884, now reprinted in Gildersleeve 1992: 291–305.
12. A good concise account is in Benne 2005: 46–68.
13. Gildersleeve 1992: 95; Ritschl 1879: 24.
14. Wolf 1869: 882.
15. From "Autobiographisches aus den Jahren 1868/69," quoted in Westphalen 1986. Of course, these invectives have a longer history. See, for example, Hummel 2002.
16. Ritschl 1879: 25.
17. Ritschl 1879: 3. The fact that this lecture was reprinted in the Brockhaus *Conversations-Lexicon,* vol. 3, 1833, as the entry for "Philology" shows the cultural authority given to Ritschl's programmatic statements.
18. Ast 1808: 3.
19. Ast 1808: 6.
20. Humboldt 1967: 257 (emphasis his). On this passage in more detail, see also Güthenke 2010.
21. For the prevalence of organic imagery, and its particular use as a key to describing and constructing cultural autonomy, see also Vick 2002.
22. See for example Pfeiffer 1976; this same line, the first half of the nineteenth century marked by neohumanism, the second half by positivist historicism, is also found in the revised New Pauly, the standard classics encyclopedia (Kuhlmann and Schneider 2013). For the problematic continuities between the new humanism of the 1920s and the postwar situation of classics, including its very recent past, see now Elsner 2013.
23. Dainat 2010; Harloe 2013: 193–196; Espagne 2010.
24. On Gesner's seminar, see Legaspi 2008; on the seminar as the quintessential locus of the new research university and its practices, Leventhal 1986 and Clark 2006; on evidence research as an important component of the university even before the eighteenth century, Haugen 2007; on the relationship of Heyne and Wolf, most recently and with further bibliography, Harloe 2013.
25. In detail, see the chapter by Grafton in this volume, and the introduction by Grafton, Most, and Zetzel in Wolf 1986.
26. Timpanaro 2005: 74, and the chapter by Montanari in this volume.
27. Harloe 2013: 137–159.

28. Most recently on Bentley's intellectual biography and critical practice, see Haugen 2011.
29. Norman 2011.
30. Wolf 1869: 874 explicitly makes reference to "the quarrel at our neighbours" as part of his history of justification of classical study.
31. For comment on the relative absence of the term "philology" before the eighteenth century, see also Zetzel in this volume.
32. More readily accessible and usually quoted as Wolf 1869; for sketches of the piece before 1807, see Markner and Veltri 1999.
33. Ritschl 1879: 3.
34. Wolf 1869: 810–811.
35. The first to use the term "Wissenschaft des Altertums" (as a translation of *science de l'antiquité*) is probably Heyne; see Harloe 2013.
36. On the narrowing down and the exclusion of Oriental (and Jewish) cultures, see Grafton 1999; Harloe 2013: 197–198 suggests that this limitation was not introduced in 1807 but was already visible in earlier comments. On the status of Oriental studies in Germany generally and on their development, see Marchand 2009.
37. Wolf 1869: 887.
38. One could begin with Wolf himself, who above and beyond his committed Hellenism also had a strong interest in Latin humanism, reprinting, for example, the works of Marc Antoine Muret (1526–1585). An important recent start is Holzer 2013, who deals with a cultural Romanism within and beyond the academy; see in that book also her concise account of Wolf's ambivalent positioning of Roman culture both in conjunction with and in contrast to Greece (84–88). On the history of Latin philology in the latter half of the nineteenth and the early twentieth century, see very usefully Schmidt 1995.
39. Wolf 1869: 823–24.
40. Hegel 1986: 550, as quoted in Leonard 2012: 95 (emphasis added).
41. Wolf 1869: 835.
42. Wolf 1869: 835–836.
43. Grafton 1983.
44. Wolf 1869: 859. In this same paragraph Wolf begins to express anxiety about the fate of Latin in the modern world of nations as the commonly understood language of scholarship, though he quickly brings his digression back to the use of classical languages for artistic purposes.
45. Wolf 1869: 859.
46. Wolf 1869: 836.
47. See also an aside in the section that deals with material sources such as coins (854), where Wolf, in order to show their value for illuminating periods for which we lack a larger amount of direct textual sources, refers to the clever insightfulness *(Scharfsinn)* of Goethe and his friends of the arts, here with regard to numismatics, which should give a kind of Ariadne's thread to the scholar.
48. Cf. Wolf's comment a little later on: "he who is able to emulate the ancients not only in their productions but also with the artistic tools of those productions would

exceed the sphere of the *litterator* and would become an artist himself, *something which nature normally denies the scholar*" (878), emphasis added.

49. "Ego a prima aetate in lectione veterum id potissimum habui, ut mei mores emendarentur, non ut apices et puncta librorum" (Wolf 1869: 837).
50. Also, a little later: "To read and observe their [the ancients'] works will steadily rejuvenate our mind and mood, not by treating them like historically positioned characters, but instead as in the intimacy with valued and dear people. In this way they will communicate their attitudes and sentiments and thus improve the shortcomings of education in our corrupted times, lifting man above the many limitations of our age"; (Wolf 1869: 877–878).
51. Wolf 1869: 837.
52. "Es ist aber dieses Ziel kein anderes als *die Kenntniss der alterthümlichen Menschheit selbst, welche Kenntniss aus der durch das Studium der alten Ueberreste bedingten Beobachtung einer organisch entwickelten bedeutungsvollen National-Bildung hervorgeht*"; Wolf 1869: 883 (emphasis in original).
53. Wolf 1869: 887.
54. See Trabant 2009; also Mattson's edition of Humboldt's letters to Wolf, Humboldt 2004.
55. Wolf 1869: 893.
56. "Einzelnes als Einzelnes zusammenzutragen, ohne sich fester allgemeiner Grundsätze zu bemächtigen, ohne von dem Geiste, der alles Einzelne zu einem harmonischen Ganzen bildet, nur eine Ahnung zu fassen" (Wolf 1869: 894).
57. Wolf 1869: 894.
58. On Boeckh, see most recently the contributions in Hackel and Seifert 2013; Poiss 2009; Horstmann 1992. For the correlation between very long tenures of individual chairs as directors of seminars and the importance of personality as a shaping factor of the institutional landscape, see Clark 2006: 164–166.
59. Boeckh 1877: 6, in the first section, titled "The Idea of Philology, or Its Concept, Range and Highest Purpose."
60. "*Wissenschaft* altogether as a whole is philosophy, the *Wissenschaft* of ideas. According to the point of view whether to understand the universe from a material or ideal side, as nature or mind, as necessity or freedom, we arrive, aside from formal disciplines, at two different kinds of science, which we call physics and ethics. Which does philology belong to? Philology includes both, so to speak, and yet it is neither" (Boeckh 1877: 10–11).
61. Boeckh 1877: 9–10.
62. For Plato's emergence at the time and shortly before from Neoplatonist interpretation, see Tigerstedt 1974. At the same time, there is a change of emphasis away from Socrates as exceptional figure and toward Plato as coherent philosopher and "author" of Socrates.
63. Compare also Boeckh's recourse to Plato, *Phaedrus* 336e (and elsewhere), for the use and glossing of *philologos* and *philologia* as "the desire for and pleasure taken in scholarly exchange" ("die Lust zu und an wissenschaftlicher Mittheilung"), 1877: 22.
64. See, for example, Thouard 2013 and Danneberg 2013.

65. Boeckh 1877: 12.
66. Boeckh 1877: 16.
67. "Die Nachconstruction der Constructionen des menschlichen Geistes in ihrer Gesammtheit" (Boeckh 1877: 16).
68. Boeckh 1877: 86.
69. Cf. Grafton's article in this volume, on the philological method of the humanists relying in its formulation on the ancient texts themselves, which in turn were the result of philological interest and intervention. What we see in Boeckh with a much greater claim to method is in fact not so different.
70. Boeckh 1877: 25–26, with reference to Schelling's *Vorlesungen über die Methode des akademischen Studiums.*
71. Boeckh 1877: 26.
72. Harloe 2013: 172 with reference to Christian Gottlob Heyne and, before him, David Ruhnken.
73. Athenaeum fragment 255 (to the extent that we can identify the author of individual fragments in this joint project). On Schlegel's philology and hermeneutics, see Leventhal 1994.
74. Though see Poiss 2010: 152–157 (based in turn on Körner 1928) for the claim that Friedrich Schlegel's thought, by way of Schleiermacher's hermeneutics, ultimately reached into a broadly conceived task for philology as developed by Boeckh.
75. Most 1998; Poiss 2010.
76. Timpanaro 2005; Sier and Wöckener-Gade 2010; Espagne 2010 on Hermann and heroic biography; also Gurd 2005 on *ingenium* and emendation, with further commentary in Güthenke 2009.
77. For the history of text criticism, see Reynolds and Wilson 1991, as well as the contributions by Montanari and Zetzel in this volume.
78. Thus summarized in Most's introduction to Timpanaro 2005: 11. Lachmann gained fame for his method with an edition of Lucretius (1850), which however has precedent in the work of Johan Nicolai Madvig, F. W. Ritschl, and especially Jacob Bernays's own edition of Lucretius (1847).
79. Most in his introduction to Timpanaro 2005 mentions the euphoric attempts to apply Lachmann's method to the developing field of Indo-European linguistics, attempts that were followed by a growing sense of disillusionment and skepticism (11–12). Lachmann was criticized in his own time, for example by the French medievalist Joseph Bédier, who focused his critique on Lachmann's usual bipartite division of a manuscript's stemma, a regularity he thought had likely more to do with the method shaping the outcome rather than the nature of most manuscript traditions. On Indo-European linguistics, known as comparative philology in the nineteenth century, see the chapter by Chang in this volume.
80. Wolf 1985: 43–44; translated by A. Grafton, G. W. Most, and J. Zetzel. (also quoted in Timpanaro 2005: 71–72); emphasis added.
81. Ritschl 1879b: 29.
82. See the chapter by König in this volume; also in Schwindt 2009. It is worth noting his reference to the so-called Lille school and its articulation of a new philology of "insistent reading." Many of the philologists of that generation and particular

school, such as Jean Bollack and Heinz Wisman, are in terms of their training and interests associated with a transfer of German philological precepts to a different, French national context, which suggests the power of movement and de- (or re-) contextualization for a new flourishing of philology's critical potential.

13. The Intelligence of Philological Practice

This essay grew out of a Tuesday Colloquium (Dienstagskolloquium) at the Wissenschaftskolleg zu Berlin in 2009, and the ideas here are expanded in a book about Rilke and the theory of philological praxis (Kōnig 2014a) at Wallstein publishing houses in Göttingen. It was translated by Daniel Smyth, as are all the sources quoted except where otherwise noted.

1. Ovid, *Metamorphoses,* 11.1–55; 10, 86–144; 10.8–85.
2. Rilke was familiar with her mother's (Gertrud Ouckama Knoop's) account of Wera's death; compare Nebrig 2009: 609–618.
3. Rilke 1955: 769–770.
4. Rilke 1942: 124–125.
5. Rilke 1977: 29.
6. For a treatment of the central questions of philology: Pollock 2009: 931–961 (in German translation: "Zukunftsphilologie?," trans. Lena Kühn, *Geschichte der Germanistik. Mitteilungen* 35/36 [2009]: 25–50); Judet de La Combe 1997: 9–29; König 2000: 317–335; Wismann 1970: 279–280 and 462–479, 774–781; Thouard 2012a.
7. Nietzsche 1997: 5. On Nietzsche as philologist compare: Benne 2005; Wegmann 1994: 334–450.
8. Haß and König 2003; compare starting in 2007 the *Journal of Literary Theory,* ed. Fotis Jannidis, Gerhard Lauer, and Simone Winko; Danneberg and Vollhardt 1996.
9. Weimar 1989; König 2014b.
10. A peculiar sort of tenacity (namely, *Sitzfleisch*) is considered by philologists to be the primary virtue, but it is also held against them. Karl Lachmann, a classical philologist and one of the most important Germanists of the nineteenth century, refrained, as a matter of principle, from openly laying out his principles; he writes: "we've cause enough to finally earn for ourselves the respect incurred through seduluous and diligent work which has been withheld for so long (and not without reason)." (Lachmann 1820: xxi).
11. The most recent exchanges about neopragmatism (compare the controversy between McDowell and Dreyfus 2007: McDowell 2007b; Dreyfus 2007a; McDowell 2007a; Dreyfus 2007b; Pippin 2005) underscore that even immediate practical activities ("embodied coping skills" at work, e.g., in expert chess play) embody a form of rationality that can be made explicit in retrospect. Explanations of this point draw on Kant's theory of "apperception" and its devices; instead of the motto "grasping what seizes us" ("Begreifen, was uns ergreift"—Staiger 1955: 10–11), it is not what seizes one, but what one does, that we want to understand.
12. Schleiermacher 1977: 71 (comp. M. Frank from Schleiermacher's lectures of 1828). Schleiermacher 1998: 3: "Hermeneutics and criticism, both philological disciplines,

are both theories that belong together, because the practice of one presupposes the other. The former is generally the art of understanding particularly the written discourse of another person correctly, the latter the art of judging correctly and establishing the authenticity of texts and parts of texts from adequate evidence and data."

13. Schleiermacher 2012: 40. On Schleiermacher's hermeneutics, compare Szondi 1978a: 106–130.
14. Szondi 1978b: 275: "But it must not be overlooked that every artwork has its own monarchical bent—to follow a remark of Valéry's—for it seeks, through its mere existence, to obliterate all other artworks."
15. Von Wilamowitz-Moellendorff 1916: 1–25; compare Bollack 1985: 468–512.
16. Compare König and Lämmert 1993.
17. Bollack 2000; Most 1999; Smith 2008; Levi 1999: 67–77; the essay by Gruendler in this volume.
18. Compare Wismann 1996: 15–24.
19. Compare König and Wismann 2011.
20. Schleiermacher 1998: 102: "conversations about the weather"; 101–102: "Some instances fail to spark its interest at all, while others engage it completely. Most, however, fall somewhere between these two extremes."
21. Schleiermacher 1998: 8.
22. Schleiermacher 1998: 41.
23. Compare König 2004.
24. König 2012: 77–102.
25. Dilthey 1973 [1922]; compare Rodi 1985: 140–165.
26. Gadamer 1999 [1982]; compare the chapter "Language as the Medium of Hermeneutic Experience," 384–406.
27. Bollack 2010, 2003; König 2008: 119–127; Judet de La Combe 2010: 363–374; Thouard 2012b.
28. Compare Szondi 1975: 404–408.
29. Boeckh 1877: 11; compare Steinfeld 2009: 211–226.
30. König 1994: 379–403.
31. Such "unrecognition" arises from the tension among three factors. I therefore speak of a "philological triangle" that binds these three factors together: knowledge, values, and institutions (see note 30), yet this shall not be pursued further at this occasion.
32. For the methodological approach, cf. König 2006.
33. On Orpheus in general and Rilke's work in particular compare Frank 1988: 180–211; Segal 1989; Rehm 1972; Kern 1920.
34. König 2011: 21–34.
35. Rilke 1955: 790: "He [the editor] nowhere allows himself independent interpolations into the text (not even in view of such an obvious linguistic lapse as the phrase 'einer jener Tänze' in the penultimate 'Sonnet to Orpheus,' page 769, where what is certainly meant is: 'eines jener Tänze')."
36. Rilke 1997: 434–515.

37. Compare the dance sonnets II.18 (dancing as writing) and I.15 (dance as experiential expression of the girls who are mute); on the relation of dance to modern literature, compare Brandstetter 1995.
38. Thouard 2010: 327–339.
39. Gerok-Reiter 1996.
40. Gerok-Reiter 1996: 248.
41. Gerok-Reiter 1996: 248.
42. Mörchen 1958.
43. Mörchen 1958: 405.
44. On its status as a "commentary" compare below; the expository authorial function is already formulated in the book's title: ". . . erläutert von . . ." (". . . elucidated by . . .").
45. Mörchen 1958: 406.

14. Philology or Linguistics?

I want to thank Pang-Hsin Ting, Cheng-sheng Tu, and Benjamin A. Elman for reading earlier drafts of this essay, and Ting in particular for sharing his expertise in Chinese phonology with me. The concepts in this chapter were first developed for the conference on Global History of Philology (Taipei, October, 2008), which was funded by Taiwan's CCK Foundation; its final archival research and revision were funded by the Academia Sinica's Career Development Award, 2012–2016. I am indebted to both institutions. All translations in the essay are my own unless otherwise indicated.

1. Rüegg 2004: 415–453.
2. Heinrich 2002: 48–50; Eschbach-Szabo 2000: 94–97.
3. For the first year or so the institute used a French name, *Institut historique et philologigue,* at least on its letterhead.
4. "Philologie est nettement distincte de la linguistique, malgré les points de contact des deux sciences et les services mutuels qu'elles se rendent." Saussure 1922 [1916], 21.
5. Fan-shen Wang and Tu 1995: 41 and 44. On Fu's life and work and the reason Fu relocated to Berlin, see Fan-shen Wang's definitive biography; F. Wang 2000: 58.
6. In history Fu read Ernst Bernheim's work on historical method (Bernheim 1908) and Henry Thomas Buckle's English history (Buckle 1920), even translating the first five chapters of the latter. He took courses in Sanskrit with the philologist Heinrich Lüders (1869–1943), Tibetan with August Hermann Francke (1870–1930), and general phonetics. See Fan-shen Wang and Tu 1995: 51.
7. Whitney 1896 [1875]: 318.
8. Anthony Grafton points out the declining image of philology in German culture in the late nineteenth and early twentieth centuries, citing Ludwig Hatvany's popular satire of philology (and *Altertumswissenschaft* in general), *Die Wissenschaft des nicht Wissenswerten* (1908), as an illustration. Grafton 1981: 101. This is also

the major theme of Marchand 2003, especially 302–376. I thank Anthony Grafton for the two references.

9. Wolf 1831.
10. Most differences in the content of the science of antiquity between this work and Wolf's are just those of categorization. For example, although numismatics appears as a new category, it was subsumed in the study of artifacts in Wolf's formulation. See Gercke and Norden 1912.
11. Wilamowitz-Moellendorff 1982: 159–165.
12. Marchand 2003: 116–151, 341–376.
13. Bloomfield 1933: 10–12.
14. "If the study of Indian literature is to thrive, the principles of classical philology must be applied to it." August Wilhelm von Schlegel, *Indische Bibliothek* (1820–30), cited by Delbrück 1989: 28. Eva Channing's translation.
15. Bopp 1816.
16. Bopp 1974: 27–28.
17. Delbrück 1989: 113–117.
18. Scholars of German philology such as Jacob Grimm saw Luther's Bible as a landmark of modern German literature. Grimm 1819, foreword.
19. Saussure's *Cours* was published posthumously in 1916; his course on general linguistics was taught at Geneva from 1906 until his death in 1913.
20. Saussure 1922 [1916]: 13–15, 33.
21. Whitney 1896: 315.
22. Sweet 1900: 1.
23. Jespersen 1922: 65. For Jespersen, philology in its continental (that is, German) sense was rather the study of one nation. Latin philology, for example, was the study of Roman culture, not a professional study of language (64). Leonard Bloomfield, a prominent American linguist who formulated the difference between linguistics and philology in the 1930s, said that "all historical study of language [philology] is based upon the comparison of two or more sets of descriptive data. . . . In order to describe a language [the linguists' task] one needs no historical knowledge whatever; in fact, the observer who allows such knowledge to affect his description, is bound to distort his data." Bloomfield 1933: 19–20.
24. Wolf 1831: 47.
25. Müller 1862: 22; Delbrück 1880: iii–iv.
26. Bernhardi 1805: 1, 6–10.
27. Benfey 1869: 4–8.
28. Brugmann 1885: 39.
29. Gabelentz considered philology as "the science of inferior imitators (epigones), who wander with melancholy admiration through the tombstones of a dead culture *(die Wissenschaft der Epigonen, die mit Wehmüthiger Bewunderung durch die Grabstätten einer erstorbenen Cultur wandern)*." Gabelentz 1995 (first published 1891): 21. For assessments of his influence, see Hutton 1995; Elffers 2008.
30. While a college student, Fu noted in the margin on page 2r of his copy of Yan Fu's translation of John Stuart Mill's *System of Logic* that philology should be translated as *yu xue* (語學). This copy is held in the Fu Ssu-nien Library of the Institute

of History and Philology at the Academia Sinica. I thank Luo Zhitian of Beijing University for this reference. Fu kept that translation in his "Objectives," although on page 23 of the same work he translated comparative "philology" as *yanyu xue* (言語學). It was already pointed out that he translated "philology" in the name of his institute as *yuyan xue* (語言學).

31. Fan-shen Wang and Tu 1995: 52.
32. Fu's collection of Jespersen's works includes Jespersen 1904, 1917, 1918, 1922, 1923, 1924, 1925, 1933, and 1937.
33. Fan-shen Wang and Tu 1995: 52.
34. Y. R. Chao 2007: 439.
35. B. Y. Chao 2007a: 439–441.
36. B. Y. Chao 2007a: 451.
37. Y. R. Chao 2006: 3–4. This essay was published in English.
38. Y. R. Chao 2006: 3.
39. Y. R. Chao 2006: 28.
40. Y. R. Chao 2006: 38–60.
41. Y. R. Chao 2006: 44–48.
42. Y. R. Chao 2007: 395.
43. Wu 2006: 4–5.
44. Zhao and Huang 1998: 117–119.
45. Hu Shi authored the preface to Chao's textbook, which came with phonograph records for the new language, and praised him for his expertise. Zhao and Huang 1998: 117.
46. B. Y. Chao 2007a: 195; Zhao and Huang 1998: 117.
47. B. Y. Chao 2007a: 225.
48. Y. R. Chao 1921: 10.
49. Zhao and Huang 1998: 125; B. Y. Chao 2007b: 550–551.
50. Zhao and Huang 1998: 126.
51. Chao took Meillet's courses on abstract nouns and on the general theory of vocabulary and read closely his *Linguistique historique et linguistique générale* (1921). Y. R. Chao 1925: 69; B. Y. Chao 2007b: 552.
52. Zhao and Huang 1998: 127.
53. Y. R. Chao 1923.
54. Karlgren 1915.
55. Y. R. Chao 2007; Zhao and Huang 1998: 111.
56. Karlgren 1925.
57. Y. R. Chao 1926.
58. Malmqvist 2011: 33–34.
59. Malmqvist 2011: 33, 35, 39–40.
60. Malmqvist 2011: 57.
61. Quoted in Malmqvist 2011: 82–83.
62. Quoted in Malmqvist 2011: 114.
63. Fu 1980a: 253–254.
64. Fu 1927: 3.
65. Fu 1980a: 254.

66. Fu 1980d: 153.
67. Fu 1980c: 455.
68. Fu 1980b: 410.
69. The third member was Yang Zhengsheng. Fu, Gu, and Yang jointly drafted several proposals regarding the work of the institute in 1928, e.g., Fu et al. 2011a and 2011b. Fu was the sole author of the inaugural statement introducing the journal of his institute.
70. Fu 1980a.
71. Fu 1928.
72. Y. R. Chao 1928.
73. Li 1928.
74. Fu 1980d: 29–41.
75. Such as "Yixia dongxi shuo (A discourse on the western and eastern locations of Yi and Xia)" and "Zhuo dongfeng yu Yin yimin (Zhou's appointments in the east and the remnants of the Yins)." Fu 1980b; Fu 1980e.
76. Fu 1980d: 46–47.
77. Fu 1980d: 42–43.
78. *Wentong* (1898), by Ma Jianzhong, is often considered to be the first work on Chinese grammar. Professional linguistic work on a Chinese grammar was first undertaken by one of Chao's earliest students in the graduate program at Tsing Hua College, Wang Li, who then went on to training in France. Wang wrote his M.A. thesis at Tsing Hua on the grammar of ancient Chinese, a subject of his own choice. In the 1930s and 1940s he published three more works on Chinese grammar: L. Wang 1936, 1946, and 1947. His peculiar interest and distinguished achievements in Chinese grammar cannot be discussed here. It just needs to be noted that he never did his work at the Institute of History and Philology.
79. Y. R. Chao 1968.
80. Fan-shen Wang 2000.
81. Mei 1990; Ting 2000.
82. Pollock 2009: 934.

Bibliography

Introduction

Alt, Peter-André. 2007. *Die Verheissungen der Philologie.* Göttingen: Wallstein.

Auerbach, Erich. 1969. "Philology and Weltliteratur." *Centennial Review* 13: 1–17.

Barck, Karlheinz, and Martin Treml. 2007. *Erich Auerbach. Geschichte und Aktualität eines europäischen Philologen.* Berlin: Kadmos.

Berman, Russell A., and Joshua Robert Gold. 2007. "Peter Szondi and Critical Hermeneutics." *Telos* 140.

Bloch, R. Howard. 1990. "New Philology and Old French." *Speculum* 65: 38–58.

Boeckh, August. 1877. *Encyklopädie und Methodologie der gesamten philologischen Wissenschaften.* Ed. E. Bratuschek. Leipzig: Teubner.

Bollack, Jean. 2000. *Sens contre Sens: Comment lit-on?* N.p.: La Passe du Vent.

Brownlee, Marina, et al., eds. "The New Philology." *Speculum* 1990.

Burton, Robert. 2001. *The Anatomy of Melancholy.* New York: New York Review Books.

Calhoun, Craig. 2010. "Renewing International Studies: Regional and Transregional Studies in a Changing Intellectual Field." In *International and Language Education for a Global Future,* ed. D. Wiley and R. S. Glew. Lansing: Michigan State University Press, 227–254.

Canfora, Luciano. 1995. *Politische Philologie: Altertumswissenschaften und moderne Staatsideologien.* Stuttgart: Klett-Cotta.

———. 2008. *Filologia e Libertà.* Milan: Mondadori.

Chang, So-an. 2001. *Shiba shiji lixue kaozheng de sixiang huoli: Lijiao lunzheng yu lizhi chongxing* [Debating Neo-Confucian ritual orthodoxy: evidential studies and the reconstruction of social relations in eighteenth-century China]. Taipei: Institute of Modern History, Academia Sinica.

Clark, William. 2006. *Academic Charisma and the Origins of the Research University.* Chicago: University of Chicago Press.

Dainat, Holger. 2010. "Klassische, Germannische, Orientalische Philologie." In *Geschichte der Universität Unter den Linden 1810–2010,* ed. Heinz-Elmar Tenorth. Berlin: Akademie Verlag, 319–338.

de Man, Paul. 1986 (1982). "The Return to Philology." In *The Resistance to Theory.* Minneapolis: University of Minnesota Press.

Dilthey, Wilhelm. 2002. *The Formation of the Historical World in the Human Sciences.* Princeton, N.J.: Princeton University Press.

Frahm, Eckart. 2011. *Babylonian and Assyrian Text Commentaries: Origins of Interpretation.* Munster: Ugarit-Verlag.

Grafton, Anthony. 1981. "*Prolegomena* to Friedrich August Wolf." *Journal of the Warburg and Courtauld Institutes* 44: 101–129.

———. 1991. *Defenders of the Text: The Traditions of Scholarship in an Age of Science.* Cambridge, Mass.: Harvard University Press.

Gumbrecht, Hans Ulrich. 2002. *Vom Leben und Sterben der grosser Romanisten.* Munich: Hansen.

———. 2003. *The Powers of Philology: Dynamics of Textual Scholarship.* Champaign-Urbana: University of Illinois Press.

Gurd, Sean, ed. 2010. *Philology and Its Histories.* Columbus: Ohio State University Press.

Holquist, Michael. 2000. "Forgetting Our Name, Remembering Our Mother." *Proceedings of the Modern Language Society* 115 (7): 1975–1977.

Horstmann, Axel. 1992. *Antike Theoria und Moderne Wissenschaft: August Boeckhs Konzeption der Philologie.* Frankfurt am Main: Peter Lang.

Hummel, Pascale. 2009. *Metaphilology: Histories and Languages of Philology.* Paris: Philologicum.

Jacob, Christian. 1999. "From Book to Text: Towards a Comparative History of Philologies." *Diogenes* 186, vol. 47 (2): 5–22.

König, Christoph, ed. 2009. *Das Potential europäischer Philologien.* Gottingen: Wallstein.

König, Christoph, and Denis Thouard, eds. 2010. *La philologie au présent: Pour Jean Bollack.* Villeneuve-d'Ascq: Presses universitaires du Septentrion.

König, Christoph, et al., eds. 2009. *Geschichte der Germanistik* v. 35–36.

Lerer, Seth. 1996. *Literary History and the Challenge of Philology: The Legacy of Erich Auerbach.* Palo Alto, Calif.: Stanford University Press.

Leventhal, Robert S. 1994. *The Disciplines of Interpretation: Lessing, Herder, Schlegel and Hermeneutics in Germany, 1750–1800.* Berlin: de Gruyter.

McGann, Jerome. 2009. "Our Textual History." *Times Literary Supplement,* November 20, 13–15.

———. 2011. "On Creating a Usable Future." *Profession* [n.v.]: 182–195.

———. 2013. "Philology in a New Key." *Critical Inquiry* 39 (2): 327–346.

Most, Glenn. 1997. "Classical Scholarship and Literary Criticism." In *The Cambridge History of Literary Criticism,* vol. 4, *The Eighteenth Century,* ed. H. B. Nisbet and C. Rawson. Cambridge: Cambridge University Press, 742–757.

———, ed. 1997–2002. *Aporemata. Kritische Studien zur Philologiegeschichte: Collecting Fragments; Editing Texts; Commentaries; Historicization; Disciplining Classics.* Göttingen: Vandenhoeck und Ruprecht.

Nietzsche, Friedrich. 1980a [1881]. *Morgenröte.* In *Sämtliche Werke: kritische Studienausgabe in 15 Bänden*, vol. 3, ed. Giorgio Colli and Mazzino Montinari. Munich: Deutscher Taschenbuch Verlag. Trans. J. M. Kennedy, New York, The Macmillan Company, 1913.

———. 1980b [1895]. *Antichrist*. In *Sämtliche Werke: kritische Studienausgabe in 15 Bänden*, vol. 6, ed. Giorgio Colli and Mazzino Montinari. Munich: Deutscher Taschenbuch Verlag. Trans. H. L. Menken, New York, Knopf, 1918.

Nippel, Wilfried. 1997. "Philologenstreit und Schulpolitik: Zur Kontroverse zwischen Gottfried Hermann und August Boeckh." In *Geschichtsdiskurs,* vol. 3, *Die Epoche der Historisierung,* ed. W. Küttler et al. Frankfurt: Fischer, 244–253.

O'Donnell, James J. 2002. Review of Jan Ziolkowski, *On Philology* (1990). *Bryn Mawr Classical Review,* January 19.

Olender, Maurice. 1992. *The Languages of Paradise: Race, Religion, and Philology in the Nineteenth Century.* Cambridge, Mass.: Harvard University Press. (First published in French, 1989.)

Patterson, Lee. 1994. "The Return to Philology." In *The Past and Future of Medieval Studies,* ed. John van Engen. South Bend, Ind.: University of Notre Dame Press, 231–244.

Pollock, Sheldon. 1993. "Deep Orientalism? Notes on Sanskrit and Power beyond the Raj." In *Orientalism and the Post-Colonial Predicament,* ed. C. Breckenridge and P. van der Veer. Philadelphia: University of Pennsylvania Press, 76–133.

———. 2009. "Future Philology? The Fate of a Soft Science in a Hard World." *Critical Inquiry* 35 (4): 931–961.

———. 2011. "Crisis in the Classics." *Social Research: An International Quarterly* 78 (1): 21–48.

Said, Edward. 2004. "Return to Philology." In *Humanism and Democratic Criticism.* New York: Columbia University Press.

Schestag, Thomas. 2007. "Philology, Knowledge." *Telos* 140: 28–44.

Schlegel, Friedrich. 1959–90. *Kritische Ausgabe.* Ed. E. Behler et al. 18 vols. Paderborn: Schönigh.

Schwindt, Jürgen Paul, ed. 2009. *Was ist eine philologisiche Frage?* Frankfurt: Suhrkamp.

Sukthankar, V. S. 1944. *Sukthankar Memorial Volume,* vol. 1, *Critical Studies in the Mahābhārata.* Poona: V. S. Sukthankar Memorial Edition Committee.

Szondi, Peter. 1967. "Über philologische Erkenntnis." In *Hölderlin Studien.* Frankfurt: Insel.

———. 1986. *On Textual Understanding and Other Essays.* Manchester: Manchester University Press.

Tenorth, Heinz-Elmar, ed. 2010. *Geschichte der Universität Unter den Linden 1810–2010: Praxis ihrer Disziplinen.* vol. 4. *Genese der Disziplinen. Die Konstitution der Universität.* Berlin: Akademie Verlag.

Trautmann, Thomas, ed. 2009. *The Madras School of Orientalism.* New York: Oxford University Press.

Tu, Chin-I, ed. 2005. *Interpretation and Intellectual Change: Chinese Hermeneutics in Historical Perspective.* New Brunswick, N.J.: Transaction.

Utz, Richard. 2009. "Englische Philologie vs. English Studies: A Foundational Conflict." In *Das Potential europäischer Philologien,* ed. Christoph König. Göttingen: Wallstein, 34–44.

Vico, Giambattista. 2001. *New Science.* London: Penguin.

Vöhler, Martin. 2002. "Christian Gottlob Heyne und das Studium des Altertums in Deutschland." In *Disciplining Classics—Altertumswissenschaft als Beruf,* ed. G. Most. Göttingen: Vandenhoeck und Ruprecht.

Whitney, W. D. 1911. "Philology." In *Encyclopedia Britannica.* 11th ed. New York: Encyclopedia Britannica Company, 21: 414–438.

Winters, Margaret E., and Geoffrey S. Nathan. 1992. "First He Called Her a Philologist and Then She Insulted Him." In *The Joy of Grammar,* ed. D. Brentari, et al. Amsterdam: John Benjamins, 351–367.

Yu, Ying-shih. 2003. *Zhu Xi de lishi shijie: Songdai Shidaifu zhengzhi wenhua de yanjiu* [Zhu Xi's historical world: A study of the political culture of Song literati]. Taipei: Yunchen wenhua.

Zini, Fosca Mariani. 2013. "Une philologie sans philologie: Giambattista Vico et la grammaire humaniste." *Geschichte der Germanistik* 43/44: 58–69.

Ziolkowski, Jan. 1990. *On Philology.* University Park: Pennsylvania State University Press.

Chapter 1

Bastianini, Guido. 2001. "Osservazioni sul Papiro di Teramene." In *POIKILMA. Studi in onore di Michele R. Cataudella.* La Spezia: Agorà Edizioni, 81–87.

Bastianini, Guido, and Claudio Gallazzi. 2001. *Papiri dell'Università degli Studi di Milano–VIII. Posidippo di Pella. Epigrammi (P. Mil. Vogl. VIII 309).* Ed. G. B. and C. G., with the collaboration of Colin Austin. Milan: LED.

Boudon Millot, Véronique, and Jacques Jouanna. 2010. *Galien. Ne pas se chagriner.* Ed. and trans. V. B. M. and J. J., with the collaboration of Antoine Pietrobelli. Paris: Les Belles Lettres.

Broggiato, Maria. 2001. *Cratete di Mallo. I frammenti.* Ed. with an introduction and notes by M. B. La Spezia: Agorà Edizioni; reprint, Rome: Edizioni di Storia e Letteratura 2006.

Cassio, Albio Cesare. 2002. "Early Editions of the Greek Epics and Homeric Textual Criticism in the Sixth and Fifth Centuries BC." In *Omero tremila anni dopo. Atti del Congresso Genova 6–8 luglio 2000,* ed. Franco Montanari, with the collaboration of Paola Ascheri. Rome: Edizioni di Storia e Letteratura, 105–136.

Conte, Gian Biagio. 2013. *Ope ingenii. Esperienze di critica testuale.* Pisa: Edizioni della Normale.

Dickey, Eleanor. 2007. *Ancient Greek Scholarship: A Guide to Finding, Reading, and Understanding Scholia, Commentaries, Lexica, and Grammatical Treatises, from Their Beginnings to the Byzantine Period.* Oxford: Oxford University Press.

Fantuzzi, Marco. 2005. "Euripides (?) *Rhesus* 56–58 and Homer *Iliad* 8.498–501: Another Possible Clue to Zenodotus' Reliability." *Classical Philology* 100: 268–273.

Führer, Rudolf, and Martin Schmidt. 2001. "Homerus redivivus [on: Homerus, *Ilias,* recensuit Martin L. West, vol. 1, Stutgardiae et Lipsiae: Teubner 1998]." *Göttingische Gelehrte Anzeigen* 253: 1–32.

Garofalo, Ivan, and Alessandro Lami. 2012. *Galeno. L'anima e il dolore. De indolentia. De propriis placitis.* Ed. I. G. and A. L. Milan: BUR.

Haslam, Michael. 1997. "Homeric Papyri and Transmission of the Text." In *A New Companion to Homer,* ed. Ian Morris and Barry Powell. Leiden: Brill, 55–100.

Janko, Richard 1992. *The Iliad: A Commentary.* General editor Geoffrey Stephen Kirk. Vol. 4. *Books 13–16.* Cambridge: Cambridge University Press.

———. 2002. "Seduta di chiusura." In *Omero tremila anni dopo. Atti del Congresso Genova 6–8 luglio 2000,* ed. Franco Montanari, with the collaboration of Paola Ascheri. Rome: Edizioni di Storia e Letteratura, 653–671.

Kotzia, Paraskevi, and Panagiotis Sotiroudis. 2010. "Galenou, *Perì alypías.*" *Hellenica* 60: 63–150.

Kouremenos, Theokritos, George Parássoglou, and Kyriakos Tsantsanoglou. 2006. *The Derveni Papyrus.* With introduction and commentary by T. K., G. P., and K. T. Florence: Olschki.

Lessico dei Grammatici Greci Antichi (LGGA). Directed by Franco Montanari. Codirected by Fausto Montana, Lara Pagani, and Walter Lapini. www.aristarchus.unige.it/lgga.

Ludwich, Arthur. 1884–85. *Aristarchs Homerische Textkritik.* Vols. 1–2. Leipzig: Teubner.

Manetti, Daniela. 2006. "La terminologie du livre: à propos des emploi d'*hyphos* et *edaphos* dans deux passages de Galien." *Revue des études grecques* 119: 156–171.

———. 2012a. "Galeno e la *ekdosis* di Ippocrate: una nota testuale." In *Harmonia. Scritti di filologia classica in onore di Angelo Casanova,* ed. Guido Bastianini, Walter Lapini, and Mauro Tulli. Florence: Firenze University Press, 475–481.

———. 2012b. "Galeno ΠΕΡΙ ΑΛΥΠΙΑΣ e il difficile equilibrio dei filologi." In *Studi sul "De indolentia" di Galeno,* ed. D. M. Pisa: Fabrizio Serra Editore, 9–22.

———. Forthcoming. "Medicine and *Exegesis.*" In *Companion to Ancient Scholarship,* ed. Stephanos Matthaios, Franco Montanari, and Antonios Rengakos. Leiden: Brill.

Manetti, Daniela, and Amneris Roselli. 1994. "Galeno commentatore di Ippocrate." *Aufstieg und Niedergang der römischen Welt: Geschichte und Kultur Roms im Spiegel der neueren Forschung* 37 (2): 1529–1635.

Matthaios, Stephanos, Franco Montanari, and Antonios Rengakos. 2011. *Ancient Scholarship and Grammar: Archetypes, Concepts and Contexts,* ed. S. M., F. M., and A. R. Trends in Classics—Supplementary Volumes 8. Berlin: de Gruyter.

———, eds. Forthcoming. *Companion to Ancient Scholarship.* Leiden: Brill.

Meijering, Roos. 1987. *Literary and Rhetorical Theories in Greek Scholia.* Groningen: E. Forsten.

Montana, Fausto. 2012. *La filologia ellenistica. Lineamenti di una storia culturale.* Pavia: Pavia University Press.

Montanari, Franco. 1993. "L'erudizione, la filologia, la grammatica." In *Lo spazio letterario della Grecia antica,* vol. 1, bk. 2. Rome: Salerno Editrice, 235–281.

———. 1994. *La philologie grecque à l'époque hellénistique et romaine.* Entretiens sur l'antiquité classique 40. Entretiens préparés et présidés par Franco Montanari. Vandoeuvres: Fondation Hardt pour l'étude de l'Antiquité Classique.

———. 1998. "Zenodotus, Aristarchus and the *Ekdosis* of Homer." In *Editing Texts—Texte Edieren,* ed. Glenn W. Most, "Aporemata" 2. Göttingen: Vandenhoeck und Ruprecht, 1–21.

———. 2000a. "Demetrius of Phalerum on Literature." In *Demetrius of Phalerum: Text, Translation and Discussion,* ed. William W. Fortenbaugh and Eckart Schütrumpf. Rutgers University Studies in Classical Humanities 9. New Brunswick: Rutgers University Press, 391–411.

———. 2000b. "Ripensamenti di Aristarco sul testo omerico e il problema della seconda *ekdosis.*" In *Poesia e religione in Grecia,* Studi in onore di Giulio Aurelio Privitera, a cura di Maria Cannatà Fera e Simonetta Grandolini. Naples: Edizioni Scientifiche Italiane, 479–486.

———. 2002a. "Alexandrian Homeric Philology. The Form of the *Ekdosis* and the *variae lectiones.*" In *Epea Pteroenta. Beiträge zur Homerforschung,* Festschrift für Wolfgang Kullmann zum 75. Geburtstag, ed. Michael Reichel and Antonios Rengakos. Stuttgart: Franz Steiner Verlag, 119–140.

———. 2002b. "Callimaco e la filologia." In *Callimaque,* Entretiens sur l'antiquité classique 43. Entretiens préparés et présidés par Franco Montanari and Luigi Lehnus. Vandoeuvres: Fondation Hardt pour l'étude de l'Antiquité Classique, 59–97.

———. 2002c. *Omero tremila anni dopo. Atti del Congresso Genova 6–8 luglio 2000.* Ed. F. M., with the collaboration of Paola Ascheri. Rome: Edizioni di Storia e Letteratura.

———. 2004. "La filologia omerica antica e la storia del testo omerico." In *Antike Literatur in neuer Deutung,* Festschrift für Joachim Latacz, ed. Anton Bierl, Arbogast Schmitt, and Andreas Willi. Munich: K. G. Saur Verlag, 127–143.

———. 2009a. "*Ekdosis* alessandrina: il libro e il testo." In *Verae Lectiones. Estudios de crítica textual y edición de textos griegos,* ed. Manuel Sanz Morales and Myriam Librán Moreno, Exemplaria Classica, Anejo 1. Huelva-Cáceres: Universidad de Huelva, 143–167 (plates. 1–8).

———. 2009b. "Un papiro di Eschine con correzioni *(P.Oxy. 2404):* Considerazioni sull'*ekdosis* alessandrina." *Archiv für Papyrusforschung* 55: 401–411.

———. 2011. "Correcting a Copy, Editing a Text: Alexandrian *Ekdosis* and the Papyri." In *From Scholars to Scholia: Chapters in the History of Ancient Greek Scholarship,* ed. Franco Montanari and Lara Pagani, Trends in Classics—Supplementary Volumes 9. Berlin: de Gruyter, 1–15.

———. 2012. "The Peripatos on Literature. Interpretation, Use and Abuse." In *Praxiphanes of Mytilene and Chamaeleon of Heraclea: Text, Translation, and Discussion,* ed. Andrea Martano, Elisabetta Matelli, and David Mirhady. Rutgers University Studies in Classical Humanities 18. New Brunswick: Rutgers University Press, 339–358.

———. Forthcoming. "*Ekdosis.* A Product of the Ancient Scholarship." In *Companion to Ancient Scholarship,* ed. Stephanos Matthaios, Franco Montanari, and Antonios Rengakos. Leiden: Brill.

Nagy, Gregor. 2000. Review of *Homeri Ilias,* recensuit Martin L. West, vol. 1 (Stutgardiae et Lipsiae: Teubner, 1998). *Bryn Mawr Classical Review,* September 12.

———. 2003. Review of Martin L. West, *Studies in the Text and Transmission of the Iliad.* Munich: K. G. Saur Verlag 2001, *Gnomon* 75: 481–501.

———. 2004. *Homer's Text and Language.* Urbana: University of Illinois Press.

———. 2010. *Homer the Classic*. Center for Hellenic Studies, Washington, D.C: Harvard University Press.

Nardelli, Jean-Fabrice. 2001. Review of *Homeri Ilias,* recensuit Martin L. West, vol. 2 (Monachii et Lipsiae: K. G. Saur Verlag, 2000). *Bryn Mawr Classical Review,* June 21.

Nickau, Klaus. 1972. "Zenodotos (3)." *Real-Encyclopädie der Classischen Altertumswissenschaft* X A: 23–45.

———. 1977. *Untersuchungen zur Textkritische Methode des Zenodotos von Ephesos*. Berlin: de Gruyter.

Nünlist, René. 2009. *The Ancient Critic at Work: Terms and Concepts of Literary Criticism in Greek Scholia*. Cambridge: Cambridge University Press.

Pagani, Lara, and Serena Perrone. 2012. "Le *ekdoseis* antiche di Omero nei papiri." In *I papiri omerici. Atti del convegno internazionale di studi, Firenze 9–10 giugno 2011,* ed. Guido Bastianini and Angelo Casanova. Florence: Istituto Papirologico "G. Vitelli," 97–124.

Pasquali, Giorgio. 1920. *Filologia e storia*. Florence: Le Monnier.

Pfeiffer, Rudolph. 1968. *History of Classical Scholarship from the Beginning to the End of the Hellenistic Age*. Oxford: Clarendon Press.

Rengakos, Antonios 1993. *Der Homertext und die hellenistischen Dichter*. Stuttgart: Franz Verlag.

———. 2001. "Apollonios Rhodius as a Homeric Scholar." In *A Companion to Apollonius Rhodius,* ed. Theodore D. Papanghelis and Antonios Rengakos. Leiden: Brill, 193–216.

———. 2002a. "The Hellenistic Poets as Homeric Critics." In *Omero tremila anni dopo. Atti del Congresso Genova 6–8 luglio 2000,* ed. Franco Montanari, with the collaboration of Paola Ascheri. Rome: Edizioni di Storia e Letteratura, 143–157.

———. 2002b. Review of *Studies in the Text and Transmission of the Iliad.* (Munich: K. G. Saur Verlag, 2001). *Bryn Mawr Classical Review,* November 15.

———. 2012. "Bemerkungen zum antiken Homertext." In *Homer, gedeutet durch ein großes Lexicon,* ed. Michael Meier-Brügger. Berlin: de Gruyter, 239–252.

Rizzo, Silvia. 1973. *Il lessico filologico degli umanisti*. Rome: Edizioni di Storia e Letteratura.

Roselli, Amneris. 2010. "Libri e biblioteche a Roma al tempo di Galeno: la testimonianza del *de indolentia*." *Galenos* 4: 127–148.

———. 2012. "Galeno e la filologia del II secolo." In *Vestigia notitiai. Scritti in memoria di Michelangelo Giusta,* ed. Edoardo Bona, Carlos Levy, and Giuseppina Magnaldi. Alessandria: Edizioni dell'Orso, 63–80.

Schmidt, Martin. 1997. "Variae lectiones oder Parallelstellen: was notierten Zenodot und Aristarch zu Homer?" *Zeitschrift für Papyrologie und Epigraphik* 115: 1–12.

Sforza, Ilaria. 2000. "Nota su un verso dei papiri tolemaici dell'*Iliade*." *Analecta Papyrologica* 12: 25–34.

Stramaglia, Antonio. 2011. "Libri perduti per sempre: Galeno, *De indolentia* 13; 16; 17–19." *Rivista di Filologia e di Istruzione Classica* 139: 118–147.

Thiel, Helmut van. 1991. *Homeri Odyssea*, recensuit H. v. T. Hildesheim: Olms.

———. 1992. “Zenodot, Aristarch und Andere.” *Zeitschrift für Papyrologie und Epigraphik* 90: 1–32.

———. 1996, 2010[2]. *Homeri Ilias*, recensuit H. v. T. Hildesheim: Olms.

———. 1997. “Der Homertext in Alexandria.” *Zeitschrift für Papyrologie und Epigraphik* 115: 13–36.

Turner, Eric Gardner. 1980. *Greek Papyri: An Introduction.* Oxford: Clarendon Press.

Turner, Eric Gardner, and Peter J. Parsons. 1987. *Greek Manuscripts of the Ancient World.* 2nd ed., rev. and enl. P. J. P. *Bulletin of the Institute of Classical Studies* Suppl. 46.

Valk, Marchinus van der. 1949. *Textual Criticism of the Odyssey.* Leiden: A. W. Sijthoff.

———. 1963–64. *Researches on the Text and Scholia of the Iliad,* I–II. Leiden: Brill.

West, Martin L. 1998–2000. Homeri *Ilias*, recensuit Martin L. West. Vol. 1, Stutgardiae et Lipsiae: Teubner; vol. 2, Monachii et Lipsiae: K. G. Saur Verlag.

———. 2001a. “Response by M. L. W. on Nagy and Nardelli.” *Bryn Mawr Classical Review*, September 6.

———. 2001b. *Studies in the Text and Transmission of the Iliad.* Munich-Leipzig: K. G. Saur Verlag.

———. 2002. “Zenodotus’ Text.” In *Omero tremila anni dopo. Atti del Congresso Genova 6–8 luglio 2000,* ed. Franco Montanari, with the collaboration of Paola Ascheri. Rome: Edizioni di Storia e Letteratura, 137–142.

West, Stephanie. 1967. *The Ptolemaic Papyri of Homer.* Köln: Westdeutscher Verlag.

Chapter 2

Adams, J. N. 2013. *Social Variation and the Latin Language.* Cambridge: Cambridge University Press.

Broggiato, M., ed. 2001. *Cratete di Mallo, I frammenti.* La Spezia: Agorà.

Chin, Catherine M. 2008. *Grammar and Christianity in the Late Roman World.* Philadelphia: University of Pennsylvania Press.

Crawford, M. H., et al. 1996. *Roman Statutes.* Bulletin of the Institute of Classical Studies Supplement 64. London: Institute of Classical Studies.

Delvigo, Maria Luisa. 1987. *Testo virgiliano e tradizione indiretta: Le ubscri probiane.* Pisa: Giardini.

Deufert, M. 2002. *Textgeschichte und Rezeption der plautinischen Komödien im Altertum.* Berlin: de Gruyter.

Dillon, J. 2012. Review of Luna and Segonds. *Proclus: Commentaire sur le Parménide de Platon, Tome III. Bryn Mawr Classical Review* 2012.05.26.

Ferri, R. 2003. Review of Deufert, *Textgeschichte. Bryn Mawr Classical Review* 2003.09.07.

Frier, Bruce W. 1989. *A Casebook on the Roman Law of Delict.* Atlanta: Scholars Press.

Funaioli, H. 1969. *Grammaticae Romanae Fragmenta.* Stuttgart: B. G. Teubner.

Gibson, Roy K., and Christina Shuttleworth Kraus, eds. 2002. *The Classical Commentary: Histories, Practices, Theory.* Leiden: Brill.

Goulet-Cazé, Marie-Odile, ed. 2000. *Le Commentaire entre tradition et innovation.* Paris: Vrin.

Harries, Jill. 2006. *Cicero and the Jurists.* London.

Henderson, John. 2004. *Morals and Villas in Seneca's Letters.* Cambridge: Cambridge University Press.

———. 2009. "Do They Even Know It's Christmas Time? Macrobius' Meta Philological Association." In *Metaphilology: Histories and Languages of Philology,* ed. Pascale Hummel. Paris: Philologicum, 29–45.

Herzog, Reinhart, and Peter Lebrecht Schmidt, eds. 2002. *Handbuch der lateinischen Literatur der Antike* I: *Die Archaische Literatur,* ed. Werner Suerbaum. Munich: C. H. Beck.

Holtz, L. 1975. "Le Parisinus latinus 7530, synthèse cassinienne des arts libéraux." *Studi Medievali* 16: 97–152.

———. 1981. *Donat et la tradition de l'enseignment grammatical.* Paris: CNRS.

Hummel, Pascale. 2009. "History of History of Philology: Goals and Limits of an Inquiry." In *Metaphilology: Histories and Languages of Philology,* ed. Pascale Hummel. Paris: Philologicum, 7–28.

Jones, C. P. 2009. "Books and Libraries in a Newly-Discovered Treatise of Galen." *Journal of Roman Archaeology* 22: 390–397.

Kaster, Robert A. 1988. *Guardians of Language.* Berkeley: University of California Press.

———, ed. 1995. *Suetonius de Grammaticis et Rhetoribus.* Oxford: Clarendon Press.

Keil, H., ed. 1961. *Grammatici Latini.* Hildesheim: Olms.

Law, Vivien. 1982. *The Insular Latin Grammarians.* Woodbridge: Boydell Press.

Lenel, O. 1889. *Palingenesia Iuris Civilis.* Leipzig: Tauchnitz.

Maine, Henry Sumner. 1931. *Ancient Law.* Oxford: Oxford University Press.

Mette, H. J. 1952. *Parateresis: Untersuchungen zur Sprachtheorie des Krates von Pergamon.* Halle: M. Niemeyer.

Most, Glenn W., ed. 1999. *Commentaries—Kommentare.* Göttingen: Vandenhoek and Ruprecht.

Pasquali, Giorgio. 1962. *Storia della tradizione e critica del testo.* 2nd ed. Florence: Felice Le Monnier.

Passalacqua, Marina. 1978. *I Codici di Prisciano.* Rome: Edizioni di Storia e Letteratura.

Pecere, Oronzo. 1982. "La ubscription di Statilio Massimo e la tradizione delle Agrarie di Cicerone." *Italia Medioevale e Umanistica* 25: 73–123.

Pfeiffer, Rudolf. 1968. *History of Classical Scholarship from the Beginnings to the End of the Hellenistic Age.* Oxford: Clarendon Press.

Reynolds, L. D., ed. 1983. *Texts and Transmission.* Oxford: Clarendon Press.

Robins, R. H. 1995. "The Authenticity of the *Technê:* The *status quaestionis.*" In *Dionysius Thrax and the Technê Grammatikê,* ed. V. Law and I. Sluiter. Münster: Nodus, 13–26.

Schulz, Fritz. 1946. *History of Roman Legal Science.* Oxford: Clarendon Press.

Tarrant, R. J., ed. 2012. *Virgil: Aeneid Book XII.* Cambridge: Cambridge University Press.

Timpanaro, Sebastiano. 1986. *Per la storia della filologia virgiliana antica.* Rome: Salerno Editrice.

———. 2001. *Virgilianisti antichi e tradizione indiretta.* Florence: Olschi Editore.

———. 2005. *The Genesis of Lachmann's Method.* Trans. Glenn W. Most. Chicago: University of Chicago Press.

Wieacker, Franz. 1988. *Römische Rechtsgeschichte* I. Munich.

Zetzel, James E. G. 1973. "*Emendavi ad Tironem:* Some Notes on Scholarship in the Second Century C.E." *Harvard Studies in Classical Philology* 77: 225–243.

———. 1980. "The Subscriptions in the Manuscripts of Livy and Fronto and the Meaning of *Emendatio.*" *Classical Philology* 75: 38–59.

———. 1981. *Latin Textual Criticism in Antiquity.* New York: Arno Press.

———. 2002. Review of Timpanaro, *Virgilianisti antichi e tradizione indiretta. Bryn Mawr Classical Review* 2002.02.09.

———. 2004. Review of Gibson and Kraus, *The Classical Commentary: Histories, Practices, Theory. Journal of Roman Studies* 94: 205–207.

———. 2005. *Marginal Scholarship and Textual Deviance.* Bulletin of the Institute of Classical Studies Supplement 84. London: Institute of Classical Studies.

Chapter 3

Abramson, Shraga. 1989. "Ketivat ha-Mishnah (Al Da'at Geonim ve-Rishonim)." In *Tarbut ve-Hevrah be-Toldot Yisrael Bi-yemei Ha-Benayim: Qovetz Maamarim le-Zikhro shel Hayyim Hillel Ben-Sason,* ed. Reuven Bonfil and Menahem Ben-Sason. Jerusalem: Makhon Shazar. 27–52.

Auerbach, Eric. 1948. *Mimesis: The Representation of Everyday Life in Western Literature.* New Haven, Conn.: Yale University Press.

Baumgarten, Al. 2005. *The Flourishing of Jewish Sects in the Maccabean Era: An Interpretation.* Atlanta, Ga.: Society of Biblical Literature.

Bernstein, Moshe J., and Shlomo Koyfman. 2005. "The Interpretation of Biblical Law in the Dead Sea Scrolls—Forms and Methods." In *Biblical Interpretation in Qumran,* ed. Mathias Henze. Grand Rapids, Mich.: W. B. Eerdmans, 61–87.

Bokser, Barukh. 1983. "Rabbinic Responses to Catastrophe: From Continuity to Discontinuity." *Proceedings of the American Academy for Jewish Research* 50: 37–61.

Boyarin, Daniel. 1990. *Intertextuality and the Reading of Midrash.* Bloomington: Indiana University Press.

———. 2007. "Hellenism in Jewish Babylonia." In *Cambridge Companion to Rabbinic Literature,* ed. Charlotte Elisheva Fonrobert and Martin S. Jaffe. Cambridge: Cambridge University Press, 336–363.

———. 2009. *Socrates and the Fat Rabbis.* Chicago: University of Chicago Press.

Cohen, Boaz. 1966. *Jewish and Roman Law: A Comparative Study.* 2 vols. New York: Jewish Theological Seminary.

Cohen, S. Y. 1984. "The Significance of Yavneh: Pharisees, Rabbis and the End of Jewish Sectarianism." *Hebrew College Annual* 55: 27–53.

Daube, David. 1992. "Negligence in the Early Talmudic Law of Contract." Reprinted in *The Collected Works of David Daube,* vol. 1, *Talmudic Law,* ed. Calum M. Carmichael. Berkeley: University of California Press, 305–332.

Elman, Yaakov. 1993. " 'It Is No Empty Thing': Nahmanides and the Search for Omnisignificance." *Torah U-Madda Journal* 4: 1–83.

———. 1994. *Authority and Tradition: Toseftan Baraitot in Talmudic Babylonia*, Yeshiva University Press, NY.

———. 1999. "The Contribution of Rabbinic Thought towards a Theology of Suffering." In *Jewish Perspectives on the Experience of Suffering.*, ed. S. Carmy. Northvale, N.J.: Jason Aaronson, 155–212.

———. 2003. "Marriage and Marital Property in Rabbinic and Sa Elman sanian Law." In *Rabbinic Law in Its Roman and Near Eastern Context,* ed. C. Hezser. Tübingen: Mohr-Siebeck, 227–276.

———. 2004a. "Acculturation to Elite Persian Norms in the Babylonian Jewish Community of Late Antiquity." In *Neti'ot David,* ed. E. Halivni, Z. A. Steinfeld, and Y. Elman. Jerusalem: Orhot, 31–56.

———. 2004b. "Order, Sequence, and Selection: The Mishnah's Anthological Choices." In *The Anthology in Jewish Literature,* ed. D. Stern. New York: Oxford University Press, 53–80.

———. 2004c. "Rava ve-Darkei ha-Iyyun ha-Eretz Yisraeliyyot be-Midrash ha-Halakhah." In Merkaz *u-Tefutzah: Eretz Yisrael veha-Tefutzot bi-Ymei Bayit Sheni, ha-Mishnah veha-Talmud,* ed. Y. Gafni. Jerusalem: Merkaz Shazar, 217–242.

———. 2005. "Cultural Aspects of Post-redactional Additions to the Bavli." In *Creation and Composition: The Contribution of the Bavli Redactors (Stammaim) to the Aggadah* (TSAJ 114), ed. Jeffrey Rubenstein. Tübingen: Mohr-Siebeck, 383–416.

———. 2006a. "R. Yosef be-ᶜIdan Ritha." *Bar Ilan Annual* 30–31, *Memorial Volume for Prof. M. S. Feldblum,* 93–104.

———. 2006b. "Yeshivot Bavel u-Vatei Din Parsiyyim bi-Tequfah ha-Amoraít veha-Batar Amorait, in E. Ettinger, ed., *Yeshivot u-Vatei Midrashot*, Jerusalem: Makhon Shazar, 2006, 31–55.

———. 2007a. "The Emergence of Omnisignificant Avestan Interpretation in the Work of Abarg on the Herbedestan." Paper presented at the Thirty-Eighth Convention of the Association of Jewish Studies, Toronto, December 15.

———. 2007b. "Ma'aseh be-Shtei Ayarot: Mahoza u-Pumbedita Ke-Meyatzgot Shtei Tarbuyot Hilkhatiyyot." In *Torah li-Shemah: Mehqarim be-Madacei ha-Yahadut li-khvod Prof. Shamma Yehudah Friedman.* Jerusalem: Bar Ilan UP, in association with Makhon Shechter le-Mada'ei Ha-Yahadut, 3–38.

———. 2007c. "Middle Persian Culture and Babylonian Sages: Accomodation and Resistance in the Shaping of Rabbinic Legal Tradition." In *Cambridge Companion to Rabbinic Literature,* ed. Charlotte Elisheva Fonrobert and Martin S. Jaffe. Cambridge: Cambridge University Press, 165–197.

———. 2007d. "The Socioeconomics of Babylonian Heresy." *Jewish Law Association Studies* 17: 80–126.

———. 2010. "Toward an Intellectual History of Sasanian Law: An Intergenerational Dispute in Hērbedestān 9 and Its Rabbinic Parallels." In *The Talmud in Its Iranian* Context, ed. Carol Bakhos and Rahim Shayegan. Tübingen: Mohr-Siebeck, 21–57.

———. 2012. “The Emotional Palette of the Grodno School: *Ye’ush* and *Hefqer.*” In *Rav Shalom Banayikh: Essays Presented to Rabbi Shalom Carmy by Friends and Students in Celebration of Forty Years of Teaching,* ed. Hayyim Angel and Yitzhak Blau. Jersey City: Ktav, 95–128.

———. Forthcoming. “Contrasting Intellectual Trajectories: Iran and Israel in Mesopotamia.” In *Encounters by the Rivers of Babylon,* ed. Uri Gabbay and Shai Secunda. Tubingen: Mohr Siebeck.

Epstein, I., ed. 1935–1948. *The Babylonian Talmud* (16 volumes). London: The Soncino Press. Cited according to Seder: Mo’ed, Nashim, Nezikin, Kodashin etc.

Epstein, Y. N. 1965. *Mavo le-Nusah ha-Mishnah.* 2 vols. Jerusalem: Magnes.

Fishbane, Michael. 1985. *Biblical Interpretation in Ancient Israel.* Oxford: Oxford University Press.

Friedman, Shamma Y. 2010. “Al Derekh Heqer ha-Sugyah.” In *Talmudic Studies: Investigating the Sugya, Variant Readings and Aggadah.* New York: Jewish Theological Seminary, 4–36.

Gafni, Isaiah. 2007. “Rabbinic Historiography and Representations of the Past.” In *Cambridge Companion to Rabbinic Literature,* ed. Charlotte Elisheva Fonrobert and Martin S. Jaffe. Cambridge: Cambridge University Press, 295–312.

Halbertal, Moshe. 1997. *Interpretative Revolutions in the Making: Values as Interpretative Considerations in Midrashic Halakhah* [Hebrew]. Jerusalem: Magnes.

Halivni, David Weiss. 1982. *Meqorot u-Mesorot Moed I: Shabbat.* New York: Jewish Theological Seminary.

———. 1986. *Midrash, Mishnah, and Gemara: The Jewish Predilection for Justified Law.* Cambridge, Mass.: Harvard University Press.

———. 1991. *Peshat and Derash: Plain and Applied Meaning in Rabbinic Exegesis.* New York: Oxford University Press.

———. 2012. *Meqorot u-Mesorot Neziqin IV; Sanhedrin, Shevu’ot, Makkot, Avodah Zarah, Horayot.* Jerusalem: Magnes.

Harris, Jay M. 1995. *How Do We Know This? Midrash and the Fragmentation of Modern Judaism.* Albany: State University of New York Press.

Haut, Irwin H. 1989–90. “Some Aspects of Absolute Liability under Jewish Law, and Particularly, under View of Maimonides.” *Diné Israel* 15: 7–61.

Havelock, Eric A. 1963. *Preface to Plato.* Cambridge, Mass.: Harvard University Press.

Hezser, Catherine. 2007. “Roman Law and Rabbinic Legal Composition.” In *Cambridge Companion to Rabbinic Literature,* ed. Charlotte Elisheva Fonrobert and Martin S. Jaffe. Cambridge: Cambridge University Press, 270–294.

Hirshman, Marc. 2006. “Aggadic Midrash.” In *The Literature of the Sages, Second Part: Midrash and Targum, Liturgy, Poetry, Mysticism, Contracts, Inscriptions, Ancient Science and the Languages of Rabbinic Literature,* ed. Shmuel Safrai et al. Assen: Royal Van Gorcum, 107–132.

Hoffmann, David Zvi. 1970. *Mesillot le-Torat ha-Tannaím*, Jerusalem: Carmiel.

Mechilta de-Rabbi Ishmael. Jerusalem: Wahrmann.

Horovitz, H. S., and I. E. Rabin, eds. 1970.

Jacobs, Louis. 1981. *Teyku: The Unsolved Problem in the Babylonian Talmud: A Study in the Literary Analysis and Form of the Talmudic Argument.* New York: Cornwall Books.

Jaspers, Karl. 1965. *The Origin and Goal of History.* New Haven, Conn.: Yale University Press.

Kahana, Menahem I. 2006. "The Halakhic Midrashim." in *The Literature of the Sages, Second Part: Midrash and Targum, Liturgy, Poetry, Mysticism, Contracts, Inscriptions, Ancient Science and the Languages of Rabbinic Literature,* ed. Shmuel Safrai et al. Assen: Royal Van Gorcum, 3–106.

Kalimi, Isaac. 2005. *An Ancient Israelite Historian: Studies in the Chronicler, His Time, Place and Writing.* Assen: Royal Van Gorcum.

Kalmin, Richard. 2006. *Jewish Babylonia between Persia and Roman Palestine.* New York: Oxford University Press.

Klawans, Jonathan. 2010. "Josephus, the Rabbis, and Responses to Catastrophe, Ancient and Modern." *Jewish Quarterly Review* 100: 278–309.

Knohl, Israel. 2003. *The Divine Symphony: The Bible's Many Voices.* Philadelphia: Jewish Publication Society.

Kugel, James. 1981. *The Idea of Biblical Poetry: Parallelism and Its History.* New Haven, Conn.: Yale University Press.

Lauterbach, J. Z. 1965. Mekilta de-Rabbi Ishmael. Philadelphia: Jewish Publication Society.

Libson, Gideon. 2003. *Jewish and Islamic Law: A Comparative Study of Custom during the Geonic Period.* Cambridge, Mass.: Islamic Legal Studies Program, Harvard Law School.

Melamed, E. Z., ed. (Epstein, J. N.). 1957. *Prologomena ad Litteras Tannaiticas: Mishna, Tosephta et Interpretationes Halachicas* [Hebrew]. Jerusalem: Magnes.

Milgram, Jonathan. 2012. "Prolegomenon to a New Study of Rabbinic Inheritance Law on the Fiftieth Anniversary of Yaron's *Gifts In Contemplation of Death.*" *Jewish Law Association Studies* 23: 181–192.

Moscovitz, Leib. 2002. *Talmudic Reasoning: From Casuistics to Conceptualization* (TSAJ 89). Tübingen: Mohr Siebeck.

———. 2003. " 'Designation in Significant': An Analysis of the Conceptual Sugya in bSanh 47b–48b." *Association of Jewish Studies Review* 27: 227–252.

Neusner, Jacob. 1982. *Judaism: The Evidence of the Mishnah.* Chicago: University of Chicago Press.

———. 1992. *The Tosefta: An Introduction.* Atlanta: Scholars Press.

Noam, Vered. 2010. *From Qumran to the Rabbinic Revolution: Conceptions of Impurity* [Hebrew]. Jerusalem: Yad Izhak Ben-Zvi.

Novak, David. 1990. "Maimonides and the Science of the Law." *Jewish Law Association Studies* 4: 99–134.

Rubenstein, Jeffrey L. 1997. "On Some Abstract Concepts in Rabbinic Literature." *Jewish Studies Quarterly* 4: 33–73.

———. 2002. "The Rise of the Baylonian Rabbinic Academy: A Reexamination of the Talmudic Evidence." *Jewish Studies: An Internet Journal* 1: 55–68.

———. 2003. "The Thematization of Dialectics in Bavli Aggadah." *Journal of Jewish Studies* 54: 71–84.

Schiffman, Lawrence H. 1994. *Reclaiming the Dead Sea Scrolls: The History of Judaism, the Background of Christianity, the Lost Library of Qumran.* Philadelphia: Jewish Publication Society.

Schremer, Adiel. 2001. "'[T]He[Y] Did Not Read in the Sealed Book': Qumran Halakhic Revolution and the Emergence of Torah Study in Second Temple Judaism." In *Historical Perspectives: From the Hasmoneans to Bar Kokhba in Light of the Dead Sea Scrolls: Proceedings of the Fourth International Symposium of the Orion Center for the Study of the Dead Sea Scrolls and Associated Literature*, ed. D. M. Goodblatt, A. Pinnick, and D. R. Schwartz. Studies on the Texts of the Desert of Judah, 37. Leiden: E. J. Brill, 105–126.

Shemesh, Aharon. 2009. *Halakhah in the Making: The Development of Jewish Law from Qumran to the Rabbis*. Berkeley: University of California Press.

Soloveitchik, Haym, *Wine in Ashkenaz in the Middle Ages: Yeyn Nesekh—A Study in the History of Halakhah* [Hebrew], Jerusalem: Zalman Shazar Center for Jewish History, 2008.

Strack, H. L., and G. Stemberger. 1991. *Introduction to the Talmud and Midrash*. Edinburgh: T & T Clarke.

Strauch-Schick, Shana. 2001. "Intention in the Babylonian Talmud: An Intellectual History." Ph.D. diss., Yeshiva University.

Sussman, Yaakov. 1990. "Ve-shuv Yerushalmi Neziqin." In *Mehqerei Talmud* I, ed. Yaakov Sussman and David Rosenthal. Jerusalem: Magnes, 55–133.

Ta-Shema, Israel. 2000. *Talmudic Commentary in Europe and North Africa, 100–1400*, 2 vols. [Hebrew]. Jerusalem: Magnes.

Urbach, E. E. 1980. *Ba'alei ha-Tosafot: Toldoteihem, Hibbureihem, Shitatam*. 2 vols. Jerusalem: Mosad Bialik.

———. 1984. *The Halakhah: Its Sources and Development* [Hebrew]. Jerusalem: Massadah.

Walton, John H. 2006. *Ancient Near Eastern Thought and the Old Testament: Introducing the Conceptual World of the Hebrew Bible*. Grand Rapids, Mich.: Baker Academic.

Watson, Allen. 1995. *The Spirit of Roman Law*. Athens: University of Georgia Press.

———, ed. 1998. *The Digest of Justinian*. 4 vols. Rev. ed. Philadelphia: University of Pennsylvania Press, 1998.

Chapter 4

PRIMARY SOURCES

Abū Hiffān. 1953. *Akhbār Abī Nuwās*. Ed. ʿA. A. Farrāj. Cairo: Maktabat Miṣr.

Abū Nuwās. 1989. *Dīwān*, vol. 4. Ed. G. Schoeler. Wiesbaden: Harrassowitz.

Abū Tammām. 1987. *Dīwān*. Ed. M. ʿA. ʿAzzām. 4 vols. Cairo: Dār al-Maʿārif.

Abū ʿUbayda. 1962. *Majāz al-Qur'ān*. Ed. Fuat Sezgin. 2 vols. 1954; reprint, Cairo: Maktabat al-Khānjī.

al-Aṣmaʿī. [1414] 1994. *Su'ālāt Abī Ḥātim al-Sijistānī li-l-Aṣmaʿī wa-radduhū ʿalayhi Fuḥūlat al-shuʿarā'*. Ed. M. ʿA. Salāma. Cairo: Maktabat al-Thaqāfa al-Dīniyya.

al-Ḥuṣrī. 1969–70. *Zahr al-Ādāb*. Ed. ʿA. M. al-Bijāwī. 2 vols. Cairo: ʿĪsā al-Bābī al-Ḥalabī.

Ibn ʿAbdrabbih. [1359–72] 1940–53. *al-ʿIqd al-farīd.* Ed. Aḥmad Amīn et al. 7 vols. Cairo: Maṭbaʿat Lajnat al-Taʾlīf wa-l-Tarjama wa-l-Nashr.
Ibn al-Anbārī, Abū l-Barakāt. [1386] 1967. *Nuzhat al-alibbāʾ fī ṭabaqāt al-udabāʾ.* Ed. M. A. Ibrāhīm. Cairo: Dār Nahḍat Miṣr.
Ibn al-Jarrāḥ. [1372] 1953. *al-Waraqa.* Ed. M. ʿA. ʿAzzām and ʿA. A. Farrāj. Cairo: Dār al-Maʿārif.
Ibn Manẓūr. 1955–56. *Lisān al-ʿarab.* 15 vols. Reprint, Beirut: Dār Ṣādir, n.d.
———. [1343] 1924. *Akhbār Abī Nuwās, taʾrīkhuhū, nawādiruhū, shiʿruhū, mujūnuhū.* Ed. M. ʿA. Ibrāhīm and ʿA. al-Shirbīnī. Cairo: Maṭbaʿat al-Iʿtimād.
Ibn al-Muʿtazz. [1375] 1956. *Ṭabaqāt al-shuʿārāʾ.* Ed. ʿA. A. Farrāj. Cairo: Dār al-Maʿārif.
———. [1399] 1979. *Kitāb al-Badīʿ.* Ed. I. Kratchkovsky. 1935; reprint, Baghdad: Maktabat al-Muthannā.
Ibn al-Nadīm. [1430] 2009. *Fihrist.* Ed. A. F. al-Sayyid. 2 pts. in 4 vols. London: al-Furqan Islamic Heritage Foundation.
Ibn Rashīq. [1353] 1934. *al-ʿUmda fī maḥāsin al-shiʿr wa-ādābihī wa-naqdihī.* Ed. M. M. ʿAbdalḥamīd. Reprint, Beirut: Dār al-Jīl [1401] 1981.
al-Iṣbahānī, Abū l-Faraj. [1401] 1981. *al-Aghānī.* Various editors. 25 vols. [1374] 1955; reprint, Beirut: Dār al-Thaqāfa.
al-Jumaḥī, Muḥammad b. Sallām. [1394] 1974. *Ṭabaqāt fuḥūl al-shuʿarāʾ.* Ed. M. M. Shākir. 2 vols. Cairo: Maṭbaʿat al-Madanī.
al-Khaṭīb al-Baghdādī. [1422] 2001. *Taʾrīkh Baghdād.* Ed. B. ʿA. Maʿrūf. 17 vols. Beirut: Dār al-Gharb al-Islāmī.
al-Lughawī, Abū al-Ṭayyib. 1954. *Marātib al-naḥwiyyīn.* Ed. M. A. Ibrāhīm. Cairo: Maṭbaʿat Nahḍat Miṣr.
al-Marzubānī. [1415] 1995. *al-Muwashshaḥ fī maʾākhidh al-ʿulamāʾ ʿalā l-shuʿarāʾ.* Ed. M. Ḥ. Shamsaddīn. Beirut: Dār al-Kutub al-ʿIlmiyya.
Qudāma b. Jaʿfar. N.d. *Naqd al-shiʿr.* Ed. M. ʿA. Khafājī. Beirut: Dār al-Kutub al-ʿIlmiyya.
al-Sīrāfī. [1374] 1955. *Akhbār al-naḥwiyyīn al-baṣriyyīn.* Ed. Ṭ. M. al-Zaynī and M. ʿA. al-Khafājī. Cairo: Muṣṭafā al-Bābī al-Ḥalabī.
al-Ṣūlī. 1937. *Akhbār Abī Tammām.* Ed. Kh. M. ʿAsākir, M. ʿA. ʿAzzām, and N. al-Hindī. Beirut: al-Maktab al-Tijārī li-l-Ṭibāʿa wa-l-Tawzīʿ wa-l-Nashr.
———. [1355] 1936. *Ashʿār awlād al-khulafāʾ wa-akhbāruhum.* Ed. J. H. Dunne. [1401] 1982; reprint, Beirut: Dār al-Masīra.
———. 1934. *Akhbār al-shuʿarāʾ al-muḥdathīn.* Ed. J. H. Dunne. [1401] 1982; reprint, Beirut: Dār al-Masīra.
al-Ushnāndānī [1389] 1969. *Maʿānī al-shiʿr.* Ed. ʿI. al-Tanūkhī. Damascus: Wizārat al-Thaqāfa wa-l-Siyāḥa wa-l-Irshād al-Qawmī.

CRITICAL LITERATURE

Arberry, Arthur J. 1955. *The Koran Interpreted.* London: Macmillan.
Bauer, Thomas. 1998. *Liebe und Liebesdichtung in der arabischen Welt des 9. und 10. Jahrhunderts.* Wiesbaden: Harrassowitz.

———. 2003. "Literarische Anthologien der Mamlūkenzeit." In *Die Mamlūken: Studien zu ihrer Geschichte und Kultur. Zum Gedenken an Ulrich Haarman (1924–1999),* ed. S. Conermann and A. Pistor-Hatam. Hamburg: EB-Verlag, 71–122.

———. 2005. "Arabische Kultur." In *Rhetorik: Begriff-Geschichte-Internationalität,* ed. G. Ueding. Tübingen: Max Niemeyer, 283–300.

Bohas, Georges, Jean-Patrick Guillaume, and Djamel Kouloughli. 2006. *The Arabic Linguistic Tradition.* 1990; reprint, Washington, D.C.: Georgetown University Press.

Boustany, Said. 1969. "Ibn Thawāba." In *Encyclopaedia of Islam,* new ed. Leiden: Brill, 3: 955–956.

Bürgel, J. Christoph. 1974. "'Die beste Dichtung ist die lügenreichste.' Wesen und Bedeutung eines literarischen Streites des arabischen Mittelalters im Lichte komparatistischer Betrachtung." *Oriens* 23–24: 7–102.

Carter, Michael G. 2004. *Sībawayhi.* Oxford: Tauris.

Cooperson, Michael. 2000. *Classical Arabic Biography: The Heirs of the Prophets in the Age of al-Maʾmūn.* Cambridge: Cambridge University Press.

Fleischhammer, Manfred. 2004. *Die Quellen des Kitāb al-Aġānī.* Wiesbaden: Harrassowitz.

Genette, Gérard. 1982. *Palimpsestes: la littérature au second degré.* Paris: Éditions du Seuil.

Gilliot, Claude. 2011. "The 'Collections' of the Meccan Arabic Lectionary." In *The Transmission and Dynamics of the Textual Sources of Islam: Essays in Honor of Harald Motzki,* ed. N. Boekhoff-van der Voort et al. Leiden: Brill, 105–133.

Gilliot, Claude, and Pierre Larcher. 2004. "Language and Style of the Qurʾān." In *Encyclopedia of the Qurʾān,* ed. J. D. McAuliffe, 5 vols. Leiden: Brill, 3: 109–135.

Gruendler, Beatrice. 1993. *The Development of the Arabic Scripts: From the Nabatean Era to the First Islamic Century According to Dated Texts.* Atlanta: Scholars Press.

———. 2005a. "Meeting the Patron. An *Akhbār* Type and Its Implications for *Muḥdath* Poetry." In *Ideas, Images, Methods of Portrayal: Insights into Arabic Literature and Islam,* ed. S. Günther. Wiesbaden: Harrassowitz, 51–77.

———. 2005b. "Verse and Taxes: The Function of Poetry in Selected Literary *Akhbār* of the Third/Ninth Century." In *On Fiction and Adab in Medieval Arabic Literature,* ed. P. Kennedy. Wiesbaden: Harrassowitz, 85–124.

———. 2006. "Arabic Alphabet: Origin." In *Encyclopedia of Arabic Language and Linguistics,* ed. Kees Versteegh, 4 vols. Leiden: Brill, 1: 148–165.

———. 2007. "The Reconstruction of the *Qaṣīda* in Performance and Reception." In *Classical Arabic Humanities in Their Own Terms. Festschrift for Wolfhart Heinrichs on His 65th Birthday,* ed. B. Gruendler. Leiden: Brill, 325–389.

———. 2008. "Abstract Aesthetics and Practical Criticism in Ninth-Century Baghdad." In *Takhyīl: The Imaginary in Classical Arabic Poetics,* ed. M. Hammond and G. J. van Gelder. Oxford: Gibb Memorial Trust, 196–220.

———. 2009. "*Tawqīʿ* (Apostille): Verbal Economy in Verdicts of Tort Redress." In *The Weaving of Words: Approaches to Classical Arabic Literature,* ed. L. Behzadi and V. Behmardi. Beirut-Wiesbaden: Ergon, 101–129.

———. 2010. "Abū Tammām." In *Encyclopaedia of Islam, THREE,* ed. G. Krämer, D. Matringe, J. Nawas, and E. Rowson. Leiden: Brill. www.brillonline.nl/subscriber/entry?entry=ei3_SIM-0035.

———. 2011. *Book Culture before Print: The Early History of Arabic Media.* Occasional Papers, Margaret Weyerhaeuser Jewett Chair of Arabic. Beirut: American University of Beirut.

Gully, Adrian. 2006. "Two of a Kind: Ibn Hishām al-Anṣārī on *Naḥw* and Ibn al-Athīr on *Balāgha.*" In *Grammar as a Window onto Arabic Humanism: A Collection of Articles in Honour of Michael G. Carter,* ed. L. Edzard and J. Watson. Wiesbaden: Harrassowitz, 84–107.

Gutas, Dimitri. 1998. *Greek Thought, Arab Culture: The Graeco-Arabic Translation Movement in Baghdad and Early ʿAbbāsid Society (2nd–4th/8th–10th Centuries).* London: Routledge.

Hammond, Marlé, and Geert Jan van Gelder, eds. 2008. *Takhyīl: The Imaginary in Classical Arabic Poetics.* Oxford: Gibb Memorial Trust.

Heinrichs, Wolfhart. 1973. "Literary Theory: The Problem of Its Efficiency." In *Arabic Poetry: Theory and Development,* ed. Gustav E. von Grunebaum. Wiesbaden: Harrassowitz, 19–69.

———. 1974. " 'Manierismus' in der arabischen Literatur." In *Islamwissenschaftliche Abhandlungen Fritz Meier zum sechzigsten Geburtstag,* ed. R. Gramlich. Wiesbaden: Harrassowitz, 118–128.

———. 1984. "*Istiʿārah* and *Badīʿ* and Their Terminological Relationship in Early Arabic Literary Criticism." *Zeitschrift zur Geschichte der Arabisch-Islamischen Wissenschaften* 1: 180–211.

———. 1987. "Poetik, Rhetorik, Literaturkritik." In *Grundriß der arabischen Philologie,* vol. 2, *Literaturwissenschaft,* ed. H. Gätje. Wiesbaden: Harrassowitz, 177–207.

———. 1991. "Mubālagha." In *Encyclopaedia of Islam,* new ed. Leiden: Brill, 7: 277–278.

———. 1992. "Muwalladūn." In *Encyclopaedia of Islam,* new ed. Leiden: Brill, 7: 808.

———. 1994. "Muslim b. al-Walīd and *Badīʿ.*" In *Festschrift Ewald Wagner zum 65. Geburtstag.* Band 2, *Studien zur arabischen Dichtung,* ed. W. Heinrichs and G. Schoeler. Beirut-Stuttgart: Franz Steiner, 211–245.

———. 1995. "The Classification of the Sciences and the Consolidation of Philology in Classical Islam." In *Centers of Learning: Learning and Location in Pre-modern Europe and the Near East,* ed. J. W. Drijvers and A. A. MacDonald. Leiden: Brill, 120–139.

———. 1998. "Takhyīl." In *Encyclopaedia of Islam,* new ed. Leiden: Brill, 10: 129–132.

Hussein, Ali. 2004. "Classical and Modern Approaches in Dividing the Old Arabic Poem." *Journal of Arabic Literature* 35: 297–328.

Jacobi, Renate. 1970. "Dichtung und Lüge in der arabischen Literaturtheorie." *Der Islam* 49: 85–99.

———. 1991. "Mufaḍḍaliyyāt." In *Encyclopaedia of Islam,* new ed. Leiden: Brill, 7: 306–308.

Larkin, Margaret. 2005. "Abu Tammam." In *Dictionary of Literary Biography,* vol. 311, *Arabic Literary Culture, c. 500–925,* ed. S. Toorawa and M. Cooperson. Detroit: Thomson and Gale, 33–52.

Leder, Stefan. 1987. "Prosa-Dichtung in der *akhbār* Überlieferung. Narrative Analyse einer Satire." *Der Islam* 64: 6–41.

———. 1997. "al-Ṣūlī." *Encyclopaedia of Islam,* new ed. Leiden: Brill, 9: 846–848.

Leemhuis, Frederik. 2004. "Readings of the Qur'ān." In *Encyclopedia of the Qur'ān,* ed. J. D. McAuliffe, 5 vols. Leiden: Brill, 4: 353–363.

Lewin, Bernard. 1968. "Ibn al-Muʿtazz." In *Encyclopaedia of Islam,* new ed. Leiden: Brill, 3: 892–893.

Massignon, Louis. 1992. "Nawbakht." In *Encyclopaedia of Islam,* new ed. Leiden: Brill, 7: 1043–1044.

Motzki, Harald. 2001. "The Collection of the Qur'ān: A Reconsideration of Western Views in Light of Recent Methodological Developments." *Der Islam* 78: 1–34.

Musawi, Muhsin Jasim. In press. "The Medieval Islamic Republic of Letters." *Mamluk Studies.*

Najjār, Ibrāhīm. 1997. *Shuʿarāʾ ʿabbāsiyyūn mansiyyūn,* 2 pts. in 7 vols. Beirut: Dār al-Gharb al-Islāmī.

Nasser, Shady. 2013. *The Transmission of the Variant Readings of the Qur'ān: The Problem of Tawātur and the Emergence of Shawādhdh.* Leiden: Brill.

Neuwirth, Angelika. 1987. "Koran." In *Grundriß der arabischen Philologie,* vol. 2, *Literaturwissenschaft,* ed. H. Gätje. Wiesbaden; Harrassowitz, 96–135.

———. 1996. "Vom Rezitationstext über die Liturgie zum Kanon: Zu Entstehung und Wiederauflösung der Surenkomposition im Verlauf der Entwicklung eines islamischen Kultus." In *The Qur'ān as Text,* ed. S. Wild. Leiden: Brill, 69–105.

Nippel, Wilfried. 1997. "Philologenstreit und Schulpolitik: Zur Kontroverse zwischen Gottfried Hermann und August Böckh." In *Geschichtsdiskurs,* vol. 3, *Die Epoche der Historisierung,* ed. W. Küttler, J. Rüsen, and E. Schulin. Frankfurt a. M.: Fischer, 244–253.

Ouyang, Wen-Chin. 1997. *Literary Criticism in Medieval Arabic-Islamic Culture: The Making of a Tradition.* Edinburgh: Edinburgh University Press.

Pellat, Charles. 1987. "Mālik b. Dīnār." In *Encyclopaedia of Islam,* new ed. Leiden: Brill, 6: 266–267.

Pollock, Sheldon. 2009. "Future Philology? The Fate of a Soft Science in a Hard World." *Critical Inquiry* 35: 931–961.

Reinert, Benedikt. 1990. "Der Concetto-Stil in den islamischen Literaturen." In *Orientalisches Mittelalter,* ed. W. Heinrichs. Wiesbaden: Aula, 366–408.

Schoeler, Gregor. 1973. "Die Einteilung der Dichtung bei den Arabern." *Zeitschrift der Deutschen Morgenländischen Gesellschaft* 123: 9–55.

———. 1992. "Schreiben und Veröffentlichen. Zu Verwendung und Funktion der Schrift in den ersten islamischen Jahrhunderten." *Der Islam* 69: 1–43.

———. 2009. *The Genesis of Literature in Islam: From the Aural to the Read.* In collaboration with and trans. S. M. Toorawa. Edinburgh: Edinburgh University Press. Rev. ed. of Schoeler, *Écrire et transmettre dans les débuts de l'islam* (2002). Paris: Presses Universitaires de France.

———. 2010–11. "The Genres of Classical Arabic Poetry: Classifications of Poetic Themes and Poems by Pre-modern Critics and Redactors of *Dīwāns.*" *Quaderni di Studi Arabi* 5–6: 1–48.

Sezgin, Fuat. 1967. *Geschichte des arabischen Schrifttums.* Vol. 1. *Qur'ānwissenschaften, Ḥadīth, Geschichte, Fiqh, Dogmatik, Mystik bis 430 H.* Leiden: Brill.

———. 1975. *Geschichte des arabischen Schrifttums.* Vol. 2. *Poesie bis 430 H.* Leiden: Brill.

Sourdel, Dominique. 1968. "Ibn al-Djarrāḥ." In *Encyclopaedia of Islam,* new ed. Leiden: Brill, 3: 750.

Sperl, Stefan. 1989. *Mannerism in Arabic Poetry.* Cambridge: Cambridge University Press.

Stetkevych, Suzanne P. 1991. *Abū Tammām and the Poetics of the ʿAbbāsid Age.* Leiden: Brill.

Szondi, Peter. 1967. *Hölderlin-Studien. Mit einem Traktat über philologische Erkenntnis.* Frankfurt a. M.: Insel Verlag.

Troupeau, Gérard. 1962. "La grammaire à Bagdad du IX au XIIIe siècle." *Arabica* 9: 397–405.

van Gelder, Geert Jan. 2004. "Muḥdathūn." In *Encyclopaedia of Islam,* new ed. Leiden: Brill, Supplement, 637–640.

———. 2013. *Classical Arabic Literature: A Library of Arabic Literature Anthology.* New York: New York University Press.

Zolondek, Leon. 1961. "The Sources of the *Kitāb al-Aġānī.*" *Arabica* 8: 294–308.

Chapter 5

PRIMARY SOURCES

Aitareyabrāhmaṇa with the commentary of Ṣaḍguruśiṣya. 2 vols. Ed. Kasinathsastri Agase. Pune: Anandashrama, 1930–1977.

Amaruśataka with the commentary of Arjunavarmadeva. 3rd ed. Ed. Durgaprasad and Vasudeva Laxman Sastri Panasikar. Bombay: Niraya Sagar Press, 1916.

Apāṇinīyaprāmāṇyasādhana of Nārāyaṇa Bhaṭṭa. Ed. and trans. E. R. Sreekrishna Sarma. Tirupati: Sri Venkateswara University Oriental Research Institute, 1968.

Brāhmaṇasarvasvam of Halāyudha. Ed. Durgamohan Bhattacharyya. Calcutta: Sanskrit Sahitya Parisad, 1960.

Jñānadīpikā of Devabodha: *Ādiparvan.* Ed. R. N. Dandekar, Pune: Bhandarkar Oriental Research Institute, Poona, 1941; *Bhīṣmaparvan.* Ed. S. K. Belvalkar, 1947; *Sabhāparvan.* Ed. R. D. Karmarkar, 1949.

Kāmasūtra of Vātsyāyana with the *Jayamaṅgalabhāṣya.* Ed. Damodar Lal Gosvami. Varanasi: Chowkhambha Sanskrit Series Office, 1900.

Kumārasambhava of Kālidāsa with the commentaries of Aruṇagirinātha and Nārāyaṇapaṇḍita. 3 vols. Ed. T. Ganapati Sastri. Trivandrum: Travancore Government Press, 1913–1914. Trivandrum Sanskrit Series 27, 32, 36; with the commentary of Vallabhadeva. Ed. M. S. Narayana Murti. Wiesbaden: Steiner, 1980.

Mahābhārata with the *Bhāratabhāvadīpa* of Nīlakaṇṭha. 6 vols. Ed. Ramachandrashastri Kinjawadekar. Pune: Chitrashala Press, 1929–1933.

Mahābhāratatātparyanirṇaya with the commentary of Vādirājatīrtha. Ed. V. Prabhanjanacharya. Bangalore: Sri Vyasa Madhwa Seva Pratisthana, 1999.

Meghadūta of Kālidāsa with the commentary of Vallabhadeva. Ed. E. Hultzsch. London: Royal Asiatic Society, 1911; with the commentary of Mallinātha. Ed. K. Parab. Bombay: Nirnaya Sagar Press, 1902.

Mīmāṃsādarśanam. 6 vols. Ed. Vasudev Abhyankar. Pune: Anandashrama Press, 1970.

Ṛgbhāṣyam of Ānandatīrtha with the *Ṭīkā* of Jayatīrtha, the *Mantrārthamañjarī* of Rāghavendratīrtha, etc. Vol. 1. Ed. K. T. Pandurangi. Bangalore: Dvaita Vedanta Studies and Research Foundation, 1999.

Ṛgvedabhāṣya of Skandasvāmin (First Aṣṭaka). Ed. C. Kunhan Raja. Madras: University of Madras, 1935; with the commentary of Veṅkaṭamādhavārya. Ed. K. Sambasiva Sastri. Trivandrum: Government Press, 1929.

Śiṣupālavadha of Māgha with the commentary of Vallabhadeva. Ed. Ram Chandra Kaka and Harabhatta Shastri. Reprint, Delhi: Bharatiya Book Corporation, 1990.

Śṛṅgāraprakāśa of Bhoja. 2 vols. Ed. Rewaprasad Dwivedi. New Delhi: Indira Gandhi National Centre for the Arts, 2007.

SECONDARY SOURCES

Acharya, Diwakar. 2006. "A Brief Note on Harṣapāla's Commentary on the Prakrit Kāvya *Setubandha*." *Newsletter of the Nepal German Manuscript Conservation Project* 2: 2–4.

Auerbach, Erich. 1967. "Giambattista Vico und die Idee der Philologie." In *Gesammelte Aufsätze der Romanischen Philologie*. Bern: Francke, 233–241.

Balbir, Nalini. 2009. "Les lecteurs Jaina Śvetāmbara face à leur canon." In *Écrire et transmettre en Inde classique,* ed. G. Colas and G. Gerschheimer. Pondichery: École française d'extrême-orient, 43–62.

Bhattacharya, Ram Shankar. 1990. "Use of Manuscripts in Textual Criticism by Our Commentators." In *Sampādana ke Siddhānta aur Upādāna,* ed. V. V. Dwivedi et al. Sarnath, Varanasi: Central Institute of Higher Tibetan Studies, 219–228.

Bronner, Yigal, and Lawrence McCrea. 2012. "To Be or Not to Be Śisupāla." *Journal of the American Oriental Society* 132 (3): 427–455.

Busch, Allison. 2011. *Poetry of Kings: The Classical Hindi Literature of Mughal India.* New York: Oxford University Press.

Bynum, Caroline Walker. 1984. "Did the Twelfth Century Discover the Individual?" In *Jesus as Mother.* Berkeley: University of California Press, 82–109.

Canfora, Luciano. 2008. *Filologia e Libertà.* Milan: Mondadori.

Colas, Gérard. 1999. "The Criticism and Transmission of Texts in Classical India." *Diogenes* 47 (2): 30–43.

———. 2011. "Relecture des techniques de correction dans les manuscrits indiens." In *Lieux de Savoir 2: Les mains de l'intellect,* ed. C. Jacob. Paris: Albin Michel, 509–535.

Colas, Gérard, and Gerdi Gerschheimer, eds. 2009. *Écrire et transmettre en Inde classique.* Pondichery: École française d'extrême-orient.

Cox, Whitney. 2014. "Snakes versus Eagles: Vedāntadeśika as Polemical Philologist." In *Philological Encounters*. Berlin: Wissenschaftskolleg zu Berlin/Forum Transregionale Studien.

Cutler, Norman. 1992. "Interpreting *Tirukkuṟaḷ:* The Role of Commentary in the Creation of a Text." *Journal of the American Oriental Society* 112 (4): 549–566.

———. 2003. "Three Moments in Tamil Literary Culture." In *Literary Cultures in History: Reconstructions from South Asia,* ed. Sheldon Pollock. Berkeley: University of California Press, 271–322.

Dandekar, R. N. 1990. "Commentators of the *Ṛgveda:* A Recapitulation." *Bulletin of the Deccan College Post-graduate & Research Institute* 50: 157–168.

De, S. K. 1955. "Some Commentators on the *Meghadūta.*" *Our Heritage* 3 (1): 15–28.

D'Intino, Silvia. 2008. "Meaningful Mantras: The Introductory Portion of the *Ṛgvedabhāṣya* by Skandasvāmin." In *Śāstrārambha: Inquiries into the Preamble in Sanskrit,* ed. W. Slaje. Wiesbaden: Harrassowitz, 149–170.

Dodson, Michael. 2007. "Contesting Translations: Orientalism and the Interpretation of the Vedas." *Modern Intellectual History* 4 (1): 43–59.

Dundas, Paul. 1996. "Somnolent Sūtras: Scriptural Commentary in Śvetāmbara Jainism." *Journal of Indian Philosophy* 24 (1): 73–101.

Edgerton, Franklin, ed. 1944. *The Sabhāparvan.* Pune: Bhandarkar Oriental Research Institute.

Fisher, Elaine. 2013. "A New Public Theology: Sanskrit and the Religious Landscape of Early Modern South India." Ph.D. diss., Columbia University.

Galewicz, Cezary. 2009. *A Commentator in Service of the Empire: Sāyaṇa and the Royal Project of Commenting on the Whole of the Veda.* Vienna: Sammlung de Nobili, Institut für Südasien-, Tibet- und Buddhismuskunde der Universität Wien.

Gode, P. K. 1940. "Textual Criticism in the Thirteenth Century." In *Woolner Commemoration Volume (in memory of the late Dr. A. C. Woolner),* ed. Mohammad Shafi. Lahore: Mehar Chand Lachhman Das, 106–108.

Gonda, Jan. 1975. *Vedic Literature (Saṃhitas and Brāhmaṇas).* Wiesbaden: Harrassowitz.

Goodall, Dominic. 2001. "Bhute 'āha' iti pramādāt: Firm Evidence for the Direction of Change Where Certain Verses of the *Raghuvaṃśa* Are Variously Transmitted." *Zeitschrift der Deutschen Morgenländischen Gesellschaft* 151 (1): 103–124.

———. 2009. "Retracer la transmission des textes littéraires à l'aide des textes 'théoriques' de l'Alaṅkāraśāstra ancien." In *Écrire et transmettre en Inde classique,* ed. G. Colas and G. Gerschheimer. Pondichery: École française d'extrême-orient, 63–77.

Goodall, Dominic, and Harunaga Isaacson, eds. 2003. *The Raghupañcikā of Vallabhadeva, Being the Earliest Commentary on the Raghuvaṃśa of Kālidāsa.* Vol. 1 [all published]. Groningen: Egbert Forsten.

Griffiths, Paul. 1999. *Religious Reading.* New York: Oxford University Press.

Gune, P. D. 1927. "Sāyaṇa's Commentary: Its Composition." In *Sir Asutosh Mookerjee Silver Jubilee Volumes.* Calcutta: Calcutta University Press, 3:467–477.

Israel, Jonathan, ed. 2007. *Spinoza: Theological-Political Treatise.* Cambridge: Cambridge University Press.

Jaddipal, Virupaksa V., ed. 2008. *Kirātārjunīyam (Traisargikam): Nṛsiṃha-Prakāśavarṣa-Jonarājakṛtābhiḥ ṭīkābhiḥ vibhūṣitam.* Delhi: Amar Granth Publications.

Kaster, Robert. 2010. "Scholarship." In *The Oxford Handbook of Roman Studies,* ed. A. Barchiesi and W. Scheidel. Oxford: Oxford University Press, 492–504.

Kunhan Raja, C. 1930. "The Commentaries on Rigveda and Nirukta." *Proceedings and Transactions of the Fifth Indian Oriental Conference, Lahore,* vol. 1. London: Arthur Probsthain.

———. 1936. "The Chronology of the Vedabhāṣyakāras." *Journal of Oriental Research, Madras* 11: 256–268.

Lanman, Charles Rockwell, ed. 1891. *The Whitney Memorial Meeting.* Boston: Ginn.

McCrea, Lawrence. 2009. *The Teleology of Poetics in Medieval Kashmir.* Cambridge, Mass.: Harvard University, Dept. of Sanskrit and Indian Studies.

———. 2010. "Poetry in Chains: Commentary and Control in the Sanskrit Poetic Tradition." In *Language, Ritual and Poetics in Ancient India and Iran,* ed. D. Shulman. Jerusalem: Israel Academy of Sciences and Humanities, 231–248.

Minkowski, Christopher. 2005. "What Makes a Work 'Traditional'? On the Success of Nīlakaṇṭha's *Mahābhārata* Commentary." In *Boundaries, Dynamics and Construction of Traditions in South Asia,* ed. F. Squarcini. Florence: Firenze University Press, 179–206.

———. 2010. "I'll Wash Your Mouth Out with My Boot: A Guide to Philological Argument in Mughal-Era Banaras." In *Epic and Argument in Indian Sanskrit Literary History,* ed. Sheldon Pollock. Delhi: Manohar, 117–141.

Nance, Richard. 2011. *Speaking for Buddhas: Scriptural Commentary in Indian Buddhism.* New York: Columbia University Press.

National Museum of India. 1964. *Manuscripts from Indian Collections: Descriptive Catalogue.* New Delhi: National Museum.

Oertel, Hanns. 1930. *Zur indischen Apologetik.* Stuttgart: Kohlhammer.

Peterson, P. 1890. *Handbook to the Study of the Rigveda,* Pt. 1. Bombay: Government Central Book Depot.

Pollock, Sheldon. 1989. "The Idea of *Śāstra* in Traditional India." In *The Śāstric Tradition in the Indian Arts,* ed. A. L. Dallapiccola and S. Zingel-Avé Lallemant. Wiesbaden: Steiner, 17–26.

———. 2003. "Sanskrit Literature from the Inside Out." In *Literary Cultures in History: Reconstructions from South Asia,* ed. Sheldon Pollock. Berkeley: University of California Press, 39–130.

———. 2004a. "The Transformation of Culture-Power in Indo-Europe, 1000–1300." *Medieval Encounters* 10 (1–3): 247–278.

———. 2004b. "A New Philology: From Norm-Bound Practice to Practice-Bound Norm in Kannada Intellectual History." In *South-Indian Horizons: Felicitation Volume for François Gros,* ed. J.-L. Chevillard. Pondichery: Institut français de Pondichéry/École française d'extrême-orient, 389–406.

———. 2005. *The Ends of Man at the End of Premodernity.* Amsterdam: Royal Netherlands Academy of Arts and Sciences, Stichting J. Gonda-Fonds.

———. 2006. *The Language of the Gods in the World of Men: Sanskrit, Culture, and Power in Premodern India.* Berkeley: University of California Press.

———. 2009. "Future Philology? The Fate of a Soft Science in a Hard World." In *The Fate of the Disciplines,* ed. J. Chandler and A. Davidson. Special issue, *Critical Inquiry* 35 (4): 931–961.

———. 2010. "What Was Bhaṭṭa Nāyaka Saying? The Hermeneutical Transformation of Indian Aesthetics." In *Epic and Argument in Sanskrit Literary History,* ed. Sheldon Pollock. Delhi: Manohar, 143–184.

———. 2011. "The Languages of Science in Early Modern India." In *Forms of Knowledge in Early Modern South Asia,* ed. Sheldon Pollock. Durham, N.C.: Duke University Press, 19–48.

———. Forthcoming a. "Philology in Three Dimensions." *postmedieval* 5 (4).

———. Forthcoming b. *Reader on Rasa: An Historical Sourcebook in Classical Indian Aesthetics.* New York: Columbia University Press.

Preisendanz, Karen. 2008. "Text, Commentary, Annotation: Some Reflections on the Philosophical Genre." *Journal of Indian Philosophy* 36 (5–6): 599–618.

Quisinsky, M., and P. Walter, eds. 2007. *Kommentarkulturen: Die Auslegung zentraler Texte der Weltreligionen, ein vergleichender Überblick.* Cologne: Böhlau.

Raghavan, V. 1942. "Uḍāli's Commentary on the Rāmāyaṇa." *Annals of Oriental Research* 6 (2), Sanskrit sec., 1–4.

Richards, John. 1997. "Early Modern India and World History." *Journal of World History* 8 (2): 197–209.

Salomon, Richard. 2009. "The Fine Art of Forgery in India." In *Écrire et transmettre en Inde classique,* ed. G. Colas and G. Gerschheimer. Pondichery: École française d'extrême-orient, 107–134.

Sarup, Lakshman. 1946. "Mādhava, Son of Śrī Veṅkaṭārya, and Sāyaṇācārya." In *B. C. Law Volume,* vol. 2, ed. B. R. Bhandarkar. Pune: Bhandarkar Oriental Research Institute, 34–37.

Schoening, J. 1996. "Sūtra Commentaries in Tibetan Translation." In *Tibetan Literature: Studies in Genre,* ed. J. Cabezón and R. Jackson. Ithaca, N.Y.: Snow Lion, 111–124.

Skilling, Peter. 2001. "Vasubandhu and the Vyākhyāyukti Literature." *International Journal of Buddhist Studies* 23 (2): 297–350.

Slaje, Walter. 2007. "Der Sanskrit-Kommentar." In *Kommentarkulturen: Die Auslegung zentraler Texte der Weltreligionen, ein vergleichender Überblick.* ed. M. Quisinsky and P. Walter. Cologne: Böhlau, 69–97.

Snell, Bruno. 1960. *The Discovery of the Mind.* New York: Harper.

Tubb, Gary A., and Emery B. Boose. 2007. *Scholastic Sanskrit: A Manual for Students.* New York: American Institute of Buddhist Studies, Columbia University.

Unni, N. P. 1987. *Meghasandeśa of Kālidāsa.* Delhi: Bharatiya Vidya Prakashan.

von Hinüber, Oskar. 2007. "Buddhistische Kommentare aus dem alten Indien: Die Erklärung des Theravāda-Kanons." In *Kommentarkulturen: Die Auslegung zentraler Texte der Weltreligionen, ein vergleichender Überblick.* ed. M. Quisinsky and P. Walter. Cologne: Böhlau, 96–114.

Whitney, W. D. 1874. "The Translation of the Veda." In Whitney, *Oriental and Linguistic Studies, First Series.* New York: Scribner's, 100–132.

———. 1893. "The Native Commentary to the Atharva-Veda." In *Festgruss an Rudolf von Roth,* ed. E. Kuhn. Stuttgart: Kohlhammer, 89–96.

Woodside, Alexander. 2006. *Lost Modernities.* Cambridge, Mass.: Harvard University Press.

Chapter 6

Baibu congshu jicheng. 1965–68. Ed. Yan Yiping et al. Taibei: Yiwen yinshu guan.

Betti, Emilio. 1980. "Hermeneutics as the General Methodology of the *Geisteswissenschaften.*" In *Contemporary Hermeneutics: Hermeneutics as Method, Philosophy, and Critique.* London: Routledge, 51–94.

Bottéro, Françoise. 1996. *Sémantisme et classification dans l'écriture chinoise. Les systèmes de classement des caractères par clés du Shuowen jiezi au Kangxi zidian.* Paris: Instituts des Hautes Études chinoises.

———. 2004. "Chinese Characters versus Other Writing Systems: The Song Origin of the Distinction between 'Non-compound' Characters and 'Compound Characters.'" In *Meaning and Form: Essays in Pre-modern Chinese Grammar,* ed. Takashima Ken'ichi. Munich: Lincom, 1–16.

Chen, Junmin. 1986. *Zhang Zai zhexue sixiang ji qi guanxue xuepai* [Zhang Zai's philosophical thought and his Guanxue school]. Peking: Renmin chunbanshe.

Feuillas, Stéphane. 1996. "Rejoindre le ciel. Nature et morale dans le Zhengmeng de Zhang Zai." Ph.D. diss., Paris.

Friedrich, Michael, Michael Lackner, and Friedrich Reimann. 1996. *Chang Tsai. Rechtes Auflichten. Cheng meng. Übersetzt aus dem Chinesischen, mit Einleitung und Kommentar.* Hamburg: Meiner, xxxv.

Genette, Gérard. 1982. *Palimpsestes. La littérature au second degré.* Paris: Seuil.

Hamburger, Jeffrey F. 2009. "Haec figura demonstrat: Diagrams in an Early Thirteenth-Century Parisian Copy of Lothar de Segni's 'De missarum mysteriis.'" *Wiener Jahrbuch für Kunstgeschichte* Band LVIII *(Neue Forschungen zur Buchmalerei): 7–77.*

Hargett, James M. 2009. "Two Recently Published Histories on the Song Dynasty." *China Review International* 16 (3): 293–304.

Huang, Chün-chieh. 2001. *Mencian Hermeneutics: A History of Interpretations in China.* Piscataway, N.J.: Transaction.

Kristeva, Julia. 1980. *Desire in Language: A Semiotic Approach to Literature and Art.* New York: Columbia University Press.

Lackner, Michael. 1996. "La position d'une expression dans un texte: explorations diagrammatiques de la signification." *Extrême-Orient, Extrême.Occident* 18: 35–49.

———. 2000. "Was Millionen Wörter nicht sagen können: Diagramme zur Visualisierung klassischer Texte im China des 13. bis 14. Jahrhunderts." *Zeitschrift für Semiotik,* Band 22 (Heft 2): 209–237.

———. 2007. "Diagrams as an Architecture by Means of Words: The *Yanji tu.*" In *Graphics and Text in the Production of Technical Knowledge in China: The Warp and the Weft,* ed. Francesca Bray, Vera Dorofeeva-Lichtmann, and Georges Métailié. Leiden: Brill, 341–382.

———. 2011. "Les diagrammes d'analyse textuelle: une pratique savante de la tradition chinoise." In *Les lieux de savoir II. Les mains de l'intellect,* ed. Christian Jacob. Paris: Albin Michel, 824–844.

Ledderose, Lothar. 2001. *Ten Thousand Things: Module and Mass Production in Chinese Art.* Princeton, N.J.: Princeton University Press.

León-Portilla, Miguel. 1990. *Aztec Thought and Culture: A Study of the Ancient Nahuatl Mind.* Norman: University of Oklahoma Press.

Makeham, John. 1997. "The Earliest Extant Commentary on Lunyu: Lunyu Zheng shi zhu," *T'oung Pao,* 2nd ser., vol. 83, fasc. 4/5: 260–299.

———. 2003. *Transmitters and Creators: Chinese Commentators and Commentaries on the Analects.* Cambridge, Mass.: Harvard University Press.

Mou, Zongsan. 1971. *Zhide zhidue yu Zhongguo zhexue* [Intellectual intuition and Chinese philosophy]. Taibei: Xuesheng shuju.

Ommerborn, Wolfgang. 1996. *Die Einheit der Welt. Die Qi-Theorie des Neo-Konfuzianers Zhang Zai.* Bochum: Grüner.

Plaks, Andrew. 2004. *Ta Hsueh and Chung Yung: The Highest Order of Cultivation and On the Practice of the Mean.* London: Penguin Classics.

Smith, Kidder, Jr., Peter K. Bol, Joseph A. Adler, and Don J. Wyatt. 1990. *Sung Dynasty Uses of the I Ching.* Princeton, N.J.: Princeton University Press.

Steinfeld, Thomas. 2009. "Skepsis. Über August Böckh, die Wissenschaft der unendlichen Approximation und das Glück der mangelnden Vollendung." In *Was ist eine philologische Frage?,* ed. Jürgen Paul Schmidt. Frankfurt: Suhrkamp, 216–218.

Szondi, Peter. 1995. *Introduction to Literary Hermeneutics.* Cambridge: Cambridge University Press.

Tillman, Hoyt. 1992. *Confucian Discourse and Chu Hsi's Ascendancy.* Honolulu: University of Hawaii Press.

Wang, Bo. 1965–68. *Yanji tu* [Diagrams that explore the initial stages]. In *Baibu congshu jicheng,* ed. Yan Yiping et al. Taibei: Yiwen yinshu guan, No. 645.

Xu, Qian. 1965–68. *Du sishu congshuo* [Collected readings of the Four Books]. In *Baibu congshu jicheng,* ed. Yan Yiping et al. Taibei: Yiwen yinshu guan. No. 81.

Zhang, Zai. 1978. *Zhang Zai ji* [Collected works of Zhang Zai]. Peking: Zhonghua shuju.

Zhou, Chunjian. 2007. "Xu Qian yu Du sishu congshuo [Xu Qian and the 'Du sishu congshuo']." *Zhongguo dianji yu wenhua* 63 (4): 50–55.

Zhu, Xi. 1983. *Sishu zhangju jizhu* [Collected commentaries on chapters and paragraphs of the Four Books]. Peking: Zhonghua shuju.

———. 1985. *Zhuzi yulei* [Master Zhu's collected sayings]. Peking: Zhonghua shuju.

Chapter 7

Allen, Don Cameron. 1970. *Mysteriously Meant.* Baltimore: Johns Hopkins University Press.

Apianus, Petrus. 1540. *Astronomicum Caesareum.* Ingolstadt: Apianus.

Baron, Hans. 1988. *In Search of Florentine Civic Humanism.* 2 vols.. Princeton, N.J.: Princeton University Press.

Beazley, J. D. 1907. *Herodotus at the Zoo.* Oxford: Blackwell.

Bentley, Jerry. 1983. *Humanists and Holy Writ.* Princeton, N.J.: Princeton University Press.

Berosus, 1545. *Antiquitatum libri quinque.* Antwerp: Steelsius.

Bianca, Concetta. 1995. "La terza edizione moderna dei *Commentari* di Pio II." *Roma nel Rinascimento* 12: 5–16.

Biondo, Flavio. 2005. *Italy Illuminated.* Ed. and trans. Jeffrey White. Cambridge, Mass.: Harvard University Press.

Botley, Paul. 2004. *Latin Translation in the Renaissance.* Cambridge: Cambridge University Press.

Brown, Patricia. 1996. *Venice and Antiquity.* New Haven, Conn.: Yale University Press.

Bussi, Giovanni Andrea. 1978. *Prefazioni alle edizioni di Sweynheym e Pannartz prototipografi romani.* Ed. Massimo Miglio. Milan: Il polifilo.

Campanelli, Maurizio. 2001. *Polemiche e filologia ai primordi della stampa: Le Observationes di Domizio Calderini.* Rome: Storia e Letteratura.

Campano, Giannantonio. 1502. *Opera.* Venice.

Canfora, Davide. 2001. *La controversia di Poggio Bracciolini e Guarino Veronese su Cesare e Scipione.* Florence: Olschki.

Casciano, Paola. 1980. "Il ms. Angelicano 1097, fase preparatoria per l'edizione del Plinio di Sweynheym e Pannartz (Hain 13088)." In *Scrittura biblioteche e stampa a Roma nel Quattrocento: Aspetti e problemi, atti del seminario 1–2 giugno 1979,* ed. Concetta Bianca et al. Vatican City: Scuola Vaticana di paleografia, diplomatica e archivistica, 383–394.

Coltman, Viccy. 2006. *Fabricating the Antique: Neoclassicism in England, 1760–1800.* Chicago: University of Chicago Press, 13.

Cosenza, Mario, ed. and trans. 1910. *Petrarch's Letters to Classical Authors.* Chicago: University of Chicago Press, 4.

Curran, Brian. 2007. *The Egyptian Renaissance.* Chicago: University of Chicago Press.

Davies, Martin. 1999. *Aldus Manutius.* Tempe: Medieval and Renaissance Texts and Studies.

Decembrio, Angelo. 2002. *De politia litteraria.* Ed. Norbert Witten. Munich: Saur.

De Landtsheer, Jeanine. 2001. "Justus Lipsius *De militia Romana:* Polybius Revived or How an Ancient Historian Was Turned into a Manual of Early Modern Warfare." In *Recreating Ancient History,* ed. Karl Enenkel et al. Leiden: Brill, 101–122.

Donati, Gemma. 2000. *Pietro Odo da Montopoli e la biblioteca di Niccolò V con osservazioni sul "De* orthographia *di Tortelli."* Rome: Roma nel Rinascimento.

Dunkelgrun, Theodore. 2012. "The Multiplicity of Scripture." Ph.D. diss., University of Chicago.

Festus. 1471–72. *De verborum significatu*. Ed. Pomponio Leto. Rome: Georg Lauer.

Filetico, Martino. 2000. *In corruptores latinitatis*. Ed. Maria Agata Pincelli. Rome: Storia e Letteratura.

Franklin, Julian. 1963. *Jean Bodin and the Sixteenth-Century Revolution in the Methodology of Law and History*. New York: Columbia University Press.

Frazier, Alison. 2005. *Possible Lives*. New York: Columbia University Press.

Friedman, John Block. 1970. *Orpheus in the Middle Ages*. Cambridge, Mass.: Harvard University Press.

Fussner, F. Smith. 1962. *The Historical Revolution*. London: Routledge.

Gaissr, Julia. 1993. *Catullus and His Renaissance Readers*. Oxford: Clarendon.

———. 2008. *The Fortunes of Apuleius and the Golden Ass*. Princeton, N.J.: Princeton University Press.

Garin, E. 1988. *Ermetismo del Rinascimento*. Rome: Editori Riuniti.

Gilmore, Myron. 1963. *Humanists and Jurists*. Cambridge, Mass.: Harvard University Press.

Ginzburg, Carlo. 1999. *History, Rhetoric and Proof*. Hanover, N.H.: University Press of New England.

Grafton, Anthony. 1983–1993. *Joseph Scaliger*. 2 vols. Oxford: Clarendon.

———. 2007. *What Was History?* Cambridge: Cambridge University Press.

Grafton, Anthony, and Brian Curran. 1995. "A Fifteenth-Century Site Report on the Vatican Obelisk." *Journal of the Warburg and Courtauld Institutes* 58: 234–248.

Hall, Edwin. 1991. *Sweynheym and Pannartz and the Origins of Printing in Italy*. McMinnville, Ore.: Bird and Bull Press for Phillip J. Pirages.

Harth, H. 1967. "Niccolò Niccoli als literarischer Zensor: Untersuchungen zur Textgeschichte von Poggios 'De avaritia.'" *Rinascimento* NS 7: 29–53.

Haskell, Francis. 1993. *History and Its Images*. New Haven, Conn.: Yale University Press.

Jorink, Eric. 2006. *Het "boeck der natuere": Nederlandse geleerden en de wonderen van Gods Schepping, 1575–1715*. Leiden: Primavera Pers.

Kallendorf, Craig, ed. 2002. *Humanist Educational Treatises*. Cambridge, Mass.: Harvard University Press.

———. 2007. *The Other Virgil: "Pessimistic" Readings of the Aeneid in Early Modern Culture*. Oxford: Oxford University Press.

Kantorowicz, E. H. 1957. *The King's Two Bodies*. Princeton, N.J.: Princeton University Press.

Kelley, Donald. 1970. *Foundations of Modern Historical Scholarship*. New York: Columbia University Press.

Kenney, E. J. 1974. *The Classical Text*. Berkeley: University of California Press.

Kretzmann, Norman, et al., eds. 1982. *The Cambridge History of Later Medieval Philosophy*. Cambridge: Cambridge University Press.

Levine, Joseph. 1999. *The Autonomy of History*. Chicago: University of Chicago Press.

Linde, J. Cornelia. 2010. "Lorenzo Valla's Textual Criticism of Livy." *Neulateinisches Jahrbuch* 12: 191–224.

———. 2011. "Lorenzo Valla and the Authenticity of Sacred Texts." *Humanistica Lovaniensia* 60: 35–63.

———. 2012. *How to Correct the Sacra Scriptura? Textual Criticism of the Bible between the Twelfth and the Fifteenth Century.* Oxford: Society for the Study of Medieval Languages and Literatures.

Lowry, Martin. 1979. *The World of Aldus Manutius.* Oxford: Blackell.

Mandowsky, Erna, and Charles Mitchell. 1963. *Pirro Ligorio's Roman Antiquities* London: Warburg Institute.

Martinelli, Lucia Cesarini, and Alessandro Perosa, eds. 1996. *Le postille di Lorenzo Valla all' 'Institutio Oratoria' di Quintiliano.* Padua: Antenore.

McCuaig, William. 1989. *Carlo Sigonio.* Princeton, N.J.: Princeton University Press.

McLaughlin, Martin. 1995. *Literary Imitation in the Italian Renaissance: The Theory and Practice of Literary Imitation in Italy from Dante to Bembo.* Oxford: Clarendon Press.

Merrill, E. T. 1910. "On the Eight-Book Tradition of Pliny's Letters in Verona." *Classical Philology* 5: 175–188.

Miglio, Massimo, and Orietta Rossini, eds. 1997. *Gutenberg e Roma.* Naples: Electa Napoli.

Miller, Peter. 2007. *Momigliano and Antiquarianism.* Toronto: University of Toronto Press.

Minnis, Alastair. 1988. *Medieval Theory of Authorship: Scholastic Literary Attitudes in the Later Middle Ages.* 2nd ed. Philadelphia: University of Pennsylvania Press.

Minnis, Alastair, and A. B. Scott with David Wallace, eds. 1991. *Medieval Literary Theory and Criticism c. 1100–c. 1375.* Rev. ed. Oxford: Clarendon Press.

Momigliano, Arnaldo. 1950. "Ancient History and the Antiquarian." *Journal of the Warburg and Courtauld Institutes* 13: 285–315.

———. 1973. *Polybius between the English and the Turks.* Oxford: Blackwell.

Monfasani, John. 1988. "The First Call for Press Censorship: Niccolò Perotti, Giovanni Andrea Bussi, Antonio Moreto and the Editing of Pliny's *Natural History.*" *Renaissance Quarterly* 41: 1–31.

Mulsow, Martin. 2002. *Das Ende des Hermetismus.* Tübingen: Mohr Siebeck.

de Nolhac, Pierre. 1907. *Pétrarque et l'humanisme.* 2nd ed. Paris: Champion.

Ogilvie, R. M. 1964. *Latin and Greek: A History of the Influence of the Classics on English Life from 1600 to 1918.* London: Routledge.

Panofsky, Erwin. 1960. *Renaissance and Renascences in Western Art.* Copenhagen: Russak.

Patrizi, Francesco. 1560. *Della historia diece dialoghi.* Venice: Arrivabene.

Prins, Yopie. Forthcoming. *Ladies' Greek: Translations of Tragedy.* Princeton, N.J.: Princeton University Press.

Quillen, Carol. 1998. *Rereading the Renaissance: Petrarch, Augustine, and the Language of Humanism.* Ann Arbor: University of Michigan Press.

Refe, Laura, ed. 2004. *Le postille del Petrarca a Giuseppe Flavio.* Codice Parigino Lat. 5054. Florence: Le lettere.

Reynolds, L. D., and N. G. Wilson. 1991. *Scribes and Scholars.* 3rd ed. Oxford: Clarendon Press.

Rhenanus, Beatus. 1551. *Rerum germanicarum libri III.* Basel: Froben and Episcopius.

Rizzo, Silvia. 1973. *Il lessico filologico degli umanisti.* Rome: Storia e Letteratura.

Rossi, Paolo. 1984. *The Dark Abyss of Time.* Trans. Lydia Cochrane. Chicago: University of Chicago Press.

Rowland, Ingrid. 1998. *The Culture of the High Renaissance: Ancients and Moderns in Sixteenth-Century Rome.* Cambridge: Cambridge University Press.

Scalamonti, Francesco. 1996. *Vita Kyriaci Anconitani.* Ed. and trans. Charles Mitchell and Edward Bodnar. Philadelphia: American Philosophical Society.

Scaliger, Joseph. 1598. *De emendatione temporum,* 2nd ed. Leiden: Plantin-Raphelengius.

Schwarz, W. 1955. *Principles and Problems of Biblical Translation.* Cambridge: Cambridge University Press.

Shewan, Alexander. 1911. *Homeric Games at an Ancient St. Andrews.* Edinburgh: J. Thin.

Siraisi, Nancy. 1981. *Taddeo Alderotti and His Pupils.* Princeton, N.J.: Princeton University Press.

———. 1987. *Avicenna in Renaissance Italy.* Princeton, N.J.: Princeton University Press.

———. 1990. *Medieval and Early Renaissance Medicine.* Chicago: University of Chicago Press.

Smalley, Beryl. 1960. *English Friars and Antiquity in the Early Fourteenth Century.* Oxford: Blackwell.

Smith, Christine. 1992. *Architecture in the Culture of Early Humanism.* Oxford: Oxford University Press.

Stenhouse, William. 2005. *Reading Inscriptions and Writing Ancient History.* London: Institute of Classical Studies.

Stray, Christopher, ed. 2007. *Oxford Classics: Teaching and Learning, 1800–2000.* London: Duckworth.

Ullman, B. L. 1955. *Studies in the Italian Renaissance.* Rome: Storia e Letteratura, 1955.

———. 1960. *The Origin and Development of Humanistic Script.* Rome: Storia e Letteratura.

———. 1963. *The Humanism of Coluccio Salutati.* Padua: Antenore.

Valla, Lorenzo. 2007. *On the Donation of Constantine.* Trans. G. W. Bowersock. Cambridge, Mass.: Harvard University Press.

Varro. 1471–72. *De lingua latina,* ed. Pomponio Leto. Rome, Georg Lauer.

Vat. Lat. 1595.

Vat. Lat. 1660.

Wallbank, M. V. 1979. "Eighteenth-Century Public Schools and the Education of the Governing Elite." *History of Education* 8: 5.

Weiss, Roberto. 1988. *The Renaissance Discovery of Classical Antiquity,* 2nd ed. Oxford: Blackwell.

Weststeijn, Thisjs. 2007. "Spinoza Sinicus: An Asian Paragraph in the History of the Radical Enlightenment." *Journal of the History of Ideas* 68: 537–561.

Chapter 8

ʿAbd al-Laṭīf. *Dībācha/Mirʾāt al-Mathnavī/Mathnavī–i Mawlavī.* Library of the Majlis-i Shūrā-yi Millī, Tehran, Ms. 5261/66809.

———. 1886. *Laṭāyif al-Maʿnavī min Ḥaqāyiq al-Mathnavī.* Kanpur: Naval Kishore Press.

———. India Office Library, London, Ms. 1101/I.O. Islamic 382.

———. 1887. *Laṭāyif al-Ḥaqāyiq min Nafāyis al-Daqāyiq* [Sublime Truths of the Refined Subtleties]. Lucknow: Naval Kishore Press.

———. [1876] 1905. *Laṭāyif al-Lughat.* Lucknow: Naval Kishore Press.

———. *Nuskha-i Nāsikha,* Maulana Azad Library, Aligarh, Aligarh Muslim University Ms., Subhanallah Collection, No. 5514–54/891; Raza Library, Rampur, India, Ms. no. 2005/04, New ACC, 432; Library of the Majlis-i Shūrā-yi Millī, Tehran, Ms. 5261/66809.

Abū l-Faḍl. 1896. *Inshā-yi Abū l-Faḍl.* Vol. 1. Lucknow: Naval Kishore Press.

———. 1920. *Inshā-yi Abū l-Faḍl.* Vol. 3. Lahore: Taj Book Depot.

———. 2002. *The Akbarnama of Abu-l-Fazl.* Trans. H. Beveridge. Delhi: Low Price Publications.

Afshār, Īraj, et al. 1989. *Fihrist-i Kitābkhāna-i Majlis-i Shūrā-yi Millī.* Tehran: Chāpkhānah-i Majlis, Volume 16, No. 5261.

Ahmad, Nazir. 2002. *Maqālāt-i Nadhīr.* New Delhi: Ghalib Institute.

Ahmad, Nazir, and Kabir Jayasi. 2004. *Qand-i Pārsī.* Vol. 2. Ed. Sayyid Ḥasan ʿAbbās. Tehran: Bunyād-i Mawqūfāt-i Duktūr Maḥmūd Afshār Yazdī, 44–62.

Ahmed, Tariq. 1982. *Religio-Political Ferment in the N.W. Frontier during the Mughal Period.* Delhi: Idarah-i Adabiyat-i Delli.

Ahuja, N. D. 1967. "Abd al-Latîf al-'Abbâsî and His Account of Punjab." *Islamic Culture* 41 (2): 93–98.

———. 1973. "An Indian Memoirist, Traveller, Epistologist and Commentator of Mughal Period (17th Century)." *Punjab University Research Bulletin* 4 (1) (April): 147–172.

Akbarābādī, Valī Muḥammad. 2004. *Mathnavī–i Mawlavī mawsūm ba Makhzan al-Asrār.* Vols. 1 and 3. Ed. Najīb Māyil Haravī. Tehran: Qaṭra.

Akber, Muhammad Siddiq. 1970. "Khidmāt-i Mullā ʿAbd al-Laṭīf ʿAbbāsī Gujarātī dar Tatabbuʿāt-i Mathnavī-i Mawlānā Jalāl al-Dīn Muḥammad Rūmī." Ph.D. diss., University of Punjab.

Alam, Muzaffar. 2011. "The Debate Within: A Sufi Critique of Religious Law, Tasawwuf and Politics in Mughal India." In *Religious Cultures in Early Modern India: New Perspectives,* ed. Rosalind O'Hanlon and David Washbrook, London: Routledge, 8–39.

Alavi, Seema. 2008. *Islam and Healing. The Loss and Recovery of Indo-Muslim Medicine: A History and Its Legacy, 1650–1900.* New Delhi: Permanent Black and Palgrave MacMillan.

Ali, M. Athar. 1985. *The Apparatus of Empire: Awards of Ranks, Offices and Titles to the Mughal Nobility, 1574–1658.* Delhi: Oxford University Press.

———. 1997. *The Mughal Nobility under Aurangzeb.* Delhi: Oxford University Press.

Ali, Sayyid Akbar. 1957. "Life and Works of ʿAbd-al-Latif ʿAbbasi of Gujarat." *Islamic Culture* 31 (1) (January): 39–54.

Ansari, N. H. 1985. "Lata'if al Lughāt." In *The Growth of Indo-Persian Literature in Gujarat,* ed. M. H. Siddiqui. Baroda: University of Baroda, 32–45.

Beale, Thomas William. 1894. *An Oriental Biographical Dictionary.* Rev. Henry George Keene. London: W. H. Allen.

Blochmann, H. 1868. "Contributions to Persian Lexicography." *Journal of the Asiatic Society of Bengal* 37, Pt. 1: 32–72.

Bürgel, J. C. 1988. *The Feather of Simurgh: The "Licit Magic" of the Arts in Medieval Islam.* New York: New York University Press.

———. 1994. " 'Speech Is a Ship and Meaning the Sea': Some Formal Aspects in the *Ghazal* Poetry of Rūmī." In *Poetry and Mysticism in Islam,* ed. Amin Banani et al. Cambridge: Cambridge University Press, 44–69.

De Bruijn, J. T. P. 1983. *Of Piety and Poetry: The Interaction of Religion and Literature in the Life and Works of Ḥakīm Sanāʾī of Ghazna.* Leiden: E. J. Brill.

Desai, Z. A. 1985. "A 17th-Century Persian Littérateur and Islamic Scholar of Gujarat." In *The Growth of Persian Literature in Gujarat,* ed. M. H. Siddiqi. Baroda: University of Baroda, 11–20.

———. 1999. "A Foreign Dignitary's Ceremonial Visit to Akbar's Tomb: A First-Hand Account." In *Akbar and His Age,* ed. Iqtidar Alam Khan. New Delhi: Northern Book Centre and Indian Council of Historical Research, 188–197.

Ethé, Hermann. 1937. *Catalogue of Persian Manuscripts in the India Office Library.* Rev. and completed by Edward Edwards. Oxford: Clarendon Press.

Gabbay, Alyssa. 2010. *Islamic Tolerance: Amir Khusraw and Pluralism.* London: Routledge.

Groff, Peter, and Oliver Leaman. 2007. *Islamic Philosophy A–Z.* Edinburgh: Edinburgh University Press.

Gulchīn-i Maʿānī, Aḥmad. 1990. *Kārvān-i Hind.* Mashhad, Iran: Āstān-i Quds-i Riḍavī.

Habib, Irfan. 1999. *The Agrarian System of Mughal India, 1556–1707.* Rev. ed. Delhi: Oxford University Press.

Hadi, Nabi. 1995. *Dictionary of Indo-Persian Literature.* New Delhi: Indira Gandhi National Centre for the Arts.

Hamadānī, Muḥammad Ṣādiq. 1988. *Kalimāt al-Ṣādiqīn.* Ed. M. Salīm Akhtar. Lahore: Intishārāt al-Quraysh.

Hanaway, William L. 1998. "Classical Persian Literature." *Iranian Studies* 31 (3–4) (Summer/Fall): 543–559.

Haravī, Qāṭiʿī. 1979. *Majmaʿ al-Shuʿarā-i Jahāngīrshāhī.* Ed. Muhammad Saleem Akhtar. Karachi: Institute of Central and West Asian Studies, University of Karachi.

Husain, Qazi Sajjad, ed. and trans. 1974. *Mathnavī-i Mawlānā-yi Rūm.* Delhi: Sabrang Kitab Ghar.

Ivanow, Wladimir. 1924. *Concise Descriptive Catalogue of the Persian Manuscripts in the Collection of the Asiatic Society of Bengal.* Calcutta: Asiatic Society of Bengal.

Kambūh, Muḥammad Ṣāliḥ. 1967–72 *Shāh Jahān Nāma.* Ed. Ghulam Yazdani and Waheed Quraishi. 3 vols. Vol 1. Lahore: Majlis-i Taraqqī-i Adab.

Khāfī Khān, Muḥammad Hāshim. 1868–74. *The Muntakhab al-Lubāb of Khāfī Khān.* 3 vols. Vol. 2. Calcutta: Asiatic Society.

Khan, Alim Ashraf. 2001. *Shaykh ʿAbd al-Ḥaqq Muḥaddith Dihlavī: Ḥayāt va ʿilmī khidmāt.* Delhi: Islamic Wonders Bureau.

Khatoon, Rehana. 2007. "ʿAbd al-Laṭīf ʿAbbāsī Gujarāti awr Masnavī-i Mawlānā-i Rūm." Unpublished article courtesy of the author.

Kinra, Rajeev. 2011a. "Make It Fresh: Time, Tradition, and Indo-Persian Literary Modernity." In *Time, History, and the Religious Imaginary in South Asia,* ed. Anne C. Murphy. London: Routledge, 12–39.

———. 2011b. "This Noble Science: Indo-Persian Comparative Philology, c. 1000–1800." In *South Asian Texts in History: Critical Engagements with Sheldon Pollock,* ed. Yigal Bronner, Whitney Cox, and Lawrence McCrea. Ann Arbor, Mich.: Association for Asian Studies, 359–385.

Lāhawrī, ʿAbd al-Ḥamīd. 1865–72. *Bádsháh Námah.* 2 vols. Vol. 1. Calcutta: Asiatic Society.

Lāhawrī, Khalīlallāh ibn Fatḥallāh Ḥārithī Yamanī. *Safīna-i Baḥr al-Muḥīṭ.* Staatbibliothek, Berlin, Ms. Orient. Fol. 248.

Lāhawrī, Muḥammad Riḍā. 2002. *Mukāshafāt-i Riḍavī dar Sharḥ-i Mathnavī-i Maʿnavī.* Ed. Riḍā Rūḥānī. Tehran: Surūsh.

Lewis, Franklin. 2000. *Rūmī: Past and Present, East and West.* Oxford: Oneworld.

Losensky, Paul. 1998. *Welcoming Fighani: Imitation and Poetic Individuality in Safavid-Mughal Ghazal.* Costa Mesa, Calif.: Mazda.

Melville, Charles. 1998. "Hamd Allah Mustawfi's *Zafarnamah* and the Historiography of the Late Ilkanid Period." In *Iran and Iranian Studies: Essays in Honor of Iraj Afshar,* ed. Kambiz Eslami. Princeton, N.J.: Zagros, 1–12.

Motlagh, Khaleghi, and T. Lentz. 1989. "Bāysonḡorī *Šāh-nāma.*" In *Encyclopaedia Iranica,* online ed., www.iranicaonline.org/articles/baysongori-sah-nama.

Mudarris Raḍavī, Muḥammad Taqī. 1965. *Taʿlīqāt-i Ḥadīqat al-ḥaqīqa, mushtamil bar āyāt, aḥādīth, maʾākhidh-i qiṣaṣ va tamthīlāt va kalimāt-i mashāyikh, bi-inḍimām-i tafsīr va tawḍīḥ-i abyāt-i mushkila.* Tehran: Muʾassasah-i Maṭbūʿātī-i ʿIlmī.

Munami, Shamim. 2008. "Ṣūba-i Bihār: Qadīm-tarīn dildāda-i Mawlānā Rūm" [Bihar: The earliest admirers of Mawlana rum]. In *Rūmī and His Message,* ed. Imtiyaz Ahmad. Patna: Khuda Baksh Oriental Public Library, 18–25.

Mustawfī, Ḥamdallāh. 2001. *Ẓafarnāma.* Ed. Mahdī Madāyinī. Tehran: Pizhūhishgāh-i ʿUlūm-i Insānī va Muṭālaʿāt-i Farhangī.

Nizami, K. A. 1950. "Shattari Saints and Their Attitude towards the State." *Medieval India Quarterly* 1 (2): 56–70.

———. 1964. *Ḥayāt-i Shaykh ʿAbd al-Ḥaqq Muḥaddith Dihlavī.* Dihlī: Nadvat al-Muṣannifīn.

O'Hanlon, Rosalind, and David Washbrook. 2011. *Religious Cultures in Early Modern India: New Perspectives.* London: Routledge.

Pertsch, Wilhem. 1888. *Verzeichniss der persischen Handschriften der Königlichen Bibliothek zu Berlin.* Handschriften-verzeichnisse der Königlichen Bibliothek 4. Berlin: A. Asher.

Pūrjavādī, Naṣrallāh, and Nuṣratallāh Rastgār. 1999. Introduction to *Ẓafarnāma-i Ḥamdallāh Mustawfī: Bah inḍimām-i Shāhnāma-i Abū l-Qāsim Firdawsī (bah taṣḥīḥ-i Ḥamdallāh Mustawfī): Chāp-i ʻaksī az rū-yi nuskha-ʼi khaṭṭī-i muvarrakh-i 807 Hijrī dar Kitābkhāna-ʼi Birītāniyā (Or. 2833).* Facsimile ed. of the British Library manuscript of Mustawfi's Zafarnamah together with Mustawfi's edition of Shahnamah. Tehran: Markaz-i Nashr-i Dānishgāhī.

Rieu, Charles. 1966. *Catalogue of the Persian Manuscripts in the British Museum.* Vol. 2. London: Trustees of the British Museum.

Rizvi, S. A. A. 1978–1983. *History of Sufism*, 2 vols. Delhi: Munshiram Manoharlal.

Rosenthal, Franz. 1947. *The Technique and Approach of Muslim Scholarship.* Analecta Orientalia 24. Roma: Pontificium Institutum Biblicum.

Rūmī, Jalāl al-Dīn. 1925–1940. *The Mathnawi of Jalalu'ddin Rūmī.* Ed. with critical notes, translation, and commentary, by Reynold A. Nicholson from the oldest manuscripts available. 8 vols. Leiden: E. J. Brill.

———. 1974. *Mathnavī-i Mawlānā-yi Rūm.* Ed. and trans. Qazi Sajjad Husain. Delhi: Sabrang Kitab Ghar.

———. 1990. *Mathnavī*. Muqaddama va taḥlīl, taṣḥīḥ-i matn bar asās-i nuskha-hā-yi zamān-i Mawlānā va nazdīk ba zamān-i ū, muqāyasa bā chāphā-yi maʻrūf-i Masthnavī, tawḍīḥāt va taʻlīqāt-i jāmiʻ va fihrist-hā az Muḥammad Istiʻlāmī. 2nd ed. Tehran: Kitābfurūshī-i Zavvār.

———. 2004. *The Masnavi, Book One.* Trans. with introduction and notes by Jawid Mojaddedi. Oxford: Oxford University Press.

———. 2007. *The Masnavi, Book Two.* Trans. with introduction and notes by Jawid Mojaddedi. Oxford: Oxford University Press.

———. N.d. *Mathnavī.* Online Persian text based on the DVD ed. of A. Surūsh, based on the Konya manuscript. Kitāb-khānah-yi āzād-i Fārsī. http://rira.ir/rira/php/?page=view&mod=classicpoems&obj=book&id=50&ord=1.

Sachau, Eduard, and Hermann Ethe. 1889–1954. *Catalogue of Persian, Turkish, Hindustani and Pushtu Manuscripts in Bodleian Library.* 3 vols. Vol. 1. Oxford: Clarendon Press.

Sarkar, Jadunath. 1919. "Travels in Bihar, 1608 A.D." *Journal of the Bihar and Orissa Research Society* 5 (4): 597–603.

———. 1928. "A Description of North Bengal in 1609 A.D." *Bengal Past and Present* 41 (69–70): 143–146.

Schimmel, Annemarie. 1992. *A Two-Colored Brocade: The Imagery of Persian Poetry.* Chapel Hill: University of North Carolina Press.

Şerif b. Seyyid Mehmed b. Şeyh Burhan. 1961. *Miftāh al-Jafr.* Topkapı Sarayı Müzesi Kütüphanesi türkçe Yazmalar Kataloğu, Fehmi Edhem Karatay. Istanbul: Topkapi Sarayi Müzesi.

Shahrastānī, Muḥammad ibn ʻAbd al-Karīm. 1984. *Muslim Sects and Divisions.* Trans. A. K. Kazi and J. G. Flynn. London: Kegan Paul International.

Sharma, Sunil. 2005. *Amir Khusraw: The Poet of Sultans and Sufis.* Oxford: Oneworld.

Shekhar, Chander. 1989. "The Critical Study of the *Mathnawi*s of Amir Khusrau Dehlavi." Ph.D. diss., Department of Persian, University of Delhi.

Stephenson, J., trans. 1911. *The First Book of the Ḥadīqatu' l-ḥaqīqat; Or, The Enclosed Garden of the Truth, of the Ḥakīm Abū' l-Majd Majdūd Sanā'ī of Ghazna.* Calcutta: Baptist Mission Press.

Storey, C. A. 1953. *Persian Literature: A Bio-Bibliographical Survey.* Vol. 1, pt. 2. London: Luzac.

Watt, William Montgomery. 1985. *Islamic Philosophy and Theology.* Edinburgh: Edinburgh University Press.

Winter, Tim, ed. 2008. *The Cambridge Companion to Classical Islamic Theology.* Cambridge: Cambridge University Press.

Chapter 9

Ahmed, Shahab, and Nenad Filipovic. 2004. "The Sultan's Syllabus: A Curriculum for the Ottoman Imperial *Medreses* Prescribed in a *Fermān* of Qānūnī I Süleymān, Dated 973 (1565)." *Studia Islamica* 98/99: 183–218.

ʿĀmilī, Zayn al-Dīn. [1547] 2006. *Munyat al-murīd fī adab al-mufīd wa l-mustafīd.* Ed. Riḍā al-Mukhtārī. Beirut: Dār al-Amīrah.

Berkes, Niyazi. 1964. *The Development of Secularism in Turkey.* Montreal: McGill University Press.

Berkey, Jonathan. 1988. *The Transmission of Knowledge in Medieval Cairo: A Social History of Islamic Education.* Princeton, N.J.: Princeton University Press.

Būrsalī, Meḥmed Ṭāhir. 1914–28. *ʿOsmānlī Müellifleri.* Istanbul: Maṭbaʿa-yi ʿĀmire.

Chamberlain, Michael. 1994. *Knowledge and Social Practice in Medieval Damascus, 1190–1350.* Cambridge: Cambridge University Press.

Efendī, ʿAbd ül-Raḥīm. 1656. *Ajwibah ʿan tisʿ masā'il.* MS, Princeton University Library, Princeton, N.J., Yahuda 4070, fols. 18b–39a.

Eickelman, Dale F. 1985. *Knowledge and Power in Morocco: The Education of a Twentieth-Century Notable.* Princeton, N.J.: Princeton University Press.

Elder, Earl Edgar. 1950. *A Commentary on the Creed of Islam: Saʿd al-Dīn al-Tāftāzānī on the Creed of Najm al-Dīn al-Nasafī.* New York: Columbia University Press.

Elman, Benjamin A. 2001. *From Philosophy to Philology: Intellectual and Social Aspects of Change in Late Imperial China.* UCLA Asian Pacific Monograph Series. Los Angeles: UCLA International Institute.

El-Rouayheb, Khaled. 2004. "Sunni Muslim Scholars on the Status of Logic, 1500–1800." *Islamic Law and Society* 11: 213–232.

———. 2008. "The Myth of 'The Triumph of Fanaticism' in the Seventeenth-Century Ottoman Empire." *Die Welt des Islams* 48: 196–221.

Ephrat, Daphna. 2000. *A Learned Society in a Period of Transition: The Sunnī ʿUlama' of Eleventh-Century Baghdad.* New York: State University of New York Press.

Ghazālī, Abū Ḥāmid. [1111] 1937. *Al-Mustaṣfā min ʿilm al-uṣūl.* Cairo: al-Maṭbaʿah al-Tijāriyyah al-Kubrā, 1937.

———. [1111] 1967. *Iḥyāʿ ʿulūm al-dīn.* Cairo: Mu'assasat al-Ḥalabī, 1967.

Ghazzī, Badr al-Dīn. [1526] 2006. *al-Durr al-naḍīd fī adab al-mufīd wa l-mustafīd.* Ed. Nash'at al-Miṣrī. Giza: Maktabat al-Taw'iyah al-Islāmiyyah.

Gruendler, Beatrice. 2013. "Les versions de *Kalila wa-Dimna:* Une transmission et une circulation mouvantes." In *Énoncés sapientiels et littérature exemplaire: Une intertextualité complexe,* ed. M. Ortola. Nancy: Éditions Universitaires de Lorraine, 385–416.

Grunebaum, Gustav von, and Theodora M. Abel. 1947. *Az-Zarnūjī's Instruction of the Student: The Method of Learning.* New York: King's Crown Press.

Hallaq, Wael. 1990. "Logic, Formal Arguments and Formalization of Arguments in Sunni Jurisprudence." *Arabica* 87: 315–358.

Hirschler, Konrad. 2012. *The Written Word in the Medieval Arab Lands.* Edinburgh: Edinburgh University Press.

Hourani, Albert. 1962. *Arabic Thought in the Liberal Age 1798–1939.* Cambridge: Cambridge University Press.

———. 1981. *The Emergence of the Modern Middle East.* Berkeley: University of California Press.

Huff, Toby. 1993. *The Rise of Early Modern Science: Islam, China, and the West.* Cambridge: Cambridge University Press.

Ibn Jamā'ah, Badr al-Dīn. [1273] 2008. *Tadhkirat al-sāmi' wa l-mutakallim fī adab al-'ālim wa l-muta'allim.* Ed. Muḥammad al-'Ajamī. Beirut: Dār al-Bashā'ir al-Islāmiyyah, 2008.

Ḳara Ḫalīl. [1694] 1871. *al-Risālah al-'awniyyah fī īḍāḥ al-ḥāshiyah al-Ṣadriyyah.* Istanbul: al-Maṭba'ah al-'āmirah.

Khiyārī, Ibrāhīm. [1672] 1969. *Tuḥfat al-udabā' wa salwat al-ghurabā'.* Ed. Rajā' Maḥmūd al-Sāmarrā'ī. Baghdad: Wizārat al-Thaqāfah.

Klein, Denise. 2007. *Die osmanischen Ulema des 17. Jahrhunderts. Eine geschlossene Gesellschaft?* Berlin: Klaus Schwartz Verlag.

Kramers, Johannes Hendrick. 1993. "Münedjdjim Bashi." In *Encyclopaedia of Islam,* 2nd ed. Brill: Leiden, 7:572.

Lewis, Bernard. 1961. *The Emergence of Modern Turkey.* London: Oxford University Press.

Lowry, Joseph, and Devin Stewart. 2009. Introduction to *Essays in Arabic Literary Biography, 1350–1850,* ed. J. E. Lowry and D. J. Stewart. Wiesbaden: Harrassowitz Verlag, 1–12.

Messick, Brinkley. 1993. *The Calligraphic State: Textual Domination and History in a Muslim Society.* Berkeley: University of California Press.

Metcalf, Barbara. 1978. "The Madrasa at Deoband: A Model for Religious Education in Modern India." *Modern Asian Studies* 12: 111–134.

Müneccimbaşī, Aḥmed b. Lütfullāh. 1691a. *Fayḍ al-ḥaram fī ādāb al-muṭāla'ah.* MS, Süleymaniye Kütüphanesi, Istanbul, Laleli 3034, fols. 160b–188b.

———. 1691b. *Fayḍ al-ḥaram fī ādāb al-muṭāla'ah.* MS, Süleymaniye Kütüphanesi, Istanbul, Nafiz Paşa 1350, fols. 1b–22a.

Musawi, Muhsin. 2007. "Abbasid Popular Narrative: The Formation of Readership and Cultural Production." *Journal of Arabic Literature* 38: 261–292.

Nauert, Charles G. 2006. *Humanism and the Culture of Renaissance Europe*. Cambridge: Cambridge University Press.

Reichmuth, Stefan. 2004. "Bildungskanon und Bildungreform aus der Sicht eines islamischen Gelehrten der Anatolischen Provinz: Muḥammad al-Sajaqlī (Saçaqlızāde, gest. um 1145/1733) und sein *Tartīb al-ʿulūm*." In *Words, Texts and Concepts Cruising the Mediterranean Sea,* ed. R. Arnzen and J. Thielmann. Leuven: Peeters, 493–522.

———. 2009. *The World of Murtaḍā al-Zabīdī (1732–1791): Life, Networks and Writings*. Oxford: Gibb Memorial Trust.

Repp, Richard Cooper. 1986. *The Müfti of Istanbul: A Study in the Development of the Ottoman Learned Hierarchy*. London: Ithaca Press.

Rosenthal, Franz. 1947. *The Technique and Approach of Muslim Scholarship*. Rome: Pontificium Institutum Biblicum.

———. 1970. *Knowledge Triumphant: The Concept of Knowledge in Medieval Islam*. Leiden: E. J. Brill.

Sāçaḳlīzāde, Meḥmed Marʿaşī. [1716] 1988. *Tartīb al-ʿulūm*. Ed. Muḥammad al-Sayyid Aḥmad. Beirut: Dār al-Bashāʾir al-Islāmiyyah.

Sanūsī, Muḥammad b. Yūsuf. [1490] 1899. *ʿUmdat ahl al-tawfīq wa l-tasdīd bi-sharḥ ʿAqīdat ahl al-tawḥīd*. Cairo: Jarīdat al-Islām.

Şeyḫī, Meḥmed. [1724] 1989. Veḳāyiʿü l-fużalāʾ. In *Şeḳaʾiḳ-i Nuʿmaniye ve Zeyilleri*. Istanbul: Çağrı Yayınları.

Spevack, Aaron. 2010. "Apples and Oranges: The Logic of the Early and Later Arabic Logicians." *Islamic Law and Society* 17: 159–184.

Taftāzānī, Saʿd al-Dīn. [1390] 1974. *Sharḥ al-ʿAqāʾid al-Nasafiyyah*. Ed. Klūd Salāmah. Damascus: Wizārat al-Thaqāfah.

Ṭāşköprüzāde, Aḥmed. [1542] 1968. *Miftāḥ al-saʿādah wa miṣbāḥ al-siyādah*. Ed. Kāmil Kāmil Bakrī and ʿAbd al-Wahhāb Abū l-Nūr. Cairo: Dār al-Kutub al-Ḥadīthah.

Touati, Houari. 2007. "Pour une histoire de la lecture au Moyen Âge musulman: A propos des livres d'histoire." *Studia Islamica* 104/105: 11–44.

Ṭūsī, Naṣīr al-Dīn. [1274] 1957–58. *Sharḥ al-Ishārāt wa l-tanbīhāt*. Tehran: Maṭbaʿat al-Ḥaydarī.

Uğur, Ali. 1986. *The Ottoman ʿUlemā in the mid-17th Century: An Analysis of the Vaḳāʾiʿü'l-Fużalā of Meḥmed Şeyḫī*. Berlin: Klaus Schwartz Verlag.

Zarnūjī, Burhān al-Dīn. [1203] N.d. *Taʿlīm al-mutaʿallim ṭuruq al-taʿallum*. With the commentary of Ibrāhīm b. Ismāʿīl (*fl.* 1587). Cairo: Dār Iḥyāʾ al-Turāth al-ʿArabī.

Zilfi, Madeline. 1977. "The Diary of a Müderris: A New Source for Ottoman Biography." *Journal of Turkish Studies* 1: 157–173.

———. 1983a. "Elite Circulation in the Ottoman Empire: Great Mollas of the Eighteenth Century." *Journal of the Economic and Social History of the Orient* 26: 309–327.

———. 1983b. "The *Ilmiye* Registers and the Ottoman *Medrese* System Prior to the Tanzimat." In *Contributions à l'histoire économique et sociale de l'Empire ottoman,* ed. J-L. Bacqué-Grammont and P. Dumont. Louvain: Peeters.

———. 1988. *The Politics of Piety: The Ottoman Ulema in the Postclassical Age (1600–1800)*. Minneapolis: Bibliotheca Islamica.

———, 1993. "Sultan Süleymān and the Ottoman Religious Establishment." In *Süleymān the Second and His Time,* ed. H. Inalcik and C. Kafadar. Istanbul: Isis Press.

Chapter 10

Chao, Yuan-ling. 1995. "Medicine and Society in Late Imperial China: A Study of Physicians in Suzhou." Ph.D. diss., University of California, Los Angeles.

Dai Zhen. 1974. *Dai Zhen wenji* [Dai Zhen's essays]. Hong Kong: Zhonghua Bookstore.

Elman, Benjamin A. 1979. "Ch'ing Schools of Scholarship." *Ch'ing-shih wen-t'i* 4 (6): 1–44.

———. 1983. "Philosophy *(I-li)* versus Philology *(K'ao-cheng):* The *Jen-hsin Tao-hsin* Debate." *T'oung Pao* 59 (4–5): 175–222.

———. 1985. "Criticism as Philosophy: Conceptual Change in Qing Dynasty Evidential Research." *Tsing Hua Journal of Chinese Studies,* Taiwan n.s. 17: 165–198.

———. 1992. "The Changing Role of Historical Knowledge in Southern Provincial Civil Examinations During the Ming and Qing." *Journal of Social Sciences and Philosophy* (Academia Sinica, Taiwan, Sun Yat-sen Institute for Social Sciences & Philosophy) 5 (1): 265–319.

———. 2000a. *A Cultural History of Civil Examinations in Late Imperial China.* Berkeley: University of California Press.

———. 2000b. "The Transformation of the Civil Service Curriculum between 1250 and 1400 and the Role of the Yuan Dynasty in Classical Studies." In *Conference Volume on Yuan Dynasty Classical Studies,* organized by Lin Qingzhang et al. Taipei: Institute of Chinese Literature and Philosophy, Academia Sinica, Taiwan, 23–69.

———. 2001. *From Philosophy to Philology: Intellectual and Social Aspects of Change in Late Imperial China.* 2nd ed. Los Angeles: UCLA Asia Institute Monograph Series.

Guangdong xiangshi lu [Record of the Guangdong provincial civil examinations]. 1794. Provincial report. Beijing Palace Archives.

Guo Shaoyu. 1963. *Qing shihua* [Qing works on poetry discussions]. Shanghai: Guji Press.

———. 1983. Preface to *Qing shihua xubian* [Qing works on poetry discussions, continuation]. Shanghai: Guji Press.

Hanson, Marta. 2002. "The *Golden Mirror* in the Imperial Court of the Qianlong Emperor, 1739–1743." *Early Science and Medicine* 8 (2): 112–147.

Henderson, John. 1986. "Qing Scholars Views of Western Astronomy." *Harvard Journal of Asiatic Studies* 46 (1): 121–148.

———. 1991. *Scripture, Canon, and Commentary: A Comparison of Confucian and Western Exegesis.* Princeton, N.J.: Princeton University Press.

Horng, Wann-sheng. 1993. "Chinese Mathematics at the Turn of the Nineteenth Century." In *Philosophy and Conceptual History of Science in Taiwan,* ed. Lin Cheng-hung and Fu Daiwie. Dordrecht: Kluwer Academic Publishers, 167–208.

Hu, Mingjie. 1998. "Merging Chinese and Western Mathematics: The Introduction of Algebra and the Calculus in China, 1859–1903." Ph.D. diss., Princeton University.

Huang Yinong. 1993. "Qingchu tianzhujiao yü huijiao tianwenjia de zhengdou" [The struggle between Catholic and Muslim astronomers in the early Qing]. *Jiuzhou xuekan* 5 (3): 47–69.

Hummel, Arthur et al. 1942. *Eminent Chinese of the Qing Period.* Washington, D.C.: Government Publishing House.

Jami, Catherine. 1994. "Learning Mathematical Sciences during the Early and Mid-Qing." In *Education and Society in Late Imperial China, 1600–1900,* ed. Benjamin A. Elman and Alexander Woodside. Berkeley: University of California Press, 223–256.

Kondo Mitsuo. 1967. *Shin shisen* [Selections of Qing poetry]. Tokyo: Shūeisha.

Li Tiaoyuan. 1881. *Danmo lu* [Record of skilled civil examination papers]. In *Hanhai* [Seas of writings], Qing ed.

Li Yan and Du Shiran. 1987. Translated by John N. Crossley and Anthony W.-C. Lun. *Chinese Mathematics: A Concise History.* Oxford: Clarendon Press.

Liang Zhangju. 1963. "Dui'an suibi" [Random writings by Liang Zhangju]. In *Qing shihua,* ed. Guo Shaoyu. Shanghai: Guji Press.

———. 1976. *Shilü conghua* [Collected sayings on regulated verse]. Taipei: Guangwen shuju.

Libu tiben [Memoranda including memorials from the Ministry of Rites]. 1765. Ms. Ming-Qing Archives, Academia Sinica, Taiwan. Ninth month, fifth day.

Lin Qingzhang. 1990. *Qingchu de qunjing bianweixue* [Study of forged classics in the early Qing]. Taipei: Wenjin Press.

Liu, James J. Y. 1962. *The Art of Chinese Poetry.* Chicago: University of Chicago Press.

Liu, James T. C. 1973. "How Did a Neo-Confucian School Become the State Orthodoxy?" *Philosophy East and West* 23 (4): 483–505.

Martzloff, Jean-Claude. 1996. *A History of Chinese Mathematics.* New York: Springer.

Peterson, Willard. 1986. "Calendar Reform Prior to the Arrival of Missionaries at the Ming Court." *Ming Studies* 21: 45–61.

Qian Daxin. 1804. *Shijia zhai yangxin lu* [Record of self-renewal from the Ten Yokes Study]. Taipei: Guangwen Bookstore reprint.

———. 1968. *Qianyan tang wenji* [Collected essays of the Hall of Subtle Research]. 8 vols. Taipei: Commercial Press.

Qinding Da-Qing hui-dian shili [Collected statutes and precedents in the great Qing]. 1968. Taipei: Zhonghua Bookstore.

Qingchao xu wenxian tongkao [Comprehensive analysis of civil institutions of the Qing dynasty, continuation]. 1936. In *Shitong* [Ten comprehensive encyclopedias]. Shanghai: Commercial Press.

Reynolds, L. D., and N. G. Wilson. 1968. *Scribes and Scholars: A Guide to the Transmission of Greek and Latin Literature.* London: Oxford University Press, 1968.

Schirokauer, Conrad. 1977. "Neo-Confucians under Attack: The Condemnation of *Weihsueh.*" In *Crisis and Prosperity in Sung China,* ed. John Haeger. Tucson: University of Arizona Press, 163–198.

Schwab, Raymond. 1984. *The Oriental Renaissance: Europe's Rediscovery of India and the East, 1680–1880.* Translated by Gene Patterson-Black and Victor Reinking. New York: Columbia University Press.

Siku quanshu zongmu [Catalog of the complete collection of the four treasuries]. 1974. Compiled by Ji Yun et al. Reprint, Taipei: Yiwen Press.

Sivin, Nathan. 1995. "Why the Scientific Revolution Did Not Take Place in China—or Didn't It?" Reprinted in Sivin, *Science in Ancient China: Researches and Reflections.* Aldershot, England: Variorium, 7:45–66.

Sun Xingyan. 1990. "Ni kechang shishi qing jian yong zhushu zhe" [Memorial recommending the use of scholia in examination compounds testing literati]. In *Qingdai qianqi jiaoyu lunzhu xuan* [Selections of writings on education from the early Qing period], ed. Li Guojun et al., 3 vols. Beijing: People's Education Press.

Tang Chih-chün and Benjamin A. Elman. 1987. "The 1898 Reforms Revisited." *Late Imperial China* 8 (1): 205–213.

Von Glahn, Richard. 2004. *The Sinister Way: the Divine and the Demonic in Chinese Religious Culture.* Berkeley: University of California Press.

Wang Mingsheng. 1960. Preface to *Shiqishi shangque* [Critical study of the Seventeen Dynastic Histories]. Taipei: Guangwen Bookstore Reprint.

Wang Zhenyuan. 1991. *Qingshi xuan* [Selections of Qing poetry]. Taipei: Luojun wenhua Co.

Xu Liwang. 2010. "Bu Qingdai jinwen jingxue fuxing yuanyu Shangshu fang 'jiangyi'—Jianlun jinwen jingxue zai Kang-Yong-Qian sanchao de diwei" [Critique of the view that Qing dynasty New Text classical studies revived due to the lectures in the Upper Study of the emperor—comprehensively evaluating the status of New Text classical studies during the three reigns of Kangxi, Yongzheng, and Qianlong]. *Fudan xuebao* [Social sciences] 5: 132–140.

Yu, Pauline. 1997. "Canon Formation in Late Imperial China." In *Culture and State in Chinese History: Conventions, Accommodations, and Critiques,* ed. Theodore Huters et al. Stanford: Stanford University Press, 83–104.

Yü, Ying-shih. 1975. "Some Preliminary Observations on the Rise of Ch'ing Confucian Intellectualism." *Tsing Hua Journal of Chinese Studies* 11: 125.

Zhang Xuecheng. 1936. *Zhangshi yishu* [Bequeathed works of Mr. Zhang Xuecheng]. Shanghai: Commercial Press.

Chapter 11

Bitō Masahide. 1977. "Mitogaku no tokushitsu." In *Nihon shisō taikei,* vol. 53, *Mitogaku,* ed. Bitō et al., Tokyo: Iwanami Shoten, 556–582.

Burns, Susan L. 2003. *Before the Nation: Kokugaku and the Imagining of Community in Early Modern Japan.* Durham, N.C.: Duke University Press.

Flueckiger, Peter. 2011. *Imagining Harmony: Poetry, Empathy, and Community in Mid-Tokugawa Confucianism and Nativism.* Stanford, Calif.: Stanford University Press.

Haga Ya'ichi. 1982a. "Kokugakushi gairon." In *Haga Ya'ichi senshū,* vol. 1. ed. Haga Ya'ichi Senshū Iinkai, Tokyo: Kokugakuin Daigaku, 5–61.

———. 1982b. "Kokugaku to ha nani zo ya." In *Haga Ya'ichi senshū,* vol. 1, ed. Haga Ya'ichi Senshū Iinkai, Tokyo: Kokugakuin Daigaku, 147–164.

Hansen, Wilburn. 2008. "The Dao of Nineteenth-Century Japanese Nativist Healing: A Chinese Herbal Supplement to Faith Healing." *Early Modern Japan* 2008: 92–103.

Harootunian, Harry. 1988. *Things Seen and Unseen: Discourse and Ideology in Tokugawa Nativism.* Chicago: University of Chicago Press.

Hirata Atsutane. 1981. "Isō Chūkeikō." In *Shinshū Hirata Atsutane zenshū,* vol. 14, ed. Hirata Atsutane Zenshū Kankōkai, Tokyo: Meicho Shuppan, 507–552.

Keichū. 1977. *Man'yō daishōki.* Vol. 1 of *Keichū zenshū,* ed. Hisamatsu Sen'ichi. Tokyo: Iwanami Shoten .

Kin Bunkyo. 2010. *Kanbun to Higashi Ajia: Kundoku no bunkaen.* Tokyo: Iwanami Shoten.

Kobayashi Hideo. 1977. *Motoori Norinaga.* Tokyo: Shinchōsha.

Kojima Noriyuki. 1968. "*Kojiki* kundoku no shūhen." *Bungaku* 36: 37–41.

Koyasu Nobukuni. 2000. *Norinaga mondai to ha nanika.* Tokyo: Seidosha.

Kurano Kenji and Takeda Yūkichi, eds. 1958. *Kojiki.* In *Nihon kotenbungaku taikei,* vol. 1, ed. Kurano Kenji and Takeda Yūkichi. Tokyo: Iwanami Shoten.

Lurie, David. 2011. *Realms of Literacy: Early Japan and the History of Writing.* Cambridge, Mass.: Harvard University East Asia Center.

Moroyama-machi machi-shi henshū iinkai. 1975. *Gonda Naosuke sensei den.* Moroyama: Kyōdō Kankō.

Motoori Norinaga. 1968a. *Kojikiden.* Vols. 9–12 of *Motoori Norinaga zenshū,* ed. Ono Susumu. Tokyo: Chikuma Shobō .

———. 1968b. *Tamakatsuma.* In *Motoori Norinaga zenshū,* vol. 1, ed. Ono Susumu, Tokyo: Chikuma Shobō, 31–450.

Nakai, Kate Wildman. 1988. *Shogunal Politics: Arai Hakuseki and the Premises of Tokugawa Rule.* Cambridge, Mass.: Council on East Asian Studies, Harvard University.

Nishihata Biten. 1990. *Kodai Chōsengo de Nihon no koten ha yomeruka.* Tokyo: Yamato Shobō.

Nishimiya Kazutami. 1988. *Nihon jōdai no bunka to hyōki.* Tokyo: Kazuma Shobō.

Ono Susumu et al. 1990. "Nikkan gekiron shinpojiumu: Man'yōshū ha hontō ni Chōsengo de yomeru ka." *Shūkan Asahi,* February 9: 110–113; February 16: 124–128; February 23: 116–120.

Ooms, Herman. 1985. *Tokugawa Ideology: Early Constructs, 1570–1680.* Princeton, N.J.: Princeton University Press.

Ōta Seikyū. 1968. *Nihon kagaku to Chūgoku shigaku.* Tokyo: Shimizu Kōbundō Shobō.

Saigō Nobutsuna. 1975. *Kojiki chūshaku.* Vol. 1. Tokyo: Heibonsha.

Sakai, Naoki. 1991. *Voices from the Past: The Status of Language in Eighteenth-Century Japanese Discourse.* Ithaca, N.Y.: Cornell University Press.

Tachibana Moribe. 1967a. *Itsu no chiwake.* Vol. 3 of *Tachibana Moribe zenshū (shintei),* ed. Tachibana Jun'ichi. Reprint, Tokyo: Tokyo Bijutsu.

———. 1967b. *Nan-Kojikiden.* In *Tachibana Moribe zenshū (shintei),* vol. 2, ed. Tachibana Jun'ichi, Reprint, Tokyo: Tokyo Bijutsu, 1–298.

———. 1967c. *Yamabiko zōshi.* In *Tachibana Moribe zenshū (shintei),* vol. 8, ed. Tachibana Jun'ichi, Reprint, Tokyo: Tokyo Bijutsu, 11–128.

Ueda Akinari. 1990. *Ashikariyoshi.* In *Ueda Akinari zenshū,* vol. 1, ed. Hino Tatsuo et al., Tokyo: Chūō Kōronsha, 15–52.

Yasumoto Biten. 1991. *Shin Chōsengo de Man'yōshū wo kaidoku dekinai.* Tokyo: JICC Shuppankyoku.

Yi Yong-hui. 1989. *Mō hitotsu no Man'yōshū.* Tokyo: Bungei Shunji.

Chapter 12

Ast, Friedrich. 1808. *Grundriss der Philologie.* Landshut: Krüll.

Baertschi, Annette, and Colin King, eds. 2009. *Die modernen Väter der Antike. Die Entwicklung der Altertumswissenschaften an Akademie und Universität im Berlin des 19. Jahrhunderts.* Berlin: de Gruyter.

Benne, Christian. 2005. *Nietzsche und die historisch-kritische Philologie.* Berlin: de Gruyter.

Boeckh, August. 1877. *Encyclopädie und Methodologie der Philologischen Wissenschaften.* Ed. Ernst Bratuschek. Leipzig: Teubner.

Clark, William. 2006. *Academic Charisma and the Origins of the Research University.* Chicago: University of Chicago Press.

Dainat, Holger. 2010. "Klassische, Germanische, Orientalische Philologie." In *Geschichte der Universität Unter den Linden 1810–2010: Praxis ihrer Disziplinen,* ed. Heinz-Elmar Tenorth, Genese der Disziplinen. Die Konstitution der Universität 4. Berlin: Akademie-Verlag, 319–338.

Danneberg, Lutz. 2013. "Kunst, Methode und Methodologie bei Boeckh." In *August Boeckh. Philologie, Hermeneutik und Wissenschaftspolitik,* ed. Christiane Hackel and Sabine Seifert. Berlin: Berliner Wissenschaftsverlag, 211–242.

Elsner, Jaś. 2013. "Paideia: Ancient Concept and Modern Perception." *International Journal of the Classical Tradition* 20 (4): 136–152.

Espagne, Michel. 2010. "De Heyne à Lachmann. Biographies héroïques de philologues allemands." In *La philologie au présent: Pour Jean Bollack,* ed. Ch. König and D. Thouard. Villeneuve-d'Ascq: Presses universitaires du Septentrion, 127–139.

Feuerhahn, Wolfgang, and Pascale Rabault-Feuerhahn, eds. 2010. *La fabrique international de la science. Les congress scientifiques de 1865 à 1945.* Revue Germanique Internationale 12. Paris: CNRS.

Gildersleeve, Basil. 1897. "My Sixty Days in Greece." *Atlantic Monthly* 79 (472) (February): 199–212; 79 (473) (March): 301–312; 79 (475) (May): 630–642.

———. 1987. *The Letters of Basil Lanneau Gildersleeve.* Ed. W. W. Briggs, Jr. Baltimore: Johns Hopkins University Press.

———. 1992. "The Spiritual Rights to Minute Research" (1895). In *Selected Classical Papers of Basil Lanneau Gildersleeve,* ed. W. W. Briggs, Jr. Atlanta: Scholars Press, 93–105.

Grafton, Anthony. 1983. "Polyhistor into *Philolog:* Notes on the Transformation of German Classical Scholarship, 1780–1850." *History of Universities* 3: 159–192.

———. 1999. "Juden und Griechen bei Friedrich August Wolf." In *Friedrich August Wolf. Studien, Dokumente, Bibliographie,* ed. Reinhard Markner and Giuseppe Veltri. Stuttgart: Steiner, 9–31.

Gurd, Sean Alexander. 2005. *Iphigenias at Aulis: Textual Multiplicities, Radical Philology.* Ithaca, N.Y.: Cornell University Press.

Güthenke, Constanze. 2009. "Shop Talk. Reception Studies and Recent Work in the History of Scholarship." *Classical Receptions Journal* 1: 104–115.

———. 2010. "The Potter's Daughter's Sons: German Classical Scholarship and the Language of Love circa 1800." *Representations* 109: 122–147.

Hackel, Christiane, and Sabine Seifert, eds. 2013. *August Boeckh. Philologie, Hermeneutik und Wissenschaftspolitik.* Berlin: Berliner Wissenschaftsverlag.

Harloe, Katherine. 2013. *Winckelmann and the Invention of Antiquity: Aesthetics and History in the Age of Altertumswissenschaft.* Oxford: Oxford University Press.

Haugen, Kristine Louise. 2007. "Academic Charisma and the Old Regime." *History of Universities* 22 (1): 199–228.

———. 2011. *Richard Bentley. Poetry and Enlightenment.* Cambridge, Mass.: Harvard University Press.

Hegel, G. W. F. (1986). *Vorlesungen über die Ästhetik I-III. Werke*, vols. 13–15. Frankfurt: Suhrkamp.

Hoesel-Uhlig, Stefan. 2004. "Changing Fields: The Directions of Goethe's *Weltliteratur.*" In *Debating World Literature,* ed. Christopher Predergast. London: Verso, 26–53.

Holzer, Angela. 2013. *Rehabilitationen Roms. Die römische Antike in der deutschen Kultur zwischen Winckelmann und Niebuhr.* Heidelberg: Winter.

Horstmann, Axel. 1992. *Antike Theoria und moderne Wissenschaft. August Boeckhs Konzeption der Philologie.* Frankfurt a. M.: Lang.

Humboldt, Wilhelm von. 1967. "Über das Studium des Alterthums, und des griechischen insbesondere." In Humboldt, *Gesammelte Schriften,* vol. 1, ed. Königlich-Preussische Akademie der Wissenschaften. Berlin: de Gruyter, 255–281.

———. 2004. *Briefe an Friedrich August Wolf.* Ed. Philip Mattson. Berlin: de Gruyter.

Hummel, Pascale. 2002. *Moeurs érudites: Etude sur la micrologie littéraire (Allemagne, XVIe–XVIIIe siècles).* Geneva: Droz.

Körner, Josef. 1928. "Friedrich Schlegels 'Philosophie der Philologie,' mit einer Einleitung herausgegeben." *Logos* 17: 1–72.

Kuhlmann, Peter, and Helmut Schneider. 2013. "Classical Studies from Petrarch to the 20th Century." In *Brill's New Pauly Supplements I,* vol. 6, *History of Classical Scholarship. A Biographical Dictionary,* ed. Peter Kuhlmann, Helmut Schneider, and Brigitte Egger. Brill Online, http://referenceworks.brillonline.com/entries/brill-s-new-pauly-supplements-i-6/classical-studies-from-petrarch-to-the-20th-century-classicalstudies.

Leersen, Joop. 2006. "Nationalism and the Cultivation of Culture." *Nations and Nationalism* 12: 559–578.

Legaspi, Michael C. 2008. "The Quest for Classical Antiquity at Eighteenth-Century Göttingen." *History of Universities* 24 (2): 139–172.

Leonard, Miriam. 2012. *Socrates and the Jews: Hellenism and Hebraism from Moses Mendelssohn to Sigmund Freud.* Chicago: University of Chicago Press.

Leventhal, Robert S. 1986. "The Emergence of Philological Discourse in the German States, 1770–1810." *Isis* 77: 243–260.

———. 1994. *The Disciplines of Interpretation: Lessing, Herder, Schlegel and Hermeneutics in Germany, 1750–1800.* Berlin: de Gruyter.

Marchand, Suzanne. 1996. *Down from Olympus: Archaeology and Philhellenism in Germany, 1750–1970.* Princeton, N.J.: Princeton University Press.

———. 2009. *German Orientalism in the Age of Empire: Religion, Race, and Scholarship.* Cambridge: Cambridge University Press.

Markner, Reinhard, and Giuseppe Veltri, eds. 1999. *Friedrich August Wolf. Studien, Dokumente, Bibliographie.* Stuttgart: Steiner.

Most, Glenn. 1998. "Karl Otfried Müller's Edition of Aeschylus' *Eumenides*." In *Zwischen Rationalismus und Romantik: Karl Otfried Müller und die antike Kultur,* ed. W. M. Calder III and R. Schlesier. Hildesheim: Olms, 349–373.

Norman, Larry F. 2011. *The Shock of the Ancient: Literature and History in Early Modern France.* Chicago: University of Chicago Press.

Paulsen, Friedrich. 1885. *Geschichte des gelehrten Unterrichts auf den deutschen Schulen und Universitäten vom Ausgang des Mittelalters bis zur Gegenwart, mit besonderer Rücksicht auf den klassischen Unterricht.* Leipzig: Veit.

Pfeiffer, Rudolf. 1976. *History of Classical Scholarship from 1300 to 1850.* Oxford: Oxford University Press.

Poiss, Thomas. 2009. "Die unendliche Aufgabe. August Boeckh als Begründer des Philologischen Seminars." In *Die modernen Väter der Antike. Die Entwicklung der Altertumswissenschaften an Akademie und Universität im Berlin des 19. Jahrhunderts,* ed. Annette Baertschi and Colin King. Berlin: de Gruyter, 45–72.

———. 2010. "Zur Idee der Philologie. Der Streit zwischen Gottfried Hermann und August Boeckh." In Karl Sier and Eva Wöckener-Gade, *Gottfried Hermann (1772–1848). Internationales Symposium in Leipzig 11.–13. Oktober 2007.* Tübingen: Narr, 143–163.

Reynolds, L. D., and N. E. Wilson. 1991. *Scribes and Scholars: A Guide to the Transmission of Greek and Latin Literature.* Oxford: Oxford University Press.

Ritschl, F. W. 1879a. "Ueber die neueste Entwicklung der Philologie." In *Kleine philologische Schriften,* ed. Wachsmuth, vol. 5. Leipzig: Teubner, 1–18.

———. 1879b. "Zur Methode des Philologischen Studiums (Bruchstücke und Aphorismen)." In Kleine philologische Schriften, ed. Wachsmuth, vol. 5. Leipzig: Teubner, 19–32.

Schmidt, Peter Lebrecht. 1995. "Zwischen Anpassungsdruck und Autonomiestreben: Die deutsche Latinistik vom Beginn bis in die 20er Jahre des 20. Jahrhunderts." In *Altertumswissenschaft in den 20er Jahren. Neue Fragen und Impulse,* ed. Helmut Flashar. Stuttgart: Steiner, 115–182.

Schwindt, Jürgen Paul, ed. 2009. *Was ist eine philologische Frage? Beiträge zur Erkundung einer theoretischen Einstellung.* Frankfurt/M.: Suhrkamp.

Sier, Karl, and Eva Wöckener-Gade, eds. 2010. *Gottfried Hermann (1772–1848). Internationales Symposium in Leipzig 11.–13. Oktober 2007.* Tübingen: Narr.

Stephens, Susan, and Phiroze Vasunia, eds. 2010. *Classics and National Cultures.* Oxford: Oxford University Press.

Thouard, Denis. 2013. "Eine Encyclopädie zwischen Ethik und Hermeneutik. Boeckh und Schleiermacher." In *August Boeckh. Philologie, Hermeneutik und*

Wissenschaftspolitik, ed. Christiane Hackel and Sabine Seifert. Berlin: Berliner Wissenschaftsverlag, 107–124.

Tigerstedt, E. N. 1974. *The Decline and Fall of the Neoplatonic Interpretation of Plato: An Outline and Some Observations.* Helsinki: Societas Scientariarum Fennica.

Timpanaro, Sebastiano. 2005. *The Genesis of Lachmann's Method.* Ed. and trans. Glenn W. Most. Chicago: University of Chicago Press.

Trabant, Jürgen. 2009. "Humboldt, eine Fussnote? Wilhelm von Humboldt als Gründergestalt der modernen Altertumswissenschaft." In *Die modernen Väter der Antike. Die Entwicklung der Altertumswissenschaften an Akademie und Universität im Berlin des 19. Jahrhunderts,* ed. Annette Baertschi and Colin King. Berlin: de Gruyter, 25–44.

Turner, R. S. 1983. "Historicism, Kritik, and the Prussian Professorate, 1790–1840." In *Philologie und Hermeneutik im 19. Jahrhundert II,* ed. Marise Bollack et al. Göttingen: Vandenhoeck und Ruprecht, 450–477.

Vick, Brian. 2002. "Greek Origins and Organic Metaphors. Ideals of Cultural Autonomy in Neohumanist Germany from Winckelmann to Curtius." In *Journal of the History of Ideas* 63 (3): 483–500.

Welcker, Friedrich Gottlieb. 1861. "Über die Bedeutung der Philologie, gelesen in der vierten Versammlung deutscher Philologen und Schulmänner zu Bonn, am 1. Oktober 1841." In Welcker, *Kleine Schriften.* Bonn: Weber, 1–16.

Westphalen, Klaus. 1986. *Professor Unrat und seine Kollegen. Literarische Porträs des Philologen.* Bamberg: C. C. Buchner.

Wolf, Friedrich August. 1869. "Darstellung der Alterthums-Wissenschaft." In *F. A. Wolf: Kleine Schriften in lateinischer und deutscher Sprache,* ed. G. Bernhardy, 2 vols. Leipzig: Waisenhaus, 2:808–895.

Wolf, Friedrich August. 1985. *Prolegomena to Homer* (1795). Trans. with introduction and notes by Anthony Grafton, Glenn W. Most, and James E. G. Zetzel. Princeton, N.J.: Princeton University Press.

Chapter 13

Benne, Christian. 2005. *Nietzsche und die historisch-kritische Philologie.* Monographien und Texte zur Nietzsche-Forschung 49. Berlin: de Gruyter.

———. 2007. "Zwischen Hermeneutik und Dialektik: Die Ethik der Kritik bei Schleiermacher." In *Schleiermacher, Romanticism, and the Critical Arts: A Festschrift in Honor of Hermann Patsch,* ed. Hans Dierkes, Terrence N. Tice, and Wolfgang Virmond. New Athenaeum 8. New York: Mellen, 169–186.

Boeckh, August. 1877. *Encyklopädie und Methodologie der philologischen Wissenschaften.* Leipzig: Teubner.

Bollack, Jean. 1965–69. *Empédocle.* 4 vols. Paris: Editions de minuit.

———. 1985. "M. de W.-M. (en France). Sur les limites de l'implantation d'une science." In *Wilamowitz nach 50 Jahren,* ed. William M. Calder III, Hellmut Flashar, and Theodor Lindken. Darmstadt: Wissenschaftliche Buchgesellschaft, 468–512.

———. 2000. *Sens contre sens. Comment lit-on? Entretiens avec Patrick Llored.* Genouilleux: La passe du vent.

———. 2003. *L'écrit. Une poétique dans l'œuvre de Celan.* Paris: *Presses universitaires de France.*

———. 2010. *L'Œdipe roi de Sophocle. Le texte et ses interpretations.* 4 vols. Rev. ed. with new afterword. Villeneuve d'Ascq: Septentrion.

Brandstetter, Gabriele. 1995. *Tanz-Lektüren. Körperbilder und Raumfiguren der Avantgarde.* Frankfurt am Main: Fischer Taschenbuch Verlag.

Danneberg, Lutz, and Friedrich Vollhardt, eds. 1996. *Wie international ist die Literaturwissenschaft? Methoden- und Theoriediskussion in den Literaturwissenschaften: Kulturelle Besonderheiten und interkultureller Austausch am Beispiel des Interpretationsproblems (1950–1990).* Stuttgart: Metzler.

Dilthey, Wilhelm. 1973 [1922]. *Gesammelte Schriften.* Vol. 1. *Einleitung in die Geisteswissenschaften. Versuch einer Grundlegung für das Studium der Gesellschaft und der Geschichte.* Ed. Bernhard Groethuysen. 7th ed. Stuttgart: Teubner.

Dreyfus, Hubert L. 2007a. "The Return of the Myth of the Mental." *Inquiry* 50 (4): 352–365.

———. 2007b. "Response to McDowell." *Inquiry* 50 (4): 371–377.

Frank, Manfred. 1988. "Rilkes Orpheus." In Frank, *Gott im Exil. Vorlesungen über die Neue Mythologie.* Frankfurt am Main: Suhrkamp, 180–211.

Gadamer, Hans-Georg. 1999 [1982]. *Truth and Method* (1960). Trans. rev. by Joel Weinsheimer. 2nd rev. ed. Reprint; London: Continuum.

Gerok-Reiter, Annette. 1996. *Wink und Wandlung. Komposition und Poetik in Rilkes "Sonette an Orpheus."* Studien zur deutschen Literatur 140. Tübingen: Niemeyer.

Haß, Ulrike, and Christoph König, eds. 2003. *Literaturwissenschaft und Linguistik von 1960 bis heute.* Marbacher Wissenschaftsgeschichte 4. Göttingen: Wallstein.

Judet de La Combe, Pierre. 1997. "Sur la relation entre interprétation et histoire des interprétations." In *Théorie de la littérature,* ed. Christoph König. Revue germanique international 8. Paris: Presses Universitaires de France, 9–29.

———. 2010. "'L'École de Lille': Une concentration diasporique." In *La philologie au présent. Pour Jean Bollack,* ed. Christoph König and Denis Thouard. Cahiers de philologie 27. Villeneuve d'Ascq: Septentrion, 363–374.

Kern, Otto. 1920. *Orpheus. Eine religionsgeschichtliche Untersuchung. Mit einem Beitrag von Josef Strzygowski, einem Bildnis und zwei Tafeln.* Berlin: Weidmannsche Buchhandlung.

König, Christoph. 1994. "Wissen, Werte, Institutionen." *Jahrbuch der Deutschen Schillergesellschaft* 38: 379–403.

———. 2000. "Kritische Philologie heute." In *Literaturwissenschaft und Wissenschaftsforschung,* ed. Jörg Schönert. Germanistische Symposien. Berichtsbände 21. Stuttgart: Metzler, 317–335.

———. 2004. *Engführungen. Peter Szondi und die Literatur.* Marbacher Magazin 108, 2nd rev. ed. Marbach: Deutsche Schillergesellschaft.

———. 2006 [2001]. *Hofmannsthal. Ein moderner Dichter unter den Philologen.* Marbacher Wissenschaftsgeschichte 2. Göttingen: Wallstein.

———. 2008. "Ungebärdiges Lesen. Laudatio für Jean Bollack (zur Ehrenpromotion durch die Universität Osnabrück 2007) (Unbridled Reading)." *Lendemains* 33 (129): 119–127.

———. 2011. "Le français de Paul Valéry dans les poèmes tardifs en allemand de Rilke." In *France—Allemagne, regards et objets croisés. La littérature allemande vue de France—La littérature française vue de l'Allemagne,* ed. Didier Alexandre and Wolfgang Asholt. Tübingen: Narr, 21–34.

———. 2012. "Das verlorene Unaussprechliche. Wittgensteins Bemerkungen über das Gedicht *Graf Eberhards Weißdorn* von Ludwig Uhland." In *Wittgenstein übersetzen,* ed. Matthias Kroß and Esther Ramharter. Berlin: Parerga, 77–102.

———. 2014a. "O komm und geh": Skeptische Lektüren der "Sonette an Orpheus" von Rilke. Göttingen: Wallstein.

———. 2014b. *Philologie der Poesie. Von Goethe bis Peter Szondi.* Berlin, Boston: de Gruyter.

König, Christoph, and Eberhard Lämmert, eds. 1993. *Literaturwissenschaft und Geistesgeschichte 1910 bis 1925.* Frankfurt am Main: Fischer Taschenbuch Verlag.

König, Christoph, and Heinz Wismann, eds. 2001. *La lecture insistante—autour du Jean Bollack.* Paris: Albin Michel.

Lachmann, Karl. 1820. *Auswahl aus den Hochdeutschen Dichtern des dreizehnten Jahrhunderts.* Berlin: Reimer.

Levi, Jean. 1999. "Pratiques divinatoires, conjectures et critique rationaliste à l'époque des Royaumes Combattants." In *Divination et rationalité en Chine ancienne,* ed. Karine Chemla, Donald John Harper, and Marc Kalinowski. Extrême-Orient, Extrême-Occident 21. Paris: Presses Universitaires de Vincennes, 67–77.

McDowell, John. 2007a. "What Myth?" *Inquiry* 50 (4): 338–351.

———. 2007b. "Response to Dreyfus." *Inquiry* 50 (4): 366–370.

Mörchen, Hermann. 1958. *Rilkes Sonette an Orpheus, erläutert von Hermann Mörchen.* Stuttgart: Kohlhammer.

Most, Glenn W., ed. 1999. *Aporemata. Kritische Studien zur Philologiegeschichte.* Vol. 4. *Commentaries—Kommentare.* Göttingen: Vandenhoeck und Ruprecht.

Nebrig, Alexander. 2009. "Die Aufzeichnungen über die Krankheit und den Tod von Wera Ouckama Knoop. Eine Quelle der 'Sonette an Orpheus' (1923)." *Zeitschrift für Germanistik* 19 (3): 609–618.

Nietzsche, Friedrich. 1997. *Daybreak: Thoughts on the Prejudices of Morality.* Ed. Maudemarie Clark and Brian Leiter. Trans. R. J. Hollingdale. With an introduction by Michael Tanner. Cambridge: Cambridge University Press.

Ovidius Naso, Publius. 2012. *Metamorphoses.* Ed. William S. Andersen. Berlin: de Gruyter.

Pippin, Robert. 2005. "Leaving Nature Behind (On John McDowell's Mind and World)." In Pippin, *The Persistence of Subjectivity.* Cambridge: Cambridge University Press, 58–75.

Pollock, Sheldon. 2009. "Future Philology? The Fate of a Soft Science in a Hard World." *Critical Inquiry* 35 (4): 936–961. (In German translation: "Zukunftsphilologie?" Trans. Lena Kühn. Geschichte der Germanistik. *Mitteilungen* 35/36: 25–50.)

Rehm, Walther. 1972. *Orpheus. Der Dichter und die Toten. Selbstdeutung und Totenkult bei Novalis—Hölderlin—Rilke.* Darmstadt: Wissenschaftliche Buchgesellschaft.

Rilke, Rainer Maria. 1942. *Sonnets to Orpheus.* Trans. M. D. Herter. New York: Norton.

———. 1955. *Sämtliche Werke.* Vol. 1. *Gedichte, erster Teil.* Ed. Ernst Zinn. Wiesbaden: Insel.

———. 1977. *Die Briefe an Gräfin Sizzo. 1921–1926.* Ed. Ingeborg Schnack. Frankfurt am Main: Insel.

———. 1997. *Sämtliche Werke.* Vol. 7. *Übertragungen.* Ed. Walter Simon, Karin Wais, and Ernst Zinn. Frankfurt am Main and Leipzig: Insel.

Rodi, Frithjof. 1985. "Diltheys Kritik der historischen Vernunft—Programm oder System?" *Dilthey-Jahrbuch für Philosophie und Geschichte der Geisteswissenschaften* 3: 140–165.

Schleiermacher, Friedrich. 1977. *Hermeneutik und Kritik.* Ed. Manfred Frank. Frankfurt am Main: Suhrkamp.

———. 1998. *Hermeneutics and Criticism and Other Writings.* Ed. and trans. Andrew Bowie. Cambridge: Cambridge University Press.

———. 2012. *Kritische Gesamtausgabe.* Sec. 2. Pt. 4. *Vorlesungen zur Hermeneutik und Kritik.* Ed. Wolfgang Virmond. Berlin: de Gruyter.

Segal, Charles. 1989. *Orpheus. The Myth of the Poet.* Baltimore: John Hopkins University Press, 1989.

Smith, Richard J. 2008. *Fathoming the Cosmos and Ordering the World: The Yijing (I-Ching, or Classic of Changes) and Its Evolution in China.* Charlottesville: University of Virginia Press.

Staiger, Emil. 1955. *Die Kunst der Interpretation. Studien zur deutschen Literaturgeschichte.* Zürich: Atlantis.

Steinfeld, Thomas. 2009. "Skepsis. Über August Böckh, die Wissenschaft der unendlichen Approximation und das Glück der mangelnden Vollendung." In *Was ist eine philologische Frage?,* ed. Jürgen Paul Schwindt. Frankfurt am Main: Suhrkamp, 211–226.

Szondi, Peter. 1975. "Bemerkungen zur Forschungslage der literarischen Hermeneutik." In Szondi, *Studienausgabe der Vorlesungen,* vol. 5, *Einführung in die literarische Hermeneutik,* ed. Jean Bollack. Frankfurt am Main: Suhrkamp, 404–408.

———. 1978a. "Schleiermachers Hermeneutik heute." In Szondi, *Schriften,* ed. Jean Bollack, newly edited in 2011 with an afterword by Christoph König. Frankfurt am Main: Suhrkamp, 2:106–130.

———. 1978b. "Über philologische Erkenntnis." In Szondi, *Schriften,* ed. Jean Bollack, newly edited in 2011 with an afterword by Christoph König. Frankfurt am Main: Suhrkamp, 1:263–286.

Thouard, Denis. 2010. "Die Vergegenständlichung des Geistes. Simmels Hermeneutik der Objektivität." *Internationales Jahrbuch für Hermeneutik* 9: 327–339.

———. 2012a. *Herméneutique critique: Bollack, Szondi, Celan.* Lille: Presses Universitaires du Septentrion.

———. 2012b. "Philologie wider Philologie. Bemerkungen zur 'Schule von Lille.'" *Geschichte der Germanistik* 41/42: 18–31.

Weimar, Klaus. 1989. *Geschichte der deutschen Literaturwissenschaft bis zum Ende des 19. Jahrhunderts.* München: Fink.

Wegmann, Nikolas. 1994. "Was heißt einen 'klassischen Text' lesen? Philologische Selbstreflexion zwischen Wissenschaft und Bildung." In *Wissenschaftsgeschichte der Germanistik im 19. Jahrhundert,* ed. Jürgen Fohrmann and Wilhelm Voßkamp. Stuttgart: Metzler, 334–450.

Wilamowitz-Moellendorff, Ulrich von. 1916. "Einleitung." In Wilamowitz-Moellendorff, *Die Ilias und Homer.* Berlin: Weidmannsche Buchhandlung.

Wismann, Heinz. 1970. "Le métier de philologue." *Critique* 276: 462–479 and 279/280: 774–781.

———. 1996. "Propositions pour une lecture d'Hésiode." In *Le métier du mythe. Lectures d'*Hésiode, ed. Fabienne Blaise, Pierre Judet de La Combe, and Philippe Rousseau. Cahiers de philologie 16. Villeneuve d' Aseq: Septentrion, 15–24.

Chapter 14

Benfey, Theodor. 1869. *Geschichte der Sprachwissenschaft und orientalischen Philologie in Deutschland.* München: J. G. Cotta.

Bernhardi, August Ferdinand. 1805. *Anfangsgründe der sprachwissenschaft.* Berlin: bei Heinrich Frölich.

Bernheim, Ernst. 1908. *Lehrbuch der historischen Methode und der Geschichtsphilosophie: Mit Nachweis der wichtigsten Quellen und Hilfsmittel zum Studium der Geschichte.* Leipzig: Duncker & Humblot.

Bloomfield, Leonard. 1933. *Language.* New York: Holt.

Bopp, Franz. 1816. *Über das Conjugationssystem der Sanskritsprache in Vergleichung mit Jenem der griechischen, lateinischen, persischen und germanischen Sprache.* Frankfurt am Main: In der andreäischen Buchhandlung.

———. 1974. *Analytical Comparison of the Sanskrit, Greek, Latin and Teutonic Languages, Shewing the Original Identity of Their Grammatical Structure.* Amsterdam: John Benjamins.

Brugmann, Karl. 1885. *Zum heutigen Stand der Sprachwissenschaft.* Strassburg: K. J. Trübner.

Buckle, Henry Thomas. 1920. *History of Civilization in England.* New York: Humphrey Milford.

Chao, Buwei Yang. 2007a. "The Autobiography of a Chinese Woman." In *Zhao Yuenren Quanji* [The complete works of Chao Yuen Ren]. Beijing: The Commercial Press, 15–1:1–335.

———. 2007b. "Family of Chaos, Put into English by Her Husband Yuen Ren Chao." In *Zhao Yuenren Quanji* [The complete works of Chao Yuen Ren]. Beijing: Commercial Press, Vol. 15 bk. 2:1–777.

Chao, Yuen Ren. 1921. "The First Green Letter." Self-published.

———. 1923. *Guoyin Xinshiyun* [The new book of rhymes]. Shanghai: Commercial Press.

———. 1925. To Bernhard Karlgren. W46–294, carton 5. Yuen Ren Chao Papers, Bancroft Library, University of California, Berkeley.

———. 1926. To Bernhard Karlgren. W46–294, carton 5. Yuen Ren Chao Papers, Bancroft Library, University of California, Berkeley.

———. 1928. *Xiandai Wuyu De Yanjiu* [Studies in the modern Wu dialects]. Beijing: Tsing Hua xuexiao yanjiuyuan.

———. 1968. *A Grammar of Spoken Chinese.* Berkeley: University of California Press.
———. 2006. "The Problem of the Chinese Language (1916)." In *Linguistic Essays by Yuenren Chao,* ed. Zong-ji Wu and Xin-na Zhao. Beijing: Commercial Press, 1–60.
———. 2007. "Yuen Ren Chao's Autobiography: First 30 Years, 1892–1921." In *Zhao Yuenren Quanji* [The complete works of Chao Yuen Ren]. Beijing: Commercial Press, Vol. 15 bk. 1:337–488.
Delbrück, Berthold. 1880. *Einleitung in das Sprachstudium: Ein Beitrag zur Geschichte und Methodik der vergleichenden Sprachforschung.* Leipzig: Breitkopf und Härtel.
———. 1989. *Introduction to the Study of Language: A Critical Survey of the History and Methods of Comparative Philology of the Indo-European Languages.* Trans. Eva Channing. New ed. Amsterdam: John Benjamins.
Elffers, Els. 2008. "Georg von der Gabelentz and the Rise of General Linguistics." In *Ontheven aan de tijd: Linguïstisch-historische studies voor Jan Noordegraaf bij zijn zestigste verjaardag,* ed. Lo van Driel and Theo Janssen. Amsterdam: Stichting Neerlandistiek VU.
Eschbach-Szabo, Viktoria. 2000. "Die Frühzeit der neueren japanischen Sprachforschung: Vom Kokugaku zum Kokugogaku." In *History of the Language Sciences: An International Handbook on the Evolution of the Study of Language from the Beginnings to the Present,* ed. Sylvain Auroux. Berlin: Walter de Gruyter, 93–101.
Fu, Ssu-nien. 1927. "Fakan Ci (Inauguration of the weekly)." *Zhongshan Daxue Yuyan Lishi Yanjiusuo Zhoukan* [Weekly of the Institute of Philology and History, Zhongshan University] 1 (1): 3.
———. 1928. "Bensuo Duiyu Yuyanxue Gongzuo Zhi Fanwei Yu Zhiqu [The areas and objectives of this Institute's work on languages]." *Lishi Yuyan Yanjiusuo Jikan* [Bulletin of the Institute of History and Philology] 1 (1): 114–117.
———. 1980a. "Lishi Yuyan Yanjiusuo Gongzuo Zhi Zhiqu [Objectives of the work at the Institute of History and Philology]." In *Fu Ssu-nien Quanji* [The complete works of Fu Ssu-nien]. Taipei City: Lianjing, 4:253–266.
———. 1980b. "Yixia Dongxi Shuo [The Eastern and Western origins of Yi and Xia]." In *Fu Ssu-nien Quanji* [The complete works of Fu Ssu-nien]. Taipei City: Lianjing, 3:822–893.
———. 1980c. "Yu Gu Jiegang Lun Gushishu [Discussion with Jiegang Gu on ancient historical works]." In *Fu Ssu-nien Quanji* [The complete works of Fu Ssu-nien]. Taipei City: Lianjing, 4:454–494.
———. 1980d. "Zhongguo Gudai Wenxueshi Jiangyi (1928) [Lecture notes on the history of ancient Chinese literature]." In *Fu Ssu-nien Quanji* [The complete works of Fu Ssu-nien]. Taipei City: Lianjing, 1–182.
———. 1980e. "Zhou Dongfeng Yu Yin Yimin [Zhou's appointments in the East and the remnants of the Yins]." In *Fu Ssu-nien Quanji* [The complete works of Fu Ssu-nien]. Taipei City: Lianjing, 3:158–167.
Fu, Ssu-nien, Jiegang Gu, and Zhensheng Yang. 2011a. "Fu Ssu-nien, Gu Jiegang, and Yang Zhensheng to the Academia Sinica, April 30, 1928." In *The Letters of Fu*

Ssu-nien, ed. Fan-sen Wang, Kuang-che Pan, and Cheng-shang Wu. Taipei City: Institute of History and Philology, Academia Sinica, 115–126.

———. 2011b. "Fu Ssu-nien, Gu Jiegang, and Yang Zhensheng to Cai Yuanpei and Yang Quan, May 5, 1928." In *The Letters of Fu Ssu-nien,* ed. Fan-sen Wang, Kuang-che Pan, and Cheng-shang Wu. Taipei City: Institute of History and Philology, Academia Sinica, 128–133.

Gabelentz, G. V. D. 1995 (1891). *Die Sprachwissenschaft: Ihre Aufgaben, Methoden und Bisherigen Ergebnisse.* London: Routledge/Thoemmes.

Gercke, Alfred, and Eduard Norden, eds. 1912. *Einleitung in die Altertumswissenschaft.* 3 vols. Leipzig: B. G. Teubner.

Grafton, Anthony. 1981. "Prolegomena to Friedrich August Wolf." *Journal of the Warburg and Courtauld Institutes* 44: 101–129.

Grimm, Jacob. 1819. *Deutsche Grammatik.* Göttingen: bei Dieterich.

Heinrich, Patrick. 2002. *Die Rezeption westlicher Linguistik im modernen Japan bis Ende der Shôwa-Zeit.* München: Judicium Verlag.

Hutton, Chris. 1995. Introduction to *Die Sprachwissenschaft: Ihre Aufgaben, Methoden und Bisherigen Ergebnisse.* London: Routledge/Thoemmes.

Jespersen, Otto. 1904. *Phonetische Grundfragen.* Leipzig: B. G. Teubner.

———. 1917. *Negation in English and Other Languages.* København: Andr. Fred. Høst.

———. 1918. *Chapters on English.* London: George Allen and Unwin.

———. 1922. *Language: Its Nature, Development and Origin.* London: George Allen and Unwin.

———. 1923. *Growth and Structure of the English Language.* 4th ed. New York: D. Appleton.

———. 1924. *The Philosophy of Grammar.* London: George Allen and Unwin.

———. 1925. *Mankind, Nation and Individual from a Linguistic Point of View.* Oslo: H. Aschehoug.

———. 1933. *The System of Grammar.* London: George Allen and Unwin.

———. 1937. *Analytic Syntax.* London: George Allen and Unwin.

Karlgren, Bernhard. 1915. "Études sur la phonologie chinoise." Ph.D. diss., University of Uppsala.

———. 1925. "To Yuen Ren Chao." W46–294, carton 5. Yuen Ren Chao Papers, Bancroft Library, University of California, Berkeley.

Li, Fang-kuei. 1928. "Mattole, an Athabaskan Language." Ph.D. diss., University of Chicago.

Malmqvist, N. G. D. 2011. *Bernhard Karlgren: Portrait of a Scholar.* Bethlehem, Pa.: Lehigh University Press.

Marchand, Suzanne L. 2003. *Down from Olympus: Archaeology and Philhellenism in Germany, 1750–1970.* Princeton, N.J.: Princeton University Press.

Mei, Tsu-Lin. 1990. "Zhongguo Yuyanxue De Chuantong Yu Chuangxin [The tradition and innovation of Chinese linguistics]." In *Xueshushi Yu Fangfaxue De Xingsi* [Reflections on the history of scholarship and methodology]. Taipei City: Institute of History and Philology, Academia Sinica, 475–500.

Müller, F. Max. 1862. *Lectures on the Science of Language.* New York: Scribner.

Rüegg, Walter. 2004. "Theology and the Arts." In *Universities in the Nineteenth and Early Twentieth Centuries (1800–1945),* ed. Walter Rüegg. Cambridge: Cambridge University Press, 393–458.

Saussure, Ferdinand de. 1922 [1916]. *Cours de Linguistique Générale.* 2nd ed. Paris: Payot & Cie.

Sweet, Henry. 1900. *The Practical Study of Languages.* New York: Holt.

Ting, Pang-Hsin. 2000. "Zhongguo Yuyanxue Yu Chao Yuen Ren [Chinese Linguistics and Yuen Ren Chao]." In *Wenhua De Kuizeng* [Cultural gifts]. Beijing: Peking University Press, 431–436.

Wang, Fan-shen. 2000. *Fu Ssu-Nien: A Life in Chinese History and Politics.* New York: Cambridge University Press.

Wang, Fan-shen, and Cheng-sheng Tu, eds. 1995. *Fu Ssu-nien Wenwu Ziliao Xuanji* [Collection of documents on and by Fu Ssu-nien]. Taipei City: Fu Ssu-nien xiansheng beiling jinian choubeihui.

Wang, Li. 1936. "Zhongguo Wenfaxue Chutan [A preliminary study on Chinese Grammar]." *Tsing Hua Xuebao* [Tsing Hua journal of Chinese studies] 11 (1): 21–78.

———. 1946. *Hanyu Yufa Gangyao* [Principles of Han grammar]. Shanghai: Kaiming Bookstore.

———. 1947. *Zhongguo Xiandai Yufa* [Modern Chinese grammar]. Shanghai: Commercial Press.

Whitney, William Dwight. 1896. *The Life and Growth of Language: An Outline of Linguistic Science.* New York: D. Appleton.

Wilamowitz-Moellendorff, Ulrich von. 1982. *History of Classical Scholarship.* London: Duckworth.

Wolf, Friedrich August. 1831. *Vorlesung über die Encyclopädie der Alterthumswissenschaft.* Leipzig: Lehnhold.

Wu, Zongji. 2006. Foreword to *Linguistic Essays by Yuenren Chao,* ed. Zongji Wu and Xinna Zhao. Beijing: Commercial Press, 1–7.

Zhao, Xinna, and Peiyun Huang, eds. 1998. *Zhao Yuanren Nianpu* [The annals of Yuen Ren Chao]. Beijing: Commercial Press.

Contributors

MUZAFFAR ALAM George V. Bobrinskoy Professor, South Asian Languages and Civilizations, University of Chicago

SUSAN L. BURNS Associate Professor of Japanese History and East Asian Languages and Civilizations, University of Chicago

KU-MING KEVIN CHANG Associate Professor of History and Philology, Academia Sinica, Taiwan

BENJAMIN A. ELMAN Gordon Wu '58 Professor of Chinese Studies, Princeton University

YAAKOV ELMAN Herbert S. and Naomi Denenberg Chair in Talmudic Studies, Yeshiva University

KHALED EL-ROUAYHEB Professor of Islamic Intellectual History, Harvard University

ANTHONY GRAFTON Henry Putnam University Professor of History, Princeton University

BEATRICE GRUENDLER Professor of Arabic Language and Literature, Yale University

CONSTANZE GÜTHENKE Associate Professor of Classics and Hellenic Studies, Princeton University

CHRISTOPH KÖNIG Professor für Neue deutsche Literatur, Universität Osnabrück

MICHAEL LACKNER Professor of Chinese Studies, Universität Erlangen

FRANCO MONTANARI Professor of Ancient Greek Literature, Universita' degli Studi di Genova

SHELDON POLLOCK Arvind Raghunathan Professor of Sanskrit and South Asian Studies, Columbia University

FAN-SEN WANG Vice President and Distinguished Professor of History and Philology, Academia Sinica, Taiwan

JAMES E. G. ZETZEL Anthon Professor of Latin, Columbia University

Index

Abaye, 73, 83, 84, 85–91
ʿAbbas, Ihsan, 10
Abbasid: dynasty 101, 106; elite, 112
Abbasid period, 14, 18, 94, 97-98, 102
ʿAbd al-Laṭīf ʿAbdallāh ʿAbbāsī Gujarātī, 13, 20, 200; origin of quest to study Rūmī, 178–179; life and works of, 179–181, 363nn6–10; on significance of *Mathnavī*, 181–183, 191; on significance of own work, 185–186, 193–194; lexicography of, 188–190. *See also Mathnavī* (Rūmī)
abgad, 95
Abū al-Shīṣ, 104
Abū l-ʿAbbās Aḥmad Ibn Thawāba. *See* Ibn Thawāba, Abū l-ʿAbbās Aḥmad
Abū l-Faḍl, 178, 190
Abū Nuwās, 108–109
Abū Tammām, 100, 105–108, 110–112
Abū ʿUbayda, 93
Academia Sinica, 22, 312, 325
Ad familiares (Cicero), 163, 168
Aelius Paetus Catus, Sextus, 49–51, 53, 61, 62
Aeneid (Virgil), 56, 167
Aeschines, 31
Aeschylus, 155
Against Ctesiphon (Aeschines), 31
Aitareya Brāhmaṇa, 131
Akhbār Abī Nuwās (Abū Hiffān, Ibn Manẓūr), 350nn85, 87; excerpts from, 109
Akhbār Abī Tammām (al-Ṣūlī), 103, 105–06, 110–111, 348n51
Akhbār/khbar, 94, 102–104, 110, 112
Alam, Muzaffar, 13, 20, 178–200
alaṅkāraśāstra, 115
alaukika, 116
Alberti, Leon Battista, 165, 169, 172
Alexander Aetolus, 28
Alexandrian Library & Museum, 25, 28, 52
Alexandrian philology, 25–27, 52; *ekdosis* in, 27–36; authenticity in, 33–34, 36, 38, 338n62; textual criticism in, 36–44. *See also* Hellenistic age
allegorical representation, 45–46, 112, 157–158, 162, 228, 248, 258
Altertumswissenschaft. See German classical philology *(Altertumswissenschaft)*
Altphilologie, 6, 13
Amaru, 122
Amaruśataka (Amaru), 122
American Journal of Philology, 264, 331, 375n11
American Philological Association, 264, 331, 334n29, 375n11
anagignoskein/anagnosis, 27
Analects (Chinese Classic), 138, 142, 227, 328
analogical exegesis, 59–64, 76, 82, 107, 109, 211, 261
Analysis of Characters as an Explanation of Writing (Xu), 227
Ānandavardhana, 351n3
ancient textual philology, 12–15, 19–20; of Homer, 27–36; conjecture *vs.* comparative variants in, 38–43; influence on culture, 156; in medieval Italy, 158–159; Wolf on, 272–273. *See also* humanist philology; *specific types*
Andhra scholarship, 117
Anfangsgründe der Sprachwissenschaft (Bernhardi), 318
animal prohibitions in rabbinic law, 67, 68, 71, 72, 77–78

Annales (Ennius), 51, 52
Annals (*Chunqiu,* Chinese Classic), 226, 233, 234–235, 236–238, 328; *Gongyang Commentary,* 237–238; *Zuo Commentary,* 238
Annius, 173–174
antiquarian philology, 317
Anūshirvān, Kisrā, 101
Anyang archaeological excavation, 327, 330
Apāṇinīyaprāmāṇyasādhana (Nārāyaṇa Bhaṭṭatīri), 123
Apollonius Rhodius, 25
Arabia, pre-Islamic, 96
Arabian Peninsula, 96
Arabic, classical, 92–93
Arabic language, 10, 13, 92–97, 188, 345n1, 346n21
Arabic philology: in the Bavli, 76–77; *vs.* poetics, 92, 96–97, 103–107, 110–112, 349n56; Qur'ān in, 92–93; authenticity in, 94–95; poet biographies and, 102–103; tradition of, 198–199
Arabic poetics/literary criticism, 18; on modern poetry, 93, 96–107, 347n34; on ancient poetry, 93–97; *vs.* philology, 103–107, 110–112, 349n56; as a discipline, 104–107, 112; grammarians criticism in, 107–110
ʿarabiyya, 14, 18, 92–93, 98, 104, 107
Arabs 93, 95. *See also* Bedouin(s)
Aristarchus of Samothrace, 25, 26, 28, 35–36, 39, 40, 52
Aristonicus, 26
Aristophanes of Byzantium, 25, 35–36, 52
Aristotle, 101, 155, 156
Arjunamiśra, 117
Arjunavarmadeva, 122
ars grammatica, 339n3
Ars Maior (Donatus), 59
Ars Minor (Donatus), 59
Aruṇagirinātha, 125–127
Asaṅga, 128
Asconius Pedianus, Quintus, 53, 341n27
Ashikari yoshi (Ueda), 256
al-ʿAskarī 102
al-Aṣmaʿī, 99, 102
Asokan edicts, 15
Assaying of Poetry (Qudāma), 101
Ast, Friedrich, 269
astronomy, 173, 176, 240–241
Atesh, Ahmed, 10
athetein/athetesis, 34, 36, 336n30, 336n32, 337n33
Ātmānanda, 130
al-ʿAttābī, 109
Attic Nights (Gellius), 53, 55, 60
Auerbach, Erich, 4, 5, 66
Augustine, Saint, 61, 140
Augustus, 26
authenticity of works: in Alexandrian philology, 33–34, 36, 38, 338n62; in Roman philology, 53–54, 170–173; in Arabic philology, 94–95; in Sanskrit philology, 128; in Chinese philology, 147, 152; of *Mathnavī* verses, 186–187, 199, 365n30. *See also* forgery; textual criticism
authorial philology, 14, 18
authority of works: in Sanskrit philology, 124, 128; of *Nuskha-i Nāsikha,* 194–198
awareness: in German classical philology, 7; in rabbinic philology, 90, 91; in Vedic philology, 131–132; in Chinese philology, 143, 232, 330; in German classical philology, 266. *See also* intention
Awrāq (al-Ṣūlī), 102–103
axial age, 64
Aztec philology, 139–140

Babylonian Talmud (the Bavli), 64, 70, 71, 73–77, 80, 81, 83–91
badīʿ, 18–19, 100, 102, 104, 105, 349n63
Badīʿ (Ibn al-Muʿtazz) 101, 104, 349nn62–64. *See also* muḥdath poetry
balāgha, 19. *See also* faṣīḥ
Banū Nawbakht, 106, 350n72
Bashshār b. Burd, 105, 107
Bava Batra, 78
Bava Metzia, 63–64, 78, 80, 90
Bava Qamma, 81–82
Bavli. *See* Babylonian Talmud (the Bavli)
Baydabā', 101
Beazley, J. D., 155
Bédier, Joseph, 9, 222
Bedouin(s): as language experts, 92, 94; poetry, 93–95. *See also* Arabs
beherah, 90
Bellum Punicum (Naevius), 51, 52
Benedict of Nursia, 61
Benfey, Theodor, 318
Bengal scholarship, 117
Bentley, Richard, 271
Bergstraesser, Gotthelf, 10
Bernhardi, August Ferdinand, 318
Betti, Emilio, 139
Bhāravi, 117
Bhaṭṭa Nāyaka, 351n3

Bhaṭṭatīri, Melpputtūr Nārāyaṇa, 1
Bhaṭṭojī Dīkṣita, 123
Bhavabhūti, 124
Bhoja, 124, 351n3; *Śṛṅgāraprakāśa,* 117
Bible. *See* Christian Bible; Hebrew Bible
biblical philology. *See* rabbinic philology
bid'a, 97, 100
Bildung, 268–270, 275–276
Biographies of Astronomers and Mathematicians (Ruan), 241
Biondi, Flavio, 172
Bloomfield, Leonard, 327, 382n23
Blumenberg, Hans, 307
Boeckh, August, 7, 13, 266–267, 276–281, 295
Boeotia (Varro), 54
Bollack, Jean, 5, 293, 296, 309
Book of the Covenant, 75
Book of the New Style (Ibn al-Mu'tazz), 101, 104
Book of the Sheet, The (Ibn al-Jarrāḥ), 102
Book of the Sheets, The (Awrāq) (al-Ṣūlī), 102–103
Book of the Wars of the Lord, 63
book production: in Hellenistic age, 27–33; and textual commentary, 55, 341n24; in Arabic culture, 95; in fifteenth century Italy, 160–161; effects on medieval scholarship, 164–165
Bopp, Franz, 315
Boulliau, Ismael, 3
British education of classical studies, 154–156
Brugmann, Karl, 315, 318
Bruni, Leonardo, 159, 160
Brush Talks from the Dream Book, 241
buddhavacana, 128
Buddhist scripture, 128
Budé, Guillaume, 162
Burns, Susan L., 11, 15, 21, 245–263
Burton, Robert, 3
Bussi, Giovanni Andrea, 164, 165, 166
But-khāna, 179, 198, 363n6
Buxtorf, Johann, 176

Caecilius, 55–56
Caesar, Julius, 159, 166
Calderini, Domizio, 168
Callimachus, 25, 52
Campano, Giannantonio, 164
Cangjie pian (Li), 138
Canon of Avicenna, 157
Carmina Saliaria, 61
Cārullāh, Veliyüddīn, 223
Centre de recherche philologique, 5
Chandragomin, 124
Chang, Ku-ming Kevin, 22, 260, 311–331
Change (*Yijing,* Chinese Classic). See *Classic of Changes* (*Yijing,* Chinese Classic)
Chao, Yuen Ren, 312, 319–325, 327–331
Charisius, 59
Chavannes, Éduoard, 324
Cheng Duanli, 137–138
Cheng Yi, 228
Chen Kui, 137
Chen Yinke, 327, 330
Chinese language, 137–138, 144, 313–314, 320–328
Chinese philology, 19; evidential studies, 11, 20, 226, 229–230, 234–244, 312, 326, 328–330; development of, 137–139, 225–226; knowledge in, 145–152, 359n32; diagrams interpreting *Zhongyong,* 146–153, 359n31; authenticity in, 147, 152; of Classics, 226–231; Song Learning, 230–236, 239–240; Han Learning, 230–239, 243–244; poetry in, 232–234; Old Text *vs.* New Text debates, 236–239, 243–244; medical, 239–240; mathematical, 240–241, 242; Fu and, 312–313, 316–319; Chao and, 319–325; history and, 325–326
Chinese scholarship, 11, 15, 16, 20, 22, 225–226, 232–236, 313, 314, 320, 326, 328
Chomsky, Noam, 329
Christian Bible, 65, 155, 157, 176
Christian Bible (Luther), 316, 382n18
Christian philology, 17–18, 53, 61, 140
Chronicles, 63, 66–67, 343n7
chronological system, ancient, 173–174, 176
Chrysoloras, Manuel, 160
Cicero, 17, 46, 48, 55, 57, 158–159
Ciceronian, The (Erasmus), 160
City of God (Augustine), 165
Classes of [Modern] Poets (Ibn al-Mu'tazz), 102; excerpt from, 104
Classic of Changes (*Yijing,* Chinese Classic), 143, 144, 152, 153, 226, 233, 234, 235, 248
Code of Justinian, 69
collation of texts: of *Mathnavī,* 13, 179, 183–184, 186–188, 191; in Alexandrian philology, 26, 30, 32, 38, 40–41, 55; in Sanskrit scholarship, 118; in Ottoman philology, 219, 220; in German classical philology, 282
commentary. *See* textual commentary
comparative literature, 2, 3, 8, 375n9

emendatio, 46, 47, 275
emendation: in Alexandrian philology, 29, 31, 38, 41; in Roman philology, 50, 56; in rabbinic philology, 83; in Sanskrit philology, 118, 120–124; in Chinese philology, 138, 139; in humanist philology, 167–169
enarratio, 46, 47
Encyclopedia and Methodology of All the Philological Sciences (Boeckh), 7, 277, 280
encyclopedia as term, 267, 268, 274
Encyclopedia Britannica, 8
Engi shiki, 254
English schooling of Latin and Greek, 154–155
Ennius, Quintus, 51, 52
Enūma Eliš, 63
ephexis, 8
epic commentaries, Sanskrit, 117, 118–120, 353nn22, 23
Epic of Gilgameš, 65
epistemology of philology, 23, 287–291
Epistles (Seneca), 48
Erasmus, Desiderius, 16, 160
Eratosthenes, 6, 25
Ethé, Hermann, 196–197
Études sur la phonologie chinoise (Karlgren), 323–324
Etymologische Forschungen auf dem Gebiete der Indogermanischen Sprachen (Pott), 315
euphonic change of Japanese language, 249–250
Euripides, 155
European philology: modern, 4, 6, 9–10, 16, 19–20; ancient *(See specific regional type)*
Eurydice, 158, 285
evidential scholarship: in China, 11, 20, 226, 229–230, 243–244, 312, 326, 328–330; in Japan, 12; in Ottoman Empire, 209, 211
exegesis. *See* hermeneutics; textual criticism
Exegesis in Verse (Kumārila), 116
Exodus, 63, 64, 67–68, 71, 72, 75, 157
Explanatory Rewriting of the Qur'ān (Abū ʿUbayda), 93

fair copy of *ekdosis,* 35, 38
faṣīḥ, 94
Festus, Sextus Pompeius, 59, 60, 166
Filetico, Martino, 167
Fishbane, Michael, 68
Five Classics (Chinese), 226–227, 232–236, 239
Five Ways *(Zhongyong),* 147–152
forgery: in Arabic poetry, 95; in Sanskrit epics, 122; of Annius, 173–174; of *Mathnavī,* 186–187; in Chinese Classics, 227; in Japanese medical philology, 259. *See also* authenticity of works
Foundations of Poetry (Thaʿlab), 101
Four Books (Chinese Classics), 228, 232–236
Fu Sinian. *See* Fu Ssu-nien
Fu Ssu-nien, 312–316, 325–331

Gabelentz, Georg von der, 318, 382n29
Gadamer, Hans-Georg, 140, 293, 295
Galen, 36–38 *(De indolentia),* 101, 156–157, 162, 342n35
Gaonic period in Jewish history, 64, 84
Gellius, Aulus, 53, 55, 168, 342n37
genealogy of Mughal scholars, 195, 197
Genesis, 63, 76
German classical philology *(Altertumswissenschaft),* 9, 21–22, 334n29; controversy of, 13; *ekdoseis* in, 27–38; interpretations of, 38–44; commentaries in, 155–157; tensions in nineteenth century, 265–266, 374n6; modernity and, 265–271; *Einseitigkeit* in, 267, 268, 272, 279, 280; *Bildung* in, 268–270, 275–276, 288; development of, 270–272, 314–316, 329; limitations of, 272–276
German national literature *(Germanistik),* 316, 333n14
Gerok-Reiter, Annette, 306–308
Geschichte der Germanistik, 333n14, 345
Geschichte der Philologie, 314
Gesner, Johann Mattias, 270
gharaḍ, 101, 348n43
Ghazālī, 215
al-Ghazzī, Badr al-Dīn, 219–220
Gildersleeve, Basil, 264–266, 267
glossai, 28
Gnomon of the Zhou Dynasty and Classic of Computations, 240
Goethe, 274–275, 375n9, 376n47
Gonda Naosuke, 259
Gongyang Commentary. See *Annals (Chunqiu,* Chinese Classic)
Grafton, Anthony, 10, 19, 154–177, 274
grammar: Arabic, 93–97, 113, 351n99; Chinese, 146, 329, 384n78
grammarians: in Alexandria, 26–35; *vs.* philologists, 46, 48, 57–59, 62, 340n4, 342n37; origin of Roman, 49–51; Latin, 59–61; Arabic philology and, 94, 96, 98, 101, 106–111; in Germany, 316–317, 329

Grammatici Latini (Keil), 58
grammatikoi, 26
Grandgent, Charles H., 320
Granet, Marcel, 313
graphe, 12–13, 27
graphein, 27
Great Chain of Academic Being, 2–3
Great Learning (Chinese Classic), 227
Greek philology, 25–44, 52, 53, 154–155, 160–161. *See also* Hellenistic age
Gregory of Tours, 61
Grimm, Jacob, 316, 382n18
Grimm brothers, 316
Gruendler, Beatrice, 13–14, 18, 92–113, 400–401
Grundriss der arabischen Philologie (Heinrichs), 401
Grundriss der Philologie (Ast), 269
Grundriss der vergleichenden Grammatik der indogermanischen Sprachen (Brugmann and Curtius), 315
Guarino of Verona, 166
Gu Jiegang, 244, 326, 328
Guoyu xin shiyun (Chao), 322
Güthenke, Constanze, 7, 21, 264–284, 314
Gu Yenwu, 326

ha-Amosni, Shimon (or Nehemiah), 75
Ḥadīqa (Sanā'ī), 178, 180
Ḥadīqat al-Ḥaqīqa (Sanā'ī), 180
Haga Ya'ichi, 260–262
hagigah offering, 68
hakhlili, 77
Han Learning, 230–239, 243–244
Harivaṃśa, 119
Harrison, Edward, 154
Haslam, Michael, 31
ḥaswī, 208–209
Hebrew Bible, 63–66, 68; duplication in, 71; accuracy of, 140; British education in, 155; medieval studies of, 161–162; accuracy of, 176. *See also* rabbinic philology; *specific sections*
Heidegger, Martin, 293, 295
Heinitz, Wilhelm, 322
Heinrichs, Wolfhart, 104, 349n63, 401
Hellenistic age, 12–13, 25–26, 272–273. *See also* Greek philology
Hermann, Gottfried, 13, 281–282
hermeneutics, 278, 280; Sanskrit, 115; Vedic, 132; in Chinese philology, 139; definition of, 289, 292–293, 379n12; as theory of philological praxis, 291–292; types of, 292–293; philosophy of, 294–298; conflicts of, 305–310. *See also* textual criticism
Herodotus, 26, 155, 160
Heyne, Christian Gottlob, 6, 270
Hezekiah, 89
Hillel, 76
Himalaya, 125–126
Hippocrates, 156
Hirata Atsutane, 257, 259, 261
Hirshman, Marc, 65
History (Livy), 55
History of Great Japan (Tokugawa Mitsukuni), 248–249
Homer, *ekdosis* of, 27–36
Huang Gan, 137
Hu Anguo, 236
Hui Dong, 230, 232
humanist philology: in medieval Italy, 159, 162–163, 169; historical revolution in, 163, 176–177; in fifteenth-seventeenth centuries, 163–166; emendation in, 167–169; authenticity in, 170–174, 222–223. *See also* ancient textual philology
Humboldt, Wilhelm von, 2, 267, 269, 275
Hu Shih/Hu Shi, 321
Hu Wei, 230
Hyginus, 56
hymns, biblical philology of, 53, 61
hyperbole: Arabic, 101, 109, 348n44, 349n64
hypomnema/hypomnemata, 28, 36, 337n41

Ibn al-Aʿrābī, 100
Ibn al-Jarrāḥ, 102, 103, 348n49
Ibn al-Muʿtazz, 100–104, 111–112, 348n50
Ibn Jamāʿah, Badr al-Dīn, 203, 204–207, 213
Ibn Mujāhid, 93
Ibn Qutayba, 102
Ibn Ṭabāṭabā', 101
Ibn Thawāba, Abū l-ʿAbbās Aḥmad, 106
Ibrāhīm b. Abī Muḥammad al-Yazīdī, 108–109
Ibrāhīm Dihlavī, 189
idolatry in rabbanic law, 86–87
Iḥyā' ʿulūm al-dīn (Ghazālī), 215
ilḥāqī, 186, 199, 367n54
Iliad (Homer), 30, 33
illness in rabbinical law, 88
imitation. *See* forgery
Indian classical languages, 4, 9, 15

Indian philology. *See* Sanskrit philology
Indian scholarship, 14, 16, 117, 123, 125, 351n3
individuality, 291–295
Indo-Persian scholarship, 198–200
insistent reading, 284, 290–291, 296, 305, 309, 378n82
"Inspiration of the Sanctuary," The (Müneccimbāşī), 202
Institute of History and Philology, Academia Sinica, 22, 312, 325–327, 328, 330
Instructing the Student in the Pathways of Learning (Zarnūjī), 203
intention: in Alexandrian philology, 30, 33; in rabbinic philology, 81–82, 85–87, 90, 91; in Arabic poetry, 101; in Chinese philology, 122, 143, 244; in Ottoman philology, 203, 208, 209, 221; in nativist philology, 246, 256, 259
interpolation: in Alexandrian philology, 35, 37; in Sanskrit philology, 119, 122; of *Mathnavī,* 186–187, 190, 197–199
interpretation of texts. *See* hermeneutics
isnād, 103
Israelite scholarship, ancient, 63–66
Italian scholarship, 158, 159
Itsu no chiwake (Tachibana), 258
iudicium, 46
Ivanov, Aleksei Ivanovich, 324

Jahāngīr, 178, 188
Jāhilī, 93. *See also* poetry: Arabic pre-Islamic
Jain scripture, 15, 117, 128
James, Arthur Lloyd, 322
Jāmī, ʿAbd al- Raḥmān, 181–182, 216
Jāmiʿ al-duwal (Müneccimbāşī), 202
Japan: scholarship in, 11, 15; Korean influences on, 245–246; Chinese influence on, 252, 259; national literature movement in, 260–261, 263
Japanese language, 249–256
Japanese philology. *See* nativist philology
Jaspers, Karl, 64
Jayatīrtha, 131
Jespersen, Otto, 317, 319, 382n23
Jewish philology. *See* rabbinic philology
Jiao Xun, 242
Ji Yun, 236
Jñānadīpikā (Devabodha), 117, 119
Jones, Daniel, 322
Jones, Stephen, 322
Judah. *See* R. Judah
Judaism, 63–64, 69, 71
al-Jumaḥī, 102
jurisprudence: in India, 14; in Islamic scholarship, 182, 205; in Ottoman education, 205, 208, 209, 211, 214–216, 370n77
al-Jurjānī, ʿAbdalqāhir, 102, 221, 223
Justinian, 61–62, 79, 156

Kālidāsa, 117, 121
Kalimi, Isaac, 67
Kāmasūtra, 126–127
Kamo no Mabuchi, 251, 253, 256
kana, 21
kangaku, 255
Kang Youwei, 237, 238–239
Kant, Immanuel, 141, 288, 289
kaozheng, 12, 20, 239, 312. *See also* evidential scholarship
Ḳara Ḫalīl Tīrevī, 221–222, 223
Karlgren, Bernhard, 323–325
Kashmiri scholarship, 117
Kātyāyana, 123
kāvya, 116, 118, 133
al-Kawthari, Muhammad Zahid, 10
Keichū, 250, 253
Kerala scholarship, 117, 123, 125
Key to the Sciences (al-Sakkākī), 113
Khālid b. Yazīd b. Mazyad, 100
al-Khalīl, 94
Khān Mashhadī, Lashkar, 180, 194
Kin Bunkyō, 249
al-Kisāʾī, 93
Knoop, Wera Ouckama, 285. See also *Sonnets to Orpheus* (Rilke)
knowledge (concept): in Chinese philology, 145–152, 359n32; acquisition of, 201–207, 207–212, 370n84; historicity of, 294–296
Kobayashi Hideo, 262
Kojiki, 21, 245, 247, 249–250, 252–253
Kojikiden (Motoori), 252–259, 261–263
Kojima Noriyuki, 254
kokugaku, 11, 12, 21, 245, 255
Kong Jihan, 241
König, Christoph, 5, 21, 284, 285–310
Konjekturalkritik, 39
Korean influence on Japan, 15, 241, 245–246, 247
Koshiseibun (Hirata), 257
Koyasu Nobukuni, 246
Kristeva, Julia, 145
Kugel, James, 70

Kumārasambhava (Kālidāsa), 121, 122, 125–127
Kumārila, 132
kundoku, 249, 250–251, 254

Lachmann, Karl, 9, 282, 379n10
Lachmann method, 43, 54, 282, 378n78, 379n10
Lackner, Michael, 11, 15, 19, 137–153, 226, 247, 257
Laḥn al-ʿāmma, 97
lakṣyagranthas, 122
Latin classical studies: translation as theory in, 16; grammar, 59–61, 169; in England, 154–156; Wolf on, 272–273, 376n38, 376n44
Latin Language (Varro), 60
laukika, 116
Learning of the Way. See *daoxue*
Lebanese scholarship, 10
L'École de Lille, 5
lectio, 27, 46
Lectures on Altertumswissenschaft (Wolf). See *Darstellung der Alterthumswissenschaft* (Wolf)
legal philology: rabbinic, 18, 65–70, 77–82, 85, 90–91; Roman, 49–51, 53, 61–62, 69, 156–158, 162; Chinese, 232, 233, 234
legere, 27
leshon hedyot, 63–64
lexeis, 28
lexicography, Arabic, 94, 96, 98
lexicography of ʿAbd al-Laṭīf, 188–190
Liao Ping, 238–239
Library of Alexandria, 25, 28
Li Fang-kuei/Li Fanggui, 327
Life and Growth of Language (Whitney), 319
limitation of modern philology, 267, 272–276, 278, 281, 289–291, 376n36
linguistics, 3, 22; decline of, 2; rise of discipline of, 8–10, 315–316, 334n27, 334n32; Qur'ānic scholarship and, 14, 92–93; in Ottoman education, 211; Lachmann method in, 282; in China, 319-325, 327, 329, 331; divorce from philology, 311–318, 327, 329, 331. *See also specific languages*
Linguistic Society of America, 330, 334n27
linguistique, 22
Lipsius, Justus, 175
Li Rui, 242
Li Shanlan, 243
Lishi yuyan yanjiusuo. *See* Institute of History and Philology, Academia Sinica
Listenwissenschaft, 64
literary criticism (and theory), 3, 8, 9. *See also* textual criticism
literary genre, Arabic 98–99, 347n26
literati, Arabic, 108, 110
living philology, 317
Livy, 55, 157, 158, 164
Li Ye, 240
logic in Ottoman education, 208–216
Lucilius, Gaius, 51, 52
lugha, 18
Lundell, Johan August, 324
Lunyu (Chinese Classic). See *Analects* (Chinese Classic)
Luther, Martin, 316
Lycophron, 28

Madhva, 120, 130
Madras School of Orientalism, 334n31
Maffei, Scipione, 228
Mahābhārata (Nīlakaṇṭha), 13, 117, 118–120, 130
Mahāyāna Buddhism, 128
Mahozan school in Babylonia, 81, 83, 84, 89
majālis, 95
Makeham, John, 138
Mallinātha, 119, 122
Mammaṭa, 123
Mandarin. *See* Chinese language
al-Manṣūr, 99
Man'yō daishōkī (Keichū), 250
Man'yōshū, 21, 249–252, 254
Man'yōshū (Yi). See *Mō hitotsu no Man'yōshū* (Yi)
Man'yōshū Man'yōkō (Kamo), 251
Martianus Capella, 13, 45
Martini, Martino, 176
al-Marzubānī, 95, 346n11
Maspero, Henri, 313, 324
Mathematical Astronomy of the Chongzhen Reign, 240
Mathematical Manual of Xie Chawei, 240
mathematical philology in China, 229, 239–242
Mathnavī (Rūmī), 13, 20; significance of, 178, 181–183; collation of, 183–184, 186–188; symbolism of six and, 184–185, 365n25; authenticity of verses, 186–187, 199, 365n30; textual commentary of, 188–191; poetic criticism of, 191–194

Matociis, Giovanni de, 158
meat prohibition in rabbinic law, 67, 68, 71, 72, 77–78, 85–86
medical philology: in medieval times, 156–157, 162; in China, 239–240; in Japan, 259–260
Meghadūta, 119
Mei Juecheng, 240, 242
Meillet, Antoine, 322
Mei Wending, 240, 241, 242
Memento to the Listener and Speaker of the Manner of the Scholar and the Student, The (Ibn Jamāʿah), 203, 204–206
Mencius (Chinese Classic), 227
Mercury (god), 45–46
Mesopotamian scholarship, 63
Messick, Brinkley, 207
Metamorphoses (Ovid), 285
metaphilology, 5
metaphor, Arabic, 100, 109
el-Mevlevī, Aḥmed ibn Lütfullāh, 202
micut, 75
Middle Eastern scholarship, 10, 13
midrash aggadah, 65, 68–69
midreshei aggadah, 70
midreshei halakhah, 70
Milesian Tales (Sisenna), 59
milk prohibition in rabbinic law, 67, 68, 71, 72, 77–78, 85–86
Mīmāṃsā, (Mīmāṃsā discipline), 14, 115, 127, 129, 131, 132
mimesis, 66
Mir'āt al-Mathnavī (ʿAbd al-Laṭīf), 181, 196–197
Mishnah, 18, 64, 69, 73, 77–82, 85
mishnaic law, 77–82
mishneh torah, 64
modernization and philology, 9–11, 133–134
Mohaghegh, Mehdi, 10
Mō hitotsu no Man'yōshū (Yi), 245–246
Montanari, Franco, 13, 17, 25–44
Montfaucon, Dom Bernard de, 228
monuments and relics, authenticity of, 172–173
Mörchen, Hermann, 307–308
Moscovitz, Leib, 84–85, 88, 90
Motoori Norinaga, 11, 21, 252–257, 260–263
al-Mubarrad, 105–106, 111–112
mudhākarah, 212, 213
al-Mufaḍḍal al-Ḍabbī, 99
Mughal philology: origin of, 178–179; scholar environment and, 180, 182, 183, 186, 189, 194–198; *Mathnavī's* significance in, 181–183. See also *Mathnavī* (Rūmī)
muḥaddith/muḥaddithūn, 93
Muhammad, Prophet 92
Muḥammad, Jalāl al-Dīn, 197, 198
muḥdath poetry (muḥdathūn), 100, 102, 104, 348n50, 349n63. *See also* poetry: Arabic Abbasid, modern (muḥdath)
mülāzemets, 218
Müller, F. Max, 318
Müneccimbāşī, 202, 208–212, 213, 223
muqābala, 13, 179
Murāri, 124
Murray, Gilbert, 155
Muslim b. al-Walīd, 105, 108
Mustawfī, Ḥamdallāh, 198, 367n64
muṭālaʿah, 202, 204, 206, 207, 208–210, 214–215
muwallad, 101, 348n42
al-Muwaswis, Muṣʿab, 103
Mysteries of Eloquence (ʿAbdalqāhir al-Jurjāanī), 102

Naevius, Gnaeus, 51, 52
Nafisi, Sa'id, 10
Nāgārjuna, 128
naḥw (uṣūʿ al-naḥw), 18, 94, 97. *See also* grammar: Arabic
naïve philology, 288, 296, 309
Nan-Kojikiden (Tachibana), 258
Nanni, Giovanni, 173–174
Nārāyaṇa Bhaṭṭatīri, Melpputtūr, 123, 124, 134, 136
narratology, 66
nativist philology, 11, 21; origin of, 245–247, 251–252; *Kojikiden* and, 252–255; response to Motoori, 255–258, 261–263; ancient text origins, 258–260; revival by Haga, 260–262. *See also* Japan
Natural History (Pliny), 158
New Testament, 155, 161–162
Niccoli, Niccolò, 169
Nicholson, R. A., 196–197, 367n54
Nickau, Klaus, 28
Nietzsche, Friedrich Wilhelm, 7–8, 267, 287
Nihon shoki, 247–248, 254, 258
Nīlakaṇṭha Caturdhara, 13, 118–119
Nirukta, 129, 130, 132
nondiscursive praxis of philology, 288, 294–298, 309–310
Nonius Marcellus, 60
nontextual evidence, authenticity of, 172–173, 175

Notes on the Mathematical Heritage, 240
numerus versuum (of Homer), 35, 36
Nuskha-i Nāsikha (ʿAbd al-Laṭīf): production of, 180–191, 193–194; significance of, 194–195, 198–199; textual criticism of, 196–197; modern copy of, 199. See also *Mathnavī* (Rūmī)

obelos, 33, 36, 336n30, 336n32, 337n33. *See also* Zenodotus as *diorthotes*
Octavius Lampadio, Gaius, 51, 52
Odyssey (Homer), 30, 33
officia, 46, 339n3
Ogyū Sorai, 250, 252
Old Testament. *See* Hebrew Bible
Olympia, Greece, 264–265
omnisignificance of rabbinic literature, 70–78, 86, 90–91
On the Agrarian Law (Cicero), 55
On the Study of Antiquity, and of Greek Antiquity in Particular (Humboldt), 269
ope ingenii, 26, 38
Opium War, 225, 243
oral-aural learning in Ottoman education, 201–207, 370n84
oral transmission in Sanskrit, 117, 352n7
Orpheus, 158, 285, 298–305
Ottoman philology, 10, 20; knowledge acquisition in, 202–212; schools of law in, 204, 208; rational sciences in, 208–209, 211, 213–220; reform of, 217–219, 223–224, 371n102; deep reading in, 221–222
ou graphein, 36, 336n32, 337n33
Ouyang Xiu, 153
Ovid mythologies, 157, 285
Oxford classical studies, 154–155

paideia, 27, 28
Paleographica graeca (Montfaucon), 228
paleography, 30, 227–228, 230, 234, 353n23
Pali scholarship, 128
Pāṇini, 114, 123–124
Panofsky, Erwin, 163, 170
papyri, *ekdosis* examplars, 29–32
Parsons, Peter J., 32
Pārvatī, 125–127
paschal sacrifice, 67–68
Passy, Paul, 322
Patañjali, 123, 124
'Pataphilology (mythological twin), 46, 57–58, 62
patria potestas, 69
Patrizi, Francesco, 175
Pelliot, Paul, 313–314, 324
Pentateuch, 63–66, 70–71
Pergamene criticism, 49
Pericles, 154
Perotti, Niccolò, 165
Persian philology. *See* Mughal philology
Persians (Timotheus), 30
peshat/peshut, 76
peshi'uta, 81–82
Petrarca, Francesco, 158–159
Pfeiffer, Rudolph, 27–28, 38, 40
Pharisees, 65, 69
philologia, 12–13, 340n4
philological arts, origins of, 13, 14, 15, 18–19
Philology (mythological twin), 45–46, 57–58, 62
philology as conceptual category, 12–16, 22–23, 25–27, 40–44; modern definitions of, 46–48, 114, 132–136, 139–140, 266–269, 277–278, 340n4; *vs.* grammarians, 57–59, 62, 342n37. *See also* philosophy: of philology
philology as discipline: rise and fall of European, 1–11, 22–23, 311, 334n27, 334n29; subdisciplines of, 3, 8, 15; metaphilology, 5; global categories of, 12; of ancient texts, 12–15, 52; origin of, 17, 25; of dramatic works, 28, 53; of modern texts, 52; specialized research of, 265, 267–270, 274; limitations of, 267, 272–276, 278, 281, 289–291, 309, 376n36; refinement of modern, 281–284; praxis of, 287–291, 309–310; divorce from linguistics, 311–325, 327, 329, 331; critics of, 382n23, 382n29. *See also* textual criticism; *specific type of philology in different regions and ages*
philosophy: of philology, 7–8, 12–16, 48, 84–91, 278–280; of hermeneutics, 139, 141, 294–298; Chinese, 141; in Ottoman education, 210, 213, 214, 221
phonetics: Sanskrit, 15; European language, 315, 317, 319–320, 322, 324–326, 381n6; Chao and, 319–320, 324–325; Karlgren and, 324
phonology: Arabic, 94; Chinese 230, 234, 323–327, 329–330
Pietro Odo of Montopoli, 167
P.Ilias 12 (Homer), 30
Plato, 155, 277–278, 280, 377n62
PLaur. III/278, 31
Plautus, Titus Maccius, 47, 53, 59, 315
Pliny, 158, 166
Plutarch, 160, 164

P.Odyssey 31, 30
Poems by a Thousand Authors, 234
poetic criticism: Arabic, 94–110; Roman, 158; Persian, 191193; Chinese, 234; Japanese, 245–246, 251; German, 298–309; Sanskrit, 352n7
poetry: Qur'ānic scholarship and, 14; Arabic, 14, 18–19; Greco-Hellenic, 26–31, 52, 341n18; Arabic pre-Islamic, 93–94, 97, 99, 102–105, 110; Arabic poetic genres, 98, 347n26; Arabic Abbasid, modern (muḥdath), 101–106, 110–112; secular, 115–116; Sanskrit, 116–117; Chinese, 232–234; German, 286. *See also specific titles*
Poetry (Chinese Classic), 226, 232–234, 235
Poggio Bracciolini, 159, 160, 163, 169
Poiss, Thomas, 281
Poliziano, Angelo, 168
Pollock, Sheldon, 1–24, 96, 114–136
Pomponio Leto, 166, 167
Pope Nicholas V, 160
Porphyry, 156
poshe'a, 82
Posidippus, papyrus of, 31
Pott, August Friedrich, 315
POxy. 2404, 31
Prakrit scripture, 15, 128, 352n10
Prinsep, James, 15
Probus, Marcus Valerius, 56
Prolegomena ad Homerum (Wolf), 44, 270
Proverbs, 64
Ptolemy I Soter, 25, 28, 160
Ptolemy II Philadelphus, 25, 28
Pumbedita (Babylonia), 83, 88
Pumbeditan school, 80, 81, 83–84, 88, 344n64

al-Qazwīnī, 113
Qian Daxin, 229, 235, 244
Qieyun (Xu), 138
Qin Jiushao, 240
quality of Arabic poetry, 98–100
Qudāma b. Jaʿfar, 101, 348n44
Qumran Dead Sea Texts, 64–65, 68–69
Qur'ān: scholarship of, 14, 65; as source of Arabic language, 92–93; Rūmī and, 182; in Ottoman education, 203, 204, 205, 208, 209; verses on Allah's origins, 364n23
qurrā', 93

Rabbah b. Avuha, 83, 84
Rabbah of Pumbedita, 81, 83, 84
rabbinic philology: roots of, 14, 18, 19, 63–66, 71–73; legal, 67–69, 77–82; classic literature in, 69–70; omnisignificance in, 70–78, 86, 90–91; conceptualization in, 81, 84–90. *See also* Hebrew Bible
Rāghavendratīrtha, 131
Raghuvaṃśa, 118–119
R. Akiva, 75
Rāmāyaṇa commentaries, 117, 120
rasa, 125–126, 355n55
R. Ashi, 74
al-Rashīd, 99
rational sciences in Ottoman education, 208–209, 211, 213–220
Rava, 65, 73, 81, 82, 83, 84, 87–91
Rāvaṇa, 130
Rav of Sura, 79, 83
rāwī/ruwāt, 94. *See also* transmission/transmitters of Arabic language
R. Dimi, 76–77
reading, philological: in Greek philology, 26–28, 30–32, 34, 36–43; in Sanskrit tradition, 124–127; deep reading, 207–213, 221–222; insistent reading, 284, 290–291, 296, 305, 309, 378n82
recension: systematic, 54, 117, 282, 283; of Sanskrit epics, 118–120, 129–130, 353nn22, 23, 356n59; of *Mathnavī,* 196. *See also* editing *vs.* correcting ancient texts
Record of Ritual (*Liji,* Chinese Classic). See *Rituals* (Chinese Classic)
Reformation, 19
Rengakos, Antonios, 40
repetition in rabbinic literature, 71–74
R. Hananiah, 89
rhetoric as discipline, 19, 159
R. Hisda, 83
R. Hoshaya, 89
R. Huna, 79, 83
rhyme books, Chinese language, 322–323
ribbuy, 75
Rilke, Rainer Maria, 285–286, 298–306
Rilkes Sonette an Orpheus (Mörchen), 307
R. Ishmael, 75
Ritschl, Friedrich, 267–268, 375n17
ritual law, Hebrew, 67–69
Rituals (*Liji,* Chinese Classic), 142, 226, 233, 234
Rituals of Zhou. See *Rituals* (*Liji,* Chinese Classic)
R. Jeremiah, 87
R. Joseph, 83, 84
R. Judah, 77, 79–80, 83
R. Nahman, 81, 83, 84, 89

Rolandello, Francesco, 165
Roman culture: histories, 55, 157–158; legal education in, 156; authenticity of antiquities from, 171–173
Roman philology: classes of, 17; origins of, 45, 48–54; authenticity in, 53–54, 170–173; textual commentary in, 54–57; Latin grammar in, 57–60; Palestinian law in, 79–84
Romanus, Julius, 59
Rosenthal, Franz, 20
Rousselot, Jean-Pierre, 322, 324
R. Papa, 84, 89
R. Shimon, 75
R. Simeon, 89
Ruan Yuan, 229, 241
Rūmī, Jalāl al-Dīn, 13, 20, 178, 190. *See also* *Mathnavī* (Rūmī)
R. Yannai, 89
R. Yohanan, 79, 89, 90
R. Zeira, 89

Sāçaḳlīzāde, Meḥmed, 213–217, 221, 223, 370n77
Sachphilologie, 13, 97–98, 281
Ṣadguruśiṣya, 130
Śākaṭāyana, 124
al-Sakkākī, 113
Salutati, Coluccio, 159, 160, 166
Samuel of Nehardea, 79, 83
Sanā'ī, 178
Sanskrit philology: early evidence of, 114–117; recension in, 117–120; emendation in, 120–124; reading, 124–127; of Vedic canon, 127–132; authenticity in, 128; comparative philology and, 132–136, 315
Sanskrit scholarship, 9, 13, 16, 19, 115
Sapir, Edward, 319, 327
Sasanian Book of a Thousand Decisions, 79
śāstras, 115
Satires (Lucilius), 51
Saussure, Ferdinand de, 312, 316–317, 331
Sāyaṇa, 129–132, 136, 357nn68, 69
Scaliger, Joseph, 166, 175, 176, 272
Schlegel, Friedrich, 7, 13, 21, 280
Schleicher, August, 315
Schleiermacher, Friedrich, 21, 278, 289, 291–293
Schwartz, Arthur, 45, 62
scribere/scriptura, 27
Scripture, Edward Wheeler, 322
Scripture, Holy. *See* Hebrew Bible; Qur'ān
Sea Mirror of Circular Measurement (Li), 240
Second Temple, destruction of, 68–70, 79
sefer ha-berit, 64
semeion/semeia, 33–34, 35
Seneca, 48
Şerif b. Seyyid Mehmed, 198, 367n65
Servius, 55, 59, 60
Setubandha commentary, 352n10
Seven Liberal Arts of Philology, 45
Shāh Jahān, 178, 180, 181, 194
Shang civilization, 330
Shemesh, Aharon, 68
Shoku Nihongi, 254
Shortcut to Higher Learning (Nonius Marcellus), 60
Shuowen (Xu), 138
Sībawayhi, 93, 346n7
Sima Qian, 249
ṣināʿat al-adab, 12, 14
Sinology, 313–314, 324–325. *See also* Chinese language
Śiva, 125–127
Śivadāsa, 125
six, symbolism of number, 184–185, 365n25
Sizzo, Margo, 286
Skandasvāmin, 130
Snell, Bruno, 114
Society for Classical Studies, 331, 334n29
Society for the Study of *Another Man'yōshū,* 246
Socrates, 156, 377n62
Song Learning, 230–236, 239–240
Sonnets to Orpheus (Rilke), 285–286, 298–305
Sophocles, 155, 273
Spinoza, Benedict de, 1, 6, 135
Sprachwissenschaft, 316–319, 329
Spring and Autumn Annals (Chinese Classic). See *Annals* (*Chunqiu,* Chinese Classic)
Śrīharṣa, 124
Śṛṅgāraprakāśa (Bhoja), 117, 352n11
Statilius Maximus, 55
Stilo Praeconinus, Lucius Aelius, 49, 53
stimulant factor, 125
Strabo, 160
studiosus philologiae, 6
Study of Confucius as Institutional Reformer (Kang), 239
subscriptions of medieval texts, 55, 166
Suetonius, 49, 51, 56
Ṣūfī Māzandarānī, Muḥammad, 179
al-Ṣūlī, 98, 100, 102, 103–108, 111, 348n51, 349n54

Sun Xingyan, 236
Swaminatha Iyer, U. V., 9–10, 334n31
Sweet, Henry, 317
syngramma, 28
Synthesis of Books and Illustrations Past and Present, 240
Syriac language, 4
Systematic Treatise on Computational Methods, 241
Szondi, Peter, 8, 98, 140, 293, 294

Tachibana Moribe, 257–258, 261
Tadhkirat al-sāmiʿ wa l-mutakallim fī adab al-ʿālim wa l-mutaʿallim (Ibn Jamāʿah), 203, 204–206
Taftāzānī, 215, 221, 216223
tahshiya wa tashrih, 20
Taiping Rebellion, 225, 235, 243
takhyīl, 102, 348n45
Taʿlīm al-mutaʿallim ṭuruq al-taʿallum (Zarnūjī), 203
Talmud of the Land of Israel, 64, 68, 69, 80
talmuds, Jewish. *See* Babylonian Talmud (the Bavli); Yerushalmi, the
Tama no mihashira (Hirata), 257
Tamil scholarship, 9–10, 334n31, 352n13
tannaim, 79
tannaitic era of Jewish history, 79, 82, 83
tanqīḥ, 13, 179
Taqrīr al-qawānīn al-mutadāwalah fī ʿilm al-munāẓarah (Sāçaḳlīzāde), 214
Tartīb al-ʿulūm (Sāçaḳlīzāde), 213
Taṣḥīf, 97
taṣḥīḥ, 13, 20, 179
al-Tawwazī, 100
teacher-student learning: in Arabic lexicography 93–94; in Ottoman education, 201–207, 370n84
Ten Commandments, 75
Ten Computational Classics, 240
Textbook on Phonetics, 319
Textgeschichte, 271
textual commentary, 371n93; Sanskrit, 19, 115–120, 127–130; Alexandrian, 28, 36; Roman, 50, 51, 54, 55; rabbinic, 73, 86; Arabic, 97, 346n20; Chinese, 138, 142, 144, 153, 226, 236, 238; humanist, 156–157, 159, 162, 170, 174; on *Mathnavī,* 181, 182, 188–194, 197, 199; of *Mathnavī,* 188–191, 193–194; Ottoman, 209–212, 216; historical, 290, 293, 295, 297
textual criticism: in Alexandrian philology, 27, 36–44; axiom of, 47; in Roman philology, 54–57; in Arabic philology, 93–98; in Sanskrit philology, 115, 120–124; in classical philology, 155–157; of *Mathnavī,* 191–193; in nativist philology, 253–254; limitations of, 281–282. *See also* hermeneutics
Thaʿlab, 101, 105–106
theodicy, 84, 90
theology, 7, 84, 162, 210, 214, 216
Theon, 26
Thiel, Helmut van, 28
Thirteen Modes (R. Ishmael), 75–76
Three Virtues *(Zhongyong),* 147–152
Thucydides, 154, 155, 160
Timotheus, 30
Timpanaro, Sebastiano, 282
Tokugawa Mitsukuni, 248–249
Tokugawa scholarship, 15, 247
Torah of Moses, 67
torts in Jewish law, 81–82
Tosafists, 71
Tosefta, 69–70
translation: as concept, 12, 16, 286–287; of Bible, 18, 77, 155, 316; in Arabic philology, 96, 97; in Sanskrit culture, 118, 128, 353n16; in ancient textual philology, 156–157, 160, 162, 164; of *Mathnavī,* 188, 190, 196, 198; in nativist philology, 249, 254; of The Sonnets to Orpheus, 286
transmission/transmitters of Arabic language, 92–97, 100, 349n63. *See also* rāwī/ruwāt; isnād
Treatise on Cold Damage Disorders, 239
Tripertita (Aelius Paetus Catus), 49–50
"Triplets" (song), 45, 62
truth, defining, 16–18, 23, 135–136, 143, 144
Tryambaka Makhin, 120
Tu Cheng-sheng, x
Turkey: scholarship in, 10
Turner, Eric Gardner, 32
Twelve Tables of the Law, 50

Über das Conjugationssystem der Sanskritsprache in Vergleichung mit Jenem der griechischen, lateinischen, persischen und germanischen Sprache (Bopp), 315
Ueda Akinari, 255, 256–257, 261
Ueda Kazutoshi, 311
al-ʿulūm al-adabiyya, 14, 18–19, 113, 351n96
ʿUmāra b. ʿAqīl, 110
Umayyad period, 98, 101
understanding of texts. *See* hermeneutics

Universal Ways and Virtues *(Zhongyong),* 147–152
University of Göttingen, 6
'Uthmān, 92

Vādirāja, 120–121
vākyaśāstra, 115
Valeriano, Pierio, 168
Valéry, Paul, 289, 299, 306
Valla, Lorenzo, 123, 161, 162, 163, 164, 170–171
Vallabhadeva, 117, 121, 136, 352n9, 354n28
Varadarāja, Udāḷi, 117, 120
varia lectio (variae lectiones), 12–13, 17, 27, 36–44
variants, conjecture *vs.* comparative, 54; of ancient texts, 38–43; in Roman philology, 54, 56; in Sanskrit philology, 118–121, 127, 353n15; in Western philology, 168; of *Mathnavī,* 183–184, 186–188, 365n30; in Ottoman philology, 221–223. *See also* authenticity of works; *ekdosis*
varietas, 27
Varro, Publius Terentius, 46, 53–54
Vasubandhu, 128
Vedic canon, 14, 351n3; philology of, 115–116, 127–132; origin of, 128, 133, 356n66
Vico, Giambattista, 7, 135
Vidyāsāgara, 119
Virgil, 17, 55–57, 58, 167
Vopadeva, 124
vulgata, 30, 31, 35, 36
Vyāsa, 124

Wang Bo, 147, 149–150
Wang Fan-Sen, viii, xi
Wang Lai, 242
Wang Li, 384n78
Wang Mingsheng, 230
Weiss, David Halivni, 87
Welcker, Friedrich Gottlob, 266, 267
Wentong (Ma), 384n78
Wenze (Chen), 137
West, Martin, 28–29, 41, 42
Western colonial influences on philology, 9–11
Western philology. *See specific regional type*
Whitney, William Dwight, 8, 135, 314, 317, 358n83
Wilamowitz-Moellendorff, Ulrich, 314
Winckelmann, Johann Joachim, 268, 273, 275
Wink und Wandlung (Gerok-Reiter), 306–307
Wissenschaft, 277, 377n60
Wolf, Friedrich August, 6, 7, 16, 44, 266–267, 270–276, 314, 318
word philology, 138, 257–258
Wortphilologie, 13, 97, 281

Xenophon, 155
Xu Qian, 141, 147, 149, 150, 151–152
Xu Shen, 227
Xu Shou, 243

Yamabiko zōshi (Tachibana), 257
Yamazaki Ansai, 247–248
Yang Guangxian, 242
Yanjitu (Wang), 150
Yan Ruoju, 1, 229, 326
Yardstick of Poetry (Ibn Ṭabāṭabā'), 101
Yerushalmi, the, 64, 70, 73–75, 81, 85
Yijing (Chinese Classic). See *Classic of Changes* (*Yijing,* Chinese Classic)
Yi Yong-hui, 245, 263
Yu, Pauline, 233

ẓāhirī, 208–209
al-Zarnūjī, Burhān al-Dīn, 203–205, 213, 215, 216, 219
Zenodotus as *diorthotes,* 25, 28–29, 33–43, 336n30, 336n32, 337n33
Zetzel, James E. G., 13, 17, 45–62
Zhang Binglin, 326
Zhang Xuecheng, 230, 232
Zhang Zai, 19, 140–146, 153, 358n12
Zhang Zhongjing, 259
Zhao Yuanren. See Chao Yuen Ren
Zhengmeng (Zhang), 140–146
Zheng Xuan, 138, 232
Zhongyong (*Doctrine of the Mean,* Chinese Classic), 143–144, 147, 227
Zhu Shijie, 240
Zhu Xi, 137, 146, 147, 149, 152, 228, 229, 247
Zinn, Ernst, 299
Zoroastrian scholarship, 72, 81
al-Zubayr b. Bakkār, 103
Zuo Commentary. See *Annals* (*Chunqiu,* Chinese Classic)